Human Service Organizations

Human Service

Organizations
A Book of Readings

Yeheskel Hasenfeld
and Richard A. English

Ann Arbor
The University of Michigan Press

Acknowledgments

Grateful acknowledgment is made to the following journals and publishers for permission to reprint copyrighted materials:

Administrative Science Quarterly, for the following articles: Richard O. Carlson, "Succession and Performance among School Superintendents"; Jerald Hage and Michael Aiken, "Routine Technology, Social Structure, and Organization Goals"; Robert W. Hawkes, "The Role of the Psychiatric Administrator"; Sol Levine and Paul E. White, "Exchange as a Conceptual Framework for the Study of Interorganizational Relationships"; Eugene Litwak and Lydia F. Hylton, "Interorganizational Analysis: A Hypothesis on Co-ordinating Agencies"; William R. Rosengren, "Structure, Policy, and Style: Strategies of Organizational Control"; Dorothy E. Smith, "Front-Line Organization of the State Mental Hospital." Reprinted by permission of the authors and the publisher.

The American Sociological Association, for the following articles: Michael Aiken and Jerald Hage, "Organizational Interdependence and Intra-Organizational Structure"; Ronald G. Corwin, "Strategies for Organizational Innovation" Edward Gross, "Universities as Organizations: A Research Approach"; Yeheskel Hasenfeld, "People Processing Organizations: An Exchange Approach"; Mark Lefton and William R. Rosengren, "Organizations and Clients: Lateral and Longitudinal Dimensions"; Charles Perrow, "The Analysis of Goals in Complex Organizations." These articles are reprinted by permission of the authors and publisher from *American Sociological Review.* Howard S. Becker, "The Teacher in the Authority System of the Public School." Reprinted by permission of the author and publisher from *Journal of Educational Sociology.* Yeheskel Hasenfeld, "Organizational Dilemmas in Innovating Social Services: The Case of the Community Action Centers." Reprinted by permission of the author and publisher from *Journal of Health and Social Behavior.*

Appleton-Century-Crofts, for Ronald G. Corwin, "The Formulation of Goals in the Public Schools." Reprinted by permission of Appleton-Century-Crofts, Educational Division, Meredith Corporation, from *A Sociology of Education.*

Harvard Educational Review, for Anthony Oettinger and Sema Marks,

The Society for Applied Anthropology, for Robert A. Stallings, "Hospital Adaptations to Disaster: Flow Models of Intensive Technologies." Reprinted by permission from *Human Organization.*

The Society for the Study of Social Problems, for Robert A. Scott, "The Factory as a Social Service Organization," and "The Selection of Clients by Social Welfare Agencies: The Case of the Blind." Reprinted by permission of the author and publisher from *Social Problems.*

The University of Chicago Press, for the following articles reprinted from *The American Journal of Sociology:* Jerald Hage and Michael Aiken, "Program Change and Organizational Properties." Copyright 1967 by the University of Chicago; S. R. Klatsky, "Organizational Inequality: The Case of the Public Employment Agencies." © 1970 by The University of Chicago. All rights reserved; Eugene Litwak, "Models of Bureaucracy Which Permit Conflict." Copyright 1961 by the University of Chicago; Julius A. Roth, "Some Contingencies of the Moral Evaluation and Control of Clientele: The Case of the Hospital Emergency Service." © 1972 by The University of Chicago. All rights reserved; Mayer N. Zald, "Organizational Control Structures in Five Correctional Institutions." Copyright 1962 by the University of Chicago; Mayer N. Zald, "The Power and Functions of Boards of Directors: A Theoretical Synthesis." © 1969 by The University of Chicago. All rights reserved.

The University of Wisconsin Press, for Michael E. Borus, John P. Brennan, and Sidney Rosen, "A Benefit-Cost Analysis of the Neighborhood Youth Corps." © 1970 by the Regents of the University of Wisconsin. Reprinted by permission of the authors and publisher from *The Journal of Human Resources.*

Foreword

As Secretary of Health, Education, and Welfare during 1968–69, I had the responsibility and privilege of "running" probably the biggest and most diverse human service organization in the world.

This stimulating book by Professors Hasenfeld and English will be helpful, I believe, for administrators as well as for students who will have responsibility in the future for the increasing demand for effective human services.

The organization of this book should contribute to an understanding of the complexity, societal pressures and demands, and distinctive problems of human service organizations. The editors in identifying some of the key dimensions of human service organizations and their interrelationships have provided a unique conceptual framework for the analysis and understanding of these organizations. This framework should also assist in the identification of gaps in our knowledge about human service organizations and should point the way for additional research, theory, and policy development.

Formulating and administering policies and programs in a large or complex human service organization is a challenging and demanding responsibility. It is best to be an optimist if one occupies a key policy or management position in such an organization. There is a continuing dilemma created by conflicting expectations facing human service organizations. On the one hand, society expects that these organizations will solve our many social and individual problems, while on the other hand there is a lack of effective service technologies to deal with such problems. It should be kept in mind that if society's expectations for human service organizations are set higher than individual and group performance can produce realistically, the result is usually frustration, disappointment, and despair of clients, practitioners, and managers as well as the general populus. The balance between achieving excellence and high quality performance in the delivery of services and the actual level of personal and organizational competence is a never-ending attempt at incremental change.

To enhance the well-being of individuals in the present-day environment and the immediate years ahead will require, it seems to me, that human service organizations play a more diversified and increased role in the lives of more people. Any organization which attempts to provide meaningful human services has substantial limitations. This is true even when such services are provided by competent personnel who are committed to quality services and who are critical of both the means and ends involved in providing specific services.

There are many valid criticisms of existing human service organizations just as there are of marriage, the family, governments, the banking system, and the post office. These institutions inherently will encounter continuous problems given environmental changes which render past service demands and solutions obsolete. We must learn, therefore, how to adapt these institutions to suit our changing needs.

Despite temporary setbacks, it seems inevitable that public funding of human service organizations will continue to increase in the future. The long-term trend has been in that direction. Approximately twenty-five percent of the gross national product is now being expended for health, education, and welfare programs—public and private. We must learn how to utilize these vast amounts in a better way than we have in the past. We will have to seek both new goals and better means to achieve these goals. We will have to recruit new kinds of personnel. We will need to fund innovative ways to deliver both old and new services. This is a gigantic task.

There are probably more creative and participatory roles in human service organizations today than ever before and it is likely that there will be more of these kinds of roles in the future. Adequate preparation for these necessary and demanding roles is essential in helping individuals attain the highest levels of self-fulfillment and in making the institutions of our society aid in this objective.

WILBUR J. COHEN

Preface

This volume provides a collection of the essential literature currently available on the administration and organization of human service organizations. The criteria utilized in the selection of writings for this volume led to the inclusion of articles which: (a) focus on a key issue that is unique to human service organizations; (b) offer a basic understanding of the effects of such an issue on the delivery of client services; (c) offer guidelines for administrators of human service organizations; (d) are grounded in and supported by empirical research.

The theoretical and empirical issues surrounding the organization and administration of human service organizations are rapidly emerging as a unique field of inquiry in such disciplines as sociology, social work, education, and public health. A significant body of theoretical essays and empirical studies is developing which attempts to identify the particular organizational and administrative problems that human service organizations encounter, and which set them apart from other types of organizations.

A central issue that underlies most studies on human service organizations is the concern with the characteristics and quality of service delivery systems. These studies attempt to identify the major organizational parameters which give rise to particular client service patterns and the impact of such patterns on the clients themselves. As such, these studies provide invaluable information for administrators, practitioners, and educators, as well as students of human service organizations.

The editors have intended this reader for both graduate and undergraduate students in the fields of sociology, social work, education, public health, and community mental health. The range of studies selected reflects the organizations that are the focus of study by students in each of the above fields. Since courses on the organization and administration of human service organizations are offered in almost all the above disciplines, the reader is geared specifically to the content of these courses. It offers a framework around which such courses can be organized.

The conceptual framework for this volume is set forth in the introductory chapter. Here we identify and analyze the distinctive attributes of human service organizations. This description and analysis is facilitated by a classification of human service organizations which gives special attention to their functions and domains.

Our discussion of the distinctive attributes and problems of human service organizations serves as a guide for the organization of this volume. Our approach is to first examine the external social and environmental factors that determine the inputs to human service organizations such as resources, legitimation, clients, and technology. We next examine the ways in which these organizations formulate their goals and establish a service technology as they interact with their environment. The internal structure and division of labor of human service organizations are dealt with as a function of organizational goals and technology. We then proceed to examine the core activities of human service organizations, namely their relations with clients. Having established basic service modalities we explore how human service organizations develop exchange relations with other organizations and the mechanisms they use to assess their own performance. Finally, we focus on the critical issue of change and innovation in human service organizations.

Our major purpose is to provide an understanding of human service organizations as organizations. In assuming a sociological approach our task is not to disregard the individual to whom we give attention throughout the volume, but to foster an understanding of human service organizations since they have important consequences for the well-being and general welfare of people.

We are indebted to a number of people who have assisted us in the preparation of this volume. We would like to thank our colleagues Irwin Epstein and John Tropman who read the entire manuscript and provided invaluable criticisms and comments, and Yosef Katan of Hebrew University who read portions of the manuscript and offered critical observations. We owe considerable debt and gratitude to Eugene Litwak, Henry J. Meyer, Rosemary C. Sarri, and Robert D. Vinter for their intellectual stimulation that helped to shape our perspectives and concerns about human service organizations. In particular we recognize with deep appreciation Phillip Fellin, Dean of the University of Michigan School of Social Work, who facilitated our labors through his encouragement and provision of resources.

For typing and retyping initial drafts of this volume, obtaining permissions from authors and publishers, and coordinating myriad clerical details, Margaret Lemley deserves our praise, as well as our gratitude. Helen Hasenfeld as a wife and friend patiently and understandably accepted the stresses and demands of our work. Her encouragement when the going was rough enabled us to successfully achieve our goal. Finally, we acknowledge to the reader that the order of our names in the editorships in no way reflects seniority, rather the loss of a tossed coin.

YEHESKEL HASENFELD
RICHARD A. ENGLISH

Contents

Introduction

Human Service Organizations: A Conceptual Overview

One of the hallmarks of the modern society has been the vast proliferation of formal organizations explicitly designed to process and change people. This trend reflects, on the one hand, the shift of socialization and social control functions from primary groups such as the family to the state, and on the other hand it reflects the development of complex people-processing and people-changing techniques that can no longer be implemented in small social units.

Inevitably, every person conducts transactions, voluntarily or involuntarily, with a whole range of organizations whose explicit purpose is to shape, change, and control his behavior as well as confirm or redefine his social and personal status. Examples of such organizations are the public schools, hospitals, welfare agencies, employment placement offices, and police departments. We shall denote the set of organizations whose primary function is to define or alter the person's behavior, attributes, and social status in order to maintain or enhance his well-being as "human service" organizations. These organizations are differentiated from other bureaucracies by two fundamental characteristics: (a) their input of raw material are human beings with specific attributes, and their production output are persons processed or changed in a predetermined manner, and (b) their general mandate is that of "service," that is, to maintain and improve the general well-being and functioning of people.

The indispensability of human service organizations in modern society is due to the functions these organizations fulfill both at the societal level and the individual level. At the societal level, human service organizations have three major functions. First, these organizations assume major responsibilities in the socialization of the members of society into various future roles they may occupy. This is exemplified in such organizations as schools, social and recreation centers, universities, and various youth serving agencies. Second, human service organizations serve as major social control agents by identifying individuals who fail to conform to their role prescriptions, and by removing them, at least temporarily, from these role positions. In doing so, these organizations enable the continuous functioning of the various social institutions without serious disruptions. Examples of such organizations are law enforcement agencies, hospitals, correctional institutions, and social service agencies. Third, these organizations assume a social integration function by providing the means and resources for the individual to become integrated in the various social units with which he affiliates. Through such mechanisms as resocialization, therapy, material assistance, and counseling, human service organizations attempt to prevent social disintegration and facilitate and restore the integration of the individual in society.

At the individual level, human service organizations provide critical resources not available elsewhere, that enable individuals to improve, maintain, and restore their well-being and personal welfare. It is through these organizations that the individual can acquire an education, obtain medical services, receive help at times of personal crises, and receive material resources to meet basic needs. The individual is not dependent solely on his ascriptive and particularistic ties with various social networks to obtain such resources. Rather, human service organizations employ universalistic criteria that, at least theoretically, enable every individual to obtain services when he needs them. Moreover, as highly organized and rational systems vested with the necessary tools and expertise, human service organizations can, in general, provide these resources and services in a far more efficient and effective way than primary groups such as the family. In short, these organizations respond to and provide some of the basic human needs to the members of society. Their effectiveness in doing so leads, according to Etzioni (1968), to a reduction of social alienation and inauthenticity.

Some Public Criticisms of Human Service Organizations

Although we are witnessing a tremendous growth in the number and range of human service organizations, there is a discernible collateral increase in the dissatisfaction and criticism by the public who transact with such organizations about their performance, patterns of service, and effectiveness. While various types of human service organizations encounter such public pressures differentially, there is growing evidence that these organizations experience some form of a "consumer revolt."

For example, public schools have come under sharp criticism from both professionals and parent groups concerning their patterns of teaching and, indeed, their very organization. Social service agencies are being accused of withholding services from those who need them most. Hospitals face a public outcry for seeming inefficiency, rising costs of treatment, and insensitivity to the needs of patients.

Four major themes can be identified in the growing public protest toward human service organizations: (a) failures to respond to the needs of the populations they claim to serve, as indicated by the discrepancy between professed objectives and actual performance; (b) the service techniques employed in such organizations are inconsistent and ill-organized, failing to demonstrate their effectiveness in achieving the desired service outcomes; (c) the mechanisms these organizations develop to transact and work with their clients are dehumanizing, degrading, and insensitive to their individual attributes and needs; (d) human service organizations are ill-managed, wasteful, and inefficient, thus consuming an ever-increasing share of public and private resources.

Although the validity of these themes of protest must await empirical examination, we propose that their existence reflects some inherent structural problems that confront human service organizations, in contrast with other bureaucracies. Failure to recognize the particular parameters that shape the structure and patterns of the service delivery system of such organizations can lead the naïve observer of human service organizations to conclude that they are irrational and dysfunctional social entities. Equally, insensitivity to the existence of these parameters by executive and administrative cadres within such organizations could result in the adoption of administrative decision-making patterns that are irrelevant and ineffective.

We should make explicit our approach to the study of human service organizations. Clearly, we take the position that these organizations are vital tools in meeting some basic human needs and problems. Moreover, we accept the notion that the development of these organizations in modern society has resulted in significant and often dramatic improvements in the welfare and well-being of people. This, undoubtedly, can be attributed, in part, to the growth of knowledge and expertise in human services, and to the organization of these services in formal organizations that pursue norms of rationality.

Since critical human needs are and will increasingly be met through human service organizations, we are committed to the objective of facilitating the effectiveness, efficiency, and responsiveness of these organizations to the needs of actual and potential clients. Therefore, the purpose of this essay and the articles that follow is to identify the unique attributes of these organizations; the parameters that shape their modes of operation; and the structural barriers that hinder the pursuit of the above objectives. In taking a critical perspective we hope to contribute to the better understanding of human service organizations; to identify some of the gaps in knowledge and research on these organizations; and to point out the issues that must be addressed in order to enhance their effectiveness.

Accordingly, we shall attempt to identify and analyze the distinctive attributes of human service organizations and the particular parameters that distinguish them from other types of bureaucracies. In doing so, we shall first suggest a classification of these organizations that groups them into sub-types in order to highlight the unique characteristics of each type in relation to the others.

A Classification of Human Service Organizations

It is useful to classify human service organizations along key dimensions in order to highlight their distinctive functions and domain, to identify the unique organizational dilemmas they must resolve, and to differentiate them from other types of organizations. Accordingly, we shall offer two typologies: the first refers to the domain and function of human service organizations, and the second to the relations between these organizations and their clients. Such a classification scheme obviously presents ideal types, and the reader needs to bear in mind that the dimensions offered should be seen as continua.

Moreover, the purpose of the typology is primarily descriptive, that is, to point out how the location of each organization along a set of dimensions creates a dominant structural dilemma that preoccupies much of the administrative decision-making processes in each organizational type.

A Typology of the Function and Domain of Human Service Organizations

Although the overall societal mandate of human service organizations is to improve, enhance, and maintain the well-being and general welfare of people, each organization addresses itself to a particular class of clients offering a predominant type of service. Hence, a basic dimension of the typology that is crucial for the understanding of such organizations is the nature of the clients they serve. At one end of the continuum are those organizations whose primary mandate is to maintain and enhance the well-being of people perceived to be adequately functioning in society. At the other end are organizations mandated to ameliorate and remedy the ill or deviant state of people perceived to be malfunctioning in society. The location of any particular organization along this continuum may be quite problematic since it depends on the public definition regarding the degree of "normalcy" of the clients served.

Such a definition, however, may vary widely among the public concerned with the services of the organization, a fact which underscores a fundamental problem that human service organizations encounter in defining their domain.

A second dimension relates to the services offered by the organization, namely whether it is people changing or people processing (Hasenfeld, 1972). People-changing organizations attempt to alter directly the attributes or behavior of their clients through the application of various modification and treatment technologies. People-processing organizations, on the other hand, attempt to change their clients not by altering basic personal attributes, but by conferring upon them a public status and relocating them in a new set of social circumstances. They do so through the use of a classification-disposition system, which may define the clients, for example, as "acceptable for admission," "juvenile delinquent," or "underachiever." Needless to say, people-changing organizations cannot operate without having their clients processed either internally or by other people-processing organizations. In either case, human service organizations can thus be classified by their predominant function. In table 1, we see that the cross-classification of these two dimensions produces four types of organizations as illustrated by specific types of agencies.

TABLE 1

A Typology of the Function and Domain of Human Service Organizations

		Predominant Function	
		People Processing	*People Changing*
Type of Clients	Normal Functioning	*Type I* University Admissions Office, Employment Placement Service	*Type II* Public School Y.M.C.A.
	Malfunctioning	*Type III* Juvenile Court, Diagnostic Clinic	*Type IV* Prison, Hospital

One important difference among these organizations is in the type of clients they serve. When the clients of the organization are defined as functioning normally, the dilemma of the organization is to determine what should be the desired outcomes of its services. This is so because the clients (or their representatives) are more likely to assume the role of a consumer whose wishes, tastes, and desires must be taken into serious account by the organization.

In contrast, as the organization moves to serve clients defined as malfunctioning, they are perceived to be less capable of defining appropriate service objectives for themselves. Moreover, there is an increasing agreement on what should be the desired outcomes, namely the amelioration of the ill or deviant state of the clients. Rather, the issue of who should be served becomes the critical dilemma. The organization must determine not only the degree of the clients' malfunctioning, but also whether the organization can effectively respond to it.

In contrast to the first class of organization, these organizations must also cope with the consequences of the very definition of the clients as malfunctioning. Often these consequences imply resistance to change, rejection by other social units, isolation from society, low self image, hostility, and the like.

Structurally, people-processing organizations must develop effective mechanisms to link the clients processed with the external units that are their recipients. Hence, the patterns of service delivery of these organizations are particularly influenced by the external relations they develop (Hasenfeld, 1972). The effectiveness of people-changing organizations, on the other hand, is determined by the treatment or change technologies which they develop and operate. Thus, a key structural and administrative issue in these organizations is the implementation of effective change technologies.

A Typology of Organization-Client Relations

The most distinctive feature of human service organizations is that the relations between the organizations and their clients, which are independent of the type of clients served, are central to their structure. The importance of these relations is an obvious consequence of their mandate, since staff-client relations become the most important tool with which each organization attempts to achieve its service goals. One dimension in these relations is the degree of the organizational interest in the client's personal biography (Lefton and Rosengren, 1966). At one extreme are organizations whose interest is limited to very few and distinct aspects of the client's biography. At the other extreme are organizations whose interest in the client's biography is very extensive.

A second dimension refers to the compliance system the organization employs vis-à-vis its clients. Following Etzioni (1961), we distinguish between three types of compliance systems—normative, utilitarian, and coercive. The cross classification of these two dimensions produces six types of organization-client relations as illustrated in table 2.

Organizations that delimit their interest in the client's biography face the inherent problem of isolating a specific set of client attributes from the rest of his biography. The problem is twofold: to determine what are the relevant attributes and to avoid the tendency of the staff to incorporate additional attributes in the service process as a way of reducing uncertainty in their intervention efforts. In contrast, organizations whose interest in the client's biography is extensive are in constant search for relevant and significant client attributes. The staff in such organizations always face the potential danger of missing or ignoring relevant data about the client. Hence, they are highly dependent on the client's cooperation in disclosing information about himself.

The compliance system used by the organization also raises distinctive structural issues that must be resolved. A normative compliance system is highly dependent on the ability of the staff to develop effective interpersonal relations with the clients and to serve as models for identification. A utilitarian system requires that the organization controls the necessary resources that are desired by the client. A coercive compliance system must ensure that the client will not escape the system, or develop mechanisms to counteract and neutralize the coercive measures.

Having identified different types of human service organizations, we shall now turn to discuss some of the key variables that influence and shape their distinct character.

TABLE 2

A Typology of Organization—Client Relations

		Interest in Client's Biography	
		Limited	Extensive
	Normative	*Type I*	*Type II*
		University	Treatment oriented mental hospital
Client's Compliance System	Utilitarian	*Type III*	*Type IV*
		Medical clinic	Nursing home
	Coercive	*Type V*	*Type VI*
		Police	Correctional institution

Distinctive Attributes and Problems of
Human Service Organizations

Although human service organizations differ in functions and client populations served, they all have characteristics and problems that distinguish them from other classes of formal organizations. In the following discussion we shall identify some of the key characteristics and problems facing such organizations, setting them apart from other types of formal organizations.

A. *The raw materials of human service organizations are human beings.*

In contrast with most other bureaucracies, the raw materials to be worked upon in human service organizations are not value neutral (Perrow, 1965). Quite the contrary, the persons being processed and changed are vested with cultural values and have a social and moral identity. Moreover, they are self-activating entities whose responses are determined not only by what is being done to them, but also by their own desires, motivations, attitudes, and past learning. Except for extreme situations of behavioral control, much of the success of the change processes contemplated by the organization is influenced by the willingness of the persons who participate in them. This fundamental fact has profound implications as to the organizational and administrative character of human service organizations.

First, the organization is constrained in its choices of change techniques by the value system prevalent in the social milieu in which it functions. For example, school personnel are prohibited from using corporal punishment as a mechanism to control behavior. Hospitals cannot perform surgical procedures without the consent of the patient or his family. More important, however, is the fact that every decision made by the organization in relation to its clients involves a value or moral component in the sense that it affects the self-identity of the clients and the moral judgment of the clients by others (Goffman, 1961). In other words, each organizational decision that relates to the career of its clients involves decisions by both the organization and the persons themselves concerning their moral rights and present and future moral worth. Hence, each human service organization must maintain an ideological system which provides its personnel with reference points in coping with the moral components of their decision-making processes. Consequently, human service organizations will vary by the types of moral assessments they develop and the moral categories they employ for their clients.

Second, and related to the above, the clients processed and

changed by human service organizations also have identifiable social locations and social affiliations which cannot be ignored by the organization. On the contrary, since the activities of the organization have direct implications for the present and future social position of its clients, it becomes highly sensitive to the clients' "social background." In human service organizations, the clients' social background serves as a critical indicator of the type of processing and changes they require, their potentials for change, and the desired outcomes. Moreover, the clients' affiliation and reference social groups exert considerable influence on their motivational and behavioral patterns which must be considered by the organization if its techniques are to be effective. Thus, the organization is constrained to minimize the potential conflict between the clients' ascriptive affiliation and social status and the consequences and implications of its activities on these affiliations and status. It also must develop mechanisms to buffer itself from the clients' social ties considered to be detrimental to the attainment of the service objectives. Such buffers may include the physical and social isolation of the clients from their social affiliations; the development of boundary roles to mediate between the organization and social groups to which the clients belong; and the design of organizational activities to serve only clients having similar social affiliations.

Third, every human service organization must develop mechanisms to cope with the self-activating properties of its clients in order to insure that its processing and change technologies are not neutralized and rendered ineffective. These mechanisms are usually expressed in the form of a compliance system whose basis of power may be coercive, utilitarian, or normative, or any mixture of each (Etzioni, 1961). The choice of the compliance system will be influenced partly by the value system of the larger social milieu and the moral assessment system developed by the organization itself.

B. *Goal definitions in human service organizations are problematical and ambiguous.*

Organizations such as factories and banks whose raw materials are inanimate objects are more likely than human service organizations to obtain the consensus of their task environment and their own personnel as to their output goals. In human service organizations the definitions of goals are primarily commitments to certain values, norms, and ideologies. Thus, a key characteristic of human service organizations is that their goal definitions are ideological in nature. Organizations define their goals in relation to a given task environment. For human service organizations the task environment is composed of a multitude of social groups and other formal organizations that have interest in, or relations with the clients. Yet each social group or organization defines its own expectations as to what should be done for, or to, the clients on the basis of its particular value system, location in the social stratification system, and interests. The difficulties in obtaining the consensus of the task environment increase when (a) the population served by the organization is defined as malfunctioning and (b) the organization attempts to deal with a wide range of attributes of the persons it handles. Both instances raise the probability of disagreements among various interest groups as to the desired outcomes. Thus, for example, the medical hospital is likely to obtain greater consensus for its goals than the psychiatric hospital. Similarly, the vocational training school can obtain a better agreement for its output goals than the public school.

Facing a task environment with multiple, and often conflicting, expectations and interests in its product raises a major dilemma for the human service organization in defining its goals. For example, in attempting to define its goals, the juvenile court encounters diverse interest groups which have influence on its domain and mandate (Vinter and Sarri, 1966). Among these groups are: (a) the police, which is concerned with the punishment and removal from the community of youngsters with high "delinquency risk"; (b) public schools that rely on the court to handle serious discipline problems; (c) professional and humanitarian citizen groups that pressure the court to adopt rehabilitative and preventative goals; (d) legislators who see the court as a device to implement various social controls over youngsters; and (e) parents who rely on the court to resolve conflicts with their children.

Human service organizations employ a wide range of strategies with differential consequences in defining their goals: (a) the organization may define its output goals in abstract and intangible terms that would be acceptable to its various constituents. Yet in so doing, the organization is increasing the likelihood of goal displacement in which organizational means become ends in themselves (Warner and Havens, 1968) and decreasing internal coherence and consistency; (b) related to the above, the organization may define its output goals through searching for the "lowest common denominator" of the various interest groups in its task environment. In so doing, however, the human service organization reduces the potential value of its product and increases the likelihood of becoming marginal; (c) the organization may pursue multiple goals to appease the conflicting interests it encounters. Such a strategy has the advantage of increasing the basis of the organization's legitimacy, but, at the same time, it increases the problems of internal integration and the probability of competition and conflict among the units implementing each goal; (d) the organization may define its output goals to conform to the expectations of those interest groups upon whom it is most dependent. This strategy, however, does not diminish the potential pressures from other groups, and can reduce the basis of the organization's legitimacy. Most important, however, it limits the freedom of the organization to respond to new environmental exigencies.

The lack of consensus as to the goals of the organization is also experienced internally. Members of the organization bring into it varied external status characteristics, reflecting many different values and attitudes of the social groups with whom they are affiliated. These affect their conceptions about the clients. Such attitudes and conceptions concerning the people with whom they work are of critical importance, since the technology of the human service organization is based in part on direct and planned manipulation of the interpersonal relations between staff and clients. The human service organization, in contrast with other bureaucracies, is limited in its ability to neutralize the personal ideologies of its members. Consequently, staff groups which are differentiated by their organizational location, occupational and professional training, and social background, are likely to develop their own ideologies toward the clients—the objects of their work. Thus, the greater the occupational and professional diversity in the organization, the greater are its difficulties in developing an internal consensus toward the output goals. The potential lack of internal consensus is further intensified as the service technology of the organization becomes more complex, thus requiring the skills of different professional groups.

In general, human service organizations are likely to experience an internal process of negotiations between conflicting ideologies, in which each ideological group seeks a locale within the organization where its conceptions about the organizational goals can be expressed (Strauss, et al., 1964). Although the organizational leadership may attempt to achieve an ideological homogeneity through its staff recruitment and selection process, it can be (at best) only partially successful. This is especially the case as the complexity of the organization increases. Typically, organizational efforts to develop an internal consensus result in an emerging definition of the organizational goals as a mixture of, and a compromise between, the various ideologies represented among the staff. However, this adds to the ambiguity and inconsistency in the definition of the organizational goals.

Finally, human service organizations must cope with the personal goals of their clients, as these will also affect the goal definitions of the organization (Wheeler, 1966). The problem here is dual. First, the personal goals of the clients may deviate markedly from the goals of the organization. This is particularly evidenced in human service organizations whose main function is resocialization and where the client population has been defined as malfunctioning or deviant. Second, these personal goals cannot be easily converted to some common denominator or scale which enabled the organization to respond in a uniform fashion.

The personal goals of the clients receive their expression through interaction with the staff of the organization. It is here that the potential clash between the two sets of goals is most ominous. The interactive process is directed, in part, by the need of the staff and the client to reach a common ground enabling the interaction to continue. It is within this negotiation process that the clients' goals may clearly influence the organizational output goals. A key organizational mechanism to minimize such influence is the maintenance of an assymetric balance of power between staff and clients, in which the latter are placed in a relatively powerless position. This assymetry increases as the potential for disagreement between the staff service goals and clients' personal goals increases. Thus, for example, patients in a psychiatric hospital are likely to have less power than patients in a general hospital, and clients of a public welfare agency tend to have less power than clients in an adult education center.

Another basic organizational mechanism to avoid the conflict between clients' personal goals and the organizational goals are intake and "cooling out" procedures. Both are designed to select clients whose personal goals conform to the goals of the organization, rejecting those who fail to accept them. Organizations that have little control over their intake are more likely to develop "cooling out" mechanisms (Carlson, 1964). Yet excessive use of these mechanisms tends to undermine the legitimation of the organization. On the one hand, it narrows considerably its domain and, on the other, it produces a large group of potential and actual clients who feel themselves deprived of the services of the organization. Hence, human service organizations encounter continuous pressures from their clients to redefine their organizational goals, further adding to their instability and indeterminance.

C. *The technology of human service organizations is indeterminant.*

A technology of an organization can be defined as a series of procedures designed to transform the raw material from one state to another in a predetermined manner. The technology is based on a body of knowledge that ensures, within certain limits, the success of the transformation process, enabling the training of personnel to perform the necessary tasks (Perrow, 1967). The level of determinancy of the technology is thus a function of three major variables: (a) the extent to which the desired outcomes are tangible and well defined, (b) the degree of stability and invariability of the raw material, and (c) the knowledge available and the degree of its completeness about cause-effect relations in the raw material.

The degree to which the technical system lacks any, or more of, these conditions, the more it becomes nonroutine and indeterminant. Obviously, the above conditions are less likely to exist in human service organizations. No doubt, human service organizations vary markedly in the degree of indeterminancy of their technologies, which is influenced by the degree of technical innovation and development. Thus, for example, the technologies employed in the medical hospital are comparatively far more determinant (with notable exceptions) than those employed in the psychiatric hospital. Yet, we suggest that human service organizations, as a category of organizations, are distinctly characterized by the fact that they experience a high level of uncertainty in all of the three elements that compose their technologies.

Already we have noted that human service organizations are far from achieving consensus on the desired outcomes for their clients. Moreover, these desired outcomes are likely to be stated in an abstract and intangible manner, particularly as they relate to the nonphysical aspects of the clients. Part of the problem is clearly technical, due to the lack of valid and reliable measurement procedures to assess the attributes of the clients which the organization wishes to change. Consider, for example, the problem of measuring such attributes as mental health, intellectual functioning, or nondeviant behavior. Thus the organization encounters difficulties, not only in specifying the desired outcomes, but in assessing the transformation process itself.

The problem is partly related to, and magnified by, the inherent variability and unpredictability of the state of the clients. The technical system in human service organizations must cope with large variations in the attributes of the persons it processes as well as with their self-activating properties. Hence the clients, as raw materials, present a high degree of uncertainty to the organization. To reduce such uncertainties, which are very costly to the organization, it may employ several strategies: (a) employ a system of stereotypes or "normal cases" which classifies clients into a small set of defined categories, and proceed with the assumption that all members of a given stereotype function in the same manner (Scheff, 1966); (b) develop an intake process that attempts through its screening methods to reduce the variability of those clients accepted for service; (c) develop a technical system that addresses itself to a very narrow set of the clients' attributes, ignoring all others.

The crucial point to note in these strategies, and others that could be deployed, is that the organization develops a series of working assumptions about the clients that are then reified in its technology, although the factual validity of these assumptions may vary considerably.

Finally, and most important, the body of knowledge about cause-effect relations available to most human service organizations is at best partial and inconclusive. This is particularly the case when a body of knowledge relates to the nonphysical attributes of the persons being processed and changed. Although the "technological revolution" has increased this body of knowledge, human service organizations still grope very much in darkness when their task is to change the attributes and behavior of people. This is due not only to the partial and fragmented development or reliable and valid knowledge, but also to the problems of translating abstract and complex principles into actual operating procedures. (For example, the problem of operationalizing the need to maintain high motivation among students for effective learning.) Moreover, many of these principles or change models assume that the organization can control and neutralize so-called "exogenous" variables, which it rarely can.

Given the above conditions, it is not surprising to note that the technical system in human service organizations tends to be indeterminant and limited in its ability to demonstrate the successful transformation of the people it processes. This fact constrains the organization from developing a coherent and functional work structure that would serve the requirement of the technology.

D. Staff-client relations are the core activities in human service organizations.

Although this fact is self-evident, it has profound implications in defining the unique character of human service organizations. Probably more than any other variable, the patterns of staff-client relations are the best indicator of the social climate and distinctiveness of the organization. Staff-client relations in human service organizations can be differentiated by a number of variables that define their pattern: (a) duration of the relations, (b) frequency with which these relations occur, (c) intensity of the interaction, (d) scope or range of clients' attributes it covers, and (e) the number of participants in the relationship. In general, it can be said that human service organizations attempting to achieve major changes in their clients will be characterized by long, frequent, and intensive staff-client relations covering a wide range of the clients' attributes.

The function of staff-client relations is dual: change and control. That is to say, the major mechanism employed to achieve change in clients is direct manipulation of the interpersonal relations between the staff and its clients. The greater the amount of changes sought, the more critical becomes the role of these interpersonal relations. At the same time, however, the use of interpersonal relations to influence the clients also serves a control function designed to elicit their conformity and compliance to the change efforts. Moreover, part of the control function is the monitoring of the clients' performance. Hence a key aspect of staff-client relations is surveilance, and the greater the need of it the more frequent and intense are these relations.

However, the dual function of staff-client relations may produce internal inconsistencies, since each calls for a different usage and manipulation of the relationship. The client is never sure whether the purpose of the interaction that the staff initiates is for monitoring or change purposes. Consequently, there is always a basic element of ambivalence in these relations. It is heightened by the fact that not only can the staff use the relationship to influence clients, but similarly clients can use the relationship to influence the staff. That is, clients can manipulate their relations with the staff in order to elicit desired staff responses. For example, clients can control the degree to which they cooperate with the staff or the extent to which they communicate with them. Hence staff members also face an element of ambivalence in their interaction with their clients since they are never sure in what way the client is manipulating the relationship or for what purpose.

Thus, the relative powerlessness of clients in human service organizations also serves as a device to minimize the clients' counter-influence. The social distance that is maintained between the two serves a similar purpose. However, the greater the social distance, the more difficult it becomes for the staff to develop meaningful interpersonal relations with clients that could be intense enough to achieve desired client changes. The debate, for example, of whether to employ as change agents persons who are experientially, socially, and culturally close to the clients is partly related to the question of the desired social distance between staff and clients.

In this context, we should point out that human service organizations are undergoing a gradual, yet dramatic, change in the patterning of their relations with clients. Reflecting a wider social process of the extension and exercise of citizenship rights by previously disenfranchised social groups, clients are less willing to assume a powerless and passive role vis-à-vis the organization. The challenge to the perceived omnipotence of human service organizations has come particularly from those client populations likely to be defined as deviant. Consequently, they have experienced a greater social distance between them and the staff in these organizations. Hence clients are beginning to use more effectively self-activating properties in order to influence the organization to respond to their personal goals. The organizing of clients as pressure groups, and their demands to participate in organizational decision-making processes, are some manifestations of the changes in organization-client relations. Human service organizations that encounter such pressures find that existing mechanisms to elicit the compliance of clients are becoming ineffective. In fact, they are moved to develop compliance systems based on normative consensus and social bonds between staff and clients, and to reshape their goals to reflect the personal goals of clients.

These pressures introduce a great deal of instability and uncertainty into the organization. First, they undermine the authoritative and presumed expert position of the staff, consequently reducing their ability to function as change agents. Second, they increase the vulnerability of the organization to external influences and counter-pressure groups, thus resulting in the diversion of crucial resources from the service functions to management and semi-political functions.

It is at present difficult to assess the consequences of these processes. It is clear, however, that they will make human service organizations more responsive to the needs of clients; at the same time, there is the danger that change technologies will become "politicized" in the sense that their ideological components will increase rather than decrease.

The greater the reliance of the organization on interaction between staff and clients to achieve desired outcomes, the more problematical becomes the control and supervision of the staff. To ensure that the goals of the organization are being met and that staff-client relations are not abused, the organization must monitor the content of the interaction between staff members and clients. Yet the visibility of the interaction itself, let along its content, is very low. Attempts to increase the visibility of the interaction clearly reduce potential effectiveness, as well as to raise basic moral and legal questions. Human service organizations are often characterized as "front-line organizations," in the sense that much of the action that occurs between staff and clients is removed from the control and support systems of the organization, and the latter are highly dependent on the feedback from the staff at the "front" (Smith, 1965).

Thus we find that human service organizations, in contrast with other bureaucracies, encounter unique problems in monitoring the activities of their staff. A major source of strain in these organizations is the pressure by administrative personnel for greater monitoring as opposed to the counter-pressure of the staff for greater freedom and discretion which they perceive to be an essential prerequisite for forming effectve relations with clients.

To resolve the monitoring and control problems, human service organizations resort to several strategies. First, they attempt to employ professional staff members whose extensive training and socialization, and identification with professional norms, ensures that their interaction with clients will be guided by professional standards and structured solely for the attainment of the desired outcomes. In so doing, however, the organization must cope with a whole series of problems that arise from the employment of professionals in bureaucracies, an issue which we shall not deal with here. Second, they develop extensive recording and record-keeping systems, the function of which is to obtain as much information as possible from the staff and make them accountable for its reliability and validity. However such a record-keeping system renders the organization's management cumbersome, costly, and burdensome to its communications channels. It is not surprising, therefore, to find that human service organizations suffer from an information overload, yet the actual use of information may be unrelated to its quantity (Wheeler, 1969). Third, they develop patterns of close supervision so that the staff report at very frequent intervals to their supervisors. The cost to an organization utilizing such a procedure is that a significant portion of staff time is devoted to supervisory sessions which may lead to structural rigidity.

E. *Human service organizations increasingly rely on professional staff.*

The need of human service organizations to rely on professionals to implement their service goals emanates from two sources. First, the nature and complexity of the human problems these organizations attempt to respond to necessitates the application of a codified set of practice principles that are grounded in a scientific and abstract knowledge base. Second, the organizational mandate of service, that is, the enhancement of the clients' well-being, requires the employment of personnel who have a strong orientation and commitment to the ideal of service. It can be readily seen that these requirements are embodied in the two central qualities of the professions (Goode, 1969).

Nevertheless, human service organizations vary considerably in the number of professionals they employ, and the roles and authority positions these professionals occupy in the organization. At one extreme we find organizations such as the prison or public welfare department which are almost devoid of professionals, while at the other extreme we find the medical hospital and the psychiatric clinic which are totally controlled by professionals. Several interacting factors may account for the number and position of professionals in human service organizations. First, as the organization becomes more committed to service goals which necessitate intimate knowledge of the clients' private world, the greater its reliance on a professional cadre. Second, when organizational ideologies about the clients emphasize their individuality, variability, and instability, coupled with the belief that the clients have the potential to be changed, cured, or helped, the more likely are professionals to occupy a prominent position in the organization. Third, when the service technologies adopted by the organization require the application of a complex body of abstract and scientific knowledge, the greater the dependence of the organization on professionals. Finally, the organizational need for professional staff increases when it seeks to achieve changes in its clients by methods that have been defined by society to be within the exclusive domain of certain professions such as medicine and law.

The employment of professionals also serves a crucial latent function to many human service organizations, namely the enlistment of professional prestige and expertise to legitimize the organization and its operations (Vinter, 1963). The organization draws upon the societal legitimation accorded to the profession, the public acceptance of the profession's expertise, and its authority in making decisions about clients. The reliance on professional staff thus increases the autonomy of the organization by buffering and insulating it from various external pressures, while at the same time lending it the prestige of the professionals it employs. The rights that the organization claims to have to intervene in the lives of its clients may be based, to a large measure, on the license and monopoly given by society to its professional staff to do so.

The reliance on professionals to enhance the legitimation of the organization may, however, result in certain unanticipated consequences, the most important of which is excessive isolation from the public which the organization claims to serve. When the sentiments, needs, and problems of the public served by the organization are communicated to it mostly through the screening and interpretation of professionals committed to specific service ideologies, the organization's service goals may become incongruous with the needs of its public (Cloward and Epstein, 1965). Furthermore, the commitment of the organization to certain professional ideologies tends to exclude other alternative approaches to serve the clients unless they are compatible with the practices of the dominant professions in the organization (Vinter, 1963).

Finally, the employment of professionals by human service organizations to enhance their legitimation does not guarantee that professional norms and standards will in fact prevail in the organization. That is, the professionals may be coopted to accept patterns of service delivery that are contrary to professional norms. This is particularly so when the professionals do not participate in the organization's executive leadership or have limited contact and identification with their professional reference groups.

The employment of professionals in human service organizations raises a series of complex administrative and professional issues resulting from the inherent incompatibility between professional and bureaucratic principles. In essence the conflict evolves around the question of authority and autonomy. As Scott (1966, p. 270) points out, "the professional expects to be allowed maximum discretion in the selection of means for achieving desired results, being constrained in his operations only by internalized norms which indicate accepted procedures." The organization in contrast, expects its personnel to identify and maintain loyalty to its goals and hold in abeyance their personal judgment in favor of organizational rules and procedures in selecting appropriate means. In human service organizations the dilemma is heightened by the fact that the professional may face counter pressures from three subsystems—the client, the organization, and the profession—each of which has its distinct preference of goals and means (Billingsley, 1964). The resolution of the conflict between bureaucratic and professional principles will depend on the authority and control structure developed in the organization. Both Litwak (1961) and Goss (1961) suggest that when the organization can clearly separate administrative duties and professional tasks, and develop a dual authority and control system (bureaucratic for administrative duties and collegial for professional tasks), the conflicts between the two orientations can be resolved.

Nevertheless, the proposed organizational model assumes that the profession in question is highly developed and well established such as medicine and law. Yet, many human service organizations rely heavily on semi-professions such as social work, education, and nursing. The semi-professions are characterized by either lack of a systematic theoretical knowledge base; lack of monopoly over their field of practice; or fragmented professional associations (Toren, 1969). As a result, the semi-professional is likely to be under greater bureaucratic controls and to be more acquiescent to administrative authority than the full-fledged professional. The counter balance provided by professional ideals and competencies to the bureaucratic omnipotence over clients may therefore be lacking. Moreover, the aspirations of the semi-professionals to raise their occupational status may result in a phenomenon of "over professionalization," whereby the semi-professionls claim professional privileges while lacking the expertise that must precede them. One result of "over professionalization" is the preoccupation of the semi-professionals with their status in the organization which could lead to rigidity and maintenance of excessive social distance from their clients particularly those from lower social classes (Walsh and Elling, 1968). A second consequence may be seen in the attempt to delegate "dirty work," (i.e., daily transactions with clients) to subordinates and other low status personnel.

Finally, "over professionalization" has also contributed to the increasing shortage of manpower in human service organizations, particularly since professional education is of long duration.

A significant unanticipated consequence of the increased professionalization of human service organizations has been the alienation of clients, particularly the impoverished and the lower classes from the services provided by these organizations. The professionalized human service technologies have produced selective criteria that result in preference of middle class and well-educated clients. Moreover, the sense of alienation has been reinforced by those aspiring professions which could not demonstrate convincingly their expertise such as social work and education.

The movement to employ nonprofessionals by human service organizations is partly an effort to increase the responsiveness of these organizations to lower class and impoverished clients. The employment of indigenous nonprofessional staff, in particular, has been advocated as a linking mechanism between the organization and its alienated and unserved clients.

The utilization of indigenous workers raises many complex issues which cannot be dealt with in this context. It should be noted, however, that this movement has introduced new structural strains in human service organizations in terms of the roles the indigenous worker will assume, his relations with the professional staff, and his place in the organizational authority structure (Katan, 1973).

F. *Human service organizations lack reliable and valid measures of effectiveness.*

A key derivative of the technological problems encountered by human service organizations is their difficulty in developing reliable and valid measures of effectiveness (Vinter, 1963). As indicated earlier, these difficulties arise from two sources: (a) lack of clear and operative definitions of the desired outcomes and (b) inadequate knowledge about cause-effect relations. The first constraint results in the problem of defining what ought to be the criteria for effectiveness. The second constraint limits the ability of the organization to evaluate and measure the consequences of the actions it takes in altering the attributes, behavior, or position of its clients. In addition, one must also consider the problems raised by the nature of the raw material itself. Being such a complex and variable entity, the organization can rarely control enough attributes of the clients in order to measure the specific consequences of its intervention procedures. Furthermore, the consequences of the organization's change efforts can be adequately assessed, by and large, only after the clients have exited. Yet at that point the ability of the organization to measure its outcomes is diminished considerably, while the costs of doing so increase.

Consequently, human service organizations tend to develop extrinsic rather than intrinsic measures of effectiveness (Thompson, 1967, pp. 83–98). Such measures can embrace several types: (a) measures of means rather than ends, such as number of clients processed per time unit, number of manpower hours invested in the clients; (b) measures of efficiency rather than effectiveness, such as costs per client served, speed of service; (c) measures based on the subjective evaluation by staff and testimonies of clients; and (d) measures that are indirectly related to the product goals of the organization. In the case of a psychiatric hospital, for example, it could be the amount of research done, while in the public school it could be the number of students winning national scholarship contests.

The inherent weakness in the use of extrinsic measures is that they cannot provide unambiguous and specific answers to the question of organizational effectiveness. Also, such measures can be readily challenged. As a result, the organizational claims for competence tend to be precarious; the lack of valid and reliable measures of effectiveness could potentially undermine legitimacy, particularly as the public pressures for accountability increase. Concomitantly, the reliance on extrinsic measures increases the probability of goal displacement, as the organization gears its activities so that it can score well on these measures.

Looking back over the series of issues and problems that human service organizations encounter as a type of bureaucracy, we can recast them as structural barriers to the pursuit of norms of rationality. It is not surprising, therefore, that human service organizations have benefitted only marginally from the "new science of management" and the development of sophisticated management tools such as operations research, and management information systems. These new management techniques are based on assumptions which often cannot be met in human service organizations. Recent efforts to apply such tools to human service organizations—hospitals, police departments, and schools—point to the immense organizational complexities and uncertainties to which they must address themselves. The success of these tools has been limited to the more routine and peripheral aspects of the organization. However, full cognizance and understanding of the unique parameters that shape the service delivery system of human service organizations may enable the development of a "new science of human service management" that is applicable to these organizations.

References

Billingsley, A. 1964. "Bureaucratic and Professional Orientation Patterns in Social Casework." *Social Service Review* 38 (December): 400–407.

Carlson, R. O. 1964. "Environmental Constraints and Organizational Consequences: The Public School and its Clients." Pp. 262–76 in *Behavioral Science and Educational Administration*. Chicago: National Society for the Study of Education.

Cloward, R. A., and Epstein, I. 1965. "Private Social Welfare's Disengagement from the Poor: The Case of Family Adjustment Agencies." Pp. 623–43 in M. Zald (ed.), *Social Welfare Institutions: A Sociological Reader*. New York: Wiley.

Etzioni, A. 1961. *A Comparative Analysis of Complex Organizations*. Glencoe, Ill.: Free Press.

Goffman, E. 1961. *Asylums: Essays on the Social Situation of Mental Patients and Other Inmates*. New York: Doubleday.

Goode, W. J. 1969. "The Theoretical Limits of Professionalization." Pp. 266–313 in A. Etzioni (ed.), *The Semi Professions and Their Organization*. New York: The Free Press.

Goss, M. E. 1961. "Influence and Authority among Physicians in an Out Patient Clinic." *American Sociological Review* 26 (February): 39–50.

Hasenfeld, Y. 1972. "People Processing Organizations: An Exchange Approach." *American Sociological Review* 37 (June): 256–63.

Katan, Y. 1973. "The Utilization of Indigenous Workers in Human Service Organizations." in this volume.

Lefton, M., and Rosengren, W. R. 1966. "Organizations and Clients: Lateral and Longitudinal Dimensions." *American Sociological Review* 31 (December): 802–10.

Litwak, E. 1961. "Models of Bureaucracy That Permit Conflict." *American Journal of Sociology* 67 (September): 173–83.

Perrow, C. 1965. "Hospitals: Technology, Structure, and Goals." Pp. 910–71 in J. March (ed.), *Handbook of Organizations*. Chicago: Rand McNally.

————. 1967. "A Framework for the Comparative Analysis of Organizations." *American Sociological Review* 32 (April): 194–208.

Scheff, T. J. 1968. *Being Mentally Ill.* Chicago: Aldine.

Scott, W. R. 1966. "Professional in Bureaucracies-Areas of Conflict." Pp. 265–74 in H. M. Vollmer and D. L. Mills (eds.), *Professionalization.* Englewood Cliffs, N.J.: Prentice-Hall.

Smith, D. 1965. "Front Line Organizations of the State Mental Hospital." *Administrative Science Quarterly* 10 (December): 381–99.

Strauss, A. et al. 1964. *Psychiatric Ideologies and Institutions.* New York: Free Press.

Thompson, J. D. 1967. *Organizations in Action.* New York: McGraw-Hill.

Toren, N. 1969. "Semi Professionalism and Social Work: A Theoretical Perspective." Pp. 141–95 in A. Etzioni (ed.), *The Semi Profession and Their Organization.* New York: Free Press.

Vinter, R. D. 1963. "Analysis of Treatment Organizations." *Social Work* 8 (July): 3–15.

Vinter, R. D., and Sarri, R. C. 1966. "The Juvenile Court: Organization and Decision Making." Pp. 173–320 in *Juvenile Court Hearing Officers Training Manual,* Vol. II. Ann Arbor: The University of Michigan, Institute of Continuing Legal Education.

Walsh, J. L., and Elling, R. H. 1968. "Professionalization and the Poor-Structural Effects and Professional Behavior." *Journal of Health and Social Behavior* 9 (March): 16–28.

Warner, K. W. and Havens, A. E. 1968. "Goal Displacement and Intangibility of Organizational Goals." *Administrative Science Quarterly* 12 (March): 539–55.

Wheeler, S. 1966. "The Structure of Formally Organized Socialization Settings." Pp. 51–116 in O. G. Brim and S. Wheeler (eds.), *Socialization after Childhood.* New York: Wiley.

————. 1969. *On Record: Files and Dossiers in American Life.* New York: Russell Sage Foundation.

Chapter I

Theoretical Orientations to Human Service Organizations

Human service organizations have reached a high level of bureau-cratization and differentiation from other types of organizations and have come to play a vital role in modern society. Although the analysis of these organizations is a recent phenomenon, it follows a long tradition of theoretical and empirical studies on governmental, political, and in-dustrial organizations, and has its intellectual antecedents in both classical and contemporary perspectives on organizations.

Two major trends can be identified in the development of orga-nizational theory. The first is concerned with the impact of organizations on people mainly as recipients of goods and services. The second focuses on the roles of people as participants or members in organiza-tions. Neither of these approaches considers both dimensions. The theories of human service organizations are compelled to take into ac-count both the impact of organizations on people as recipients of serv-ices, and people as members of organizations. This is particularly the case since human service organizations are distinguished by two basic attributes: (1) the purveyors and recipients of services are both mem-bers of the same organization and (2) the provision of organizational services requires the interaction between the purveyors and the recipi-ents of services.

The first tradition, the classical approach, concerns itself with the phenomenon of bureaucracy in industrial societies and its relationship to problems of democracy and individual freedom. The major theorists in this tradition are Marx, Weber, and Michels.

In Marxist critique of industrial society the concept of bureauc-racy is conceived as the state itself through which the dominant social class exercises its power and domination over other social classes. There-fore, bureaucracy for Marx is only one instance of the general process of alienation. Thus, with the abolition of social classes in modern industrial societies, bureaucracy as the instrument of the capitalist class will wither away and die (Mouzelis, 1968, pp. 8–15).

Unlike Marx, Max Weber was not only concerned with bureaucracy as governmental or public administration, but with the increasing bureaucratization of all social institutions in modern industrial societies. It is in the latter context that Weber, in contrast to Marx, confronts the problems of alienation and freedom. No longer is class domination considered the central problem of industrial society, but bureaucratic domination. While Weber was concerned about the inevitability of bureaucratization in all social institutions, he firmly held the view that monocratic bureaucracy was the most efficient, precise, and rational means of organization. Hence, in Weberian bureaucracy the organizational dimension comes into sharp focus (Gerth and Mills, 1958, pp. 46–50).

Bureaucracy for Weber is a specific type of legal-rational authority as distinguished from organizations of people bound together through charismatic or traditional authority. His ideal type of bureaucracy was the large-scale organization with the following dimensions: a high degree of specialization, hierarchical authority structure, impersonal relationships between organizational members, appointment of officials on the basis of merit and technical knowledge, a priori specification of job authority, separation of policy and administrative decisions, and rules to govern relations not specified by the above dimensions (Weber, 1947, pp. 329–34).

Robert Michels (1949) was concerned explicitly with the omnipotence of organizations and their founders, and the ways in which organizational elites divorce themselves from the people they were organized to serve. In his well-known "Iron Law of Oligarchy" ("iron because it is presumably without exceptions, and oligarchy because the rule of a few is imposed," Etzioni, 1964, p. 11), Michels maintained that a few leaders will inevitably dominate the organization and put their interests in preserving the organization and their leadership positions above the interests of the members. Thus, Michels concluded from his studies of European Socialist parties and labor unions that all large-scale organizations tend to displace their official goals and develop bureaucratic structures which hinder the development of internal democracy.

In the post-Weberian development of organizational analysis, an organization came to be viewed as an adaptive organic whole rather than solely a rational-legal system. Gouldner (1959, pp. 405–6) has called this the natural-system model of organizational analysis. From this perspective the organization is not only conceived as a purposively designed instrument to achieve specific goals, but a cooperative system which seeks to survive and maintain its own equilibrium. Further, this quest for survival, according to this model, may continue even after the attainment of organizational goals (Selznick, 1948; Etzioni, 1964).

The social scientists who conceptualized organizations as adaptive social structures were helped in their study of organizations by the "structural-functional" perspective (Gouldner, 1954; Bendix, 1956; Blau, 1956 and 1963; Lipset, Trow, and Coleman, 1956; Selznick, 1966; Merton, 1968; Parsons, 1956). Although using Weber (and to some degree Marx) as their principal foundation, as Etzioni (1964) points out, the structuralist approach had its major dialogue with the human relations approach. In contrast to the human relations approach (as we shall see later in our discussion of the human relations approach) the structuralists enlarged the study of organizational analysis to include the consequences of external pressures on the organization, the conflict between organizational needs and personal needs, informal and formal relations, and the effects of the environment on the organization (Etzioni, 1964, p. 41). Their empirical studies indicate that the response of the organization to these pressures may result in unanticipated consequences, goal displacement and patterns of organizational structure which significantly deviate from monocratic Weberian bureaucracy.

In shifting the unit of analysis from the individual and the group to the structure of the organization as a whole, the structuralists also expanded the scope of organizational analysis to include not only economic and industrial organizations, but also prisons, schools, social welfare agencies, and hospitals.

In the second tradition, scientific management, the concern shifted from ways in which the organization could serve people to ways people could serve the organization. Taylor, the father of scientific management, believed that for every organizational task in industry there is one best way of performance or way of doing a job which could be scientifically determined (Taylor, 1911; Copley, 1923). Once these laws were identified a careful delineation of requirements for each worker's job could be made, thus ensuring effectiveness and the maximization of productivity as defined by management.

Taylor's conception of organization encouraged and required careful selection and matching of worker with tasks, close supervision and control of the worker, and the application of economic incentives to reinforce or elicit worker initiative and cooperation. His theory of individual motivation regarding the worker's desire to obtain the highest possible wages and management's desire for profit making were considered to provide a mutuality of interest between worker and management. Since greater productivity created opportunities for the worker to increase his earnings, management likewise was able to enhance his profits. Scientific management assumed that if you controlled people you could likewise control their productivity. That is, the worker was viewed as an instrument of production that could be manipulated as a nonsocial object.

The human relations theorists (Mouzelis, 1968, pp. 97–119 and Whyte, 1969, pp. 7–10) realized that the problem was far more complex, and that management must address itself to styles of supervisors and leadership, workers' sentiments, motivations, morale, and social relations as they affect work performance. The human relations approach was, therefore, social psychological as expressed in its emphases on leadership styles, group participation in decision making, job satisfaction, and morale in industrial organizations (Mayo, 1945; Roethlisberger and Dickson, 1939; Lewin, 1952). We should point out, however, that contemporary social scientists writing in the tradition of the human relations approach abandoned its earlier narrow focus and gave attention to problems of intergroup relations, interest groups, organizational structure, and authority (Mouzelis, 1968, pp. 108–12).

Like Taylor and the ideas expressed in the scientific management approach, earlier writings in the human relations approach to organizational theory also asserted that there was one best way to organize work relations in order to increase productivity. Essentially, it required a form of organization that permitted the worker's autonomy; that provided for participatory democracy in decision making related to the worker's tasks; and in general, cognizance of related aspects of the informal dimensions of the organization. Once these conditions were established, the likelihood of greater individual motivation and task involvement were believed to have been maximized.

In reaction to the neglect of rational aspects of organizational behavior in the human relations approach, and the scientific management theorists' extreme emphasis on rational behavior in organizations, decision-making theorists (Simon, 1957; March and Simon, 1958) made at least two major contributions to organizational analysis. First, they attempted to integrate the human relations and scientific management's polar conceptualizations of affective and rational aspects of organizational behavior. Second, they focused their analysis on problem-solving and decision-making activities in organizations. The individual as a participant in the organization remained the unit of analysis, but the emphasis shifted to his role as a decision maker. Decision making is analyzed as an outcome of the interaction of rational as well as affective processes. This approach to organizational theory has led to an emphasis on information processing systems, communications, problem-solving and decision-making processes in organizations.

The human relations perspective of organizational analysis developed a set of normative prescriptions designed to resolve the inevitable problems between the individual and the organization (Likert, 1962). In so doing, the early human relations theorists attempted to develop an ideal model of organization in which there is "a perfect balance between the organization's goals and the workers' needs" (Etzioni, 1964, p. 40).

The structuralist in rejecting a normative approach to the study of organizations made explicit the inevitable strains and conflicts in organizations. Moreover, recent developments in organizational theory have begun to make explicit the political character of organizations. Thus, emphasis is given to the problems of power and conflict as these social processes relate to the distribution of and control over resources, people, decision and policy making, and the development of organizational goals (Mouzelis, 1968).

In this brief overview of the two major traditions of organizational analysis (classical and scientific management) and their past traditions, we have attempted to show how the object of analysis shifted from the impact of bureaucracy on people to the role of people in bureaucracy. With the contemporary convergence of these various approaches to organizational theory, the organization itself is given primacy as the object of analysis in which these two concerns are taken into account. This is particularly the case with the increasing interests in the study of human service organizations.

The unique position and role which the clients occupy in human service organizations has set forward a new dimension to organizational analysis. This perspective takes into account the fact that not only are those who have primary responsibility for the delivery of services members of the organization, but those who consume the services occupy temporary membership in the organization. Although there are qualitative differences between staff and client membership statuses in human service organizations, the student, the patient, the client, and the inmate are all recipients of services as well as temporary members of the organization providing the service. Because of this unique feature of human service organizations, attention is focused on the organization-client relationship and many of its resultant strains and tensions, particularly those embodied in the differential career patterns, commitments and motivations of clients, and problems of scope of membership and intensity of involvement (Rosengren and Lefton, 1970).

The four theoretical articles presented in this chapter are mainly in the tradition of the synthesis that has taken place in organizational analysis and the perspectives described above. They each deal with a particular type of human service organization and examine some of the unique problems confronting these organizations.

Vinter focuses his analysis on the conceptualization of health and welfare organizations which he calls treatment agencies as distinguished from socialization agencies. They differ in three substantive ways: (1) the presumed nature of their clienteles; (2) the changes they seek in their clienteles; and (3) the contrasting valuation accorded each type of organization by the larger society. Vinter points out that these two types of organizations belong to a larger class of organizations referred to as people-changing organizations and serve the major functions of socialization and social control. They differ from other types of organizations by their substantive goals and the nature of the changes they seek to affect in their clientele as well as the primacy given to this change effort as an organizational goal. Thus Vinter stresses the unique goal orientation of people-changing organizations and the problems that such goals create for the organization as the critical distinctive characteristic of people-changing organizations as contrasted with other types of organizations.

Finally, his cogent discussion of the unique problems and dilemmas that confront treatment organizations, namely, their use of human relations technologies, reliance on professionals, consequences for clients, and evaluation of performance, further assist an understanding of these organizations.

Bidwell provides a conceptual overview of the organizational character of public elementary and secondary schools. He identifies several unique characteristics of these schools as organizations and some of their special problems. From his review of empirical literature on public schools, Bidwell considers the following characteristics as significant in the analysis of school systems as organizations: (1) the recruitment nature of the student-client role; (2) the professionalization of school staff; (3) the pressures and constraints in dealing with variability in student abilities and accomplishments; (4) the requirements for rationalization of procedures in dealing with students; and (5) the controlling powers of external groups such as local constituencies and governmental agencies.

Hasenfeld's selection makes explicit the distinction between people-changing and people-processing organizations. People-processing organizations, by his definition, are those organizations designed to achieve changes in their clients by conferring a public status upon them and relocating them in a new set of social circumstances. He distinguishes such organizations from people-changing organizations in four ways: (1) by their type of product (clientele); (2) technology; (3) the locus of technology; and (4) the relative duration of staff-client encounters.

He presents a framework for analyzing the ways in which the

external environment influences the client classification and disposition functions of people-processing organizations. Using an exchange or transactional perspective to organizational analysis, he explores and identifies the various patterns in which people-processing organizations relate to their environments; the conditions under which the organizations' dependence upon its market units will tend to increase or decrease; and traces the significance of the organizations' power-dependence relationship with the environment to people-processing organizations' classification-disposition functions.

Parsons provides a theoretical perspective on the mental hospital as a type of people-changing organization. He begins his analysis by giving primacy to the goal of the mental hospital which is "to cope with the consequences for the individual patient and for patients as a social group, of a condition of mental illness." Using the goal of the mental hospital as a reference point, he describes how the nature of the clientele served creates certain social responsibilities for the hospital. These social responsibilities then become components of the overall goal. These components are classified under four headings: (1) custody; (2) protection; (3) socialization; and (4) therapy. He uses this classification to analyze the different functions of the hospital as an organization and to distinguish it from other types of organizations.

Following his discussion of the goals of the hospital and the value system in which it operates, Parsons identifies four functions of the hospital. These functions are: (1) the legitimation of the operation of the hospital in the community; (2) the processes involved in dealing with the recipients of the hospital's services; (3) the processes of acquiring facilities necessary for carrying out its functions; and (4) the ways in which the hospital is integrated into the community in which it operates. Within the context of these four functions, he systematically points out the internal and external features and problems unique to the mental hospital as an organization.

References

Bendix, R. 1956. *Work and Authority in Industry.* New York: John Wiley and Sons.

Blau, P. M. 1956. *Bureaucracy in Modern Society.* New York: Random House.

————. 1963. *The Dynamics of Bureaucracy.* Chicago: The University of Chicago Press.

Copley, F. B. 1923. *Frederick W. Taylor, Father of Scientific Management.* New York: Harper and Brothers.

Etzioni, A. 1964. *Modern Organizations.* Englewood Cliffs, N.J.: Prentice-Hall, Inc.

Gerth, H. H., and Mills, C. W. (eds. and trans.) 1958. *From Max Weber: Essays in Sociology.* New York: Oxford University Press .

Gouldner, A. W. 1954. *Patterns of Industrial Bureaucracy.* New York: The Free Press.

————. 1959. "Organizational analysis," in Robert K. Merton, Leonard Broom, Leonard S. Cottrell, Jr. (eds.) *Sociology Today: Problems and Prospects.* New York: Basic Books, Inc.

Lewin, K. 1952. "Group decision and social change," in G. E. Swanson, T. M. Newcomb, and E. L. Hartley (eds.) *Readings in Social Psychology.* New York: Holt, Rinehart and Winston, Inc.

Likert, R. 1962. *New Patterns of Management.* New York: McGraw-Hill.

Lipset, S. M., Trow, M. A., and Coleman, J. S. 1956. *Union Democracy.* Glencoe, Ill.: The Free Press.

March, James G., and Herbert A. Simon. 1958. *Organizations.* New York: Wiley and Sons.

Marx, K. 1909. *Capital: A Critique of Political Economy.* Chicago: Charles H. Kerr.

Mayo, E. 1945. *The Social Problems of an Industrial Civilization.* Boston: Graduate School of Business Administration, Division of Research.

Merton, R. K. 1968. *Social Theory and Social Structure.* New York: The Free Press.

Michels, R. 1949. *Political Parties.* Glencoe, Ill.: The Free Press.

Mouzelis, N. P. 1968. *Organization and Bureaucracy: An Analysis of Modern Theories.* Chicago: Aldine Publishing Co.

Parsons, T. 1956. "Suggestions for a sociological approach to theory of organizations," *Administrative Science Quarterly* 1:63–85.

————. 1960. *Structure and Process in Modern Societies.* Glencoe, Ill.: The Free Press.

Roethlisberger, F. J., and Dickson, W. J. 1939. *Management and the Worker.* Cambridge, Mass.: Harvard University Press.

Rosengren, W. R., and Lefton, M. (eds.). 1970. *Organizations and Clients: Essays in the Sociology of Service.* Columbus, Ohio: Charles E. Merrill Publishing Co.

Selznick, P. 1966. *T. V. A. and the Grass Roots.* New York: Harper and Row Publishers.

————. 1948. "Foundations of the theory of organization," *American Sociological Review* 13:25–35.

Simon, Herbert A. 1957. Administrative Behavior. 2nd ed. New York: Macmillan.

Stammer, O. (ed.). 1971. *Max Weber and Sociology Today.* Translated by Kathleen Morris. New York: Harper and Row Publishers.

Street, D., Vinter, R. D., and Perrow, C. 1966. *Organization For Treatment: Comparative Study of Institutions for Delinquents.* New York: The Free Press.

Taylor, F. W. 1911. *Scientific Management.* New York: Harper and Row Publishers.

Weber, M. 1947. *The Theory of Social and Economic Organizations.* Translated by Kathleen Morris. New York: Harper and Row Publishers.

Whyte, W. F. 1969. *Organizational Behavior: Theory and Application.* Homewood, Ill.: Richard D. Irwin, Inc. and the Dorsey Press.

Analysis of Treatment Organizations

Robert D. Vinter

Sociological study of the formal organization has successively included such diverse types as the government bureau, business corporation, law firm, and military organization. Extension of organizational analysis into the health and welfare field has been extremely limited; it has just begun with respect to the mental hospital and the prison. Within this framework there are as yet no adequate studies of the public welfare agency, child guidance clinic, youth-serving recreation agency, probation office, juvenile court, or family service or adoption agency. This mode of analysis proceeds by comparing different types of organizations to gain better understanding of each, and then examines the interrelations among their major operational features. Gradually the knowledge thus available will permit deliberate redesign of organizational conditions to achieve more effective services. This preliminary statement is limited to direct-service health and welfare organizations, which are given the general term "treatment" agencies.

We will begin with consideration of the larger category of "people-changing" organizations and the two major types that compose this category: socialization and treatment agencies. We will then examine the distinctive features of treatment organizations. Finally, we will address certain problems that confront treatment and other complex organizations, namely, use of human relations technologies, reliance on professionals, consequences for clients, and evaluation of performance.

People-Changing Organizations

Treatment agencies are part of a larger class of organizations responsible for changing people. The university and military academy, guidance clinic and mental hospital, probation office and correctional institution are all examples of organizations in this general class. Viewed broadly, the major functions of people-changing organizations are socialization and social control. In each instance a specific population is dealt with in ways calculated to insure the preservation of dominant values and patterns.

Organizations in this general class can be distinguished from all others on the basis of their substantive goals. To some extent every or-

Reprinted from *Social Work* 8 (July, 1963):3–15.

ganization must bring about certain changes in those who participate in it: newcomers must be socialized into appropriate behavior patterns, proper loyalties and attitudes must be induced, persons must be managed, their activities co-ordinated, and so on. These changes are, however, essentially instrumental and incidental to the main purposes of most organizations; they are necessary but do not in and of themselves constitute goal achievement. For schools, mental hospitals, prisons, and the like, the major goal *is* that of changing persons in ways distinctive to each, and the extent to which the organization achieves such change is a primary criterion of its effectiveness.

The nature of the change sought, as well as its primacy as a goal, also differentiates these from other organizations. A scope and permanence of change is customarily attempted that pervades the behavior of persons and endures beyond the period of their affiliation with the organization. People-changing organizations are usually concerned with effecting new and diffuse modes of behavior, new self-images or personalities—in sum, with altered persons in changed statuses. Finally, the behavioral modes or altered personalities sought by people-changing organizations are invested with a moral quality that does not infuse the limited modifications sought by other organizations. Thus, the proper education of youth is imbued with quasi-sacred meanings, while the rehabilitation of criminals or the mentally ill touches on basic societal values.

Question can be raised about whether certain organizations included in this analysis, particularly the prison or custodial mental hospital, are concerned with people-changing. Substantive goals serve as the basis of our classification, not whether organizational strategies are judged as likely to achieve lasting change or the rates of change are actually achieved. The latter are questions of effectiveness and should be addressed in empirical terms. The author asserts that an organization has people-changing as a goal under one or more of these conditions: (1) when such a mandate is specified by its goal-setting agents, (2) when changing clientele is professed as a goal in the organization's formal statement of purpose, (3) when a significant proportion of organizational resources is allocated to the tasks of changing its clientele or to the personnel assigned to such tasks. More often than not all these conditions, in various balances, are met by specific treatment organizations.

The goal of changing clientele need not be the agency's only (or even its dominant) goal, since complex organizations typically possess a hierarchy of goals whose priorities change over a period of time. Most adult prisons adhere to deterrence as a primary goal (i.e., confinement and punishment of inmates in order to forestall future offenses by these or other persons), yet there is ample evidence that they are increasingly committed to the goal of rehabilitation. Insofar as custody and confinement are aimed at preventing future commission of offenses by felons, the prison is engaged in the task of changing people. The prison's coercive and archaic practices of inducing change are not assumed, on an a priori basis, to vitiate the goal itself. Distinctions must be made, therefore, not only between goals and effectiveness but also between ends and means. This mode of analysis has the benefit of directing attention to the *consequences for the organization* of treatment as a goal: publics pose different expectations of achievement, new élites contend for dominance, and ideologies and strategies must be redefined. Failure to accomplish the goal, or even persistent reluctance to implement its imperatives, subjects the organization to new strains.[1]

Socialization and Treatment Organizations

The two major types of people-changing organizations, socialization and treatment agencies, can be differentiated in at least three ways: the presumed nature of their clienteles, the changes they seek, and the contrasting valuation accorded each by the larger society. Socialization organizations, primarily schools and youth-serving agencies, seek to prepare individuals for adequate performance of their social roles. The persons worked with are perceived as moving along normal developmental gradients. It is generally assumed that these persons are motivated to change and that the essential task is to provide appropriate learning opportunities. Other conditions in most of their life situations are generally presumed to be benign and unlikely to impede change.[2]

Treatment organizations, in contrast, seek to resolve problems of deviance; they serve persons who have demonstrated that they are *not* moving along normal gradients and, for one reason or another, are not adequately performing conventional social roles. Delinquents and criminals, emotionally disturbed persons, and the chronically unemployed are regarded as possessing defective attributes or as improperly motivated and oriented. Their behavior is disapproved; conditions in their past or present life situations are believed to be adverse and likely to impede change efforts.

These distinctions, while stated in very broad terms, characterize dominant views shared among the general public about the clientele and tasks of these two types of organization and underlie differences in the valuation and resources each receives. Schools enjoy legitimation and resources in far greater measure than those awarded to prisons, mental hospitals, and the like. This seems due in part to the persistence of adverse public sentiment regarding various forms of deviance. Concern for public safety, revulsion with many types of misconduct, and fear of the bizarre are responses often directed at the behaviors of treatment organization clientele, especially criminals and the mentally ill. In former eras such problems were dealt with by scourging, harsh repression, exile, or even death. Persons who persisted in deviant behavior were excluded from the community, which then "closed ranks" against them.[3]

The rise in humanitarianism has muted these more extreme attitudes of past eras. Harsh and repressive measures for coping with deviant behavior are less often utilized, while insistence on protection of the community has been balanced by a new optimism about the potentials of rehabilitation. These trends have significantly altered the societal mandates given treatment agencies, although they still enjoy a far less favorable status than do socialization organizations.

Public attitudes toward specific deviancy patterns are, of course, highly differentiated. The degree of jeopardy for others, the age and sex of the deviant, and the normative areas in which behavior violates expectations are among the conditions that shape public response to the deviancy. In an important sense, however, the many forms of deviance are perceived as alike. In this society, largely oriented toward individual achievement, fulfillment of conventional roles tends to be regarded as the responsibility of the individual. Conformity and deviance, like success and failure, are seen as matters of personal volition and as somehow inhering in the character and willfulness of each individual.

Negative attitudes toward the behavior to be changed are easily expanded to include the organization responsible for the changing. Rehabilitation goals are consequently more precarious than educational goals, and the treatment organization must expend greater energy in justifying its programs and gaining support for its purposes. Persisting belief that the deviant *intentionally* violates expectations produces a continuous strain toward punitive and exclusionary measures and a reluctance to allocate generous resources in support of the treatment organization. Differences in resource allocation between socialization and treatment agencies also derive from more rational considerations about gains and losses for the community: the conditions of survival may be seen as set more by the effectiveness of education than of treatment.

These elements in belief and valuation serve to define the essential nature of the client populations and the mandates for change. They provide not only the cultural context but also the restraints and imperatives that shape organizational effort. And finally, these perspectives are deeply intertwined in the technologies utilized by treatment organizations.

Change-Oriented Technologies

The means for change utilized among organizations concerned with deviance range all the way from coercive repression to manipulative persuasion. Organizations at both these extremes use human relations technologies and emphasize that the basic task of people-changing is accomplished through *deliberate structuring of staff-client relations.* The operational strategies of each, however, are based on quite different assumptions about the causes and cures of deviance, how much of what kind of change is possible, and how to achieve this change. The range of change-oriented strategies can be illustrated by comparing that used by the mental health clinic with that of the prison.

The technology of the clinic focuses on *manipulation of affect and cognition through persuasive communication.* Change objectives are ambitiously defined and refer primarily to intrapersonal modifications. Emphasis is placed on development of intimate interpersonal relations, on inducements, volition, and high communication between staff and clients. Clients are perceived essentially as wanting to change, or only persons sufficiently motivated are selected for service. Despite the clinic's use of quasi-standardized diagnostic categories, its clients are seen as more different than alike, requiring careful assessment and individualized response to their unique attributes. The major personnel tasks involve ability to manage affect, to respond unconventionally in "charged" situations, and to maintain warm and trustful but impersonal relations. These nonroutinized tasks constitute an esoteric and complex technology, and the necessary staff competencies must be secured through specialized training.

The prison, at the other extreme, focuses on *coercion and the application of negative sanctions.* Change objectives are minimally defined; they emphasize secure containment and limited accommodations to the official system rather than intrapersonal reorientation. Relations between staff and clients (in this case inmates) are distant and formal, based on the principle of domination and submission. Since clients are perceived as more alike than different, they can be handled by use of standardized procedures and in large groups. Clients are typically seen as opposed to change and as united in solidary opposition to official purposes. Here, too, affect is a problem, but it is dealt with by means of constant supervision, forced deference, and a protective architecture. Personnel are expected to follow the rules and routines, to manage men without increasing their opposition, and to maintain social distance from the clients. Such basic capabilities can be found on the open labor market, and skill can be gained through experience.

Some of the beliefs underlying these contrasting strategies are traditional and include major elements of folklore; others are derived from newer behavioral theories and professional philosophies. Although more crystallized or sophisticated, these views are directly analogous to those cited as shared among the general public. Both public and professional belief systems tend to emphasize that *individual* attributes are at issue in deviancy patterns. Only recently and in small measure have these beliefs about the characterological bases of derivancy been infused by understanding of the situational and social forces that induce nonconformity. The target unit among most treatment organizations continues, therefore, to be the individual person, usually abstracted and sometimes removed from his local environment, rather than the immediate social conditions that may have generated or shaped his performance problems.

Treatment technologies can be considered in large part as action correlates of these prevailing belief systems. Thus, the classification and diagnostic systems utilized in treatment agencies have their origins in such beliefs and, in turn, they categorize clients for organizational effort.[4] As indicated, all treatment organization technologies assert the crucial importance of staff-client relations in achieving change. There are three major dimensions along which these relations vary, permitting notation of significant differences among agencies.

How Treatment Organizations Vary

1. *Standardization of procedures.* Every treatment organization makes some differentiation among its clientele and adapts activity accordingly. These distinctions may be relatively crude and result merely in assigning persons to categories that are then handled uniformly and *en masse.* Segregation of prisoners among types of security units and separation of "front" and "back" ward programs are examples, respectively, among prisons and mental hospitals. At this extreme clients are subjected to the same general regimes and are expected to accommodate themselves appropriately. At the other extreme the organization may design its approaches with regard to the unique characteristics and "needs" posed by each client. Staff are then required to discriminate in their perceptions and actions, to encourage differentiated client behavior, and to respond accordingly.

Relative emphasis on client categorization rather than individualization—on universalistic rather than particularistic orientations—can be seen as conditioned by the balance of accommodations the organization is willing to make for, rather than demand from, the clientele. This balance, in turn, is often viewed as a consequence of organizational size and the pressure of managerial requirements, especially within residential institutions. The necessity of caring for and co-ordinating the activities of a large number of people on a twenty-four-hour basis does create pressures for routinization. Findings from a comparative study of juvenile institutions make clear, however, that the use of standardized group management procedures is not determined simply by size, but by choice among alternative technologies.[5] When clients are viewed as more alike than different they can conveniently be handled routinely and in the aggregate.[6]

2. *Balance of gratifications and deprivations.* In some organizations the stress on deprivations is such that the client has little to gain but much to lose. Pessimism about the degree of change that is feasible and belief that client motives are antagonistic support use of repressive means. In other organizations the stress on gratifications is such that the client has much to gain and little to lose. Material and social inducements are offered for compliance with the official system and willing participation in the processes of change. Rewards and inducements are more likely to be utilized when the client's motives are regarded as positive or when he can terminate affiliation with the agency of his own volition. The problem of developing and sustaining client commitment and compliance will be discussed later.

3. *Complexity of change techniques.* Treatment organizations vary in the range and complexity of techniques utilized to cause change among clients. Some present only a limited range of approaches, while others use a wide repertoire of techniques. Limited approaches are more likely to be utilized when the client personality is conceived in essentially simplistic terms or the deviance is not regarded as severe. Use of multiple measures and esoteric techniques serves to increase, respectively, the organization's co-ordination requirements and its dependence on specialized personnel.

The author's thesis is that treatment organizations may be differentiated with respect to these important technological dimensions: implications of each for staffing patterns as well as for clients have been hinted at. Before proceeding with consideration of these organizations' reliance on professionals, the indeterminancy of treatment technologies must be noted. The final section of this statement will deal with this problem; here it need only be observed that neither agencies nor professionals concerned with deviance have succeeded in creating technologies that achieve high levels of demonstrable effectiveness. This limitation has contributed to the precariousness of treatment organizations and has heightened their dependence on professional cadres.

Reliance on Professional Personnel

The rise of treatment agencies has been accompanied by the emergence of service professions concerned with the same problems of deviance and dependence. Treatment organizations increasingly rely on these professions to compose their élite cadres and to implement their goals. Social work, psychiatry, and clinical psychology have been the most numerous professions among organizational personnel, with psychiatric nursing, teaching, and a variety of "counseling" or "therapy" specialties also found in some contexts.

The most obvious reason for dependence on professionals is that they possess the technical competencies necessary for guiding interpersonal relations. Their expertise is directly relevant to the task of people-changing through staff-client transactions. Treatment organizations have also gained a relatively stable labor market by reliance on the professions.[7] The precarious goals and values of treatment organizations are defended by professional groups and additional legitimation is gained as the more or less prestigious professions are able to mediate directly with various public sectors in commanding resources for the organizations.[8] Finally, and most importantly, professionals are needed to certify that clients are able to resume conventional roles because they have been treated, rehabilitated, or the like.[9]

Reliance on the service professions has had other consequences than mere implementation of agency purposes. A question about who has captured whom arises once the primary tasks of the organization are defined as requiring professional expertise. Performance of these tasks may then become the exclusive responsibility of professionals, or at least subject to their direct control. When professionals can be induced to serve in limited numbers and in lower-echelon "line" positions, the general perspectives of the organization may remain relatively unaffected. When, however, professionals are presented in large numbers and assume élite positions, dependence on them brings with it limiting commitment to particular ideologies and strategies of change. Alternative approaches are thus denied the organization except as these are mediated through the profession.[10] The risk is that the approaches defined by one or another profession may not be sufficient for achievement of treatment goals, yet the organization is no longer as free to pursue alternative means.

A second problem posed by reliance on professional cadres is that the treatment organization may become primarily a context for professional practice, which is something different from being a goal-oriented enterprise. Internal arrangements may be shaped to serve the interests or convenience of professional practitioners. The medical hospital is an example of a formal organization largely adapted to professional requirements; many of its problematic aspects and the criticisms directed at these are conditions by this fact.[11]

The service professions are variously dependent on treatment organizations as contexts for practice. It would be expected that the broader the opportunities for practice—as among different organizations, or wholly outside any organization—the less a profession's dependence on and accommodation to a single type of organization. Thus, psychiatrists are better able than others to assert their claims with respect to the treatment organization: in addition to their greater prestige, psychiatrists are sought by many types of treatment agencies, while they typically maintain some anchorage in private practice. Social workers and teachers, however, are members of largely bureaucratized professions and have few opportunities for practice independent of organizations. Being in relatively scarce supply, social workers are still able to influence some of the terms of affiliation with any particular treatment agency. One measure of this is their concentration in certain agencies considered as more favorable contexts for professional practice.[12]

It must be noted that not all treatment organizations have accepted professional claims to crucial competencies. Most of those in the corrections sector, and especially prisons, have refrained from a thoroughgoing commitment to the professions. Similarly, relatively few professionally trained social workers are employed within public assistance agencies. One explanation for these patterns may be that neither the prison nor the public assistance agency should be considered a treatment organization as it has been defined. If they are not concerned with changing people, they do not require these professional competencies. Another explanation may be that both organizations are, in fact, concerned with effecting change, but social workers do not have the appropriate skills. There is probably some truth in each of these statements. Many of the difficulties evident in the limited employment of social workers in these two contexts arise from the dominance of other than change goals (e.g., custodialism and deterrence in the prison) as well as from limitations in professional technologies.

As treatment agencies become more complex they tend to employ members of several—sometimes many—professional groups. This presents new problems in defining the appropriate division of effort and allocation of authority among these groups. Competing claims are presented with respect to the essential competencies, preferred tasks, and appropriate statuses within the organization.[13]

Controlling Professional Behavior

Finally, professionals in treatment organizations also assert the principle of autonomy in exercise of their special skills. They value independence and initiative in the use of these skills, especially in the primary areas of *decisions about and transactions with clientele*. The more complex and estoteric the technology utilized, the less possible it becomes to control behavior directly through administrative rules or close supervision. The treatment organization must, nevertheless, insure that staff behavior is in conformity with its general purposes, and that staff actions are co-ordinated. Certain mechanisms are developed, therefore, to achieve the necessary controls while respecting professional claims to autonomy. Four of these control mechanisms are:

1. *Commitment to organizational goals.* When the agency can neither precisely specify the task to be performed (because of its complexity) nor closely observe performance (because of autonomy claims), it can seek control by demanding greater commitment to its general purposes. Ideological conformity to the values and goals of the organization can be scrutinized among staff and taken as an approximation of direct control.[14] Thus, the organization can rely on members of a profession known to espouse similar values, select individuals who seem most committed to its particular ends, and encourage overt manifestations of staff dedication. Unfortunately, high ideological commitment tends to increase doctrinairism and parochial perspectives among treatment agency personnel. These, in turn, impede pragmatism and rationalism in organizational operation and innovation.

2. *Maximizing colleague controls.* Acknowledgment of the legitimate authority of officials primarily because they are in superior positions is not a tenet of professionalism, yet practitioners are strongly oriented to collegial relations. They value their reputations among members of their own profession, seek colleague support and advice, and respond to the judgments of those recognized as more expert than themselves. The organization, however, cannot always adjust its administrative hierarchy to parallel the gradations of competence accepted among its professional personnel. Even when this is possible, persons in higher positions tend to be viewed as *senior* colleagues, who can offer recommendations but should not issue directives.[15] The organization may, therefore, increase the opportunities for interchange among per-

sonnel with respect to crucial decisions and actions. While providing reassurance that the less proficient will be guided by the more expert, such interchange also supports ideological commitment and conformity. Staff meetings and case conferences are examples of decision-making procedures that increase colleague controls.

Emphasis on colleague controls presents several difficulties for the agency. Professionals may spend inordinate proportions of time in consultation with colleagues, weighing views on clients, considering alternative procedures, and reviewing processes of client change.[16] There are also difficulties in defining who should be included and excluded in such collective decision-making. Thus, the extension of equalitarianism contemplated by certain of the "team" practices and the "therapeutic milieu" philosophies must eventually encompass all operative personnel. Ultimately, the excessive communication requirements and the erosion of administrative authority may severely limit the organization's capacity to perform its basic service tasks.[17]

3. *Segregation of tasks and roles.* Insistence on semi-independent performance is most characteristic of professional personnel, primarily with respect to activities involving their core competencies. Other tasks may be assigned to nonprofessionals, for whom conventional administrative procedures are more appropriate. Role separation as one approach permits the organization to differentiate its control procedures among personnel in accordance with the type of task. By establishing dual hierarchies of authority, one set of control procedures may be used for professionals, with another set for ward attendants, secretarial personnel, and so on. Furthermore, professionals are assigned many secondary activities that they do not perceive as requiring core competencies, and which can be governed by conventional administrative procedures (e.g., record-keeping). The latter pattern results in the establishment of dual lines of authority to control personnel in different *phases* of their work.[18] Thus, professionals in hospitals and universities seem willing to accept the exercise of administrative authority over certain of their activities, while relying on professionally defined controls for other activities. The problem with each of these dual authority structures, whether they divide only the tasks or both staff and tasks, is that of unclear and debatable boundaries between the phases of agency activity governed by each.

4. *Superordination of professions.* Control of staff performance and co-ordination among professional subgroups has also been attempted by giving greater authority and pre-eminence to members of one profession. In general and mental hospitals all other groups are subordinated to the medical profession, whose members direct and

oversee activities. This arrangement can suffice only when there is one profession to whose superior knowledge and skill others defer, and when such deference within the organization is generally condoned among the professions. Nurses and social workers, for example, have long acknowledged the pre-eminence of medicine and have experienced less strain in being subordinated to control by physicians and psychiatrists. In contrast, clinical psychology has no tradition of subordination and acknowledges the superior wisdom of psychiatry in far less degree. Subordination of psychologists to psychiatrists is consequently accompanied by tension.[19] Similarly, there are challenges within the correctional field when other personnel are subordinated to social workers, while within courts social workers are often skeptical of the legal profession's pre-eminence.

The superordination of professions has only transitory usefulness for control of performance in treatment organizations. On the one hand, the press toward attainment of full professional stature impels each subgroup to affirm the authenticity of its own special knowledge and competence. On the other hand, enlargements in the knowledge base of each profession jeopardize continued dependence on another group.

Given the contemporary status of professions and their relative monopoly of certain competencies, the treatment agency has little choice but to rely upon them, although this dependence has mixed consequences for organizational performance. Once professionals are introduced within the agency, special mechanisms are required for their co-ordination and control. Reciprocally, however, it is probable that the long-term development of the professions is shaped crucially by their movement into treatment agencies. At the very least the tenets of independent entrepreneurial professionalism must give way to the demands of practice within bureaucratic contexts. Study of such patterns among treatment organizations offers special opportunities for pursuit of more general questions about emerging forms of professionalized bureaucracies.

Consequences for Clients

Let us now turn our attention to clients, and to certain of the effects for them induced by the patterns of treatment organizations. It was noted earlier that the treatment agency seeks to modify the personalites, statuses, or behavior patterns of its clientele. Pupils, patients, and prisoners are simultaneously the raw material on which and with whom the organization works, persons whose interests must be served, and—in their changed condition—the "products" of organized activity. Clientele frequently sustain affiliation with these organizations over extended periods and acquire formal statuses within them, since change cannot be effected by means of transitory or peripheral involvement.

The essential strategy of all treatment organizations is the design of client experiences calculated to result in relinquishment of non-conformist patterns of conduct, disapproved values, and deviant identi-ties. New and more acceptable modes of behavior must be presented to the client and he must be trained in them. Relations between staff and clients are of crucial significance since the former must both *represent* the new modes to clients and directly *manage* the learning of them. A number of conditions may and often do adversely affect the desired relations between staff and clients, thereby curtailing treatment effects. Thus, persons may sometimes be involuntary client members of the organization, they may be opposed to the official change objectives and wish to remain deviant, and they may be alienated from many aspects of the organization.

One source of client resistance or alienation may be the various conceptions of them and of their problems that have previously been identified. These are, in balance, less than positive conceptions and may be resisted as they are made manifest through the person's experience as a client. Observers of correctional programs have noted, for example, the origins of inmate opposition in their attempt, by "rejecting the rejectors," to preserve at least minimally adequate self-images.[20] Ac-ceptance of the fact that one's condition or behavior is disapproved by others and commitment to the objectives of treatment are made more difficult by the negative characterological implications associated with certain prevailing conceptions of deviance.

Difficulties in mobilizing client commitment to change may be aggravated by a client's initial experiences within the treatment orga-nization. Although the goals of the agency are defined at least partially in terms of the client's well-being, he must assume a status in which he is accorded least power, least prestige, and fewest rewards. Acceptance of the client status and role may require a radical shift from the person's conventional situation. Furthermore, motivation and allegiance of per-sons at the lowest ranks cannot be maintained—as in many other types of organizations—through promotion and advancement opportunities for those who perform most capably. (Parenthetically, it should be noted that socialization organizations, such as schools and youth-serv-ing agencies, typically promote their clientele through the ranks and actively recruit the most promising among these for eventual member-ship in the staff system.)

Adverse conceptions of clientele, nonvoluntary change, low

status within the organization, and lack of advancement opportunities are problematic conditions that may be offset for persons if the remainder of their experiences as clients is essentially positive. It is at this point that the treatment technology becomes most important. If clients are handled in largely routinized ways that ignore or deny their individuality, and if they are subjected to deprivations rather than inducements, further resistance and antagonism would be expected. Under these circumstances is found, moreover, the crystallization of client resistance into a kind of collective opposition working against the goals of treatment. The custodial prison is often cited as a prime example of these adverse conditions, and the prison's change potentials, correctly, are questioned.

Most other types of treatment organizations present certain degrees of these problems, however, and their demonstrated success rates are also less than desirable. Thus, the use of standardized routines that vitiate individuality can be seen in the "red tape" associated with agency intake, decision-making, and referral processes; in the adherence to formal and often arbitrary rules and procedures; and in the lack of staff spontaneity and warmth in direct contact with clients.[21] Each of these conditions can be justified in terms of other organizational requirements, yet their net effect on clients must be regarded as dubious. Similarly, one may question whether the gratifications and inducements mediated through staff-client relations in many agencies are sufficiently potent to accomplish desired change. Evidence of how difficult it is to sustain a client's commitment to change, when he is free to disengage himself at will, can be seen in the high "dropout" rate of open treatment agencies.[22]

Evaluating Effectiveness

All treatment organizations—indeed, all people-changing organizations—encounter difficulties in evaluating their effectiveness. Relatively speaking, it is much easier to judge the success of a manufacturing corporation, since it can be stated, for example, in terms of the quantity of goods produced and sold at certain levels of profit. Profit and production goals can more easily be translated into operational codes, and objective measures exist for assessing results. Direct comparisons can thus be made among many such organizations.

Treatment organizations cannot so easily refer, however, to numbers of persons changed with such and such degrees of success. The clinic can, of course, cite how many clients were served or the *per capita* costs of this service. Yet these facts say little about effectiveness, and it is difficult to describe the ways in which clients have been helped or served. There is far less certitude in such statements, little agreement about the most appropriate terms, and even less public understanding of what is meant.

There are three basic sources of difficulty in judging success of treatment organizations: (1) The change goals of each are sufficiently ambiguous that they do not provide clear guides either for designing strategies or for assessing results. What precisely is meant by "mental health," "rehabilitation," and "better social functioning"? Change objectives that refer to people are perhaps necessarily ambiguous or statable only in very general terms. (2) Whatever the balance of particular purposes for a given treatment agency, specific operational implications are not readily derivable from the statement of tasks and therefore remain contentious. Treatment procedures and practices are as yet indeterminate and of uncertain validity. Practitioners of these healing arts can neither obtain nor offer clear guidelines for action, and the consequences of their efforts remain only partially demonstrable. Evaluation cannot, therefore, as in certain other enterprises, center on the operational processes of the agency without begging the question of outcomes. (3) Treatment organizations are largely deprived of information about a person's performance *after* termination of client status. This problem is aggravated for agencies that deal with persons removed from their local environments, such as mental hospitals, since there are fewer means for gaining knowledge about the client's behavior after his discharge. For all treatment agencies, however, the effects of the organization's interventions tend to be confounded with the influences of other social systems in which clients live. The resources necessary for follow-up studies are seldom available, and even when they are it is difficult to factor out the specific impact of the organization.

Limitations in objective assessment of effectiveness have important consequences for the treatment organization. They induce emphases on intraorganizational behavior, pressures toward goal displacement, and a tendency toward self-justifying doctrine rather than rational planning. Since follow-up or "outside" information is relatively unavailable, change in a client is assessed more in terms of his responses to agency expectations and his relations with other personnel than in terms of his capability for conventional social role behavior. The model patient or prisoner is one who conforms to the rules and routines; the model clinic client is one who keeps his appointments and learns to reveal himself and to communicate using the language of therapy. Such organizationally valued changes may not merely be irrelevent to community performance requirements, but in extreme form may result in a client's "trained incapacity" to function adequately outside the agency (e.g., "institutionalization" in the mental hospital).[23] The task of the treatment organization is to define roles and changed modes of behavior for clients that directly intersect with performance requirements of conventional life in the community. This becomes more difficult insofar as clients are abstracted from their local environments and the agency ignores or lacks knowledge of their immediate social situations. Disjunctures between organizational experiences and community life reduce the relevance of change processes and increase the difficulty of clients' reintegration.

Displacement of goals may be evidenced in two directions: one toward overconcern with means and the other toward emphasis on secondary objectives. Limited measures of achievement encourage an imbalance of concern between goals and the procedures that supposedly are instrumental to them. The risk, as has been noted, is that the treatment organization becomes essentially a context for professional practice rather than a goal-directed enterprise. Among agencies that do not rely upon professionals, goal displacement is more likely to take the form of overvaluing organizational stability. Rule adherence, efficiency, administrative convenience, and preservation of good order become watchwords in the absence of independent measures of effectiveness.

These tendencies combine to engender a high degree of doctrinairism throughout the entire range of treatment organizations. Belief systems become self-validating, routines are not objectively assessed, and ideological commitment is pervasively inculcated. Charismatic leaders emerge since they offer coherence and guidance in otherwise ambiguous situations. Similarly, personnel in treatment organizations develop strong feelings that only "insiders," immersed in the rhetoric and reality of the agency, can adequately appreciate its processes and accomplishments.

Deprived of confident knowledge about goal attainment, the treatment organization encounters difficulties in assuring external publics that it is both competent and effective. Defense of its precarious values becomes more difficult when these are transformed so that they can be fully appreciated only among the sophisticated. The capability of the agency to certify that its clients have been changed is reduced, as external publics maintain their "closed ranks" even against those who have been rehabilitated. Yet, paradoxically, the growing prestige of the service professions has made it somewhat easier to interpret organizational activity in terms of professional practice. Less professionalized agencies, however, experience new difficulties as support diminishes for the traditionalistic values they embody.

Perhaps a more serious problem is that of a planned innovation and technological advance among organizations that are less oriented toward utilitarian criteria. Growing rationalism in the larger society has affected the treatment organization: its former stratagems are now less serviceable in the competition for scarce resources, and there is increasing public reluctance to accept its claims without objective evidence. Reasoned choice among alternative courses of action and development of more effective measures are thus rendered difficult when crucial knowledge about consequences is lacking.

Notes

1. See, for example, Milton Greenblatt, Richard H. York, and Esther L. Brown, *From Custodial to Therapeutic Patient Care in Mental Hospitals* (New York: Russell Sage Foundation, 1955); Richard McCleery, *Policy Change in Prison Management* (East Lansing, Mich.: Michigan State University Press, 1957): Talcott Parsons, "The Mental Hospital As a Type of Organization," in Milton Greenblatt, Daniel J. Levinson, and Richard H. Williams, eds., *The Patient and the Mental Hospital* (Glencoe, Ill.: The Free Press, 1957).

2. This view has been changing in recent years, with greater recognition of sociocultural conditions impeding the education of some youth and concern about their doubtful motivations, especially within the lower economic strata. *See* Frank Riessman, *The Culturally Deprived Child* (New York: Harper & Bros., 1962).

3. For an analysis of such public studies, *see* Elaine and John Cumming, *Closed Ranks: An Experiment in Mental Health Education* (Cambridge, Mass.: Harvard University Press, 1957), pp. 91–150. *See also* Julian L. Woodward, "Changing Ideas on Mental Illness and Its Treatment," *American Sociological Review,* Vol. 16, No. 4 (August 1951), pp. 443–454.

4. For an analysis of contrasting diagnostic systems, their ideological sources and technological consequences, *see* Rosemary Sarri, "Organizational Patterns and Client Perspectives in Juvenile Correctional Institutions: A Comparative Study." Unpublished Ph.D. thesis, University of Michigan, 1962.

5. Robert D. Vinter *et al., The Comparative Study of Juvenile Institutions: A Research Report* (Ann Arbor, Mich.: University of Michigan Press, 1961). Chapter IX. Certain of the concepts and ideas presented here have been developed in a four-year comparative study of juvenile institutions, supported by NIMH Grant M-2104.

6. Litwak observes that organization emphasis on impersonal relations and general rules is more likely to occur when the events at issue are uniform rather than nonuniform. Our point is that *definitions* of the uniformity of events (here human events) vary among people-changing organizations. Eugene Litwak, "Models of Bureaucracy Which Permit Conflict," *American Journal of Sociology,* Vol. 57, No. 2 (September 1961), pp. 177–184.

7. One aspect of organization-profession interdependence has been the organization's assumption of training responsibilities for the profession.

8. The more prestigious the profession, the greater capacity to legitimate treatment organizations. One would expect, therefore, to find a scale of preeminence within organizations corresponding to the relative ranking of professions in the larger

society. This appears to be the case with respect to psychiatry, whose higher prestige relative to the other professions mentioned is a matter of common knowledge. *See* Raymond G. Hunt, Orville Gurrslin, and Jack L. Roach, "Social Status and Psychiatric Service in a Child Guidance Clinic," *American Sociological Review*, Vol. 23, No. 1 (February 1958), pp. 81–83.

9. *See* Frances G. Scott, "Action Theory and Research in Social Organization," *American Journal of Sociology*, Vol. 64, No. 4 (January 1959), pp. 386–395.

10. Erving Goffman, *Asylums: Essays on the Social Situation of Mental Patients and other Inmates* (Garden City, N.Y.: Doubleday & Co., 1961). *See especially* "The Medical Model and Mental Hospitalization," pp. 321–386.

11. It is recognized that hospitals vary and that increasingly they are assuming characteristics not dictated by professional requirements. *See* Robert N. Wilson, "The Physician's Changing Hospital Role," *Human Organization*, Vol. 18 (1959–1960), pp. 177–183; and Charles B. Perrow, "Organizational Prestige: Some Functions and Dysfunctions," *American Journal of Sociology*, Vol. 66, No. 4 (January 1961), pp. 335–341.

12. *Salaries and Working Conditions of Social Welfare Manpower in 1960* (New York: National Social Welfare Assembly, undated). *See especially* Table 18, p. 39.

13. Alvin F. Zander, Arthur R. Cohen, and Ezra Stotland, *Role Relations in Mental Health Professions* (Ann Arbor, Mich.: University of Michigan Press, 1957). *See* Chapter IV.

14. *See* Lloyd E. Ohlin, "Conformity in American Society Today," *Social Work*, Vol. 3, No. 2 (April 1958), pp. 58–66.

15. For a fuller discussion of these problems, *see* Robert D. Vinter, "The Structure of Service," in Alfred J. Kahn, ed., *Issues in American Social Work* (New York: Columbia University Press, 1959), pp. 260–265.

16. For example, Lind found that, in two welfare organizations, personnel in the unit with the higher level of professionalization spent significantly more time conferring about cases and were also more dependent on colleagues (here including the immediate supervisor). Roger M. Lind, "Organizational Structure and Social Worker Performance." Unpublished Ph.D. thesis, University of Michigan, 1962.

17. Blau and Scott present a cogent critique of these and related devices used by treatment organizations. Peter M. Blau and W. Richard Scott, *Formal Organizations* (San Francisco: Chandler, 1962), pp. 189–191.

18. See Amitai Etzioni, "Authority Structure and Organizational Effectiveness," *Administratice Science Quarterly*, Vol. 4, No. 1 (June 1959), pp. 43–68: and Robert Wilson, *op. cit.*

19. *See* Zander *et al., op. cit.*

20. Lloyd W. McCorkle and Richard R. Korn, "Resocialization Within Prison Walls," *The Annals*, Vol. 293 (May 1954), pp. 88–98.

21. *See* Goffman, "The Moral Career of the Mental Patient," *loc. cit.*, pp. 125–170.

22. *See* Dorothy Fahs Beck, *Patterns in Use of Family Agency Service* (New York: Family Service Association of America, 1962). Chart 19, p. 20.

23. J. K. Wing, "Institutionalism in Mental Hospitals," *British Journal of Clinical Psychology*, Vol. 1, No. 1 (1962), pp. 38–51.

The School as a Formal Organization

Charles E. Bidwell

The central purpose of this study is to move toward a formulation of the organizational character of schools. The article reviews the greater portion of the existing research literature which speaks to the organizational nature of schools, attempts to abstract from the findings certain generic attributes of school organization, and, in conclusion suggests how these attributes may be related systematically.

One of the major difficulties inherent in this effort is the diversity of schools. Consider, for example, the great differences between the structures and central activities of elementary schools and universities and between the public and private varieties of each of these school types. The author has deliberately chosen in this study to consider only public elementary and secondary school systems. In part, this choice was forced by the almost complete absence of empirical research dealing with any other kind of school. Even taxonomic descriptions, comparing the attributes of types of schools, are lacking. In addition, however, the choice arose from the conviction that the most generic organizational attributes of schools should be equally evident in schools of any type, so that the outcomes of this discussion will be broadly relevant to studies of all kinds of schools.

The hope is that the ideas developed can serve as a starting point for badly needed comparative studies of school types, to be refined and modified as the differential characteristics of varieties of schools are revealed. At least what is said will be applicable to the most numerous category of school organizations, within which, certainly, there is sufficient variation to permit more than simple descriptive accounts.

This choice imposes three especially important limitations upon the discussion. First, only schools with child and adolescent student bodies are considered, so that the effects upon a school of preadult or adult students are not treated. Second, the parent-clients of the schools under analysis do not pay fees and are part of the schools' public constituencies. Thus, variability resulting from differences in the source of support of types of schools is not explored. Third, only day schools are

Excerpted from James G. March, ed., *Handbook of Organizations* (Chicago: Rand McNally and Company, 1965), pp. 972–78.

considered; public elementary and secondary boarding schools are, at least in this country, almost nonexistent. As a result, the characteristics of those schools which are "total institutions" must be ignored. (For a treatment of such schools, centered on their effects upon students, see Goffman, 1961).

To set the frame for the discussion, three basic assumptions concerning the nature of public elementary and secondary school systems as organizations have been made. First, it is assumed that school systems are client-serving organizations, that is, that they are social units specifically vested with a service function, in this case the moral and technical socialization of the young.

From this assumption, it follows that the central goal of any school system is to prepare its students for adult status, by training them in the knowledge and skills, and by indoctrinating them in the moral orientations, which adult roles require. Given school systems, then, set their more specific goals within these limits, for example, by giving varying weight to technical and moral socialization, by spelling out the content of socialization, or by emphasizing more or less heavily preparation for common, or for certain differentiated, adult roles.

Second, it is assumed that the role structure of a school system contains a fundamental dichotomy between student and staff roles. In Nadel's (1957, pp. 35–41) terms, the student role is a recruitment role; staff roles are achievement roles. Young persons are compelled to enter school systems as students simply because of their placement in certain age-grades, without reference to specific performances. Furthermore, since students are to be socialized to adult life, the central activities of this role are not directly relevant to the immediate interests or lives of its incumbents. From the point of view of the student, participation in these activities is likely to be foreign to his own preferences, yet he cannot opt for or against participation. From the point of view of the school system, it cannot selectively recruit its clientele: educational services more often than not must be provided to student-clients who do not desire them and may not be able to profit from them. Yet the school system is expected to bring all students to some minimal level of accomplishment.

Staff members, on the other hand, enter their roles voluntarily, on the basis of prior performance. The two chief categories of staff roles are teacher and administrator. To the incumbents of these roles, the school system offers incentives, at the least a salary, in return for contributions of trained competence. This exchange is signified by the specific contractual relation of the school system and its teaching and administrative staffs.

These two main categories of staff roles are professionalized. To become a teacher, one must, in principle, have completed specialized training, have been licensed, and have demonstrated at least potential expertise. (But the professionalization of the role of teacher is by no means secure. Most states issue temporary teaching certificates, for which the training requirements are slight. The presence in a school system of numbers of teachers holding such certificates may countervail the effects of professional norms on teachers' orientations and performance. These norms and their effects are discussed later.) The requirements for entrance to administrative roles include these same professional elements, since administrators typically are drawn from the teaching ranks, but in most cases additional special training is demanded, or at least evidence of administrative aptitude displayed while a teacher. In more complex school systems, other professional roles, e.g., school psychologist, are found. These roles, too, are entered on the bases of training, license, and technical competence.

Another category of staff roles lacks these characteristics. These roles are nonprofessional, for example, clerical or maintenance positions. While these are achievement roles, the abilities for which the school system contracts are relatively undifferentiated, and the performance criteria for entrance are typical of such occupations.

Third, it is assumed that school systems are to some degree bureaucratic. That is, they display at least in rudimentary form the following characteristics:

1. a functional division of labor (e.g., the allocation of instructional and coordinative tasks to the school-system roles of teacher and administrator);

2. the definition of staff roles as offices, that is, in terms of recruitment according to merit and competence, legally based tenure, functional specificity of performance, and universalistic, affectively neutral interaction with clients;

3. the hierarchic ordering of offices, providing an authority structure based on the legally defined and circumscribed power of officers, a system of adjudication of staff disputes by reference to superiors, and regularized lines of communication;

4. operation according to rules of procedure, which set limits to the discretionary performance of officers by specifying both the aims and modes of official action.

Involved here is the further assumption that rationalized activities are necessary for school-system functioning. Rationalization appears to be essential for two reasons. First, the school system is responsible for a uniform product of a certain quality. This uniformity requirement is of a distinctive kind. It sets a minimum, but not a maximum, level for student accomplishment. As for the minimum standard, all students, by the time they leave school, must have acquired rudimentary competence for adult citizenship, that is, for enacting roles common to all adult members of the society. Students also are to be prepared for differential roles, most notably in the occupational sphere. Categories of graduates thus display varying kinds and degrees of acquired competence, but within each of these categories, their preparation must again reach at least a minimum standard.

Yet the recruitment nature of the student role means that any given cohort of students probably contains marked variations of ability, both in kind and degree. To provide services which have uniform outcomes means that the school system must devise consistent methods of assessing the ability of its students at various stages of their school careers and consistent procedures for socializing them according to these assessments. In other words, while at any point in time the members of a cohort of students may vary in their readiness for socialization, so that methods of socialization also must vary at this time point according to these individual differences, the school system must routinize the variability of its service procedures. Essentially, this means that procedures must be selected universalistically on the grounds of variable student aptitude, for all students of given kinds and levels of ability must undergo similar forms of socialization.

Second, socializing children and adolescents for adult roles is massive and complex. Thus, school systems deal with students over long periods of time and must provide educational services which comprise coherent sequences of increasingly differentiated and demanding socialization tasks. As the roles for which students are trained have become more complex and specialized (see Parsons & White, 1961, pp. 109–115) and as, in the United States, the school-leaving age has been raised so that most students remain in school systems for periods of 10 to 12 years, the coordination of educational activities so that they are coherent and sequential moves more and more to the center of school-system administration.

At the same time, the typical educational technology requires persisting interaction between an individual teacher and his students. Such interaction permits the teacher to assess subtle variations in student performance and to adjust instructional methods accordingly, in a way which would not be possible were the student to move over very short periods of time from one teacher to another. Moreover, persisting relations between teacher and student would appear to be necessary to the massive form of socialization which is required in bringing students from childhood to adulthood (see Strauss, 1959, pp. 89–131). The interpersonal bonds which develop over longer periods of time may both legitimize the technical competence of the teacher and provide him with powerful affective resources useful in motivating and sanctioning students. One may note here a potential strain between the definition of the teacher role as an office and the nature of the functions allocated to it, a point discussed later.

Given this aspect of the educational technology, the division of labor in school systems is both temporal and functional. Over time, the activities of the school usually are divided into nine-month periods, the school year, or four and a half month periods, the semester, in which a teacher continues to be responsible for the instruction of the same group of students. In elementary schools, in which the content to be learned is relatively undifferentiated, the temporal dimension, in fact, is the one significant basis for the divison of labor. The teacher interacts with only one classroom group, in all phases of instruction, for a school year or a semester. In junior and senior high schools, where the curriculum is more specialized, the functional principle is important, with teachers instructing several classroom groups in a single subject-matter area, but their relationship to each of these student groups persists over the customary semester or school-year periods.

Thus, the temporal division of labor is tied to the age-grade placement of students. They are categorized as client aggregates into school grades or classes which in modern Western countries correspond to each age-grade represented in the student body. Students are assigned as class or grade units to members of the teaching staff. This close correspondence of school grades and age-grades is not typical of other times and places, suggesting that it arises as school systems become routinized, so that students must be moved through the system in batches and cannot be assigned to school grades individually on the basis of achievement.

The problem of dealing with variability in student abilities and accomplishments, during a school year, thus is vested in the classroom teacher, and one important component of his professional skill is ability to handle day-to-day fluctuations in the response to instruction by individual students and collectively by the classroom group. At the same time, his bureaucratic office is a means by which the school-system administration can insure the teacher's adherence to universalistic criteria in these decisions. Consequently, an important facet of school-system organization is the autonomy granted to—or perhaps demanded by— the teacher as a professional to make discretionary judgments about procedures to be used during the time a student group is in his charge.

Teacher autonomy is reflected in the structure of school systems, resulting in what may be called their structural looseness. The teacher works alone within the classroom, relatively hidden from colleagues and superiors, so that he has a broad discretionary jurisdiction within the boundaries of the classroom. Similarly, the school units of a school system are relatively autonomous, so that the teaching and administrative personnel of a school also enjoy broad discretionary powers concerning the procedures to be employed during the period of time that students are assigned to that school. The school is to a substantial degree a self-contained organizational unit, with a defined population from which students are drawn (the school district in a one-school system or the attendance area for each school within a multischool system). The principal and teachers usually retain at least some control, often substantial, over curricula and teaching methods. Moreover, even though the system itself recruits teachers, they usually cannot be assigned to a school without the principal's consent. Thus, school systems must operate by coordinating, in the interests of sequence and uniformity, not simply spatially dispersed, but structurally discrete and relatively independent subunits.

In short, both the temporal division of labor and the structural looseness of school systems reinforce the professional basis of school-system activities—the discretion of staff members and subunits to determine what services are to be provided and how this is to be done. But the school system cannot rely entirely on such judgments, since a uniform product must be attained and since the movement of students from grade to grade, and thus from classroom to classroom and school to school, within the system must be sequential. To put the point somewhat differently, the product of each classroom and school unit must be uniform with respect to the next stage of the student career. Even if activities within the classroom and school units of the system are not routinized, the movement of students from one unit to the next must be.

Maintaining this routinization, therefore, is a principal task of school-system administration. Insuring the object of administrative control is the universalistic and thus uniform assessment of student accomplishment and the subsequent determination of institutional procedures, also universalistic solely in response to student differences in this measured performance. Such control (system-wide) can be achieved in at least three ways: the interweaving of staff orientations with professional norms and local school-system policies, thus maximizing the commitment of teachers and school principals to goals and methods of procedure, in addition to recruiting teachers and principals with such commitments; the establishment of standards of student accomplishment prerequisite to movement from grade to grade, that is, examinations which constrain the performance of teachers as well as of students; and the bureaucratization of school and classroom activities by rules of procedure which restrict the discretionary autonomy of classroom teachers or school staffs. One especially might expect such rules to center on examination, i.e., on the universalistic assessment of student progress during, as well as at the end of, a year or semester. Here may lie an important source of conflict between bureaucratic principles and the nature of the teaching technology as it tends to particularize the student-teacher relation through the development of interpersonal bonds. (For a discussion of the effects of achievement and ability testing on societies and school systems, see Anderson, 1962.)

All three modes of control in the service of rationalization are evident in the operation of any school system, although school systems presumably vary in the salience of any one and in the way they are combined. The important point here is to note that both the looseness of system structures and the nature of the teaching task seem to press for a professional mode of school-system organization, while demands for uniformity of product and the long time span over which cohorts of students are trained press for rationalization of activities and thus for a bureaucratic basis of organization.

One way in which school systems seem to differ from the classical bureaucratic structure—the looseness of articulation between subunits —has already been noted. They also differ in another important respect. Despite the functional and temporal differentiation of teaching activities, the teaching cadre typically does not contain specialized teacher offices. Thus, teachers' salaries usually are tied to training and seniority rather than to function or position. Within the teaching cadre there is no bureaucratic career. The administrative cadre, however, does contain specialized offices, corresponding to functional allocations—principal, director of elementary education, and superintendent, for example. Salary is tied to official rank, and the internal career line of a school system thus consists of movement into and through the administrative ranks.

With respect to their bureaucratization, it should also be noted that school systems vary widely. The simplest form of school-system organization is a single school unit with a small student body, a few teachers, and an administrator. More typically nowadays, school systems are complexes of school units, both elementary and secondary (although some school systems are restricted to elementary or secondary education), each with its own subadministrator (principal) and teaching staff, overlaid with a system-wide administrative cadre. In moderately complex systems, this administrative cadre consists of a chief administrator (superintendent), responsible for the direction of all system activities, and his immediate "staff." In more complex systems, there may be intervening administrative echelons for directing instructional activities (e.g., district superintendents, or directors of elementary or secondary education), multiple hierarchies for providing auxiliary professional and nonprofessional services (e.g., a director of psychological services and his staff, or a business manager who directs maintenance personnel), and a large number of "staff" positions and agencies attached to the superintendent's office.

It was argued above that school systems are "required" to produce uniform outcomes of a given level of quality, and that this is a powerful constraint toward bureaucratization. The source of this constraint is external and arises from the fact that school systems not only are client-serving, but also are agents of public welfare. They are, in fact, an arm of the state government (Edwards, 1955, pp. 23–46) and as such must be responsible to the apparatus of government and to a public constituency. Thus, they must respond to public definitions of the nature of adequate service and service outcomes while they attempt to maintain sufficient latitude for professional staff judgments concerning what procedures, and what outcomes, best serve their public trust. The constraining force of public constituencies is enhanced by the responsibility of school systems to use efficiently the public funds from which they are supported. Consequently, one would expect that school administrators and their subordinates must balance three criteria in determining lines of action: professional norms and standards, public wishes, and fiscal efficiency. The latter two are likely to be inextricably linked.

These external pressures gain immediacy because the state function of education in the United States has been delegated to local units of school government, usually the school district, which comprise the immediate public constituency of the school and elect, or through some other governmental unit appoint, a lay board of education vested with over-all authority for system policies and operations, and for establishing the budget. The chief school administrator, the superintendent, legally is the executive officer of the board, so that authority flows from the board to the superintendent and thence down the system hierarchy. One would expect, then, that an important aspect of the functioning of school systems is conflict between lay-board and professional-staff judgments and efforts at its resolution within the legal limits of school-board and superintendent authority.

At the same time, however, the states retain certain general policy, supervisory, and advising functions related to local school districts, exercised through state-level and regional school bureaucracies, especially state departments of education and the offices of county school superintendents. These agencies may constrain and limit both board and staff actions. Since their personnel usually are drawn from the ranks of professional educators, they may act as power resources for local school staffs vis-à-vis school boards.

Finally, the local public constituencies of school systems may intervene directly in school-system operations, independently of the school board. This is especially likely because the parents of students, the "indirect" clients, are also among the school system's constituents and may act in this dual capacity as they interact with teachers or school principals concerning the affairs of their children. The existence of an indirect clientele thus opens school systems at the subunit levels—school and classroom—to the public constituency. As will be seen, the nature of the local community served by the school system may also affect its openness to external constraints.

In short, several aspects of school systems as organizations which appear to be significant for their analysis have been identified: the recruitment nature of the student-client role, the professionalization of school staffs, the essential variability of procedures, the requirements for rationalization of procedures, and the controlling powers of local constituencies and higher governmental agencies.

References

Anderson, C. A. "Dilemmas of Talent-Centered Educational Programmes, U.S.A." In *Yearbook of Education,* 1962. New York: Harcourt, Brace, and World. 1962, pp. 445–57.

Edwards, N. *The Courts and the Public Schools* (revised). Chicago: University of Chicago Press. 1955.

Goffman, E. "On the Characteristics of Total Institutions." In *Asylums,* Garden City, New York: Doubleday Anchor. 1961, pp. 1–124.

Nadel, S. F., *The Theory of Social Structure.* Glencoe, Illinois: Free Press. 1957.

Parsons, T. and White W., "The Link Between Character and Society." In S. M. Lipset & L. Lowenthal (eds.), *Culture and Social Character.* New York: Free Press. 1961, pp. 89–135.

Strauss, A., *Mirrors and Masks.* Glencoe, Illinois: Free Press. 1959.

People Processing Organizations: An Exchange Approach

Yeheskel Hasenfeld

The study of formal organizations whose function is to change the lives of people occupies a prominent position in organizational literature. At the theoretical level, studies have concentrated on conceptualizing such organizations (Goffman, 1961; Vinter, 1963; Lefton and Rosengren, 1966; Wheeler, 1966). At the empirical level, studies on organizations such as schools (Cicourel and Kitsuse, 1963), hospitals (Roth, 1963; Strauss *et al.*, 1964), and correctional institutions (Street, Vinter and Perrow, 1966) have increasingly focused on the effects of organizational characteristics on the fate of the people they serve.

Scant theoretical attention has been paid, however, to the emerging importance of those organizations whose explicit function is not to change the behavior of people directly but to process them and confer public statuses on them. Examples of such organizations are a diagnostic clinic, a university admissions office, an employment placement office, a credit bureau, or a juvenile court. We shall denote these as "people-processing" in contrast to "people-changing" organizations. These organizations shape a person's life by controlling his access to a wide range of social settings through the public status they confer; and they may define and confirm the individual's social position when his current status is questioned.

Moreover, processing functions (i.e., classifying, conferring public statuses, and disposing of clients), are an integral part of the technology of people-changing organizations (e.g., Freidson, 1965; Scheff, 1966: 169–187; Scott, 1969). For example, the rationale for the treatment of the psychiatric or physically disabled patient is based on the "ill" status conferred on him. As people-changing organizations increase in size and complexity, these processing functions are likely to be delegated to distinct sub-units or organizations. Yet, the organization's requirements in defining the structure and content of their people-processing functions has not been systematically formulated and explored.

This paper analyzes people-processing organizations by focusing on the exchange relations they develop with their environment, and by tracing the effects of such relations on the structure and content of their

Reprinted from *American Sociological Review* 37 (June, 1972):256–63.

people-processing functions. Environment here means the organizational network within which the organization seeks to attain its goals. (Dill, 1958; Evan, 1966). These organization-environment relations are emphasized for two reasons. First, the core technology of such organizations consists of a set of boundary roles which define the input of clients to the organization and mediate their placement in various external units. Second, the effects of these relations on the development of the organization's technology and its clients' careers is a relatively neglected area of study.[1]

This study identifies systematically key parameters which influence the exchange relations people-processing organizations develop with their environment. In turn, it derives a series of propositions about the effects of such exchange relations on the processing of clients which it illustrates with findings from studies on such organizations.

The Characteristics of People-Processing Organizations

People-processing organizations can be defined by the nature of their "product" and of their processing technology. Their major "product" is people with changed statuses and locations in various community systems. Vinter and Sarri (1966) analyze the processing technology into four major tasks:

1. The client's attributes and situation must be assessed to determine whether he is legitimately subject to official action;
2. The client's attributes and situation must be explored to determine appropriate action alternatives;
3. Choices must be made from among these alternatives; and
4. Once an alternative has been chosen, the person's relocation in a new social set must be managed.

Thus, the core technology of people-processing organizations is the classification and disposition of clients.

Again, this organization does not try directly to alter the behavior of people who enter its jurisdiction, as is the case with people-changing organizations. Rather, it produces changes by identifying and defining the person's attributes, social situation, and public identity, which in turn typically results in both societal and self-reactions. It is through these anticipated reactions of significant others that the organization tries to change its clients' social position and future behavior.

Thus, for example, when a diagnostic center "diagnoses" the client's problems, it is presumed that the therapists who receive the diagnosis will determine the nature of the change efforts to be used. Or when an employment placement agency determines that a client qualifies for a certain job or training program, the client's very definition gains him access to the job or program, and thus alters his situation, prospects, and skills.

Furthermore, unlike people-changing organizations, people-processing organizations are organized so that the anticipated reactions to the statuses they confer occur mainly outside their boundaries. That is, those expected to respond to the classified person by working with him or trying to change him are located in an organization external to the definers'. Similarly, the technological activities of such organizations occur primarily at their boundaries. That is, staff activity consists of transactions with clients and their dossiers at input, negotiations with them on a classification-disposition status at output, and exchanges with potential external recipients of the clients. In contrast, the technology of people-changing organizations is more likely to be insulated from the environment and the organization's boundary transactions, particularly as the intensity of the change efforts increases (Wheeler, 1966: 79–80). Finally, since staff-client encounters in people-processing organizations are not organized to change the client's behavior directly, their relative duration tends to be shorter than in people-changing organizations. Table 1 summarizes some distinct differences between people-processing and people-changing organizations.

TABLE 1

Differences Between People-Processing & People-Changing Organizations

Variable	People-Processing	People-Changing
Type of product	Altered status	Behavioral change
Technology	Classification-disposition	Socialization-resocialization
Locus of technology	Organizational boundary	Intra-organizational
Relative duration of staff-client encounter	Short term	Long term

Given these distinguishing characteristics, people-processing organizations must develop direct and systematic links with external recipient units or markets. We shall denote such formally organized external units "market units." They are thus an integral part of the larger organizational network to which the processing organization is linked. In fact, the network order is based partly on the predictability of the responses of the network's market units to the output of the processing organization.

Furthermore, given the unique product of such organizations, their claims of service effectiveness depend, in part, on the response of the receiving units to the clients' statuses. An employment placement agency's effectiveness is measured largely by its ability to classify and refer applicants to potential employers whose responses will agree with the conferred status (Blau, 1963:37–44). In short, the market's reactions to the products of people-processing organizations are crucial to their survival and effectiveness.

Exchange Relations and Classification-Disposition Systems

It is proposed that the classification-disposition systems of processing organizations will reflect the constraints of their exchange relations with market units. We assume that under the norms of rationality (Thompson, 1967), such organizations will try to develop systems sensitive to the needs of their market units in order to optimize the units' receptivity to their output.

We can analyze the way processing organizations respond, adapt and manage their relations with market units with a power-dependence paradigm. As Thompson (1967:30) defines it:

> An organization is dependent on some element of its task environment (1) in proportion to the organization's need for resources or performance which the element can provide and (2) in inverse proportion to the ability of other elements to provide the same resource or performance.

In general, the more a processing organization depends on a given market unit for accepting its product, the more its classification-disposition system will respond to the constraints and contingencies of that market unit.

Given this paradigm, the analysis of the exchange relations between the processing organization and each of its market units must focus on:

(a the conditions which lead to dependence on a market unit, and
(b the countervailing forces the organization can mobilize to enhance its independence.

The following conditions tend to increase a processing organization's dependence on a given market unit:

(a Enforced dependency on the market unit by externally controlling agents such as legal statutes, parent organizations, and other regulatory groups.
(b High discretion exercised by the market unit over its own intake.
(c Greater need for the client services provided by the market unit.

(*d* Greater prestige of the market unit as a validator of the processing organization's goals and performance.

(*e* Scarcity of knowledge about potential and alternative market units.

The following conditions tend to increase a processing organization's independence of a given market unit:

(*a* Freedom permitted the organization by its externally controlling agents to develop exchange relations.

(*b* Possession of strategic resources needed by potential market units.

(*c* Availability of alternative market units offering similar client services.

(*d* Development of a self-validating organizational ideology.

(*e* An effective intelligence system about alternative market units.

The conditions that increase or decrease the organization's dependency on its market units are summarized in Table 2 and will be discussed in some detail below. Clearly, in the organization's exchanges with its market units all the above conditions may operate simultaneously. For discussion and illustration, however, they will be treated separately.

Dependency vs. Freedom Imposed by External Policies

In analyzing processing organizations' market relations, one must fully recognize the constraints, requirements, and privileges of policy-regulating external units. The funding agency, the parent organization, the legislative unit and the like, may exert direct and indirect influence on two levels: (a) relations with market units; (b) policies vis-a-vis clients.

Policy regulations may restrict the type or range of market units that the organization can use, and may further stipulate the conditions of such transactions. To comply with these policies the organization will have to incorporate such stipulations in the classification-disposition process. For example, government sponsored manpower agencies are often restricted in the type of employers or training programs they can use for their clients (Levitan and Mangum, 1969). These constraints, in turn, limit the type and range of occupational categories staff can use to classify and refer their clients.

Moreover, external policies may even specify the attributes that potential clients must have to qualify for certain market units. Such policies curtail a staff's discretion and may rigidly restrict the number of classification-disposition categories they can confer on clients. Such is the case for public welfare departments which are controlled by extensive restrictive policies of this kind (Keith-Lucas, 1957).

TABLE 2

Conditions Which Increase Dependence v. Countervailing Powers

Condition of Dependence	Countervailing Power
Dependence imposed by external policies	Freedom permitted by external policies
Intake discretion of market unit	Possession of strategic resources
Need for client services of market unit	Availability of alternative client services
Market unit as validator of organizational goals	Development of self-validating organizational ideologies
Intelligence deficiencies about alternative market units	Intelligence effectiveness about alternative market units

External policy units may also require specific information about the clients' attributes and situations, and the need to collect such information thus invariably has consequences for the classification-disposition system. Official classifications, at least, will tend to be constrained to reflect these information requirements.

On the other hand, external policies may give much latitude to the processing organization's relations with external units, enhancing its independence. With such freedom it can select the market units most compatible ideologically and can control the type of clients it serves. Scott (1969) in his study of blindness agencies notes, for example, that the near absence of external policy regulations enabled these agencies to select both programs and clients most compatible with their treatment ideologies.

Intake Discretion vs. Possessing Strategic Resources

Market units can be distinguished by the amount of intake discretion they use in accepting or refusing a processing organization's products. The greater the discretion the greater the processing organization's dependency on these units, a situation reflected, for example, in the relationship between the employment placement office and potential employers. Consequently, the organization's classification-disposition system is more likely to adhere to these units' intake criteria. Nevertheless, when the organization possesses resources essential to these units, it can potentially offset the effects of such dependency. When it is a major supplier of clients, controls economic resources, or largely validates a market units' claims for competence, it is in a better bargaining position with them. For example, while the private physician depends on the psychiatric hospital to accept his referred patients, he may also validate the hospital's claim for competence, and thus be only partly constrained by its intake discretion. Mishler and Waxler (1963) found that the psychiatric hospitals they studied were far more likely to accept patients referred by private physicians, though the hospitals added rules to their classification systems on age, previous hospitalization and presence of a relative.

On the other hand, market units having little intake discretion tend to require a minimal set of criteria of their clients for entry (e.g., the public shool, the mission shelter, the city's general hospital, etc.). When a significant proportion of the market is composed of units with little intake discretion, one would expect the classification-disposition system used by the processing organization also to have a few relatively global typification rules which are insensitive to the client's attributes and situation. Since the relative lack of intake discretion decreases its dependency on the market unit, the processing organization is less likely to expend resources and energies to develop an elaborate classification system vis-a-vis the unit. In Scheff's (1966:128–155) study of psychiatric screening of patients to a state mental hospital, the screening psychiatrists used very few and gross classification-disposition procedures partly because the hospital used minimal intake discretion. Sudnow (1965) describes a similar pattern in the procedures of the public defender's office.

Under these conditions, however, the market units may try to develop various tacit agreements with the processing organization to control their intake informally. When these occur, the formal classification-disposition system takes on classification criteria which may make it irrelevant in the actual routing of classified persons. Thus, for example, correctional institutions receiving young offenders from a state diagnostic center may tacitly agree with the center to consider additional classification-disposition criteria such as space availability, age, and race, which neutralize such other criteria as offender's psychological and social adjustment problems (Dickson, 1967).

Need for Market Unit Services vs. Available Alternatives

The need for a given market unit largely depends on the changes in social position or future behavior the processing organization seeks for its potential clients, and the nature of the demands of potential clients. The more functionally specific its processing tasks the more dependent the organization on other units' specialized services. Yet, the availability of other market units providing comparable services increases a staff's discretion. The organization is in a stronger bargaining position with these units and hence may develop its classification-disposition system somewhat independently of them.

Hence when the organization needs the services of a given market unit having few counterparts, we would expect its system to correspond to constraints imposed by the market unit. On the other hand, having alternative services available potentially frees the organization from such restrictions.

Lacking such units, the organization is under pressure to control either its intake, or its output of clients, or both. Hence, its system may accept only clients for whom disposition resources are available. Similarly, if the organization cannot control its client intake, it is likely to confer a temporary or "holding" status on clients for whom few alternative market units are available. Such a status links the person to the organization, yet defines him as unready for disposition. A study of employment placement agencies indicated that clients for whom employment opportunities were not available were more likely to be classified as requiring counseling than clients similar to them for whom employment opportunities were available (Hasenfeld, 1970).

As we shall note later, the effectiveness of an organization's intelligence system also crucially influences the effective range of available alternatives.

Market Units as Validators of Organizational Goals vs. Self-validating Organizational Ideologies

Potentially, the organization's products are critical to validating its goals, and organizations go to great lengths to use a variety of product measures as indices of their effectiveness and efficiency. For people-processing organizations, the product is placement of a client in one of several market units. Market units differ in their importance in validating an organization's claims of success. This difference is based on: (a) the type of effectiveness and efficiency measures the organization must use with its regulatory groups, and (b) the prestige, importance and amount of crucial resources the market unit controlls in the organizational network.

Hence, the greater the organization's dependence on a market unit for validating its goals, the more will it try to devise a classification-disposition system that will assure placing its clients positively in such a unit. For example, state rehabilitation agencies tend to be evaluated by the number of successful job placements; so they are likely to limit the entry of seriously debilitated clients into their programs (Levine and White, 1961:590–592). Similarly, Reiss and Bordua (1967:32–40) suggest that since police departments depend on prosecutors and courts to validate their claim of competence, the criteria they use for disposition of suspects are partly defined through negotiations with these offices.

The proposition, however, is based on the assumption that an organization's critical product for validating its goals is a "placed" client. An organization's usefulness may rest, however, on other products or side payments (Cyert and March, 1963:29) just as critical to its survival as placing clients, if not more so. It may be a source of employment for members of important political groups, or a training ground for jobs considered important by external validating groups. Ohlin's (1960) analysis of the role of interest groups in influencing correctional objectives points up the importance of side payments. These side payments may neutralize the influence of recipient market units. In fact, they may make the processing organization unconcerned with the market unit's response to its clients. Under these circumstances one may find that its classification-disposition system is insensitive to market conditions and that major disjunctures occur between the two.

Similarly, organizations may develop self-validating ideologies as buffers against negative feedback from their market units. Self-validating ideologies are internally generated belief systems about an organization's effectiveness that negate assessment criteria used by external groups, or those based on evaluation of outcomes. Thus, Eaton (1962) found, for example, that treatment-oriented social work agencies were hostile toward evaluative research and preferred symbolic research based, in part, on staff beliefs about treatment outcomes.

Such ideologies minimize the organization's dependence on its market units to validate its goals. A potentially unanticipated consequence of such ideologies is a staff's biased perception of the type and range of market units that could effectively serve its clients. Such perception, in turn, they foreclose potential transactions with a greater variety of market units. Consequently, its classification-disposition system might respond less to market contingencies than to the self-validating belief system.

Intelligence Effectiveness vs. Intelligence Deficiency

Finally, we propose that organizational intelligence about the environment to potential market units is crucial in determining the range and scope of the exchange relations that people-processing organizations can develop. Such an intelligence system's importance stems from the fundamental fact that enviromental stimuli elicit organizational responses only when transformed into bits of information (Dill, 1958). As Wilensky (1967) suggests, the organization's intelligence system profoundly affects the ways an organization interprets its environment and responds to it.

For people-processing organizations the functions of an effective intelligence system would be to:

(*a* determine the various intake criteria used by potential market units;
(*b* search and identify new market possibilities;
(*c* monitor changes in market conditions regarding intake selection; and
(*d* provide feedback to the processing organization about its success or failure in disposing of its clients.

Moreover, an intelligence system's effectiveness will be determined not only by the amount and accuracy of its information but also by the extent it disseminates this information among staff who are processing clients.

The greater the effectiveness of the intelligence system the wider the range of market units likely to be considered and the less the organization will depend on a few market units. Hence, its classification-disposition system will become more elaborate, and have varied and specific typification rules. In contrast, an organization experiencing intelligence deficiencies must rely on the few market units that use only minimal intake discretion, or those whose intake criteria are well known in the community. Hasenfeld (1971) noted that the lack of adequate and valid information about community resources by the staff of community action centers serving the poor led, in part, to using market units already well known to the poor themselves. Under these conditions the classification-disposition system will become simplified, and be characterized by a few global typification rules.

Conclusions

We have tried to define and develop a perspective on people-processing organizations that emphasizes the effect of the external environment on the classification and disposition of clients. We have suggested that these core activities occur at such organizations' boundaries and are expressed in the form of continuous transactions with clients and other organizations. We suggest, therefore, that an exchange or transaction view of formal organizations provides a potent model for analyzing such organizations and their core activities, particularly in explaining the various patterns of people-processing such organizations develop. This study identifies some key inter-organizational features which determine the power-dependence relations between the processing organization and its environment, and traces their significance for such an organization's system for classifying and disposing of clients.

Our study is inevitably limited in its scope, and does not address itself to several key variables that clearly influence clients' careers in processing organizations. Among these are the role of the clients and their resources in negotiating with the organization; the characteristics of the organizational processing technologies; and the social position, training and orientation of personnel in such organizations. Nevertheless, the study systematically derives a series of testable propositions about the effects of the organization's power-dependence relations with its market units on client management patterns in people-processing organizations.

Notes

1. Some of the studies which address themselves explicitly to this issue are Reiss and Bordua (1967); Ohlin (1960); Carlson (1964); Levine and White (1961).

References

Blau, P. M. 1963. *The Dynamics of Bureaucracy*. Chicago: University of Chicago Press.

Carlson, R. O. 1964. "Environmental Constraints and Organizational Consequences: The Public School and its Clients." Pp. 262–276 in *Behavioral Science and Educational Administration*. Chicago: National Society for the Study of Education.

Cicourel, A., and John Kitsuse. 1963. *The Educational Decision Makers*. Indianapolis: Bobbs-Merrill.

Cyert, Richard M., and James G. March. 1963. *The Behavioral Theory of the Firm*. Englewood Cliffs: Prentice-Hall.

Dickson, D. 1967. "Reception: Organization and Decision Making in a Juvenile Corrections Reception Center." Working paper No. 33. Center for Research on Social Organization, the University of Michigan.

Dill, W. 1958. "Environment as an influence on managerial autonomy." *Administrative Science Quarterly* 2 (March):409–433.

Eaton, J. W. 1962. "Symbolic and substantive evaluation research." *Administrative Science Quarterly* 6 (March):421–442.

Evan, W. M. 1966. "The Organization-Set: Toward Theory of Interorganizational Relations." Pp. 171–191 in James D. Thompson (ed.), *Approaches to Organizational Design*. Pittsburgh, Pennsylvania. The University of Pittsburgh Press.

Freidson, E. 1965. "Disability as Social Deviance." Pp. 71–79 in Marvin B. Sussman (ed.), *Sociology and Rehabilitation*. Washington, D.C.: American Sociological Association.

Goffman, E. 1961. *Asylum: Essays on the Social Situation of Mental Patients and Other Inmates*. New York: Doubleday.

Hasenfeld, Y. 1970. "People Processing Organizations and Client Careers: A Study of Four Anti-Poverty Organizations." Unpublished Ph.D. Dissertation. The University of Michigan.

―――. 1971 "Organizational dilemmas in innovating social services: The case of the community action centers." *Journal of Health and Social Behavior* 12 (September):208–216.

Keith-Lucas, A. 1957. *Decisions About People in Need: A Study of Administrative Responsiveness in Public Assistance*. Chapel-Hill: University of North Carolina Press.

Lefton, Mark, and William R. Rosengren. 1966. "Organizations and clients: Lateral and longitudinal dimensions." *American Sociological Review* 31 (December):802–810.

Levine, S., and Paul White. 1961. "Exchange as a conceptual framework for the study of interorganizational relationships." *Administrative Science Quarterly* 5 (March):583–601.

Levitan, S. A., and Garth L. Mangum. 1969. *Federal Training and Work Programs in the Sixties*. Ann Arbor, Michigan: Institute of Labor and Industrial Relations.

Mishler, E. G., and Nancy E. Waxler. 1963. "Decision process in psychiatric hospitalization: Patients referred, accepted, and admitted to a psychiatric hospital." *American Sociological Review* 28 (August):576–587.

Ohlin, L. 1960. "Conflicting Interests in Correctional Objectives." Pp. 111–129 in Richard A. Cloward et al. (eds.), *Theoretical Studies in the Social Organization of the Prison*. New York: Social Science Research Council.

Reiss, A. J., and David J. Bordua. 1967. "Environment and Organization: A Perspective on the Police." Pp. 25–55 in David J. Bordua (ed.), *The Police: Six Sociological Essays*. New York: Wiley.

Roth, J. 1963. *Timetables*. Indianapolis: Bobbs-Merrill.

Scheff, T. J. 1966. *Being Mentally Ill*. Chicago: Aldine.

Scott, R. A. 1969. *The Making of Blind Men: A Study of Adult Socialization*. New York: Russell Sage Foundation.

Strauss, A., L. Schatzman, R. Bucher, D. Ehrlich, and M. Saleshin. 1964. *Psychiatric Ideologies and Institutions*. New York: Free Press.

Street, D., R. D. Vinter, and C. Perrow. 1966. *Organization for Treatment*. New York: Free Press.

Sudnow, D. 1965. "Normal Crimes: Sociological Features of the Penal Code in a Public Defender's Office." *Social Problems* 12 (Winter):255–276.

Thompson, J. D. 1967. *Organization in Action*. New York: McGraw-Hill.

Vinter, R. D. 1963. "Analysis of Treatment Organization." *Social Work* 8 (July):3–15.

Vinter, R. D., and Rosemary C. Sarri. 1966. "The Juvenile Court: Organization and Decision Making." Pp. 173–320 in *Juvenile Court Hearing Officers Training Manual*, Vol. II. Ann Arbor: The University of Michigan, Institute of Continuing Legal Education.

Wheeler, S. 1966. "The Structure of Formally Organized Socialization Settings." Pp. 51–116 in O. G. Brim and S. Wheeler (eds.), *Socialization After Childhood*. New York: Wiley.

Wilensky, H. 1967. *Organizational Intelligence*. New York: Basic Books.

The Mental Hospital
as a Type of Organization

Talcott Parsons

The purpose of this study is to attempt to delineate, in very broad terms, the type of social organization which is characteristic of mental hospitals, above all which distinguishes them from other types of organization prominent in industrial societies—business firms, governmental administrative agencies, universities, etc. There is, of course, a wide range of variation to be found within the category of mental hospital. Mention will be made of this range in a number of connections, but the main emphasis will be on the hospital as a type relative to other types.

What I am here calling an "organization" is a type of collectivity to be distinguished from a variety of others. It is defined by the relatively clear primacy of a specific collective goal (or, in Bernard's term, an "organization purpose"). It includes such sub-types as business firms, research laboratories, administrative agencies, etc. From it should be clearly distinguished *communities* such as the household and the group subject to a common political jurisdiction, *ascriptive solidarities* such as kinship groups and ethnic groups, and *associations* which operate to integrate the interests of their members relative to a common focus of pressure or interest, responsibility or opportunity.[1]

I shall begin this analysis by a characterization of the goal of the organization. Then I shall deal with the other aspects of its structure in the light of the functional problems which must be met by an organization oriented to the given type of goal in a given type of social situation.

The goal of a mental hospital, put broadly, is *to cope with the consequences for the individual patient and for patients as a social group, of a condition of mental illness.* Illness in turn is a state of impaired psychic functioning of the individual which is institutionally defined as not the individual's "fault" or responsibility, which exempts him from various ordinary obligations but which is also institutionally defined as an undesirable state.

Reprinted from Milton Greenblatt, Daniel J. Levinson, and Richard H. Williams, eds. *The Patient and the Mental Hospital* (Glencoe, Ill.: The Free Press, 1957): pp. 108–29.

The Goal of the Mental Hospital

The goal of the hospital is here purposely defined as "coping" with the consequences of illness in order not to exclude what is usually called the custodial function. But custodial care is, in the light of the institutional definition of illness, a second best, to be accepted only insofar as the preferable goal, namely, recovery from the state of illness, is not technically possible or is excessively costly. The institutional definition of the role of illness, through exempting the sick person on certain levels from responsibility for his condition, by implication institutionalizes his obligation to accept help in coping with it. This may be the help of an individual, as in the private practice of medicine, or of an organization. It is the latter case which is of interest here.

Within this framework, what are the crucial criteria of *mental* illness? In the case of somatic illness the focus of the disturbance seems to center in the relations between the body as a system and the personality. Somatic illness is in the first instance an "intra-individual" phenomenon, and only secondarily a social phenomenon in that the functioning of the individual in his social relationships may be impaired through the ramifications of the central disturbance.[2] Thus the primary focus of an acute infection is impairment of organic functioning. Naturally it may prevent the individual from carrying out his occupational responsibilities.

In the case of mental illness, on the other hand, the focus of disturbance is in the relations between the *personality* of the individual and the *social* system or systems in which he participates. The etiological or diagnostic factors may of course be mainly somatic. The crucial issue, however, is the problem occasioned by the presence in the community of a person in this condition. A mentally ill person is then, in my view, a person who by definition cannot get along adequately with his fellows, who presents a problem to them directly on the behavioral level. The many forms this malfunctioning can take need not be gone into here.

The *goal* of the mental hospital can be more precisely defined in terms of a complex of social responsibilities. These responsibilities derive from the problems raised by the actual or potential deviant behavior of the individual who is ill. For present purposes the responsibilities may be classified under four headings: (1) Custody; (2) protection; (3) socialization; and (4) therapy. These are, then, components of the over-all goal of the hospital.

The custodial responsibility is to meet the "needs" of the sick individual in his state of illness, rather than in an earlier prepathological state or in a hypothetical state of recovery. Of course, the hospital does not necessarily shoulder this whole burden alone. The financial aspect of it may be borne by the family, by political authority through taxation, or by charity through various welfare devices. But a major component of "taking care" of the individual is a function of the hospital; in the case of seriously deteriorated patients this extends to the most elementary matters.[3]

The word *protective* has been chosen to designate the second main component of the hospital's goal; perhaps it is too narrow in its connotations but no more adequate one suggests itself. What is meant is the responsibility to manage the individual's integration in the social system, again in his state of illness and not in a hypothetical state of recovery. The most obvious specific reference is to protection both of others and of himself against harm that he might do. Here it should be remembered that suicide is regarded as a *social* offense, and that frustration of suicide attempts is regarded as socially justified. Protection of others against violence is clearly involved.

These obvious cases do not, however, exhaust what is here meant by protection. More broadly, it is protection of the social interests which are jeopardized by the illness of the patient. Illness is a deviant condition characterized by withdrawal or by aggression against self or others. With reference not to the personality needs but to the social roles of the sick person, there is a social interest in preventing harm and in making other provision for the role-functions from which the individual withdraws because of his illness. As in the case of custodial care, only part of this function is performed by the hospital, but it may be a particularly important part.

The third function or goal-component of the hospital I have referred to as "socialization." By this I mean that *in relation to the patient,* preliminary to anything which can legitimately be called therapy as such, it is necessary to make the patient a full "member" of the hospital organization. Especially important here is the internalization of the hospital's values. The base on which this process operates is, of course, the general institutionalization of the values of health in the society and the definition of the illness as a deviation from health. There is further specification of what is meant by mental as distinct from somatic illness. But there is a double problem of socialization with respect to any particular patient. One aspect concerns his accepting the idea that his condition is justifiably defined as mental illness. This is particularly important in the case of a large proportion of psychotic patients who tend to resist this definition strenuously. A second aspect concerns acceptance of hospitalization in this particular hospital, i.e., acceptance of the *role* of patient.

The fact that there is often an element of compulsion in the establishment of the relation again makes for peculiarly acute psychological difficulties. For many patients, the hospital remains subjectively a prison. In this case socialization into the role of patient is not successfully accomplished.

The fourth function or goal-component of the hospital, and the one generally regarded as primary, is therapy. By therapy I mean a complex of processes oriented toward the recovery of the patient from his illness. The pathological features must be eliminated or at least reduced so that the individual is either put in a state of "normal" psychosomatic balance or is enabled to perform a "normal" set of social roles, or both. It would follow from the above approach that "social adjustment" should play a particularly important part in the evaluation of therapy.

These four may be treated as subgoals of the more general goal which was defined above as "coping with the consequences of the individual's state of mental illness. This classification can be used to analyze the different functions of the hospital as an organization. It must, however, always be understood that a situational reference is involved in any imputation of function. In this case the reference is to the state of mental illness itself. Different types of illness will require different types of custodial care, of protection, of process of socialization and of therapy. Obviously one of the most important distinctions is that between the types of illness for which hospitalization is indicated and those for which it is not. Clearly a large part of the indication has to do with the importance of the first three functions.

Again, different types of hospital care can be analyzed in terms of the balance they provide between the different functional components or subgoals. It has been common to speak of the distinction between "custodial" and "therapeutic" emphases. For certain purposes this distinction is useful, but for others it is too simple. The term custodial, as used in this context, tends to suggest a residual category which includes all three of the non-therapeutic components which have been outlined. Furthermore, although therapeutic *primacy* is ordinarily the ideal, and custodial primacy may not be regarded with favor, the other three are always to some degree necessary functions and should therefore not be treated as reprehensible. The problem of their proper integration with each other and with therapy in relation to different classes of cases is a way of stating the problem of the formulation of policy for the mental hospital.

The classification can also serve to relate the hospital to other types of organization in the society and in this way throw its special characteristics into relief by contrast. Thus schools have certain important resemblances to hospitals, but differ from them in the clear primacy of socialization functions—socialization, to be sure, usually in different roles than that of patient, but still socialization. Custodial and protective, and even therapeutic components may, however, also be present in the functions of schools. A prison, in the dominant tradition, clearly gives primacy to the protective function, especially in its negative aspects, while, particularly recently, there has been a tendency to define it in the direction of the school—as an agency of resocialization—but also again with at least therapeutic undertones. Finally, various hospitals for chronic diseases, homes for the aged, etc., have primarily custodial functions.

The Relations of the Mental Hospital to the Wider Community

For general theoretical reasons,[4] I shall follow the procedure of dealing with the value system as the major point of reference for the analysis of the structure and functioning of any social system. A hospital like any collectivity must be treated as a subsystem of a society. The value system of the collectivity then must be treated as a derivative of the values of the society as a whole.

As an organization, the hospital's value system, like that of other organizations, is concerned primarily with the definition of its goal and secondarily with the definition of the institutional patterns (norms or rules) within which the pursuit of the goal should be sought. The goal is to cope with the consequences of the states of human individuals we call mental illness. This goal is linked with the more general value system of the society through the patterns of valuation of the individual personality. American societal values put a primary emphasis on achievement, and it is chiefly because mental illness hinders effective achievement that in our society it is defined as an undesirable state. Even the custodial and protective components of the goal fit from this point of view. Relieving others of the responsibility for custodial care of the patient frees them for more important achievement (partly through relieving them of psychological "strain") and the protective function includes protection of the conditions of effective achievement for others. Other important components of the American value system are also relevant here. Thus the "welfare" of the individual is positively valued and this includes his own states of satisfaction or "happiness." Hence unnecessary suffering on the part of anybody is condemned.

Using the value system of the organization as a reference point, let me try to spell out its implications for the functioning of the organization in the various contexts in which it operates. The first essential distinction in the classification of these contexts is between *external* functions, relating the organization to the rest of the society, and *internal* functions, relating the various structural parts of it to each other. The present section will be devoted to the external functions.

These functions may be classified under four main headings: (1) the *legitimation* of the operation of the hospital in the community; (2) the processes involved in dealing with the *recipients* of the hospital's services, the patients and, above all, their families; (3) the processes of acquiring the *facilities* necessary for carrying out its functions; and (4) the ways in which the hospital is *integrated into the community* in which it operates.

Legitimation. With respect to legitimation, we presume that organizations like the mental hospital could not function at all if they were not legitimized in terms of the wider value system of the society. But even if the broad pattern of this legitimation is "given" in the culture of the society, its specification and maintenance with reference to the particular hospital do not occur automatically, but require specific mechanisms.

The relevant mechanisms concern the ensuring of community "confidence" in the hospital. This will include the "community standing," the reputation for responsibility of the elements in the community who sponsor the hospital and take responsibility for the integrity and technical competence of its administration. It will also include the utilization of the relevant professional groups, particularly the medical profession, not simply in a technological sense, but as guarantors of the bona fide character of the operation. The formula in general is that if reputable medical personnel associate themselves with the hospital it must be "all right." More specifically, these processes include the diffuse area of "public relations," the mechanism by which the "right" of the organization to operate and the appeal to give it support are established."

Relations to Recipients of Hospital Services. The second context brings out one of the most distinctive features of the mental hospital as an organization, namely, that the primary recipients of its services, the patients, are served through being taken directly into the organization as members. One of the primary jobs of the hospital staff is to select patients for *admission* and correspondingly to decide about discharge. Perhaps the closest analogy in our society is the residential school or college. The most striking contrast is with the ordinary commercial relationships where a customer is not in any comparable sense "admitted" to membership in the firm which produces or sells the commodity he buys.

We may then raise a series of questions about hospital admission: What are the criteria of admission? What is the form taken by payment for service if any? Is any counterservice expected of the patient other than a payment? If so, is any reward provided for effective performance of this counterservice?[5]

The services produced by the mental hospital stem from the components of the hospital goal discussed above. They are simultaneously services to the individual patient and to the social groups of which he is a member, notably his family. The protective and custodial services benefit the groups to which he is related, and also himself in that he is protected "against himself" and taken care of where he cannot take care of himself. Still more obviously is this true of therapeutic services. The socialization services are justified particularly as a condition of effective performance of the other three.

On this background it is understandable that the primary criterion of admission to the hospital is *need* in the particular sense defined by being mentally ill; conversely, the criterion of discharge is cessation of the need.

With respect to "payment" for service the obvious principle is one of reciprocity. The hospital needs financial support, and those who accept its services are expected to contribute to this in proportion to their capacity. This leads to the well-known principle of the sliding scale, which applies to professional and charitable services generally. It is true that many of our mental hospitals are free to the beneficiaries, being supported out of taxation. However, even in state hospitals an attempt is usually made to get some payment from the family if they can afford it. Moreover, like many other tax-supported services, mental hospitals are in fact paid for on an indirect sliding scale through progressive taxation. The difference from the more familiar sliding scale is that the taxpayer contributes to the support of mental hospitals whether members of his family are patients in them or not—as he does to public schools. This may be interpreted as a transfer of the obligation of "care" from the family to a higher-order ascriptive solidarity or community.

Let us now take up the other side of the total "boundary transaction" of the hospital with the recipients of its services. The question is whether the patient (and/or his family) "contributes" anything to the functioning of the mental hospital. The answer is unequivocally yes. There is a limiting type of somatic illness where the sick individual is simply an object being "operated upon" by the therapeutic personnel. The only coöperation required of him then is to allow himself to be treated in this way; similarly with certain extreme psychoses. But corresponding to the fact that in mental illness the focus of disturbance is behavioral, is the fact that therapy is a process of social interaction.[6] The positive role of the patients is an essential aspect of the process. His coöperation must be enlisted, he must be adequately motivated to "do his part" toward recovery. Therapy is cooperative "work." It is not too far-fetched to think of the patient as being in a sense "employed" to play a role in this enterprise. This is particularly conspicuous for the hospitalized patient whose primary "job" is to get well.

The contributory (work) aspect of the role of patient is most clearly brought out in the therapeutic component of the hospital function. It is, however, also present with respect to the custodial component. It is very general practice, and thought to be therapeutically helpful, for the patient to do as much for himself as he can, to work and even in a sense "earn his keep." Indeed, one prominent deviant tendency in mental hospitals is for the organization to become a kind of special industrial enterprise. With respect to the protective function, the contributory factor is made clear in that negative sanctions are systematically applied to the "disturbed" patient who requires special protective measures. At the very least, assignment to the disturbed ward puts such an individual in a low position in the status-hierarchy of the hospital. Hence we can say that coöperation in minimizing the protective measures necessitated for the hospital is actively solicited and systematically rewarded. This is conspicuous in the case of the hospitals which experiment self-consciously with minimization or even complete elimination of traditional protective practices. Similar considerations apply to the socialization factor.

Finally, what "payment" does the patient receive from the hospital for his coöperative contribution? Clearly it is not a money payment, which is understandable in that the recipient of the service and the contributor tend to be the same person or unit. Moreover, he is usually financially deficit relative to the hospital; except in some private hospitals, the patient pays at best only part of what it costs to provide the service. With money payment eliminated, the "payment" takes the form of symbolic rewards. These in turn are of two main interconnected types: One is the approval of the staff, when they indicate that the patient is "doing a good job"; the other is the system of more or less well-defined privileges (and their obverse, deprivations) which deliberately or not are manipulated in relation to the patient's conduct. Ward assignment is particularly crucial in this respect, but also going-out privileges and things of that sort.

We may sum up the aspect of the hospital's functioning which is concerned most directly with relations to patients and their connections. Its most distinctive feature is the "admission" of the patient to a kind of "membership" in the organization, which takes the form of physical residence on the hospital premises and subjection to the authority and control of the hospital authorities. This special status is also formalized in that leaving the hospital involves a formal act of discharge by these same authorities.

The status of the hospital patient is thus in certain but different respects analogous to two others which are familiar in our society; precisely because of the analogies the differences are illuminating. The first of these is the *customer* who purchases goods or services offered on the market, making a money payment for them; the second is the *employee* of an organization who enters into a contract of employment. The hospital is performing a complex of services, which fit into the general paradigm of the division of labor. But it does this by taking its "customers" directly into its organization, thereby establishing with them the kind of solidary tie which goes with common membership in an organization. In this it is similar to the residential school or college. In both cases payment is in general adjusted according to the sliding scale principle which symbolizes the common collectivity membership to which reference has been made.

The analogy to the contract of employment centers on the expectation that the patient will actively cooperate in the performance of the function of the hospital, above all, by "trying" to get well and to help the therapeutic agents toward this goal. Here, however, he is not given money remuneration, but is "paid" in a variety of attitudinal and status rewards which are graded in the organization of the hospital.

It is further significant that these two aspects, the role of "customer" and of "employee" are not differentiated, as in the case of the economic division of labor, but are fused in the same concrete role. The cases in which this fusion does and does not occur seem to define a major line of distinction between types of social organization. The type case of the separation of the two role-relations is the provision of goods and services to the consumer by "commercial" productive units. The case of fusion includes not only the hospital and the school, but, above all, the two great super-ordinate collectivity structures of historic societies, the state and the church which "purvey" services only to their own members. It is also notable that kinship units are universally included in this type.

What is the significane of the fact that the hospital, although its functions from the societal point of view is highly specialized, belongs on the fused relation, collective solidarity side of this particular analytical line? Why are services of this type not purveyed, as Herbert Spencer thought they should be, on strictly commercial principles?

I shall here suggest a tentative answer on one of several possible levels. It is true that in societal terms the function of the mental hospital is specific and specialized; its concern is only with health, not with economic production, maintaining political order, or any of a variety of other social interests. But if in societal terms this function is specific, in terms of the personality of the patient this is not so. A disturbance of personality functioning which an legitimately be said to constitute mental illness, must be considered to be highly *generalized* through the personality; this is one main reason why it cannot be remedied by ordinary processes of "teaching."

The implication of the generalization of the disturbance constituting mental illness is that only through *diffuse* commitments to therapeutic agencies can an adequate therapeutic relationship become established. In seeking therapeutic help the individual cannot restrict his obligation to the agency with which he establishes a relationship, to a sector of his motivational structure which has been delineated in advance, as he can in inquiring about a purchase; he must be ready to follow the therapeutic problem wherever it may lead.

This diffuseness of commitment to therapeutic agencies is intimately connected with the relations between mental illness and the regressive components of the structure of personality. Since all individuals have gone through roughly the same order of socialization, deeper disturbances involve the more regressive levels, which are the origins of the whole range of later, more differentiated parts of the personality.

If a therapeutic agency is to meet the requirements of its function, it must provide adequate objects of transference. The primary socializing agents for the earlier stages, which hence are relevant transference objects for the deeper levels of regression, have always been family figures. Hence the therapeutic agency must, in certain crucial aspects, produce a situation similar to that of the child in the family.

Seen in this light, taking the patient into the hospital and thereby attenuating his ties with other collectivities, takes on a special significance. The most important feature of the pre-Oedipal child's social role was the confining of his most significant relationships and hence objects of cathexis to the narrow circle of the family. Furthermore he was in a dependent status within the family. In these respects (but by no means all respects) it can be seen that the individual's status as hospital patient constitutes a repetition of his status as a child in the family. This seems to be a primary significance of hospitalization as a symbolic change of status; it takes the individual out of a responsible adult position in his family of procreation and occupation and puts him into a dependent, childlike position in another collectivity which is analogous to his family of *orientation*.[7]

The Acquisition of Facilities. Let us turn now to the third of the four main boundary-processes between the hospital and its environment —the acquisition of the facilities needed to carry out the hospital's functions. In a modern society with developed monetary institutions, there are, for any organization, three main categories of facilities. On one level, the generalized facility par excellence is financial resources.[8]

Rather special conditions obtain with respect to the financing of the mental hospital: these can be brought out particularly through contrast with the business firm. A minority of hospitals are financed by the charges for service paid by patients. But even here the sliding scale usually prevails and financing purely on this basis is possible only for a few hospitals catering to the higher income groups.

Generally, financial resources must be raised mainly from sources other than payment by the patient. The essential underlying basis is the social value judgment that health is a "right" of the individual. It is considered an obligation of society, through political organization or through voluntary contribution, to provide hospitalization regardless of the individual's ability to pay. Essentially, then, this phase of the financing of hospitals is an extension of the principle of the sliding scale.

In this respect again a broad line runs through the whole of the social structure. The hospital stands on one side of the line, along with government, education, religion, and the family, while organizations devoted primarily to economic production stand on the other. The care of illness is regarded as the positive responsibility of certain elements of the population; it cannot be left to the "self-interest" of entrepreneurs and the "wishes" of those needing it.

Two main types of organization are predominant in this field: The first, the relatively autonomous type in which a private board of trustees assumes the responsibility of adequate financing as well as certain authority over the conduct of the organization; the second, in which the hospital is a unit in a larger organizational system, usually that of a government character, though sometimes of religious bodies.

The essential point seems to be that there must be some effective organizational intermediary between the ultimate sources of financial resources and the operative parts of the organization. This intermediary organization must be "trusted" by the ultimate sources of funds, e.g., private donors or legislative bodies which vote funds, and to justify this trust it must have some, but not too much, control over the uses to which the funds are put.

The concrete facilities for which money funds are spent, are divided into two categories, namely, physical facilities and personnel.

Though there may be special features of the conditions of acquisition of physical facilities for mental hospitals, they do not loom very large and do not warrant further discussion in this brief chapter.

The problem of the *acquisition of personnel* through employment is far more complex and provides many special problems of great concern to students of the hospital and persons bearing responsibility in this field. It will not be possible to go into more than a few of these problems, those of the broadest sociological interest. Perhaps these can be conveniently classified as those touching three classes of personnel; namely, professional, administrative, and a category best called "service."

It is the key position of certain professional groups that more than anything else distinguishes the occupational role structure of the mental hospital. Of these the psychiatrists occupy the central position, but they stand at the center of a complex of professional groups including nurses, social workers, occupational therapists, and, lately, in increasing numbers, psychologists and sociologists.

The acquisition of the services of these professional persons involves a special type of labor market. It is characterized by patterns very much like the sliding scale in the payment for services—indeed, in the individual fee-for-service case, the two coincide. The salary of the professional man is analogous to the old conception of "just price" and differs sharply from the economist's standard of "marginal productivity." Its determination is particularly conditioned by the need to provide favorable opportunities for exercise of special technical competence in a highly responsible situation.

Administrative roles and the recruitment of personnel for them present special problems in types of organization primarily devoted to the provision of professional services to a category of persons; in this respect the hospital is, of course, similar to the university and a few other organizational types. There is a built-in dilemma here. The goal of the organization is defined in terms of the professional service and only the professional man is competent to evaluate the service given and the competence of those who do it, as well as the adequacy of the conditions and facilities provided. However, the technical expert—certainly the psychiatrist—is not, as such, a competent expert on the functioning of organizations, and yet organization which is beyond his professional competence is required to provide the setting for adequate performance of his functions. Someone must exercise administrative authority on the basis of a number of considerations, of which psychiatric technicalities are only a part, and in these spheres the administrator must be in a position sometimes to overrule the professionally competent personnel.

Hence such organizations involve an unstable balance between two different types of authority: the organizational executive and the professional specialist.

No fully stable solution of this dilemma seems to have been found. An important feature of the mental hospital, however, is that the clearly paramount role on the professional side is played by *one* type of professional specialist, namely, the psychiatrist. In the university on the other hand, the faculty comprises a wide diversity of professional types in many substantive fields. This difference probably has something to do with the strong tendency for hospitals to place physicians in the positions of primary administrative responsibility.

As a general rule, the psychiatrist who becomes superintendent, particularly of a large mental hospital, does little practicing of psychiatry in this capacity, and it is open to question how far his "understanding" of psychiatry and psychiatrists by virtue of being one is an essential positive asset in his strictly administrative capacity. The respect in which his psychiatric standing is clearly important is in the symbolization of psychiatric (medical) control of the hospital. This clearly serves to mitigate staff anxieties generated by their being placed under administrative control through which some professional autonomy must be sacrificed. Correspondingly, the relative frequency with which non-academic people are made university presidents is probably associated with the greater diversity of the total faculties of a university (including professional faculties) as compared with the professional staff of a hospital.

For reasons such as this, what are felt to be the relevant qualifications of hospital administrators are highly unstructured and the features of the particular situation and particular personalities tend to weigh very heavily. One tendency has been to try to establish an independent profession of hospital administrators including special programs of technical training for them. It is, however, difficult to define the qualifications and the appropriate training and it remains to be seen how successful this attempt will prove to be.

There are many categories of hospital personnel that are neither professional nor administrative and that present few special problems, e.g., kitchen personnel or those taking care of buildings and grounds. The major point seems to be the influence of the special atmosphere which attaches to the mental hospital (as distinguished from other types of organizations) and which may very well lead to a selectivity in the types of people available for such jobs.

There is, however, one category of great importance—because of contact with patients—namely, the *attendant*. In terms of both qualifications and authority, his role is defined residually. He has responsibility in the direct care and management of patients, and yet he has no professional qualifications and no special competence other than that derived from direct experience. His role is clearly of great importance and because of the cost of professional personnel, a good deal of responsibility tends to be left in his hands. Until recently the role has often been defined mainly by practical exigencies rather than by any clear conception of positive function.

Selectivity in recruitment is likely to be more pronounced for aides than for other categories of nonprofessional personnel. It is rather special personalities who can tolerate spending most of their working time in intimate contact with mentally ill people without the stabilization of their motivations provided by a well-defined professional role. Fortunately, some of these problems are coming to be studied, but at present relatively little can be said about this vital area. The most important point seems to be that the mental hospital is dependent on a specially selected set of lower-order occupational personnel, drawn on an unknown basis from the local community in which the hospital is situated.[9]

Integration into the Larger Community. The fourth major boundary-process of an organization concerns the mechanisms by which, indirectly, its procedures are made acceptable to the community at large. This above all involves its adherence to values and to patterns of organization and operation which (a) are generalizable beyond particular organizations, or (b) are considered to be justified by the particular circumstances of the particular case or type of organization.

Besides the direct role of the values which has already been noted, there are three major complexes of (hospital-community) integrative mechanisms. They may be called the *"contract"* complex, the *"authority"* complex, and the *"universalistic rule"* complex. Let me discuss each of these briefly in turn.

The central feature of the complex that I have called *contractual* is this: It defines the obligations of loyalty to the organization that are assumed by the providers of facilities to it, and by those employed by it. The essential problem of integration of the organization with the rest of the community is to maintain patterns of procedure consonant with those operative in the community at large. The obvious cases are those patterns defining the nature and extent of the responsibility of elements in the community for making provision for the care of the mentally ill, and the patterns defining the categories of personnel who are competent to carry on this function and their status in the community. We have already noted the importance of observing the standards of training and competence which transcend any particular organization's personnel needs in their scope. It is notable that these standards have by no means remained unchanged over a period and are continually undergoing modification, through formal provisions and informally.

The relation of institutional standards in this field to the processes of change may be illustrated by the problem of introducing new professional groups which in turn will introduce new procedures in the functioning of the hospital. One of the interesting recent cases is the social scientist. Making a place for this new type of role, as distinguished from new incumbents in established role-types, involves institutional change. Though it may be "spearheaded" in particular organizations, it can never become firmly established without being generalized with respect to the functions of a category of organizations.

It was said that the contractual complex particularly concerns definition of the scope of loyalty of personnel (and providers of facilities) to an organization. This point is illustrated by the case of professional personnel; here a professional person has a dual responsibility in his occupational capacity—first to the organization (and through it to patients), and second to the professional group of which he is a member. Any organization must necessarily combine the services of a *plurality* of occupational categories with different types of competence, training, etc. Correspondingly, the members of a given occupational category will be employed in a plurality of different organizations. These two bases of structure in the occupational world cross-cut and interpenetrate with each other. Their integration requires mechanisms which transcend both the particular organization and the particular professional group. The institutionalization of the contract of employment is such a mechanism.[10]

The second important complex of institutional integration of the organization in its social environment is what we have called the *authority* complex. It concerns the relations of the organization to patients and, secondarily, to operative personnel. The essential point is that, to carry out its functions, the organization must be given some order of control over the human situations in which this is done. But the patterns involved can never be the concern only of the hospital itself; they must be integrated into the relevant pattern system of the society as a whole. This is particularly crucial to the legitimation and hence community tolerance of the mental hospital because it exercises compulsion and because it exposes the patient to exploration and manipulation of concerns usually regarded as extremely personal and private.

Here, corresponding to the fact that the psychiatrist is a member both of the hospital organization and of his wider professional group, is the important fact that the patient is a member both of the hospital and of various outside solidary groups, notably his family. Not only is the family's permission necessary for the patient's commitment in the first place, but it retains a legitimate concern with what happens to him in the hospital. Hence the conditions of commitment and the exposure to various kinds of treatment need to be institutionally regulated on a basis transcending the practices and exigencies of the particular organization. As in the professional case, the patterns here are by no means completely stable but are undergoing continual adjustment and change. The shifting line between the treatment of certain types of behavior as criminal and as evidence of mental illness is a case in point. Different types of authority are exerted in the prison and in the hospital. This institutionalization thus incorporates the institutionalized definitions of the nature of mental illness, and relates these to maintenance of balance between the protective, the custodial, the socialization, and the therapeutic functions of the hospital.

It is thus not surprising that mental hospitals are especially conspicuously involved in two institutional complexes that serve to integrate them in the community. The first is the direct use of *legal legitimation* of their functions through legal commitment. Generally speaking, we may say that in a relatively "individualistic" society like our own, the resort to formal legal authorization of action means that the situation is felt to be actually or potentially explosive, that protection is needed in case of trouble. The relation is, of course, a two-way one; the hospital is in need of protection, but at the same time the use of compulsion is a matter of public concern and cannot be left to the unregulated discretion of private organizations.

The second involvement is with the informal authority of the *medical profession*. From the sheer point of view of technical contribution to the therapeutic function—to say nothing of the other functions of the hospital—it is by no means easy to draw the lines between contributions which are inherently medical and those which are not. Only the narrowest of medical partisans would claim that the M.D. degree conferred a complete monopoly of relevant competence, and that absence of it excluded a person from any contribution. Factors other than the sheer technical competence of medical personnel would seem to determine in part the tremendous emphasis placed on the legitimating role of the physician in the authority exercised by mental hospitals. This emphasis in effect says that physicians may avail themselves of the coöperation and assistance of other groups, professional and nonprofessional, but it is legitimate to hold the physican responsible for the outcome, and he delegates his responsibility at his own risk. The basis of this seems to lie essentially in the institutionalized confidence that the general population rests in the physician as both a competent and an ethically responsible custodian of the interests of individuals who may in any way be defined as ill. Given the potential explosiveness in so many directions of the phenomena of mental illness, this is a great protection for the hospital; it can always say that physicians are in the last analysis responsible. It is also a mechanism by which a type of "public" control other than the legal is imposed on the hospital—only if reputable physicians will take responsibility, will the organization be trusted in the community.

Both the contractual complex and the authority complex define in relatively specific ways what is to be expected of the mental hospital as an organization and thus the conditions under which it will be tolerated or supported in the community. But there is an even more general level of expectations that transcends the particularities even of this *type* of organization. With due regard to its special functions and needs, the organization must observe community standards of "good practice." Compulsion and personal investigation of patients is necessary but it must not be carried farther than technical requirements dictate. Patients must not be subjected to unnecessarily harsh discipline or other deprivations. Employees in all categories must be treated "fairly" by community standards. Administration must be honest. The catalogue could be carried further. Suffice it to say that conformity with the general social standards of acceptable conduct is an essential condition of smooth functioning of any organization in a community setting.

The Internal Structure and Processes of the Mental Hospital

I have reviewed the values of the mental hospital as an organization and the principal processes and patterns of its interchange with individuals and collectivities in its social environment. It remains to say something about its internal structure and functioning.

Socialization and Values. The value system has its internal as well as its external aspects. It is assumed, in the broad way in which we can speak of social system values generally, these two aspects are shared by all categories of personnel who are involved in the functioning of the hospital, including patients. It should not, however, be lightly assumed that the implementation of the value system, not in the technological and administrative senses, but in the sense of motivational commitment, takes place "automatically" and presents no problems.

We presume that such organizations could not function at all if they were not legitimized in terms of the value system of the larger society and various of its subsystems, including persons in roles which have little to do directly with mental hospitals. But at the same time any particular mental hospital represents specification of the more general community values having to do with its functions and position in the community. It cannot be assumed that just the right order of commitment exists in advance in the personnel who become, in one or another capacity, members of the organization.

Thus a hospital, like any other organization, performs functions of socialization for all categories of its personnel as well as for its patients. Sociologically, the process of socialization and the mechanisms by which it proceeds should be analyzed by the same basic paradigm used for any process of socialization (Parsons and Olds, chap. 4 in Parsons and Bales, 1955). (There are, however, peculiarities. Since socialization theory has, above all, been worked out in connection with the socialization of the child, appropriate allowances must be made for differences in the situations of adults in two types of roles, namely, the occupational roles of hospital personnel and the role of patient.)

Personnel, of course, break down into a variety of subcategories and attempting to discuss each would lead too far afield. Suffice it to say that there must be frustration of previous "unrealistic" expectations, and that in relation to the disturbance resulting, there must be "permissiveness" in allowing for the "inexperience" of new people. There must be supportive factors in the situation, but this support must not go so far as permanently to legitimize and reward the patterns of deviant behavior of the new person. There must be adequate rewarding of proper behavior as people begin to "catch on." To keep an eye on the functioning of these socialization mechanisms is by no means the least important task of persons in posts of administrative responsibility.

In the case of the patient, role socialization is closely connected with therapy as a total process. However, it seems to me that a careful attempt to disentangle this element from the specifically therapeutic process would be well worthwhile. This is perhaps particularly true of hospitalized patients, so many of whom have been subjected to compulsion in the admission process, where the normal ambivalence about acceptance of the role of patient may be greatly accentuated. Here it should of course be remembered that the hospital and its personnel do not stand alone as agents of such socialization but that the attitudes and roles of family members and others may be of crucial significance.

Routine Technical Functions. Besides socialization, the most important set of functions which may be classed as direct implementation of the organization's value system, are its routine technical functions. From the point of view of the theory of organization as such, the performance of activity directly implementing the organizational goal is not directly a matter of policy-making or any other aspect of administration, but should be thought of ideally as routinized under the control of the organization. Only when something "goes wrong" or when technical innovations have to be introduced do "policy questions" come to be involved.[11]

Once operating on a satisfactory basis, the function of the organization as such in relation to these technical processes is to maintain favorable conditions for their stable, continuing operation, including the flow of patients into and out of the established relational "slots," the replacement of personnel, and the flow of facilities. The basic distinction between technical and organizational functions is intimately related to the distinction between professional and executive roles. Professional roles as such are, in a setting of organization, generally operative or technical roles.[12]

The results of technical performance do not accrue most directly to the responsible administration of the hospital in the policy-oriented sense, but rather to the aspect or part of the administration most concerned with the maintenance of an effective system of facilities for the performance of technical function. There may be postulated a kind of exchange in this sense between administration and technically operative personnel.

Another main direction of involvement of the technical subsystem concerns the most direct ways in which the responsible administration can implement its commitment to the value of the organization, i.e., to its therapeutic goals. This is done by the allocation of authorizations and responsibilities among the operative echelons. On the one side, the powers and authority of administration must be legitimized. This legitimation cannot be directly derived from the individual technical competence and moral integrity of the administrative personnel, since their direct functions are not as such operative. The primary focus of legitimation must rather lie in recognition of the exigencies which make organization necessary so that its cost is justified. On the other side, within the framework of an established organization, the administration takes responsibility for adjusting the allocation of responsibilities among the operative groups. This is done, above all, through the fact that the administration is in a position to provide facilities and authority which greatly enhance the probabilities of *successful* performance by the operative personnel.

The Integration of "Administrative" and "Operative" Systems. Discussion of the functions of operative units in relation to administration has brought out the fact that the internal structure of the hospital often tends to be polarized in terms of these two structural elements. This general tendency with respect to all organizations is, I think, accentuated in the case of the hospital by the prominence of professional services in the situation. In the nature of the case, professional services are concentrated at the operative level. Even though administrative personnel are often professionally qualified people, we have suggested that this is to a large extent explained by the importance of symbolic integration between the two parts of the organization.

In order to clarify this subtle relationship, let us look at some of the internal problems from the point of view of the responsible administration. It may be suggested that their primary function is the making of policy decisions which bind the organization as such. But as we have noted, these are not technically operative policy decisions; the latter belong in the operative subsystems. They are rather decisions which concern the affairs of the organization as a whole. Externally they concern matters of the numbers and types of patients to be admitted, finance, and personnel recruitment, integration of the organization in the community, public relations, etc. Internally they concern the authorization and enforcement of measures to implement the organization's commitments relative to the outside situation.

Internally these administrative functions, besides the one treated under the heading of socialization, break down into three main categories. The first is the category most directly concerned with the internal implementation of its goal-commitments. On theoretical grounds it may be said that such decisions are concerned in the first instance with maximizing the *integration of the organization,* that is, enlisting the loyalty of its personnel to the organization. Broadly, in a "good" organization, this will be assured most effectively through belief in the "rightness" of the decisions taken. But such decisions have consequences which bear unevenly on the different groups within the organization. This unevenness and the related processes of shifting of responsibilities and rewards are the sources of the integrative *problems* associated with policy decisions. Repercussions are then mediated to the personality level by the institutionalization of rules of fairness in the distribution of responsibilities and rewards. The prime base in the structure of organization for the acceptance of the consequences of policy decisions, on the other hand, is the institutionalization of authority.

The problem directly relevant to the mental hospital is the nature of the authority pattern appropriate to such an organization, and its relation to the mobilization of support for policy decisions. The primary key to this in turn lies in the prominence of high-level, professional personnel in the operative echelons of the organization. They are objects of administrative authority, and the pattern of authority must give adequate recognition to their special technical competence, and hence responsibility on the appropriate operating levels, and to their professional integrity and right to autonomy. These conditions seem to make for two main phenomena. One is the relative sharpness of the distinction between "purely administrative" questions (those on which it is felt unnecessary to consult professional personnel) and questions which do involve the professionals. (In the university, for example, the tendency is to treat budgetary questions as "purely administrative.") The second phenomenon is the strong mitigation of the "authoritarian" tendency of many organizations in favor of a "collegial" principle. This will generally mean taking leading members, at least of the professional staff, more or less fully into the decision-making process, thus blurring the distinction between administrative and operative elements in the organization.

A second major focus of the administrative function lies in the *maintenance of adequate facilities*. Externally, as we pointed out, this concerns financing and recruitment of personnel. Internally it is the maintenance and improvement of the patterns of allocation and organization necessary to provide the facility-base for operative performance. Responsibilities relative to "housekeeping" functions, and to the organization of "auxiliary" personnel, should be treated here. It is particularly important to keep clearly in mind the nature of the subsystems which make up the larger organization. Control of many auxiliary personnel in their operative functions is placed in the hands of these subsystems; thus the nurse is supposed to act largely under the authority of the physician. But responsibility for the organizational framework within which the subsystems work must be taken by the administration of the hospital.

What is particularly distinctive of the mental hospital in this context? If one major thing could be pointed out, it is the great importance of what, relative to the manifest level of organizational administration, are the *latent* functions of facilities and their organization. That patients should be adequately fed and housed, that there should be adequate facilities and personnel for their "care" in the protective and custodial senses, goes without saying; on this level, the problems of the mental hospital are similar to those of other organizations. But because these provisions of facilities constitute the environment of the therapeutic process, the ways in which they are arranged may, because of the symbolic meanings they acquire, become of great significance for the hospital function itself through their effect on the conditions of patients. This is perhaps the main point at which a conflict may arise between the needs of the hospital as an organization and its therapeutic functions for patients. Obviously also for this reason this is a prominent possible focus of conflict between administration and operative therapeutic subsystems.

The third major focus of the administrative function is the one already discussed, the adjustments in the *allocation of responsibilities* in relation to the legitimation of its exercise of authority. What is required here is to earn the "confidence" of the operating personnel through insuring opportunity for successful achievement. This is a higher order of basis for securing the loyal coöperation of the organization than that involved in support for policy decisions in the usual sense. I am discriminating two different factors in what is often called "satisfaction" of personnel with the administration. On the one hand, there is the problem of support for the current commitments which have varying consequences for different elements within the organization. Here the emphasis is on the *relative* burdens and rewards received as a consequence of such decisions. The other component is the shared attitudes of legitimation of the over-all conduct of the administrative function, not taken mainly in distributive terms.

Again we may ask what is particularly distinctive of the mental hospital in this respect as compared with other types of organizations? I think it can be said that this is particularly important in defining the basis of the independent position of the professional component of the hospital personnel. The central pattern is the definition of the psychiatrist as *par excellence* the competent expert in the diagnosis and therapy of mental illness, and hence in the functions of hospital administration insofar as they facilitate effective functioning on the part of the psychiatric staff. The focus here is on the attitudes of the psychiatric staff in their capacity as responsible members of their *professional group,* rather than in terms of their specific hospital positions.

Very closely involved here is the relation between the functions and prerogatives of the psychiatrists and those of other categories of personnel in the hospital. The balance of functional contribution of the several groups has to be regulated in terms of a value system broader than that of the hospital as such. We find here the primary articulation with the institutionalized patterns of science: The basic cultural definitions of health and illness, the balance of the different components in the etiology and therapy of illness, the definition of "medicine" and its boundaries, etc. The shift in recent years toward taking greater cognizance of the "behavioral sciences," and hence the question of including some of their subject-matter in medicine, is an illustration of the dynamic elements involved in this balance of adjustment.

It may prove illuminating to illustrate the uses of the above analysis by a brief discussion of a rather common type of "pathology" of the larger mental hospital. The difficulty of preventing such hospitals from leaning heavily in the direction of custodial and protective primacy is well known. I should like to bring out one of the less appreciated factors in reinforcing this tendency. I have emphasized throughout the key position of the psychiatrist, not only as the primary operative agent of the therapeutic process itself, but as the focus of the legitimation of the functions of the hospital as a whole.

The tendency manifested in the selection of psychiatrists as superintendents is widely diffused through hospital organization. Psychiatrists are by and large the most expensive members of the hospital staff. Most large mental hospitals stand, for obvious reasons, in a chronic state of budgetary deficiency. In such a situation there is an economically understandable trend to replace the services of psychiatrists with those of less expensive personnel—nurses, social workers, psychologists, and aides. At the same time, because of the symbolic importance of the psychiatrist's legitimating role, there is a tendency, within sub-units of the hospital, to put psychiatrists in positions with a large component of administrative responsibility, i.e., as heads of services, etc.

The outcome of all this is both a scarcity of psychiatric service and a deflection of what there is into administrative rather than operative functions. The result places the psychiatrists in a difficult position. They are held responsible for the operative conduct of the hospital's therapeutic function, but because they are spread so thin and have so little direct contact with patients they are, to a large extent, not implementing this responsibility but are delegating it to nonpsychiatric personnel.

This situation may well have something to do with the sensitivity of the psychiatric component of the staff to the prerogatives of their position of authority, the well-known insistence that the psychiatrist be recognized unequivocally as "captain" of the therapeutic team. The simple fact is that a level of responsibility is often imputed to them which they are not in a position to implement successfully, and in this situation, protection against being challenged from below or outside, serves to mitigate the strain.

At the same time, the auxiliary personnel (such as nurses and aides) to whom responsibility is delegated may have tendencies in the direction of a custodial emphasis. This is, first, because they are often formally forbidden to assume therapeutic responsibilities. But because they stand in close operative relations to the daily lives of patients, they have a strong vested interest in the smooth functioning of the hospital or at least their ward. Once patients are well socialized into such a community, they may easily get too well-adjusted to be brought over a therapeutic hump. There is no one to apply the kind of pressure necessary to upset the balance of the "good institutional cure."

Conclusions

This study has been more in the nature of a prolegomenon than of a satisfactory, full analysis of the mental hospital as a type of social organization. It has attempted, in outline form, to apply a general paradigm of the principal elements of an organization to the case of the mental hospital. The impression given by the attempt is perhaps a little pedantic. But its justification lies in taking a step toward being more systematic than has been the custom in studies in this area. An attempt to go farther will have to aim at *placing* the relationship of the hospital, both in its relations to the outside community and in its internal exigencies, to other types of organization, and of collectivity structure. This placing cannot be in terms of specific "points" but rather of ranges within which the relevant features of the hospital can be expected to fit in relation to other types of organization. Why the hospital should fall within a given range and differ in this respect from other types of organization must then be related to the nature of its functions, to the types of patients it must deal with and how, to the types of personnel it employs, to the modes of its financial support, to its "public relations," and to the many internal exigencies of the sort we have attempted to outline.

Above all, I wish to emphasize that the sociology of the mental hospital is heavily dependent on the extent to which the peculiarities of the hospital as an organization can be systematically related to those of other types of organization which differ from it. This cannot be derived from the study of mental hospitals alone, but only from its place in the comparative study of the whole range of types of organization.

Notes

1. This sentence refers to a classification of types of collectivity which has not as yet been published. The concept of organization as used here has been set forth in Talcott Parsons (1956). A number of reference points for the following discussion will be taken from this paper. In the mental hospital as an organization I am particularly indebted to Stanton and Schwartz (1954).

2. What I refer to here is the *focus* of disturbance. Etiologically and diagnostically, of course, the source may lie in any features of the total individual as a system in his environment, in biochemical factors of his metabolism, or in various features of his personality. The two problems are analytically distinct.

3. It should be realized that this function is by no means peculiar to the mental hospital: it is shared with the general hospital. Here too the individual is often incapacitated for much of ordinary self-care and must be "taken care of." Relieving the family of the burden of such care constitutes one of the important functions of hospitals of either sort. Whether or not such care has any therapeutic significance is a secondary question in the present context. On this general question in relation to the family cf. Parsons and Fox, 1953.

4. Cf. Parsons, Bales and Shils, 1953, chap. V, for the general rationale of this procedure.

5. It will be noted that the logical paradigm I am employing here is that familiar in economics in relating four "flows" to each other; namely, the provision of goods or services to customers, payment for them, the provision of labor services for production, and the payment of wages. What I am trying to do is adapt a general paradigm of goal-attainment in social systems to the special case of the hospital. For the general paradigm cf. Parsons and Smelser, 1956, chap. 2.

6. This applies literally of course to psychotherapy. Questions must be raised in relation to chemotherapy, surgical and shock treatment.

7. The above argument has been couched in terms of the therapeutic component of the hospital's function. But it can be seen that similar considerations apply to the custodial and protective functions. For the child, both functions are performed in the first instance by his family, and we have here a transfer from the family of procreation to the hospital as an equivalent of the family of orientation. Again, the regressive significance in relation to childhood is clear. Socialization into the role of patient, on the other hand, is the process of psychological adaptation to the new status—the prerequisite of therapy.

8. This statement should not be taken to imply that financial resources alone constitute a sufficient basis for acquiring adequate concrete facilities. Other particularly important conditions are legitimation of the goals of the organization and validation of its position in the community—which will be discussed. But given a satisfactory state in these respects—and the "acceptance" of the organization by its potential customers—adequate financial resources constitute an effective means of mobilizing the specific facilities needed.

9. It has been noted that a substantial proportion of hospital aides are former patients. This is probably a significant fact, indicating that there is a tendency for persons with the experience of mental illness to hang together. Also, discharged persons who would have difficulty finding employment in the general labor market are often taken care of this way.

10. For reasons of space this discussion has been confined to the institutionalization of the contract of employment as such. It could, however, be generalized to include the commitment of financial resources to the organization. This has been omitted as it seems to present less distinctive features than the employment side because of the special professional character of mental hospital personnel. Cf. Parsons and Smelser (1956, chap. 3) for a broader discussion.

11. Of course policy decisions have to be taken with respect to the treatment of particular patients or categories of them. These involve policy for the therapeutic subsystem responsible for the particular patients, not for the hospital as a total organization.

12. As noted in the footnote above, however, this need not be true of the subsystem within which the specifically professional function is performed. Here the professional expert is specifically charged with the *responsibility* of carrying out

a technical function and as such is responsible for the policy decisions involved in its implementation.

References

Parsons, T. "A sociological approach to the theory of organization, I and II," *Administrative Science Quarterly,* 1956, 1, 63–86 and 225–239.

Parsons, T., Bales, R. F. & Shils, E. *Working papers in the theory of action.* Glencoe, Ill.: Free Press, 1953, chap. V.

Parsons, T. & Fox, Renee. "Illness, therapy and the modern urban American family," *Journal of Social Issues,* 1953, 8, 31–44.

Parsons, T. & Olds, J., in Parsons, T., & Bales, R. F. *Family, socialization and interaction process.* Glencoe, Ill.: Free Press, 1955, chap. IV.

Parsons, T., & Smelser, N. *Economy and society.* Glencoe, Ill.: Free Press, 1956, chaps. 2 and 3.

Stanton, A. H. & Schwartz, M. S. *The mental hospital.* New York: Basic Books, 1954.

Chapter II

Human Service Organizations and Their Environment

As open systems, human service organizations maintain continuous interchanges with their environment for the attainment of necessary inputs, the disposition of their outputs, and the maintenance of the organization as a viable system.

The organizational environment can be conceptualized as a set of all the elements external to the organization which affect its structure and operations and which are, in turn, affected by the activities of the organization (Hall and Fagen, 1956). This definition implies, therefore, that the environment presents a series of constraints, contingencies as well as opportunities to the organization in shaping its character. Analytically, the organizational environment may be differentiated into three subsystems—ecological, sociocultural, and economic-political.

The ecological subsystem denotes the characteristics of the geographic area within which the organization functions. These include, among others, the physical and geographic patterns of the area, the demographic composition of the population, and the nature and availability of resources in the area.

The sociocultural subsystem refers to the social stratification patterns, the level of technological development and organization, and the system of values and norms that prevail in the community in which the organization functions.

The economic-political subsystem denotes the set of social units on whom the organization depends for the procurement of necessary resources and the maintenance of its mandate and legitimization. These include the beneficiaries of the organization's services; suppliers of clients, fiscal resources, staff and equipment; regulatory groups that oversee the activities of the organization; other organizations offering needed complementary services; and competing organizations.

These three interacting environmental subsystems set limits and influence the attributes of the organization in the following critical areas: (a) the cultural and normative framework within which the organization must function; (b) the legitimation of the organization in the community; (c) the procurement of necessary resources (e.g., technical knowledge, personnel, funds); (d) the input of the raw material (i.e., clients) to be worked upon; and (e) the disposition of its products. Generally, we can define as hospitable that environment which enables the organization to attain a high level of autonomy in selecting the parameters in each of the above areas. In contrast, a hostile environment severely limits the ability of the organization to choose the desirable attributes and protect them. The impact of the environment on the organization is also a function of its texture. By texture we refer to (a) the extent to which the environment is composed of other formal organizations, and (b) the degree of complexity and rate of change in the environment. The more the environment is characterized by the existence of other formal organizations and a high degree of complexity and change, the greater its influence on the organization (Terreberry, 1967).

The relative importance of various elements in the environment on the functioning of the organization is determined by the definition of its domain, namely the type of human needs or problems it covers, the population it serves and the services it renders (Levine and White, 1961). In other words, the claims which the organization makes in these areas determine which parts of the environment will be relevant in affecting the characteristics of the organization. For example, the domain of the public school defines its relevant environmental context to include such variables as the sociocultural composition of the area from which the school draws its students, the governmental agencies that provide its resources, the pool of potential teachers for the school, the educational institutions that will absorb the graduates of the school, the health and welfare agencies that provide complementary services, etc.

The character that the organization will develop through its interchanges with the environment will depend largely on its ability to exploit opportunities presented by the environment and to adapt to its constraints and contingencies. The process of adaptation may involve several interrelated facets. First, the organization may attempt to enhance its position through changes in the definition of its domain and goals. Second, the organization may influence and change elements in the environment. Third, the organization may move into a more hospitable environment. Failure to undertake any of these or related activities will result in a state of organizational precariousness (Clark, 1956).

The nature of the organization's adaptation and ability to enhance its autonomy is determined by the power-dependence relations that exist between it and critical elements in the environment (Thompson, 1967). The more the organization is dependent on the resources controlled by an external unit without possessing countervailing powers (e.g., control over resources the external unit needs) the greater the influence of that unit over the organization. The organization, thus employs a variety of tactics to enhance its independence vis-à-vis its environment. These may include competition, cooptation, bargaining, and coalition formation (Thompson and McEwen, 1958) all of which will have differential consequences on the formation of the organizational domain and the nature of its operations.

Human service organizations face some distinct problems vis-à-vis their environment which are not shared by many other types of organizations. First, because the goals of human service organizations are value ladened and reflect ideological commitments, the sociocultural context within which the organization functions has particular impact on the definition of its goals. The value system that prevails in the community will set significant limits on the range of service ideologies the organization can select. The lesser the congruency between the two, the more precarious will be the legitimation of the organization in the community. Second, because the raw material of human service organizations are clients, they always present a strong environmental influence on the operations of the organization. Even when the organization controls the input of clients it cannot effectively neutralize the ties of the clients with their community. Hence, the social milieu of the clients becomes one of the major sources of environmental control over the organization.

Third, most human service organizations are nonprofit and typically deficit operating agencies. Often their product is not saleable or negotiable on the market. Consequently, the ability of most human service organizations to produce "profit" which can then be used to purchase needed resources is nonexistent. As a result, human service organizations are likely to be dependent on external units for the procurement of resources without having sufficient countervailing powers vis-à-vis these units. This state of dependency characterizes many human service organizations, and indicates the powerful role that external units have in shaping the policies and service patterns of these organizations.

Articles in this chapter provide examples of the influence of the ecological, sociocultural, and economic-political subsystems of the environment on human service organizations' access to resources, their definitions of their inputs and outputs, and their responses to external interest groups. Klatzky's article on the differential capabilities of public employment agencies to secure economic resources points to the fact that agencies in wealthier states are more likely to obtain a higher share of Federal tax funds than agencies in poorer states. This is due to the ability of wealthier states to pay higher salaries and provide unemployment benefits to a greater proportion of their unemployed which in turn increases their share of Federal tax funds. Moreover, wealthier states place greater emphasis on unemployment compensation functions while poorer states tend to emphasize employment placement functions. Such a differential emphasis, in turn, maintains the above noted inequality.

Herriot and Hodgkins point to the impact of the sociocultural environment on the inputs and outputs of public high schools. Using a national sample of public high schools, the authors show that the degree of modernization and the social class structure of the communities in which the schools are located significantly influence the quality of their teachers and effectiveness of the schools' educational output. The authors thus, point to some key environmental constraints upon the potential effectiveness of human service organizations.

The importance of the relations between the organization and key community groups is illustrated in Ohlin's study. He proposes that the economic-political environment is composed of interest groups each of which attempts to influence the activities of the human service organization in the direction of its vested interests. Through the institutionalization of watchdog rules, these interest groups attempt to place the activities of the correctional institution under their scrutiny, and when the activities of the institution affect their interests, they exert influence on the organization. As a result, the goals and activities of the correctional institution reflect the conflicting pressures of the interest groups and the shifts in their relative power and influence on the organization.

References

Clark, B. 1954. "Organizational Adaptation and Precarious Values." *American Sociological Review* 21:327–36.

Hall, A. D., and Fagen, R. E. 1965. "Definition of System." *General Systems* I:18–28.

Levine, S., and White, P. E. 1961. "Exchange as a Conceptual Framework for the Study of Interorganizational Relations." *Administrative Science Quarterly* 5:583–601.

Terreberry, S. 1968. "The Evolution of Organizational Environments." *Administrative Science Quarterly* 12:590–613.

Thompson, J. D., and McEwen, W. J. 1958. "Organizational Goals and Environment." *American Sociological Review* 23:23–31.

Thompson, J. D. 1967. *Organization in Action*. New York: McGraw-Hill.

Organizational Inequality: The Case of the Public Employment Agencies

S. R. Klatzky

Introduction

The recent reemphasis on environmental factors as important determinants of an organization's development and operations has led to the more specific proposition that some organizational environments are more limited than others in terms of the resources which they can make available to the organizations within their jurisdictions.[1] Differential access to resources, in turn, sets limits on the tasks which organizations can perform and the ways in which those tasks are performed. Access to resources may be limited by the fact that a particular organization is in competition with others of the same type for the same limited resources—money, raw materials, customers, or other necessities. If the organizations in question are approximately equal in their command of resources, active competition may occur, with the balance of favor shifting back and forth from one organization to another. Alternatively, the organizations may be arranged in a stable hierarchy within which each organization has little probability of changing its relative position. In the latter case, there must be a process by which the relative competitive advantages and disadvantages of the organizations are maintained and reinforced over time.

Although the statements above seem obvious, very few students of organizations have actually studied this process by comparing the members of a set of organizations in order to isolate the mechanisms which maintain (or reduce) the advantages of some organizations over others. This study, while necessarily limited in scope, is one attempt to make this kind of comparison. More specifically, it is an attempt to show how differences in the economic characteristics of states are related to the fiscal resources allocated to the state employment agencies, and, in turn, how this differential allocation affects the operations of the agencies.

Functions of State Employment Agencies

The state employment agencies have two major functions. First, there are those (hereafter referred to as UC functions) which center around

Reprinted from *American Journal of Sociology* 76 (November, 1970):474–91.

unemployment compensation—the payment of benefits to those individuals who constitute the "insured unemployed" (about which more will be said later). Second, there is the set of tasks centering around the provision of "employment services" (hereafter referred to as ES functions). The primary task within this set is the provision of free job-placement services. In addition, the Employment Services division has such duties as providing employment counseling; providing special services to young people, veterans, and older workers; conducting labor-market studies and furnishing labor-market information; supplying industrial services to employers, labor organizations, and others (see Haber and Kruger 1964, pp. 41–42).

Each state program is autonomous with respect to the other states and in some part, with respect to the federal government. Although all of them must operate within certain broad limits set by the federal government, there is room for considerable variation in structure and in policies. There is, however, at least one important area in which the state programs are dependent on the federal government and, indirectly, upon one another: financing. In accordance with the Social Security Act of 1935, funds for the operation of the employment agencies are provided by a federal tax on all employers who employ a minimum of eight persons for twenty or more weeks a year.[2] Ninety percent of the money collected in this way within each state goes directly to the state program for use in paying unemployment compensation. The other 10 percent is sent to the federal government, where it is pooled and redistributed in order to finance the states' total employment services program and the administrative aspects of their unemployment-compensation program. Since the amount of money to be pooled and redistributed is limited, each state must submit a budget justifying its requests for funds. The money is then allocated by the federal government according to criteria which are not completely specified and which vary from year to year. Some of the reasons for this variation will be discussed below. The important point at the moment, however, is that there is variation between states, not only in the amount of money which they get from the federal government, but also in the rate of return of federal funds to the state for tax dollars collected from employers in that state. That is, if each state program were completely independent, then the money collected from employers within a state would be used by that state alone. The fact that the tax is federal rather than state means that some of the funds collected in one state may be used to finance the programs in another state.[3] The competitive position of a state can thus be measured by the ratio of federal funds allocated to a state to federal taxes collected within that state.

Differences in Allocation

This ratio does, in fact, become a bone of contention between the states. Some states seem to get a consistent rate of return greater than 100 percent.[4] As a starting point in attempting to explain the sources of this variation, we can examine the factors cited by the Federal Bureau of Employment Security to account for the variation. These factors include: (1) the highest overhead costs of sparsely settled states with widely scattered local offices; (2) differences among states in work load due to differences in rates of unemployment; (3) differences among states in salary rates; (4) differences among states in rents and other nonpersonal costs; (5) differences among states in the relative complexity of the state law, since states which cover more employers than are covered by the federal tax have higher administrative costs; (6) differences among states in intensity of programs of the Employment Service for youth, veterans, minority groups, and older workers (these items are paraphrased from Haber and Murray [1966, pp. 413–14]). Although the rationale for redistribution of funds presumably is based, at least in part, on the premise of equalization of the burdens of the program in states with unequal capacities to finance it, the fact remains that most of the factors cited above appear to work to the advantage of wealthier states; some, in obvious ways and others, in ways which are more subtle. Although we do not have measures of the last three factors mentioned above, it seems likely that wealthier states would have higher rents and would cover more employers than would poorer states although they might or might not have more intensive employment services, depending on how those are measured.

If the median income level in a state[5] is used as an indicator of state wealth, then we can analyze the effect of state wealth and the effects of the first three factors mentioned above on the ratio of federal funds allocated to taxes collected (hereafter referred to as the fund ratio) to see whether the factors offered as explanations for variation in the ratio do, in fact, affect it. The effect of the first factor, sparse settlement of states and consequent scattering of local offices, can be estimated by the correlation of population density with the fund ratio for 1963. This correlation and the intercorrelations of all variables used in this paper are presented in table 1. The correlation between population density and the fund ratio for 1963, however, is .009, so that it seems unlikely that sparse population is a factor in explaining differences among states in the fund ratio.[6]

The second factor cited—differences in work load, due to differences in rates of unemployment—is somewhat more complicated to

TABLE 1
Intercorrelations of Nine Variables

Variables	1	2	3	4	5	6	7	8	9
1. Median state income, 1960	—	—	—	—	—	—	—	—	—
2. Percentage unemployed, 1960	.213	—	—	—	—	—	—	—	—
3. Insured unemployed per population	.549	.586	—	—	—	—	—	—	—
4. Average interviewer's salary	.533	.360	.499	—	—	—	—	—	—
5. Benefit positions per 1,000 insured unemployed	.340	−.006	.068	.090	—	—	—	—	—
6. Applications per employee	−.667	−.168	−.457	−.279	−.429	—	—	—	—
7. Potential weeks of benefit duration	.300	.196	.319	.119	.031	−.361	—	—	—
8. Population density, 1960	.130	−.112	.023	.002	.246	−.066	.342	—	—
9. Funds allocated per taxes collected	.157	.604	.524	.493	.217	−.249	.119	.009	—

measure. It is not clear whether the fund ratio is affected more by actual unemployment or by insured unemployment; and there is frequently considerable difference between the two. Although the actual levels of unemployment are unavailable by state for noncensus years, we do have the percentage unemployed by state in 1960.[7] The correlation between this variable and the number of insured unemployed per population by states in 1966 is .586, indicating that insured unemployment explains only about 35 percent of the variance in actual unemployment.[8] This figure is not inconsistent with other data which indicate that insured unemployment has accounted for approximately 40–50 percent of total unemployment in each of the years from 1956 to 1964 (see Haber and Murray 1966, p .20).

The difference between actual and insured unemployed is important insofar as the fund ratio is concerned. If disproportionate amounts of money are allocated to states because of their high levels of actual unemployment, this could be justified in terms of the equalization principle. Those states which have the highest levels of unemployment need a greater proportion of the federal funds. Actual levels of unemployment are slightly related to state income (the correlation is .213) and may reflect the existence in some of the wealthier states of higher levels of industrialization with consequent fluidity in employment. Whatever advantage this gives to wealthier states can be justified on the grounds that it does not stem from a previously existing advantage that those states had. In this case, access to certain resources does not increase the probability of access to other resources. However, the same cannot be said for insured unemployment. Its correlation with state income is .549; and even when actual unemployment is controlled, the partial correlation between income and insured unemployment is still .535. Thus actual unemployment (1960) can account for virtually none of the correlation between insured unemployment and income. This correlation probably reflects, in part, the fact that wealthier states can most easily afford to provide unemployment coverage to some categories of employees excluded by the federal government. For example, they can afford to extend coverage to employees in firms smaller than the minimums set by the federal government. (For a discussion of the categories excluded by the federal government, see Haber and Murray [1966, pp. 143–69].)

Another reason sometimes cited to explain why wealthier states have higher levels of insured unemployed is that they include only those people who have not already exhausted their unemployment benefits. Since wealthier states can afford to provide benefits for a longer period than can the poorer states, they will have higher levels of insured unemployed (Haber and Murray 1966, p. 23). However, examination of the data shows that the number of weeks of potential benefit duration explains only a very small part of the correlation between state income and the rate of insured unemployed. If the correlation between the latter two variables (.549) is decomposed into the direct effect of income on insured unemployed and the indirect effect which operates through potential weeks of benefit duration, the direct effect is .500, and the indirect effect is .049, a negligible amount.[9] Whatever the major intervening variables between state income and insured unemployed may be, the fact remains that wealthier states have higher levels of insured unemployment; and this correlation still exists when actual unemployment is controlled.

If we can assume that wealthier states are in a better position to provide unemployment insurance for a greater proportion of their citizens, then we can ask: does this advantage, in turn, lead to an advantage in their ability to obtain a disproportionately large share of the federal funds allocated?[10] Before turning to this question, however, there is another factor which is presumed to affect the fund ratio. This factor is the differences in salaries paid by the various states. It stands to reason that states with higher median incomes would budget higher salaries for employment-agency personnel; and, in fact, the correlation between the average salary paid to employment interviewers and the median state income is .533.[11] Of course it is not inevitable that the Bureau of Employment Security will grant a state's budgetary request for higher salary payments just because other salaries in the state are higher. However, the Federal Bureau of Employment Security has deliberately instituted a "comparability policy to assure that State Employment Service salaries are in line with comparable positions in other departments of State government" (U.S. Department of Labor 1966, p. 16). If salary differences among states are taken into account in redistributing the federal funds, then high-income states have another advantage in obtaining more federal funds per the funds which employers in their state contribute.[12]

We turn now to the question: what effect do the factors discussed above actually have on the fund ratio? Specifically: (1) what is the direct effect of state income? (2) what are the direct effects of the rate of actual unemployment, the rate of insured unemployment, and the salary levels in different states, and (3) to what extent do the indirect effects of mechanisms such as insured unemployment and salaries, which both stem from prior advantages of wealthy states, counteract or reinforce the direct negative effects of state income on the fund ratio?

As table 2 shows—directly, at least—the pooling and redistribution of federal funds do work to the advantage of the poorer states. The direct effect (measured by the beta weight) of median income on the fund ratio is $-.264$, whereas the original zero-order correlation conceals a set of indirect effects which contradict the direct effect and whose combined effects exceed the direct negative effect of income. Each of the other three variables in the regression has a sizable direct positive effect on the fund ratio; all of the standardized regression coefficients except that for insured unemployment are greater than twice their standard errors and that for insured unemployment is almost twice as great. Although actual unemployment increases a state's share of the funds allocated ($b^* = .370$), both insured unemployed and higher salaries have strong positive effects on the fund ratio even when actual unemployment is controlled (the b^*'s are .270 and .365, respectively). Just as important, however, are their indirect effects. If state wealth as measured by median income is regarded as causally prior to the other three variables, then the correlation between income and the fund ratio can be decomposed into the direct effect of income and its indirect effects, operating through each of the other three variables. To do this, we use the following equation (which is one of the normal equations):

$$r_{y1} = b^*_{y1.234} + b^*_{y2.134}r_{12} + b^*_{y3.124}r_{13} + _{y4.123}r_{14}.$$

TABLE 2
Regression of Fund Ratio on Four Independent Variables

Independent Variables	Zero-Order Correlations	Standardized Regression Coefficients	Partial Correlations
Median state income, 1960	.157	−.264*	−.275
Percentage unemployed, 1960 . . .	.604	.370*	.383
Insured unemployed per population .	.524	.270†	.251
Average interviewer's salary	.493	.365*	.382
		Multiple R = .710	

*Coefficient is greater than twice its standard error.
†Coefficient is between 1-1/2 and two times its standard error.

TABLE 3
Decomposition of Correlation Between Median State Income and Fund Ratio

Direct effect	−.264
Indirect effect due to:	
Percentage unemployed, 1960	.079
Insured unemployed per population	.148
Average interviewer's salary	.195
Total = zero-order correlation	.158

If income is considered x_1 and the fund ratio is y, then $b^*_{y1.234}$ represents the direct effect of income, while the other terms in the equation represent the indirect effects of the other variables, each of which consists of the product of the direct effect (b^*) of that variable and the correlation of that variable with income. These effects are shown in table 3. The indirect effects show that even if we ignore that portion of the indirect effect of income which travels through actual unemployment (since it can plausibly be argued that wealthier states need this advantage due to their higher levels of industrialization and consequent higher actual unemployment), the indirect effects due to insured unemployment and salaries alone more than compensate for the direct negative effects of income (.343 versus − .264). In other words, even when one allows for the greater need of wealthier states for administrative funds because of more actual unemployment, wealthier states are still left with a slight advantage in obtaining a disproportionate share of the federal pool of resources.

Stratification and Task Emphasis

Thus far we have described only one aspect of the stratification system within which a particular group of organizations operates. That is, we have described the process by which differential possession of certain resources (economic affluence) creates or increases the probability of access to other resources (federal funds). However, differences in resources also exert constraints upon the internal processes of organizations. In the case of the employment agencies in particular, differences in state wealth lead to the emphasis of certain tasks at the expense of others. Of the two major tasks which all of the agencies have—paying unemployment compensation to those eligible to receive it and providing a placement service for those seeking jobs—one might expect, in the absence of any other information, that wealthier states would emphasize the latter function. Unemployment might be seen as less of a problem in wealthier states, and jobs would be more readily available, so that the importance of the employment agency as an intermediary between employer and employee in a highly fluid labor market would be increased. However, we also know that wealthier states have higher levels of insured unemployment, so it should not be surprising to find that wealthier states place relative emphasis on unemployment compensation rather than employment services. And, indeed, if we measure the relative emphasis on UC functions versus ES functions, we find that high-income states do place greater relative emphasis on unemployment functions.

One measure of the relative emphasis on UC functions is the number of positions allocated to functions related to unemployment benefits per number of insured unemployed in the state.[13] Although increases in this variable indicate high unemployment-compensation overhead costs, they simultaneously indicate that a state is allocating a disproportionate amount of its resources (in the form of positions) to UC functions by comparison with the allocations of other states. If an agency has fifteen benefit positions per 1,000 insured unemployed, it obviously places greater emphasis on unemployment functions than does a state which only has eight benefit positions for the same number of insured unemployed. Using this measure of UC emphasis, we find that high-income states have more benefit positions per 1,000 insured unemployed than do the low-income ones (the correlation between this variable and median state income is .340). We find an even stronger relationship between income and another measure of task emphasis. This measure is the number of job applications filled out per agency employee.[14] An application requires an interview in which a job seeker informs an employment service interviewer of his availability and qualifications for referral to job openings. Ideally, we would wish to have the number of applications per ES interviewer; but since this information was not available, we have used the cruder measure of applications per employee. This variable should work the opposite of the variable discussed above—benefit positions per 1,000 insured unemployed—since increases in magnitude in this variable indicate a relatively greater emphasis on at least some ES functions by comparison with other states. In fact, the two variables are negatively correlated ($r = -.429$). Using this variable, we find a strong indication that wealthier states deemphasize employment security functions since the correlation between state income and applications per employee is $-.667$.

Given the fact that wealthier states have higher rates of both actual and insured unemployment, one might expect the effect of state income on ES or UC task emphasis to be mediated by either or both of these two variables. That is, it might be that wealthy states place disproportionate emphasis on UC functions because of the disproportionate burdens imposed by their high levels of insured or actual unemployment. This, of course, would not eliminate the causal relationship between state wealth and UC emphasis because, as we have argued, a state's affluence and its consequent ability to insure a greater proportion of the unemployed are a major cause of higher levels of insured unemployment. In fact, however, the relationship between state income and each of the task-emphasis variables is maintained even when actual and insured unemployment are both controlled, as table 4 shows. In the case of benefit positions per 1,000 insured unemployed, the relationship is actually strengthened slightly when the other variables are controlled ($r = .340; b^* = .435$).

Assuming the validity of the finding that high-income states emphasize UC tasks at the expense of ES tasks, we can go on to postulate possible explanations for this situation. The organizational literature is rich with studies of cases in which organizational goals become modified, deemphasized, or displaced due to constraints both internal and external to the organization.[15] These studies have tended to focus on differences among the characteristics of the tasks or goals themselves, which cause some tasks to have a higher probability of successful completion than others. However, this study emphasizes the differences among organizations which share the same tasks. Very little has been written on the causes of systematic variation among organizations of a given type in the extent to which they emphasize or deemphasize the tasks which they all have in common. This may reflect the fact that some of the most pressing constraints to which organizations must adapt are

TABLE 4

Regressions of Two Indicators of Task Emphasis on Median State Income, Insured Unemployment per Population, and Percentage Unemployed

Independent Variables	Zero-Order Correlations	Standardized Regression Coefficients	Partial Correlations
Regression of Benefit Positions per 1,000 Insured Unemployed			
Median state income, 1960	.340	.435*	.360
Insured unemployed per population .	.068	−.173	−.126
Percentage unemployed, 1960	−.006	.003	.003
		Multiple R = .369	
Regression of Applications per Employee			
Median state income, 1960.	−.667	−.586*	−.549
Insured unemployed per population .	−.457	−.167	−.153
Percentage unemployed, 1960	−.168	.055	.059
		Multiple R = .677	

*Coefficient is greater than twice its standard error.

those that are constant across all organizations of a single type. On the other hand, it is often the case that some of these constraints vary in their severity and in their relevance to different organizations within a single type. An example of this variation is the fact that mental hospitals differ in the extent to which they have continuing relationships with other agencies and organizations (e.g., sheltered workshops) which act as receiving agencies or markets for the disposal of released patients. Variation in the ability of mental hospitals to "market" released patients should, it can be argued, affect emphasis on treatment goals versus custodial goals.

In the case of the employment agencies, there are several possible reasons for the relationship between state wealth and emphasis on unemployment compensation. One such factor might be that social expectations for an adequate unemployment compensation program are higher in states in which most people receive adequate wages. In other words, relative deprivation mechanisms require unemployment support in these states. Another factor might be the relative lack of need for an extensive ES placement service since most of the unemployment is due to temporary layoffs and movement from one job to another. In such cases, there may be a tacit agreement between the employment agency and employees that the latter can collect unemployment compensation without actually seeking or requiring help in seeking another job, as they are formally required to do.[16] The needs of employers in high-income states may also play an important part in increasing the emphasis on UC functions. Since the money for unemployment benefits comes from a tax on employers, the unemployment agency is accountable to the needs of employers as well as employees. By tiding people over through temporary periods of unemployment, the employment agency allows industries some flexibility with regard to layoffs and buildups of labor in slack and busy periods without their having to worry about the possibility that the skilled labor force which they have developed will drift away to other firms or other states. This would be particularly important in wealthy industrialized states in which firms might otherwise be forced to compete more actively for the available labor force.[17] Still another factor in the positive relationship between state income and UC emphasis may be the simple fact that wealthy states find it easier to succeed at their UC tasks than do poorer states. Poor states do not have the economic base which supplies the tax money for unemployment compensation. Since little satisfaction and little organizational power can be generated by emphasizing goals which have a low probability of success, poor states are more likely to emphasize the ES tasks which are not so completely hampered by lack of state resources.

Although we cannot at the present time test the validity of the hypotheses proposed in the preceding paragraph, there is one further explanation which can be tested and which relates to the findings in the first half of this study. It may be that a disproportionate emphasis on UC functions which finds expression in high UC overhead costs has feedback effects on the ability of a state to obtain a disproportionate share of the federal funds allocated, that is, effects which go beyond those contributed by the mechanisms such as higher rates of insured unemployment, and higher salaries. The appropriate test of this question would be to add the variable, benefit positions per 1,000 insured unemployed, to the original regression of the fund ratio presented in table 2 of this study and test to see whether this variable adds significantly to the variance explained by the original four variables. This test is presented along with the regression coefficients for all variables in this second regression in table 5. The results show that the contribution of a disproportionate

TABLE 5

Regression of Funds Allocated per Taxes Collected on Five Independent Variables and Test of Significance of Increment in Variance Explained by Adding Benefit Positions per 1,000 Insured Unemployed to the Model Presented in Table 2*

Independent Variables	Zero-Order Correlations	Standardized Regression Coefficients	Partial Correlations
Average interviewer's salary	.493	.392†	.434
Median state income, 1960	.157	−.405†	−.407
Percentage unemployed, 1960	.604	.365†	.406
Benefit positions per 1,000 insured unemployed	.217	.301†	.395
Insured unemployed per population .	.524	.317†	.313
		Multiple R = .762	

*The model presented in table 2 is referred to below as model 1. The model presented in this table (table 5) is referred to as model 2:

$$F = \frac{R^2_{\text{model 2}} - R^2_{\text{model 1}}/df_{\text{model 2}} - df_{\text{model 1}}}{1 - R^2_{\text{model 2}}/N - k_{\text{model 2}} - 1} = \frac{.581 - .504/1}{1 - .581/45} = 8.55$$

$$Pr(F \mid n_1 = 1, n_2 = 45 \mid \geq 7.24) = .01$$

†Coefficient is greater than twice its standard error.

allocation of positions to benefit related functions is indeed significant in its effect on a state's ability to obtain a greater return on the money contributed to the federal funds. The contribution made by this variable is almost 8 percent of the explained variance (.581–.504). If the applications-per-employee variable is added to this model, however, it does not independently contribute a significant amount.[18] This suggests that it is the overhead aspect of benefit positions that increases its share of federal funds rather than the UC emphasis per se. However, it is not inevitable that high-income states have higher UC overhead costs. In fact, one might expect the opposite; that wealthy states would be able to operate their UC programs more economically than poorer states because of the economies made possible by wealth (e.g., wealthy states can afford computers which can eliminate some positions).

What, then, are the implications of the finding that unemployment agencies in wealthy states emphasize unemployment functions and therefore have higher UC overhead costs? One might take this to indicate that these agencies make a deliberate choice to focus on unemployment functions in order to increase their share of the federally allocated tax funds. What is far more likely is that state agencies are maintained in a fairly stable relationship with the federal government from year to year as far as their budgets are concerned. In fact, according to Haber and Murray (1966, p. 403), "There has been a tendency to use an historic basis to develop the amounts for unmeasurable functions and overhead costs in each state's annual grant; that is, the state must show why it has increases over the previous year's costs." Whether agencies in high-income states originally emphasized UC functions for various reasons and therefore had higher overhead costs which enabled them to obtain proportionately more money or whether the self-sustaining cycle began at some other point has all of the earmarks of a chicken-egg argument. Only longitudinal data could show that this is actually a stable relationship over time. However, the evidence available on budget decisions indicates that budgets are altered only slightly from year to year and the changes that are made are only "marginal changes" from previous budgets.[19] As Crecine (1967, p. 789) points out, "Only small portions of the budget are reconsidered from year to year and consequently, once an item is in the budget, its mere existence becomes its 'reason for being' in succeeding budgets." If the budgetary process operates this way in employment agencies, then it is indeed likely that those states which got larger shares of federal money last year are likely to do so this year also and next year as well.

Summary and Conclusions

This study has attempted to describe the hierarchically differentiated system within which a set of organizations operates. This system, like many other stratification systems, allows organizations with greater access to some resources to obtain greater access to other resources.[20] Employment agencies exist in environments which differ greatly in economic resources. This variation affects the salaries which employment agencies can pay and the proportion of unemployed people that their programs can insure. Both of these factors, in turn, affect the allocation of the federal tax collected by the states and redistributed by the Bureau of Employment Security. Although the direct effect of state wealth is to reduce the share of this tax money which a state receives, the indirect advantage which agencies in wealthy states have in terms of their higher salaries and higher rates of insured unemployment (even with actual unemployment held constant) more than makes up for the negative direct effect, leaving the high-income states with a small net advantage.

The stratification system in which organizations are involved also affects the tasks which they pursue. Employment agencies in wealthier states place disproportionate emphasis on unemployment compensation tasks, whereas those in poorer states emphasize placement services. Several reasons can be advanced for this difference, not the least important of which is that emphasis on unemployment functions, which wealthier states can more easily afford, has feedback effects on the share of federal tax money which a state receives. Although this is undoubtedly due to a stable pattern built up over a period of time rather than to any deliberate attempt on the part of state agencies to get more money from the federal government, the fact remains that the system functions in such a way as to reward agencies which place disproportionate emphasis on unemployment functions, and this, in turn, provides an incentive for states to maintain this emphasis.

Since the stratification system affects the task emphasis in these organizations and task demands, in turn, influence organizational structure, it is very likely that the stratification system of government organizations has further indirect, if not direct effects on organizational structure and internal processes. For example, unemployment-compensation tasks are much more routine and repetitious than employment-service tasks. Procedures for the former can thus be more standardized, lower levels of expertise might be required, some of these tasks can be automated, and so on.

The consequences of organizational stratification are not limited to those which affect organization structure. The services which organizations can perform for their clients are also limited by the position of the organizations in their stratification hierarchy. By virtue of residence in one state rather than another, for example, the opportunities of individuals are limited by factors which constrain the organizations which serve them. By comparing these organizations, we can begin to estimate the importance of a major source of variation in the life chances of individuals.

APPENDIX A
Fund Ratios for States Grouped by Regions

New England:		West Virginia	. . . .	.853
Maine	.904	North Carolina	. . . . . .	.687
New Hampshire	.880	South Carolina	. . . . . .	.784
Vermont	1.531	Georgia	. . . .	.639
Massachusetts	.847	Florida	. . . .	.718
Rhode Island	1.455	East South Central:		
Connecticut	.723	Kentucky	. . . .	.837
Middle Atlantic:		Tennessee	. . . .	.633
New York	1.062	Alabama	. . . .	.846
New Jersey	.825	Mississippi	. . . .	1.268
Pennsylvania	.943	West South Central:		
East North Central:		Arkansas	. . . .	1.486
Ohio	.637	Louisiana		.878
Indiana	.500	Oklahoma	. . . .	1.250
Illinois	.606	Texas		.780
Michigan	.814	Mountain:		
Wisconsin	.595	Montana		1.723
West North Central:		Idaho		2.113
Minnesota	.729	Wyoming		1.833
Iowa	.715	Colorado		.938
Missouri	.649	New Mexico		1.412
North Dakota	1.998	Arizona		1.622
South Dakota	1.240	Utah		1.875
Nebraska	.719	Nevada		1.516
Kansas	.755	Pacific:		
South Atlantic:		Washington		1.081
Delaware	.702	Oregon		1.176
Maryland	.892	California		1.045
District of Columbia . .	1.187	Alaska		3.376
Virginia	.511	Hawaii		1.069

Notes

1. See, for example, Thompson's (1966, chap. 3) discussion and that of Stinchcombe (1965). For other recent studies which explicitly consider the importance of environment as a determinant of organizational structure, operations, or interorganizational relations, see Emery and Trist (1965), Aiken and Hage (1968), Lawrence and Lorsch (1967), Seashore and Yuchtman (1967), Litwak and Hylton (1962), and Thompson and McEwen (1961).

2. There have been minor modifications in these parameters over the years, but the law has remained basically the same. For a discussion of these changes, see Haber and Murray (1966, p. 107).

3. Some of the state agencies resent this arrangement and feel that they deserve all the taxes which are collected in their state. See Haber and Murray's discussion (1966, pp. 413–14).

4. The fund ratio by state in several different years can be found in Haber and Kruger (1964, p. 92). The source for the variable used in this study, however, is Haber and Murray (1966, p. 412). They present the fund-ratio data for 1963, which were the most recent data readily available. The values for this variable, by states grouped in regions, can be found in Appendix A of this study.

5. The source of data on median state income is U.S. Bureau of the Census (1962, p. 4). The data are for the year 1960.

6. The fact that population density is also unrelated to the other causal variables makes it very dubious that it could be an indirect cause of variation in the fund ratio. Population density was obtained from U.S. Bureau of the Census (1962, p. 2). The data are for the year 1960. All of the correlations used in this article can be found in table 1. It should be noted that these correlations are somewhat inexact estimates of the true values for two reasons. One is that the data on different variables span a range of years from 1960–66. If we can assume (as we have done) that the underlying relationships remain fairly stable over such a time period, then it does not matter that the values on particular variables have changed in this period so long as those of other variables changed accordingly. Whenever possible we tried to get data as close to 1966 as possible. For variables obtained from the Census, however, this was impossible. Even if all the variables were available each year, it would not be clear what the true causal interval should be since the effects of some variables probably operate over a different time span than those of others. A second, more minor, inaccuracy is due to the fact that one case is missing on one variable, average interviewer's salary (described below). For all other variables, $N = 51$, which includes all states plus Washington, D.C. The zero-order correlations and regressions are computed by a program which computes univariate statistics on the basis of all cases present on each variable, while bivariate statistics are computed only on the basis of cases present on *both* variables. This has the effect of producing a correlation which is usually very slightly lower than that which would be obtained by a pairwise-present method. In the case of variables correlated with average interviewer's salary, this factor seems to affect the relevant correlations by approximately .006 (as estimated by comparing several cases in which we also had correlations computed by a pairwise-present method).

7. This variable was obtained from U.S. Bureau of the Census (1962, p. 4).

8. The numerator of the variable, insured unemployed per population, was obtained from U.S. Department of Labor (1967, p. 8). It is the number of average weekly insured unemployed for the full year 1966. The closest approximation we could obtain to the size of the potential labor force by state in 1966 was the 1965 population estimate obtained from the *Rand McNally Commercial Atlas* (1967, p. 30). Needless to say, this variable is a crude estimate of the underlying variable. It is affected, for example, by differing age compositions of different states.

9. The formula for this decomposition is $r_{y1} = b^*_{y1.2} + b^*_{y2.1} r_{12}$, where $b^*_{y1.2}$ is the direct effect of variable 1 on variable y; and $b^*_{y2.1} r_{12}$ is the indirect effect which operates through variable 2. See also the discussion below. The variable, average duration of benefits (potential for insured claimants)—referred to above as average number of weeks of potential benefit duration—was obtained from U.S. Department of Labor (1967, p. 8). These are data for the year 1966.

10. Findings which support this assumption are those of Dye (1966, p. 134), who finds that for various types of federal expenditures, "Wealthier states provide much better benefits than poorer states, and yet poorer states tend to spend larger shares of their personal incomes for health and welfare services." Dawson and

Robinson's study (1965, pp. 371–410) bears on the question raised here also. They found that the relationship (rank-order correlation) between state income and welfare expenditures has declined in the period between 1941 and 1960; and they attribute this decline to the equalizing effect of increased federal participation over this period. However, their findings refer only to the direct effect of state income, whereas we are concerned with indirect effects as well.

11. The variable, average interviewer's salary, was obtained from Division of State Merit Systems (January 1965a, b; January 1966, p. 6), "Employment Interviewers." It is an average based on data from the three review periods ending on the dates listed above.

12. One might argue that the advantage of paying higher salaries for obtaining federal funds is more apparent than real since the funds so obtained in the states which pay higher salaries are also inflated, and their purchasing power is therefore reduced. To the extent this is true, the payment of higher salaries cannot be seen as a mechanism which reinforces prior advantages of wealthy states. However, one might also point out that since these states are, in fact, wealthier, they can more easily afford to shoulder the burdens of inflated currency without being compensated for it by the federal government. We have no way of knowing whether differences in the cost of living compensate for differences in salaries and, consequently, for differences in federal fund allocation. However, the reader should keep this problem in mind when interpreting the meaning of findings involving salaries.

13. This variable was obtained from an original memo by the deputy director of Unemployment Insurance Service, Bureau of Employment Security, to all regional directors of the Unemployment Insurance Service, dated November 3, 1965. Subject: "Management Improvement and Cost Reduction in the UIS." The data are for financial year 1965.

14. The numerator for this variable is the number of new applications averaged for four different months in 1966—March, June, September, and December. The data were averaged to compensate for seasonal variation. Data for March were obtained from the Bureau of Employment Security, form ES209, item 1, new applications, process code 100. Data for the other three months were obtained from *Employment Security Statistics*, U.S. Department of Labor, Manpower Administration, Bureau of Employment Security.

15. See, e.g., Selznick's classic study of the TVA (1966); Clark (1961); Sills (1961); Zald and Denton (1963); Rapoport and Rapoport (1957); and Scheff (1962).

16. On the requirements for receiving unemployment compensation, see Haber and Murray (1966, p. 419) and Haber and Kruger (1964, pp. 96–97). For an informative discussion of various types of violations of requirements, see Becker (1953, chap. 3).

17. The importance of keeping together a skilled labor force in slack periods is suggested by E. A. G. Robinson (1958, pp. 85–86).

18. By putting benefit positions per 1,000 insured unemployed into the model before applications per employee, we are making the assumption that unemployment functions are more basic and crucial than employment services. This assumption seems warranted in light of what we know about the employment agencies. See, e.g., Haber and Murray's (1966, p. 419) discussion of the reasons that placement services get undermined due to the dominance of UI functions.

19. See, e.g., the studies done by Crecine (1967) and Wildavsky and Hammond (1965).

20. This aspect of stratification systems constitutes part of Tumin's critique (1966) of the functional analysis of stratification.

References

Aiken, Michael, and Jerald Hage. 1968. "Organizational Interdependence and Intra-Organizational Structure." *American Sociological Review* 33 (December): 912–30.

Becker, Joseph M. 1953. *The Problem of Abuse in Unemployment Benefits.* New York: Columbia University Press.

Clark, Burton R. 1961. "Organizational Adaptation and Precarious Values." In *Complex Organizations,* edited by Amitai Etzioni. New York: Holt, Rinehart & Winston.

Crecine, John P. 1967. "A Computer Simulation Model of Municipal Budgeting." *Management Science* 13 (July):786–815.

Dawson, Richard E., and James A. Robinson, 1965, "The Politics of Welfare." In *Politics in the American States,* edited by Herbert Jacob and Kenneth N. Vines. Boston: Little, Brown.

Division of State Merit Systems, 1965a. *State Salary Ranges* (January), Washington, D.C.: Department of Health, Education and Welfare.

———. 1965b. *State Salary Ranges* (July). Washington, D.C.: Department of Health, Education and Welfare.

———. 1966. *State Salary Ranges* (January). Washington, D.C.: Department of Health, Education and Welfare.

Dye, Thomas R. 1966. *Politics, Economics, and the Public.* Chicago: Rand McNally.

Emery, F. E., and E. L. Trist. 1965. "The Causal Texture of Organizational Environments." *Human Relations* 18: 21–32.

Haber, William, and Daniel H. Kruger. 1964. *The Role of the United States Employment Service in a Changing Economy.* Kalamazoo, Mich.: W. E. Upjohn Institute for Employment Research.

Haber, William, and Merrill G. Murray. 1966. *Unemployment Insurance in the American Economy.* Homewood, Ill.: Irwin.

Lawrence, Paul R., and Jay W. Lorsch. 1967. *Organization and Environment.* Boston: Division of Research, Graduate School of Business Administration, Harvard University.

Litwak, Eugene, and Lydia F. Hylton. 1962. "Interorganizational Analysis: A Hypothesis on Co-ordinating Agencies." *Administrative Science Quarterly* 6 (March): 395–420.

Rand McNally & Co. 1967. *Commercial Atlas and Marketing Guide.* 98th ed. Chicago: Rand McNally.

Rapoport, Robert N., and Rhona S. Rapoport. 1957. " 'Democratization' and Authority in a Therapeutic Community." *Behavioral Science* 2:128–33.

Robinson, E. A. G. 1958. *The Structure of Competitive Industry.* Digswell Place: James Nisbet.

Scheff, Thomas J. 1962. "Differential Displacement of Treatment Goals in a Mental Hospital." *Administrative Science Quarterly* 7: 208–17.

Seashore, Stanley E., and Ephraim Yuchtman. 1967. "Factorial Analysis of Organizational Effectiveness." *Administrative Science Quarterly* 12 (December): 377–95.

Selznick, Philip. 1966. *TVA and the Grass Roots*. New York: Harper & Row.

Sills, David L. 1961. "The Succession of Goals." In *Complex Organizations,* edited by Amitai Etzioni. New York: Holt, Rinehart & Winston.

Stinchcombe, Arthur. 1965. "Social Structure and Organizations." In *Handbook of Organizations,* edited by James G. March. Chicago: Rand McNally.

Thompson, James D. 1966. *Organizations in Action*. New York: McGraw-Hill.

Thompson, James D., and William J. McEwen. 1961. "Organizational Goals and Environment." In *Complex Organizations,* edited by Amitai Etzioni. New York: Holt, Rinehart & Winston.

Tumin, Melvin M. 1966. "Some Principles of Stratification: A Critical Analysis." In *Class, Status, and Power,* edited by Reinhard Bendix and Seymour Martin Lipset. 2d ed. New York: Free Press.

U.S. Bureau of the Census. 1962. *County and City Data Book*. Washington, D.C.: Government Printing Office.

U.S. Department of Labor. 1966. "Strengthening Personnel in the Employment Service System." *Employment Service Review* 3 (February): 15–18.

———. *Unemployment Insurance Statistics* (February). Washington, D.C.: Bureau of Employment Security.

Wildavsky, Aaron, and Arthur Hammond. 1965. "Comprehensive versus Incremental Budgeting in the Department of Agriculture." *Administrative Science Quarterly* 10 (December): 321–46.

Zald, Mayer N., and Patricia Denton. 1963. "From Evangelism to General Service: The Transformation of the YWCA." *Administrative Science Quarterly* 8: 214–34.

Social Context and the School: An Open-System Analysis of Social and Educational Change

Robert E. Herriott and Benjamin J. Hodgkins

Theoretical Considerations

Formal Education in Modern Societies

The importance of education in modern societies is readily acknowledged in most literature dealing with social change and development. Educational variables are also frequently used in cross-cultural studies as indicators of the degree of development of a society (e.g., Shannon, 1959; Cattell et al.; 1952; Schnore, 1961). The effect of modern development on the role of formal education, however, has for the most

Excerpted from *Rural Sociology* 34 (June, 1968):149–66.

part been considered primarily in a speculative manner. Its existence has usually been assumed from the demonstrated fact that as societies become more modern, literacy rates and the educational level of the population rise. The "why" and "how" of this covariation too often remains unspecified. It is our view that the underlying feature of this relationship between modernization and education is the *dependence* of technological development on the social institution of formal education; a dependence important not only in terms of the transmission of technical knowledge,[1] but also in terms of the development of an instrumental orientation amenable to the implementation of that knowledge (Gerth and Mills, 1946:426–434).

In modern societies, the only formal and systematic attempt to instill this instrumental orientation occurs in formal education. Couched in terms of achievement based on universal standards of performance, and effectively neutral evaluation in specific role contexts, mass formal education generally places the neophyte in a social milieu quite unlike his limited family experiences, but not unlike the social context in which he will spend his adult life.[2] By "adjusting" to the school milieu over a period of years, the student internalizes the instrumental orientation to social relationships necessary for successful performance as an adult in a rapidly modernizing society.[3] Thus, the institutional role of education can be viewed in terms of the social needs of modern industrialized society as they are reflected in the technical requirements and values associated with modern life.[4]

Although several bases undoubtedly exist for examining the dynamics of this process, the insights of Max Weber on education as a bureaucracy seem particularly relevant. Weber suggests that "a rational and bureaucratic (modern) structure" of education best corresponds to the "ideal" means for imparting specialized training (Gerth and Mills, 1946:426). Thus, as a society becomes more modern, the formal education system tends to become increasingly rational and bureaucratic in nature.

If one views formal education within a modern society in this manner (as being rationally constituted to fulfill an institutional role), it is relevant to ask how the inputs, structural characteristics, and outputs of formal education vary with the degree of modernization. To the extent that inputs and structural characteristics approach the bureaucratic ideal, the outputs of the educational system may be expected to approximate the needs of modern society, thereby resulting in an "effective" formal educational system. With regard to inputs, for example, both the number and type of students in societies at early stages of modernization generally are not determined rationally in terms of modern social needs. The formal educational system of such societies tends, in Weber's terms, to emphasize a "pedagogy of cultivation" for the elite and not the specialized training and orientation necessary for modern life (Gerth and Mills, 1946). Many ex-colonial African states are examples of this phenomenon (see Ashby, 1964). In such cases the effectiveness of the formal system is low.

Such a view of the relationship between the degree of modernization and the effectiveness of education has generally been used to compare societies, but it can also be applied within a modern society. There is research, for example, which suggests that the process of modernization varies *within* American society in a manner similar to the variations more frequently noted among societies (Allen and Bentz, 1965; Anderson and Bowman, 1955; Gillin, 1955). If this is indeed the case, it seems reasonable to expect similar variation in the effectiveness of the formal education system in terms of its development toward an ideally rational bureaucratic form.

The School as a Social System

Historically, the study of the school *as a social organization* has been a neglected area of empirical research (Gross, 1956:64; Bidwell, 1965: 972). Although many reasons exist for this oversight, of particular importance has been the tendency of past analysts of the school to utilize conceptual models derived from economic or social psychological assumptions (e.g., Burkhead, 1967; Barker and Grump, 1964). In such instances the results have been somewhat disappointing from a sociological perspective, because the fundamentally social nature of the school as a formal organization has been overlooked.

To overcome this limitation, we have chosen to consider the relationship of modernization and education utilizing a general systems approach which focuses on education at the organizational level. At this level, the institutional role of education may be identified as the extrinsic *genotypic* function of the organization, the "purpose" of the organization vis-à-vis the larger society.[5] For systems theory generally, and organizational analysis in particular, the concept of "purpose" is a complex, but highly relevant one. By purpose we do not imply an ultimate goal or end, nor do we mean the conscious intent of the organization's membership. Rather, organizational purpose vis-à-vis the larger society refers to the state of organizational behavior consistent with its social institutional role. Thus, if we acknowledge the economic institution's social role as primarily that of distributing goods and services, the "purpose" of business organizations may be defined accordingly. So also, if the primary social purpose of the institution of education in modern society is that of transmitting technical skills and an appropriate orientation for their implementation in adult life, the school as a social organization can be viewed analytically as a purposive organization consistent with that institutional role.

A second characteristic of importance to our systems approach is the perception of the school as an *open* social system. As described by Buckley (1967), Allport (1960), and von Bertalanffy (1962), an open system is a set of elements: (1) in mutual interaction, (2) characterized by an input and output in energy, (3) existing in a homeostatic state wherein its input and output will not appreciably affect its form, (4) manifesting an increasing complexity over time, and (5) displaying a high degree of interaction with its environment. It is this final characteristic that is of particular importance in the discussion and analysis to follow, where we shall attempt to articulate the effects of interaction with the environment on the structure and functioning of educational organizations.

The Environment of American Public Schools

To understand the dependence of the American public schools, as a social organization, on its environment, it is helpful to consider sociocultural changes in American society, attendant to the modernization process. These changes can best be viewed in terms of changes in ideology and values.[6] Briefly, the most modern sectors of American society may be characterized ideally as manifesting a universalistic value orientation, wherein instrumental performance on the part of the individual is valued and status granted based on achievement. Beliefs about the worth of individual performance in terms of abilities, effort, and rewards are extolled in terms of their contribution to the larger society.[7] In contrast, less modern sectors of American society tend to have traditional values and ideology, characterized as expressing a particularistic value orientation, in that individuals, objects, or situations are appraised in a unique and relative sense rather than in terms of universal achievement. In these sectors ideology is focused on the sacredness of past events and the desirability of traditional behavior.[8]

If the above assumptions hold, the criteria sensitizing the organization to feedback from its environment will vary from one sociocultural context to another. The effect of this on the public school can be anticipated in somewhat the following manner. In the more modern sectors of American society, universal values and ideology will lead to an emphasis on the larger sociocultural needs of society. Such an emphasis will be reflected in the concern for the school regarding its production and adaptation relative to the standards of the larger society. Conversely, the more traditional sectors of society will be more attuned to particularistic values and ideas associated with their local environments. In such settings, school-community relations and the internal stability of the organization will be of paramount concern in the school to the probable detriment of meeting the standards of the larger society.

Further insight into the effects of differing sociocultural contexts on the school as an open system can be gained by considering the different adaptation of schools within different sociocultural contexts. We would expect schools in the more modern sectors of American society to have more complex structures consistent with a more highly specialized division of labor among their membership. In contrast, schools in more traditional areas would be less specialized, and would evidence a greater permeability from their local sociocultural environment.

There are, of course, many additional ways in which variability in the sociocultural context of schools could influence their organizational structure and functioning. The preceding discussion is illustrative rather than exhaustive. We would now like to present a brief empirical test of selected aspects of our general reasoning.

Methodological Considerations

Research Design

During the past several years we have conducted a study exploring the general thesis noted above that the more modern the sociocultural context in which American public schools are located, the more modern their structure, inputs, and outputs (Herriott and Hodgkins, 1969). In this study we wish to report some specimen results of the larger inquiry dealing with three context variables, one input variable, and one output variable, and focusing on public senior high schools. The two hypotheses we will test are as follows:

I. *The more modern the sociocultural context of American public senior high schools, the more specialized their inputs.*

II. *The more modern the sociocultural context of American public senior high schools, the more effective their outputs.*

The three sociocultural contexts we will consider are each major social dimensions within American society: (1) region, (2) metropolitan area, and (3) school neighborhood. Elsewhere we have developed at length a discussion of how each dimension can be subdivided into social settings of differing degrees of modernity (Herriott and Hodgkins, 1969:ch. 9). For the sake of brevity we shall simply assert that a region composed of the U. S. Census divisions of New England, Middle Atlantic, East North Central, Pacific, and Mountain can be characterized as being more modern than one composed of the West North Central, West South Central, East South Central, and South Atlantic. We shall further assert that the central cities of the Standard Metropolitan Statistical Areas (SMSAs) of the Bureau of the Census are more modern than are the rings of SMSAs, which are more modern than non-SMSA settings. Finally, we shall assert that school neighborhoods which are largely white-collar in their adult composition are more modern than those predominantly blue-collar or farm.

Our measure of the specialization of organizational input for senior high schools focuses on the specialized training of the school's faculties. It is measured by the proportion of full-time faculty members who hold at least a Master's degree. The measure of effectiveness of organizational output focuses on the production of students seeking further formal education consistent with the requirements of the larger society. It is represented by the proportion of previous tenth graders who, after the twelfth grade, go directly on to some form of further schooling. Such a measure of output takes into account not only graduates who go on, but also adjusts for the former tenth graders who have dropped out.

A sample of three- and four-year public senior high schools was obtained from data collected by the U. S. Bureau of the Census during the 1965–66 school year as one phase of the Equality of Educational Opportunity (EEO) survey of the U. S. Office of Education.[9] To accomplish one of the minor objectives of the EEO survey, the October 1965 educational supplement of the monthly Current Population Survey (CPS) of the Bureau of the Census was expanded to learn the enrollment status of the 28,000 persons age 6–19 in the CPS national sample of households.[10]

In addition to learning the enrollment status of these individuals, the CPS also learned the identity of the elementary or secondary school then being attended by the enrollees and last attended by the non-enrollees. In this way, the 10,500 public and private elementary and secondary schools most recently attended by these 28,000 persons were identified.

A precoded questionnaire was then mailed to the chief administrative officer of each school. It requested information about the school relevant to an exploration of educational opportunity (e.g., type of control, number of students in attendance, percentage of students who are Negro, percentage who are Catholic, etc.). Completed questionnaires were returned by 7771 (73 percent) of the schools, of which 6333 were public and 1212 Roman Catholic.[11] The test of the current two hypotheses involves only 1124 *public* three- and four-year senior high schools, drawn from this sample.

Test of Specimen Hypotheses

To test Hypothesis I, the mean proportion of teachers holding at least a Master's degree was computed within each of 12 sociocultural context categories defined jointly by the two regional, three metropolitanizational, and two social class categories noted earlier.[12] As predicted by the hypothesis, the largest proportion of such teachers (52.6 percent) is found in the most modern context (that characterized as being of high social class, in the central city, and in the more modern region); and the smallest proportion (29.8 percent) is found in the least modern sociocultural context (that characterized as being of low social class, in nonmetropolitan areas, and in the less modern region) (Table 1). In addition, for all six possible social class context com-

TABLE 1
Mean Percent of Senior High School Teachers with at least
a Master's Degree by Sociocultural Context

Region	Metropoli-tanization	Social Class	Mean Percent	Number of Schools
More Modern				
	Central City	High	52.6	109
		Low	43.3	98
	Ring	High	47.9	233
		Low	38.1	142
	Nonmetropolitan	High	37.4	59
		Low	32.4	65
Less Modern				
	Central City	High	44.7	45
		Low	34.8	32
	Ring	High	40.9	89
		Low	33.6	50
	Nonmetropolitan	High	34.9	74
		Low	29.8	128
	All Contexts		40.6	1124

parisons (holding constant both region and metropolitanization), the high social class category has a larger percentage of teachers with at least a Master's degree than does the low social class category. For all four possible metropolitanization context comparisons (holding constant both region and social class), the central city has a higher proportion of teachers with at least a Master's degree than does the ring, which in turn has a higher proportion than do the nonmetropolitan areas. Further, for all six possible regional comparisons (holding constant both metropolitanization and social class), the more modern region has a higher proportion of such teachers than does the less modern region (Table 1).

In order to summarize independent main effects of each of these three sociocultural context variables on the organizational input of schools, a least-squares regression analysis was performed with dummy main effects and interaction terms pivoted on the least modern sociocultural contexts (see Table 2 for all operational definitions).[13] The results of this analysis are presented in Table 3, and serve to clarify what was suggested in Table 1. Each sociocultural context makes a significant independent contribution to the explanation of variation in organization input, whereas none of the interaction terms is significant (Table 3). Thus Hypothesis I receives clear support.

To test Hypothesis II, the mean proportion of former tenth-grade students going directly on to any form of further formal schooling was computed within each of the 12 sociocultural contexts. Although the mean of 62.1 percent for the most modern of these contexts is clearly greater than that of 47.1 percent for the least modern, the results are not as systematic as in the case of organizational input (Table 4). Nevertheless, for all six possible social class context comparisons (holding constant both region and metropolitanization), the high social class category has a larger percentage of students going on to further schooling than does the low social class category. For five of six regional comparisons (holding constant both metropolitanization and social class), the more modern region has a higher proportion of such students than does the less modern region. However, the pattern varies greatly across the four possible metropolitanizational context comparisons (holding constant both regional and social class). For the high social class schools of the less modern region, the predicted relationship is observed, but for the low social class schools of the same region just the opposite occurs. For schools in both high and low social class contexts of the more modern region, the ring has the highest proportion of students going on, followed by the central city, and then by nonmetropolitan areas. With respect to the organizational output of schools,

TABLE 2
Definition of Dummy Sociocultural Context Main Effects and Interaction Terms

Original Variable			Dummy Variable	
Variable	Category	Symbol	Value	Interpretation
Main Effects				
Region	NE, MA, ENC, M, P	R_1	1	Modern
	SA, ESC, WSC, WNC	—	0	Not Modern
Social Class	35-100% White-collar	S_1	1	High Social Class
	0-34% White-collar	—	0	Not High Social Class
Metropolitanization	Central City	—	0	Not Ring
	Ring	M_1	1	Ring
	Non-SMSA	—	0	Not Ring
Metropolitanization	Central City	M_2	1	Central City
	Ring	—	0	Not Central City
	Non-SMSA	—	0	Not Central City
Interaction Terms				
Region – Ring	$R_1 = 0, M_1 = 0$	—	0	
	$R_1 = 0, M_1 = 0$	$R_1 M_1$	1	
	$R_1 = 1, M_1 = 1$	—	0	
	$R_1 = 1, M_1 = 0$	$R_1 M_1$	1	
Region – Central City	$R_1 = 0, M_2 = 0$	—	0	
	$R_1 = 0, M_2 = 1$	$R_1 M_2$	1	
	$R_1 = 1, M_2 = 1$	—	0	
	$R_1 = 1, M_2 = 0$	$R_1 M_2$	1	
Region – Social Class	$R_1 = 0, S_1 = 0$	—	0	
	$R_1 = 0, S_1 = 1$	$R_1 S_1$	1	
	$R_1 = 1, S_1 = 1$	—	0	
	$R_1 = 1, S_1 = 0$	$R_1 S_1$	1	
Ring – Social Class	$M_1 = 0, S_1 = 0$	—	0	
	$M_1 = 0, S_1 = 1$	$M_1 S_1$	1	
	$M_1 = 1, S_1 = 1$	—	0	
	$M_1 = 1, S_1 = 0$	$M_1 S_1$	1	
Central City –	$M_2 = 0, S_1 = 0$	—	0	
Social Class	$M_2 = 0, S_1 = 1$	$M_2 S_1$	1	
	$M_2 = 1, S_1 = 1$	—	0	
	$M_2 = 1, S_1 = 0$	$M_2 S_1$	1	

Unstandardized regression equation:
$$\hat{Y} = a + r_1 R_1 + s_1 S_1 + m_1 M_1 + m_2 M_2 + (r_1 m_1)(R_1 M_1) + (r_1 m_2)(R_1 M_2) + (r_1 s_1)(R_1 S_1) + (m_1 s_1)(M_1 S_1) + (m_2 s_1)(M_2 S_1).$$

Where:
$\hat{Y}$ = predicted mean on the dependent variable for the ith cell.
a = predicted mean for the pivotal (least modern) cell.
r_1, s_1, m_1, and m_2 = unstandardized regression coefficients for the main effects.
$(r_1 m_1)$, $(r_1 m_2)$ ... $(m_2 s_1)$ = unstandardized regression coefficients for the interaction terms.

there is clearly an interaction between metropolitanizational context and the other two sociocultural contexts.

In order to summarize the independent main and interactional effects of each of the three sociocultural contexts on the organizational output of schools, we performed a least-squares regression analysis again. These results, presented in Table 5, clarify what was suggested in Table 4. Although the independent main effects of regional and

TABLE 3

Eighth-order Unstandardized Regression Coefficients for the Relationship of
Sociocultural Context and Percent of Senior High School Teachers
with at least a Master's Degree

Sociocultural Context Variable[a]	Coefficients (N = 1124)
Main Effects	
Modern Region (R_1)	7.0*
Ring (M_1)	6.5*
Central City (M_2)	10.3*
High Social Class (S_1)	9.1*
Interaction Terms	
R_1M_1	−1.6
R_1M_2	−2.7
R_1S_1	−0.4
M_1S_1	−1.8
M_2S_1	−2.0
Predicted Mean for Least Modern Cell	29.9
F-Ratio	14.8*
Multiple R	.33

[a]See Table 2 for the operational definition of each variable.
*p < .05.

TABLE 4

Mean Percent of Senior High School Tenth-grade Entrants Later Going Directly on to
Any Post-secondary Education, by Sociocultural Context

	Sociocultural Context			Number
Region	Metropolitanization	Social Class	Mean Percent	of Schools
More Modern				
	Central City	High	62.1	94
		Low	41.6	90
	Ring	High	64.4	221
		Low	50.6	135
	Nonmetropolitan	High	51.6	56
		Low	50.0	60
Less Modern				
	Central City	High	59.6	42
		Low	38.5	27
	Ring	High	57.7	82
		Low	43.2	42
	Nonmetropolitan	High	56.7	62
		Low	47.1	98
	All Contexts		54.3	1009

TABLE 5
Eighth-order Unstandardized Regression Coefficients for the Relationship of
Sociocultural Context and Percent of Senior High School Tenth-grade Entrants
Later Going Directly on to Any Post-secondary Education

Sociocultural Context Variable[a]	Coefficients (N = 1009)
Main Effects	
Modern Region (R_1)	5.2*
Ring (M_1)	2.6*
Central City (M_2)	−0.9
High Social Class (S_1)	18.1*
Interactions	
$R_1 M_1$	−4.1*
$R_1 M_2$	−1.9
$R_1 S_1$	1.6
$M_1 S_1$	−4.4*
$M_2 S_1$	−7.8*
Predicted Mean for Least Modern Cell	47.9
F-Ratio	24.8*
Multiple R	.43

[a]See Table 2 for the operational definition of each variable.
*p<.05.

social class context are each significant, the effect of the metropolitanizational context is primarily through its interaction with the other
two contexts (Table 5). Nevertheless, considerable support for Hypothesis II is apparent. Also noteworthy is the rather strong interaction effect of the central city in combination with low social class
($M_2 S_1$). The suppressing effect of the urban ghetto on education output can be clearly seen.

Summary

Specimen hypotheses were proposed regarding the relationship of the
sociocultural context of schools to organizational inputs and outputs.
Specifically, it was hypothesized that the more modern the sociocultural context in terms of region, metropolitanization, and social class:
(a) the more specialized the inputs, and (b) the more effective the output. Results of an analysis of 1124 public three- and four-year senior
high schools supported our input hypothesis. The output hypothesis
was supported for region and social class contexts. However, it was
not supported for metropolitanization. Subsequent analysis revealed
that although the region and social class context effects upon school
output were direct, the effect of metropolitanization was primarily
through its interaction with social class.

Discussion

This study has reported some specimen results of an analysis of the relationship between the school as a social organization and the sociocultural context in which it exists. The larger study of which this is a part provides many additional examples of the relationship of the sociocultural contexts of schools to their organizational structure and functioning. Although the empirical portion of all of our analyses utilizes data collected for other purposes and possesses the usual shortcomings of such secondary analysis, we believe the results have implications for theortical, methodological, and substantive concerns.

On the theoretical level, we have endeavored to set forth a model of the school in society that incorporates two major concepts not generally considered simultaneously by those interested in the sociological study of education and social change. These are "modernization" and "open social system." We feel that our efforts to integrate these two concepts have been worthwhile for they have helped us to focus on some important aspects of the effects of social change on the school in contemporary American society. We expect we have just begun to scrape the surface in this endeavor. An elaboration and extension of our consideration of the American public school as an open social system within sociocultural contexts of varying modernity can be carried out, and can shed additional light on the relationship of modernization to education.

With respect to methodology, we believe we have avoided two major limitations of past sociological research on the school as a formal organization; the tendency to overgeneralize from case studies of a few schools, and the use of students as the unit of analysis when the primary focus is on the school. By combining, within a large sample of schools, the span of survey research and the parsimony of multivariate regression statistics, we were able to examine systematically relationships between variables conceptualized, measured, and analyzed *at the level of the school itself*. This approach also appears to warrant elaboration and extension.

Perhaps the most crucial result of our total effort is the support this research offers for the hypothesis that the sociocultural context has a systematic influence on the school. By identifying an important characteristic of a school's environment (the extent to which that environment has been influenced by the modernization process), inputs and outputs have been shown to vary systematically from one sociocultural context to another. Our total findings suggest that the issue of environmental effects on the school is not whether the social context influences the organization, but rather what *aspects* of the sociocultural context have an influence on the school and in what *manner* that influence is expressed.

There are many substantive implications from our findings for both basic and applied concerns. For example, our total research effort suggests that the question of "inequality of educational opportunity" probably needs to be reconsidered with greater emphasis on the organization-community relationship—past research has tended to focus primarily on the individual's potential for educational attainment. If the logic of our model holds, significant changes in the structure and functioning of the American public school are greatly dependent on the sociocultural context in which the school exists. The pouring of extraordinary money, teacher talent, curricula, etc. into public schools in "depressed areas" undoubtedly has a useful short-run effect; but if our interpretations are correct, it will prove inadequate in the long run without significant changes in the values and ideology of the sociocultural context in which the school exists as an open social system.

Perhaps even more important are implications related to the old argument of the school's role as an agent of change within the larger American society. This issue must be recast when the school is viewed as an open social system, for within such a framework there is a high degree of reciprocity between school and environment. However, this reciprocity is severely constrained by the ideology and values dominant in the sociocultural context in which the school is controlled. We would argue that the community probably permits the school to be a change agent only to the extent that it wants to be so changed. The widely cited lack of success of the school as an agent of change in the urban ghetto speaks clearly to the school's dependence as an organization on sociocultural factors currently beyond its control.

If our reasoning and interpretations are valid, the reform of public schools in the less modern areas of America through local initiative is likely to be a very slow and sporadic process. On the other hand, future efforts to reform public schools in the less modern sections of American society from a central (primarily federal) level are likely to be greatly resisted and eventually evaded by the more traditional sociocultural context in which such schools are located. On the basis of reasoning and data in addition to that presented above, we expect that the greatest change in the structure and functioning of the American public school in less modern areas will come not from local, state, or federal initiative focused directly upon the schools, but rather from external forces that can modify the sociocultural context in which these schools exist. We suspect that until the local environment which supports, maintains, and controls the American public school can be changed, little widespread change can be made in the structure of the school itself.

Notes

1. For a most interesting discussion of this relationship, see Keyfitz (1963).

2. For an excellent discussion of the distinction between family and school as socializing agencies, see Dreeben (1968: esp. chs. 2, 3).

3. Interestingly enough, examples of the successful end product of this experience are not seen as particularly desirable by many contemporary writers. We refer here to the negative connotations surrounding the "white-collar man," the "organization man," or the "bureaucrat." And yet, as many students of the problem have argued, this type of personality configuration seems necessary in order to operate within the modern complex bureaucratic milieu.

4. Durkheim has expressed essentially the same view in defining education's role in society, although the meaning of his definition has never been systematically explored for modern society. Durkheim defines this role as ". . . to arouse and to develop in the child a certain number of physical, intellectual and moral states which are demanded of him by both the political society as a whole and the special milieu for which he is specifically destined" (Durkheim, 1950:71).

5. Following Katz and Kahn (1966:62), we are distinguishing here between *intrinsic* functions necessary for the maintenance of the organization, and *extrinsic* functions which are performed by the organization as a part of a larger social system. *Genotypic* in this instance refers to the primary function as determined by the organizations' institutional role.

6. We are using ideology and values in the Parsonian sense, i.e., an *ideology* is a ". . . system of beliefs held in common by members of a collectivity," with some level of commitment as an aspect of group membership; *values* are ". . . of a shared symbolic system which serves as . . . criterion of standard(s) of selection among the alternatives of orientation which are intrinsically open in a situation. . . ." See Parsons (1951: 349, 12).

7. These generalizations are derived essentially from Parsons' discussion (1951:132–91) of the "Universalistic-Achievement Pattern."

8. An excellent discussion of traditional society is set forth in Hoselitz (1963: 11–31).

9. For the larger study of which this was a minor part, see Coleman et al. (1966).

10. For the results of this research, see Nam et al. (1966: sec. B–F). This report has been summarized in Coleman et al. (1966: ch. 6).

11. Neither the target sample nor the resulting one is in any sense a random probability sample of American schools. However, the sample is large (approximately six percent of all American schools). An extensive analysis of non-response has been conducted, and suggests that whatever bias may exist within the sample has led to an underestimate of relationships rather than to an overestimate. See Herriott and Hodgkins (1969: Appendix A).

12. The operational definition of sociocultural context categories is as follows:
   1. Region: (a) more modern—New England (NE), Middle Atlantic (MA), East North Central (ENC), Pacific (P), Mountain (M); (b) less mod-

ern—South Atlantic (SA), East South Central (ESC), West South Central (WSC), and West North Central (WNC).

2. Metropolitan: (a) Central city of SMSA; (b) Ring of SMSA; (c) Non-SMSA.

3. Social class: (a) High—35–100% white-collar fathers as estimated by the school principal; (b) Low—0–35% white-collar fathers. (The split was made at the median across all 7771 schools in the larger study.)

13. For a technical discussion of this procedure, see Suits (1957); Davies (1961); Melichar (1965); Johnston (1963). For social science applications, see for example, Orcutt et al. (1961:216–31); Morgan et al. (1962); or Wilson (1963: 217–35).

References

Coleman, James S., et al. 1966. *Equality of Educational Opportunity.* Washington, D.C.: U.S. Government Printing Office.

Davies, M. 1961. "Multiple linear regression analysis with adjustment for class differences." *Journal of the American Statistical Association* 56 (September): 729–735.

Herriott, Robert E., and Benjamin J. Hodgkins. 1969. *Sociocultural Context and the American School: An Open-Systems Analysis of Educational Opportunity.* Washington, D.C.: U. S. Department of Health, Education, and Welfare, USOE Final Report No. 602972, January.

Hoselitz, Bert F. 1963. "Main concepts in the analysis of the social implication of technical change." Pp. 11–31 in Bert F. Hoselitz and Wilbert E. Moore (eds.), *Industrialization and Society.* New York: UNESCO.

Johnston, J. 1963. *Econometric Methods.* New York: McGraw-Hill.

Melichar, Emanuel. 1965. "Least-squares analysis of economic survey data." Paper presented at the annual meeting of the American Statistical Association, Philadelphia.

Morgan, James N., Martin H. David, Wilbur J. Cohen, and Harvey E. Brazer. 1962. *Income and Welfare in the United States.* New York: McGraw-Hill.

Nam, Charles B., A. Lewis Rhodes, and Robert E. Herriott. 1966. *Inequalities in Educational Opportunities: A Demographic Analysis of Educational Differences in the Population.* Tallahassee: Florida State University.

Orcutt, Guy H., Martin Greenberger, John Korbel, and Alice M. Rivlin. 1961. *Microanalysis of Socioeconomic Systems: A Simulation Study.* New York: Harper & Brothers.

Parsons, Talcott. 1951. *The Social System.* Glencoe, Ill.: The Free Press.

Schnore, Leo F. 1961. "The statistical measurement of urbanization and economic development." *Land Economics* 37 (August): 229–245.

Suits, Daniel B. 1957. "Use of dummy variables in regression equations." *Journal of the American Statistical Association* 52 (December): 548–551.

Wilson, Alan B. 1963. "Social stratification and academic achievement." Pp. 217–235 in A. Harry Passow (ed.), *Education in Depressed Areas.* New York: Columbia University, Bureau of Publications, Teachers College.

Conflicting Interests
In Correctional Objectives

Lloyd E. Ohlin

Definition of Interest

Organizational activities and change are here seen as responsive to
influences from a network of competing or cooperating interest groups
located inside and outside the correctional agency. The term *interest*
is used to denote a line of current or future activity in which a person
or group has invested its action resources and expectations. A group
maintaining a certain interest becomes a *correctional interest group*
when its activities conflict with, merge with, or otherwise engage the
activities of a correctional agency in such a way as to focus the attention
of both parties on the juncture of interests. An incident disclosed during
the research on which this study is based will illustrate the meaning
of these terms.

The warden of a maximum-security prison sought to introduce
a shoe factory to provide more work for the inmates and to give them
some training in a trade. He also thought this would be a self-sustaining
and even profitable industry for the prison, since the state-use law
would permit him to sell the shoes to all state institutions, which were
then purchasing shoes for inmates from private manufacturers. It
seemed to be an excellent choice of a prison industry from the standpoint of the interests of the state, the institution, and the inmates.
Elaborate plans were drawn up for the new industry, and negotiations
for equipment were under way, when rumblings of dissatisfaction from
several shoe-manufacturing and wholesale companies and a labor union
began to reach the prison administration. There were threats that the
prison's competition with the free market and with free labor would be
made a public issue. Political pressures to reconsider the proposal began
to be felt by the administrators. The project was soon abandoned in
favor of another industry that offered less challenge to influential groups.

In this case the shoe companies, the labor union, and apparently
some political figures had an established *interest* in existing arrangements for the private purchase of shoes for inmates of state institutions.

Reprinted from R. Cloward et al., *Theoretical Studies in the Social Organization of the Prison* (New York: Social Science Research Council 1960): pp.
111–29.

A *correctional interest group* was created when the proposal to establish a prison shoe factory threatened to disrupt these arrangements.

The term interest group is used here more broadly than in current political science literature, where the term is often used interchangeably with pressure group to designate an association organized to exert influence in behalf of its members.[1] In this paper all groups are regarded as pursuing interests. They seek to influence one another when the pursuit of their interests seems to require it, and especially when the intersection of their interests promises either to impede or promote a projected line of activity. There are many channels through which groups seek to protect their interests, and all groups use them. However, as interests become diversified and the necessity to exert influence becomes an accepted part of routine operations, groups tend to set up their own specialized divisions to deal with public relations or form associations with other groups for this purpose. These associations serve "watchdog" or reporting functions for their membership and become fronts for the mobilization and exertion of influence.[2] This differentiation of functions is viewed here as part of the routine operations of all groups; the difference lies not in the nature of the pressure group activities but in the degree of their specialization.[3]

In this analysis of how the correctional organization acquires its form and its objectives, the idea of a variety of largely independent interest groups involved in a network of related activities that interlock with those of the correctional organization is of crucial importance. These groups operate on what Mills has called "the middle levels of power."[4] Knowledge of how these interest groups are created, how they may be assessed in relation to each other and the correctional agency, and how they influence correctional practice is essential in understanding the pressures and problems of correctional administration.

Formation of Interest Groups

One type of interest group emerges when it sees existing or possible activities of the correctional program as means for achieving its own objectives. Its interests are served through the promotion, development, and support of particular correctional activities. For example, in jails, prisons, and reformatories inmate leaders constantly press for control over routine administrative decisions about work and cell assignments, food distribution, record keeping, and other operations. The acceptance of such "help" by officials results in the sharing of authority with inmate leaders and confers on them additional power to exact recognition and conformity from their fellow inmates. Similarly, control of the correctional system by leaders of a political party as a resource for discharging political obligations through patronage or favored treatment of certain offenders represents a conversion of the correctional system to special interests.

Other interest groups are formed when innovations in correctional practice threaten their existing activities or plans. They are interested in preventing the development of activities unfavorable to them.

Correctional interest groups also may be created indirectly through obligations to groups that are directly involved with correctional agencies. The emergent interest groups serve to strengthen the efforts of their allies. Search for support of this kind is a prominent and often decisive feature of correctional crisis situations.[5]

The process by which correctional interest groups are created tends to focus their attention only on those correctional activities that directly affect them. No group devotes equal attention to all aspects of correctional organization. Control over different correctional decisions is differentially distributed among various groups in terms of their interest and capacity to exert influence. For example, each phase of prison organization—the custodial, industrial, agricultural, educational, religious, therapeutic, administrative, and maintenance activities—manages to arouse its own structure of interested groups both inside and outside the prison walls. Some groups, such as the inmates, staff, state welfare or public safety office, parole authorities, prisoners' aid societies and other reform groups, have diversified involvements in a number of correctional functions. Certain business groups are primarily concerned with prison policies for the purchase and use of consumer goods; others, with the prison industrial and agricultural activities which produce goods for sale to other state agencies. Policemen, judges, and prosecutors express concern about security and release practices and sometimes share with welfare, civic, religious, and reform groups interest in the rehabilitative features of prison operation. Educational groups, personnel managers' associations, labor unions, and manufacturing and trade associations occasionally express support of or opposition to certain vocational and job-training programs of the prison. At times of severe prison crisis, however, these disparate interest groups often join in loose coalitions of criticism or defense to enforce broad mandates of prison management which would serve their common interests.

Assessment of Interest

This article draws its perspective from theoretical assumptions implicit in an action-situation framework of analysis. Persons and groups maintaining correctional interests perceive one another primarily in terms of the actions that each must take in order to achieve his own interests. Effective action requires (1) accurate knowledge of the orientation of other interest groups and (2) realistic assessment of the dimensions of these interests that are relevant to the pursuit of one's own.

Orientation of Interest Groups

Close observation of one another's activities is necessary to obtain accurate information about the interests of potential allies or rivals. There appear to be two principal means for acquiring such information: (1) the everyday contacts involved in discharging the routine tasks of the correctional program; (2) the institutionalization of a watchdog role either inside or outside the organization, with appropriate channels for communicating observations to the centers of decision.

A major share of the observing, assessing, and reporting on correctional activities occurs as an incidental part of the routine contacts that representatives of interest groups maintain with correctional organizations. Enforcement agencies, especially in rural areas, learn very quickly about changes in parole selection or supervision practices. They know personally the offenders dealt with and need no specialized observation unit to report when their interests appear to be violated. In some states the law requires the parole board to notify the sentencing judge, the prosecuting attorney, and the complaining witness when an offender whom they had caused to be sent to prison is being considered for parole. Parole authorities usually notify police officials of the release of a paroled offender to their jurisdiction. Offenders, through special writs claiming abuses in the prison system or while undergoing conviction for new crimes, become sources of factual reports on prison life and practices to the criminal agencies involved. The sources of observation and reporting are as numerous as the points of contact between persons identified with different correctional interest groups.

Of greater interest from a theoretical standpoint are the various ways in which interest groups institutionalize the watchdog role. Four devices are commonly employed: visible or secret liaison agents; a public relations unit; a special watchdog association or committee; and representation on a controlling or advisory board or commission.

Liaison. A rather common maneuver is to install an agent or liaison unit that is in the pay of one group within the organization of another. When this is done formally, a common channel for handling routine contact and closer coordination of services may result. The justification of this practice in terms of facilitating communication and joint activity should not obscure the importance of the observing, assess-ing, and reporting functions that are an integral part of the job. The agent is expected to note and report current or proposed activities that challenge the interests of his employer.

In one correctional system the parole authority permanently maintained a parole agent at the police headquarters of the largest city in the state to carry on liaison activities with the police department, the courts, and the prosecutor's office. This liaison officer was well-accepted by the enforcement agencies, since he was sympathetic to their prob-lems. As part of his duties, he reported to the parole agencies his observa-tions on enforcement practices that touched on their concerns. The parole administrators used his knowledge of enforcement agencies to appraise possible reactions to proposed changes in the parole program. In another correctional system the police department of the largest city in the state maintained a permanent liaison unit of three policemen in the state parole agency. They used its files for enforcement purposes and represented the enforcement viewpoint in many routine decisions of the agency. Through this unit, police headquarters and district stations were kept well-informed of the parole supervision activities that related to various aspects of the police function.

Occasionally, the watchdog function is performed by persons who observe and report in secret. Paid informers are in this category. The bitterly hated *rat* or *stool pigeon* in the inmate society is regarded as serving the interests of the prison administration in this way. Resent-ment arises not only from an obvious threat to the plans and interests of inmate leaders, but also from great moral indignation at the sub-version of otherwise reliable cues to the management of social inter-action: the informer makes a claim for full recognition as a *good con* while simultaneously serving concealed interests of opposing groups and undermining the inmate solidarity that he invokes to achieve his advantage. Although most correctional officials also publicly express dislike for the informer, few refuse to use the information obtained or to reward him appropriately.

A distinction should be made between the role of the informer and the secret agent. The latter takes on the guise of the "insider" when, in fact, all his past and future commitments are to the interests of the outside group. At least one side in the conflict has confidence in him, whereas the *stool pigeon* is regarded by both groups as having betrayed interests which he once openly avowed and has never publicly re-nounced.

Public Relations. Organizations in the correctional field appear to devote considerable attention to problems of public relations. Very often public relations programs are deliberately used to serve watchdog functions as well as the manifest purpose of mobilizing public support.

In one state system a correctional administrator trained in social work undertook to introduce a series of new proposals to reorganize the correctional system over a relatively short time. During the period of change he spent much time traveling about the state, explaining the program to his own staff and other groups, sampling and gauging their reactions, and mobilizing support for his proposals; at the same time he sought to identify sources of resistance and to find ways to immobilize them. He gave hundreds of speeches criticizing the existing system and calling for a bold program of innovation implementing the philosophy and principles of social work. He addressed civic and humanitarian groups with welfare interests, businessmen, labor unions, personnel managers, religious groups, fraternal organizations, police, sheriffs, judges, prosecuting attorneys, and state and local bar associations. He talked with leaders of all these groups and urged members of his staff to do the same; from them he regularly received reports on the sentiments and reactions of interested groups. Possible sources of resentment and resistance were identified and dealt with before any general consolidation of opposing interests could take place. These communicating, watching, assessing, mobilizing, and compromising operations of the correctional administrator and his staff led to the institutionalization of a whole series of correctional reforms with no serious public conflict.

Apparently, the customary educational and informational functions of a public relations program not only provide a legitimate channel for gaining access to, and stimulating reactions from, other groups, but also furnish an excellent screen for observation and assessment of their interests. The watchdog role quickly becomes an accepted part of a fully developed program of public relations.

Special Associations. Many groups interested in correctional activities have more pressing interests. When several groups share an incidental concern about correctional activities, they can facilitate avoidance of duplication, economy of operations, and effectiveness of observation and reporting of relevant matters by pooling resources and maintaining an association to carry out the watchdog role. Many local prisoners' aid societies have been formed by coalitions of humanitarian and welfare interests. Such specialized associations report on the care and treatment of inmates of jails, workhouses, reformatories, prisons, and state farms or work camps, and watch the handling of persons in police lockups and juvenile institutions. They observe the activities of probation and parole organizations as well, always alert for violations of the welfare interests that they serve and for crucial spots in which to attempt reforms. Similarly, bar associations usually maintain special committees that periodically inspect correctional activities or investigate complaints, particularly as they relate to the problems of civil rights.

Over the last thirty years, many privately supported crime commissions have been established in major cities of the United States. Such organizations specialize in observing and reporting on the handling of crime and correctional problems by official agencies. Similar functions are performed by permanent legislative committees on correctional activities. In addition to promoting new legislation on correctional matters, they are expected to make periodic inspections of the operation of correctional agencies. Such committees differ from the special investigating committees that are appointed during periods of correctional crisis. The latter do not carry on a watchdog function but have the more limited objective of protecting political and other interests during the resolution of the crisis.

Watchdog organizations operate under relatively constant pressure to demonstrate success by uncovering and reporting violations of the interests of their supporting bodies. One assumption implicit in their organization is that correctional agencies are continually strained toward such violations, which will occur in hidden and informal ways, if not by formal directive. Insofar as the security and rewards of the association's staff depend on its alertness in uncovering "abuses" of correctional authority, the influence of the association on the development of correctional policy often becomes disproportionate to the pressure that the supporting interests would be disposed to exert by themselves. The watchdog association thus poses a special problem for the correctional administrator, who must find ways of neutralizing the concentration of influence that it represents.

Boards. The watchdog function may be institutionalized through representation of correctional interest groups on boards or commissions that have advisory or controlling authority over correctional activities. Such boards frequently have control over budgetary recommendations to legislatures and certain powers of inspection and appointment. Members are usually appointed by the governor, for specified periods that may be terminated at his pleasure. They represent a variety of business, professional, religious, and civic groups with acknowledged interests in correctional activities. Through political influence, groups especially concerned with correctional activities are thus enabled to secure strategic points of vantage, both for influencing the development of correctional programs and for maintaining vigilant contact with current operations.

Attributes of Interest

The correctional administrator needs to appraise accurately at least three attributes of the relations of a group to its correctional interests: advertency, saliency, potency.

Advertency. Interest groups vary in the degree of alertness that they sustain over any given period toward their own involvements in correctional activities. When potentially hostile interests are not aroused, the correctional administrator frequently can make changes of program that could not be undertaken at times of correctional crisis. The state of advertency of interest groups seems to set tolerance limits on what the correctional administrator may do.

These limits, however, are difficult to assess. The correctional administrator must do some careful testing before he can be sure of negotiating a desired change with safety to himself and to his organization. Tradition has such strong influence in correctional organizations that reform administrators are often tempted to dispose swiftly of practices whose only apparent justification is that "we've always done it that way." Many correctional practices do persist for a time after the supporting interest structure has disintegrated, but it is perilous for the administrator to assume that all routinized procedures are of this sort. The routine activities of correctional organizations represent solutions of past conflicts of interest. It may be a mistake to assume without investigation that these routines no longer are supported by an active structure of interested groups. The following incident illustrates this point.

A new warden was brought into a maximum-security prison to undertake limited reform measures which the state administration was under pressure to initiate. During his first year in office he became concerned about the work at the quarry, which was losing money for the prison and was an industrial and training liability. He believed that the money lost on the quarry operation could be spent much more fruitfully on some other industrial enterprise which would serve equally well to keep the inmates busy and at the same time provide some vocational or trade training. Although the quarry operation appeared to have continued simply of its own momentum for many years, the proposal that it be abandoned gave rise to strong protests from surrounding counties that had been obtaining free gravel from the quarry for use on rural roads. The prison was deeply entrenched in the political patronage system in the area, and local politicians had long expressed a genuine proprietary interest in the way the prison was run. Expressions of great dissatisfaction with the proposal quickly came from them as well as from the state capital. Some of the guards who had been taking work crews out to the quarry had become accustomed to this assignment over the years and expressed reluctance about giving up the fresh air and sunshine of the quarry job for duty inside. Similar expressions were received from older inmates who enjoyed working outside rather than in the cellhouses or the other industries, and who were well aware that not much work was required of them in the quarry. The proposal to shut down the quarry was abandoned.

Saliency. The saliency of correctional interests varies with the scope and importance of the group's activities that are circumscribed by them. When only a few or relatively insignificant activities of the group are affected, the saliency of interests is low and the attention of the group to correctional activities is likely to be quite sporadic and of limited duration.

Advertency and saliency should not be confused: they are different attributes of group interests. In any practical situation the correctional administrator estimates the degree of advertency of group interests by answering the question, "How concerned is this group about what we are doing?" He assesses the alertness and knowledge of the group through cues provided by his liaison, public relations, or other channels for getting information. In assessing the saliency of the group's interests, he tries to determine how much of a stake it has in the correctional program, that is, how many of the group's activities will be affected by a change in correctional practice, how seriously these activities will be disrupted, and how central they are to the welfare of the group.

Potency. The potency of correctional interests lies in the group's readiness to mobilize as much power as it can, or as it needs, to realize these interests. When there is conflict between competing interest groups over an area of correctional practice, pressures develop to form coalitions capable of mobilizing and exerting superior power. The power of a correctional interest group lies in its ability to interfere with the activities of a correctional organization or to apply sanctions—penalties or rewards—to its members. Interference may consist of active harassment or simply noncooperation in a situation involving mutual obligations. For example, powerful sanctions, such as appointments, promotions, and pay, are means to political control of correctional activities. Business, professional, or other groups capable of mobilizing political influence may work through these channels in order to develop correctional programs favorable to their interests. In contrast, inmates generally resort to direct interference, such as hunger strikes, riots, sabotage by overconformity to orders, or refusal to work, as means of exerting influence on correctional practice.

Assessing the individual power of these interest groups is not enough. All groups develop commitments, obligations, and influence with other groups which can be mobilized in times of crisis. The total network of interests in which a group is involved becomes the appropriate basis for assessing the potency of its interests. The directorate of interests to which most state correctional systems seem most responsive is that in control of the dominant political party in the state. Even an established civil service system frequently affords relatively little protection against the power of a direct political assault on the correctional, organization. In political parlance, the concepts of "clout,"[6] "connection," and "sponsor" generally signify hidden linkages to influential persons and groups which are most difficult to uncover. Nevertheless, in most states survival or development of the correctional organization depends more on the astuteness of the administrator in assessing and dealing with these networks of political influence than on any other factor. In assessing the significance of interest group power for himself and his organization, he seeks to answer the question, "How can they hurt us or help us?"

In this section certain factors involved in the assessment of interest have been identified. A prerequisite for accurate judgment is the establishment of reliable channels for collecting information about the activities of relevant interest groups. In addition to the casual accumulation of such knowledge through routine work contacts between groups, four means of institutionalizing the functions of observing and reporting were described. Use of such channels should reveal not only the direction of the correctional interests of groups, but also the advertency, saliency, and potency of these interests. This assessment is a basic part of the administrative task. The security of the correctional system is as much a reflection of the accuracy with which the administrator evaluates the sources of criticism and defense as it is of his ability to cope with them.

Tactics of Influence

An adequate theory of the organization and development of correctional activities implies knowledge of how interest groups exert their influence on them. There are two principal mechanisms for the achievement of control by correctional interest groups: representation among correctional personnel, and the use of sanctions.

Representation in the Correctional Organization

The correctional administrator has many reference groups to which he is committed, and with whose interests, objectives, and systems of action, he has become identified. The term *commitment* denotes certain limitations on his actions that he accepts as a condition for maintaining his relations with particular persons or groups. Some of these groups have interests limited to only a few of his activities; others are concerned with much of his public and private behavior. During his career the administrator acquires commitments to certain moral and ethical group values which are presumed to control or guide his conduct. The extent to which his work reflects and implements these values is inspected by his friends and relatives, the criminal offenders under his care, his employees and professional colleagues and other interest groups with which he is affiliated. During his academic or vocational training, the administrator has taken on commitments to educational and professional groups which favor particular correctional programs. He looks to these groups for professional identity and often relies on them for status, prestige, employment opportunities, and other career rewards. Furthermore, he is indebted to those responsible for his appointment, whether through channels of civil service or political patronage.

This direct representation in the correctional system through commitments accepted by correctional board members, administrators, or other agency personnel is eagerly sought by interest groups. It minimizes the need for institutionalized forms of observation, and may give the maximum advantage in contests involving the development of correctional policy. Group interests are indirectly represented when they correspond with those of other groups to which the administrator is committed, or when correctional activities that serve the interests of one of his reference groups serve others as well. This incidental service or latent interest becomes an important source of strength at times of crisis, when a coalition in defense of the challenged correctional policy or program must be formed.

Use of Sanctions

The power to support or to penalize the correctional administrator and members of his organization is the means through which the interests of opposition groups secure recognition, as well as the means through which groups succeed initially in placing committed representatives of their interests in the organization. Use of sanctions by an interest group involves rewarding or penalizing correctional personnel, or taking action to support or sabotage the correctional program.

Personnel Sanctions. Perhaps the strongest controls over the actions of correctional personnel lie in the power to make appointments or to offer tangible rewards, such as promotion, pay increases, tenure, maintenance. As a consequence, conflict about the form and development of correctional policies frequently is diverted to the struggle for control of personnel operations. The adoption of a civil service system may be viewed as an effort to set up alternative channels for exerting such control in opposition to the traditional political patronage. New criteria for selection and appointment of personnel under civil service become major weapons in the control of correctional operations. The struggle of correctional and welfare groups to raise personnel standards is largely an effort to gain further command over correctional policies. For example, as the social work movement gains strength in the correctional field, the pressure to get civil service examinations and job requirements stated in terms of training and experience in social work gradually results in the recruitment of persons committed to social work as a profession and a framework for correctional decisions. Quite different persons would be recruited through a political patronage system or even a strong civil service system in which examinations were prepared by police authorities or correctional officials without training in social work.

Because of the vulnerability of most state correctional systems to personnel controls outside the administrators' reach, the relative power of interest groups to influence correctional decisions becomes partly a function of their ability to influence key areas of decision about personnel. Since these areas are generally controlled by political and legislative figures who mediate many divergent interests, the influence of correctional interest groups is often obscured. Nevertheless, the training and commitments of the personnel appointed, the actions and backgrounds of the persons selected for promotion and pay increases, and the rationale of dismissals testify to the relative power of the competing interest groups and their tactics of influence.

Certain undercover tactics—such as bribes, threats of public exposure, private gifts, personal and political favors—are unquestionably used by some interest groups to gain competitive advantage. Since the effectiveness of these tactics depends on secrecy, they are inappropriate for controlling routine decisions and are more likely to be used to affect strategic and unique decisions. This is also true of mutual obligations arising from personal loyalty or friendship, which share some of the features of political "clout" (cf. page 144 supra). "Clout" is expendable and so is husbanded as a resource or influence for special occasions. The play of interests through these networks of personal obligation is exceedingly complex. They are important for mobilizing appropriate pressures for special actions but become too extended and unreliable for channeling routine efforts.

Program Sanctions. The correctional administrator who ignores the ways in which his decisions or the activities of his organization violate the expectations of correctional interest groups may find that it becomes impossible for him to carry out his program. Opposition groups may attack it directly through various forms of sabotage. Key personnel may be induced to take jobs elsewhere. Certain agencies, such as the police and the courts, with which he has routine dealings may be persuaded to invoke obsolete rules or to elaborate requirements that introduce delays and confusion in the operations of his organization. Personnel managers and employers in the community may be led to default on agreements to hire parolees or to donate supplies and assistance for the prison's vocational training program. Petitions from local groups may result in restrictions on the development or operation of the prison's honor farm, trusty, or work-camp program. The administrator may be forced to allocate excessive amounts of staff time to security functions, with corresponding curtailment of the rehabilitation program. Heavy bureaucratic demands for extra reports and alternative plans for development may divert staff attention and effort from his own plans for the organization.

The correctional administrator and his staff are engaged in a great variety of activities which depend for their success on the prompt and coordinated fulfillment of expectations by other agencies with which he is routinely in contact. This essential reliance on other groups makes the correctional agency's program subject to sabotage by these groups either through active harassment or simple noncooperation. Correctional interest groups in control of these agencies or capable of influencing them have a strategic advantage: they can force correctional personnel to take account of their interests or suffer crippling damage to their own program and possibly to their careers.

In addition to making direct attacks on the correctional program, interest groups can exploit the necessary reliance of correctional agencies on legislative enactments and appropriations for maintaining or developing their programs. The legislative arena provides many excellent opportunities for the trading of influence and the mobilization of support by interest groups that are actively obstructing the correctional program. A group's capacity to obstruct the program is often matched by its power to facilitate legislative approval of it. The besieged administrator of a correctional agency, threatened with destruction of his program, is extremely vulnerable to interest groups with sufficient legislative influence to hamper or aid his cause. The temptation if not the necessity of winning the support of such groups in defense of the correctional program is apparent.

The public relations program of a correctional organization is also especially vulnerable to the application of sanctions. All correctional agencies seek to present a public image of their work that will create a favorable climate for its development. The agency is represented as engaged in an orderly and humanitarian way in the protection of society and the rehabilitation of criminal offenders. The difficulty is that effective control and treatment of offenders constitute a hazardous task, which no one really knows how to carry out efficiently within the limits imposed by the values of a democratic society. There is a normal quota of failures and errors, which those in the field expect but find difficult to explain to outsiders. Consequently, there is always a discrepancy between the image of correctional practice presented to the public and the facts known to insiders. This discrepancy is a condition of special vulnerability in the public relations program. On almost any occasion a correctional interest group can point to the discrepancy and cause the correctional organization considerable public embarrassment. The threat does not lie so much in the discomfort created by the disclosure as in the possibility that it may precipitate a more general crisis for the agency, by virtue of coincidence with the antagonisms of other groups.

It is apparent that areas of special vulnerability facilitate the use of sanctions against a correctional agency. These are areas where the administrator or his staff lack control over what happens—where they are forced to rely on the cooperation of other persons or groups, in order to assure the security and growth of the agency. Since the attention of interest groups involves only segments of the agency's program, except in severe crises, relatively limited compromises are usually sufficient to elicit supportive rather than hostile maneuvers. The pressures in this situation lead to efforts in two directions: concentrated effort to build a structure of interest group commitments in which the organization can maintain a stable and secure course; deviance from earlier commitments in order to make limited compromises for further security. Gradually a problem arises because the increment of new objectives and interests for the organization comes in conflict with the old. Schisms and crises, which the limited compromises sought to prevent, are created. One pattern of organizational change is that by successive compromises conflicts in the external environment are built into the organization itself.

Establishment of Correctional Objectives

Interest groups constitute the basic organizational structure which gives form and content to correctional activities. The power and influence of interest groups are not static, however, but change with their fortunes over time. These shifting interests and varying pressures are reflected in the correctional organization's own activities. The old, routinized ways of doing things gradually create problems. These problematic situations become the focus of new conflicts of interest, out of which new patterns of activity emerge. Sometimes these situations pose basic dilemmas, which cannot be solved by limited compromises or informal adjustments. When there is much at stake and the power of the conflicting interests is relatively balanced, an issue may become public. It becomes a public issue in the sense that it captures the attention of others whose interests are not immediately involved in its solution. The competing interest groups permit a public issue to develop because of their respective stakes in the solution and because they must go beyond their own numbers to gain support for their positions. In this process of seeking support interest groups on both sides of the issue become instruments for the formation of larger correctional opinion groups or publics.

Correctional opinion groups are made up of persons who are organized to express the same views about correctional activities. But persons who act together in this way need not *do* the same thing when they are involved in a correctional crisis. For example, in one situation a police group and a social work group voiced similar public criticism of a probation and parole administration, although they were committed to quite different objectives and favored different patterns of correctional activity and organization.

In general, "making an issue public" is a hazardous undertaking for a correctional organization and for many of the interest groups that support its activities. Often the opinion groups which are formed are difficult to control. The issue concerning a particular correctional activity may be broadened to relate to many, or even all, of the activities of the organization. When this occurs the organization is likely to undergo a crisis experience, from which it may emerge with a new correctional administration and a new mandate which will control the direction of its future development. The group interests behind the activation of public opinion groups try to mobilize greater support by making other persons and groups aware of interests of their own that are affected by the actual or proposed correctional activity. This effort initiates a complex process, in which the direction of change and the shifts of power and influence are not always controllable.

The interest groups that successfully mobilize widespread favorable public opinion are most likely to wield the greatest influence in the determination of correctional policies and programs. Generally, the most influential interest groups have ready access to the agencies of mass communication. Interest groups with a great diversity of interests in addition to those relating to correctional activities are also more likely to be able to mobilize a strong opinion group. In fact, the power of an interest group over a correctional administrator and his organization's activities directly reflects the group's ability to secure supporting statements from the leaders of other important groups in the community—groups that have prestige, status, and access to communication channels where their statements carry weight and authority. It is largely through direct access to the institutions of communication and through many links with crucial interest groups that national organizations, such as the National Probation and Parole Association, achieve influence over the direction of correctional development.

It is becoming increasingly apparent that a basic struggle is developing between the adherents of a *protective* philosophy and the adherents of a professional *social work* philosophy for power to control the correctional field. In some states this conflict has already posed major crises for correctional organizations. The capacity to create a supporting structure of opinion groups has been an important critical weapon in this struggle for control, and both sides have exhibited the ability to exploit their strategic advantages.

Adherents of a protective approach to correctional work have the major advantage of being in control of most of the penal institutions and probation and parole systems in the country. Furthermore, the historic development of the protective ideology out of a combination of enforcement and welfare interests has permitted its adherents to straddle conflicts that must be squarely faced by protagonists of the social work approach. Correctional groups oriented to protective functions find it relatively easy to ally themselves with closely related occupational groups, such as the police and public prosecutors, and usually find it easy to gain their support because of the apparent conflict of enforcement interests with social work practice and ideology. The complex linkage of interests that has grown out of many adaptations successfully made in the past provides a source of strength which is difficult to challenge.

Adherents of a social work philosophy also possess certain tactical advantages in the struggle for control of the correctional field. They are closely identified with the social work profession, which plays a leadership role in the pervasive humanitarian welfare-movements of our day. Well-known educators, citizens with high prestige, personnel of other agencies which are part of the broad social-welfare movement, all share with the social worker in corrections certain understandings and goals. This identification, combined with the cultural drift in mass opinion toward welfare objectives, enables the social work in corrections to mobilize powerful interest groups in defense of his position. In addition, he is equipped with a missionary ideology that provides him with a well-rationalized philosophy of work and a set of principles, techniques, and skills to implement this philosophy. In any struggle for control of an organization, the social worker is much more likely to have at hand a comprehensive program for correctional action. Furthermore, the social work movement has developed over time broadly mobilized interest groups with which it has won similar struggles about other social problems. There are, in other words, latent opinion groups which can be quickly rallied in support of welfare objectives, through skills developed in conflict situations in the past.

The conflict between the adherents of a protective ideology and of a social work philosophy is of basic importance in the development of correctional practice. The implications of these different positions for practice should be examined closely and understood. The nature of correctional work may be expected to change considerably as control passes from one group to the other. In such a period of struggle and transition, it is particularly important to understand not only the differences in the two positions and their implication for correctional practice, but also the way in which change from one system to the other takes place and the consequences for the development of the organization and for the attainment of correctional objectives. In this process of change public opinion plays a critical role. Advocates of either a protective philosophy or a social work philosophy often think that they must take into account only immediate adherents of one another's correctional views and allied groups. This study, however, has pointed to large and important networks of interests that are involved in correctional activity. Unless these are considered in developing a correctional program, it is likely to fail, and the potential value of various measures for reform will be part of the cost.

Notes

1. Cf. V. O. Key, Jr., *Politics, Parties, and Pressure Groups* (3rd ed.; New York: Thomas Y. Crowell Company, 1952), pp. 23–182.

2. Cf. E. Pendleton Herring, *Public Administration and the Public Interest* (New York: McGraw-Hill Book Company, 1936), p. 35.

3. The use of the term *interest group* in this study seems to accord most closely with that contemplated by Arthur F. Bentley, *The Process of Government* (Evanston: Principia Press of Illinois, 1908).

4. C. Wright Mills, *The Power Elite* (New York: Oxford University Press, 1956). See particularly pp. 242–268, for discussion of the relevance of the concept of interest groups to analysis of the middle ranges of power as contrasted with the

organization and expression of influence at higher and lower levels of the power structure of American society. In the research on which this article is based, attention was focused on the organization and operation of state correctional systems. No evidence was found of the centralization and coordinated use of power implicit in the concept of a "power elite" at this level. Instead there was confirmation of Mills' expectation that a theory of interest group relations would provide the most accurate statement of the organization and expression of influence throughout the middle ranges of governmental policy and decision making.

5. An analysis of the creation and use of crises by interest groups to achieve organizational change in correctional institutions appears in an unpublished paper by Lloyd E. Ohlin and Donnell M. Pappenfort, "Crisis, Succession and Organizational Change," presented at the annual meeting of the American Sociological Society, September, 1956.

6. This term refers to a network of acknowledged claims and mutual obligations through which one acquires access to the services of a powerful political figure.

Chapter III

Executive Leadership

Executive leadership is expressed in the formulation of policy decisions that commit the organization as a whole to the particular domain, mandate, and mode of operation. Hence the executive functions primarily at the institutional level of the organization (Parsons, 1960, pp. 16–58) where the fundamental characteristics of the organization in relation to its environment are being determined.

The motivating force guiding the decisions of the executive is the dual need to ensure the survival and growth of the organization, and to maintain and enhance its effectiveness. These needs are expressed in the continuous endeavors of the executive to: (a) develop and maintain vital and nurturing linkages between the organization and its environment, and (b) organize its internal work structure to achieve the organizational goals effectively and efficiently. Consequently, the decisions made by the executive involve major commitments, not easily reversible, in terms of values, resources, personnel, and performances, which are the main action guidelines for members of the organization. As such, these critical decisions set the parameters for the operation of the various subsystems of the organization.

Five critical decision-making areas can be identified in which executive leadership may play a crucial role in determining outcomes: (a) formulation of the basic service mission of the organization within the context of the opportunities, constraints and contingencies presented by the environment; (b) negotiations and mediation between the organization and external interest groups in order to gain legitimation and procure necessary resources; (c) selection of the service technologies to carry out the mission of the organization; (d) development and maintenance of the internal structure of the organization to implement its various tasks; and (e) initiation and implementation of changes in the organization in the face of new opportunities, constraints, and contingencies confronting it.

The ability of the executive to direct or redirect the organization as a whole in each of these areas is determined not only by his personal skills but also by the degree of autonomy he has to make major policy decisions. A crucial administrative skill, in this regard, is the ability of the executive to assess accurately the degree of maneuverability he has to pursue his objectives for the organization. It can be easily noted then, that the executive has to make decisions in a relatively high state of uncertainty and risk. In fact, an endemic dilemma in the role of the executive is how to optimize his decision-making processes in the face of continuous pressures from the external environment as well as from within the organization. Moreover, the potential costs as well as pay offs in each alternative to be chosen are often high. Thus, the executive is preoccupied with assessing the opportunities and the constraints that are present in each area of decision making and in forecasting the potential consequences of selecting among alternatives. In this sense the executive must adopt a futuristic outlook since his ability to forecast trends and shape the organization accordingly will determine its viability and effectiveness.

The nature of the executive leadership and the functions it performs vary significantly with the stage of development of the organization (Perrow, 1961). At no time in the life of an organization is the role of an executive more critical than in the founding stage. The executive, in this stage, shapes the character of the organization by defining its mission (Selznick, 1959) and by selecting its social base. This process involves the formation of relations with power centers in the community, development of administrative ideologies, and the recruitment of personnel committed to these ideologies. The charisma of the executive at this stage of organizational development will be a major factor in determining the extent of the institutionalization of the organization.

The second stage in the organizational development is the establishment of its technical core and the formalization of its activities. Hence, the technical-administrative skills of the executive are of key importance in creating the technical competence of the organization. The rise of technocrats to leadership positions in the organization typifies this stage of the development.

The third stage of development is the expansion and differentiation of the organization's division of labor. The role of the executive as coordinator and mediator among the various work units emerges during this stage. The executive must assign tasks to different units; develop channels of communication and patterns of coordination among units; establish mechanisms of control and supervision; and mediate and resolve conflicts that arise among various interest groups within the organization.

The fourth stage of development is the establishment of mechanisms and procedures to increase stability and predictability in the organization (Katz and Kahn, 1966, pp. 87–89). The executive role is that of a caretaker and mediator. In this position the primary functions of the executive are to protect the organization from external pressures and resolve conflicts that arise internally without altering the basic patterns of the organization.

Finally, as the organization faces new challenges that require important changes in its structure and operations, the executive role is that of an innovator and reformist. At this stage of the organization's development executive succession may become an acute and critical issue since the needed reforms often call upon new executive talents and skills. Promotion of an "insider" may result in increased bureaucratization (Gouldner, 1954) and greater resistance to change, while the hiring of an "outsider" may narrow the base of support for the changes offered by the executive.

Although the organization may follow various patterns of development and not necessarily in the sequence described above, the key point to note is that different executive skills are called upon at each stage. Thus, the same executive although effective at one stage of the organization's development may become quite ineffective at other stages.

In this context, leadership style is an important variable in shaping the role of the executive, particularly in terms of the initiative and risks he is willing to undertake. Accordingly, we can distinguish between a proactive versus a reactive executive. A proactive executive is guided by the motivation to actively influence and shape the external environment of the organization as well as its internal structure in order to fulfill the organization's mission. Hence, he tends to be an initiator, an innovator, and a change-oriented person. Moreover, the proactive executive is willing to engage in high risk taking behavior. In contrast, the reactive executive is preoccupied with maintaining the status quo, and his decisions are primarily in response to pressures generated either from without or from within the organization. The reactive executive is mainly motivated to maintain the adaptiveness of the organization and to avoid risk taking behavior.

Some of the issues facing the executive receive an added and particular emphasis in human service organizations. First, the lack of consensus about the goals of the organization and the potential disagreement about the values it should adopt complicate the process of institutionalization. The executive must formulate a service ideology which explicitly or implicitly involves moral assumptions about the persons to be served, their position in society, and the mandate of the organization in intervening in their lives. Thus, the executive must be particularly sensitive to the prevailing attitudes and conflicting interests in the community, and his role may be highly politicized in this context. The organizational ideology formulated by the executive will reflect the political position of the organization in the community, and will be subject to frequent challenges.

Second, when the choice of service technologies cannot be based on clear and objective effectiveness and efficiency criteria, the executive must make the choice which in turn has far reaching consequences to the service modalities of the organization. Moreover, to ensure the implementation of the desired technologies, the executive needs to recruit staff members who share and identify with his ideology.

Third, the more complex and indeterminant the service technology the more likely the organization to select its executive on the basis of his demonstrated competence as a change agent, i.e., therapist, doctor, or teacher. This pattern can be observed in agencies employing indeterminant technologies such as the psychiatric hospital, the child guidance clinic, and the experimental school. However, the organization may, as a result, suffer from lack of other important executive skills. The development of an executive cadre in which the various executive skills are pooled together is one of the current trends to ensure the effectiveness of the executiveship. In the final analysis, executive leadership is measured by its success in maintaining and promoting the vitality of the organization.

The articles in this chapter address themselves to the various functions of executiveship in human service organizations. Hawkes identifies three linking roles that the psychiatric administrator assumes: (a) between the organization and the resources of legal and political support; (b) between the organization and sources of technical and professional support; and (c) between the organization and the population to be served. In each of these roles the administrator must use different negotiation skills, often not related to his professional training. yet, his linking role between the hospital and these subsystems, provides the executive with crucial intelligence that is typically not available to other members of the organization. Thus the power of the executive in the organization is enhanced.

One key mechanism of external control of the organization is the board of directors. A major task for the executive is to execute the policies of the board in the organization as well as influence the board to accept organizationally generated policies. Zald provides a review and synthesis of this issue, particularly in terms of the executive's influence over the board and the board's control of the executive. He indicates the functions of the board and suggests hypotheses regarding the conditions which increase the power of the board over the executive and vice-versa. Of particular importance is his identification of the critical phases in the organization's life cycle in which the board comes to assume a crucial role in affecting the character of the organization.

Carlson examines the crucial question of executive succession. Studying the succession of school superintendents, Carlson advances the proposition that when the school board is seeking change within the system an outsider will be brought in as superintendent. In contrast, when the board wishes to maintain the status quo it will appoint an insider. Carlson concludes by implying that school boards cannot afford to have an insider followed by an insider since such a succession pattern will suppress any innovation in the school system.

Finally, the selection from Street, Vinter, and Perrow examines the functions of the executive within the organization in terms of goal selection and delegation of authority. The authors indicate how the selection of correctional goals involves a series of moral commitments as well as beliefs about the causes, nature, and cure of deviant behavior. These beliefs are internally reinforced through the delegation of power to those subunits in the institution that are most oriented or most crucial to the implementation of the goal commitments.

References

Gouldner, A. 1954. *Patterns of Industrial Bureaucracy*. The Free Press of Glencoe.

Katz, D., and Kahn, R. L. 1966. *The Social Psychology of Organizations*. New York: John Wiley and Sons, Inc.

Parsons, T. 1960. *Structure and Process in Modern Societies*. The Free Press of Glencoe.

Perrow, C. 1961. "The analysis of goals in complex organizations." *American Sociological Review* 26:856–66.

Selznick, P. 1957. *Leadership in Administration*. New York: Harper and Row.

The Role of the Psychiatric Administrator

Robert W. Hawkes

In recent years the mental hospital has been viewed as a small social system.[1] Its social structure has been depicted as a complex of interrelated roles. This type of analysis has shed light on many of the more vexing problems of hospital organization. However, this approach[2] has somewhat neglected the fact that the hospital is a complex special purpose organization which is intimately related to a larger social environment.[3]

Another line of inquiry has been pursued by investigators interested in social class. Recently they have shown a close relationship between class affiliation and the type of treatment received by people who are classified as mentally ill.[4] This nexus directs our attention to an empirical connection between the operation of the hospital organization and the social system of which it is a part. But it does not provide us with an adequate theoretical linkage between the two phenomena.[5]

By focusing on the role of the psychiatric administrator in this paper one can begin the job of constructing theoretical links between the hospital and its social environment. In addition, administrative behavior not fully explained by the small-social-system approach can be accounted for.

The empirical evidence for this study is based on my observations, gained during nearly two years of research on the administrative process in mental hospitals as it operated in one state's system and affected one of the state's hospitals. I was given every opportunity to attend all formal meetings and many informal meetings. These data were augmented by interviews, systematic observations, and repeated conversations with strategic administrative personnel. Here I present the framework that was developed during that research, with illustrative material aimed at clarifying the framework.

Role Identity

The role of the psychiatric administrator is identified and conditioned by the unique juncture of three sets of relationships;[6] for our purposes,

Reprinted from *Administrative Science Quarterly* 6 (June, 1961): 89–106.

they are unchanging and exclusive of the personal interpretation that may be given the role by a particular incumbent:

1. His relationship with sources of political, legal, and financial support, which make his office locally legitimate and endow it with organizational authority.

2. His relationship with sources of technical and professional support, which give him professional authority, provide him with a hospital staff, and involve him in reciprocal rights and obligations with neighboring medical facilities.

3. His relationship with the problem population (potential or actual patients plus the nonhospital persons involved).

These three sectors of the administrator's role imply three sets of contracts. By making these contracts analytically explicit, we will have a framework on which to build hypotheses about the administrator's role.

Contract 1: The Administrator and the Sources of Legal, Economic, and Political Support

These sources are the state political hierarchy and the legislature in the case of the state mental hospitals, the board of trustees and potential donors in the case of private hospitals. The contract between the administrator and the source group might be stated as follows: The administrator will carry out the functions of administering an organization for the care and treatment of patients, and the economic and political group will pay him, and, by allowing him to occupy the office of superintendent, give him legitimate authority within the designated hospital organization.

One of the unique features of this contract is its quantitative emphasis. Not only the amount of money to be paid to the administrator for his services, but also the amount that will be allocated to the hospital, is generally made explicit. Implicit is some assumed number of patients to be treated. While little direct evidence supports this point, indirect evidence bears it out. Hospital budget requests estimate the number of patients to be cared for in a given year, and the moneys are allocated largely on that basis. Statistical reports are given in terms of number of patients treated, admitted, discharged, etc. I attended many staff meetings at which the hospital superintendent compared statistically the hospital's current performance with its past performance. At other staff meetings, the performances of different hospitals were compared in terms of patient-staff ratios. Such emphasis on statistical counting leads one to suspect that the administrator is expected to treat some minimum number of patients within a given fiscal time period.

Another point that distinguishes Contract 1 is the pressure exerted on the administrator to conform to certain nonmedical role standards: he must deal with the source group not only on the basis of his professional role as licensed psychiatrist, but also on the basis of his personal achievements and attributes. This is necessary because the source group is composed largely of nonmedical individuals whose professional role definitions and role behavior may be quite different from his. Two illustrations of this may be found in observations of how an administrator was selected and of the administrator's behavior vis-à-vis this source group.

During a period when a new administrator was sought, I observed that the search process seemed to be influenced by considerations of how well or how forcefully the prospective administrator could represent the interests of the hospital to judges, legislators, and the other key laymen in the hospital's political and economic environment. For instance, in the course of many conversations between the author and one of the strategic people involved in choosing a new superintendent, this person constantly stressed the need for the superintendent to present the hospital's "case" with vigor. The terms "reformer," "fighter," and "progress" were continually used. What a man could do by way of organizational achievement seemed paramount. Of the many candidates available who enjoyed excellent professional reputations in psychiatry, the one finally selected had, above all, an outstanding record in dealing with the economic and political problems of psychiatric administration.[7]

In associations with the source group, a group made up mainly of his social and/or economic peers, the administrator was observed to drop certain intraprofessional behavior patterns to conform more with the behavior patterns of the political and financial decision makers. At meetings consisting of medical residents and staff, the administrator and others would use the title "Doctor" in addressing each other, while at interprofessional meetings, which included both medical men and laymen (such as state financial officers, foundation representatives, journalists, lawyers, educators), the administrator and others present dropped the use of titles—indeed, first names were the rule. At the all-medical meetings held at the hospital, the administrator would preside; at the interprofessional meetings the person who was considered the host would preside. At the hospital meetings the superintendent could veto courses of action proposed. He often played the role of a stern father chiding his children, and as the person with the highest status he generally had the last word—both literally and figuratively. In contrast, at the interprofessional meetings, the superintendent played the part of the genial "good fellow," shaking hands with those present and interspersing his serious comments with topical quips. Instead of the administrator having the "last word," it was the host who summed up at the end of these meetings—although this summary was a recapitulation and not a final approval as in the case of the medical meetings.

Contract 2: The Administrator and the Sources of Technical and Professional Support

The referent sources here are the groups which give the administrator membership, training, and technical assistance in the field of psychiatric medicine. In return for such support the administrator not only abides by the general ethics of medicine, but has the implicit obligations of employing medically approved types of treatment and personnel and of upholding the medical status system. We consider this a contract, because, in exchange for his continuing privileges and rights as a doctor, the administrator is expected to continue to behave in certain ways prescribed by his medical reference groups. Failure to follow these prescribed ways can bring serious repercussions. I shall give illustrations, based on my observations, to exemplify the implicit parts of the contract.

That intraprofessional role obligations are the main determinant of choice of treatment and personnel seems indicated by the fact that whenever economically possible, administrators employ treatment and personnel currently in vogue in the psychiatric profession. This is so despite the fact that the effectiveness of various treatments and personnel—past and present—has not been clearly established on scientific grounds. The administrator therefore chooses treatment and personnel legitimatized by the medical profession. As has been shown, this is the contract obligation that the administrator accepts in relation to the medical profession. The following brief account illustrates the point that despite considerations of seniority, personnel less approved medically are replaced by personnel more approved medically.

Several years ago occupational therapy and group psychotherapy were techniques new to the hospital under observation. These techniques were introduced into the hospital by an attendant with administrative approval. It should be noted that an attendant has little if any formal medical status. As these therapeutic techniques became more central to the treatment program of the hospital, they were put under the direction and control of more legitimatized, higher-status medical personnel. An occupational therapy department which consisted of several registered occupational therapists was established, and group psychotherapy was administered by several resident psychiatrists. The attendant who introduced occupational therapy and group psychotherapy was gradually eased out of the administration of these programs as the more legitimatized medical personnel were put in charge. Thus as new therapies became more important to the hospital the administration gave their direction and control to legitimatized medical personnel.

That the administrator implicitly agrees to support the intraprofessional status system has already been partly illustrated in detailing certain intraprofessional "rules of the game" under Contract 1. Another common example of this, which I observed on numerous occasions, occurred when a seasoned nurse would patiently follow the instructions of relatively inexperienced first-year resident psychiatrists. The residents' orders were generally carried out, even though the nurse had more information about the patient and might have recommended a different course of action.

It should be noted in passing that the hospital administration studied was well aware of this communication problem. It held numerous meetings to try to find a way to relax the relatively rigid role behavior generated by the clearly delineated statuses of the medical profession. The aim of the administration was to encourage communication based on the staff member's knowledge rather than on his status.

Thus we see that professionally designated statuses are a larger determinant of role behavior in this contract than in Contract 1. In this second contract, the administrator is operating within a semiautonomous professional social system with many of its own rules.[8]

Contract 3: The Administrator and the Problem Population

The problem population includes not only patients and potential patients, but also families and friends of patients, referral agencies, physicians, and others—in short, all of those community members outside of the hospital who directly participate in the inflow and outflow of patients. The contract here may be stated as follows: The administrator will provide hospital service to the mentally ill, and, in return, the relevant population will allow some of its members to be treated as mentally ill and follow the procedures laid down for them by the administrative authority of the hospital.

This is perhaps the most vague and yet the most complex relationship of the three. Without populations in need or desirous of the services of a mental hospital, the role of hospital administrator would become nonfunctional to the community.[9]

John and Elaine Cumming touched on this subject in their book *Closed Ranks, An Experiment in Mental Health Education.*[10] In describing the failure of a program to change community attitudes toward mental illnesses in general, and the mentally ill in particular, they showed that community attitudes will remain largely unchanged without some significant community support. Indeed it is only in the recent past that the community has allowed the mental hospital administrator to redefine his role. Formerly he was assigned the role of chief custodian over many unwanted citizens. Today, in part as a consequence of the mental health movement, he may be recognized by the community as an integral part of the medical organization needed for the treatment of mental illness.

Without community acceptance of the administrator's role, the relationship between the administrator and the economic, political, and legal sources of support would tend to disintegrate, although the second contract—the administrator's relationship to the medical profession—might remain intact. Restated, the psychiatric administrator might remain a doctor and seek a more willing population, but he could not remain administrator for a particular problem population without its implicit consent.

This third contract is characterized by an impersonality that stems from two sources. First, the amount of personal contact between the administrator and each relevant individual in the populace is relatively brief, if it exists at all. Even if the administrator manages to spend a good deal of time talking with people whom his hospital serves—or might serve—the amount of time spent with each one will be of such short duration that little in the way of a personal relationship is likely to develop. Second, and this is especially true of the state hospital, it is likely that the administrator will stand much higher on the socioeconomic ladder than most members of the relevant problem population. He therefore will be viewed primarily in terms of his office and professional status rather than as a familiar person. Many patients in the hospital who were interviewed knew of the existence of the hospital superintendent; they knew his title and name, but few could recognize him, or the assistant superintendent, or the clinical director.

Boundary Positions of the Administrator

In considering the boundaries linking the hospital with the outside community, a boundary, for our purposes, is defined as an area of *interaction* between members and nonmembers of an organization, and is marked by inputs and/or outputs. Thus a boundary in the financial sphere of operation would include, for example, interaction between the administrator and such "outside" persons as a board of trustees, and it would be marked by the input of money and of organizational authority for the administrator. A boundary in the medical sphere of operation would include interaction between the administrator and medical groups outside the hospital, and would be marked by the input of personnel, approved treatment procedures, and medical authority. A boundary in the patient sphere of operation—and this is the most important boundary of all—is primarily interaction between hospital staff and problem population, and is marked by patient admission (input) and discharge (output).

Having examined the three sectors of the administrator's role, we can see that each touches on these boundary operations, either directly or indirectly, and that much of his role definition comes from elements found *outside* the hospital—elements in the nonmember area of the boundary.

We now aim to show how the administrator, operating within his role on the financial and medical boundaries of the hospital, influences the primary boundary transaction—the formal *raison d'être* for the hospital: the input and output of patients. This boundary activity lends unique power possibilities to the administrator's role.

Administrator's Influence on Patient Input

The major inputs of a mental hospital are money, personnel, authority and patients (who would be considered raw material in an industrial enterprise). Here, our concern is with input of patients: how, how many, and what kind of patients will be admitted to the hospital. Although the administrator does not decide these questions directly, he does influence decisions about them, and these decisions are made, for the most part, *outside* of the hospital.

For example, the general trend of patient input is determined by hospital-community relations. The presence in a given community of home care programs, out-patient facilities, psychiatric wards in general hospitals, family service agencies, and the like, influences the rate and types of patients admitted to a given mental hospital. While these facilities are generally developed outside the domain of the hospital, the administrative hierarchy of the hospital can influence their development and/or operation by recommendations and influence. Such influence, if exercised, is exerted outside of the hospital on community leaders, for example, who make the decisions to raise money in order to maintain or change existing community psychiatric facilities or even provide for new ones. Since personnel is often recruited, the administrator, again operating largely outside of the hospital, may recommend and actually recruit many of the personnel needed to operate such community facilities.

Another illustration of the administrator's influence on patient input is found with respect to hospital facilities. The rate of patient admission is partly determined by the availability of facilities, and facilities are largely determined by the availability of funds. Decisions about the amount of money and materials allocated to the hospital are made *outside* the hospital in the state legislature, state bureaucracy, and/or board of trustees. The administrator, acting as a kind of pressure "group" will influence these decisions by his requests for continued maintenance or the expansion of hospital facilities, operative budget, and personnel. Again we see that the administrator, acting outside the hospital in his relations with the political and economic source group, affects patient input.

It should be noted here that this process of budgetary allocation is highly complex and seems to operate on several levels. Ideas for more efficient and humane patient intake originated generally either with ancillary personnel or at the hospital superintendent's level and involved relatively small amounts of money. Ideas relevant to major expansion of facilities generally originated on the superintendent's level or in the state commissioner's office and involved large amounts of money. Therefore, ideas relevant to reorganized procedures for patient admission had a time horizon of one or two fiscal years, whereas ideas relevant to capital expansion had a time horizon of up to ten years. The initial negotiation often consisted of a "debate" between the superintendent, who wanted better admissions procedures and an expansion of facilities, and representatives of the fiscal control section of the state mental health department who advocated holding the line at the level of last year's budget. In general, the final figure that went into a request for a given year's appropriation for a particular hospital was a compromise between the current needs and future plans of that hospital and the estimated climate of legislative receptiveness to appropriations for mental health in general. The actual budgetary allocation largely determined the number and kind of patients that the hospital could admit and care for.

The administrator also affects patient input through his dealings with the technical and professional source group—the group that supplies personnel to the hospital. Since the administrator may greatly influence the selection of personnel, and since the personnel in charge of admissions exercise control with respect to patients (as will be shown later, this applies to discharge even more), the administrator is indirectly affecting patient input.

There are two mechanisms through which the administrator exercises control over the selection of personnel: (1) In the short run he accepts or vetoes the replacement of specific personnel, such as intake social workers and resident psychiatrists. (2) In the long run he may reduce or promote the use of certain types of personnel, who may emphasize different criteria of mental health and illness. This point is best illustrated by the increase in the number of social workers in mental hospitals, performing more intake functions and participating in discharge arrangements. These social workers brought more emphasis on family relations into admission and discharge decisions. It must be stated that the administrator does not always have boundary transactions as the explicit aim of the type of action described above. Here the aim was nominally to allow psychiatrists more time with patients in the hospital. The effect, however, was to alter the input-output relations of the hospital.

Thus by exercising authority in one boundary of the organization, the administrator can influence transactions in other boundaries. Note that much of the actual process of the selection of personnel goes through channels which take the administrator outside the organization: colleagues outside the hospital, conventions, professional associations, and the like. Thus the administrator's influence over many decisions regarding patient input is conditioned largely by factors outside of the hospital.

Administrator's Influence on Patient Output

The chief output of a mental hospital is treated patients. While the discharge of a mental patient is generally legitimatized by the doctor who is in charge of the case, the process is very complex and involves the opinions of ancillary personnel, the readiness of family and friends to accept the patient, and many other social relationships. Actual discharge rarely involves the administrator directly, except perhaps in unusual cases where he operates in a purely medical capacity. Much of what was said regarding the administrator's role in admissions, however, is also applicable to discharge: allocation of resources and selection of staff personnel may greatly affect particular discharges. Furthermore, because of the greater uncertainty involved in discharge as compared to admission, the administrator is able to affect the boundary of patient output even more than that of input. This uncertainty in discharge evolves from the fact that the criteria of health are less specific and more difficult to apply than are the criteria of illness. This relative absence of medical or technical criteria in discharge permits greater administrative intervention, albeit indirect, in the discharge process.

In recent years, hospital administrators have enlarged their influence on discharge by, in effect, enlarging the discharge boundary. This has been done through elaborated rehabilitation procedures. I observed the development of rehabilitation programs at four mental hospitals; at only one was there a later development—and it was smaller in scope—with respect to admission procedures. These enlarged rehabilitation facilities include special wards and other hospital areas set aside for rehabilitation functions. In addition to social workers, vocational counselors, and occupational therapists, many people with teaching abilities in such skills as typing, carpentry, and sewing were employed. Thus the administrator can broaden his control over discharge by initiating a rehabilitation program which calls for expanded facilities and staff, since facilities and staff are under his control through his activities *outside* the hospital with the economic and technical source groups.

Administrative Control Through Central Communication Position

The role of the administrator takes on a dynamic quality when we see that he can move freely between fiscal and political support and patient treatment and care. He is a participant both in the economic-political groups that provide the hospital with financial and material resources and in the professional-technical groups that provide the hospital with personnel who treat patients.

Traditionally, social scientists have viewed such roles, which are imbedded in two or more contexts, as providing role conflicts for their incumbents. This may be true of the psychiatric executive role, but the fact that this role is linked by implicit contract to both sectors also creates the possibility of increased power and control. The mental hospital administrator is able to exert control over each of the two important groups, because to each he is the only representative or main spokesman of the other one.

One instance of this can be observed in the administrator's role in setting up rehabilitation programs as discussed under patient output. In requesting funds from the economic and political groups, the administrator could speak as an expert representative of the professional-technical group, pointing to the psychiatric needs of the patients. To the medical staff, he could indicate the political and economic possibilities of bringing a given rehabilitation plan into being. If, for example, the medical staff requested different timing on instituting a rehabilitation plan, the administrator would be in a position to accept or reject such a suggestion on the basis of his knowledge of the optimal time to seek or obtain funds.

Access to vital political and economic information is a particularly important source of influence in the psychiatric profession. This can be easily seen when one considers the relative autonomy afforded doctors, not only because of the uncertainties in defining mental health, but also because of the mores of the medical profession. The hospital administrator, as a doctor, is not likely to criticize publicly or to evaluate the work of another doctor. This would seem to minimize the administrator's role in most problems involving control within the organization. But through his superior knowledge of political, legal, and financial resources and his access to them, the administrator can, in fact, control professional aspects of admission and discharge.

The administrator's situation in terms of a simple communication flow may be shown as follows:

In the above scheme communication flows to and from the administrator.

The composition and content of regularly scheduled meetings illustrates the operation of this communication structure. Shortly after I arrived in the field, I was invited to attend bimonthly meetings of all of the superintendents of the mental hospitals in the state system. At these bimonthly meetings, few doctors were present, other than the superintendents of the respective hospitals and the commissioner of mental health. The meetings were divided into morning and afternoon sessions. The morning session was devoted to a special report by someone at the host hospital. Among those present were perhaps one or more of the clinical personnel from the host hospital. At this time, the host superintendent could point to the recent performance of his hospital and could also indicate anticipated needs for technical and professional facilities and staff. Thus he communicated his hospital's accomplishments and needs not only to his colleagues but, more important, to the commissioner of mental health. The commissioner, although a psychiatrist, was nevertheless even more committed to his role in the economic and political support of the state hospitals and was further removed from the practicing technical support groups than were the hospital superintendents.

Afternoon sessions were business meetings, attended only by the commissioner of mental health, members of his fiscal group, and the superintendents of the various hospitals in the state system. These sessions dealt with broad questions of administration, such as possible future appropriations, grievance procedures, problems of recruiting types of staff, and the like. Thus no one from a given hospital except the superintendent had access to the relevant legal, political, and economic matters.

At the hospital studied, monthly medical executive committee meetings were held. Present were the hospital superintendent, the assistant superintendent, and various senior clinical personnel. These meetings were concerned primarily with allocation of personnel and, to a lesser extent, with types of treatment to be made available in the future, issues closely related to each other. One of the factors that gave the superintendent a prominent decision-making role in allocation of current resources was his superior knowledge of the possibilities of the availability of future resources.

At other intrahospital meetings, such as regular staff meetings, rehabilitation meetings, doctors' staff meetings, and morning rounds, the hospital personnel whose roles were primarily political and/or economic were rarely present. Such personnel would be those directly in charge of wages and salaries, data concerned with patient admission, discharge and "inventory," civil service technicalities, and so on. The superintendent generally met with them individually.

I also attended meetings between the hospital superintendent and the various state officials, whose concerns were mainly economic and legal. At these meetings the superintendent was generally the only member of the hospital staff present and, therefore, except for the occasional appearance of the commissioner for mental health, he was the only medical expert in attendance. He presented requests and plans for improved facilities based on the treatment needs of the patients as they were medically interpreted by the superintendent in his role as a doctor. While his conclusions were sometimes challenged, his medical premises were not.

To sum up, the administrator can exercise power and control because he has access to the complementary means of goal attainment with respect to the two groups, which are somewhat separated, yet quite interdependent.[11] It is safe to generalize that to the extent that the administrator allows or encourages communication between the two groups, to that extent he loses power and control both inside and outside of the hospital organization.

Another hospital observed in a different state system illustrates this loss of control. The superintendent adopted a "laissez-faire" policy. The hospital, as a consequence, operated as a set of semi-autonomous units. The rehabilitation unit, for example, applied directly for and received federal support; as a consequence it operated with only nominal attention to hospital policy. Thus the superintendent, in giving up his central position in the communication net, gave up effective control over the hospital. In addition he gave up effective representation of the hospital to its political and economic sources of support outside of the hospital.

A Strategy for Analysis

By examining the three contracts that identify the administrator's role, I have touched on three separate but interdependent systems, of which his role is both a product and a part and which we will call social subsystems. They are: (1) the system of economic and political support (especially visible in the case of state and federal hospitals), (2) the system of medicine and its related professions, and (3) the community system, which provides the hospital with patients. These social subsystems give us a new unit for further theorizing and research. We know that each subsystem is, in a way, separate from the other—yet overlapping; that each is part of society—yet distinguishable in terms of activities; and that each can be characterized by specific mores and socioeconomic attributes. In addition, each gives us a set of role definitions peculiar to it. These role definitions interlock so that roles are defined reciprocally within each subsystem.

Further examination of the social subsystems provides us with a more comprehensive way of studying the characteristics of organizations. They can be viewed as products of the subsystems and, in a more dynamic sense, they are the focal point of subsystems activity. It is possible to analyze the role of each member of the organization in terms of these crosscutting subsystems, but this would take us beyond the scope of this study.

Summary and Conclusions

The administrator's role has been divided into three sectors which extend beyond the confines of the hospital organization. Although the administrator does not necessarily participate directly in each sector, I have attempted to show that each has an important bearing on the definition of his role. I have tried to indicate that some of the dynamics of organization control involved in the role of the administrator can be understood in terms of his boundary position. While not participating directly in the chief input-output boundary processes of the organization—the admission and discharge of patients—nevertheless the administrator can influence them through his participation in other boundary processes. Because he stands in a position which links the input and output of (1) money and authority and (2) personnel, he can influence both of these processes and thereby exercise power and control over the admission and discharge of patients. It would seem that the administrator plays a role in three subsystems, which transcend the usual hospital limits. The hospital organization can be viewed as a product of the three subsystems and thus the administrators' role can be interpreted as a boundary-spanning link among the three subsystems.

Thus, through an analysis of the administrator's role we have made a beginning at connecting the hospital organization to its larger stratified social environment. One of the more obvious next steps is to link our social subsystems with social class and thereby derive a more complete picture of what happens inside the hospital organization as a consequence of factors that emanate outside the hospital.

Notes

1. Examples of this approach are: A. Stanton and M. Schwartz, *The Mental Hospital* (New York, 1954); I. Belknap, *Human Problems of a State Mental Hospital* (New York, 1956); and W. Caudill, *The Psychiatric Hospital as a Small Society* (Cambridge, Mass., 1958).

2. See for example the Foreword to M. Jones, *The Therapeutic Community* (New York, 1953): "When they discuss the 'therapeutic community,' they are referring only to carefully managed relationships within a closed institution," p. x.

3. The following two examples illustrate the kind of intrusion the outside world can make into a "therapeutic community." W. Caudill, in "Social Process in a Collective Disturbance on a Psychiatric Ward," describes a disturbance within the hospital and notes that a contributing factor was the matter of how patients on an open ward went into town and what they did there (in M. Greenblatt, D. J. Levinson, R. H. Williams, eds., *The Patient and the Mental Hospital* [Glencoe, 1957], pp. 438–471). "The most intense conflict at the hospital came immediately after the report of an outside firm of management consultants, who suggested, among other things, the discharge of seventeen (patients) who were unable to pay the full fee" (Stanton and Schwartz, *op. cit.*, p. 93).

4. For one of the best ecological studies that has direct relevance to a mental hospital see A. Hollingshead and F. Redlich, *Social Class and Mental Illness: A Community Study* (New York, 1958).

5. An exception to this is T. Parsons. "The Mental Hospital as a Type of Organization," Greenblatt *et al., op. cit.*, pp. 108–129.

6. We will use the terms administrator and superintendent interchangeably. The term administrator may facilitate comparisons with other administrators. Superintendent is a term used to designate the highest administrative officer in public mental hospitals. For a somewhat different, though overlapping discussion of the role of the chief administrator, or superintendent, in a state hospital see I. Belknap, *Human Problems of a State Mental Hospital* (New York, 1956), pp. 70–85.

7. Belknap, *op. cit.*, p. 80, notes that the superintendents who served the longest terms of office at Southern State Hospital were those who gave priority to the role of "efficient administrator" rather than that of "good doctor."

8. See for example, T. Parsons, "The Professions and Social Structure" in *Essays in Sociological Theory, Pure and Applied,* (Glencoe, 1949), pp. 185–199.

9. Belknap (*op cit.*, p. 139), notes that patients in a southern hospital are segregated according to sex, race, and, to a lesser extent, age. Thus what Belknap calls a "common-sense method" of classification reflects the mores of the social system in which the hospital is imbedded. It would seem that the community from which the problem population is drawn imposes rules that influence administrative decisions respecting the care of patients.

10. Cambridge: Harvard University Press, 1957.

11. While this is emphasized here as a source of power, Belknap (*op. cit.*, p. 80) points to it as an "either-or" situation, and Parsons in "The Mental Hospital as a Type of Organization" (in Greenblatt *et al.*, *op. cit.*, p. 118) points to it as an unstable dilemma: "Administrative roles and the recruitment of personnel for them present special problems in types of organizations primarily devoted to the provision of professional services to a category of persons; in this respect the hospital is, of course, similar to the university and a few other organizational types. There is a built-in dilemma here. The goal of the organization is defined in terms of the professional service and only the professional man is competent to evaluate the service given and the competence of those who do it, as well as the adequacy of the conditions and facilities provided. However, the technical expert—certainly the psychiatrist—is not, as such, a competent expert on the functioning of organizations, and yet organization which is beyond his professional competence is required to provide the setting for adequate performance of his functions. Someone must exercise administrative authority on the basis of a number of considerations, of which psychiatric technicalities are only a part, and in these spheres the administrator must be in a position sometimes to overrule the professionally competent personnel. Hence such organizations involve an unstable balance between two different types of authority; the organizational executive and the professional specialist."

The Power and Functions of Boards of Directors: A Theoretical Synthesis

Mayer N. Zald

In this theoretical synthesis of propositions about the power and influence of boards of directors our general orientation is that, in the relationships among boards (as collectivities), individual board members, and executives, each party brings to bear "resources." These resources may be based in legal rights, in monetary control, in knowledge, or even in force of personality and tradition. Resources may be crudely classified as "detachable" resources, personal characteristics, and strategic contingency situations. It is the balance of resources for specific situations and decisions that determines the attribution of relative power in the encounter between boards and executives.

It must be noted that the power of boards of directors or of individual board members does not refer to their formal voting rights. As in so many voting situations, formal voting may be irrelevant to many (though not all) of the crucial decisions. Instead, the power of board members relates to their service on and control of key committees and the extent to which other members and the management (who may also be board members) find it necessary to be bound by their perspectives and ideas.

The corporation form (as we have come to know it) was created as a means of accomplishing "desirable" ends that were beyond the capabilities of individuals. Boards of directors were created and recognized in law in order to insure continuity in the management of organizations and to fix a locus of responsibility for the control of "independent" organizations.[1] Boards are charged with the proper use of resources in pursuit of organizational goals. Directors are not personally responsible for organizational losses, but they are responsible for prudent action in behalf of the "owners" (whomever that might be).

Prudent action includes appointing and perpetuating effective management of the organization and overseeing the work of such management. This control function of the boards of directors is inward looking; the board operates as the agent of the corporation at the request of the owners (members) to oversee organizational activity.[2]

Because of their formal position of responsibility and their

Excerpted from *American Journal of Sociology* 75 (July, 1969) 97–111.

involvement in the organization, boards also develop an outward-looking function; they promote and represent the organization to major elements of the organizational set, for example, customers, suppliers, stockholders, interested agencies of the state, and the like. That is, they defend and support the growth, autonomy, and effectiveness of their agencies vis-à-vis the outside world.

Obviously, boards differ in the extent to which they perform either the external representation or internal control functions. For instance, it is likely that boards of prosperous manufacturing firms, in a competitive industry, and with unproblematic governmental relations, have less of an external representation function than welfare agencies heavily dependent on wealthy donors or on the community fund. Similarly, in small organizations in which board members have intimate knowledge, they may decide all nonroutinized expenditures, major personnel changes, markets, and types of product. In other organizations they may be restricted to formal appointment of the executive and the auditor and to setting executive salaries.

Although there is this variety, there are some relatively standard activities in which boards engage and which have implications for their potential power. First, a major concern of boards tends to be personnel. At the very least, boards usually must choose a chief operating officer and decide on his salary (if there is one). Second, boards that are not "paper boards," that actually hold meetings and discuss organizational affairs, usually review the financial condition of the organization and set financial policy (dividend rates, capital indebtedness, etc.). In some cases the rules and bylaws of the board require formal approval for all nonroutine expenditures over a stipulated amount. Finally, many boards review organizational output, its "product," markets, and comparative operating efficiency. Which of these activities are performed, and to what extent, depends on the structure of the organization, its environmental interrelations, and the sources of board member power vis-à-vis executives.

Detachable Resources a Power Base

A resource is "detachable" if it is not closely tied to the person, that is, if it is transferable. Utilizing a cross-sectional approach, we examine gross variables between organizations and between board members causing differences in the relative power of boards and individual board members.

There are two main bases of power considered. First, the relative power of board members can be based on their access to and control of relevant external resources. Second, knowledge relevant to the ongoing operations of the organization may be considered an internal organizational base of power differentially distributed between boards and executives.

External Bases of Power

External funding and facilities control.—A major source of board member control and influence stems from their control of crucial inputs of capital, raw materials, or "market." Control of external resources serves as a lever for board power when the organization finds it difficult to secure these facilities from other sources and requires this source.

The historic pattern of raising funds has seen a shift from the support of agencies by a few wealthy philanthropists to mass campaigns and community funds. When agencies were the "agents" of one or two families, or a small circle, the policies and procedures were sharply governed by these members of the board and by the chief funders. As funding shifts to the community fund or to mass drives, the power of the board *as founders* may decrease. Two corollary hypotheses can be stated for voluntary agencies: (1) *The more agencies receive contributions in small amounts from many givers, the less the likelihood of board members having power vis-à-vis the executives.* (2) *To the extent that fund-raising campaigns are based more on a sharp image of need and less on interpersonal relations of board members and fund raisers, we would expect the influence of the board member to be diminished.*

The growth of community funds has a complex relation to the structure of individual boards. The fund represents a centralized source of financial support, and the amount received from the fund can be crucial to the agencies involved.

The funds themselves allocate money through committees made up of businessmen, housewives, and professionals. To the extent that professionals dominate the funds, we would expect the boards of the agencies to become less important in interceding for the organization. However, students of these organizations suggest that there is a correlation between the prestige of the boards of agencies and their likelihood of having their requests granted a respectful hearing. Auerbach (1961) suggests that the settlement house serving a slum neighborhood but having an unknown board is less likely than the middle-class agency having a prestige ("power") board to receive a favorable hearing. The high-prestige board member may not only be generally respected but may control significant financial contributions to the fund. If Auerbach is correct, the maintenance of a prestige board facilitates relations with the community fund.

Community legitimation.—Board members may control an important external resource, a segment of community legitimation. They control community legitimation in that they "represent" diverse groups or interests which can be mobilized to affect the organization. Such organizations as boards of education and government commissions have boards either elected directly by the voters or appointed by the political executive. In general, *the more closely board members are linked to external groups, the more they "represent" community legitimation and, therefore, the more powerful they are vis-à-vis the administrative leadership.* Board members may be elected or appointed and yet not represent group interests if, for instance, appointment is "nonpartisan" and if board membership is largely symbolic. The more diverse and intense the interests in a given organization, however, the more likely the organization is to be politicized and the more likely board members are to represent community segments.

The external bases of power discussed above provide opportunities for factions to arise as groups commanding different resources contend for the definition of organizational goals and directions and for control of the organization. *The larger the number of board members having external bases of power, the more likely are coalitions of board members to arise.* Furthermore, given a number of board members with external bases of power, *the more divergent the definitions of organizational goals and policies, the more likely are the coalitions to resemble factions.*

Even if board members do represent external interests, ownership, or sources of funding, factions need not arise and board members need not attempt to influence managerial decision premises. An ideology of professionalism may lead to an effective abrogation of the role of the board. In such cases, the board serves to provide a mantle of legitimation and community justification (Kerr, 1964). Only when a given issue is defined as outside of legitimate professional competence will board members' attitudes and perspectives begin to influence decisions. Thus, Crain and Street (1966) note that, in large cities, on the issue of school policy toward desegregation, it is the board and its attitudes, not the school superintendents' professional or personal perspectives, that predict the outcome of policy debate.

Internal Resources: Knowledge

Knowledge is a "detachable" resource in that it can be acquired and lost. Detailed knowledge of the organization and its problems is a *sine qua non* of decision making. The board member or executive without knowledge has difficulty influencing the decision process, especially when there are agreed-upon goals. Knowledge can come from detailed familiarity with the specific organization or from general expertise about a given technical process.

Several conditions of organizational size, complexity, and technology condition the ability of boards to have sufficient knowledge to challenge and/or formulate lines of action. At the most general level, sufficient knowledge is a function of the degree of complexity of the organization and the technicality of its knowledge base. *The greater the complexity of the organization and the more technical its knowledge base, the lower the influence of board members.* This proposition leads us to expect, for instance, that larger organizations, with many product lines or task domains and geographically dispersed units, would have a less well-informed board than smaller, more concentrated organizations.

When an organization is small, with few plants, products, and markets, the directors can have independent knowledge of the plants, contact with the staff at several levels, and detailed acquaintance with the community and market situation. As the organization grows larger, the board member becomes increasingly dependent on the staff for his information. Furthermore, the organization is usually structured to channel information to and through the president or chief operating officer. Thus, the board becomes dependent on the executive, and one of their few outside checks becomes the balance sheet, subject to independent audit. Even accounting reports may become so complex that a high degree of familiarity and expertise is needed for their interpretation.

Of course, as the organization becomes larger and more complex, the chief operating officers also become more dependent on *their* staff. But the staff's conditions of work are directly dependent on the executive, and to some extent he is able to use them as his eyes. Even though the executive is formally appointed by the board, his greater knowledge of the full range or organizational concerns allows him to shape the kinds of information they receive and the kinds of matters they discuss.

Boards may be adapted to this imbalance in knowledge by being required to spend more time on organizational affairs (Brown and Smith, 1957, pp. 57–59). Sometimes, the appointment of "inside" board members (full-time executives) is recommended as a solution, but the independence of the officer from the chief executive cannot be assured.[3]

The relevance of knowledge to power becomes even clearer if we examine organizations in which various kinds of professionals and scientists furnish the key services of the organization. For instance, we would expect boards of directors of hospitals to be concerned mainly with financial matters while boards of educational institutions might have a greater say in personnel matters, though not curriculum matters, and finally, boards of such organizations as YMCAs might be involved in decisions about all phases of organizational activity. Where the knowledge base is esoteric, the board is not able to evaluate the requirements of the organization for new lines of endeavor, or to evaluate lines of action and personnel except in terms of fiscal matters.

Again there are adaptive solutions to the imbalance. Boards may delegate to internal committees the evaluation of projects involving technical decision criteria. Second, they may add to the board members with technical knowledge. General expertise, acquired outside of the organization, becomes a base for power.

To this point, I have offered propositions about bases of power which increase or decrease the board members' potential to influence the policies of large-scale organization, focusing on external resource control and the relative imbalance of knowledge. However, this cross-sectional approach is limited in at least two ways. First, I have played down the identities or characteristics of board members that may influence their role in boards. Second, I have ignored the process and phasing of boards that lead them to be more or less important and powerful at different times.

Personal Characteristics and Participation

Attributes attached to persons such as social status, sex, and personality are very general factors influencing how an individual will relate to others and how others will respond. While they are not "detachable" resources (at least to the same extent) as were those discussed in the last section, they are external characteristics brought into the board-executive relation from the larger society, and they affect the participation and influence of board members.[4]

Socioeconomic Status

Given the structure of American society and the function of boards in controlling property, in legitimating voluntary agencies, and in linking the activities of diverse institutions, it is not surprising that members of boards of directors tend to be selected from the higher reaches of the stratification system. While some organizations, such as YMCA's and settlement houses may dip into the middle-middle class[5] for a few board members, most board members will be drawn from the higher reaches of the socioeconomic pyramid.

The prestige and status of the board member gives him a reputation which affects others' reactions to him, and it gives him a set of expectations of how others should react to him. In general, *the higher the prestige and status of the member, the more likely other board members and staff are likely to defer to his opinions.*

Of course, reputation and generalized status do not fully determine influence. Strodtbeck, James, and Hawkins (1957) have presented data from jury deliberations indicating that the higher-status jury members are more likely to be chosen as foremen and have high rates of initial participation and, presumably, influence. However, they also note that, over time, the correlation between SES, participation, and influence declines. Generalizing from the findings of Strodtbeck et al., we might expect that, *if the only criteria for allocating influence is participation and knowledgeability, the low-status members who participate highly and are knowledgeable will become equal to the higher-status board members, even though officers will be more likely to be drawn from higher-status members.*

However, if the functions of boards involve more than just deliberation (as in the jury), the extended resources of votes controlled, access to funds, and prestige which can be used in interorganizational relations will guarantee to the higher-status board members a greater share of influence. (See the above discussion of the role of "power" boards.) Furthermore, if we compare boards composed of people of different status levels, those in higher-status boards are likely to expect a higher level of deference and influence than boards composed of people from the middle ranks (Moore 1961).

The comments above also apply to the relation of executives *to* boards as well as *among* board members. Some boards employ executives whose salaries and status may be equivalent to or higher than that of the board members (e.g., in some YMCAs and in school boards). If so, executive influence is enhanced.

Sex

Societal role definitions associated with sex also influence board member participation. Babchuk, Marsey, and Gordon (1960) found that, in a middle-sized community, women are more likely to be on boards of smaller and low prestige organizations than on the boards of the larger voluntary agencies—the hospitals and universities. Not only do women have less command of external resources—they rarely represent major bureaucratic organizations—but, on the average, they are socialized to more passive role taking. In boards with male executives, we would expect women to have less influence than men, to participate less freely in discussion, to be less assertive, and to be taken seriously to a lesser degree.

Other personal characteristics also influence board-executive interaction. The range of personality and self-presentation variables that are relevant is well known. Instead of pursuing them, the discussion turns to phases of organizational growth and change that implicate board power. In these last two sections resources have attached to the individual role occupant. But now we turn to power resources attached to the situation, that is, to the role expectations and definitions created by the ongoing social system.

Strategic Contingencies Situations

Examination of the functioning of a board over long periods of time would reveal an ebb and flow of board functions, importance, and power during different phases of organizational development and activity. Organizational phases affect the power of boards in several ways. First, at some points in the history of an organization, the formal requirements of board ratification and action require at the very least that managers get the approval of the board. Even if the board is but a rubber stamp, such periods allow some reinforcement of the image of board power. Furthermore, at such times dissident board members have a chance to crystallize board discontent with management and to express such discontent. At other times, the absence of meetings and debated issues prohibits such expression. Second, the phases of organizational development require the board to perform activities in the service of the organization—such as fund raising—that give it power over the managers. Thus some of our "cross-sectional" propositions (above) may also be implicated in the phase development of organizations.

Let us specify a number of broad organizational problems that not only require board action but also seriously implicate the responsibility of board members to debate and decide organizational matters.

The general proposition is that *it is during the handling of major phase problems, or strategic decision points, that board power is most likely to be asserted.* It is at such times, too, that basic conflicts and divisions both within the board and between the managers and the board are likely to be pronounced. Three types of broad-phase problems are discussed: life-cycle problems, choosing of successors, and fund-raising and facilities expansion.

Life-cycle Problems

Life-cycle problems are those of organization genesis, character formation and transformation, and basic identity.

Organization genesis.—When a corporate organization is newly established, or when the board as a responsible agent is being formed, a great deal of attention is likely to be paid to the formulation of policy, the roles of managers and boards, and the formation of guidelines for actions. *Boards will meet regularly and often, and it is likely that board power and influence will be continuously used and called upon.*

But qualification is in order; many business corporations develop out of individually owned firms or partnerships. If the new board does not control ownership certification, the power of the board may be relatively restricted during this period.

Character crises and transformation.—Organizations develop characters which become institutionalized in procedures and modes of handling problems. Organizational character, a term used by Selznick (1957), is the standard pattern developed for resolving recurring and basic problems and conflicts within the organization and with the organization's environment. These include such aspects of organization environment and intraorganization relations as labor policy, major product emphases, market strategies, relation to competitors, and quality-quantity emphases.

Pressures to change these aspects of character almost inevitably become issues for the board of directors. First, both legal requirements and the standard functions of boards in policy setting become obviously implicated when the major dimensions of the organization are subjected to change. Second, if these aspects of character have developed qualities of the sacred and traditional, as so often happens, changing them is likely to develop conflict. The managers will be forced both by divisions among the managers and by the awareness of concerned board members to bring such matters to the board.

In general, *the more routine and stable the organization in all its aspects—for example, labor, market, financing, etc.,—the less likely are crises of character to occur and the less likely are boards to be mobilized.*[6]

Moreover, *character crises are likely to be more difficult to solve in organizations without computational criteria*[7] *for choosing among alternatives.* For instance, voluntary welfare agencies with their ambiguous goals and unproven means are likely to have more prolonged debate on such matters than are businesses.

Identity crises[8]—Large-scale organizations have identity crises of several kinds. One is the crisis of mergers in which the existence of the organization as an organization is threatened, even though there is perpetuation of the function and the capital of the organization. A second is the threat to vanish entirely. A third identity crisis is involved in joint undertakings with other organizations. Such joint undertakings partially restrict the autonomy and independence of organizations.

Because there are often clear benefits to be gained through organizational mergers or joint undertakings, it is possible that business corporations, as a class of organizations, have a higher rate of identity crises than other kinds of organizations. However, YMCAs, orphanages, settlement houses, ethnic-based community centers, religious denominations, universities, governmental commissions, and others have all faced identity crises—problems of fission and fusion. Again, it is when issues like these are debated that boards are most fully involved and likely to have influence.

Choosing a Successor

Often the only real contact board members have with the organization is through the chief executive, and one of the prime responsibilities of boards is the choice of effective managerial leadership. In some organizations the board chooses only the chief executive, but in others the board may take an active part in appointing most upper executives. The amount of active participation in appointing upper executives is probably a good index of its power. More important here, *it is at the time of choosing a successor that board power is most mobilized* (Zald, 1965).

Succession processes can vary greatly. Of course, if a dominant executive or controlling group creates a "crown prince" or appoints the successor, then the board as such only ratifies the appointment. A crown prince appointment by a chief executive (not by a controlling ownership group) can only be effective when a retiring chief has been seen as successful. Thus, just as we suggested that the board is more likely to be active when an organization is involved in crises, so too *is it more likely to be active in choosing a successor when the organization is facing a crisis.*

The choosing of a successor often allows the basic questions of organizational mandate, character, and identity to come to the fore. Since the choice of the executive is so closely linked to decisions about organizational directions, it is natural to have a period of stock taking at that time.

Since the mobilization of board influence occurs around the time of succession, the periodicity of succession becomes of great importance. Because of deaths, age, and career patterns, some boards may be confronted fairly often with questions of succession, while others may only confront this question once in a generation. (Some Protestant denominations appoint their ministers yearly, while many larger business corporations try to arrange for ten-year terms for their chief executives.)

Notes

1. Although much of our discussion is applicable to governmental organizations, most of it is framed in terms of nongovernmental ones. Governing boards and organizations in the "public" sector tend to have less autonomy of organizational operation. Mainly discussing private organization gives our propositions a greater specificity and concreteness.

2. We usually think of boards of directors as agents of the "owners," but legally they are servants of the corporation vested with corporate control. On the ambiguities here, see Marris (1964, pp. 12–13).

3. Questions about the functions of inside directors pervade the policy-oriented literature. Wiley (1967) shows that among large corporations there is a slight tendency over time for them to have a greater proportion of outside board members. His findings are at variance with popular stereotypes.

4. Goffman (1961, p. 30) distinguishes between "external resources" and "realized resources" to discuss the exactly parallel phenomena of how external resources become determinants of interaction locally realized.

5. In our study of the Chicago YMCA, less than 10 percent of the almost 1,000 board members of the thirty-seven local departments were rated in 1961 as earning less than $8,000 a year.

6. See an interview with Cordiner (1967), former president of General Electric, for a discussion of the role of the board during GE's internal transformation of organizational structures.

7. The phrase "computational criteria" refers to known means to agreed-upon goals (see Thompson and Tuden, 1958, pp. 195–216).

8. Identity crises are subcases of character crises—i.e., those subcases in which an organization's social recognition as an entity are at stake.

References

Auerbach, Arnold J. 1961. "Aspirations of Power People and Agency Goals." *Social Work* 6 (January):66–73.

Babchuk, Nicholas, N. R. Marsey, and C. W. Gordon. 1960. "Men and Women in Community Agencies: A Note on Power and Prestige." *American Sociological Review* 25: 399–403.

Brown, Courtney C., and E. Everett Smith. 1957. *The Director Looks at His Job.* New York: Columbia University Press.

Cordiner, Ralph. 1967. An Interview with Ralph Cordiner. *Forbes* 100 (October 15):30–37.

Crain, Robert L., and David Street. 1966. "School Desegregation and School Decision-making." *Urban Affairs Quarterly* 2 (September):64–83.

Goffman, Erving. 1961. *Encounters.* Indianapolis: Bobbs-Merrill.

Kerr, Norman. 1964. "School Board as an Agency of Legitimation." *Sociology of Education* 38 (Fall):34–59.

Marris, Robin. 1964. *The Economic Theory of 'Managerial' Capitalism.* New York: Free Press.

Moore, Joan A. 1961. "Patterns of Women's Participation in Voluntary Associations." *American Journal of Sociology* 66 (May):592–98.

Selznick, Philip. 1957. *Leadership in Administration.* New York: Harper & Row.

Strodtbeck, Fred L., Rita N. James, and Charles Hawkins. 1957. "Social Status in Jury Deliberations." *American Sociological Review* 22 (December):713–19.

Thompson, J. D., and Arthur Tuden. 1958. "Strategies, Structures and Processes of Organizational Decision." In *Comparative Studies in Administration*, edited by J. D. Thompson et al. Pittsburg: University of Pittsburg Press.

Wiley, James A. 1967. "Trends in Board of Directors Structure in Industry." Unpublished paper, Vanderbilt University.

Zald, Mayer N. 1965. "Who Shall Rule: A Political Analysis of Succession in a Large Welfare Organization." *Pacific Sociological Review* 8 (Spring):52–60.

Succession and Performance among School Superintendents

Richard O. Carlson

All enduring organizations must cope with succession. To minimize dependence on individuals as such, organizations are structured around roles, offices, or jobs. Replacement of an individual, however, is potentially a significant event in the development of an organization, particularly when a key office is involved. Beyond its developmental significance, succession can be stressful for members and clients of an organization; therefore organization theory should deal with succession and organizational responses to succession.[1] This article develops and tests some propositions about succession of the chief executive in public school systems, taking the origin of the successor as a variable. Although the data have a specific setting, they may carry important implications for succession in other organizations.

With few exceptions, school superintendents are drawn from the ranks of those already employed in public schools. To obtain the superintendent's credential, they must provide evidence of successful experience as a classroom teacher. Usually by the time the credential is earned, some administrative experience has also been gained. Ultimately two alternatives are open to the would-be superintendent. One is to wait for the superintendency to become available in his own school system; the other is to seek a superintendency in some other school system.

The man who waits simply remains in his school system until the superintendency is his. His career is one of ascent up the hierarchy

Reprinted from *Administrative Science Quarterly* 6 (September, 1961): 210–27.

in one school system, although he may have changed school systems prior to becoming superintendent. The man who waits can be called an insider. He has been promoted from within. Ordinarily the insider completes his career as superintendent in the one home system. If he is removed from the superintendency before retirement age has been reached, he often takes an existing or frequently new lower-level administrative position in the same home district.

The man who does not wait, but seeks a superintendency whenever it is to be found, can be called an outsider. His career is always spread over two or more school systems. He has never served the district in which he is superintendent in any capacity other than superintendent. Ordinarily his career does not stop with one superintendency.

Insiders and outsiders differ in the importance they assign to career and place. Both have made sacrifices to obtain the superintendent's credential. The insider, however, seems to want the career of superintendent only if it can be had in a specific place, his home school system. He puts place of employment above career as superintendent. The insider is place-bound. The outsider puts career above place. He leaves the home school system and takes a superintendency elsewhere. The outsider is career-bound.

Whether to wait for the superintendency or seek it is a major decision in the career of an individual. The differences that are suggested by the commitments of place-bound and career-bound superintendents are so basic that they should be apparent in the ways in which these two types relate to their organizations. This article, taken from a larger study on administrative succession in public schools,[2] presents some evidence of these differences.

Some of the data presented relate to the job to be done by insiders and outsiders as defined by the employers. These data spell out the conditions of a successful performance in office. Other data bear on relevant personality factors of superintendents with different origins.[3] Still other data bridge the gap between personality and job, and deal with action in office. Significant events in the cycle of succession are used as the analytic scheme. This facilitates an intertwining of factors that pertain to the job to be done, personality factors, and the superintendent's acts as successor. First, attention is given to the conditions of employment of inside and outside successors. Then the concern shifts to the early activities of successors and the differences between insiders and outsiders. After the prominence gained by the two types is examined, the analysis centers on tenure of employment and succession patterns.

Continuous observations and interviews were made over a nine-month period in four school systems that had new superintendents. Leads gained from these observations and interviews were followed in lengthy interviews with an additional twenty superintendents. Data were taken from selected reports and documents, and a secondary analysis was made of raw data collected for two published studies dealing with superintendents.

Conditions of Employment

When a school board chooses a superintendent it has a free hand. Seniority rights do not infringe on the appointment. It is not reviewed at a higher level. The board can make the appointment solely in the light of what it believes will be best for the board and the school system. Under what conditions then does a school board deem it best to appoint an insider as the new superintendent? When does it prefer an outsider?

Observations and interviews in the four school systems indicate that, if the administration of the school system is perceived as satisfactory, the appointment will go either to an insider or outsider.[4] If the school board perceives the administration as unsatisfactory, the appointment will go to an outsider. This trend was evident in the districts under observation, and with histories collected on thirty-six other successions. No insider reported that the school board was unhappy with the way the schools were being administered at the time he was appointed. Typical of their responses were: "I succeeded a very successful man." "I think they were satisfied." "Now you'll always have an individual who is dissatisfied with a particular part of the school system but generally they seemed to be proud." On the other hand, in no case where the administration was considered unsatisfactory was an insider appointed.

The conditions of employment indicate that the school board will be satisfied if the insider "keeps things as they are," but they expect an outsider to make changes and are only satisfied when he does. School boards expect a creative performance from outsiders and are happy with a stabilizing performance from insiders.

It appears that the insider, because of his history in the organization, is so bound up by the internal and external interpersonal structure that if appointed at a time when changes are desired he will be unable or unwilling to make the desired changes. To gain the job as an insider, he had to give more than token support to his predecessor and his predecessor's program. To depart from this program in any major way would signal a change of "face." Such pressures seem to ensure that with an insider the organization will continue along its present path.

Not only is the school board free of a number of important constraints in the selection of the superintendent, but also it is free to determine the salary. The commitments of the insider suggest that it will be easier for the board to come to terms with him than with an outsider, since he appears more interested in making a career in the particular school system than in making a career as a superintendent. Further, from what has been said above it appears that the school board is purchasing a service requiring less creativity from the insider than from the outsider. Linking the differences in services expected with the insider's commitments, we should find that insiders accept the job on the terms of the school board while outsiders tend to take the appointment on their own terms. The outsider is in a position to bargain and win; the insider is not interested in bargaining and would probably lose if he did. Table I indicates the extent to which outsiders are able to command higher salaries than insiders. The beginning outsider receives from $1,000 to $5,000 more a year than the beginning insider. A similar but less marked difference holds true regardless of time in service.[5]

Further, in a sample of 745 superintendents, 38 marked as appropriate the response that a willingness to accept the salary was a reason for being selected for the superintendency they now held. Nine

TABLE 1
Mean Salaries of First or Second Year: Inside and Outside Successors
by School District Population*

Population of District	Mean Salary of Insiders (number)	Mean Salary of Outsiders (number)	Difference in Favor of Outsiders
500,000 and over	$19,750 (2)	$22,250 (1)	$2,500
100,000 to 499,999	14,200 (7)	19,200 (8)	5,000
30,000 to 99,999	12,400 (14)	15,000 (15)	2,600
10,000 to 29,999	10,300 (9)	11,500 (42)	1,200
5,000 to 9,999	9,450 (5)	10,450 (21)	1,000
2,500 to 4,999	6,900 (3)	8,100 (15)	1,200

*These data were obtained by a secondary analysis of raw data gathered by the American Association of School Administrators (A.A.S.A.) and the National Education Association (N.E.A.). Their report on the data can be found in *Profile of the School Superintendent* (Washington D.C.: American Association of School Administrators, 1960). I wish to express thanks to the N.E.A. and the A.A.S.A. for permission to use their raw data.

per cent of the insiders and 3 per cent of the outsiders made this acknowledgment.[6]

Administrative Responses of Successor

The definition of the situation under which insiders are appointed suggests that they will be inclined to keep things pretty much as they are,
for after all the employers are happy. The limited evidence available
demonstrates that the insider conforms to the expectation that he will
not make great changes.

The tendency for new chief executives to become preoccupied
with rules and rule making[7] has been noted in at least two other settings.[8]
New school superintendents show the same tendency. Rules formalize
internal or external commitments of an organization. They are instrumental in establishing the course of an organization and in determining
its character. Insiders acted in ways that did not alter the course or
establish new commitments. Their rule activities preserved and tight-
ened what existed. In the case of the outsiders observed, about 85 per
cent of the effort expended in rule making was in the area of new rules
—rules that filled in gaps or rules that took the place of existing ones.
Insiders, on the other hand, did not devote any significant amount of
time to new rules. Their concern for rules was in publicizing and reinforcing old rules and assessing the extent to which old rules were being
followed.

Barnard has cited the "propensity of all organizations to expand,"[9] and it has been noted that as organizations expand the administrative component tends to constitute a larger and larger per cent of
those employed in the organization.[10] There is every reason to expect
that the addition of individuals to an administrative staff will be related
to potentially identifiable organization variables, and no reason to
expect that such conditions will take place at random. Leadership
change or stability appears to be such a variable. The new chief executive is faced with the problem of loyalty and of building goals into the
social structure of the organization. It is somewhat commonplace to see
old organizations abandoned or bypassed and new ones created to
handle marked changes in orientation and goal. An old agency or organization embodies precedents for action, alliances, and personal loyalties
and can muster resistance capable of drastically restricting the full development of a new program. But often, even though new goals are
sought or weak ones emphasized, the organization cannot be cast aside;
it must be maintained. If this is the case, as it is with public schools, the
alternative is to cast aside people, bring in new ones, or both.

The conditions of employment suggest that the outsider has reason to "retool" the school system and that the insider does not. Success for the outsider tends to be defined in terms of change. For change to be realized loyalty and commitment to an idea or person must, to some extent, be diffused throughout the organization. The insider does not need to alter loyalties and commitments. For him success lies in keeping the organization committed as it is.

Such reasoning underlies two hypotheses about successors and expansion of the administrative staff. The first hypothesis is that during the early stages of the succession cycle the number of outside successors who add to their central office administrative staff will be greater than the number of inside successors who add to their central office administrative staff.[11] To test the hypothesis the succession and staffing histories of the one hundred largest school districts in California were gathered for the period from 1952 to 1956. The size of the administrative staff of the central office inherited by a new superintendent was compared with the size of the staff two years later. The administrative staff of the central office was taken as the index, for its size is less responsive to increases in numbers of pupils, and therefore more responsive to the wishes of the superintendent than is the size of the total administrative staff. If the pupil enrollment of a district is growing, as was the case with all of these districts, it must provide additional administrative personnel in its new schools. If a district adds a new school, it is not compelled to add certified administrative staff at the central office level, but when an addition is made to the *central* office administrative staff, such an addition is not as directly related to external forces as it is to the discretion of the administrative offices of the school district.

The one hundred districts had a total of thirty-five new superintendents during the four-year period. Twelve of the new superintendents were insiders and twenty-three were outsiders. Three of the twelve insiders and fourteen of the twenty-three outsiders increased the size of their central office administrative staff during their first two years in office. The statistical significance of the difference is beyond the .05 level of confidence[12] and therefore supports the hypothesis that during the early stages of the succession cycle the number of outside successors who add to their central office staff will be greater than the number of inside successors who add to their central office staff.

This hypothesis is based on the assumption that expansion of the administrative hierarchy involves discretion and that it is not directly related to the growth in enrollment. This assumption can be tested by comparing the number of additions made to the central office staffs over a specified time in school systems of "identical" size and growing at the same rate. The assumption can be considered valid if it can be demonstrated that such school districts do not exhibit an "identical" pattern in the additions to the central office administrative staff.

The second hypothesis relating successors and expansion of the administrative staff is concerned with the impact of the successor on the rate at which positions are added to the administrative staff. It tests the assumption just made and states that during the early stages of the succession cycle, outside successors will add more positions to the central office administrative staff than will "old" superintendents in comparable districts during same time span, and vice versa for insiders. Each of the thirty-five districts with new superintendents was paired with another district in which: *(a)* the type of district was the same (i.e., elementary, high school, unified) and the size and pupil growth figures corresponded year by year for the relevant time span with a difference of less than 10 per cent of the enrollment of the district with a new superintendent, *(b)* the superintendent had been in office at least four years and was therefore "old." Four districts were lost from the sample because these conditions could not be met. If more than one district met the conditions from the total population of the one hundred largest districts, the "twin" was drawn at random from among those in the qualifying group Eleven districts with inside successors and twenty districts with outside successors could be matched with a "twin."

The eleven districts with new insiders added a total of five positions at the central office level, an average of 0.45 positions per district within two years after the succession, and their "twin" districts of the same size and growth rate with "old" superintendents added fourteen such positions, an average of 1.27 positions per district over the same time span. The twenty districts with new outsiders added thirty-nine positions, an average of 1.9 positions per district within two years of the succession, and their "twin" districts with "old" superintendents added twenty-five positions, an average of 1.25 positions per district over the same time.[13]

The findings support the assumption that newness of the superintendent is a factor bearing on the discretionary act of adding to the central office administrative staff, and further substantiate the notion that outsiders increase the administrative staff more than insiders.

But the findings raise a question. What happens to the rates after the first two years in office? If the rate of additions to the staff remained the same over an extended period, it is obvious that the central office staffs of districts with insiders would become significantly smaller than central office staffs of districts with outsiders.

Ultimately there are two possibilities. One is that over the long run insiders and outsiders create about the same number of new positions, but the positions are created at different times in the succession cycle. It could be argued that, given the needs of the outsider, he creates most of the new positions early in his stay in office, whereas the insider creates them throughout his term of office.

The second possibility is that outsiders create more administrative positions in the central office than insiders. Perhaps given the conditions of employment and commitments of the two types of successors and the head start of the outsider, as shown by the data, the insider would never catch up with the outsider in the number of new administrative staff positions he creates during his term in office. The expansion rates of each may converge toward a mean, but this would still mean that there would be a difference between the number of positions added over time in "identical" districts. This suggestion further implies that, in continually growing school districts, a district might reduce the difference between the size of its central office staff and the mean size for comparable districts as it replaces an insider with an outsider, and the other way around. These explanations are speculative since data are lacking.

Prominence among Colleagues

Insiders and outsiders are called on to render different types of services to school systems. The data on rule making and staff changes indicate that the two types tend to conform to the expectations formed at the time of employment. Insiders and outsiders also differ in their prominence among colleagues.

The phrase "a comedian's comedian" is a rating one step above superior or excellent. It means that the individual has mastered the important subleties that are most readily recognized by his colleagues. An insider is not a superintendent's superintendent.

Twenty superintendents, recommended by two knowledgeable judges as being perceptive about the experiences and careers of superintendents, were each asked to name five prominent superintendents within their state. Several factors should be considered before looking at the responses. About one-third of the superintendents in the United States are insiders. They are found in districts of all sizes but hold about one-half of the superintendencies in cities of 100,000 or larger.[14] Their disproportionate representation in large systems might cause a skewing effect in the ratings. On the other hand, insiders usually complete their careers in one school district. This might, to some extent, limit their acquaintance with other superintendents.

The responses of the twenty superintendents were heavily in

favor of outsiders. Eighty-three of the one hundred votes were for twenty-nine outsiders, seventeen votes were for three insiders. (One insider received fourteen votes.)

Change and Succession Patterns

The career of many superintendents is marked by movement from district to district, and school superintendents, like city managers,[15] assert that they can hurt the profession and fail to provide proper service by moving too soon or staying too long. One highly regarded elder statesman among superintendents has remarked that he is most proud of the fact that he never left a superintendency voluntarily; he always managed to stir up enough controversy over innovations that he was asked to leave. Another superintendent has written: "If a man stays in one administrative post for very many years, he must be tremendously efficient and capable, or else resort to the practice of maintaining his job at the expense of any creditable educational performance in his district."[16]

The commitment of the insider to the community and the school district is made obvious by the fact that he stays and waits for the superintendency. It is to be expected, then, that he places lower value on mobility than the outsider and further that he is more likely to remain in the superintendency longer than the outsider.

A secondary analysis of data gathered by Seeman shows that insiders' and outsiders' attitudes toward mobility differ significantly.[17] On a scale "whose purpose was to distinguish those for whom mobility interest takes precedence over a wide range of more 'intrinsic' interests (for example, health, family, community)"[18] eleven insiders scored a mean of 69.8 and thirty outsiders a mean of 78.5.[19] The higher the score the greater the interest in mobility. Sample items state: "I wouldn't let my friendship ties in a community stand in the way of moving on to a higher position." "The executive who has his eye on the jobs up the line, just can't go all out for the group he is serving at the moment." "My goal has always been to wind up as head of a small organization that I could guide over the long pull." "If you've got a worthwhile program developing in your present position, I don't think you ought to be really tempted if a bigger job comes your way." "If you stay quite a while in one executive position, you become too concerned with keeping things as they are."[20]

Table 2 shows length of incumbency and origin of 792 superintendents. About 14 per cent of the insiders have held the job twenty or more years and about 6 per cent of the outsiders have been in one job this long. The mean time in office for insiders is ten years and for out-

TABLE 2
Origin of Superintendent and Length of Incumbency*

	Origin of Superintendent	
Years in Office	% Insiders N = 279	% Outsiders N = 513
1-2	14.3	19.8
3-4	16.5	17.7
5-9	25.1	28.2
10-14	23.6	21.4
15-19	6.8	6.8
20-24	7.2	1.8
over 25	6.5	4.0

*Secondary analysis of raw data gathered for A.A.S.A. and N.E.A. *Profile of School Superintendent.*

siders eight years. Medians are eight years for insiders and six years for outsiders.

Greater commitment to community and school district, the attitude against mobility, and the longer stay in office suggest that the insider, more than the outsider, tends to practice job perpetuation.[21]

The various comparisons between insiders and outsiders suggest the hypothesis that an organization would not be able to adapt itself and operate successfully under the impact of two successive insiders. A reputation would develop that the system was not developing an adequate program and able personnel could not be attracted. The community would complain about outmoded procedures and practices. Institutional integrity would be damaged, for the commitments of the insider suggest that he is more willing to make compromises than the outsider. In time, this could reflect on the professional standing of all administrators in the system and on the school board.

There are four possible succession patterns in school systems: insider to insider, insider to outsider, outsider to outsider, and outsider to insider. On the basis of the facts discussed above, it was expected that the pattern of insider to insider would occur rarely. In 103 successions taking place over some thirty-two years in forty-eight city school systems in California the least frequent pattern was from insider to insider: this pattern occurred only seven times. A study of succession patterns in school districts of Pennsylvania replicated the finding.[22] Table 3 gives the findings of both samples.

Since insiders show (1) high commitment to community and school district, (2) low commitment to specialized skills of the profession, (3) appointment for a stabilizing performance, (4) administrative activity tending toward maintenance of the organization, (5) lack of

TABLE 3
Succession Patterns

Type Change	California*	Pennsylvania†
Outsider to outsider	58	43
Insider to insider	7	9
Outsider to insider	22	31
Insider to outsider	16	23
Total	103	106

*Data gathered for all (48) city school districts in California from the annual directory of California Association of Secondary Administrators, *California Schools,* for the period 1926 to 1958.
†Data gathered for all (24) first- and second-class school districts and 17 third-class districts in Pennsylvania drawn at random from personnel files in the State Department of Public Instruction for the period 1922 to 1959.

proportionate place among prominent members of the profession, and (6) long tenure in office suggesting the tendency to practice job perpetuation, it would seem that a school system cannot afford to have an insider follow an insider into the superintendency. Succession patterns support this assumption.

Successor's Program and Counteracting Forces

The preceding discussion has shed some light on the differences between place-bound and career-bound school superintendents. Any full understanding of how these two types relate to their organizations must include a study of the responses of organizations to the successors. Though highly influential, the chief executive is not the master of the organization's course. A good deal is known about counteracting forces within organizations undergoing change; change that is frequently initiated by outside successors.[23] When the new leadership is committed to system maintenance as with insiders, the tracing out of counteracting forces has been ignored, although there is no reason to expect that counteracting forces will be absent.

For example inside successors may be unwilling to press for advances in salary and welfare benefits for teachers. The lower salary of an insider is not as far "out of line" with respect to teachers' salaries as is the salary of the outsider. The insider, therefore, feels less pressure to bring teachers' salaries "into line." Also, some judge school systems by how much they pay teachers. To raise teachers' salaries may be a side payment bargained for and won by outsiders, but not by insiders. Furthermore, insiders may know the teachers too well to be concerned over their salaries. In contrast, the outsider knows only the salary figures for the district, and if salaries are low he will raise them without thought of teachers as individuals.

This may have been the basis of teacher resentment in one system observed. In one of the systems involving an insider, the teachers' organization took on a more aggressive attitude than had been customary on salaries and welfare benefits. The teachers' organization assumed that to gain welfare benefits and salary increases it must work around the superintendent (which was contrary to past procedures), and deal directly with the school board. Members of the teachers' organization felt the superintendent would not "fairly" represent their case. He was disturbed. The development established a precedent and a new definition of the relationship between teachers, superintendent, and school board with possible far-reaching consequences. The consequences of the precedent, however, could not be adequately assessed during the time given to this research.

Summary and Further Implications

The basic proposition explored here is that the origin of the successor is a major variable in the study of administrative succession—that insiders, those promoted from within, and outsiders, those brought in from outside, relate to their organizations in dissimilar ways during the cycle of succession. One of the distinctive differences in the two types of school superintendents is the value put on career and place of work. Insiders are place-bound; they put place of employment above career. Outsiders are career-bound; they put career above place of employment. Insiders are called on for a stabilizing performance when employers wish to maintain the system. They are paid less and gain less prominence than the outsiders, who are called on for a creative performance when the employers desire changes in the system. Similarly, insiders act in a way that does maintain the system: they do not develop new rules and policies that alter the course of the organization; they do not prepare the organization for new ways of functioning by expanding the administrative staff. Outsiders, on the other hand, look more favorably upon mobility and occupy a superintendency for a shorter period of time. Such differences suggest that a school system, under normal circumstances, would not employ two successive insiders in the superintendency. Succession patterns over thirty years in eighty-nine school systems support the proposition.

These differences permit a tentative characterization of the two types. Their performances label the insider as an adaptive man and the outsider as an innovator. Both are conformists in the sense that their performance conforms to the expectations of their employers. The insider, however, adapts or modifies his performance to fit the office. He aims at preserving the office as it has been, which negates the possibility of bringing added status to the role. The place-bound superintendent seems to derive status from the office; he does not bring status to it. The insider is like an understudy, or a stand-in. He performs within the framework established by the predecessor rather than by creating a new framework. The performance of the outsider, on the other hand, does add something to the role. The office is modified rather than the person. His performance changes the office and the relations of others to the office; such a performance holds possibilities of increasing the status of the office.

The variable or origin used here is gross and unrefined. However, such a gross distinction is probably useful in many organizational settings. It is not necessary to leave a firm, government agency, army, or labor union to become an outsider. An outsider is simply a "stranger" in Georg Simmel's use of the term: a man unacquainted with the social realities of the particular setting. Thus the new manager from the home office is an outsider with reference to his new field office position, just as is the army officer taking command of a new post. Gouldner's "Mr. Peele" is a case in point. Peele was not an outsider with respect to the General Gypsum Company, but he was an outsider with reference to the Oscar Center Plant.[24]

School systems belong to a class of organizations that can be called "domesticated"; that is, they are not compelled to attend to all of their needs. A steady flow of clients is assured, and although they do compete for resources, support is not closely tied to quality of performance. The business firm in a competitive industry, on the other hand, can be seen as existing in a "wild" setting. It is not protected at vulnerable points as is the school system. There is probably less demand for adaptation to the environment in the protected setting and, therefore, more place-bound chief executives would be found in "domesticated" than in "wild" organizations. It should follow that the succession pattern of place-bound to place-bound executive would occur less frequently in "wild" than in "domesticated" organizations. These are purely speculative ideas, however, for adequate data are not available.

Notes

1. The meager systematic literature on succession and its consequences is largely descriptive in nature and tends to overemphasize the disruptive aspects. Propositions are seldom developed or tested. There are, however, notable exceptions. Trow has tested some propositions about succession rates in small groups, and Scheff has attempted to account for individual differences in the resistance to change

that frequently follows succession. Cf. Donald R. Trow, Membership Succession and Team Performance, *Human Relations,* 13 (1960), 259–268; and Thomas J. Scheff, "Perceptual Orientation of Staff Members toward Patients in a Mental Hospital Ward," paper read at the meeting of the American Sociological Association, August 1960.

2. The larger study, "Administrative Succession and Organizational Development" (forthcoming), was supported by a post-doctoral fellowship from the Administrative Science Center, University of Pittsburgh. I am indebted to my colleagues at the Administrative Science Center for their counsel.

3. Several researchers have gathered data on the personalities of individuals having commitments similar to those of place-bound and career-bound individuals. Marvick has written about "institutionalists" and "specialists" in a federal agency. Some differences between "locals" and "cosmopolitans" on a college faculty have been pointed to by Gouldner. And Avery has gathered data on potential "passive" and "active" managers. There seems to be a likeness among institutionalists, locals, passive managers, and insiders as well as among specialists, cosmopolitans, active managers, and outsiders. Cf. Dwaine Marvick, *Career Perspectives in a Bureaucratic Setting* (Michigan Government Studies No. 27; Ann Arbor: University of Michigan Press, 1954); Alvin W. Gouldner, Cosmopolitans and Locals: Toward an Analysis of Latent Social Roles—I and II, *Administrative Science Quarterly,* 2 (1957), 281–306, 2 (1958), 444–480; and Robert W. Avery. "Orientation toward Careers in Business: A Study in Occupational Sociology" (unpublished doctoral dissertation, Harvard University, 1959).

4. It might appear natural for school boards always to appoint an insider when things are going well. After all, the insider knows the school system's background and its history and undoubtedly is well versed in the present programs, problems, sources of support, philosophy, and personnel in the generalization and its environment. Sometimes no insider has the necessary experience or credential to be given the superintendency. Or there may be too many qualified insiders, so that selecting one from among them might invite unnecessary grievances or might deepen already existing factions. In both these cases an outsider is sought.

5. The differences in pay, conditions of employment, and other areas are not necessarily related to the quality of insiders and outsiders. The differences seem to be a function of the definition of the sitiuation. There is no reason to expect that outsiders are more capable administrators than insiders. This explanation is given support by recent research in another setting which suggests that while the University of Texas discriminates against those on the faculty with Ph.D. degrees from the University of Texas as opposed to Ph.D. degrees from other institutions in academic rank, class load, and so on, there is no difference between these two groups in scholarly production. Noting the restriction due to the sample, the author concludes "There is no reason to believe that the differential treatment of the inbred product is the result of inferior quality on his part." See Reece McGee, The Function of Institutional Inbreeding, *American Journal of Sociology,* 65 (1960), 483–488.

6. Secondary analysis of data in A.A.S.A. *Profile of the School Superintendent.*

7. The term "rule" is being used here in a broad way to include such items as definition of work day, procedures for handling paper work and people, and policy statements.

8. Oscar Grusky, Role Conflict in Organization: A Study of Prison Camp Officials, *Administrative Science Quarterly,* 3 (1959), 452–472; and A. W. Gouldner *Patterns of Industrial Bureaucracy* (Glencoe, 1954).

9. Chester I. Barnard, *The Functions of the Executive* (Cambridge, Mass., 1938), p. 159.

10. F. W. Terrien and D. L. Mills, The Effect of Changing Size upon the Internal Structure of Organization, *American Sociological Review*, 20 (1955), 11–13.

11. A somewhat similar but untested proposition to the effect that an outsider as a top executive will utilize an "assistant-to" more frequently than an insider has been advanced by Thomas L. Whisler, The "Assistant-to" in Four Administrative Settings, *Administrative Science Quarterly*, 5 (1960), 181–216.

12. This difference yielded a probability of .024 on a one-tailed test using the Fisher Exact Probability Test.

13. Both differences are statistically significant beyond the .01 level of confidence. The Wilcoxon Matched-Pairs Signed-Ranks Test was used to determine significance.

14. Secondary analysis of A.A.S.A. data, in *Profile of the School Superintendent.*

15. See George K. Floro, Continuity in City Manager Careers, *American Journal of Sociology*, 61 (1955), 204–246.

16. T. H. Bell, *The Prodigal Pedagogue* (New York, 1955), p. 149.

17. Melvin Seeman, Social Mobility and Administrative Behavior, *American Sociological Review*, 23 (1958), 633–642. I wish to express thanks to Professor Seeman for granting me access to the data gathered for his study.

18. *Ibid.*, p. 642.

19. The differences in scores on the scale of attitude toward mobility produced a z-score of 2.44 on the Mann-Whitney Test which is significant beyond the .01 level of confidence on a one-tailed test.

20. Melvin Seeman, *op. cit.*, p. 635.

21. A similar relation between performance and tenure in office has been observed about mental hospital superintendents. Belknap has written: "The superintendents have been confronted, as medical men, with a dilemma. If they conformed to the structure of the hospital as they found it, they could carry out a reasonably good, routine custodial administration. If, however, they attempted to establish modern psychiatric treatment of patients, the procedures necessary called for changes in the traditional routines. . . . But the professional training of any physician has been for at least the past hundred years in the direction of seeking and finding improvement in the condition of his patients. . . . The superintendents . . . found themselves confronted with a choice between being good doctors and poor administrators, or good administrators and poor doctors. . . . The superintendents with the longest tenure were those who apparently accepted the second horn of the dilemma and became efficient administrators" (Ivan Belknap, *Human Problems of a State Mental Hospital* [New York: McGraw-Hill Book Company, Inc., 1956; by permission], pp. 79–80).

22. Because there are a number of cases of insider to insider succession, even though fewer than chance would indicate, and because of the high possibility of detrimental consequences of such a succession pattern, it would seem fruitful to explore the conditions under which such a succession pattern occurs. Three conditions suggest themselves: (1) A lack of separation of municipal politics and school board functions may alter the setting of appointments. (2) The term in office of the first insider may not run its full course, because of death or other natural reason. (3) The insider may be a deviant member of his class. In additiion, it would be fruitful to come to a better understanding of the consequences of following the succession pattern of insider to insider.

23. See S. M. Lipset, *Agrarian Socialism* (Berkeley, 1950); Gouldner, *Patterns of Industrial Bureaucracy.*

24. Gouldner, *ibid.*

Executiveship in Juvenile Correctional Institutions[1]

David Street, Robert D. Vinter, and Charles Perrow

Executive leadership has a key influence on organizational achievement and adaptation. Above the chief administrator fans out the complex world of the parent organization, courts, official and unofficial regulatory or standard-setting groups, and publics. Below him is spread out the organization itself: chief subordinates who constitute the executive core, other personnel, and the inmates. The environment and the internal realities of the organization both exert pressures upon the executive; his behavior has crucial effects on staff performance and inmate response. Analysis of these modes of behavior is essential, therefore, to understanding operative patterns.

At least three crucial dimensions of executive leadership shape the organization. First, the executive formulates specific goals and basic policies that give meaning and direction to the enterprise. He must formulate operational aims and policies within the range of environmental mandates and constraints. Second, the executive is the key link between the organization and its environment. The most general and pervasive influences upon organizational behavior stem from external sources, and the executive has the task of mediating between these forces and organizational exigencies. He receives both mandates and resources from the environment, and external units hold him accountable for organizational performance. Third, the executive establishes the structure of roles and responsibilities within the organization that enables it to pursue its goals. He must define tasks, allocate personnel, and manage the interdependent relations that result. As part of this endeavor, the executive must delineate the competencies appropriate to staff roles and recruit persons to fill these positions.

Analysis of these three broad areas will provide a context for

Excerpted from *Organizations for Treatment* (New York: Free Press, 1966), pp. 45–49; 63–66; 93–94; 103–6.

understanding the behavior of employees and inmates. We shall explore the executives' efforts in these areas in terms of *strategies,* emphasizing thereby the dilemmas, contradictory directives, and imperatives for action that are forced by the chief administrators. Attention to the nature and consequences of executive strategies must also take into account the sources or antecedents of administrative activity, including the mandates given executives, previous experience or training, career commitments brought to these situations, and so on.

Although anecdotal accounts and isolated studies have provided insights into limited aspects of executive performance, there is little systematic knowledge about executiveship or conceptualization of its major phases. There is perhaps least understanding of how executives can harmonize internal and external requirements or balance seemingly incompatible demands, for prior studies have tended to focus on limited aspects of executive behavior rather than upon how the executive confronts the full range of problems that face him.

Executive Autonomy

In performing his role the executive is neither wholly free nor completely a prisoner. Requirements, constraints, and opportunities are presented by both the environment and the internal situation. The environment sets severe bounds on the goals the executive may formulate and the means he may use, and it restricts his resources. At the same time, he is able to select from a set of alternative cultural definitions, a range of goals and means, and a variety of possibilities for resources. Within the institution he again encounters both freedom and constraint. Traditions and the perspectives of the staff set limits, as do the types of inmate the organization receives, the size and location of the institution, and so forth. Yet the executive may retrain, discharge, or promote staff members; violate traditions or create new ones; alter intake criteria to modify the types of delinquent received; and exploit the advantages of the physical setting.

Long-established patterns of conduct may be highly resistant to change, and drastic modifications may bring anarchy or organized opposition. Furthermore, some roles are set by the experiences or training that personnel receive elsewhere: A cottage parent cannot be transformed into a psychiatrist or a psychiatrist into a classroom teacher. Others are required by law, as in legislation prescribing the provision of an academic school for the inmates. On the other hand, psychiatrists may be placed in direct charge of cottage parents or cottage parents trained to support the efforts of clinical personnel; the academic school may be integrated in a treatment program; and the support of staff may be developed for a program of planned change.

The selection of an executive presupposes that, on the basis of his background and his presentation of himself as a candidate, he will exercise his "freedom" in certain directions; he can be removed from office if he seems to exceed this expectation too far. Yet executives derive much of their autonomy from the uncertainties and contradictory pressures that play on the correctional institution and that make the expectations broad. This general condition, together with the multiplicity and segmentation of external groups that pose demands for institutional performance, offers further opportunities for executive initiative and discretion. Conflicting demands can be balanced, new coalitions of support can be nurtured, and ingenuity can be exercised in giving specific meaning and substance to ambiguous directives. Thus conditions that one executive perceives as constraining or fraught with risk may be seen by another as inviting manipulation and assertive action.

Emphasizing the freedom of action potentially available to the executive, however, does not imply that his action is highly potent or necessarily will achieve its intended purposes. A variety of forces attenuates the effects of administrative action, and a complex interplay of behaviors and difficulties surrounds and absorbs executive activity, generating unanticipated consequences. The concept of executive leadership, nevertheless, directs attention to the rational elements in organizational performance, to the relation between ends and means, and to the assessment of action strategies.[2]

Goal Definition

Definition and specification of the mission or essential productive task of the institution are primary tasks of the executive, necessary to give purpose and direction to staff activity and to earn support from external units. The executive must specify goals within the limits of the basic mandates and tasks shared by all juvenile institutions: to retain and contain committed youngsters, to provide care and sustenance, to educate those of a certain age, and to change the inmates in some respect. More important than variations in additional ends that may be asserted are the concrete definitions and relative weights accorded to these major purposes, given the lack of clarity and consensus on goals in the environment and among factions of personnel and the generality of official mandates coming from the parent organization. The primary elements of the goal definition refer to the kinds of change sought in the inmates and to the ways they should behave once such changes have been achieved.

The goal definitions actually selected have their sources in themes and models available from the general culture. When the executive chooses from among models—for example, by selecting from military, penal, religious, family, boarding-school, or residential-treatment models—he has committed himself to distinctive notions about the causes, nature, and cures of deviant behavior. He is committed as well to associated beliefs about the character of the delinquent and the nature of the delinquent population, to images of particular behavior or personality changes that are desirable and feasible, and to models of staff activity likely to induce these changes. Thus the executive's selection of one or another or combinations of these general models begins to specify major productive tasks and suggests a rationale that supports and extends the chosen alteratives. Of course, any general model requires specification, extension, and reformulation to fit the particular requirements and constraints and the press of events within and without the organization. These changes may give rise to a distinctly new institutional design.

We should expect the executive's choice to be partially conditioned by his background and personal commitments. Those chosen from professional ranks are likely to emphasize purposes and credos in keeping with their training and collegial reference groups. Others are likely to derive their orientations from more traditional sources or from experiences in other people-changing organizations like schools or adult prisons. Past traditions of the institution and the terms of succession should also have significant bearing on the executive's definition of goals. The promotion to an administrative position of a staff member who represents one faction within the organization or the appointment of a professional from another institution signifies expectations that press upon the new executive.[3]

Purposes must be communicated to various audiences inside and outside the organization. Within limits the executive may, to project the institution and its tasks to external publics, use terms different from those he employs to guide internal operations. Continuous surveillance from outside makes risky any attempt to treat the audiences as totally segregated, however. Therefore, one of the executive's continuing tasks is to formulate goals effective inside while legitimate outside.

The executives' formulations of goals provide the basis for classifying these institutions into the three basic goal types, obedience/conformity, re-education/development, and treatment. The types form a custody-treatment continuum based on the degree of complexity of beliefs about people-changing embodied in organizational goals. In the obedience/conformity institutions it was assumed that the orientations of the inmates could not be altered basically but that the inmates could be conditioned to behave properly (or would learn to conform out of fear of the consequences). In the re-education/development institutions there was greater concern for training the inmate—for developing his capabilities so he could pursue a gainful career after release. Executives in these places assumed that most inmates possessed resources that could be drawn upon and developed, thereby better equipping them for law-abiding lives, and that they were not irredeemably committed to delinquent careers. In the treatment institutions the executives assumed that deviance could be corrected only by a thoroughgoing reorientation or reconstitution of the inmate; otherwise, his unconscious identifications and other intrapersonal forces would probably lead him toward continued delinquent behavior. The treatment executives believed the inmates to have significant potentialities, however.

Toward the treatment pole of the continuum the executives sought more extensive change and had greater optimism about the organization's capacity to effect significant change. Those in the obedience/conformity institutions demanded overt compliance and submission but were relatively indifferent to other phases of behavior or argued that these would follow from changes in manifest conduct. The treatment executives sought broad changes: altered personalities, enhanced cognitive and technical skills, and improved interpersonal relations. Executives in the re-education/development institutions sought change between these extremes, moderate both in the range of attributes to be altered and in the degree of change sought.

The patterns of staff performance designed by the executives were generally commensurate with their views of the delinquent personality and its malleability. Pessimistic and simplistic views shared by the obedience/conformity executives supported relatively standardized and even coercive methods, whereas the treatment executives' greater optimism and complex views supported more differentiated and voluntaristic methods. A core difference among the executives was in their views of whether staff members were supposed to *act upon* or to *engage* inmates in the processes of change. Within the obedience/conformity institutions inmates were to be forcibly molded, controlled, and otherwise dealt with as resistant objects. Inmates of the treatment institutions, in contrast, were to be worked with and to be won over and induced to adopt new behaviors and attitudes. They were presumably responsive and ready to be engaged in the change process. In the re-education/

development institutions, the Regis executive appeared more inclined toward the former position, and the Bennett executive toward the latter.

All the executives encountered problems in specifying and assuring particular staff-inmate relations at the concrete level. None of the executives was satisfied with what he believed to be the actual patterns. For example, Jackson at Dick was worried that his personnel did not balance their strictness with enough interested concern; Mitchell at Regis doubted that his staff members were able to respond with sufficient understanding; and Taylor at Milton believed that his subordinates tended to become overinvolved with the boys. There appeaaed to be deficiencies and inconsistencies in administrators' specifications for staff-inmate relations: The "message" seemed to be difficult to comprehend or did not appear to provide adequate guidelines. Further, at all institutions executives expected personnel to behave in ways that required unusual competencies and orientations, considering the quality of personnel available. Thus at Dick personnel were expected to employ frequent coercion in ways that generated confidence, whereas at Milton non-professional personnel were to assume a high degree of detached particularism. It is important to observe that these difficulties increased across the continuum: Executive prescriptions for staff activity became more esoteric, and specifications for behavior become more ambiguous and conditional nearer the treatment pole. Treatment institution executives, therefore, faced the greatest problems in developing arrangements to assure desired staff activity.

As we expected, there was an association between goal types and executive backgrounds. All but the treatment executives had backgrounds at least partly in education. Only Mitchell at Regis, however, as a member of a teaching order, had spent all his previous career in education. The others had also been in either business and politics (Jackson of Dick), military and adult corrections work (Hanna of Mixter), or orphanage administration (Ramsey of Bennett).

Careers of the treatment executives were sharply different. None had been an educator. Both the major subordinates had clinical degrees —Taylor of Milton being a psychiatrist and Burns of Inland a clinical psychologist. Furthermore, the chief executives of both institutions had rather unconventional careers—not in total institutions or clinical professions but in journalism and public relations (Perkins of Milton) or religious, youth, and community-relations work (Wright of Inland). Experience in schools or conventional total institutions appears not to have been compatible with leadership in treatment innovations, but experience likely to build facility in relating to the environment appeared to do so.

Organization of Staff Activity

A major area of executive leadership is that of defining and managing staff activity. This area of executive effort consists of prescribing work units and patterns to implement the productive goals set for the institution. The requirements of care and sustenance, academic schooling, and rehabilitation are sufficiently complex that multiple operational units must be established. The key issues then become how these major activities are to be assigned to work units and coordinated. The overall design of staff effort directed toward implementation of goals is referred to as the organization's *technology.*

In certain respects the executive is constrained by the general division of labor and definitions of competence prevailing in society. For example, state laws compel either the establishment of academic schools and employment of qualified teachers or the use of outside schools. Even in this area, however, the primary objectives of the educational program, as well as the terms of its integration with other phases of institutional regimen, remain for decision. The existing architecture and institutional plant and the requirements for congregate living also impose certain administrative patterns while leaving undecided the question of how much the inmates should be involved in providing for their own and the institution's maintenance. Similarly, established professional disciplines claim expertise with respect to treatment tasks and press for the employment of qualified representatives, but the executive has considerable discretion over the number to be recruited, the particular duties they will be assigned, and so on.

Of no less importance than the allocation of responsibilities and personnel are prescriptions for relations among units and for degrees of power and autonomy officially given to each. The division of labor may be based on occupational roles recognized in the general culture (e.g., teachers, clinicians), or phases of the program (e.g., cottage, work, educational units), or on some combination of these. It seems inevitable that certain task units will be accorded greater power than others, commensurate with their perceived importance. The crucial operations are those designed to control and change the inmates, but any of several staff groups may be viewed as making the primary contribution to these aims.

Official plans for assuring collaboration among operating units are closely related to the executive's administrative style and definition of his own role. At one extreme he may attempt to supervise all major phases of the institutional program directly, becoming himself the chief instrument for coordination. At the other extreme he may delegate considerable authority to certain subordinates, encourage a decentralized pattern of operation ,and establish other mechanisms for inter-unit co-ordination (e.g., staff committees or teams). Some combination of these approaches is to be expected in most instances, with the executive re-serving certain tasks for closer control or investment of his own time while delegating other functions.

The scope and complexity of all but the smallest institutions pro-vide a stimulus to both delegation of authority and specialization in the executive role. External demands and pressures can readily be distin-guished from the flow of internal events, and the managerial implica-tions of each appear to be of a different order. We would expect execu-tive tasks to be frequently demarcated between external and internal processes. Further, we would think external relations so important that they would be less likely to be assigned to subordinates.

The central issue in the executive's internal strategies was the allocation of power or authority within the organization. Executives gave structural support, especially power, to the subordinates, subunits, and operational patterns they believed to be most oriented to their major goals or most crucial in implementing them. To substantiate this con-clusion we may examine the patterned differences among the three types of institutions—particularly in the investment of power in certain units, the composition of the executive core, and the executives' overall administrative style.

Personnel assigned to the cottages or living units were allocated most authority and autonomy in the obedience/conformity institutions, whereas clinicians were similarly favored in the treatment institutions. In each instance these groups could exercise greater control over de-cisions about inmates, their views were deferred to most frequently by executives, and their activities were accorded primacy relative to those of other staff units (Milton put the clinicians in direct charge of other personnel). The situation was less clear in the re-education/develop-ment institutions because the academic programs were conducted by outside schools, but a more balanced distribution of authority seemed to be intended. Teachers' assessments of inmates were accepted as signifi-cant indices of progress, and the activities of living-unit personnel were regarded as crucial to inmates' social development. Further, clinicians were assigned to perform some important functions for which they were accorded independent authority.

In all organizations the tasks, authority, autonomy, and valuation assigned to staff subunits were roughly commensurate with the execu-tive's major goals and program designs. Favored units were not neces-sarily those with the most personnel, those highest in the formal table of organization, or those best qualified under general criteria. Teachers, for example, constituted large cadres in both the obedience/conformity and treatment institutions and were relatively highly educated and well paid, but they were given relatively little authority anywhere.

Selective and unequal allocation of authority was also apparent in the executives' choice of chief assistants. At each institution the heads of major staff subunits constituted a kind of cabinet. It was accorded some recognition but actually exercised little real authority. There was, however, an executive core composed of those few subordinates with whom the chief administrator chose to work most closely and to whom he delegated most authority, regardless of formal patterns. Within this core executives at two of the institutions (Milton and Inland) formed a particularly close association or an executive "partnership" with one other person. The executive at Mixter also yielded considerable autonomy to another person, the custodially-oriented director of cottage life, relegating the assistant director to minor duties. The composition of the executive core, the use of partnerships, and the allocation of power among these persons was systematically linked to the executives' major goal commitments. To some extent they also reflected personality and idiosyncratic differences among the executives.

In general, increasing organizational size and technological complexity are likely to give rise to greater specialization and delegation of executive power. The low levels of specialization and sharing of power found in Regis and Bennett seemed to result for precisely this reason. Size and complexity also seemed to underlie the contrasting patterns at Mixter and Dick. Mixter showed greater specialization and delegation of power, apparently because it was too large to be administered without it. Dick showed less, seemingly not only because it was smaller and its executive more energetic but also because of the institution's relatively simple and routinized design. Instead of sharing in administrative power members of Dick's executive core were assigned limited authority to implement Jackson's explicit directives. Two of the members of the core, further, were trusted lieutenants who assisted in advancing his political career, a concern for which executiveship itself was largely instrumental.

Closely associated with the sharing of executive power was the administrative style by which leadership was exercised. The executives varied in their use of a directive or coordinative approach in the guidance of subordinates' activities. Those at the extremes showed the greatest contrast: Dick's executive exercised firm direction over all phases of staff performance, whereas the treatment executives tended toward the coordination of relatively autonomous subordinates. Again, the complexity of the technology appeared to have a major influence on administrative behavior, since the performance requirements at the treatment institutions were too intricate to be managed directly by the executives.[4] At such places, furthermore, the greater numbers of professional personnel probably required a coordinative administrative style because of their emphases on autonomy, rationality, and persuasion.

Perhaps most important in accounting for administrative style was the incorporation of unified interaction principles for all persons within the institution. The model of the essential staff-inmate patterns of control desired by executives was exemplified in their own behavior vis-a-vis chief subordinates and other staff members. This definition of basically similar interaction patterns increased consistency within the organization and enhanced the clarity of executive philosophies and operational designs, thereby facilitating the chief administrator's infusion of preferred orientations throughout the organization. Reliance on unified and consistent human-relations principles may be of special importance for organizations whose primary task involves changing persons through interpersonal means.[5]

Notes

1. The findings are from a comparative study of the following six types of institutions:

Dick (for Discipline)—A large public institution with no treatment program, whose staff felt no lack because of it, that concentrated on custody, hard work, and discipline.

Mixter (for Mixed Goals)—A very large public institution that to an extent emphasized both custody and treatment. It attempted some measure of treatment but presented to most boys an environment of surveillance, frequent use of negative sanctions, and other corollaries of custody. A few months after the first field study of Mixter, it established a separate small maximum security unit, *Maxwell* (for Maximum Security), in another part of the state. We were able to make some study of the early development of this unit.

Regis (for Religious and, in Latin, Rules)—A small institution run by a religious order. It emphasized full scheduling of the day's work, study, and recreational activities together with indoctrination and enforcement of the virtues of authority and religiosity. This was one of the two institutions where the inmates went off the grounds daily to attend classes with ordinary parochial or public school children.

Bennett (for Benign)—A quite small private institution that, like Regis, stressed neither modern treatment techniques nor custodialism and sent its boys off grounds to school each day. Inmates lived in a firm but rather homelike environment.

Milton (for Milieu Therapy)—A fairly large public institution. The clinical staff had much power, influenced the non-professional staff to provide the inmates with considerable freedom of behavior, and provided a round of "therapeutic experiences."

Inland (for Individual Therapy)—A small private "residential treatment center" in which the clinicians were in virtually complete control. They allowed much freedom to the inmates while stressing the use of psychotherapeutic techniques to attempt to bring about major personality change.

2. We do not assume the executive's behavior to be "rational" in any *total* sense; we accept Herbert Simon's notion of cognitive limits on rationality (*Administrative Behavior* [New York: Macmillan, 1957]) and Alvin Gouldner's assertion of the heuristic usefulness of a rational model of organization ("Organizational Analysis," in Robert Merton, Leonard Broom, and Leonard Cottrell, Jr. [eds.], *Sociology Today* [New York: Basic Books, 1959]). At the same time, starting with the concept of the organization as an institution made explicit by Selznick, we recognize the importance of non-rational, irrational, and unplanned-for elements and consequences. Much of the criticism of rationalistic theories is misdirected in that it assumes if an actor pays attention to such characteristics as system maintenance he is irrational; but the "rational" actor we see views such characteristics as constraints in undertaking calculative processes on the knowledge, albeit limited, available to him. His "true" rationality can be measured only *ex post facto* with indices of organizational effectiveness and is not assumed in our model of decision-making.

3. See Lloyd Ohlin, "Conflicting Interests in Correctional Objectives," in Richard A. Cloward, *et al.*, *Theoretical Studies in Social Organization of the Prison* (New York: Social Science Research Council, 1960), pp. 111–129; and Richard McCleery, *Policy Change in Prison Management* (Lansing: Governmental Research Bureau, Michigan State University, 1957).

4. Eugene Litwak, "Models of Bureaucracy Which Permit Conflict," *American Journal of Sociology*, 67 (September, 1961), 177–84.

5. Jules Henry, "Types of Institutional Structure," in Milton Greenblatt, Daniel J. Levinson ,and Richard H. Williams (eds.), *The Patient and the Mental Hospital* (New York: The Free Press, 1957), pp. 73–91.

Chapter IV

Organizational Goals

Similar to other formal organizations, human service organizations are deliberately structured to seek specific goals. These goals, to which the organization commits its resources and personnel, define the form and content of the service delivery system.

It is important to distinguish as Perrow (1961) does between official goals which define the general and publicly acceptable purposes of the organization, and operative goals which define what the organization actually is trying to accomplish. Operative goals limit and focus the attention of the staff to those activities which are relevant to the organization. This is done by directing the development of an administrative structure to reward actions which enhance the attainment of the goals and to discourage those which do not (Zald, 1963).

The goals the organization attempts to accomplish are multidimensional and reflect the "production," adaptation, and maintenance needs of the organization. Several types of goals can be distinguished accordingly:

a) Output goals—the goods and services the organization provides its customers and clients
b) Adaptation goals—these direct organizational activities to enhance its position in the environment and promote its growth and institutionalization
c) Maintenance or management goals—these include the activities of the organization to maintain internal stability and predictability, and optimize the functioning of its various work units
d) Derived goals—"the uses to which the organization puts the power it generates in pursuit of other goals" (Perrow, 1970, pp. 135–36)

A distinctive set of problems of human service organizations consist of the inherent ambiguities, inconsistencies, and conflicts that exist in the definition and implementation of their goals. These features of the goals in such organizations produce major dilemmas in the structuring of their activities and present a serious obstacle for their ability to pursue a norm of rationality (Thompson, 1967).

Several factors account for the problematic nature of the goals in human service organizations. First, the "raw materials" of these organizations are human beings vested with cultural values (Perrow, 1965). Organizational decisions about desired behavioral and social outcomes in clients, and the means to achieve them inherently involve moral issues and value judgments for which there is often lack of consensus among the organization's critical publics. Should the school provide a sex education program, the hospital emphasize research, or the welfare agency become an advocate on behalf of its clients? These are examples of goal decisions in which the organization encounters conflicting and ambiguous community values. Thus, in seeking to enlist the support of various interest groups in order to meet their disparate expectations, the human service organization is likely to commit itself to multiple and conflicting goals. Such commitments compete for resources and personnel, and pose problems of integration and coordination for the organization.

Second, human service organizations tend to face turbulent environments in terms of their complexity, instability of the expectations of various interest groups, and the unpredictability of the resources available to the organization. Shifts in public expectations; changes in the characteristics and demands of potential clients; the development of new intervention strategies; and changes in public and private funding patterns, present continuous uncertainties that make past organizational commitments obsolete. However, once the organization has made major investments of resources to accomplish certain goals, it becomes difficult for the organization to alter its operative goals.

Third, the potential for inconsistencies and conflicts among the various organizational goals is heightened in human service organizations since the output or service goals are particularly sensitive to changes in other organizational goals. For example, promoting organizational growth by increasing the number of clients served will have direct impact on the quality of the services even with added staff. Moreover, actions taken by the executiveship of the organization in order to survive and adapt to changing environmental contingencies may increase the discrepancies between its operative goals and the original service objectives.

Fourth, human service organizations must make choices as to the type and range of client attributes they will respond to and formulate their output goals accordingly. However, the organization cannot isolate these attributes from others characterizing the clients, and therefore, must respond to them in some manner. For example, the public school finds that it must respond to various behaviors of its students not directly related to their scholastic performance. The hospital, similarly, encounters the emotional and social problems generated by the physical illness of the patient, as well as the illness itself. Both organizations find it necessary to devote some energy to the other attributes of their clients, thus adding to the complexity in operationalizing their goals.

Finally, as we shall point out in the next chapter, many goal ambiguities found in human service organizations also stem from the indeterminant nature of the technologies employed to achieve service objectives. When the technology itself is ambiguous and fails to provide clear task definitions to the staff, the output goals of the organization are likely to become amorphous. They may be gradually replaced by goals for which well-defined technologies are available. It is not surprising to find, as Perrow (1965) indicates, that the operative goals of mental hospitals may emphasize custody rather than treatment for lack of a viable rehabilitative technology.

The goal problems identified in this discussion indicate that the frequent accusations of goal displacement in human service organizations may be oversimplistic. They fail to take into account the fact that these organizations must pursue multiple goals (Etzioni, 1960) and that in doing so they encounter unique problems that limit organizational rationality.

The articles in this section deal with many of these issues. Perrow, after cogently differentiating between official and operative goals, argues that the latter are determined by the particular problems facing the organization in its course of development. These problems or tasks, shared by all organizations are: (a) security of sufficient resource input, (b) attainment of legitimation of the organization by the community, (c) marshalling of necessary technical skills, and (d) coordination of the activities of the members of the organization and its external relations. Perrow's thesis is that those persons within the organization who are most skillful and resourceful in solving a key organizational problem, will determine the operative goals. Having suggested previously that human service organizations tend to face a turbulent environment, we can hypothesize (following Perrow) that, as environmental contingencies change, so will the nature and urgency of the problems the organization must solve. Consequently, pressures will be brought to bear on the organization in order to modify its leadership structure and operative goals.

In his selection Corwin emphasizes the role of both external constraints and past internal commitments in defining the operative goals of human service organizations. He proposes that the operative goals are the culminating result of a bargaining process among power blocks representing different ideologies and interests. Corwin hypothesizes that, when facing new sources of constraints and inducements, the public school will modify its operative goals only to the extent to which they do not conflict with previous commitments. This implies that the succession of goals envisioned by Perrow may be only partly accomplished since the solutions sought for the new problems confronting the organization are constrained by previous decisions and actions. One strategy adopted by the school to increase its maneuverability in the face of changing and conflicting community pressures is to pursue multiple goals, as is the case in the comprehensive school model. Such a solution, however, tends to reduce the power of the school by increasing the number of tasks it must now accomplish.

Scott presents a fascinating case study of the structural processes that have led to the displacement of the goals of sheltered workshops for the blind. In so doing, he points to the more general conditions which lead to goal displacement in human service organizations. Although originally established as social service agencies to meet the employment needs of the blind, the sheltered workshops gradually transformed themselves into a business enterprise, thus obfuscating their service objectives. Scott documents the economic conditions which threatened the survival of the workshops and resulted in the displacement of their goals. Interestingly, once economic considerations predominated, the social service objectives were ignored even when the external economic conditions became favorable again. Of particular importance are the mechanisms used by the workshop managers in order to minimize the strain resulting from goal discrepancies. These mechanisms essentially involved changes in the belief systems about the nature of their clients, desired behavioral outcomes, and expectations of the "normal" public which were subsequently reified. This study suggests that the belief systems developed by the human service organization concerning clients served, and its service objectives, may stem from considerations which have little to do with the welfare and well-being of the clients.

Finally, Gross proposes in his study a multi-faceted approach to the measuring of goals in human service organizations such as universities. Arguing that universities as complex systems have both product and maintenance goals, Gross suggests a methodological procedure to measure the relative emphasis universities put on output goals, adaptation goals, management goals, motivation goals, and positional goals. Of particular importance is his attempt to measure the congruency between what faculty and administrators perceive to be the existing goal emphases, and what goals they think should be emphasized. By implication,

Gross points to the multiplicity of goals human service organizations seek to accomplish; the effects of the hierarchial importance of the various goals on the operations of the organization; and the level of goal congruency as a gauge of staff attitudes toward the organization.

References

Etzioni, A. 1960. "Two approaches to organizational analysis: A critique and a suggestion." *Administrative Science Quarterly* 5:257–78.

Perrow, C. 1961. "The analysis of goals in complex organizations." *American Sociological Review* 26:856–66.

———. 1965. "Hospitals: Technology, structure, and goals," in James March (ed.) *Handbook of Organizations*. Chicago: Rand McNally.

———. 1970. *Organizational Analysis: A Sociological Review*. Belmont, California: Wadsworth.

Thompson, J. D. 1967. *Organization in Action*. New York: McGraw-Hill.

Zald, M. 1963. "Comparative analysis and measurement of organizational goals: The case of institutions for delinquents." *Sociological Quarterly* 4:206–30.

The Analysis of Goals in Complex Organizations

Charles Perrow

Social scientists have produced a rich body of knowledge about many aspects of large-scale organizations, yet there are comparatively few studies of the goals of these organizations. For a full understanding of organizations and the behavior of their personnel, analysis of organizational goals would seem to be critical. Two things have impeded such analysis. Studies of morale, turnover, informal organization, communication, supervisory practices, etc., have been guided by an over-rationalistic point of view wherein goals are taken for granted, and the most effective ordering of resources and personnel is seen as the only problematical issue. Fostering this view is the lack of an adequate distinction between types of goals. Without such clarification it is difficult to determine what the goals are and what would be acceptable evidence for the existence of a particular goal and for a change in goals.

It will be argued here, first, that the type of goals most relevant to understanding organizational behavior are not the official goals, but those that are embedded in major operating policies and the daily deci-

Excerpted from *American Sociological Review* 26 (1961): 856–66.

sions of the personnel. Second, these goals will be shaped by the particular problems or tasks an organization must emphasize, since these tasks determine the characteristics of those who will dominate the organization. In illustrating the latter argument, we will not be concerned with the specific goals of organizations, but only with the range within which goals are likely to vary. Though general hospitals will be used as the main illustration, three types of organizations will be discussed: voluntary service organizations, non-voluntary service organizations and profit-making organizations.

The Over-Rationalistic View

Most studies of the internal operation of complex organizations, if they mention goals at all, have taken official statements of goals at face value. This may be justified if only a limited problem is being investigated, but even then it contributes to the view that goals are not problematical. In this view, goals have no effect upon activities other than in the grossest terms; or it can be taken for granted that the only problem is to adjust means to given and stable ends. This reflects a distinctive "model" of organizational behavior, which Gouldner has characterized as the rational model.[1] Its proponents see the managerial elite as using rational and logical means to pursue clear and discrete ends set forth in official statements of goals, while the worker is seen as governed by nonrationalistic, traditionalistic orientations. If goals are unambiguous and achievement evaluated by cost-accounting procedures, the only turmoil of organizational life lies below the surface with workers or, at best, with middle management maneuvering for status and power. Actually, however, nonrational orientations exist at all levels, including the elite who are responsible for setting goals[2] and assessing the degree to which they are achieved.

One reason for treating goals as static fixtures of organizational life is that goals have not been given adequate conceptualization, though the elements of this are in easy reach. If making a profit or serving customers is to be taken as a sufficient statement of goals, then all means to this end might appear to be based on rational decisions because the analyst is not alerted to the countless policy decisions involved. If goals are given a more elaborate conceptualization, we are forced to see many more things as problematic.

Official and Operative Goals

Two major categories of goals will be discussed here, official and "operative goals.[3] Official goals are the general purposes of the organization as put forth in the charter, annual reports, public statements by key executives and other authoritative pronouncements. For example, the goal of an employment agency may be to place job seekers in contact with firms seeking workers. The official goal of a hospital may be to promote the health of the community through curing the ill, and sometimes through preventing illness, teaching, and conducting research. Similar organizations may emphasize different publicly acceptable goals. A business corporation, for example, may state that its goal is to make a profit or adequate return on investment, or provide a customer service, or produce goods.

This level of analysis is inadequate in itself for a full understanding of organizational behavior. Official goals are purposely vague and general and do not indicate two major factors which influence organizational behavior: the host of decisions that must be made among alternative ways of achieving official goals and the priority of multiple goals, and the many unofficial goals pursued by groups within the organization. The concept of "operative goals"[4] will be used to cover these aspects. Operative goals designate the ends sought through the actual operating policies of the organization; they tell us what the organization actually is trying to do, regardless of what the official goals say are the aims.

Where operative goals provide the specific content of official goals they reflect choices among competing values. They may be justified on the basis of an official goal, even though they may subvert another official goal. In one sense they are means to official goals, but since the latter are vague or of high abstraction, the "means" become ends in themselves when the organization is the object of analysis. For example, where profit-making is the announced goal, operative goals will specify whether quality or quantity is to be emphasized, whether profits are to be short run and risky or long run and stable, and will indicate the relative priority of diverse and somewhat conflicting ends of customer service, employee morale, competitive pricing, diversification, or liquidity. Decisions on all these factors influence the nature of the organization, and distinguish it from another with an identical official goal. An employment agency must decide whom to serve, what characteristics they favor among clients, and whether a high turnover of clients or a long run relationship is desired. In the voluntary general hospital, where the official goals are patient care, teaching, and research, the relative priority of these must be decided, as well as which group in the community is to be given priority in service, and are these services to emphasize, say, technical excellence or warmth and "hand-holding."

Unofficial operative goals, on the other hand, are tied more directly to group interests and while they may support, be irrelevant to, or subvert official goals, they bear no necessary connection with them. An interest in a major supplier may dictate the policies of a corporation executive. The prestige that attaches to utilizing elaborate high speed computers may dictate the reorganization of inventory and accounting departments. Racial prejudice may influence the selection procedures of an employment agency. The personal ambition of a hospital administrator may lead to community alliances and activities which bind the organization without enhancing its goal achievement. On the other hand, while the use of interns and residents as "cheap labor" may subvert the official goal of medical education, it may substantially further the official goal of providing a high quality of patient care.

The discernment of operative goals is, of course, difficult and subject to error. The researcher may have to determine from analysis of a series of apparently minor decisions regarding the lack of competitive bidding and quality control that an unofficial goal of a group of key executives is to maximize their individual investments in a major supplier. This unofficial goal may affect profits, quality, market position, and morale of key skill groups. The executive of a correctional institution may argue that the goal of the organization is treatment, and only the lack of resources creates an apparent emphasis upon custody or deprivation. The researcher may find, however, that decisions in many areas establish the priority of custody or punishment as a goal. For example, few efforts may be made to obtain more treatment personnel; those hired are misused and mistrusted; and clients are viewed as responding only to deprivations. The president of a junior college may deny the function of the institution is to deal with the latent terminal student, but careful analysis such as Clark has made of operating policies, personnel practices, recruitment procedures, organizational alliances and personal characteristics of elites will demonstrate this to be the operative goal.[5]

The Task—Authority—Goal Sequence

While operative goals will only be established through intensive analysis of decisions, personnel practices, alliance and elite characteristics in each organization, it is possible to indicate the range within which they will vary and the occasion for general shifts in goals. We will argue that if we know something about the major tasks of an organization and the characteristics of its controlling elite, we can predict its goals in general terms. The theory presented and illustrated in the rest of this paper is a first approximation and very general, but it may guide and stimulate research on this problem.

Every organization must accomplish four tasks: (1) secure inputs in the form of capital sufficient to establish itself, operate, and expand as the need arises; (2) secure acceptance in the form of basic legitimization of activity; (3) marshal the necessary skills; and (4) coordinate the activities of its members, and the relations of the organization with other organizations and with clients or consumers. All four are not likely to be equally important at any point in time. Each of these task areas provides a presumptive basis for control or domination by the group equipped to meet the problems involved. (The use of the terms control or dominance signifies a more pervasive, thorough and all-embracing phenomenon than authority or power.) The operative goals will be shaped by the dominant group, reflecting the imperatives of the particular task area that is most critical, their own background characteristics (distinctive perspectives based upon their training, career lines, and areas of competence) and the unofficial uses to which they put the organization for their own ends.

The relative emphasis upon one or another of the four tasks will vary with the nature of the work the organization does and the technology appropriate to it,[6] and with the stage of development within the organization.[7] An organization engaged in manufacturing in an industry where skills are routinized and the market position secure, may emphasize coordination, giving control to the experienced administrator. An extractive industry, with a low skill level in its basic tasks and a simple product, will probably emphasize the importance of capital tied up in land, specialized and expensive machinery, and transportation facilities. The chairman of the board of directors or a group within the board will probably dominate such an organization. An organization engaged in research and development, or the production of goods or services which cannot be carried out in a routinized fashion, will probably be most concerned with skills. Thus engineers or other relevant professionals will dominate. It is also possible that all three groups—trustees, representatives of critical skills, and administrators—may share power equally. This "multiple leadership" will be discussed in detail later. Of course, trustees are likely to dominate in the early history of any organization, particularly those requiring elaborate capital and facilities, or unusual legitimization. But once these requisites are secured, the nature of the tasks will determine whether trustees or others dominate. The transfer of authority, especially from trustees to another group, may be protracted, constituting a lag in adaptation.

Where major task areas do not change over time, the utility of the scheme presented here is limited to suggesting possible relations between task areas, authority structure, and operative goals. The more interesting problems, which we deal with in our illustrations below, involve organizations which experience changes in major task areas over time. If the technology or type of work changes, or if new requirements for capital or legitimization arise, control will shift from one group to another. One sequence is believed to be typical.

Voluntary General Hospitals

We will discuss four types of hospitals, those dominated by trustees, by the medical staff (an organized group of those doctors who bring in private patients plus the few doctors who receive salaries or commissions from the hospital), by the administration, and by some form of multiple leadership. There has been a general development among hospitals from trustee domination, based on capital and legitimization, to domination by the medical staff, based upon the increasing importance of their technical skills, and, at present, a tendency towards administrative dominance based on internal and external coordination. (The administrator may or may not be a doctor himself.) Not all hospitals go through these stages, or go through them in this sequence. Each type of authority structure shapes, or sets limits to, the type of operative goals that are likely to prevail, though there will be much variation within each type.[8]

 Trustee Domination. Voluntary general hospitals depend upon community funds for an important part of their capital and operating budget. Lacking precise indicators of efficiency or goal achievement, yet using donated funds, they must involve community representatives —trustees—in their authority structure. Trustees legitimate the non-profit status of the organization, assure that funds are not misused, and see that community needs are being met. Officially, they are the ultimate authority in voluntary hospitals. They do not necessarily exercise the legal powers they have, but where they do, there is no question that they are in control.

 The functional basis for this control is primarily financial. They have access to those who make donations, are expected to contribute heavily themselves, and control the machinery and sanctions for fund raising drives. Financial control allows them to withhold resources from recalcitrant groups in the organization, medical or non-medical. They also, of course, control all appointments and promotions, medical and non-medical.

 Where these extensive powers are exercised, operative goals are likely to reflect the role of trustees as community representatives and contributors to community health. Because of their responsibility to the sponsoring community, trustees may favor conservative financial policies, opposing large financial outlays for equipment, research, and education so necessary for high medical standards.[9] High standards also require more delegation of authority to the medical staff than trustee domination can easily allow.[10] As representatives drawn from distinctive social groups in the community, they may be oriented towards service for a religious, ethnic, economic, or age group in the community. Such an orientation may conflict with selection procedures favored by the medical staff or administration. Trustees may also promote policies which demonstrate a contribution to community welfare on the part of an elite group, perhaps seeking to maintain a position of prominence and power within the community. The hospital may be used as a vehicle for furthering a social philosophy of philanthropy and good works; social class values regarding personal worth, economic independence and responsibility; the assimilation of a minority group;[11] or even to further resistance to government control and socialized medicine.

Such orientations will shape operative goals in many respects, affecting standards and techniques of care, priority of services, access to care, relations with other organizations, and directions and rate of development. The administrator in such a hospital—usually called a "superintendent" under the circumstances—will have little power, prestige or responsibility. For example, trustees have been known to question the brand of grape juice the dietician orders, or insist that they approve the color of paint the administrator selects for a room.[12] Physicians may disapprove of patient selection criteria, chafe under financial restrictions which limit the resources they have to work with, and resent active control over appointments and promotions in the medical staff.

Medical Domination. Trustee domination was probably most common in the late nineteenth and early twentieth century. Medical technology made extraordinary advances in the twentieth century, and doctors possessed the skills capable of utilizing the advances. They demanded new resources and were potentially in a position to control their allocation and use. Increasingly, major decisions had to be based upon a technical competence trustees did not possess. Trustees had a continuing basis for control because of the costs of new equipment and personnel, but in many hospitals the skill factor became decisive. Some trustees felt that the technology required increased control by doctors; others lost a struggle for power with the medical staff; in some cases trustees were forced to bring in and give power to an outstanding doctor in order to increase the reputation of the hospital.[13] Under such conditions trustees are likely to find that their legal power becomes nominal and they can only intervene in crisis situations; even financial requirements come to be set by conditions outside their control.[14] They continue to provide the mantle of community representation and non-profit status, and became "staff" members whose major task is to secure funds.

It is sometimes hard to see why all hospitals are not controlled by the medical staff, in view of the increasing complexity and specialization of the doctor's skills, their common professional background, the power of organized medicine, and the prestige accorded the doctor in society. Furthermore, they are organized for dominance, despite their nominal status as "guests" in the house.[15] The medical staff constitutes a "shadow" organization in hospitals, providing a ready potential for control. It is organized on bureaucratic principles with admission requirements, rewards and sanctions, and a committee structure which often duplicates the key committees of the board of directors and administrative staff. Nor are doctors in an advisory position as are "staff" groups in other organizations. Doctors perform both staff and line functions, and their presumptive right to control rests on both. Doctors also have a basic economic interest in the hospital, since it is essential to most private medical practice and career advancement. They seek extensive facilities, low hospital charges, a high quality of coordinated services, and elaborate time and energy-conserving conveniences.

Thus there is sufficient means for control by doctors, elaborated far beyond the mere provision of essential skills, and sufficient interest in control. Where doctors fully exercise their potential power the administrator functions as a superintendent or, as his co-professionals are wont to put it, as a "housekeeper." The importance of administrative skills is likely to be minimized, the administrative viewpoint on operative goals neglected, and the quality of personnel may suffer. A former nurse often serves as superintendent in this type of hospital. Policy matters are defined as medical in nature by the doctors,[16] and neither trustees nor administrators, by definition, are qualified to have an equal voice in policy formation.

The operative goals of such a hospital are likely to be defined in strictly medical terms and the organization may achieve high technical standards of care, promote exemplary research, and provide sound training. However, there is a danger that resources will be used primarily for private (paying) patients with little attention to other community needs such as caring for the medically indigent (unless they happen to be good teaching cases), developing preventive medicine, or pioneering new organizational forms of care. Furthermore, high technical standards increasingly require efficient coordination of services and doctors may be unwilling to delegate authority to qualified administrators.

Various unofficial goals may be achieved at the expense of medical ones, or, in some cases, in conjunction with them. There are many cases of personal aggrandizement on the part of departmental chiefs and the chief of staff. The informal referral and consultation system in conjunction with promotions, bed quotas, and "privileges" to operate or treat certain types of cases, affords many occasions for the misuse of power. Interns and residents are particularly vulnerable to exploitation at the expense of teaching goals. Furthermore, as a professional, the doctor has undergone intensive socialization in his training and is called upon to exercise extraordinary judgment and skill with drastic consequences for good or ill. Thus he demands unusual deference and obedience and is invested with "charismatic" authority.[17] He may extend this authority to the entrepreneurial aspects of his role, with the result that his "service" orientation, so taken for granted in much of the literature, sometimes means service to the doctor at the expense of personnel, other patients, or even his own patient.[18]

Administrative Dominance. Administrative dominance is based first on the need for coordinating the increasingly complex, nonroutinizable functions hospitals have undertaken. There is an increasing number of personnel that the doctor can no longer direct. The mounting concern of trustees, doctors themselves, patients and pre-payment groups with more efficient and economical operation also gives the administrator more power. A second, related basis for control stems from the fact that health services in general have become increasingly interdependent and specialized. The hospital must cooperate more with other hospitals and community agencies. It must also take on more services itself, and in doing so its contacts with other agencies and professional groups outside the hospital multiply. The administrator is equipped to handle these matters because of his specialized training, often received in a professional school of hospital administration, accumulated experience and available time. These services impinge upon the doctor at many points, providing a further basis for administrative control over doctors, and they lead to commitments in which trustees find they have to acquiesce.

The administrator is also in a position to control matters which affect the doctor's demands for status, deference, and time-saving conveniences. By maintaining close supervision over employees or promoting their own independent basis for competence, and by supporting them in conflicts with doctors, the administrator can, to some degree, overcome the high functional authority that doctors command. In addition, by carefully controlling communication between trustees and key medical staff officials, he can prevent an alliance of these two groups against him.

If administrative dominance is based primarily on the complexity of basic hospital activities, rather than the organization's medical-social role in the community, the operative orientation may be toward financial solvency, careful budget controls, efficiency, and minimal development of services. For example, preventive medicine, research, and training may be minimized; a cautious approach may prevail towards new forms of care such as intensive therapy units or home care programs. Such orientations could be especially true of hospitals dominated by administrators whose background and training were as bookkeepers, comptrollers, business managers, purchasing agents, and the like. This is probably the most common form of administrative dominance.

However, increasing professionalization of hospital administrators has, on the one hand, equipped them to handle narrower administrative matters easily, and, on the other hand, alerted them to the broader medical-social role of hospitals involving organizational and financial innovations in the forms of care. Even medical standards can come under administrative control. For example, the informal system among doctors of sponsorship, referral, and consultation serves to protect informal work norms, shield members from criticism and exclude non-cooperative members. The administrator is in a position to insist that medical policing be performed by a salaried doctor who stands outside the informal system.

There is, of course, a possibility of less "progressive" consequences. Interference with medical practices in the name of either high standards or treating the "whole" person may be misguided or have latent consequences which impair therapy. Publicity-seeking innovations may be at the expense of more humdrum but crucial services such as the out-patient department, or may alienate doctors or other personnel, or may deflect administrative efforts from essential but unglamorous administrative tasks.[19] Using the organization for career advancement, they may seek to expand and publicize their hospital regardless of community needs and ability to pay. Like trustees they may favor a distinctive and medically irrelevant community relations policy, perhaps with a view towards moving upward in the community power structure. Regardless of these dangers, the number of administration dominated hospitals oriented towards broad medical-social goals will probably grow.

Multiple Leadership. So far we have been considering situations where one group clearly dominates. It is possible, however, for power to be shared by two or three groups to the extent that no one is able to control all or most of the actions of the others. This we call multiple leadership: a division of labor regarding the determination of goals and the power to achieve them.[20] This is not the same as fractionated power where several groups have small amounts of power in an unstable situation. With multiple leadership, there are two or three stable, known centers of power. Nor is it the same as decentralized power, where specialized units of the organization have considerable autonomy. In the latter case, units are free to operate as they choose only up to a point, when it becomes quite clear that there is a centralized authority. In multiple leadership there is no single ultimate power.

Multiple leadership is most likely to appear in organizations where there are multiple goals which lack precise criteria of achievement and admit of considerable tolerance with regard to achievement. Multiple goals focus interests, and achievement tolerance provides the necessary leeway for accommodations of interests and vitiation of responsibility. Many service organizations fit these criteria, but so might large, public relations-conscious business or industrial organizations where a variety of goals can be elevated to such importance that power must be shared by the representatives of each.

In one hospital where this was studied[21] it was found that multiple leadership insured that crucial group interests could be met and protected, and encouraged a high level of creative (though selective) involvement by trustees, doctors, and the administration. However, the problems of goal setting, assessment of achievement, and assignment of responsibility seemed abnormally high. While the three groups pursued separate and unconflicting operative goals in some cases, and were in agreement on still other goals, in areas where interests conflicted the goal conflicts were submerged in the interests of harmony. In the absence of a single authority, repetitive conflicts threatened to erode morale and waste energies. A showdown and clear solution of a conflict, furthermore, might signal defeat for one party, forcing them to abandon their interests. Thus a premium was placed on the ability of some elites to smooth over conflicts and exercise interpersonal skills. Intentions were sometimes masked and ends achieved through convert manipulation. Assessment of achievement in some areas was prevented either by the submergence of conflict or the preoccupation with segmental interests. Opportunism was encouraged: events in the environment or within the hospital were exploited without attention to the interests of the other groups or the long range development of the hospital. This left the organization open to vagrant pressures and to the operation of unintended consequences. Indeed, with conflict submerged and groups pursuing independent goals, long range planning was difficult.

This summary statement exaggerates the impact of multiple leadership in this hospital and neglects the areas of convergence on goals. Actually, the hospital prospered and led its region in progressive innovations and responsible medical-social policies despite some subversion of the official goals of patient care, teaching, research, and preventive medicine. The organization could tolerate considerable ambiguity of goals and achievements as long as standards remained high in most areas, occupancy was sufficient to operate with a minimum deficit, and a favorable public image was maintained. It remains to be seen if the costs and consequences are similar for other organizations where multiple leadership exists.

Application to Other Organizations[22]

Voluntary Service Organizations. Other voluntary organizations, such as private universities, social service agencies, privately sponsored correctional institutions for juveniles, and fund raising agencies resemble hospitals in many respects. They have trustees representing the community, may have professionals playing prominent roles, and with increasing size and complexity of operation, require skilled coordination of activities. Initially at least, trustees are likely to provide a character defining function which emphasizes community goals and goals filtered through their own social position. Examples are religious schools, or those emphasizing one field of knowledge or training; agencies caring for specialized groups such as ethnic or religious minorities, unwed mothers, and dependent and neglected children; and groups raising money for special causes. Funds of skill and knowledge accumulate around these activities, and the activities increasingly grow in complexity, requiring still more skill on the part of those performing the tasks. As the professional staff expands and professional identification grows, they may challenge the narrower orientations of trustees on the basis of their own special competence and professional ideology and seek to broaden the scope of services and the clientele. They may be supported in this by changing values in the community. Coordination of activities usually rests with professionals promoted from the staff during this second character defining phrase, and these administrators retain, for a while at least, their professional identity. Trustees gradually lose the competence to interfere.

However, professionals have interests of their own which shape the organization. They may develop an identity and ethic which cuts them off from the needs of the community and favors specialized, narrow and—to critics—self-serving goals. Current criticisms of the emphasis upon research and over-specialization in graduate training at the expense of the basic task of educating undergraduates is a case in point in the universities.[23] There is also criticism of the tendency of professionals in correctional institutions to focus upon case work techniques applicable to middle-class "neurotic" delinquents at the expense of techniques for resocializing the so-called "socialized" delinquent from culturally deprived areas.[24] The latter account for most of the delinquents, but professional identity and techniques favor methods applicable to the former. Something similar may be found in social agencies. Social workers, especially the "elite" doing therapy in psychiatric and child guidance clinics and private family agencies, may become preoccupied with securing recognition, equitable financial remuneration, and status that would approach that of psychiatrists. Their attitudes may become more conservative; the social order more readily accepted and the deviant adapted to it; "worthy" clients and "interesting cases" receive priority.

It is possible that with increasing complexity and growth in many of these voluntary service organizations, administrators will lose their professional identity or be recruited from outside the organization on the basis of organizational skills. In either case they will be in a position to alter the direction fostered by selective professional interests. Of course, the problem of coordinating both internal and external activities need not generate leadership seeking broadly social rather than narrowly professional goals, any more than it necessarily does in the hospital. Administrative dominance may stunt professional services and neglect social policy in the interest of economy, efficiency, or conservative policies.

Non-Voluntary Service Organizations. A different picture is presented by non-voluntary service organizations—those sponsored by governmental agencies such as county or military hospitals, city or county welfare agencies, juvenile and adult correctional agencies.[25] Authority for goal setting, regulation, and provision of capital and operating expenses does not rest with voluntary trustees, but with governmental officials appointed to commissions. In contrast to volunteers on the board of a private service organization, commissioners are not likely to be highly identified with the organization, nor do they derive much social status from it. The organizations themselves often are tolerated only as holding operations or as "necessary evils." Commission dominance is sporadic and brief, associated with public clamor or political expediency. On the other hand, the large size of these organizations and the complex procedures for reporting to the parent body gives considerable importance to the administrative function from the outset, which is enhanced by the tenuous relationship with the commissioners. Consistent with this and reinforcing it is the low level of professionalization found in many of these agencies. The key skills are often non-professional custodial skills or their equivalent in the case of public welfare agencies (and schools). Administrators are often at the mercy of the custodial staff if, indeed, they have not themselves risen to their administrative position because of their ability to maintain order and custody.

Nevertheless, professional influence is mounting in these organizations, and professional groups outside of them have exercised considerable influence.[26] Professionals may assume control of the organization, or administrators may be brought in whose commitment is to the positive purposes of the organization, such as rehabilitation of the clients, rather than the negative custodial functions. This appears to have happened in the case of a few federal penal institutions, a few state juvenile correctional institutions, and several Veterans Administration mental hospitals. Even where this happens, one must be alert to the influence of unofficial goals. The organizations are particularly vulnerable to exploitation by the political career interests of administrators or to irresponsible fads or cure-alls of marginal professionals. In summary, the sequence of tasks, power structure, and goals may be different in nonvoluntary service organizations. The importance of administrative skills with system maintenance as the overriding operative goal does not encourage a shift in power structure; but where new technologies are introduced we are alerted to such shifts along with changes in goals.

Notes

1. Alvin Gouldner, "Organizational Analysis," in Robert Merton, Leonard Broom and Leonard S. Cottrell, Jr., editors, *Sociology Today*, New York, Basic Books, 1959, p. 407.

2. A strong argument for considering changes in goals is made by James D. Thompson and William J. McEwen, "Organizational Goals and Environment: Goal-Setting as an Interaction Process," *American Sociological Review*, 23 (February, 1958), pp. 23–31.

3. A third may be distinguished: social system goals, which refers to those contributions an organization makes to the functioning of a social system in which it is nested. In Parson's terminology, organizations may serve adaptive, gratificatory, integrative, or pattern-maintenance functions. See Talcott Parsons, "Sociological Approach to the Theory of Organizations," *Administrative Science Quarterly*, 1 (June-September, 1956), pp. 63–86, 225–240. This alone, however, will tell us little about individual organizations, although Scott, in a suggestive article applying this

scheme to prisons and mental hospitals, implies that organizations serving integrative functions for society will place particular importance upon integrative functions within the organization. See Frances G. Scott, "Action Theory and Research in Social Organization," *American Journal of Sociology*, 64 (January, 1959), pp. 386–395. Parsons asserts that each of the four functions mentioned above also must be performed within organizations if they are to survive. It is possible to see a parallel between these four functions and the four tasks discussed below, but his are, it is felt, too general and ambiguous to provide tools for analysis.

4. The concept of "operational goals" or "sub-goals" put forth by March and Simon bears a resemblance to this but does not include certain complexities which we will discuss, nor is it defined systematically. See J. G. March and H. A. Simon, *Organizations*, New York: Wiley, 1958, pp. 156–157.

5. Burton Clark, *The Open Door College*, New York: McGraw-Hill, 1960.

6. For an illuminating discussion of organizations which emphasize technological differences, see James D. Thompson and Frederick L. Bates, "Technology, Organizations, and Administration," *Administrative Science Quarterly*, 2 (December, 1957), pp. 325–343.

7. Many other factors are also important, such as the legal framework, official and unofficial regulatory bodies, state of the industry, etc. These will not be considered here. In general, their influences are felt through the task areas, and thus are reflected here.

8. The following discussion is based upon the author's study of one hospital which, in fact, passed through these stages; upon examination of published and unpublished studies of hospitals; and upon numerous conversations with administrators, doctors, and trustees in the United States. Sophisticated practitioners in the hospital field recognize and describe these types in their own fashion. See Charles Perrow, "Authority, Goals and Prestige in a General Hospital," unpublished Ph.D. dissertation, University of California, Berkeley, 1960, for fuller documentation and discussion.

9. Exceptions to conservative financial policies appear to occur most frequently in crisis situations where accreditation is threatened or sound business principles are violated by run down facilities, or inefficient management. See Temple Burling, Edith M. Lentz, and Robert N. Wilson, *The Give and Take in Hospitals*, New York: G. P. Putnam, 1956, Chapters 4, 5, 6.

10. Burling *et al.*, (*ibid.*, p. 43), note that active trustees find delegation difficult.

11. Perrow, *op. cit.*, chapter 5.

12. Edith Lentz, "Changing Concepts of Hospital Administration," *Industrial and Labor Relations Research*, 3 (Summer, 1957), p. 2. Perrow, *op. cit.*, p. 86.

13. Berthram Bernhein, *The Story of Johns Hopkins*, New York: McGraw-Hill, 1948, pp. 142–148.

14. For a detailed analysis of such a shift of power, see Perrow, *op. cit.*, pp. 43–50.

15. There is a small group of doctors on the medical staff, who may or may not bring in private patients, who receive money from the hospital, either through salary or commissions—pathologists, anesthetists, roentgenologists, paid directors of the out-patient department, etc. These are members of the organization in a direct sense.

16. Oswald Hall, "Some Problems in the Provision of Medical Services," *Canadian Journal of Economics*, 20 (November, 1954), p. 461.

17. Albert F. Wessen, "The Social Structure of a Modern Hospital," unpublished Ph.D. dissertation, Yale University, 1951, p. 43.

18. Wessen notes that the doctor "sees ministering to the needs of doctors as a major function of hospitals." (*Ibid.*, p. 328).

19. Charles Perrow, "Organizational Prestige: Some Functions and Dysfunctions," *American Journal of Sociology*, 66 (January, 1961), pp. 335–341.

20. As in small group analysis, there is an increasing though belated tendency to recognize the possibility that there may be more than one leader in an organization. For a recent discussion of the problem in connection with army groups, see Hanan Selvin, *The Effects of Leadership*, Glencoe, Ill.: The Free Press, 1960, Chapters 1, 7. Amitai Etzioni goes even further in discussing "professional organizations." For a provocative discussion of goals and authority structure, see his "Authority Structure and Organizational Effectiveness," *Administrative Science Quarterly*, 4 (June, 1959), pp. 43–67.

21. Perrow, Authority, Goals and Prestige . . . , *op. cit.*, chapters 4, 10.

22. The dogmatic tone of this concluding section is, unfortunately, the consequence of an attempt to be brief.

23. Earl J. McGrath, *The Graduate School and the Doctrine of Liberal Education*, New York: Bureau of Publication, Teachers College, Columbia University, 1960.

24. Robert Vinter and Morris Janowitz, "Effective Institutions for Juvenile Delinquents: A Research Statement," *Social Service Review*, 33 (June, 1957), pp. 118–122; Donald Cressey, "Changing Criminals: The Application of the Theory of Differential Association," *American Journal of Sociology*, 56 (September, 1955), p. 116; Lloyd Ohlin and W. C. Lawrence, "Social Interaction Among Clients as a Treatment Problem," *Social Work*, 4 (April, 1959), pp. 3–14.

25. Public schools are excluded here because of the elective status of school boards; however, with some revisions, the following analysis would be applicable.

26. Thompson and McEwen note that the "importance of new objectives may be more readily seen by specialized segments (professionals) than by the general society" and argue that public clamor for change has not been the initiating force. *Op. cit.*, p. 29.

The Formulation of Goals in the Public Schools

Ronald G. Corwin

Organization is being viewed here not as a carefully coordinated entity, but as a set of sometimes tenuous coalitions. The bargaining between

Excerpted from R. Corwin, *A Sociology of Education* (New York: Appleton, Century, Crofts, 1965), pp. 433–38.

these coalitions establishes the organization's operating goals. The term "goal" has been used with reservation and caution. That term implies a sense of direction and rationality and a degree of planning which seldom exist in complex organizations. Completely rational direction is not permitted to exist in complex organizations, even though the persons in charge may themselves be rational and have a clear set of personal objectives and organizational goals in mind. Rational planning toward a goal (*e.g.* getting as many students as possible into college) is not completely permitted in the schools for two major reasons. First, there are external constraints on the school, such as a limited tax base, which restrict the ability of the school to be completely consistent. Second, other commitments made by the organization set precedents which circumscribe the number of available alternatives. Thus, Clark describes a community with a recruiting process which diverted the resources and teachers of a junior college from the vocational program to which it was officially committed to a college prep program.[1]

The internal *commitments* of an organization should be distinguished from the nonoperational *goals*. Nonoperational goals are those that are difficult to identify in practice, such as "educating each child to the best of his capacity to contribute to the society." Such goals are so abstract that it is difficult to dispute them; and because they are abstract, they provide few clues to what the schools should do to implement them. Does the above-mentioned goal imply that schools should teach vocational training? Drivers education? At best such goals set outside limits; *e.g.* the above definition would probably preclude teaching children to be criminals.

Contrasted to these nonoperational goals are the actual commitments which an organization makes. A commitment is an obligation to which an organization has pledged itself; it is more than an idle promise. The degree of commitment can be measured by the sanctions that can be invoked against the organization that fails to fulfill it, *e.g.* a school is committed by the sanction of law to serve students until age sixteen. Not all commitments are so explicitly stated, however. For example, in agreeing to accept responsibility for an adult education program, a school unwittingly may have obligated itself to place graduates of the program in the local job market—a commitment which it perhaps cannot fulfill.

Accumulated commitments constitute the organization's *operating goals*. It is these commitments, and not the nonoperational "goals," that determine the actual direction that the organization takes. Thus, a school's operating goals may be the result of its commitment to local taxpayers who want a vocational agriculture program rather than its expressed goal of preparing students for life adjustment. Or, despite its professed concern with the average and slow learner, a school may commit itself primarily to educating the gifted learners in order to demonstrate their success and obtain the support of outside groups. These commitments not only set the direction which a school *will* take, but each commitment that a school makes also limits the alternatives that it *can* take; commitments therefore limit power. As already mentioned, a comprehensive program commits the school to several different goals simultaneously. This provides flexibility, but it restricts the resources (*i.e.* money and personnel) that can be allocated to any one of its commitments and limits its power to achieve the total set of commitments. For example, every teacher, dollar, and classroom allocated to the athletic program or to driver education could otherwise have been used to improve the academic program (unless they have been donated by outside groups specifically for these purposes). This principle does not apply only when the academic program is poor, as some defendants of the nonacademic program seem to imply. It is equally true that a strong academic program is prevented from becoming even stronger by competing commitments.

It is hypothesized that the commitments of a school are the result of a bargaining process among the power blocks within the school and between those power blocks and certain outsiders who are able to exercise constraint. The implication is that the operating goals of a school are identical to the bargains made between groups in conflict.[2] The ability of a group to achieve commitment (*e.g.* to implement a program to motivate lower-class children) will, therefore, obviously depend on its power. And its power will depend to a great extent on its ability to obtain outside supporters who will be in a position to enforce compliance with whatever commitment the school makes. Thus, if a group of faculty is able to interest a federal agency in a "Gray Areas project" for the system, the school officials will be embarrassed professionally if they express a lack of interest in cooperating in the program. Although a less powerful outside agency probably could not invoke the same degree of pressure, the faculty group could rely on other outside powers such as professional organizations or militant Negro organizations.

The relationship between internally made commitments and externally imposed constraints is also part of a bargaining process. The intensified professional militancy among teachers, the increasing size and complexity of schools and the corresponding power of administrators, diversified financing, diverse sources of control over the schools, and cleavages existing among the pressure groups in most commitments, all are factors that indicate that in the near future the public schools will continue to take an increasingly militant posture toward outside pressures. The historical disposition of schools passively to adapt to outside pressures can be contrasted with the more recent evidence demonstrating the success of some schools in evading outside pressures. Schools will not become completely independent of local control, but in comparison to their historical tendency to adapt passively to external controls they seem to be showing more of a spirit of strategic resistance.

The relative strength of the schools in comparison to outside pressures will depend on the factors discussed before—the professionalization of teachers and administrators, the sources of finance and control, the institutional pattern, and the strategic advantage to the school of adapting to outside pressures. Beyond that, however, it is hypothesized that a school will be most likely to adapt to pressures which correspond with its previous commitments and do not conflict with previous commitments. Thus, schools have willingly committed themselves to the expansion of math and science courses, which fit the traditional middle-class, college-oriented curriculum; their willingness is especially also related to the fact that these courses have been supported by the Federal Government. However it can be expected that schools will be more reluctant to work for racial integration of the lower-class schools or for more effective lower-class education (even when some powerful groups push for it), because this commitment is contrary to the whole basis of prestige by which the middle-class community evaluates itself and the school (*i.e.* the instruction of "desirable" students and the ability of schools to place their graduates in "good" jobs or colleges). Using the same line of reasoning, it would appear to be easier to integrate the schools in lower-class areas of the city then in middle-class areas where more specific commitments have been made to middle-class white residents.

There are other factors, of course. For example, the existing budget alters and circumscribes a school's commitments. If that budget is increased, then the school is able to increase its total commitments. Thus federal aid for some schools, with appropriate pressure, will eventually increase the commitment that public schools are willing to make to education improvement in slum schools, since it can then be done without seriously violating their commitments to middle-class education.

Because commitments are part of a system of exchange and compromise, and because they accumulate over time, the operating goals of an organization which evolve are not necessarily consistent. The existence of simultaneous and inconsistent commitments competing for scarce resources creates dilemmas. One strategy for minimizing incipient conflicts is to focus on the commitments alternately rather than simultaneously. Thus, as suggested above, a school may stress the middle-class college program until publicity is given to its incompetent lower-class educational program, at which time the school will shift its focus of attention to that problem. Similarly, schools neglected math-science programs until the cold war and the Federal Government gave them impetus in recent years. Recently, many schools have shifted their attention away from extracurricular aspects of the program as a result of cold war pressures. In general it seems that in schools with multiple operating goals, the focus of attention will closely reflect the current demands of outside pressure groups.

Conversely, however, it follows that the visibility of a school's activities will modify the kind of demands which outside groups do make. Generally, the zone of public indifference to the school's activities is relatively high. Some of this indifference is due to the fact that the public is uninformed about school practices. It can be hypothesized, therefore, that a school's control over its commitments is inversely related to the publicity about them which is not imitiated by school authorities. Secrecy, especially secret competition, shields the organization from public scrutiny. The more the public becomes aware of practices, the more pressure will be exerted on the school to operate in terms of the values of pressure groups rather than in terms of technical criteria. The dilemma is that in shielding its problems from the public, the school contributes to public indifference, which, in turn, jeopardizes the support it can expect to receive from the public.

Using some of these principles, it is impossible to summarize much of the above discussion by elaborating on the conditions under which schools will resist and will adapt to outside pressures. First, schools are likely to adapt to outside pressures without much resistance if the outside pressures facilitate the fulfillment of previously unfulfilled commitments. The degree of resistance will vary directly with the magnitude of shift that must be made in the *priority* hierarchy of the commitments. For example, under equivalent pressures, a system that was devoting one-fifth of its resources to slum-school education will adapt to current demands to improve slum-school education more quickly than a system that was previously devoting only one-tenth of its resources. Second, a school will show more resistance to making new commitments (*e.g.* creating a preschool program) than to changing the hierarchy of priority among existing commitments. The degree of resistance to a new commitment will vary in direct relation to the extent to which it contradicts an existing one; for example, the growing concern for a special program for slum schools conflicts with the usual commitment of suburban schools to educate only an elite group.

The existence of simultaneous commitments contributes to the ability of the schools to adapt to changing outside pressures. The more commitments it has made, the more maneuverability that a school has. This principle can be compared with the previous statement that the alternatives and power of a school are limited by the number of commitments that it has made. The two statements relate to different perspectives. The conclusion that commitments limit the total power of an organization views all of the alternative commitments at a given time. On the other hand, the conclusion that the maneuverability of an organization is increased by the commitments that it has made is based on a historical view of commitments. These two principles essentially define the two major strategies available to schools. Maneuverability through increasing the available alternatives is the principle on which the comprehensive school is based; the specialized school, on the other hand, seeks to increase its power by reducing the alternatives that it must accomplish at any one time. Which of these two principles is ultimately more effective is debatable. In a specialized and changing society, does the effectiveness that comes from the ability of an organization to channel its resources to a few commitments outweigh the disadvantage of limited adaptability?

Notes

1. Burton R. Clark, *The Open Door College: A Case Study* (New York: McGraw-Hill, 1960).

2. R. M. Cyert and J. G. March, "A Behavior Theory of Organizational Objectives," in Mason Haire, ed., *Modern Organization Theory* (New York: Wiley, 1962); also, Herbert A. Simon, "On the Concept of Organizational Goal," *Administrative Science Quarterly* (June, 1964), pp. 1–21.

The Factory as a Social Service Organization

Robert A. Scott

A major theme in the sociological literature on formal organizations is a documented tendency for day-to-day policy decisions of an organization to modify, transform, and occasionally even to subvert the objec-

Reprinted from *Social Problems* 15 (Fall, 1967): 160–75.

tives for which the organization was established.[1] Systematic descriptions and analyses of such discrepancies between official and operative goals continue to be important and theoretically meaningful sociological tasks. At the same time, it is also necessary to analyze the consequences which they may have. Such analyses are important for two reasons. First, the fact that discrepancies occur between official and operative goals is of theoretical and practical interest only if they make a difference to the organization, to the persons whom it employs and processes, and/ or to the original problem situation which led to its establishment. These consequences indicate the theoretical and practical significance of the discrepancies. Second, by focusing on the consequences of goal discrepancies, rather than on the fact of their occurrence, the various terms which are used to label the process are transformed from simple descriptive concepts into useful tools of conceptual analysis.

There are several studies of goal displacement in which the effects of this process are described and analyzed. Some of these studies deal with the impact of goal discrepancies within organizations upon the original problem situations and conditions which the organizations were created to solve.[2] Other studies describe the effects of goal displacement upon such things as types of activities which organizations come to sponsor,[3] on the behavior of persons in organizationally relevant contexts,[4] and on the values and value systems of the larger environment of which the organizations are a part.[5] The findings of these studies provide an excellent base of knowledge concerning the consequences of discrepancies between official and operative goals. The purpose of the present article is to broaden this base by analyzing the consequences of goal discrepancies in one type of social welfare organization which I have studied: namely, sheltered workshops for the blind.

I will be concerned with two consequences of this process. The first I have already referred to in my discussion. It concerns the effects which goal displacement in sheltered workshops for the blind had upon the problems and conditions which first led to the establishment of these organizations. The second concerns the effects of goal displacement upon the belief systems which are shared by workers for the blind. In order to deal with this it will be necessary to clarify this aspect of organizational behavior.

All organizations which process people, and especially people who have been labeled "problems," maintain complex systems of beliefs about those whom they try to help. These belief systems consist of explanations as to why a particular trait or condition is a problem in the first place, what ought to be done about it, how human nature operates, and how to change it in desired ways. Such beliefs serve as guidelines for establishing the official goals of the helping organizations. They also serve a number of other functions as well. They often become the "window dressing" which convincingly explains and legitimates the organization's activities to the public. For individual workers, these systems of beliefs infuse the otherwise mundane and often distasteful activities of a job with a sense of purpose and nobility. As such, workers experience them as personal, deep-seated convictions about the rightness, goodness, and nobleness of their work.

Initially, systems of beliefs are simply expressions of commonly shared values and convictions about persons who fall into the problem group that concerns the organizations. Official organizational goals are derived from these shared values, and the tasks of workers in them are defined in terms of the specific contribution which they can make toward implementing these goals. If discrepancies and contradictions between official goals and operative policies of an organization arise, these belief systems are subjected to severe stresses and strains. Among the workers who perceive these discrepancies, they are experienced as psychological conflicts. There are several ways in which these conflicts can be reduced.[6]

The first, and most obvious alternative is to establish new operative policies which are consistent with the official goals of the organization. This strategy is seldom possible since operative policies are themselves determined by complex economic, social, and political forces in the environment over which organization members can exercise little influence. Indeed, in many instances the operative policies which conflict with official goals are essential for the organizations' survival. Consequently, attempts to modify operative policies so as to reduce belief system strains may have the effect of running the organization itself out of business.

A second alternative involves the development and use of collective mechanisms of defense. Organization members may simply deny or ignore contradictions and discrepancies between what the organization says it is doing and what it is in fact accomplishing. While some workers may be able to do this for sustained time periods, it is unlikely that it will be a successful means for tension resolution for all organization members for the reason that reality impinges upon at least some of them, and sooner or later one of their numbers is bound to give into it.

A third, and more workable, alternative is to change beliefs about the problems which the organization is trying to solve so as to make them consistent with operative policies. This strategy of deriving belief systems about problems of employment of the blind from the concrete policies which are necessary to keep a sheltered workshop in existence requires a periodic reconceptualization of ideas about what the blind do or do not wish to have; what they do or do not need; or what is or is not good for them. The success of this method for reducing the strains of goal discrepancies hinges on simple processes of persuasion, and on extracting testimonial evidence from workshop clients that the derived beliefs about them are in fact correct.

A fourth and equally workable alternative is to change beliefs about the contribution of "normals" to the problems of the deprived or "plighted" group. This involves altering basic conceptions about such things as the willingness of normals to be tolerant toward the blind, and their receptivity to employing the blind. As with beliefs about the problems of persons that organizations attempt to solve, beliefs about the feelings of normals are also easily changed since they, too, hinge on processes of persuasion and the accumulation of testimonial evidence.

In this study I will try to show how goal displacements which occurred in sheltered workshops produced marked changes in the belief systems of workers for the blind about the problems of employment of the blind and of the part that normals play in creating these problems.

Official Goals of Sheltered Workshops for the Blind

Sheltered workshops for the blind were originally conceived as one element of an overall attack upon the problem of employment of the blind. The essence of this problem was that while there were many blind persons who had the demonstrated capacity to work as productively as sighted workers in commercial factories, there were almost none who had the opportunity to do so. Out of a conviction that work is ennobling, and that the integration of the blind into the sighted community through work is good, workers for the blind set out a philosophy which would provide for the implementation of these beliefs.

This philosophy stated as its primary objective the full-time employment of blind persons in competitive industry. A secondary objective, in the event that competitive employment was unfeasible, was employment in sheltered workshops. Still another alternative was the program of home industries. Under this program seriously disabled blind persons could earn a modest income by assembling and finishing products brought to them at their homes by a representative of the state commission or local agency for the blind. Historically, this program has played a marginal part in employment programs for the blind. For this reason, no further mention of it will be made in this paper. Sheltered workshops specialized in the manufacture of a few standard products selected both for the ease with which they could be assembled and for their marketing potential. In sheltered workshops blind persons were taught broom and mop making, rug weaving, chair caning, willow work, and similar crafts. The program of commercial placement rested on the assumption that in every factory and industrial plant there are a number of jobs which do not require sight and which trained blind persons can perform as ably as sighted persons. Commercial employment programs had placement officers whose job was to locate such positions in industries in the community, to find interested and qualified persons who might fill them, and to train such persons for the positions. After employment was secured, the placement officer was expected to act as a liaison among the blind worker, his employer, and the sponsoring agency.[7]

The goal of full-time employment of blind persons in commercial industry was first formally stated at the annual meetings of the American Association of Workers for the Blind in 1905 by Mr. Charles Campbell, Head of the Massachusetts State Commission for the Blind. Mr. Campbell stated that the purpose of the Massachusetts Commission was "to enable blind persons to become selling agents, and when possible, to become wage earners in shops or factories for the seeing."[8] It was his belief that "every able bodied blind person . . . can find work of some kind side by side with seeing people if efforts are persistently made in this direction."[9] He went on, "It is merely a question of time before blind operatives become an accepted part of the great army of factory workers."[10] These views which were reiterated by Mr. Campbell and others during the early 1900's, have been continually expressed through the years, up through the present time, in major statements by influential people in the field of work for the blind.[11]

It was recognized, however, by most employment specialists that this goal was not always attainable. Some blind persons were so disabled that they could not compete in commercial industry; others were blinded later in life and could not make a good enough adjustment to their visual loss to be considered for commercial work. For these persons sheltered workshops were seen as most appropriate places for work. In sheltered workshops production norms were less stringent than they were in commercial industry; equipment was specially adapted to the requirements of blind operatives; piece rates were generally higher per unit of production than in commercial industry; and a minimum wage[12] was guaranteed regardless of the worker's productivity level. The principal function of the sheltered workshops was to provide a social service to blind persons. This fact was emphasized by a leading employment specialist, Mr. J. N. Smith, in the 1937 issue of the *Outlook for the Blind* (a major journal of work for the blind): "While following the methods of industry to some extent, the sheltered workshops are not and never can be businesses or industries; the welfare of the client, and not profit, is the goal."[13]

Sheltered workshops had two secondary functions. They were expected to serve as laboratories for evaluating and training blind persons for placement in commercial industry; and they were expected to absorb blind men and women who were competent to work in commercial industry but who were unable to find jobs because of adverse economic conditions.

Displacement of Goals in Sheltered Workshops for the Blind

Insofar as their social service function is concerned, sheltered workshops appear to have been doomed from their inception. This was so for several reasons.

First, because of the fact that they were created in order to provide therapeutic activity for commercially unemployable blind adults, sheltered workshops were bound to operate at a deficit. Yet, workshop founders made no systematic provision for subsidizing these deficits. The question of who would pay the difference between costs and income was either ignored or brushed off as a mundane and practical problem which would somehow solve itself. As we will see shortly, the failure of sheltered workshops to find reliable and long term sources for subsidizing their operations was a major contributing factor to the displacement of their goals.

The programmed annual deficit of sheltered workshops was aggravated by a second fact. While workshops were not created for the same reasons that commercial factories are built, they were nevertheless subject to many of the same economic principles of supply and demand which operate upon commercial enterprises. A manufacturer does not ordinarily build a factory unless he has very sound reasons for believing that there is substantial demand for his product. If his judgment is correct, his operation will expand; if he is in error, his enterprise will be liquidated. The planning of sheltered workshops was not based on this line of reasoning. They started with the premise that a social service function could be fulfilled in a factory. The items which were to be manufactured had to be easy to produce because of the physical deficiencies of the workers. The selection of goods was further constrained by the fact that there was very little capital available for the purchase of equipment and inventories. The selection of goods to be produced in sheltered workshops was not, therefore, determined by their demand or market ability, but by the contingencies of a social service function and the absence of funds for capital investments. The sale of manufactured goods was, however, very much influenced by the principles of supply and demand. Workshops originally produced items such as brooms, mops, and caned chairs. The market for caned chairs was very small indeed; the market for brooms and mops was substantially larger, but the margin of profit was very slight. In their sales campaigns, workshops were therefore forced to emphasize the fact that the products were "blind-made" in the hope that by so doing, the charitable impulses of the public would prevail over their visible disinterest in the items produced. In general, this type of appeal did not succeed.

Third, even though sheltered workshops were supposed to be social service organizations, the general agencies for the blind of which they were usually a part, had to hire industrially trained individuals to run them. Workers for the blind simply did not have the "know-how" to set up and run an orderly manufacturing concern. The necessity for using qualified persons with industrial experience to manage the shops was heightened by the fact that standard broom and mop making equipment had to be modified in order to make them operable by a blind worker. This required engineering modifications, the design of special safety equipment, and the rearrangement of standard production line activities. Only a person with training and experience in industrial factories could successfully manage such an operation. Consequently, while the primary goal of workshops was social service to industrially unemployable blind adults, the persons who were hired to implement the goals were ones whose major interests and abilities were in the operation of industrial enterprises. This situation had a number of implications. For one thing, the authority to make operative policy decisions of all types, and especially those of pay, promotion, and standards of production, was placed in the hands of workshop managers who were guided by commercial, rather than social service standards. A worker's earnings were calculated on a piece rate basis. A pay incentive system was used so that the more a worker produced, the more he earned. A worker had to produce goods at a reasonable rate in order to make any money, or even to make his going to the workshop worthwhile in the first place. In addition, high standards of production were stressed at all times, some workers being "docked" for producing poorly made items. Moreover, workshop managers measured their success by commercial standards. Their challenge was to make sheltered workshops for the blind "going operations." While they seemed to adopt the abstract concept of work as therapy, their concrete policies were based on concepts and practices which govern commercial factories.

The incompatibilities contained in the basic concept of a factory as a social service organization ultimately resulted in the displacement of the goals of this program. The story of that process is as follows.

Directors of agencies for the blind and workshop managers attempted to make up annual deficits in a number of ways. Attempts were made to prevail upon state legislators to regularly subsidize the workshops. Though subsidies were occasionally made during the early years of the shops' operation, the idea of making a permanent annual appropriation to sheltered workshops was an idea which became increasingly unpopular among legislators. This arrangement was not always welcomed by the agency and workshop personnel either, since it required constant negotiations with the frugal and sometimes capricious politicians. Many workshops conducted annual fund raising campaigns to make up the difference, but this policy was quickly abandoned because it brought workshops into direct conflict with the fund raising activities of parent agencies. One commonly adopted policy was for workshops to charge a price higher than the fair market value of the items which they produced. This policy did help to offset some of the annual deficits, but from their inception in 1900 up through World War I, sheltered workshops resembled "shoe string" operations in every respect.

Despite these problems, sheltered workshops did make some modest progress toward implementing their goals. It was generally possible for a blind person of limited abilities to secure a position somewhere in a sheltered workshop; at the same time the energetic and resourceful efforts of those responsible for the placement of more capable blind persons in commercial industry made it possible for at least some blind persons to work "on the outside." Both the commercial placement and the sheltered workshop programs enjoyed moderate success and mutual cooperation up to, during, and shortly after World War I. The Depression, however, pretty thoroughly vitiated programs of commercial placement; at the same time, it had the effect of grossly magnifying all of the basic incompatibilities contained in the idea of a factory as a social service organization. The very existence of sheltered workshops for the blind was threatened during the Depression. The policies which workshop managers had to adopt in order to save the shops eventually resulted in a displacement of their goals. In addition, these policies subverted the goals of the commercial employment program, with the consequence that the sheltered workshops ultimately exacerbated the very problems which the entire employment program for the blind had been established to alleviate.

With the Depression employment opportunities for the blind collapsed. As unemployed blind workers began to flock to agencies for the blind for assistance, they were referred to workshops for whatever jobs they could get. The workshops, however, were no better off. The bottom had dropped out of the already limited market of their products, and they were unable to find new products which could be widely sold. The policy of relying upon the charitable impulses of the public as a means for selling products and for meeting deficits became impracticable. People no longer had extra income to buy brooms and mops out of sympathy for the blind. Former commercial consumers of blind-made products were themselves out of business or no longer in need of very many products of the workshops. The workshops, therefore, were caught in the center of a series of crosspressures. The market for their goods had declined at the same time that they were being pressured to find positions in the shops for those blind persons who were laid off in industry. In addition, as their annual deficits rose, it became more and more difficult to obtain public subsidy for them. Under these circumstances the workshop managers were forced to concentrate less upon providing social services to their employees, and more upon keeping the workshops in existence. The concern of the shops shifted from social service matters to a preoccupation with business affairs. The idea of employing incompetents was transformed from a cause to a luxury. Very basic economic problems had to be solved and solved quickly if the shops were not to close down completely.

In order to survive, it was essential for the workshops to find and ensure for themselves a dependable market for their goods. The effects of the Depression on sheltered workshops drove home a very basic lesson to their managers. It was that an industrial organization of this type could ill afford to rely upon the general public as its only outlet for goods. A more dependable and predictable consumer had to be found. It was in the federal government that workshop managers found their buyer. Through an intriguing lobbying process, workshop managers succeeded in having an economic platform constructed upon which existing sheltered workshops could begin to build. This platform was the Wagner-O'Day Act, which was passed by Congress and signed by the President in 1937. The act provided that "brooms and mops and other suitable commodities hereafter produced in accordance with applicable federal specifications by or for any Federal department or agency shall be produced from such non-profit making agencies for the blind."[14] A critical phrase in the wording of this act was "and other suitable commodities," for within six months of the bill's passage five additional commodities had been added to the list, and within a few years this number was increased to 32 items.[15] This act also became the model for 16 similar laws passed by state governments.

This legislation had the intended effect of guaranteeing the shops at least a minimum amount of business each year in standard inventory items such as mops and brooms. Since the government was now bound by law to buy the products that the shops made, so long as these products met its specifications, the shops had a guaranteed outlet for many more goods than just mops and brooms. It was now possible to diversify and expand operations, and consequently to fill up the deficit which the shops were annually running. The principal unintended effect of this legislation was brought about by the fact that the government expected the commodities of the workshops to meet minimum specifications and to be delivered according to a time schedule.[16] The consequence of these specifications was to make it necessary to employ competent and efficient workers. The specifications were such that only industrially competent workers were able to produce the items in the quantity and with the quality which were necessary for government orders. The employment of industrial incompetents, therefore, became increasingly impractical. Moreover, the workshops were forced to adopt a more stringent set of business principles. The acceptance of a government contract introduced a new predictability into the schedule of workshops. Managers could now begin to anticipate and plan production schedules as these came along. This in turn led them to run the shops in a more business-like fashion than ever before. Consequently, as a result of the Wagner-O'Day Act, the social service function for which the shops had originally been established was gradually pushed further and further into the background.

Dramatic evidence of this displacement is supplied by a report which was presented to the American Association of Workers for the Blind by the manager of a sheltered workshop in the New York metropolitan area. The data which were reported were responses to a questionnaire mailed out to 25 of the major workshops throughout the country. It inquired about the policies of the management concerning matters of employment and business. It was reported that "the consensus of opinion of 25 employers of blind workers is that the maximum age at which workers should be hired should be set at 45 with an outside limit of 50 for exceptional men and women. When we take into consideration the months and even years that it takes to train a blind person to be a top notch producer, we realize that any higher age limit would tend *to reduce the years of usefulness to the workshop to such an extent that it might well be a losing proposition.*"[17] (emphasis added) The report went on, "Still another strong argument for *eliminating the incompe-*

tents from our shops is the breakdown in morale of the whole force which is sure to follow if these incompetents are allowed to remain."[18] (emphasis added) One can see emerging in this report a striking tendency toward giving precedence to what is good for the workshops over the managers' avowed responsibility to the group of people for whom the workshops were established as a social service.

The report states that the operation of the workshop should be governed by strict business standards—efficiency, production, and cost. Only competent workers should be employed. Some managers pointed to the possibility "that the saving effected in reduced costs of operation will allow for the establishment of auxiliary craftshops in which the less skilled and less competent workers may be given employment and in which they might at least be partially self-supporting."[19] Though this suggestion was followed by some agencies, the savings made by the workshops were more often used to expand the workshops than to create special craftshops.

The strength of these sentiments is revealed in some of the correspondence which accompanied the questionnaires which had been sent out. One manager observed, "We are anxious to improve the character of workers and do away with the idea that our shop is a retreat for unemployable blind who foment trouble and do not want to produce anything."[20] Another person took the position that "the blind who are physically and mentally unable to produce sufficiently to take care of their needs should not be employed in a workshop whose *main object is producing marketable merchandise*."[21] (emphasis added) The implications of this position are that the shop should *employ industrial competents,* i.e., the persons who in ordinary times worked in commercial industry. The seed of a nasty conflict between advocates of workshops and advocates of commercial employment for the blind was planted at this time.

These sentiments of workshop managers were accompanied by a belief that anything that improved the economic position of the workshops was acceptable. The extremes to which this view was taken are revealed in a speech given by Mr. S. S. Catell to workshop managers at the 1935 AAWB meeting. Mr. Catell asked the following question of shop managers, "Would it be advisable for this shop to employ a few extra broom makers *who have normal vision,* at times, when needed, to enable the shop to take larger orders, fill them promptly, and give better satisfaction to customers? The shops would then make a special effort to secure larger orders resulting in more employment for the blind worker."[22] (emphasis added) Mr. Catell was not alone in proposing this idea. Others had mentioned this matter in the report, "In the consideration of the question of who shall be employed in sheltered work-shops, some thought an investigation should be given to the hiring of more sighted workers in our shops. . . . Those who have put this policy into practice say that production is speeded up, costs are kept down, and more blind workers can be put to work."[23]

In the first few years after its passage, the Wagner-O'Day Act had only a modest impact upon the amount of business which was done by the workshops. In 1939, for example, government orders accounted for only about ten percent of the total business of workshops participating in the program. It was assumed that this figure might increase some-what, but that it would probably never exceed 20 to 25 percent of total production. The lobbyists for this preferential legislation failed to an-ticipate World War II, and the enormous increase in demands by the government for workshop produced goods.

Within the four-year period 1940–43, eighty percent of all busi-ness done by sheltered workshops for the blind was devoted to filling government orders.[24] During that period the government business with the shops amounted to more than 17 million dollars. Moreover, increased industrial demands, coupled with the generally favorable economic conditions which were brought about by the war resulted in over eight million dollars in additional sales. In a period of a few years, sheltered workshops were transformed from social service organizations to big businesses.[25]

The Consequences of Goal Displacement

The fact that operative policies subverted the official goals of sheltered workshops for the blind had two principal consequences. The first re-lated to the original problem which led workers for the blind to estab-lish a formal employment program for blind persons; the second related to the belief systems of workers for the blind about the blind and about the general public.

The economic boom during the war years, which brought about an acceleration of business for sheltered workshops, had additional con-sequences for employment opportunities for the blind. When World War II erupted, there was an acute labor shortage in the country. Em-ployers sought every able man and woman for work in factories, shops, and industrial plants in order to meet production orders. Consequently, many opportunities developed for the commercial employment of blind workers.[26]

These circumstances provided an opportunity for workshops to give consideration to their original function of providing social services to commercially unemployable blind persons. The market for goods was now guaranteed; there were plenty of commercial employment opportunities for the able-bodied blind; and general economic conditions would have made it comparatively simple to raise funds in order to overcome the deficits the workshops would inevitably run. The workshops did not follow this course.

Faced with the prospects of expanded orders for merchandise from federal and state governments, and with an improved commercial market for blind-made products, the workshops began to increase their production, drawing upon the pool of skilled and competent blind workers who had come to them during the Depression. The changing conditions were reflected in the enthusiastic statements of workshop managers concerning the business prospects of the workshops. In 1941 one manager told AAWB members, "Our workshops are now engaged in big business, and they should conduct their business in accordance with the same principles as those observed in the management of private commercial enterprise."[27] Discussions at the 1941 and 1943 conventions of the American Association of Workers for the Blind largely consisted of suggestions of ways to implement formal procedures for running the workshops as "big business." One manager was moved to comment, "I want to come directly to the special significance which with the advent of war has come to the workshops for the blind. In a sense, it is a rather curious significance; curious in that it is new to the workshops, and perhaps as yet a bit unfamiliar. But it is also a great thing, and it may be summarized in these five words: you are doing 'big business.'"[28]

Despite the generally improved conditions there nevertheless remained a disparity between production and sales. In an attempt to remedy this disparity, the services of sales experts were retained. At no point, however, did workshops have more orders than they could fill.

It seems reasonable to assume that if the shops were outproducing the markets, and there were employment opportunities for the blind in commercial industry, that workshop managers would encourage their better workers to get jobs on "the outside." If the essential problem of the workshops was the sale of their items, and not their production, one could adjust the balance of production and sales by encouraging the better workers to leave. This consideration, coupled with the philosophy which originally brought the sheltered workshops into being, leads us to ask: What efforts did agency personnel and workshop managers make to find jobs for their more productive employees? What attitude did they take toward skilled blind men and women leaving for "outside jobs"?

A characteristic attitude (in terms of the considerable support it received) was expressed by one placement manager who remarked,

"Without question, I am sure that the primary purpose of every worker for the blind is consideration for the welfare of his client. This being true, every effort should be made to secure for the client the type of work for which he is best fitted and which provides the greatest remuneration. One of the fundamental principles of economics is that labor always seeks the highest bidder for its service—this is true of the blind as well as the sighted worker. We cannot, therefore, *blame the blind worker when he deserts the sheltered workshop for more lucrative employment* . . . . In my capacity as Placement Manager, I am responsible not only for the placement of workers in private industry, but the employment of blind labor in the various departments of our own workshop, as well as in our concession stands. It is true *we have lost a number of our best workers to private industry,* but there has not been a general exodus such as that experienced in other cities and which has had such a crippling effect upon workshops, especially those engaged in filling Government orders."[29] (emphasis added)

National Industries for the Blind (NIB) itself was constantly being approached by industrialists making requests for skilled and able-bodied blind men and women. In relation to these requests the President of NIB gave the following statement of policy, "Of late there has been much discussion regarding the placement of the blind in private industry. This is a service which should be provided by the individual agencies, and it is up to each to formulate its own policies in this connection. Any inquiries which we receive relating to placement are always referred back to the agency in the territory from which the inquiry came. We have tried to devote our efforts strictly to the field of production and merchandising of blind-made products, and we expect to continue this policy in the future."[30] This ostrich-like stance assured NIB that its supply of skilled workmen would go untouched since the only men the agencies could offer were newly blinded persons who were untrained in industrial work. It is clear that the attitude expressed above, which was shared by a considerable number of other workers for the blind, mitigated against the placement, by the agencies, of blind workers in commercial industry.[31]

In short, the fundamental incompatibility contained in the idea of a factory as a social service organization was grossly exaggerated by the economic upheaval of the 1930's. The existence of the workshops was threatened by the Depression, so that managers were forced to adopt policies which ultimately led the workshops to prosper, but which also subverted their official purpose. The operative policies which were instituted in order to preserve the shops also had the effect of vitiating the primary objective of employment of the blind in commercial industry, and of exacerbating the conditions which were responsible for the establishment of the employment programs in the first place.

The second consequence of the developing discrepancy between official and operative goals was that belief systems of workers for the blind changed so that by the end of World War II, the basic notions which were expressed about blind persons (i.e., what they needed, what they wanted, how to alleviate their plight) were different from, and often contradicted the beliefs of the pioneers of employment programs for the blind.

The first fact to be recognized is that the original, official goals of employment programs, as these were stated in the early 1900's, remained the official goals through this entire process, and continue to serve this function at the present time.[32] Even during the period when sheltered workshops were enjoying their greatest expansion, workshop managers and others continued to espouse the original and official doctrines of integration of the blind with the sighted in work settings, and of the virtues of such commercial employment. For example, the Director of the Office of Vocational Rehabilitation (a federally sponsored program for retraining handicapped persons for employment), in a major address before the AAWB convention of 1941, stated that "In view of the present emergency in which employers are clamoring for qualified workers, there is presented to all rehabilitation workers, and especially to the workers in the field of work for the blind, not only a golden opportunity, but also a challenge to do their part in seeing that every blind person, who is or can be made employable, finds his proper place in our efforts to meet the defense needs of our nation."[33] These sentiments were accepted and restated by many others who were centrally concerned with employment of the blind. The discussions of special sections on commercial and workshop employment at AAWB conventions from the time of the Depression through the end of World War II suggest a widespread recognition of the fact that operative policies were not entirely in keeping with the official objectives for which employment programs were established. The frequency with which such discussions occurred and the spirited rehashing of old issues underscored the fact that workers at that time were experiencing the strains which were the products of goal discrepancies.[34]

One of the ways in which these strains were minimized was through a gradual change in beliefs of employment specialists, and most especially workshop managers, concerning the blind, the sighted, and employment problems of the blind. These changes were related to two general issues.

First, beliefs about the desirability of integration of the blind into work settings with sighted persons gradually began to change. At the beginning of this movement there was wholehearted endorsement of the idea of integration of the blind, with an elaborate set of accompanying notions about the ways in which blind and sighted persons would benefit from working together. The proceedings of AAWB meetings of the 1900–1920's reflect these beliefs in many ways. In addition to abstract and highly emotional statements of the integration philosophy, individual workers who had obtained employment in commercial establishments were invited to give testimonial statements as to the virtues of their positions. These were supplemented with statements of the experiences of commercial placement specialists.[35]

These beliefs began to undergo changes as the effects of the Depression were felt by the workshops. More and more one heard it said that while integration was a noble ideal, its applicability varied from blind person to blind person; and that there were always going to be some blind persons for whom integration was simply undesirable.[36] During and after the war, these beliefs were further transformed, so that workers were now arguing that while there was no doubt that integration was desirable for some blind workers, a majority of the blind were simply happier with their own kind. The most complete statement of this view was expressed by the manager of one of the largest sheltered workshops for the blind in the country, who compared the virtue of employment in sheltered workshops to those in commercial industry. He stated, "In the well-organized blind workshops, year round employment is practically assured, whereas in commercial industry employment quite often is seasonal, and in the case of labor curtailment, the blind worker, being less versatile, is very apt to be the first to go. The efficiently managed workshop . . . can afford to pay higher piece work rates or day labor rates for the work performed, thus offsetting in a measure, the handicap of the individual. In sighted industry, by comparison, the blind individual would have to adapt himself to the equipment at hand and accept the prevailing rate of pay. In an industrial workshop the blind worker is competing at his own level so that when he does a better job than his fellow worker, it gives him a definite lift to know that he can improve himself, increase his earning power and perhaps eventually take over a job with greater responsibility. Everything in a well-organized workshop is created to minimize the blind individual's handicap. The staff has been trained to deal with blind people. In most cases, the workers are collectively producing completed articles which are sold under the agency's label. He can, therefore, take a just pride in the things he creates. By contrast, as an employee among sighted workers, his handicap must be brought home to him in many ways—in his contacts with co-workers, in the equipment he uses, in the facilities of the factory, etc. Unquestionably, in many cases he realizes that he is just plainly being tolerated."[37] One way in which the strains created by the disparity between official and operative goals in sheltered workshops were minimized was therefore to change beliefs about what employment arrangements blind persons needed or preferred to make.

A second change which occurred related to beliefs about how sighted persons, and especially sighted employers, felt about the blind. Initially, the blind took the view that sighted individuals were kindly but misled persons whose misconceptions could be erased if they were taught the "true facts" about the blind. These beliefs were manifested in the content of AAWB programs during the first two or three decades of this century. Employers who had agreed to hire blind workers were invited to discuss their experiences; employment specialists described the success with which they had applied the "hard sell" to factory owners; and the view of blind employees about their treatment at the hands of sighted employers were also solicited. The views of workers for the blind toward the sighted were generally favorable and forgiving; no one questioned the fact that most sighted employers could be re-educated in exactly the same way and with the same success that most sighted workers for the blind had been re-educated.[38]

This view of the public and of its attitude toward the employment of the blind changed over the years. The idea began to emerge that the public in general, and employers in particular, were abysmally ignorant about the condition of blindness and of the way in which it affected individuals. There emerged over time the notion that there was in the mind of a sighted person a stereotype of the blind. This stereotype consisted of a complex set of erroneous ideas, such as the notion that the blind lived in darkness, or that they were gifted in special but undefined ways, or that they were evil, or alternatively that they were good and noble. These ideas acted as barriers which directly impeded the efforts of commercial employment specialists to place blind workers in industry. It was, therefore, the stereotype of the blind which accounted for the discrepancy between official and operative goals.[39]

There is no doubt that the stubborn, and often irrational, fears and misconceptions about blindness among sighted individuals had a sobering effect upon those who first tried to obtain industrial positions for blind persons. Many employers rejected out of hand the idea of hiring a blind person, without giving workers for the blind so much as an opportunity to present their case. Others agreed to give blind persons a chance, but then reneged at the last moment. These bitter experiences suggested that stereotypic ideas about the blind were indeed real barriers to their placement in commercial industry.

It is not the presence or absence of a stereotype which is at issue, but rather the extent of its pervasiveness. Over the years, workers for the blind have developed an increasingly rigid and elaborate conception about how sighted persons view the blind. The idea has emerged that sighted persons are unenlightened individuals, whose rigid and erroneous ideas are simply unchangeable. In fact, however, the research evidence throws this whole conception into some considerable doubt. Studies by Lukoff and Whiteman[40] and by Paske and Weiss[41] have shown that there are individual stereotypic ideas which are held by some, but not all, sighted persons; but that the idea of a stereotype of the blind, in the sense of an aggregate of misconceptions, simply does not exist. That there are particular stereotypic ideas about the blind is clear; it is equally clear that these ideas are not nearly so pervasive, elaborate, and rigid as workers for the blind would have us believe them to be.

One explanation for the development of increasingly unrealistic ideas about the feelings of sighted persons toward the blind is that such beliefs served to minimize the strains which accompanied the discrepancies between official and operative goals. By convincing themselves, and others, of the existence of the stereotype, it was possible for workers for the blind to account to themselves and others for the disparities between their official goals and the effects of the day to day policies which they made. In short, they argued that commercially employable blind persons had to be placed in sheltered workshops because commercial employers refused to hire them.

Summary

This article has described an instance of goal displacement and analyzed two consequences which this process has had. The first concerned the effects of goal discrepancies upon the original problem of employment of the blind; and the second concerned the implications of these discrepancies for the belief systems of workers for the blind about the blind, the feelings of the general public toward the blind, and the best means by which to resolve the plight of the blind. Changes in these belief systems were interpreted as responses to ideological strains which were created by discrepancies between official and operative goals.

Notes

1. Various aspects of this general tendency have been described in the following works: Amitai Etzioni, *Modern Organizations,* Englewood Cliffs, N.J.: Prentice Hall, Inc., 1964, pp. 10–14; Peter Blau and W. Richard Scott, *Formal Organizations,* San Francisco: Chandler, 1962, p. 229; Sheldon Messinger, "Orga-

nizational Transformation: A Case Study of a Declining Social Movement," *American Sociological Review*, 20 (Feb., 1955), pp. 3–10; Philip Selznick, *TVA and the Grass Roots*, Berkeley: University of California Press, 1949, Chapters 1, 2, and especially page 13; Charles Perrow, "The Analysis of Goals in Complex Organizations," *American Sociological Review*, 26 (Dec., 1961), pp. 854–866.

2. Robert Michels, *Political Parties*, Glencoe, Ill.: Free Press, 1949; Philip Selznick, *op. cit.*

3. Sheldon Messinger, *op. cit.*

4. Robert K. Merton, *Social Theory and Social Structure*, Glencoe, Ill.: Free Press, 1957, pp. 195–206.

5. Burton R. Clark, "Organizational Adaptation and Precarious Values," *American Sociological Review*, 21 (June, 1956), pp. 327–336.

6. The alternatives described in the following discussion, and the fundamental logic upon which the discussion itself is based, are parallel to the basic formulations of dissonance theory in social psychology. See: Leon Festinger, *A Theory of Cognitive Dissonance*, Evanston, Ill.: Row, Peterson, 1957.

7. For history of employment programs in this field, see: C. Esco Obermann, *A History of Vocational Rehabilitation in America*, Minneapolis: T. S. Denison and Co., Inc., 1965, especially Chapters 1, 2, and 10.

8. *AAWB Proceedings*, 1905, p. 32.

9. *AAWB Proceedings*, 1905, p. 33.

10. *AAWB Proceedings*, 1905, p. 33.

11. For additional statements of this philosophy in the 1900's, see: *Outlook for the Blind*, April, 1907, pp. 10–12; *AAWB Proceedings*, 1907, p. 101; 1920's and 1930's, see: *Outlook for the Blind*, April, 1919, p. 13; *Outlook for the Blind*, March, 1926, pp. 56–59; *Outlook for the Blind*, September, 1931, p. 83. For more recent statements of this philosophy, see: *AAWB Proceedings*, 1950, p. 59; *AAWB Proceedings*, 1962, p. 186.

12. The minimum wage paid was ordinarily quite low and did not correspond to minimum wage levels established by federal legislation.

13. John N. Smith, *Outlook for the Blind*, October, 1937, pp. 105–106.

14. Quoted from statement of this law which appeared in the *AAWB Proceedings*, 1939, p. 145.

15. *AAWB Proceedings*, 1948, p. 17.

16. These requirements were explained to workshop managers by Mr. C. C. Kleber, President of National Industries for the Blind, at the 1939 AAWB meeting as follows, "Practically every article purchased by the Federal departments is covered by a set of rigid specifications and it is of the utmost importance that these specifications be met in every detail before we can hope to supply any particular article." *AAWB Proceedings*, 1939, p. 92.

17. *AAWB Proceedings*, 1935, p. 83.

18. *AAWB Proceedings*, 1935, p. 82.

19. *AAWB Proceedings*, 1935, p. 84.

20. *AAWB Proceedings*, 1935, p. 92.

21. *AAWB Proceedings*, 1935, p. 92.

22. *AAWB Proceedings*, 1935, p. 191.

23. *AAWB Proceedings*, 1935, pp. 83–84.

24. *AAWB Proceedings*, 1943, p. 18.

25. For additional information regarding the amount of business workshops did for the federal government, see: *AAWB Proceedings*, 1947, p. 78.

26. See, for example, Hector Chevigny and Sydell Braverman, *Adjustment to Blindness*, New Haven: Yale University Press, 1950, p. 278; *AAWB Proceedings*, 1941, p. 61; *AAWB Proceedings*, 1943, p. 26.

27. *AAWB Proceedings*, 1941, pp. 17–18.

28. *Outlook for the Blind*, April, 1942, p. 121.

29. *AAWB Proceedings*, 1943, p. 124.

30. *AAWB Proceedings*, 1943, p. 58.

31. Hector Chevigny, *op. cit.*, pp. 278–279.

32. For evidence of this point, see citations listed in footnote 5.

33. *AAWB Proceedings*, 1941, p. 60.

34. See, for example: *AAWB Proceedings*, 1933, pp. 18–26, 42–46, 85–89, 122–127, 185–191, 232–236; *AAWB Proceedings*, 1935, pp. 45–50, 80–117, 223–252, 262. *AAWB Proceedings*, 1937, pp. 66–72, 73–75, 76–82, 138–139, 156–162, 180; *AAWB Proceedings*, 1939, 21, 37–45, 50–55, 214–216, 222–227, 251–256; *AAWB Proceedings*, 1941, pp. 14–18, 96–100, 130–131.

35. See, for example: *Outlook for the Blind*, 1907, pp. 18, 81, 100; *Outlook for the Blind*, 1908, pp. 10–53; *Outlook for the Blind*, 1909, pp. 156–172; *Outlook for the Blind*, 1911, pp. 4–7, 27–30; *Outlook for the Blind*, 1913, pp. 24–28; *Outlook for the Blind*, 1915, pp. 24–27, 48–51.

36. See, for example; *AAWB Proceedings*, 1941, pp. 96–101; *AAWB Proceedings*, 1939, pp. 222–228, 251–256; *AAWB Proceedings*, 1937, pp. 161–171.

37. *AAWB Proceedings*, 1950, pp. 68–69.

38. See citations listed in footnote 35.

39. For statements of the content of these stereotypes, see: Joseph S. Himes, Jr., "Some Concepts of Blindness in American Culture," in *Attitudes Toward Blindness*, New York: American Foundation for the Blind, 1951, pp. 10–22; Alan Gowman, *War Blind in American Social Structure*, New York; American Foundation for the Blind, 1957, Chap. 3.

40. Irving F. Lukoff and Martin Whiteman, *Attitudes and Blindness: Components, Correlates and Effects*, mimeo, 1963, especially Chapters 11, 12.

41. Victor Paske and Walter Weiss, *Fritidsun Der Sogelsen*, mimeo, Copenhagen, 1965.

Universities as Organizations: a Research Approach

Edward Gross

Universities are usually not viewed as formal organizations. The extant literature in the field (Riesman, 1958; Knapp and Goodrich, 1952; Knapp and Greenbaum, 1953; Barton, 1961a; Corson, 1960; Capen, 1953; Woodburne, 1958) tends to see them in one or both of two major ways: (1) as

Excerpted from *American Sociological Review* 33 (August, 1968): 518–44.

institutions, that is as being concerned with performing something essential for the society, such as educating the youth, passing on the cultural heritage, providing lines of upward mobility, and the like; (2) as communities, that is, as providing "homes" or "atmospheres" in which persons may set their own goals, such as self-fulfillment, the pursuit of truth, the dialogue at the two ends of the log,[1] and other traditional ivory-tower values. It is those who follow this latter view who feel disturbed at the "intrusion" of government money into the presumably sacred confines of the university, sacred referring here to the value of "disinterested pursuit of the truth."

However, neither of these two approaches seems to have told us much about the university, though they often reveal how professors and administrators in the university feel. Apart from the sheer paucity of research, our view is that a part of the reason is that much of what goes on in universities is not "caught" by either model, though they each explain some things. Perhaps, it was our judgment, light might be shed on universities by seeing them as organizations. In so doing, we do not mean to imply that this model should supplant the others, for a single-minded view of universities as "bureaucracies" (Cf. Stroup, 1966) is as one-sided as viewing them only as institutions or only as communities. This article is an attempt to test the usefulness of an organizational model in accounting for structural variables in universities.

Nature of the Organizational Model[2]

As Parsons (1960, chap. 1 and 1961, pp. 38–41) has noted, the distinctive feature of organizations that marks them off from other kinds of social systems is that the problem of goal attainment has primacy over all other problems. It is not the presence of a goal (or goals) as such, since all social systems will have, from time to time, goals of various kinds, but rather that the system's adequacy is judged in terms of its relative success in attaining or moving toward the goal, or its state of "readiness" to move toward or orient itself toward such a goal (Cf. Georgopoulos and Tannenbaum, 1957; Price, 1968.). The polar concept is that of "community," illustrated by such systems as a group of friends, a set of colleague peers, a gang, or a nuclear family. Such a group may develop goals (attacking another gang, having a baby) but even if it fails in the attainment of those goals, the group does not necessarily break up. It does break up when hostilities or cleavages mean that persons are no longer at home in one another's presence. On the other hand, in organizations, any failure in goal attainment (however much the members may enjoy one another's company) throws the whole system into jeopardy.[3] Of course the use of a systems approach hardly implies any lesser centrality of organizational goals, for it is through goal attainment (or the claim that such is its intent) that the organization translates its inputs into outputs, or at least legitimizes its right to operate and to call on the society for its inputs.

In spite of the central importance of "goal" in organizations, it is surprising how little attention has been given to developing a clear definition of what is meant by "goal" (Simon, 1964). Etzioni (1964, p. 6) defines an organizational goal as "a desired state of affairs which the organization attempts to realize." But this definition immediately raises the question, pointed to by many, of *whose* state of affairs it is that is desired. Theoretically, there could be as many desired states for the organization as there are persons in it, if not more. What appear to be goals from the point of view of the top administrators may not be goals at all from the point of view of those further down.

But even before one can talk about different perceptions of organizational goals, it is essential to distinguish private from organizational goals. A private goal consists of a future state that the individual desires for himself. Such a notion comes close to the psychologist's conception of a motive. This meaning may be distinguished from what a particular person desires *for the organization as a whole* (Cartwright and Zander, 1953, pp. 308–311). The latter comes closer to the notion of an organizational goal, although it still consists of something that the particular person wishes and may not at all correspond to the organization's goals. Further, it still leaves open the question of how one is to determine an organization's goals when there are differences of opinion. In a small organization there may not be much difficulty, for there the top man's personal goals for the organization *are* the organization's goals. It is this simplification which made it possible for classical economics to develop the theory of the firm (as a "person") without being concerned much about developing a precise definition of organizational goal which was any different than the goal of the entrepreneur. The firms that the classical economists were talking about were in the main small ones which had essentially no greater problem to solve than decide what price to sell its product at and how many units to produce for the market. Once organizations grow large, one must be concerned with the possibility that there will be many persons in a position to influence the goals of the organization (Cf. Cyert and March, 1963, chap. 3). In the case of ideological organizations, where personal values coincide, there may be a close correspondence between private goals for the organization and group goals. Yet in general one cannot assume that private and group goals will coincide. In fact in the typical case it is safe to say that they will not. It is consequently necessary to offer a person an inducement to participate (March and Simon, 1958, chap. 4), so that he attains his personal goal through the group goal of the organization. That is, when the organization attains its group goal, means are provided for taking care of the personal goals of the persons in it so that they will then be motivated to participate. They must be motivated to participate to the extent that they will give up their personal goals (for the moment) for the organization as a whole should these differ from organizational goals. Nevertheless in order to avoid any reification of the concept, it is necessary to emphasize that goals will always exist in the minds of certain persons. That is to say, although an organization goal is not the same thing as a personal goal nor necessarily the same as the goal that a particular person desires for an organization (as distinct from what he desires for himself), it certainly would seem that one kind of evidence on the nature of organization goals would consist of the statements of particular persons attesting what they thought the organization's goals were.

Thompson and McEwen (1958) and Parsons (1960, p. 17) have attempted to define goals in terms of system linkages. Both have seen a goal as involving some type of output to a larger society. In this sense organizations are always subsystems of larger systems, the goal of one subsystem being a means or input of a different subsystem. In the simplest case the production of automobile batteries is a goal to the firm that manufactures them but will be a means or input to an automobile manufacturing firm. Such an approach has the great value of emphasizing the need to relate organizations to one another and to the surrounding society.[4] Furthermore, when goals are defined in this manner, it becomes clear that those within organizations have only a limited amount of freedom to set the goals of the organization. They will be constrained by what outsiders can be persuaded to accept. On the other hand such an emphasis may tend to underestimate the contribution that rational decision-makers within organizations make in choosing the goals of organizations rather than being limited to the demands of the market.[5] A more serious limitation of the output approach follows from the fact that organizations have a great many outputs, both intended and unintended, many of which will be no different than functions or consequences. It becomes a problem to single out certain kinds of outputs as *the* goals of the organization. The importance of by-products in industrial organizations should alert the investigator to the danger here.

In spite of the strictures we have suggested on the definitions offered thus far, there is no doubt that they all touch on the elements of a definition of goals. Goals will exist in someone's mind and they will involve the relationship between an organization and the situation in which it is implicated.

An important contribution has been made by Etzioni (1964, pp. 16–19), in a work in which he criticizes the goal approach to the study of organizations as being too limited. To define an organization solely in terms of its goal and therefore to judge its effectiveness in terms of its degree of success in obtaining that goal is to doom the investigator to disappointment. The "metaphysical pathos" to which Gouldner (1961) has called attention—namely the pessimism of those who see men doomed forever to disappointment in their organizational hopes— Etzioni sees as being due to expecting too much. Few organizations succeed in attaining their goals to the degree that those in them will wish they could be attained. One typically must settle for a good deal less and the leaders of organizations, their hopes high, would seem to be always expecting more than they will ever receive. Rather than seeing these limited results as a consequence of man's inherent limitations or as the basis for a sad romantic lament on man's smallness in the face of his large goals, Etzioni takes the view that the definition itself may be at fault. He compares organizations to electric lights and other types of mechanical equipment which may have very low efficiencies. Much of the energy may be lost in heat. Nevertheless no one expresses great concern but rather compares one mechanical gadget to another, and discovers that one may be twice as efficient as another even though it is only 10 percent efficient, compared to the other which is 5 percent efficient.

The Problem of Support and Maintenance

Etzioni's analogy calls attention to a basic fact about organizations of all kinds: no organization can spend all of its energies on goal attainment. At least some of these energies, and perhaps a great deal, must be spent on activities which cannot easily (if at all) be shown to be contributing to goal attainment.

One of the first to point this out was Bales (1958) in his studies of task-oriented small groups under laboratory conditions. He found that two major sets of processes were in operation in these groups. The groups, on being assigned a particular task or goal, would typically begin by giving their attention to the most efficient way of moving towards that goal, which consisted of solutions to various problems which he posed to them. Very early, however, it was discovered that other kinds of activities began to make their appearance. When someone would make a proposal that a given approach be tried, others had to agree, disagree, or take no stand, and this activity began to divide the group on the basis of their estimates of the most worthwhile procedures. The consequence of such cleavage was the development of feelings toward one another or toward the solutions proposed, irritation at not having one's own views taken properly into account, as well as ordinary fatigue. It became necessary, Bales found, for the group to stop its goal-directed activity and give some attention to repairing the social damage that was being done as the group attempted to move towards the solution of the problem. A kind of "maintenance" activity was necessary, with certain persons assuming the role of "maintenance engineers," as it were, in giving attention to what Bales came to speak of as "social-emotional" needs. Such needs might be taken care of in a phase manner or in other ways. It has of course been the experience of persons who have worked with conference groups and other kinds of task-oriented groups that some time must always be given to such maintenance activities. For example, all have noticed the tendency of many meetings to begin with informal chit-chat, and to end with laughter or other kinds of activities which are related to solidarity or to satisfaction of various kinds of personal needs.

The paradox may be stated as follows: an organization must do more than give attention to goal attainment in order to attain its goals. A useful approach is that suggested by the Parsonian functional imperatives (Parsons, 1961). Whether one is prepared to agree that these and no other imperatives exist, they do represent an attempt, based on Bales' work as a matter of fact, to state a set of conditions necessary for system survival. As such they apply directly to organizations. It is noteworthy that only one of the system imperatives is goal attainment. The names given to the other imperatives are, as is now widely known, adaptation, integration, and pattern-maintenance and tension management. The import of these categories is that a good part of any system's energies must be given over to activities that do not contribute in any direct sense to goal attainment but rather are concerned essentially with maintaining the system itself.[6]

However, it does not carry one far to seek to dispose of such energies as "used up" in a manner analogous to wasted smoke coming out the stack of a steam engine, for such a view is the very one Etzioni is criticizing. It is true that some of the energy of participants is given over to support or maintenance activities. But it is also the case that such activities may, in the minds of participants, still constitute organizational goals in every sense of the term. An example is the problem of what to do with profit or money as a goal of a business. On the one hand, it is hard to imagine a discussion of the goals of a business which could go on for very long without the importance of making money being brought up as, obviously, "why we are in business." However, as Parsons (1960) has pointed out, an organization cannot legitimize its existence in society simply by making money: it must do something for the society, i.e., produce some kind of output which can be exchanged for money (or which can be used as a claim for tax or philanthropic money.) In one sense, one could insist that "money" is the means used to buy the inputs necessary to produce the output. On the other hand, one could insist that the output (or product) is the means used to get the money, which is what the enterprise is about to begin with. In our view, Etzioni (1958:309) probably offers the best solution to this dilemma when he defines economic organizations as "those whose primary aim is to produce goods and services, to exchange them, or to organize and manipulate monetary processes."

We would generalize his solution to all organizations: money is only one kind of support or maintenance activity. Any support or maintenance activity can be a goal of an organization. For the university, take the case of one activity which we designated (in our research) as a possible organization goal as follows: "Ensure the continued confidence and hence support of those who contribute substantially (other than students and recipients of services) to the finances and other material resource needs of the university." Such a goal may be ranked moderately high in a great many universities and there may be considerable agreement that it deserves this ranking. Persons may decide that this goal is a moderately important one by statements which they hear, by statements made in the catalogue or other publications of the university, by the activities of certain members of the administration and perhaps by the general concern of the faculty and others to so behave in public situations as to "represent the university" in an honorable manner. Persons who engage in behavior which secures unfavorable public attention may be criticized by their colleagues as threatening the likelihood of attaining this goal. We cannot see any useful purpose served by insisting that this goal is, after all, a *means* which enables the university to then pursue its "output" goals. This is, of course, true but it is no less a goal for all that. Deliberate attention is given to it for the entire university and the university must move toward it in the same way as it moves toward its goal of giving direct service or teaching students. The same will be true of such possible goals as "making sure that the university is run democratically," "protecting the faculty's right to academic freedom," and even "maintaining the character of the university." Indeed, the claim could be that some obvious goals are only means themselves. For instance, only by producing students with certain skills (a goal) can the university continue to "maintain its character." The latter might be considered the more basic goal.

We think that the reason for possible confusion here is that it is often assumed that only a goal which is reflected in some visible or operationally definable output deserves the name "goal." It is of course true, as Downs (1967) points out, that ideological elements often get so intimately intertwined with organizational goal statements as to make such statements relatively dubious or even useless as operational guides in the definition of organizational procedures. Hence, it is more dependable to look for specific outputs that can be pointed to as evidence of what the organization is really doing, whatever it says it is doing. However, there remain goal activities which are still goals, even though it is difficult to assign or point to outputs. Their goal character is attested by the simple fact that participants talk about them as intentions for the future of the organization, and they go ahead and try to realize those intentions. Whether they succeed often requires, for test, further

TABLE 1

Sample Goal Question

One of the great issues in American education has to do with the proper aims or goals of the university. The question is: What are we trying to accomplish? Are we trying to prepare people for jobs, to broaden them intellectually, or what? Below we have listed a large number of the more commonly claimed aims, intentions or goals of a university. We would like you to react to each of these in two different ways:

(1) How important *is* each aim at this university?
(2) How important *should* the aim be at this university?

Example: to serve as substitute parents		of abso- lutely top impor- tance	of great impor- tance	of medium impor- tance	of little impor- tance	of no impor- tance	don't know or can't say
	Is	☐	☐	☒	☐	☐	☐
	Should Be	☐	☐	☐	☐	☒	☐

A person who had marked the alternatives in the manner shown above would be expressing his perception that the aim, intention or goal, "to serve as substitute parents," *is* of medium importance at his university but that he believes it should be of no importance as an aim, intention, or goal of his university.

NOTE: "of absolutely top importance" should only be checked if the aim is *so* important that, if it were to be removed, the university would be shaken to its very roots and its character changed in a fundamental way.

verbal statements, or perhaps rather vague products, such as "the image of the organization."

In our conceptual work, we speak of goals which admit of clear outputs as "output goals." For the university, these involve the usual goals of teaching, research and community service (further subdivided, as shown below). Those which do not involve clear outputs turn out to be what we speak of as "support goals." These involve a variety of activities designed to help the organization survive in its environment, those activities which ensure that the university is run in desired ways, those designed to ensure motivated participation, and those designed to ensure the university's position in the population of universities. Further, we found it useful to list a large number of goals, assuming that all of them would be present at a given university but in differing degrees. The extent of emphasis on given goals would be our measure of the importance of that goal at a university.

Defining a University's Goals

A serious problem in studying any organization's goals is that of devising a way of describing them that will avoid the usual tendency of participants to "gloss" their own organization's goals (the confounding of ideologcal elements, as mentioned above), as well as get some measure of degree of emphasis (rather than the common assumption that something either is or is not an organization goal). For the case of the university, we wanted, furthermore, a measure which was not dependent on specific measurable outputs (which, as noted previously, are only available for some goals). Our solution was the use of the model indicated by the sample question in Table 1.

The special features of this approach are: (1) it does not ask the subject to volunteer a goal statement himself. Hence it is possible to measure degree of consensus on a particular goal statement. Asking the subject to compose a verbal statement invites the "ideological confounding" referred to above. (2) It keeps separate the subject's *perception* of what is from his feelings about what should be. It asks the respondents to serve as informants as it were, and tells the investigators how they see the university separately from the question of how they would like it to be. These are not entirely separate, of course, but it was our feeling that degree of consensus would constitute a partial control on such biases. We decided to include a goal only if the standard deviation of the scored perception was less than 1. For over half of the goals we finally used, the standard deviation is actually 0.80 or less. A given respondent may be cut off from opportunities to observe the actual im-

TABLE 2

University Goals

(A) Output Goals

Output goals are those goals of the university which are reflected, immediately or in the future, in some product, service, skill or orientation which will affect (and is intended to affect) society.

1. *Student-Expressive:* Those goals which are reflected in the attempt to change the student's identity or character in some fundamental way.

   1.1 Produce a student who, whatever else may be done to him, has had his intellect cultivated to the maximum.

   1.2 Produce a well-rounded student, that is one whose physical, social, moral, intellectual and esthetic potentialities have all been cultivated.

   1.3 Make sure the student is permanently affected (in mind and spirit) by the great ideas of the great minds of history.

   1.4 Assist students to develop objectivity about themselves and their beliefs and hence examine those beliefs critically.

   1.5 Develop the inner character of students so that they can make sound, correct moral choices.

2. *Student-Instrumental:* Those goals which are reflected in the student's being equipped to do something specific for the society into which he will be entering, or to operate in a specific way in that society.

   2.1 Prepare students specifically for useful careers.

   2.2 Provide the student with skills, attitudes, contacts, and experiences which maximize the likelihood of his occupying a high status in life and a position of leadership in society.

   2.3 Train students in methods of scholarship and/or scientific research, and/or creative endeavor.

   2.4 Make a good consumer of the student—a person who is elevated culturally, has good taste, and can make good consumption choices.

   2.5 Produce a student who is able to perform his citizenship responsibilities effectively.

3. *Research:* Those goals which reflect the dedication to produce new knowledge or solve problems.

   3.1 Carry on pure research.

   3.2 Carry on applied research.

4. *Direct Service:* Those goals which reflect the provision of services directly to the population outside of the university in any continuing sense (that is, not faculty, full-time students, or its own staffs). These services are provided because the university, as an organization, is better equipped than any other organization to provide these services.

   4.1 Provide special training for part-time adult students, through extension courses, special short courses, correspondence courses, etc.

   4.2 Assist citizens directly through extension programs, advice, consultation, and the provision of useful or needed facilities and services other than teaching.

   4.3 Provide cultural leadership for the community through university-sponsored programs in the arts, public lectures by distinguished persons, athletic events, and other performances, displays or celebrations which present the best of culture, popular or not.

TABLE 2 (cont.)

4.4 Serve as a center for the dissemination of new ideas that will change the society, whether those ideas are in science, literature, the arts, or politics.

• 4.5 Serve as a center for the preservation of the cultural heritage.

(B) Adaptation Goals

Those goals which reflect the need for the organization to come to terms with the environment in which it is located. These revolve about the need to attract students and staff, to finance the enterprise, secure needed resources, and validate the activities of the university with those persons or agencies in a position to affect them.

1. Ensure the continued confidence and hence support of those who contribute substantially (other than students and recipients of services) to the finances and other material resource needs of the university.
2. Ensure the favorable appraisal of those who validate the quality of the programs we offer (validating groups include accrediting bodies, professional societies, scholarly peers at other universities, and respected persons in intellectual or artistic circles).
3. Educate to his utmost capacities every high school graduate who meets basic legal requirements for admission.
4. Accommodate only students of high potential in terms of the specific strengths and emphases of this university.
5. Orient ourselves to the satisfaction of the special needs and problems of the immediate geographical region.
6. Keep costs down as low as possible through more efficient utilization of time, and space, reduction of course duplication, etc.
7. Hold our staff in the face of inducements offered by other universities.

(C) Management Goals

Those goals which reflect decisions on who should run the university, the need to handle conflict, and the establishment of priorities on which output goals are to be given maximum attention.

1. Make sure that salaries, teaching assignments, perquisites and privileges always reflect the contribution that the person involved is making to his own profession or discipline.
2. Involve faculty in the government of the university.
3. Involve students in the government of the university.
4. Make sure the university is run democratically insofar as that is feasible.
5. Keep harmony between departments or divisions of the university when such departments or divisions do not see eye to eye on important matters.
6. Make sure that salaries, teaching assignments, perquisites and privileges always reflect the contribution that the person involved is making to the functioning of this university.
7. Emphasize undergraduate instruction even at the expense of the graduate program.
8. Encourage students to go into graduate work.
9. Make sure the university is run by those selected according to their ability to attain the goals of the university in the most efficient manner possible.
10. Make sure that on *all* important issues (not only curriculum), the will of the full-time faculty shall prevail.

(D) Motivation Goals

Those goals which seek to ensure a high level of satisfaction on the part of

TABLE 2 (cont.)

staff and students, and which emphasize loyalty to the university as a whole.
1. Protect the faculty's right to academic freedom.
2. Make this a place in which faculty have maximum opportunity to pursue their careers in a manner satisfactory to them by their own criteria.
3. Provide a full round of student activities.
4. Protect and facilitate the students' right to inquire into, investigate, and examine critically any idea or program that they might get interested in.
5. Protect and facilitate the students' right to advocate direct action of a political or social kind, and any attempts on their part to organize efforts to attain political or social goals.
6. Develop loyalty on the part of the faculty and staff to the university, rather than only to their own jobs or professional concerns.
7. Develop greater pride on the part of faculty, staff and students in their university and the things it stands for.

(E) Positional Goals

Goals which serve to help maintain the position of this university in terms of the kind of place it is in comparison to other universities, and in the face of attempts or trends which could change its position.
1. Maintain top quality in all programs we engage in.
2. Maintain top quality in these programs we feel to be especially important (other programs being, of course, up to acceptable standards).
3. Maintain a balanced level of quality across the whole range of programs we engage in.
4. Keep up-to-date and responsive.
5. Increase the prestige of the university or, if you believe it is already extremely high, ensure maintenance of that prestige.
6. Keep this place from becoming something different from what it is now; that is, preserve its peculiar emphases and point of view, its "character."

---

portance of a goal. But not everyone is, and it is a fair assumption that the average is a reasonable estimate of what the goal really is. One can, of course, quote Samuel Johnson's famous remark that an average of the opinions of gossips is still gossip, but we do not believe we are in the presence of gossip. We do not ask for opinions, but for perceptions. In effect, we ask Professor X or Dean Y at the University of A to act as our eyes. We say: "We cannot come to the University of A to check on how you actually spend your time. So we ask you to look for us and give us a report on what you have seen." The procedure can, perhaps, be compared to asking several astronomers each to look through a telescope, and then each report what he has seen. We require consensus, not because we are sure that the average is near the truth, but because it is probably closer to the truth than any other estimate.

Finally, the "score" which a given goal received at a university provided us with a measure of the degree of emphasis it receives, whether the outputs are clearly visible or not. In any case, in the last analysis, outputs are not only measures of goals but of *success* in goal realization, a factor which confounds considerations of efficiency and effectiveness in goal measurement.

Through examination of literature on university goals by the investigators and members of the research staff, and through pre-testing among administrators and colleagues at the University of Minnesota, the 47 goal statements listed in Table 2 were secured. They are presented there in the order in which we conceptualized them. On the questionnaire, the descriptive summary statements were not, of course, present, and the goal statements were presented in a random order.

We make no special apology for the length of the list of goals. Indeed it is our belief that the study of organizations has suffered from an over-simple view of goals. Most organizations are characterized as having but one goal and many classifications that are available in the literature are based on such simplified views of organizations. We suggest that one of the reasons that such classifications have not been more helpful is that they describe very little about the organizations that they are meant to comprehend. A goal structure would seem to be more descriptive.

Organizations undoubtedly differ in the complexity of their goal structures, with universities being among the more complex. Yet every organization must grapple with adaptation, management, motivation, and positional goals, in addition to its output goals. The university in the United States is probably unique in the number of *output* goals it has, but its support or maintenance goals may not be particularly complex. A manufacturing organization may have a much shorter list of output goals, but perhaps a longer list of support or maintenance goals, depending on any special management problems it may face, difficulties in securing supplies, or various forms of competition. At the end, its list of goals might turn out to be quite as long as that faced by a university.

Finally, some might quarrel with the use of the word "goal" to describe support and maintenance activities. Of course, many maintenance and support activities are not organizational goals. By an organizational goal, as stated above, we understand a state of the organization as a whole toward which the organization is moving, as evidenced by statements persons make (intentions), and activities in which they engage. The most obvious organizational goals are, of course, what we have called "output goals," (making shoes, protecting society from criminals, healing the sick, and so forth), and it is those kinds of goals that the layman has in mind when he speaks of an organization's goals. Yet it is possible for *anything* to become an organizational goal, even such an activity as repairing broken plumbing provided it is conceived of as an organizational problem. For example, if repeated breakdowns occurred to the point where it became one of stated targets for the next year to seek funds to put in a new plumbing system, and if persons were then observed to be moving in the direction of saving money or diverting it, to make this possible, then a new organizational goal would have been created. Goals may and do change over time, but *some* kind of adaptation, management, motivation, and positional goals will always be present in every organization.

The data on goals were related to a variety of other measures, especially the power structure of universities, as well as materials on university characteristics secured from other documentary sources, as will be described below.

Methods of Data Collection

The original motivation for the research extended beyond the simple desire for reliable knowledge about universities as organizations. As educators ourselves, we were concerned by the oft-made claim that there is a widening gulf in values and interests between academic administrators and members of the faculty. The resentment of the faculty at what they feel is administrators' arrogance in thinking of themselves as the "spokesmen for the university," the general derogation of administration ("He became assistant to the provost and that was the last anyone ever heard of him." "I'm only an administrator temporarily since no one else wanted to do it," or, in the words of one, who, though Dean of Letters and Sciences at the University of Wisconsin at Milwaukee, is definitely not a "former sociologist": "Remember that Dean is a 4-letter word"), and the suspicion that administrators receive generally higher salaries than others are often matched by equally uncomplimentary sentiments from administrators. The latter accuse faculty of being little interested in students, of caring little for the university (inter-university mobility, or the "job offer" being regarded as disloyalty), and of the scarcity of persons willing to serve as "working members of the faculty" (that is, willing to serve on committees concerned with administrative matters.) We were interested in how much substance there was to the claims that such fundamental differences existed, how much of it was based on value differences, and positional differences, and how much on differing conceptions of proper role, with the faculty often conceiving of themselves as the "central figures" and the administration as "support," while administrators often conceive of themselves, in the manner of the high school principal, as simply a special kind of member of the faculty.

Because of these interests, we deliberately decided to limit our attention to educational organizations highly likely to exhibit a range of conditions of such conflict and difference. One could find many schools, e.g., a small, church-controlled liberal arts school for men only, in which there may be almost complete consensus on organizational goals and values. Hence, we deliberately excluded all colleges which were dominated by some single point of view or a commitment to a uniform task which is of such a nature as to severely limit the goal variation that can exist. Not included in our original plans, therefore, were church-controlled schools, liberal arts colleges, teacher's colleges, and technical training institutions.

Our population consisted of the nondenominational[7] universities in the United States. It is these universities, with their graduate and professional schools, that seemed certain to exhibit the kind of goal variation we were interested in. It is further in this kind of educational institutions that the "support functions" are claimed to have increased greatly and in which administrators are often accused of having attained positions of considerable power. The universities are also distinguished by the importance in them of the graduate school and, for our purposes, a graduate school is necessary to provide assurance that the goal of research will be well represented in the university.

The institutions were selected on the basis of the following criteria:

1. The Ph.D. degree must be granted in at least three of four fields (humanities, biological sciences, physical sciences, and social sciences).

2. Ph.D. degrees granted in the two least emphasized fields must come to ten percent or more of the total degrees conferred. This provision was designed to overcome any undue concentration in one field, and thus help insure the kind of diversity of goals that we were interested in.

3. There must be a liberal arts undergraduate school or college with three or more professional schools.

4. The institution must have conferred ten or more degrees during the years 1962–1963. This conservative rule enabled us to keep the number of universities studied to manageable size in view of the large number of new universities that have appeared in recent years.

We secured the data for making the above decisions from *American Colleges and Universities*, ninth edition, 1964 (appendix IV and VI).[8]

It turned out that there were seventy universities defined in this way, and we decided to include all but two of them. The two exceptions were the University of Minnesota and the University of Washington, since they were the home institutions of the investigators. They were excluded because of the involvement of the investigators in them and because the University of Minnesota was used for pretesting purposes. The list of universities turned out to be substantially equivalent to that used by Berelson (1960, pp. 280–281), with denominational, technical, and starred universities excluded, except for the addition of a small number of universities which have attained university status since the time at which his list was drawn up.

The securing of accurate data on numbers of faculty and administrators at the 68 universities proved to be an exceedingly difficult task, owing to inadequacies of catalogue information (multiple listings, variations in inclusiveness, mixing in of part-time with full-time, problems of "clinical staff," members of institutes, laboratories, and other semi-autonomous portions of universities, overseas branches, and so forth), description of duties, date of materials and other problems. We had to telephone university officers and friends at particular universities to secure many of these data. Finally, on the basis of the best information we were able to get, there were, in the spring of 1964 when our study began, the following numbers in the 68 universities: 8,828 administrators and 67,560 faculty. Although the focus of the research was on administrators, we desired a sample of faculty to serve as a basis of comparison, particularly with reference to the question of whether administrators differed, as a group, from faculty, but also to examine differential career patterns, self-conceptions, and other variables not being reported on in this study. Because of the desire to make rather detailed comparisons among administrators, we attempted to get all of the academic administrators.[9] On the other hand, since we planned only very broad groupings among the faculty (e.g., social sciences, humanities, etc.), we felt that a 10% sample would suffice. Hence, the total number surveyed consisted of 8,828 administrators[10] plus 6,756 faculty members, for a total of 15,584.

The questionnaire was very long (300 questions, requiring a minimum of 1½ hours to fill out, and often—some of the respondents wrote—requiring 3 hours), and faced the usual problems of mailed questionnaires. A variety of devices was used to stimulate response: (1) the enlistment of the endorsement or assistance of accrediting bodies and professional societies; (2) an earlier study of Deans of Business Administration at 101 universities resulted in offers from approximately one-half of the deans to stimulate interest at their own universities; (3) the president of the University of Minnesota at the time (Meredith Wilson) wrote to all presidents of member universities of the American Association of Universities that fell in our sample (approximately one-half of them) asking for their assistance. In addition, it must be remembered that we were contacting a highly literate, questionnaire-sophisticated group, on a subject of direct, immediate interest to them—their own jobs. It is also, a subject, as we have said, on which there are few data of any validity. We therefore offered the *quid pro quo* of a copy of the findings, if desired, or at least the general results which would later be published. (To our dismay we received well over 1500 requests.) Offsetting such obvious interest is the clear fact that this group is continually the target of surveyors, to the point, we were told by several, that their secretaries had standard instructions to file all questionnaires unless otherwise advised ahead of time.[11] Our final response rate for the entire questionnaire of usable replies was 50.9 percent of administrators and 40.4 percent for the faculty. A short form of the questionnaire, dealing only with careers, was sent out to non-respondents. It resulted in a total response rate for that portion of the questionnaire of approximately 76 percent. A variety of tests was employed to test the likelihood of bias. They left us with confidence that the response group was not appreciably biased at least with reference to dimensions of interest to us. The main reason for the lower than desirable response rate (actually high by usual mail questionnaire standards) appears to be the length of the questionnaire.[12]

Major Findings

The following findings are limited only to the goal analysis, the relationship of goals to the power structure, and the implications of those findings for the empirical characterization of universities in organizational terms.

In Table 3, an overall, composite ranking of the 47 goals at all 68 universities is presented. The scores there are based on unweighted means. However, subsequent analyses of the same goals making use of various weights (response rate, treating universities equally, use of single scores for entire university) produce no important shifts in goal position. As presented in Table 3, however, they do reflect the somewhat lower response rate of faculty; that is, they reflect somewhat more the perceptions and views of administrators. The column labelled "is" refers to the ranking of goals on the portion of the question (as illustrated in Table 1) that represented the answers to the "is" row (the respondent's report on his perception of how important the goal in fact is); the column labelled "should," in turn, refers to the ranking in terms of respondent's conception of how important he thought the goal *should* be.

As can be seen, the top goal at the 68 universities is perceived as being that of protecting academic freedom. Furthermore, not only do the respondents see it as in fact the top goal, but they believe that it should be the top goal. As will be shown below, this finding is of the first importance in our ability to characterize universities in organizational terms. It should further be noted that if we had elected to restrict our attention only to the usual output goals (teaching, research, service), we would never have made this discovery since we would not have thought of "protecting academic freedom" as a goal.

TABLE 3

Ranking of American Universities

"Is"	Goal	"Should"	"Is"	Goal	"Should"
1	Acad Freedom ...	1	25	Fac U Govt	19
2	U Prestige	11	26	Reward Prof	21
3	Top Qual Imp	7	27	Stud Activities	43
4	Ensur Confidence ..	26	28	Stud Success	33
5	Keep up to Date ..	6	29	Run U Demo	22
6	Train Scholarship ..	2	30	Affect Stud Perm ...	15
7	Pure Research	16	31	Assist Citizens	36
8	Top Qual All	4	32	Just Rewd Inst	13
9	Mntn Fav Apprsl ..	34	33	Devlp Pride Univ	23
10	Ensure U Goals ...	9	34	Sat Area Needs	42
11	Dissem Ideas	5	35	Mntn Bal Qualty	31
12	Applied Research ..	30	36	Will of Fac	24
13	Stud Careers	32	37	Special Training	38
14	Stud Intellect	3	38	Stud Character	12
15	Hold Our Staff ...	18	39	Educ to Utmost	37
16	Comm Cult Ldshp .	28	40	Accp Good Stud Only .	39
17	Stud Inquire	10	41	Stud Pol Rights	40
18	Encour Grad Wk ..	27	42	Devlp Fac Lylty	29
19	Preserve Heritage ..	20	43	Keep Harmony	41
20	Stud Good Citzn ..	14	44	Undrgrad Inst	44
21	Well Round Stud ..	17	45	Stud Univ Govt	46
22	Max Opportunity ..	25	46	Pres Character	47
23	Stud Objectivity ..	8	47	Stud Taste	45
24	Keep Costs Down .	35			

Paying attention, for the moment, only to the "is" list (that is the goals as listed on the table), one can characterize the "top" and "bottom" goals by the simple device of ranging the actual average scores in a single distribution, marking the distribution off in standard deviation units (from the overall mean), and asking which goals fell in the top standard deviation (of 6) and which in the bottom.

The *top goals,* then, turn out to be:

1. protect the faculty's right to academic freedom
2. increase the prestige of the university
3. maintain top quality in those programs we feel to be especially important
4. insure the continued confidence and support of those who contribute substantially to the finances and other material resource needs of the university
5. keep up-to-date and responsive
6. train students in methods of scholarship and/or scientific research and/or creative endeavor
7. carry on pure research

At the other end, the *bottom goals* are seen to be:

44. emphasize undergraduate instruction even at the expense of the graduate program
45. involve students in the government of the university
46. keep this place from becoming something different from what it is now
47. make a good consumer of the student

What is most striking about the list of top goals is that practically all of them are what we have called support goals and only one of them in any way involves students. Even that one refers to training students for research or other creative endeavors which is, after all, closely associated with what the professors consider to be important and represents a possible output to them, or to the academic field. This squares with the goal of carrying on pure research, which is also rated very high. The singular scarcity of any emphasis on goals that have anything to do with students is all the more remarkable in view of the fact that of our total of 47 goals among which respondents could choose, 18 involved direct reference to students in some way. Thus there was ample opportunity, and a result so striking as this could hardly have been produced by chance or by a sampling bias.

Supporting this general finding is the fact that students are mentioned more frequently among the goals at the bottom. The goal fourth from very bottom involves undergraduate instruction. This is quite consistent then with the finding that pure research and preparing students for research or creative careers are emphasized as top goals in American universities.

No particular pattern among the support goals is evident among the top goals although three of them are positional (increasing prestige of the university, maintaining top quality in programs felt to be important, and keeping up-to-date and responsive). As a general finding one can say that American universities, taken collectively, emphasize only pure research as an output, but put it seventh to a variety of other goals which are more concerned with the position of one's own university and the programs that it offers and with efforts to maintain a high quality at the university. At the very top they put academic freedom as a goal. Such a goal appears to be of first importance in American universities and refers to the importance in them of autonomy from outside interference of any kind. One must remember also that these findings do not refer to what people think ought to be the case, but rather to their perceptions of the way things are. The administrators and faculty at American universities believe that actually, right now, universities *do* protect the faculty's right to academic freedom more than they do any one of 46 other possibilities.

What Persons Feel the Top and Bottom Goals Ought to Be. We utilized the same procedure in selecting a top and a bottom group—one standard deviation in the distribution of means at the top, and one standard deviation at the bottom. When we did so, we found the following to be those goals that persons felt *ought* to be at the top in the American university.

1. protect the faculty's right to academic freedom
2. train students in methods of scholarship and/or scientific research, and/or creative endeavor
3. produce a student who, whatever else may be done to him has had his intellect cultivated to the maximum
4. maintain top quality in all programs we engage in
5. serve as a center for the dissemination of new ideas that would change the society, whether those ideas are in science, literature, the arts or politics
6. keep up-to-date and responsive
7. maintain top quality in those programs we feel to be especially important
8. assist students to develop objectivity about themselves and their beliefs and hence examine those beliefs critically
9. make sure the university is run by those selected according to their ability to attain the goals of the university in the most efficient manner possible

On the other hand, those goals felt to belong at the very bottom are:

45. make a good consumer of the student
46. involve students in the government of the university
47. keep this place from becoming something different from what it is now

When we examine this distribution we see that although students come out a little better, the student goals are far from being prominent. Persons felt that the faculty's right to academic freedom not only was the most important goal (as shown above) but that it ought to be the most important goal. In this list, however, two student goals came in second and third places: one referred to the same goal as had occurred in the previous table (training students in research and related activities); in addition persons felt that the goal dealing with cultivating the student's mind deserved a high amount of emphasis (although it was not perceived as in fact given that emphasis). In other words, respondents' conception of the way things ought to be is different from the way they actually are. In their view more attention should be given to cultivating the student intellect than is in fact being given.

One other student goal also was present in this top group of nine, namely the goal dealing with assisting students to develop objectivity about themselves. This goal, which did not rank high among the goals actually being emphasized was felt to be one which ought to be emphasized.

At the other end there was a feeling that involving students in the government of the university ought to be of very little importance. It would seem that those students seeking a greater share in decision-making power at the university will not receive much support from administrators and faculty. On the other hand, students might take some consolation from the fact that there is no particularly strong feeling that the faculty should be involved in the government of the university either. In general, then, students as a group are not felt to be particularly important, nor is there any strong feeling that the situation in that respect is different from what it ought to be (with one or two exceptions—training a student in research and cultivating his intellect, and assisting him to develop objectivity about himself). Nor is there evidence, either in what goals are or what they should be, to suggest that it is an important goal of the university to prepare a student for a useful career, to assist him in upward mobility, to assist him to be a good consumer, or to become a good citizen.[13]

Goal Congruence. In the case of seven goals, there is congruence between the actual position and the position that persons feel they ought to be in. Four goals are perceived to be important and our respondents feel they ought to be important. These are:

1. protect the faculty's right to academic freedom
2. maintain top quality in those programs we feel to be especially important
3. keep up-to-date and responsive

4. train students in methods of scholarship and/or scientific research and/or creative endeavor

The following three are at the bottom and our respondents feel that that is where they belong:

1. make a good consumer of the student
2. keep this place from becoming something different from what it is now
3. involve students in the government of the university

On the whole the above is rather impressive evidence that, at least at the top and bottom, there is a fairly strong sentiment that things are the way they ought to be. Four out of the seven top "is" goals and four out of the nine top "should" goals are congruent with one another. Practically all of the goals at the bottom are congruent with one another.

This generally happy[14] situation does not seem to prevail throughout the distribution. One way of examining the lack of general congruence is through "sins of goal commission" and "sins of goal omission." That is we can compare those goals which seem to be out of line with one another on the two scales. For example the goal, "to develop loyalty on the part of faculty and staff to the university, rather than to their own jobs or professional concerns," is very low on the list of the way goals are perceived to actually be (being actually 6th from the bottom). On the other hand, when we look at the list of what persons think goals ought to be we find that this goal is considerably higher up (19th from the bottom). Such goals, which persons feel ought to be given more attention than they are being given ("sins of goal omission") include in order of discrepancy of ranks:

1. produce a student who, whatever else is done to him, has had his intellect cultivated to the maximum
2. make sure that salaries, teaching assignments, and perquisites always reflect the contribution that the person involved is making to the functioning of the university
3. assist students to develop objectivity about themselves and their beliefs and hence to examine those beliefs critically
4. make sure the student is permanently affected by the great ideas of the great minds of history
5. develop loyalty on the part of the faculty and staff to the university, rather than to their own jobs or professional concerns

Looking over this list we see a relative dissatisfaction with goals which tend to be pushed to one side when the personal ambitions and the research careers of the faculty become dominant interests. There seems to be some feeling that top faculty (who are likely to be most mobile) do not have sufficient loyalty to the university. In the second neglected goal, there is probably being expressed a feeling on the part of persons who serve on committees and attempt to do their jobs that they are not sufficiently well recognized. We also see the familiar plaint of the liberal arts person that not enough attention is being given to the student's mind or to the attempt to get the student to develop insight into himself.

The "sins of goal commission" involve goals felt to be emphasized too much. Those goals, in order of discrepancy of ranks, are:

1. insure the favorable appraisal of those who validate the quality of the programs we offer
2. insure the continued confidence and support of those who contribute substantially to the finances and other material resource needs of the university
3. prepare students specifically for useful careers
4. carry on applied research
5. provide a full round of student activities

We see that although providing a full round of student activities is not emphasized as a goal (as we can see again by looking at Table 3), nevertheless there is a feeling that it is emphasized more than it ought to be. In addition persons resent the apparent emphasis on the need to satisfy outside organizations that validate programs. There is similar resistance to what might be construed as pressure from the outside in the emphasis on carrying on applied research. On the whole these are entirely consistent with the emphasis that we have already noticed on academic freedom, and on the needs and the concerns of the faculty and their own professional careers. In addition we note again that the only way in which students come into the picture here is that, while there is a general feeling that not much attention is being paid to them or should be, that in one area at least, mainly providing a full round of student activities, the relatively little attention paid is too much.

Notes

1. A metaphor of dubious authenticity. According to most authors, the phrase is attributed to President Garfield who, while a congressman, was said to have referred to the ideal university as one "with President Mark Hopkins at one end of a log and a student at the other." Eells (1962), remembering that Hopkins was a college located in New England, thought the metaphor inappropriate to the winter climate. His investigations lead to doubts that the precise phrase was ever used and that, at the very least, Garfield meant to place the log (or more likely bench) inside an enclosed building.

2. We shall use the phrase "organizational model" and the term "organization" without benefit of adjectives, such as "formal," "complex" or "large-scale," in order to avoid having to choose among them. While we agree with Blau's and Scott's (1962:6–7) criticism of such items we do not believe any one adjective avoids the problems they refer to.

3. The distinction is basically that drawn by Weber between *Vergemeinschaftung* and *Vergesellsschaftung*, which Henderson and Parsons translate in adjective form as "communal" and "associative." "A social relationship will be called 'communal' if and so far as the orientation of social action . . . is based on a subjective feeling of the parties, whether affectual or traditional, that they belong together. A social relationship will, on the other hand, be called 'associative' if and in so far as the orientation of social action within it rests on a rationally motivated adjustment of interests or a similarly motivated agreement, whether the basis of rational judgment be absolute values or reasons of expediency." (Henderson and Parsons, 1947:136.)

4. The failure to do so was one of the earliest criticisms of the classic Hawthorne studies. (See Landsberger, 1958:chap. 3.)

5. Cf. the distinction between what Alvin W. Gouldner (1959) calls a "rational" and "natural system" model.

6. Daniel Katz and Robert L. Kahn (1966:chap. 6.) seek to conceptualize such maintenance in terms of "efficiency," or the amount of energy used up to maintain the system. However, as they are quick to point out, the word "energy" may be misleading in that it implies an ability to measure inputs in quantitative terms. Quite apart from difficulties of measurement, there is the central fact that much of an organization's inputs consist not of energies alone but also of information or signals. Katz and Kahn refer to D. R. Miller's (1963) approach to these matters. A treatment which seeks to generalize this discussion to all social systems is in Buckley (1967:chaps. 3, 4.)

7. Our study also included 10 denominational (mostly Catholic) universities, which fulfilled our test for "university" in all respects. However, preliminary findings suggested strongly that they made up a universe of their own and deserved separate tabulation and analysis. We are not reporting on them here.

8. Purdue University turned out to be an exception. It was not classified as a university by the editors of that volume, yet it was the feeling of the investigators that it was excluded by a minor technicality. Consequently, it was included. Such places as M.I.T. and Cal. Tech. are automatically excluded by our criteria.

9. For example, since we desired to compare deans of medical schools with deans of pharmacy schools, and since there were only about 50 of each in the total population of schools, and allowing also for the likelihood of incomplete response, the actual numbers we end up with might easily be, say, 25 of each. We could hardly operate with a smaller number and make any sort of general statements about such positions. Hence, any sampling would have reduced such numbers too much to have been of any use. Of course, most of our examined relationships involve much larger categories. Again, we are not here reporting on such finer categories.

10. The term "administrator" is, in general, restricted to academic administrators only (excluding, for example, persons involved in buildings and grounds, room scheduling, dean of students office, student residences and dining halls, and the like). However, many coding problems were presented which required intensive search of catalogue descriptions, letters to chairmen of departments or other persons, occasional personal letters to the person himself, and other searches of documents.

When in doubt, we usually included the individual in the sample and hoped his responses to the background questions on the questionnaire would clarify his status. Unfortunately, this procedure depended on his filling out the questionnaire. One result was that our original estimates of numbers of administrators (and faculty) had later to be revised. They were not far off, however.

11. One president of a college not on our list wrote us, expressing concern that his university had not been included. It may be that one way colleges get recognized as universities is through joining the (less and less) exclusive group that routinely get questionnaired.

12. Space forbids description of the tests of bias employed. Detailed information may be secured by writing to the author, or by examining Gross and Grambsch (1968).

13. In the above discussion the term "rank" has been used loosely to refer to what is, strictly speaking, a rating on a five-point scale. In this way, we have followed the procedure in the classic North-Hatt study of occupations, and for much the same reason, persons cannot rank a list of 47 items by comparing each with all others at the same time.

14. "Happy" in the sense implied in the Durkheimian conception of social integration as a state of a society in which people do willingly what they must do. For an organization, such a state is approximated when the actual goals are what members think they should be. It is obvious that we are speaking only of administrators and faculty. We have no data from students, and the possibility, for example, that assigning them a low place in university government is "happy" for them is quite dubious, according to the news of students campus activities at the time of this writing (June, 1968).

References

Bales, Robert F. 1958. "Task roles and social roles in problem-solving groups." Pp. 437–447 in Eleanor F. Maccoby, Theodore M. Newcomb, and Eugene L. Hartley (eds.), *Reading in Social Psychology*. New York: Henry Holt.

Berelson, Bernard. 1960. *Graduate Education in the United States*. New York: McGraw-Hill.

Buckley, Walter. 1967. *Sociology and Modern Systems Theory*. Englewood Cliffs, New Jersey: Prentice-Hall.

Cartwright, Dorwin and Alvin Zander (eds.). 1953. *Group Dynamics*. Evanston: Row Peterson.

Cyert, Richard and James G. March. 1963. *A Behavioral Theory of the Firm*. Englewood Cliffs, New Jersey: Prentice-Hall.

Downs, Anthony. 1967. *Inside Bureaucracy*. Boston: Little, Brown.

Etzioni, Amitai. 1958. "Industrial sociology: the study of economic organizations." *Social Research* 25:303–324.

——— 1964. *Modern Organizations*. Englewood Cliffs, New Jersey: Prentice-Hall.

Gouldner, Alvin W. 1959. "Organizational analysis." Chap. 18 in Robert K. Merton et al. (eds.), *Sociology Today*, New York: Basic Books.

——— 1961. "Metaphysical pathos and the theory of bureaucracy." Pp. 71–82 in Amitai Etzioni (ed.), *Complex Organizations*, New York: Holt, Rinehart and Winston.

Gross, Edward and Paul V. Grambsch. 1968. *Academic Administrators and University Goals*, Washington, D.C.: American Council on Education.

Katz, Daniel and Robert L. Kahn. 1966. *The Social Psychology of Organizations*. New York: John Wiley.

Landsberger, Henry A. 1958. *Hawthorne Revisited*. Ithaca, New York: Cornell University.

March, James G., and Herbert Simon. 1958. *Organizations*. New York: Wiley.

Miller, D. R. 1963. "The study of social relation: situation, identity and social interaction." Pp. 639–737 in S. Koch (ed.), *Psychology: A Study of a Science*, Vol. 5. New York: McGraw-Hill.

Parsons, Talcott. 1960. "A sociological approach to the theory of formal organizations." *Structure and Process in Modern Societies*. New York: Free Press of Glencoe.

Parsons, Talcott, et al. 1961. *Theories of Society*. New York: Free Press of Glencoe.

Simon, Herbert. 1964. "On the concept of organization goal." *Administrative Science Quarterly* 8:1–22.

Thompson, James D., and William McEwen. 1958. "Organization goals and environment." *American Sociological Review* 23:23–50.

Chapter V

Organizational Technology

The technology which the organization employs to achieve its desired outputs is one of the key variables that affects both the goals and the internal structure of the organization. In human service organizations technology is a basic determinant of service delivery patterns in general, and of client-organization relations in particular.

The concept of technology refers to a set of systematic procedures used by the organization to bring about predetermined changes in its raw material (i.e., clients), or to move the raw material from state A to a given state B. For example, an educational technology attempts to move pupils from a state of ignorance in a given subject matter to a certain state of knowledge and proficiency. Perrow (1965, pp. 915–16) has succinctly defined attributes of a technology as follows:

1. Some knowledge of a nonrandom cause-and-effect relationship is required, that is, the techniques lead to the performance of acts which, for known or unknown reasons, cause a change under specified conditions.
2. There is some system of feedback such that the consequences of the acts can be assessed in an objective manner.
3. It is possible to secure repeated demonstrations of the efficiency of the acts.
4. There is an acceptable, reasonable, and determinant range of tolerance, that is, the proportion of the successes must be estimated, and even though the proportion might be small, it is judged high enough to continue the activity.
5. The techniques can be communicated sufficiently that most persons with appropriate preliminary training can be expected to master the techniques and perform them under acceptable limits of tolerance.

Following this definition we can distinguish three components in the technical system of every organization (Hickson, Pugh, and Pheysey, 1969): (a) the knowledge base of the technology, (b) the nature of the raw material to be worked upon, and (c) the sequence of activities and equipments used in the technology. We shall show that

279

in each component human service organizations face issues which affect their basic characteristics.

Human service organizations vary by the degree of the determinancy of their technologies, that is, the available knowledge of cause-effect relations in assessing and changing human attributes. For example, many of the medical technologies are highly determinant, while many of the technologies for changing human behavior are highly indeterminant.

When cause-effect relations are known the technology provides clear explicit courses of action for the staff to follow in achieving the desired results. This is the case, for example, in determining social security benefits, treating many diseases, or teaching a specific trade.

In contrast, organizations mandated to assess and change human behavior (e.g., mental hospitals, schools, correctional institutions), are characterized by indeterminant technologies which are incomplete, of limited reliability and validity, and occasionally even self contradictory. The staff in these organizations must perform in a state of uncertainty, lacking adequate knowledge about what techniques to employ and when, and whether these techniques will in fact produce the desired outcome. Consequently, many of the attributes of technology as outlined by Perrow may exist only partially in these organizations.

A closely related characteristic of the technology of human service organization is its complexity. The rapid advances in knowledge, on the one hand, and the increasing role of these organizations in handling complex human problems, on the other hand, force them to employ more and more complex technologies. As a result, these organizations must utilize a wide range of skills and competencies and establish elaborate linkages among the various components of their technical system. That is, the sequencing of activities and the structuring of the work flow become more problematic as the complexity of the technology increases.

These developments imply that human service organizations will encounter in varying degrees two critical technological issues. First, there are serious lacunae in the knowledge base of their technologies which result in reduced effectiveness and inability to develop a coherent internal work system. Second, human service organizations cannot easily develop a routine and programmed set of procedures for staff to follow in order to obtain the desired output. This leads to reduced efficiency and increased variability in the output of the organization.

One of the mechanisms by which human service organizations attempt to overcome lacunae in knowledge is to develop service ideologies. Rapoport (1960, p. 269) defines ideologies as "formal systems of ideas or beliefs that are held with great tenacity and emotional investment, that have self-confirming features. . . . Ideology welds observable aspects of the environment into a kind of unity by filling in gaps in knowledge with various projections that ultimately supply a coherent belief system on which action can be based and justified."

The purpose of these ideologies is to introduce some order and coherence in the work performed by the staff. Most important, however, these ideologies provide the staff with the rationalization and legitimation to take various courses of action which cannot be justified technologically, but can be defended ideologically. Furthermore, the use of ideologies enables the organization to overcome frustrations inherent in the lack of explicit means to achieve considered outcomes. Hence, the more indeterminant the organizational technology, the more elaborate are the ideologies developed and used by the staff. However, as Perrow (1965) cogently points out, ideologies cannot serve as blueprints for the appropriate flow of work and activities in the organization, and therefore, there is an inherent gap between the actual work performed by the staff and their belief system. Moreover, ideologies tend to be self-confirming and reduce the motivation to seek new knowledge and introduce technological innovations.

The complexity and often indeterminancy of the technology, coupled with the unstable and variable characteristics of clients worked upon, necessitate the adoption of nonroutine and nonprogrammed work procedures. The high administrative costs and the difficulties in structuring such procedures lead to the operation of "Gresham's law of planning" in which programmed activity tends to drive out nonprogrammed activity (Simon, 1965, p. 67). That is, the staff in human service organizations are likely to develop and emphasize routine work patterns at the expense of nonroutine and nonprogrammed tasks, unless there is a strong incentive system to counter this tendency. The organization may attempt to "routinize" its technology through the redefinition of its operative goals and ideologies, the training, socialization and supervision of its workers, and the definition of its clients.

Clients are a basic component of technology. As the raw material to be worked upon they set apart human service organizations from all other bureaucracies. First, since the clients are vested in values, they set significant normative limits on the choice and use of technologies by the organization. Second, clients tend to be highly variable and unstable, thus introducing many uncertainties and exceptions which must be coped with by the technologies. This is also a major contributing factor to the indeterminancy of human service technologies, since the high variability and instability of clients prevent the formulation of valid and reliable practice principles. One way in which human service organizations tend to reduce the variability and instability of their clients is in the development of stereotypic "normal cases" (Scheff, 1966) through which the clients are classified into broad categories assumed to have the same characteristics. A basic function of the organizational ideologies is to support such stereotypes.

Third, and most important, clients are self-activating entities potentially capable of neutralizing many of the techniques employed by the organization to change their attributes. As a result, all human service organizations face the necessity to control their clients. Inevitably, the technology of such organizations includes mechanisms of client control which vary in scope and range with the type of technology used.

Finally, the structuring of the work flow in the organization is obviously determined by the knowledge base and the characteristics of the clients. In general, the more simple and determinant the knowledge base used and the less variable and unstable the clients, the more the work flow will be structured in a serially ordered and linked set of activities. In contrast, as the knowledge base becomes more complex and indeterminant, and the clients are more variable and unstable, the selection, combination, and order of application of various techniques will be determined by feedback from the client himself (Thompson, 1967, p. 17).

The articles that follow address themselves to the various topics raised in this discussion. Stallings uses flow models to chart the sequence of activities performed by various units in the hospital as dictated by the medical technology. In contrasting the flow of activities and the linkage of the various units during normal operations and disaster situations, Stallings is able to show the degree of congruency between the internal organization of the various work units and the requirements of the technology when the inputs vary. The greater the congruency, the more efficient the organization will be to achieve its output goals. By implication, the study suggests that human service organizations may fail to serve their clients adequately if the internal work arrangements and linkages among units do not reflect and adapt to the requirements of the technology.

Aiken and Hage in a study of sixteen health and welfare agencies examine the relationship among technology, internal structure, and goals. Measuring technology in terms of "routineness" of the work done, they show that routine technology is correlated with formalized and centralized internal structure of the organization, and with less professionally trained staff. Concomitantly, organizations with a high degree of work "routineness" are more likely to emphasize efficiency and quantity of clients served, than the quality of the services.

The selection from Strauss, et al., explores the relationship between psychiatric ideologies and the organization of treatment in a mental hospital. Contrasting the somaticists with the psychotherapists, the authors show how the two approaches are expressed in the differential assumptions made about the patients and their illnesses, the type of change techniques employed, and the role of the ward staff in the treatment regime. The researchers indicate cogently that the interaction among ideologies, hospital rules and regulations, and patients results in a system of negotiated work arrangements that reflect these factors rather than a well-defined technology. In fact, it could be argued that the reliance of ideologies rather than determinant technologies reinforces a continuous negotiation process that is characteristic of the hospital's internal work arrangements.

Finally, Oettinger and Marks raise serious questions about the educational results of new teaching technologies and their consequences on the organization of the school. They cogently challenge the claims of programmed instruction methods in achieving broad educational goals. Most important, from our perspective, however, are their eloquent arguments regarding the immense organizational difficulties in adopting and implementing a highly sophisticated, complex, and expensive teaching technology. They point out that the basic conditions for the adoption of new technologies—sufficient independence from other systems, reliable research tools, and specific goals—hardly exist in the school system, and for that matter in most human service organizations. In particular, the adoption and use of various technologies in these organizations are influenced by the various interest groups that watch over the activities of the organization.

References

Hickson, D. J., Pugh, D. S., and Pheysey, D. C. 1969. "Operations technology and organization structure: An empirical reappraisal." *Administrative Science Quarterly* 14:378–97.

Perrow, C. 1965. "Hospitals: Technology, structure and goals." Pp. 915–16 in J. G. March (ed.) *Handbook of Organizations*. Chicago: Rand McNally.

Rapoport, R. 1960. *Community as a Doctor*. London: Tavistock Publications.

Scheff, T. 1966. *Being Mentally Ill*. Chicago: Aldine.

Simon, H. 1965. *The Shape of Automation for Men and Management*. New York: Harper and Row.

Thompson, J. D. 1967. *Organizations in Action*. New York: McGraw-Hill.

Hospital Adaptations to Disaster:
Flow Models of Intensive Technologies

Robert A. Stallings

A great number of models have been employed in empirical studies of formal organizations. Some have been developed explicitly and elaborately in their own right while others are more implicit in specific investigations of organizational behavior. A majority of existing organizational models, however, fall generally into three main categories. Certainly the most famous of these is Weber's classic *bureaucratic* model with its emphasis on rationality. In contrast stands the *natural systems* model which views organizations as comprised of autonomous and often competing subparts. More implicit than either of these is a *behavioristic* model emphasizing the personal meaning of interaction in an organizational setting.

Recent empirical research in such "professional organizations"[1] as hospitals has produced rather distinct consequences in the application of each of these models. In order to account for contradictory principles of disciplined compliance and professional expertise, the bureaucratic tradition has produced a *dual structural* model whose essential feature is two subsystems referred to as line and staff. Research in hospitals utilizing a natural systems approach has for the most part focused upon conflicts among various occupational groups such as physicians, administrators, nurses, technicians, and so on. And behavioristic models have led to a variety of social psychological studies on the attitudes, beliefs, and satisfactions (or dissatisfactions) of hospital personnel.

Each of these models of organization contains its own weaknesses when employed in field studies of organizational behavior. This is necessarily so since each seeks to explain only certain aspects of complex situations. Still, two important criticisms may be made of these general models when applied in analyses of adaptation to environmental changes by hospitals. With few exceptions each has led to a divison of hospitals into *nominal* or artificial subunits such as dual authority structures while ignoring more natural subdivisions. And they have produced an inherently *static* conceptualization of organizations and their behavior in that the dynamic nature of hospital processes is not adequately developed. It is suggested that both these weaknesses may be overcome through a device which will be termed a *flow model*.

Reprinted from *Human Organization* 29 (Winter, 1970): 294–302.

Deviation

Perhaps the more serious drawback in the application of existing models in the study of organizational adaptation has been a concern for nominal subparts. Most common is a focus on various occupational groupings. In professional organizations such as schools, for example, this kind of conceptualization may be most useful since the three major subunits—administration, professional staff, and maintenance—are homogeneous groups consisting of administrators, teachers, and custodians respectively. In the case of hospitals, however, distinctions of this sort may be seriously misleading. An X-ray department consists of radiologists, technicians, clerks, and typists. Treating each of these as separate units (i.e., as occupational categories) ignores potentially more important aspects of this department as a system in its own right. Even treating such a seemingly homogeneous category as nurses as an organizational subdivision may lead one to overlook the fact that the department Nursing Service involves such distinct roles as director, supervisors, clerks, etc.—all of whom are nurses.

Apart from such empirical examples, there is considerable theoretical justification to urge caution in using these approaches. Recent discussions of organizational technologies, as those by Thompson and Perrow,[2] direct attention to more meaningful subdivisions which necessarily consist of heterogeneous rather than homogeneous task roles. In short, from the standpoint of overall organizational behavior, an empirical examination of hospitals which focuses on such categories as occupation tends to break up more natural units which need to be examined—both internally and in their relationships with other units —in accounting for adaptations to environmental fluctuations.

The concept of technology has additional relevance with regard to the second major limitation of existing organizational models, that is, their inherently static view of organizational activities. Perrow has defined technology as

> the action that an individual performs upon an object, with or without the aid of tools or mechanical devices, in order to make some change in that object. The object, or "raw material," may be a living being, human or otherwise, a symbol, or an inanimate object.[3]

From an organizational standpoint the basic "raw materials" of hospitals are its patients. Hospital care cannot, however, be conceived as a static phenomenon but must be considered a *dynamic process* in which patients progress through definite—though overlapping—phases. In other words, the various subunits of the hospital (as above, best considered in terms of departments) are responsible for differing types of activities performed on these raw materials at different times during the period of hospitalization. In essence, the kind of technology which is involved in hospitals is what Thompson has labeled an "intensive technology" to indicate that "a variety of techniques is drawn up in order to produce a change in some specific object, but the selection, combination, and order of application are determined by feedback from the object itself."[4]

> The intensive technology is most dramatically illustrated by the general hospital. At any moment an emergency admission may require some combination of dietary, X-ray, laboratory, and housekeeping or hotel services, together with the various medical specialties, pharmaceutical services, occupational therapies, social work services, and spiritual or religious services. Which of these, and when, can be determined only from evidence about the state of the patient.[5]

In short, drawing upon implications of recent discussions of organizational technologies, it is contended that a model of professional organizations can be constructed which takes into account both actual operating subunits and a dynamic conceptualization of organizational processes. Such a model would appear particularly well suited to examine one type of structural adaptation to disaster situations, that is, changes in the *relationships* among these various operating subunits. Analysis of this type involves the comparison of a model constructed from hospital activities during the crisis with another constructed from that same hospital's activities under more "normal" conditions. The effects of qualitative differences between these two situations must be controlled for, however. That is, since the notion of intensive technology suggests that the arrangement of organizational parts will vary in accordance with variations in the conditions of individual patients, valid comparisons can only be made when the "normal" model is constructed for patients with the same types of injuries as those encountered in the disaster situation. Controls of this nature would highlight those adaptations due to quantitative differences in the number of inputs for such related factors as priorities and the like. Before these models are developed from an actual hospital involved in a recent disaster, however, a word about the type of data used and how they were obtained is in order.

Background and Data

The organization under examination is a 400-bed general hospital located in the suburbs of a large midwestern metropolis. When its doors opened in 1961, it became the second hospital in the area sponsored by the hospital association of a major Protestant denomination. A school of nursing, operated by the association, is located on the rear of the hospital grounds.

With little warning and devastating force, a spring tornado ground its way through seven of the suburban communities surrounding this hospital, killing 32 persons and injuring more than 400 others. During the next four hours the hospital received nearly 200 victims of this disaster. One hundred eighty-seven victims were officially treated, 58 of whom were admitted and 84 others treated and released. Nine victims were dead on arrival at the emergency room, and 37 with only minor injuries were transferred to other hospitals in the area after preliminary examination and treatment.

Data analyzed in this study were collected by field teams of the Disaster Research Center of The Ohio State University. Two sources of data were utilized. Members of a five-man team, in the area within 48 hours after the tornado touched down, conducted semistructured *interviews* with administrative officials as well as other "key" individuals at the hospital. Three weeks later, a second field team began more systematic interviewing of personnel at various levels within the organization, and a third team obtained responses from at least one high-level official in all the various departments three months after the disaster. Those interviewed included: executive director, administrator, director of nursing, chaplain, public relations director, the disaster medical committee chairman, the chief radiologist, all department heads, and four nursing supervisors as well as nearly two dozen doctors, nurses, and interns who worked in various areas of the hospital during the emergency. Respondents were asked questions pertaining primarily to the actions of their particular subunits during the emergency. Forty-two interviews were conducted, all of which were either tape-recorded or notes taken during the session read immediately into a recorder. Transcripts of these interviews were particularly useful in constructing a flow model for the emergency period.

The second major source of data consisted of *supportive materials* obtained by members of the various field teams. Of particular relevance were copies of organizational charts, post-disaster departmental critiques and evaluations, the hospital's disaster manual, and a complete set of floor plans of the building. These materials were utilized to develop a flow model of the hospital under normal circumstances.

Analysis

By adding a time dimension to the operations of technologies in hospitals and by focusing on departments as organizational subunits, a flow model of the structure of the general hospital may be developed. In constructing this model, as previously pointed out, the specific pattern may vary in relation to the type of injury a patient has received. Development of flow models for a wide variety of injuries, while informative, is not required for analysis of the types of adaptation occurring in a disaster situation. Instead, it is sufficient to construct a model for a single, non-disaster emergency case which is as similar as possible to those encountered in greater numbers during these crises. Since the specific disaster involved in this study is a tornado, the victim of an automobile accident represents an organizational input corresponding most closely with victims of this disaster. This pattern is represented in Figure 1.

The normal emergency pattern most often becomes an input into the organization upon his delivery to the emergency entrance, typically by fire or police department ambulance. Thus the first department on the sequential diagram is the emergency room. After an examination, a representative of medical records secures the patient's name, address, nature of injury, closest relatives, etc. Generally, the patient is taken next to either the X-ray department or surgery or both. (Obviously, the morgue is always a possibility throughout and need not be dealt with.) A separate cast room is available to which the patient might also be dispatched. In this hospital, all these departments are adjacent to one another in a separate emergency suite.

A patient requiring hospitalization then comes into contact with the admissions office and medical records once more, where more information is secured prior to his formal admission to the hospital. Admission means assignment to a particular ward which, further, means that several "internalistic" departments[6] become involved with the patient for the first time. Their particular sequence depends on many situational factors (e.g., the time a day, the condition of the patient, and so forth) and in any case is only of minor importance. Internalistic departments are: dietary, central supply, laundry, the chaplain's office, etc. (Of course, in the early stages of hospitalization, a revisit to surgery or X-ray remains a possibility, but over time this likelihood diminishes.) Such departments as inhalation therapy are likely to come into contact with the patient if his injury so requires. Finally, after he has recovered sufficiently to be discharged, he once again deals with medical records and the finance office (although additional contact with this latter department may also follow his release).

Other departments cannot be fixed on this flow scheme, either because they are not directly in contact with the patient at any particular time or because they are in continual contact with him throughout his hospital stay. Examples of the former are the entire educational section (except for student nurses who might work in the wards), a majority of

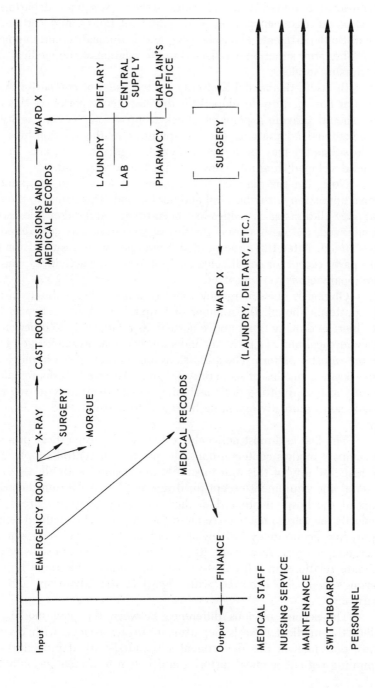

Fig. 1. Flow model for a nondisaster emergency case

administrative departments (business office, personnel department, switchboard, cashiers, payroll, and public relations), and certain internalistic departments (housekeeping and maintenance and engineering). The latter situation is reflected in the relation of the medical staff and nursing service.

By itself, this model is of only limited use. But comparison with a similar flow pattern developed for the emergency period in this disaster should provide a point of attack from which the complexity of organizational adaptations (i.e., adaptations in the relationships between subunits) may be better analyzed. Figure 2 represents such a model developed from interview data for the crisis period.

Note that the diagram traces patient flow only to the point of formal admission to the hospital and not beyond. This is due to the fact that once all disaster casualties had been treated and either released or hospitalized, the crisis period for this organization was considered to have ended. After this time normal operations were resumed for the most part (except for certain clean-up and recording activities), and no additional victims were received.

Obviously the emergency room is still the first subunit in this flow pattern. Though the number of hospital personnel active in this area increased many times above normal, its relationship to other emergency medical units (e.g., X-ray and surgery) remains unchanged from the pre-disaster pattern. The admissions office also remains in much the same position on this crisis-period diagram. The staff clerks remained on duty at the admitting desk, assigning disaster victims requiring hospitalization to already available beds and to those cleared by evacuation.

The first and most noticeable difference between these pre- and post-impact models centers around the position of central supply. It is the responsibility of this unit to supply the hospital with all necessary material and equipment except for drugs and blood. During the crisis, areas of the hospital other than the emergency treatment area (i.e., primarily the wards) made no requests for supplies. This enabled central supply to concentrate exclusively on supplying the emergency room and emergency surgery. As a result, its position shifted into an exclusive and intimate relationship with these emergency units. This same type of rearrangement also occurred with regard to the laboratory and the pharmacy.

The second obvious difference between the flow models involves the medical records department. In accordance with disaster plans, personnel in this department suspended normal procedures of compiling patient medical histories and began to attach specially de-

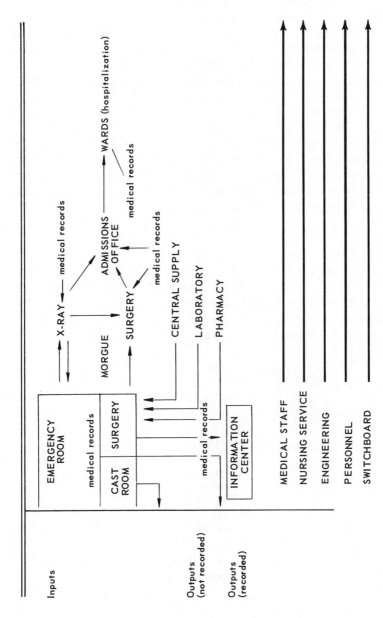

Fig. 2. Flow model for crisis period

signed disaster tags to victims as they were delivered to the emergency room. This resulted in a dispersal of departmental staff into the emergency treatment area. These persons were also complemented by non-departmental hospital personnel who joined in the tagging operations. As a unit, this department ceased to exist during the emergency period. It was not until the crisis was over (i.e., after the last remaining patients had been cleared from the emergency room) that the medical records staff began the compilation and typing of medical histories. Thus, this unit is dropped from its previous position on the flow model.

Two internalistic departments do not appear on the crisis flow model. The laundry had been closed for the day approximately one hour before the tornado struck, and all its personnel had returned home. (It is important here to point out that this disaster occurred at 5:30 p.m. when those sections of the hospital which operate only during the normal workday were closed.) There was no need to reopen this unit until the regularly scheduled work shift the following morning. Similarly, the dietary department was closed by the administrator after the last of the patients in the house had been fed their evening meals. Personnel were advised to go home in order to lessen the confusion in the building. Having completed its feeding operation, the department postponed dishwashing and other clean-up activities until the following morning.

Nor was the finance office reopened during the emergency after having closed for the day. Consequently, none of the victims who were treated and released had any contact with this office until the following morning, if at all.

The most interesting difference between the two diagrams is in the emergence of a totally new unit in the crisis model. In accordance with the organization's disaster plan, an information center was established in the hospital chapel relatively early in the crisis period. Here relatives and friends of victims brought to the hospital were counseled by the hospital chaplain as well as by over fifty ministers of all faiths who stopped in from time to time. Members of the press and mass communications networks were also restricted to this area where they were given up-to-date information on the names and conditions of victims by the public relations director and those assisting him. Also patients who had been examined and were being released were sent here for coffee and sandwiches if they had not eaten, or for religious counseling. The basic purpose for the establishment of this center, however, was to help eliminate the problem of convergence by providing a waiting area away from the emergency suite. This problem is rather common for hospitals following large scale emergencies and is discussed in more detail elsewhere.[7]

Of the various departments not directly located on this flow chart, only the controller's office (including finance, payroll, and cashiering) was inoperative as a unit during the emergency. Obviously there were few if any demands made upon it at this time. When this office did reopen the following morning, however, insurance company representatives were present in abundance to begin the third-party-payer process of financing the costs of the tragedy. Also members of the Red Cross began contacting this department as it undertook the provision of aid to disaster victims. Demands during this period were much heavier than for comparable normal periods but not such that additional personnel were needed.

Evaluation and Implications

After comparing flow models constructed from both pre- and post-impact periods, it may generally be concluded that this technique does depict structural adaptations in multiple-unit organizations subject to severely altered environments. The approach points out where adaptive rearrangements have taken place in the relationships among the various subunits of such complex structures.

While it does not provide direct indications of the nature of these adaptive rearrangements (for example, formal-informal or sanctioned-unsanctioned) nor explain why such adaptations took place, it does provide a particularly advantageous point of attack from which such questions may be analyzed. Thus the flow model is not without significant implications, of both a practical and a theoretical nature. Three such implications are discussed.

First, the flow model incorporates two perspectives essential for the understanding of modern hospital care by combining into one an *input/output* organizational model with a *process* model of medical treatment. Thus, when the various subunits of the hospital are arranged over time, they represent a series of phases through which the patient passes during his stay in the hospital. The specific arrangement of these units and the length of time spent in each particular phase vary with the individual case and are in any event of only secondary importance. Of major concern is the fact that an output from one department is also an input for the next department in the sequence. For example, a patient treated in the emergency room who requires further hospital attention becomes an input into the X-ray department, and so on.

There is hardly anything startling about this fact in the case of one individual patient. But in the context of a disaster producing large numbers of victims who move through the hospital "system" almost simultaneously, this simple input/output relationship becomes much more problematic. For example, if the X-ray department were only partially operative or badly understaffed in terms of the demands upon it, then a bottleneck may be created between patients needing orthopedic surgery, for instance, in the emergency room and the surgical staff in the operating room. The flow model depicts, for researchers and hospital administrators alike, that all departments in this sequence must be capable of handling their own particular demand inputs for the overall disaster medical response to be efficient or, more importantly, to be effective.

Secondly, in its practical applications, the flow model points out that merely mobilizing doctors and nurses in the disaster situation represents in itself an inadequate response. Focusing on departments rather than upon individuals, this model suggests that mobilization of human resources should be conducted in somewhat the same order as the units presented on the normal-period flow chart. For example, medical personnel (doctors, interns, nurses, etc.) would be contacted first, followed by X-ray personnel, members of the admissions staff, and so on.

To a large extent, this is the pattern that is followed in hospital notification plans. However, if departments are viewed as organizational components each with its own technology, it would appear that clerical personnel should be altered before certain medical and even supervisory personnel. That is, each technology requires for its full implementation the activities of all components of that particular subunit. The tasks of low-level members of a department are no less important to its overall functioning than are those of its head or supervisor. Using the X-ray department again as an example, technicians are needed to take and develop negatives. Typists and other clerical workers must identify and properly code each picture taken. Finally, a trained radiologist is needed to evaluate and diagnose the developed photograph in order to recommend proper treatment. All these tasks need to be performed if the department is effectively and rapidly to dispose of its voluminous demand-inputs. Thus, X-ray technicians and clerks may need to be contacted before a pharmacist or the head of a department such as central supply. The flow model, with its departmental focus, suggests more efficient guidelines to emergency notification systems that may be overlooked on a common-sense basis.

Reference was made above to the notion of the capability of the various departments in relation to the demand-inputs faced in a major disaster or emergency situation. At an organizational level, the Disaster Research Center has developed the concept of stress as an index of this capability-demand ratio. Under normal conditions it is assumed that the capability of an organization exists in a dynamic interrelationship with the demands upon it such that its capability is at least equal to (and most often in excess of) demands. When a change in the environment occurs, such as a natural disaster, demands are likely to increase greatly and suddenly. The capability of the organization may be reduced as well. When a situation exists such that demands exceed capability, the organization is said to experience stress.

Determining whether or not an organization as complex (i.e., composed of as many different operating units) as a general hospital has experienced stress is at best a difficult task. Demands placed upon some units may be greatly above normal and may surpass their capabilities while little or no demands may be made upon other units. By focusing on these various subunits and by viewing each as having its own demand-inputs, the flow model adds new light to the concept of stress. It can be argued that much of the confusion surrounding the application of this concept involves its assumption of a single technology. That is, capabilities and demands are related to the ability of work units to produce desired outputs. In organizations which involve only one such output, the success in producing these outcomes is relatively simple to determine. But in those organizations such as hospitals which include several technologies, each producing different kinds of outputs, such a determination is much more difficult.

As Thompson suggests, it is possible to treat various departments as units possessing distinct and discrete technologies. For each department, therefore, particular sets of demands, inputs, capabilities, and outputs may be identified. In organizations with multiple technologies the concept of stress is best applied to each technological unit (i.e., department) rather than immediately to the entire organization. Thus, the emergency room may experience stress (that is, demands may exceed its capabilities) but the X-ray department may not, and so forth.

Furthermore, the time dimension implicit in the flow model points out that not all departments will experience stress simultaneously (if, indeed, at all). Demands upon the emergency room may so exceed its maximum capability that few outputs are forthcoming. When capabilities are increased through the mobilization of personnel (among other means), larger numbers of patients are then readied for the services of other departments (e.g., X-ray admissions, the wards, etc.). These in turn may experience stress. Indeed, in the hospital examined here some subunits did not experience significant increases in demands until the following day (dietary and laundry) and even the following week (as in the business and finance offices). In short, with the use of such flow models much of the confusion surrounding the concept of organizational stress in organizations with multiple technologies can be resolved by examining the capability/demand/output relationships for each of their component parts.

Finally, this discussion of organizational stress in light of the application of flow models raises an important question for general theories of social systems. That is, given the traditional notion of interdependence of parts in social systems, how is it possible for some but not all subunits to experience stress? Or, put another way, why is it that changes in one segment of the system do *not* lead to changes in other segments of that same system? Flow model analysis has suggested at least two kinds of relationships of organizational units to the primary raw material of hospitals. *Direct* relationships are characteristic of departments such as nursing service, medical staff, X-ray, and so on. *Indirect* relationships are best illustrated by the personnel department, the business office, switchboard, public relations, and the like. Results of the data analysis show that some *but not all* directly related units underwent adaptation as a result of the increased demands of disaster as did certain of those departments only indirectly related to patient care. And along slightly different lines, identical conclusions may be drawn when the distinction is made between those departments located in the patient-flow sequence and "off-line" units such as maintenance.

At a very practical level the answer is a simple one, namely that some units of the organization are more affected than others by the increased demands of emergency situations. But on a more theoretical level the implication clearly is that traditional conceptions of system interdependence do not admit to differences of this sort. Granting that complex organizations such as hospitals may be thought of as a smaller version of large-scale social systems, flow model analysis indicates that more than one type of interdependence may exist. Results of this analysis suggest the need for closer examination of relations between subsystems over and above those characterized by input/output relationships.

Summary

The concept of flow models has been used to depict the interrelationships of subparts in organizations with intensive technologies, that is, those in which a variety of activities are selected and ordered to produce certain desired changes in raw materials. Two such models were developed for normal and emergency situations and then compared in order to determine changes in interdepartmental relationships under crisis conditions.

Results of this comparison indicate first more effective means of disaster planning in organizations with such technologies. In hospitals, for instance, the findings suggest that plans for the mobilization of various personnel are best developed along lines of departmental membership rather than in terms of such aggregate categories as occupation or position in an authority hierarchy. Also, some considerations were disclosed which shed more light on the determination of the amount of stress experienced by organizations under these conditions. In organizations with multiple functioning units as over against those with only a single operating unit, the flow model suggests that not all units will necessarily experience great increases in demands. Rather, stress at an organizational level is better thought of as some sort of overall sum of departmental evaluations on this dimension. And theoretically, traditional notions of interdependence of parts in social systems theory was called into question when it was noted that organizational subunits exhibited differential adaptations to the effects of environmental alterations. The explanation may lie in the fact that kinds of interdependency other than those of the input/output variety exist.

Two aspects of flow model analysis remain open for further investigation apart from studies of other types of organizations in differing situations. Possible changes in the *nature* of interrelationships among subunits need to be explored as well as compared. One might hypothesize, for example, that the degree of interdependency among departments will increase as input/output relationships within the organization become more problematic. And secondly, administrative and managerial processes which *coordinate* the relationships among departments need further examination. It may be that these processes require more intensive and more frequent implementation in situations of this nature. Flow models seem particularly well suited to provide more theoretical systemization for analysis of these and other aspects of organizational behavior in future research.

Notes

1. A. Etzioni, *Modern Organizations*, Prentice-Hall, Englewood Cliffs, New Jersey, 1964, p. 77.

2. J. B. Thompson, *Organizations in Action*, McGraw-Hill, New York, 1967; C. Perrow, "A Framework for the Comparative Analysis of Organizations," *American Sociological Review*, Vol. 32, 1967, pp. 194–208.

3. Perrow, *ibid.*, p. 195.

4. Thompson, *op. cit.*, p. 17.

5. *Loc. cit.*

6. Etzioni, *op. cit.*, p. 91.

7. C. E. Fritz and J. H. Mathewson, *Convergence Behavior in Disaster: A Problem of Social Control*, National Academy of Science-National Research Council, Washington, D.C., 1957.

Routine Technology, Social Structure, and Organization Goals

Jerald Hage and Michael Aiken

In the last few years, technology has become increasingly popular as an explanatory concept in organizational analysis. Blauner (1964) used it as a key factor in explaining different levels of alienation in American industry. Woodward (1965) found that types of technology affected the number of levels of management and the span of control in British industry, and Perrow (1967) has suggested several hypotheses linking this concept to different aspects of the organization's structure and goals. The purpose of this article is to explore these and other hypotheses in a study of people-processing organizations.

This kind of organization provides a particularly interesting context for the study of the association between technology and the structure and functioning of an organization. Techniques of reinforcement or interviewing are less obvious than those of machine handling. Yet rehabilitation centers, mental hospitals, family agencies, and schools have a work-flow and add value to their product, the client, just as any industrial firm does. The difficult task is to find measurable dimensions for describing this work-flow. The terms used by Blauner (1964) and Woodward (1965)—continuous process or assembly-line—are clearly not applicable to people-processing organizations. Furthermore, these categories are also limited in industry in their application: they describe only some kinds of technologies. Therefore, one task is to locate a general technological dimension that can be used not only in industry but also in people-processing organizations as well.

Part of the difficulty in finding a general variable describing technology stems from the fact that the concept subsumes many different ideas. The construct is so rich that it would be better to treat it like that of the concept of social structure—one containing many dimensions that need to be delineated and measured. Litwak (1961) has suggested one basic dimension, the uniformity of tasks. Perrow (1967:195–196) has called attention to a similar idea, the routineness of work. However, he defines this as including both the relative stability or variability of the raw material as well as how much is understood about this material. If the clients are stable and uniform and much is known about the particular process of treatment, then the organization has a routine work-

Reprinted from *Administrative Science Quarterly* 14 (1969):366–75.

flow. The teaching of reading might be a good example. In the contrasting situation of little uniformity and little understanding, we have a nonroutine work-flow. The interviewing of a psychotic might be an apt illustration. Thus, Perrow's discussion of routine vs. nonroutine actually subsumes several dimensions.

The routineness of work does not cover all aspects of the concept of technology. There are other dimensions that can be defined and measured. For example, the environment of work, such as level of noise, dirt, and layout or the amount of energy used, is frequently included under the rubric "technology" (Labovitz, 1963). It is difficult, however, to apply this across all organizations. The degree of routineness is one dimension of technology that can be applied equally to people-processing, industrial, and other kinds of organizations, and it can provide the basis for general propositions that can be tested in many organizational contexts.

The interest in technology as an independent variable stems from the recognition that the work processes of an organization provide the foundation upon which social structure is built (Perrow, 1967:195). Because of this, technology should influence the nature of that structure. That is, technology is likely to determine whether it is formalized or nonformalized, whether it has a diverse or relatively simple division of labor, and so together, the technological foundation and substructural social arrangements influence the substructure of organizational goals. As Perrow has suggested, these factors set limits on the goals that are maximized and those that are minimized. It is this connection between routine work, organizational structure, and goals that forms the focus of this article.

The intellectual problem posed here requires that the organization be treated as a unit of analysis and that properties of that unit—analytical, structured, and global (Lazarsfeld and Menzel, 1961)—be abstracted and analyzed. The routineness of the technology of the entire organization rather than the routineness of particular techniques is thus analyzed. Similarly, the concern with social structure is with the arrangement of all social positions or jobs in an organization, not just certain ones. The research design for sampling these arrangements and for measuring the complete organization as a unit of analysis are described in the next section. The specific hypotheses and findings relating the degree of routine work to structural variables and goals are then presented.

Research Design and Measurement

The data were collected in sixteen health and welfare agencies located in a large midwest metropolis during the early Spring of 1967. Ten agencies were private; six were either public agencies or branches of public agencies. These organizations were all the larger agencies that provide rehabilitation services, psychiatric services, and services for the mentally retarded as defined by the directory of the community chest. The organizations varied in size from just over twenty in a small family agency to over six hundred in one of the mental hospitals.

Procedures for Measuring Organizational Variables

A central problem in the study of organizations concerns the measurement of organizational properties or variables (Lazarfeld and Menzel, 1961: James Coleman, 1964). Organizations are composed of individuals working in various jobs which are arranged in different structural configurations and work-flow. It is these arrangements which will be described and measured in this study.

    The organization was divided into levels and departments and then job occupants were selected randomly within these categories. In other words, a stratified random sample in which the stratification was based on two key dimensions of the organization—levels and departments—was used. This procedure has several advantages: (1) it can be used in any kind of organization, irrespective of its specific goals; (2) it corresponds to the way organizations are actually structured; (3) organizational participants are likely to locate themselves in terms of different levels and departments. These criteria are not only analytical justifications, but also correspond to the reality of organizational life. Certainly the nature of work, an essential part of the problem of measuring work-flow and its routineness, is likely to vary at minimum by level and department. Therefore, the sampling procedures should attempt to reflect these basic aspects of the organization.

    Respondents within each organization were selected by the following criteria:

1. All department heads and supervisory personnel, both professional and non-professional.
2. One half of other professionals in departments of less than ten members were selected randomly.
3. One third of other professionals in departments of more than ten members were selected randomly.

Non-supervisory administrative and maintenance personnel were not interviewed because they were less likely to be involved in the establishment of organizational goals and policies. The different ratios in larger and smaller departments insured that the smaller departments would be adequately represented. All supervisory personnel at the upper levels were included because they were most likely to be key decision-makers. This stratified design resulted in 11 interviews in the smallest organizations and 62 in one of the larger.

Since the unit of analysis was the organization, the data for each organization had to be aggregated in order to calculate scores for measures of organizational structures. This was done by first computing means for each social position in the organization. A social position was defined in the same way as the sample was stratified, that is, by level and department. For example, if an organization's professional staff consisted of two departments—psychiatric and social work—and two levels—supervisors and caseworkers—then there were four social positions in this organization.

Computation of means for each social position has the advantage of avoiding the problem potentially created by the use of two sampling ratios. In effect, responses are standardized by organizational location—level and occupation—and then combined into the organizational score. Computation of means of social position also has the major theoretical advantage of focusing on the sociological perspective of organizational reality. An organization is perceived as a collection of social positions rather than an aggregate of individuals.

The second step was to compute an organizational score for each dimension by averaging the means of all social positions, as defined, in each organization. Equal weight was thus given to each social position.

The sampling procedure omitted non-supervisory and non-professional personnel, but since this was done in all organizations it represents a standardized procedure. The sampling and aggregation procedures prevent the top echelons from being underweighted, which would happen if the score was computed by equally weighing each interview in an organization.

Measurement of Routineness

Several different questions were used in constructing the measure of the routineness of work. The first of these questions is as follows: "Would you describe your work as being very routine, somewhat routine, somewhat nonroutine, or very nonroutine?" This question, together with several others developed by Hall (1963) loaded together in a factor analysis of various aspects of organizational behavior and seem to represent a separate and distinct dimension representing the routineness of work. Hall's questions were:

1. People here do the same job in the same way every day.
2. One thing people like around here is the variety of work (reversed).

3. Most jobs have something new happening every day (reversed).

4. There is something different to do every day (reversed).

Respondents replied definitely true, true, false, or definitely false to each of the questions. A factor analysis was felt to be necessary because there is a seemingly close similarity between routineness of work process and other aspects of organizational life such as the degree of job codification or specification of work procedures. This variable has different substantive content from either of the measures of formalization used.

Routineness of work measures how much variety there is in work; job codification measures how well defined the job is; rule observation measures the enforcement of the rules; job specificity measures how concrete the job description or procedural manual is. Clearly, routineness is different from the content of each of these. As a check on this measure the distribution by type or organization was examined.

The organizations included here are relatively homogeneous since most of them provide psychological, psychiatric, or rehabilitation services of one kind or another. As one might expect in such organizations, the scores tend more towards nonroutineness. That is, the organizational scores ranged from 1.31 to 2.46 on a scale that could vary from 1.00 to 4.00

The highest on routineness is a family agency in which the caseworkers use a standard client interview that takes less than fifteen minutes. The purpose of the interview is to ascertain the eligibility of clients for county, federal or state medical aid. One interviewee said: ". . . somewhat routine—Even though each patient is individual, the type of thing you do with them is the same. . . ." The organization at the other extreme is an elite psychiatric family agency in which each member is an experienced therapist and allowed to work with no supervision at all.

Information from other sources about the agencies within each organizational category reported in Table 1 suggests that the reports of the staff are relatively correct. For example, the residential treatment center that scored lowest on routineness is one in which the executive director reported that the work is so novel and innovative that his staff does not know which professional association to join because each of the existing ones is clearly inappropriate. One staff member of this organization replied:

> Highly nonroutine. No two days are alike when you are working with highly unpredictable children. We individualize very highly here; we would turn the place upside down for one child—and sometimes we do.

TABLE 1
Means and Range for Scores of Degree of Routineness
in Different Organizational Categories

Kind of Organization	Number	Mean	Range
Family agencies	6	1.83	1.31–2.46
Rehabilitation centers	3	1.80	1.59–1.94
Residential treatment homes	3	1.73	1.46–1.90
Mental hospitals	3	1.73	1.63–1.82
Department of special education	1	1.64	1.64

This organization was considering creating a new professional society. While there is little difference between degree of routineness among the three mental hospitals, the one that is least routine is an elite, private sanitorium attached to a university medical school.

In general, the range within each category of organizations is somewhat restricted except for the social casework agencies. This suggests that the sample is basically similar in terms of technology: each organization relies heavily upon some variety of psychiatric techniques. The range is greatest in the social casework agencies because it is here that the standardized interview is most likely to be found. Examination of the responses of various occupational groups in the study gives greater appreciation of the validity of the measure and of the variation in technologies. As might be expected, the higher the level within each organization, the more likely the job occupant is to report that his job is very nonroutine (Hall, 1962). A supervisor in a residential treatment center said ". . . highly nonroutine because we're dealing with a rather flexible entity, that is, a disturbed student." A case coordinator in an elite social casework agency described his job as nonroutine because: ". . . the planning requires some creativity and supervision and consultation requires the ability to relate current problems which are never routine." Finally, a supervisor in a rehabilitation center replied:

> Because of the kind of problems we have, they cannot be anticipated. Each week problems occur, so that appointments have to be changed constantly.

But at each level there are differences. The supervisors of the ancillary departments, such as business or maintenance, are more likely to state that their jobs are routine than those who head departments of social work, psychology, nursing, or teaching. One accountant said: "By the nature of accounting and statistics—it must be routine—it's mandatory in accounting." This not only suggests that the sampling procedure is indeed an appropriate one, but that staff members more removed from dealing with the clients report more routine work procedures.

Members of occupational groups that spend a lot of time with clients were more likely to perceive their work as nonroutine than those who spend short periods of time with clients. Thus nurses are more likely than either psychiatrists or psychologists to state that their work is very nonroutine. Similarly, houseparents who actually live with emotionally disturbed children are more likely to state nonroutine work than homemakers who visit homes for short periods of time.

Members of occupational groups that perform the same activities with clients without variation are more likely to perceive their work as routine than those who have greater variety in their work. For example, vocational instructors who teach standardized procedures were more likely to report their work as routine than teachers who teach verbal and written skills. One teacher in a residential treatment center said her work was nonroutine because of "working with emotionally disturbed children; from one day to the next their reaction varies." In contrast, a vocational instructor said her work was highly routine because:

> You have to have a routine or you couldn't do it. You have to make a schedule and not interfere with anyone and you have to train your girls that way.

Psychometricians were more likely to describe their work as routine than clinical psychologists. And, finally, administrative assistants were more apt to report routine work situations than assistant executive directors, even though they are on the same level of authority. The latter must supervise a variety of occupational skills.

While these examples demonstrate variations among different occupational groups and among different levels of authority in these organizations, the results of this study are not simply functions of variations in occupation and level of authority. Rather, the measure seems to have captured a characteristic of the organization itself. This contention is supported by our findings using one-way analysis of variance tests of three different independent variables: levels of authority (three), occupational groups (thirteen largest), and organization (the sixteen included here). Differences by level and occupational group were not statistically significant, but differences by organization were.

Hypotheses and Findings

Routine Work and Social Structure

Perrow (1967:198–199) begins his discussions of the impact of technology on the social structure (he uses the phrase "structure task") by noting that coordination can occur either via planning, programmed interaction, or feedback. This basic assumption, which is derived from March and Simon (1958: chapter 6) provides a basic for interpreting the possible consequences of the degree of routineness of work. If technology can be routinized, then coordination can be and probably will be planned and programmed. If it cannot, then coordination must be effected via feedback. From this flows a series of consequences for organizational social structure.

1. *Organizations with routine work are more likely to be characterized by centralization of organizational power.*

If organizational members constantly face a work situation characterized by highly varied clients' needs, then greater organizational power will accrue to organizational members who interact with the clients most frequently. It will be necessary to have constant reports from such individuals in order for adequate coordination to be accomplished. The need for feedback about client-handling and particularly about basic policies, as well as the development of new programs, will result in a decentralization of organizational decision-making (cf. Greenblatt, York and Brown, 1955). The search for new programs is presumedly a reflection of the attempt to find more adequate technology for solving the problems of the clients. But this requires a series of decisions about personnel, policies, programs, and budget allocations. The most appropriate participants in making such decisions are those who work with clients.

The findings shown in Table 2 suggest that this line of reasoning is correct. The correlation coefficient between the degree of routineness of work and participation in organizational decision-making is $-.72$; that is, the more routine the work-flow, the greater the centralization of decision-making about basic organizational issues.

It should be noted that in his original discussion, Perrow suggested four possible arrangements of an organization's power structure, corresponding to his two basic continua defining routineness: the incidence of exceptional cases and the incidence of analyzable problems. In the extreme case of nonroutine work, that is, where there is both variability in clients as well as lack of knowledge about their handling, the power structure should be polycentralized (Perrow, 1967: Figure 3). The data in Table 2 indicate that it is decentralized. (The polycentralized organization is more probable in Perrow's type 1 organization.) Actually, Perrow's own discussion of the high power of both technicians and supervisors indicates that the nonroutine organization really should be decentralized since he states that both groups will have high power.

Perrow (1967:198) makes a critical distinction between organizational power and work discretion. This corresponds to discussions of

TABLE 2

The Relationship Between Routine Work and Social Structure

Structural Variables	Pearsonian Product-moment Correlation Coefficients	p
Degree of centralization		
Degree of participation in organizational decisions	− .72	<.001
Degree of hierarchy of authority in work decisions	− .02	N.S.
Degree of formalization		
Degree of job codification	.21	N.S.
Degree of rule observation	.20	N.S.
Presence of a rules manual	.51	<.05
Presence of job descriptions	.53	<.05
Degree of specificity of job descriptions	.61	<.01
Degree of stratification		
Affect between supervisors and staff	− .09	N.S.
Distance between supervisors and staff	.19	N.S.
Degree of complexity		
Amount of professional training	− .55	<.05
Amount of professional activity	− .12	N.S.
Number of occupational specialties	− .19	N.S.

*For discussion of the construction of all the measures of the variables included here with the exception of the presence of a rules manual and job descriptions and the two measures of stratification, see Aiken and Hage, 1968.

other researchers, such as Blauner (1964), who have noted the differences between participation in basic organizational decisions about policies and participation in decisions about work appropriate to a particular job (cf. Hage and Aiken, 1967). Perrow indicates that routine work might lead both to low discretion over work decisions as well as little power in making organizational decisions. The measure of autonomy in work decisions used in this study—the hierarchy of authority—indicates that this is not necessarily the case. There was no correlation ($r = -.02$) between these two organizational characteristics. Discretion over work is evidently affected by other organizational variables, not by the degree of routineness of work.

2. *Organizations with routine work are more likely to have greater formalization of organizational roles.*

If an organization is coordinated via planning, this will be reflected in a high degree of formalization of organizational roles. Such formalization will be reflected in various types of rules and regulations defining role obligations and enactment. One way to bring about such formalization is to establish a series of written documents that specify who is to do what, when, where, and why. Routine work obviously facilitates the process of formalization by providing the stability or lack of variety in clients that makes the writing of documents containing regulations or rules more manageable. Such documents are variously called policy manuals, job descriptions or evaluation procedures.

The use of a rules manual and of job descriptions are two basic mechanisms for establishing organizational control. Aside from these indicators of formalization, the degree of specificity in job descriptions, the degree of codification of jobs, and the degree of rule observation, that is, the degree of surveillance, were measured. The major distinction between job codification and specificity of the job descriptions is one between rules and procedures; the former measures whether or not there are rules for the job occupants while the latter measures the degree to which work procedures are specified. These are complementary ideas that need not necessarily be correlated (Rushing, 1966). Indeed, each of these three dimensions was obtained in a factor analysis of several batteries of tests developed by Hall (1963). Since there is such a close connection between the idea of routineness and formalization, items in these dimensions were included in the same factor analysis, and these items loaded with separate factors. The presences of a rules manual and of job descriptions was based on staff responses to questions about each of these. The items included in the other three variables are described elsewhere (Aiken and Hage, 1968).

Routine work leads to the formalization of regulations as represented by the presence of a rules manual ($r = .51$), the presence of job descriptions ($r = .53$), and the degree of job specificity ($r = .61$), but has little impact on job codifications ($r = .21$) and rule observation ($r = .20$) although the relationships with these factors are in the predicted direction (see Table 2). This parallels the findings on the relationship between routine work, power, and discretion over work. Job codification and rule observation refer more to work regulations while the rules manual, job descriptions and job specificity reflect basic work guidelines and policies of the organization. These last three are more likely to be manifestations of the programming for the orgnaization's coordination than the other two measures.

3. *There is no relationship between the degree of routine work and organizational stratification.*

If the organization is highly programmed with routine work, there is little need for interaction; the interaction that does occur can be programmed in ritualized reports to the boss. Perrow (1967: Figure 3) hypothesizes that there is less interdependence of work groups in a routine organization. This suggests that there may be considerable social distance between levels of hierarchy or chain command. An excellent illustration of this phenomenon is found in Crozier's (1964) study of bureaucracy where there was considerable difference in the prestige of staff and supervisors in an obviously routine organization.

Two dimensions of organizational stratification, the degree of affect toward supervisors and the degree of social distance between supervisors and staff were measured. These dimensions were obtained from a factor analysis of scales developed by Seeman and Evans (1961) in their study of the stratification of medical wards. The findings indicate that there is no support for this hypothesis. There is almost no relation between the degree of affect and routineness ($r = .09$), and there is only a very weak positive relationship between routineness and social distance ($r = .19$), indicating that the direction of these relationships support the expectation of barriers developing between supervisors and staff when the work-flow is routinized, but that the strength of these relationships are not large enough to argue for support of the hypothesis.

4. *Organizations with routine work are likely to have staff with less professional training.*

Although Perrow (1967) does not discuss this dimension of organizational structure, it would appear that if the organization is coordinated by programming, there is less need for a variety of occupational specialties or for well-trained occupants. In other words, the programming of the organization allows for simplification of the social structure. As technology becomes routinized, it is less necessary for an organization to hire men with highly specialized skills. The main purpose of the assembly-line, the extreme routinization of work-flow, is to eliminate completely the need for highly skilled labor. To a lesser extent, the same principle can operate in people-processing organizations. If the interview of a client is straight-forward, for example, simply ascertaining the eligibility of the client for welfare then the organization has little need for job occupants with advanced degrees. In contrast, using psychiatric skills requires at a minimum a master's degree, and more advanced training is often desirable. To a lesser extent, the routinization of technology can affect the number of different occupational specialties as well. If little is known about the particular technology, the organization is likely to hire different specialties in the hope that something may work. As one member of a rehabilitation organization said, "We keep thinking that if we have a variety of specialists, our clients are better off, but in fact we don't know if this is really true."

Organizations with routine work have less well trained staff. The correlation between professional training and degree of routineness is −.55. But the degree of routine work has little effect on either the diversity of occupational groups in an organization (r = −.19) or on the relationship with the amount of professional activity, the third measure of complexity (r = −.12). Routine work reduces the need for expertise but does not seem to affect either the variety of job specialties or the amount of involvement in professional activities.

The routineness of work may be only a consequence of size. That is, as size of the organization increases bureaucratization might also increase, thus providing a strong pressure toward routinization of work. This would mean that many of the observed relationships between this aspect of technology and these social structural variables may simply be functions of the inevitable programming that is necessary for the co-ordination of larger organizations. Almost no relationship was found between the size of the organization and the routineness of the work process (r = .07). This finding indicates that relationships between the routineness of work and other structural properties of organizations are evidently not a function of the size of the organization. Routineness of technology should be treated as an input that can affect the social structure of an organization independently of organizational size (Pugh et al., 1969).

Routine Work and Organizational Goals

Earlier it was suggested that technology can set limits on the goals of the organization. This process presumedly occurs via the structure of the organization. As technology is routinized, the organization is co-ordinated via programming. This is likely to be accompanied by centralization of power, formalization of roles, and some lessening of the level of professionalization in the organization. In such a social structure, a limited range of goals are likely to be maximized (Hage, 1965). In such a structure the organization is likely to emphasize the goal of efficiency in preference to other goals such as morale. Similarly, organizations with routine work structures are likely to emphasize the quantity of clients serviced rather than the quality of those services.

Perrow (1967:202) suggests basically the same hypotheses, although he does not provide any rationale for them. He makes a crucial distinction between system goals and product goals. In Perrow's view, the routine organization is likely to be concerned with stability and high profits achieved via quantity of production and an avoidance of innovation. In contrast, the nonroutine organization will emphasize growth, quality, and innovation, being less concerned with making profits. While these are examples of industrial firms, they suggest consequences for people-processing organizations as well, since the referents of system and product goals can be applied to all kinds of organizations, the idea is one of service. Do the organizational decision-makers emphasize the quantity or the quality of client service? Similarly, the emphasis of efficiency is akin to the idea of profits while emphasis on new programs is akin to the idea of innovation. Thus, while the system goals included here are not exactly the same as Perrow's, they are similar in meaning and can be applied to both industrial and non-industrial organizations.

This discussion of goals, whether system or product goals, is more general than the usual discussion of goals where the referant is the specific goal of some type of organization, (cf. March, 1965; Zald and Denton, 1963). Thus, the goal of schools is to teach or socialize; the goal of hospitals is to cure; the goal of business firms is to make profits, and so on. Similarly, the measures used in this study avoid this parochial approach to the study of goals by listing basic dimensions that can be applied to any organization, whether profit-making or not, thus providing an opportunity for the development of general propositions across all kinds of organization.

Respondents in the organizations were asked in a series of six paired comparisons to select the goal their organization was emphasizing at the time of interview: (1) the effectiveness of client services, (2) the efficiency of operation, (3) the morale of the staff, or (4) the development of new programs or services.

To minimize the effect of response set, the ordering of presentation of pairs was randomized. It should be noted that these questions are designed to elicit reports about the organization's emphasis on goals. In order to measure product goals as described by Perrow, the respondents were additionally asked whether the organization placed greater emphasis on the quantity of clients served or on the quality of client service. There is the possibility that the respondents reported the organizational priorities epoused by the organizational elites rather than reporting the actual emphasis in the organization from their point of view. That is, there is the danger that they simply reported the goals desired by organizational leaders. There is no assurance that actual outputs were measured. Values about goals is a safer term to describe what was measured.

A scale was constructed for each goal such that in each of the three comparisons made, ten points were assigned if the respondent selected the goal and five points if he said half and half or gave both goals equal weight. Thus the scale for each goal varies from zero (the goal was never chosen) to thirty (the goal was chosen in each of the three pairs). A separate scale was constructed for each of the four goals.

There is no association between routineness and relative effectiveness as an organizational goal (r = .oo). This is not unexpected since the label "effectiveness" probably elicited normative responses. Most organizations strive to maximize effectiveness, but they differ in the pathways they choose; some choose to emphasize morale, others efficiency and still others new programs.

1. *Routine work is positively related to an emphasis on efficiency as a system goal.*

The routinization of the work-flow allows for the efficient handling of large numbers of clients at low cost, efficiency thereby becoming a systems goal. The notion of efficiency in nonprofit organizations is analogous to that of the profit motive in a business. Efficiency is facilitated via the formalization of regulations and careful planning of the organization. Table 3 indicates that these two organizational variables—degree of routineness and emphasis on efficiency—are related (r = .45).

TABLE 3

The Relationship Between Routine Work and Organizational Goals

System Goals	r	p
Emphasis on effectiveness	.00	N.S.
Emphasis on efficiency	.45	.10
Emphasis on morale	− .37	N.S.
Emphasis on new programs	− .05	N.S.
Product-Characteristic Goals		
Emphasis on quality	− .42	N.S.

2. *Routine work is negatively, but weakly related to morale as a system goal.*

The great strength of a routine work-flow is that it allows for the careful coordination of all the organizational tasks. But in the process, the fact that human beings are involved is frequently neglected. Thus routine work results in a lessening of emphasis on morale as a system goal. In addition, in many circumstances there is likely to be an incompatibility between the goals of morale and efficiency. Fringe benefits, higher salaries, and favorable working conditions may not be consistent with efficiency, but they affect morale. Perhaps more importantly, the pressure towards rapid, low cost production (that is, efficiency) reduces morale. Similarly, regulations which are the *sine qua non* of efficiency debilitate morale and enmesh staff members in red tape.

As expected, there is an inverse relationship between the degree of routine work and the emphasis on morale (r = −.37), but this relationship is not statistically significant. Organizations in which there is a routine work-flow are more likely to be those in which policy does not maximize high morale, at least according to the staff members in those organizations, but this is only a tendency since this relationship is not strong.

3. *There is no relationship between routine work and the development of new programs as a system goal.*

Much of the reasoning discussed above applies to this goal. New programs do not allow for an emphasis on efficiency. Similarly, routine work is the antithesis of the nature of work in the innovating organization (Wilson, 1966).

Despite the plausibility of the argument that the organization that is emphasizing new programs is one interested in innovativeness, the data do not support the hypothesis. There is no correlation between the emphasis on the development of new programs and the routineness of work ($r = -.05$). Admittedly, the development of new programs is not the only way in which organizations can innovate.

4. *Routine work is negatively, but weakly related to the quality of client service as a product goal.*

A routine work-flow allows for the gradual speed-up of the work process. The difficulty with the assembly-line and its speed of operation is the clearest example of this phenomenon, but the Blau (1965) study of records in a welfare agency illustrates the same idea in the context of people-processing organizations. The consequence of this is the maximization of the goal of quantity as opposed to quality.

The hypothesis is moderately supported by the data ($r = -.42$). The more that technology is routinized, the less the emphasis on the quality of service, and the more the emphasis on the number of clients served.

Summary and Discussion

Most of Perrow's implicit hypotheses about the relationships between the routineness of technology and dimensions of social structure receive considerable support. The more routine the organization, the more centralized the decision-making about organizational policies, the more likely the presence of a rules manual and job descriptions, and the more specified the job. While the measures of stratification used seem to measure a concept similar to Perrow's idea of interdependence, these concepts are distinct, so the lack of supporting findings here do not necessarily provide negative evidence. Although Perrow did not discuss the degree of complexity, it is interesting to note that routineness is negatively related to the amount of professional training but does not appear to have much association with other measures of complexity. Similarly, routineness does not appear to have much association with the hierarchy of authority or discretion over work decisions.

When the relationship between routineness of technology and organizational goals is examined, there are additional confirming results. In organizations with a relatively routine technology, the staff members are likely to report more emphasis on efficiency and quantity of clients than on quality of service and staff morale. There is no association between routineness of technology and the goal of innovation measured in this study.

It should be remembered that most of the 16 organizations studied were on the nonroutine side of the scale. But, precisely because it is a relatively homogeneous sample, the findings are all the more encouraging. The results do not appear to be simply a consequence of size; size has little or no relationship with routineness. While it is relatively easy to accept hypotheses about the relationship between routineness and properties of an organizational structure, it is less easy to accept the idea that the degree of routineness is the only variable involved. The size of the organization, its autonomy, and its level of financing are probably variables of equal importance.

Nor should the routineness of technology be considered as the only relevant technological dimension. Other dimensions such as the number of different kinds of technologies or the amount of organizational knowledge also need to be explored. In particular, it may be that these are more likely to be related to measures of complexity and the amount of organizational innovations.

Other input variables besides technology need to be explored in order to understand the relative importance of technology in determining social structure and in setting limits on organizational policy.

References

Aiken, Michael, and Jerald Hage. 1968. "Organizational interdependence and intra-organizational structure." *American Sociological Review* 33 (December): 912–930.

Blau, Peter. 1955. *The Dynamics of Bureaucracy*. Chicago: University of Chicago Press.

Blau, Peter, and W. Richard Scott. 1962. *Formal Organizations*. San Francisco: Chandler.

Blauner, Robert. 1964. *Alienation and Freedom: The Factory Worker and His Industry*. Chicago: University of Chicago Press.

Coleman, James S. 1964. "Research chronicle: the adolescent society." In Phillip Hammond (ed.), *Sociologist at Work*:213–243. New York: Basic Books.

Crozier, Michel. 1964. *The Bureaucratic Phenomenon.* Chicago: University of Chicago Press.

Greenblatt, Milton, Richard York, and Esther Brown, 1955. *From Custodial to Therapeutic Patient Care in Mental Hospitals.* New York: Russell Sage Foundation.

Hage, Jerald. 1965. "An axiomatic theory of organizations." *Administrative Science Quarterly* 10 (December):289–321.

Hage, Jerald, and Michael Aiken. 1967. "Relationship of centralization to other structural properties." *Administrative Science Quarterly* 12 (June):72–92.

Hall, Richard. 1962. "Intraorganizational structural variation: application of the bureaucratic model." *Administrative Science Quarterly* 7 (December:295–308.

———. 1963. "The concept of bureaucracy: an empirical assessment." *American Journal of Sociology* 69 (July):32–40.

Labovitz, Sanford. 1963. *Technology and Division of Labor.* Doctoral dissertation, University of Texas.

Lazarfeld, Paul, and Herbert Menzel. 1961. "On the relation between individual and collective properties." In Amitai Etzioni (ed.), *Complex Organizations: A Sociological Reader:* 422–440.. New York: Holt, Rinehart, and Winston.

Litwak, Eugene. 1961. "Models of bureaucracy which permit conflict." *American Journal of Sociology* 67 (September):177–184.

March, James G. 1965. *The Handbook of Organizations.* Chicago: Rand McNally.

March, James G., and Herbert A. Simon. 1958. *Organizations.* New York: Wiley.

Parsons, Talcott, and Neil Smelser. 1956. *Economy and Society: A Study in the Integration of Economic and Social Theory.* New York: Free Press.

Perrow, Charles. 1967. "A framework for the comparative analysis of organizations." *American Sociological Review* 32 (April):194–208.

Pugh, Derek, David J. Hickson, and C. Robin Hinings. 1969. "The context of organization structures." *Administrative Science Quarterly* 14 (March):91–114.

Rushing, William. 1966. "Organizational rules and surveillance." *Administrative Science Quarterly* 10 (March):423–443.

Seeman, Melvin, and John Evans. 1961. "Stratification and hospital care: I. The performance of the medical interne." *American Sociological Review* 26 (February):67–80.

Thompson, Victor. 1961. *Modern Organization.* New York: Knopf.

Wilson, James Q. 1966. "Innovation in organization: notes toward a theory." In James Thompson (ed.), *Approaches to Organizational Design:* 193–218. Pittsburgh: University of Pittsburgh Press.

Woodward, Joan. 1965. *Industrial Organization.* London: Oxford University Press.

Zald, Mayer. 1963. "Comparative analysis and measurement of organizational goals: the case of correctional institutions for delinquents." *Sociological Quarterly* 4 (Summer):206–230.

Zald, Mayer, and Patricia Denton. 1963. "From evangelism to general service: the transformation of the YMCA." *Administrative Science Quarterly* 8 (September):214–234.

The Organization of Treatment in a Psychiatric Hospital

Anselm Strauss, Leonard Schatzman, Rue Bucher,
Danuta Ehrlich, Melvin Sabshin

The Somaticists' Organization of Treatment

When organizing treatment for a patient, each psychiatrist at PPI must take into account the hospital's rules, resources, and drawbacks. He must also aim for a specific therapeutic goal: whether merely to prepare the patient sufficiently to face the outside world, to alleviate obvious symptoms, or to use the hospital visit as the first step in an extended course of therapy. Which goal he chooses depends on both his ideology and his assessment of the patient—but also his goals depend upon the types of patient he hospitalizes.

The somaticists at PPI treat mainly "depressive reactives," "psychotics," and "schizophrenics" of various types. They are hospitalized either because their behavior temporarily renders them unsuitable to remain in society or because they can be more easily treated within the hospital. Almost none has been treated previously at the doctors' offices, although they may have initially visited there. The principal therapeutic goal is to return these patients to the outside world as quickly as possible in a condition to cope with it somewhat better. The somaticist settles for minimal functioning and expects little, if any, change in personality. For these hospital patients, in contrast to office visitors, the psychiatrist dares hope only for symptomatic cure or for a generally better, although sometimes only temporary, handling of life's daily round. Meanwhile hospitalization puts maximum distance between the patient and his stressful environment, allows treatment to be efficiently organized, and permits for diagnosis if necessary.

These doctors pride themselves upon how speedily they move their patients out of the hospital: Indeed, this speed is a central feature of their treatment. They emphasized the value of this feature when talking to us. They believe that more analytically oriented psychiatrists labor with slower psychotherapeutic methods—when patients can be treated more quickly. They criticize the analysts for allowing patients to run through insurance money and claim that the doctor's duty is to effect

Excerpted from A. Strauss, et al., *Psychiatric Ideologies and Institutions* (New York: Free Press, 1964), pp. 184–87; 190–95; 297–98.

relatively quick recovery. Since many of their patients possess limited finances, this consideration buttresses the preference for short hospital stays.

In addition, they have little faith that prolonged hospital stays help patients. The hospital is not regarded as having special curative or instrumental powers: It is merely a locale where specific treatments like EST [electric shock treatment] or supportive therapy can be administered, and where the patient can temporarily be shielded from society— and *vice versa*. If the patient wishes continued therapy in office visits, so much the better, providing genuine benefit can be expected from such visits.

Let us visualize then the somatically oriented psychiatrist who brings his patient to the hospital: Where will he request that his patient be placed? In what kind of ward? His criteria for initial placement are two. A primary consideration is the patient's condition. If his behavior is quite bizarre, noisy, or in other ways difficult to control, then the proper place is in a relatively closed unit. The psychiatrist, in effect, accepts the hospital's conventional map, as the administration itself typically conceives it. But a second criterion for initial placement rests upon the consideration that one specific ward has the best arrangements for giving EST. Many patients are treated principally by that means. Furthermore, each somaticist believes he has customarily good working relationships with the personnel of that ward.

Somaticists' patients are therefore found clustered on 3EW or on one other relatively close ward. If patients are initially judged too "difficult" for these two wards, then the psychiatrists will request transfers to them after the patients' behavior has become more appropriate. They rarely use 2E, a more open ward. Sometimes they use 2N, the most open ward, as a locale from which patients finally will return home—and occasionally for patients who need only slightly different environments from their own homes plus supportive therapy.

In his favorite unit, the somaticist counts upon reliable routine nursing care for his patients, including medication when ordered. He also counts upon its staff to arrange efficiently for various diagnostic tests given at the main hospital. Indeed he has come over the years to rely upon an efficient secretary who is attached to both wards. She saves him much valuable time in dealing with the main hospital and expedites administrative details that otherwise he himself would have to handle or delegate to head nurses.

Toward his patients, his approach is distinctly medical. He is more likely to order medical tests than are most psychotherapeutically oriented men. He tends to utilize nurses in rather traditional medical fashions. He regards their functions as chiefly managerial and nursing-care. He likes to brief his nurses or give them orders with a minimum of verbal interchange. As he is rather uninterested in utilizing nurses as auxiliary to his own therapy, his picture of the nursing staff is relatively undifferentiated: He does not make fine distinctions among those who are good for certain kinds of therapy and those who are good for other kinds, those who are especially effective with certain kinds of patient and those who are not.

Since he does not believe nurses and aides are especially important therapeutic agents, he is neither particularly sensitive to their possible interference with his own therapeutic relations nor particularly apt to become annoyed or angry at the staff's psychological ineptitude—as long as the staff does not unduly disturb his patient or make the patient's environment unpleasant. In fact, if he is not entirely impervious to convert criticism of his treatment of particular patients by members of the staff, he is at least relatively protected from it by his ideological assumption that his therapy alone contributes to the patient's improvement. He is relatively oblivious to the surges of feeling that periodically run through the hospital staff, surges to which psychotherapeutically oriented psychiatrists are sensitive and with which they attempt to cope. The somaticists do not experience the full weight of this collective mood, and entire areas of conflict with the staff are therefore avoided in somatic hospital practice.

By the same token, the somaticist rarely, if ever, realizes that sometimes the staff organizes its own supplementary therapy around his patient because it believes his patient is receiving poor therapy. He can neither approve nor condemn this additional nursing effort. Occasionally he may even be brought up short against a high court of judgment, as when the nurses complain to the central administration that he is ordering EST for a very young patient. From time to time, the administration supports the complaints, and the psychiatrist must bend to the decision, having no recourse other than to withdraw his patient from the hospital.

Another aspect of his treatment ideology, however, leads him to believe that whatever the staff wishes to do by way of psychotherapy may actually be useful, for it contributes to keeping the staff happy while not actually interfering with his own program. The staff's actions may even make a patient's stay happier and more pleasant. One of these somaticists is therefore distinctly permissive; he tells those who show initiative to do with his patient what they think best, whether therapy or management is involved. His somatic colleagues tend to play along with the nurses, discussing patients when asked and probably giving the idea whether intentionally or not, that everyone is important to the total therapeutic set. They reason essentially that nurses merely contribute toward making the patient's environment more tolerable or supportive.

Sometimes the somaticist runs afoul of the staff's managerial problems. The nurses may wish to transfer a patient to a more controlling ward because she is no longer appropriate to their own. If the somaticist regards this transfer as inconvenient—and this kind of psychiatrist is on a tight time schedule—then he may bargain for another day or two on the original unit; he may even raise loud objections. More often, he is likely to abide by the staff's decision, since the transfer usually does not much inconvenience him or disturb his treatment of the patient. Sometimes too he faces the consequences of PPI's notably heterogeneous patient population. His patient, for instance, may complain that she does not wish to remain on 3EW because many noisy young people are there; generally, however, he regards the composition of any given ward as not very relevant to the patient's progress but only to her comfort and pleasure.

These psychiatrists bend every effort to remain medical men in their styles of practice. They utilize the hospital and its staff in fairly traditional ways. They believe that they are well served by the institution, for it is rather well organized to serve them, and they can take routine advantage of it—routine because they scarcely need be especially clever in their use of the hospital nor especially innovative in taking advantage of its resources. As a result, they are open to sharp criticism by other attending men and by the staff, but this criticism scarcely shakes their convicions about how a hospital can effectively be utilized.

The Psychotherapists' Organization of Treatment

Like the somaticists, these men must take into account the hospital itself in organizing individualized treatments for patients. The hospital, with its rules and regulations, its resources and its possibilities, constitutes a framework within which they must work. But they also operate in an ideological framework, generally if loosely referred to as "a psychodynamic approach." During their training they have become committed to it, largely through the supervision of analysts (or analysts in training) and through conferences, seminars, and classes.

These two frameworks together result in a typical operational procedure. With few exceptions and despite some differences in therapeutic philosophy, most ex-residents regard the hospital as if it were a *set* of differentiated therapeutic environments. They utilize and manipulate the environments into which they place patients. These environments, along with face-to-face therapy, constitute the psychotherapist's main weapons. In order to prevent the reader from assuming that such an environmental emphasis signifies the practice of *milieu*therapy, we hasten to explain what these men actually do with their patients.

The hospital, it will be recalled, consists of five wards that vary, in terms of the central administration's conception, from the most open to the most closed. The psychotherapist recognizes the administration's map and on occasion utilizes it. But the administrative map is not a therapeutic map: The latter must chart the hospital's interior space according to the therapeutic consequences that may follow from placing patients upon various wards. The hospital's interior space is not pictured in the same way by each psychiatrist, but all do picture various words according to *therapeutic* qualities and possibilities.

Here are some examples of those therapeutic dimensions. Wards can be viewed as locales in which varying amounts of "contact" are given a patient by the personnel; where he can receive varying amounts of stimulation from other patients; where he can experience varying degrees of external control over his own behavior; or where he can be confronted by varying necessities to exert control over his own behavior. Wards are locales where varying amounts of deliberately induced regression—prescribed by the psychiatrist—can be "tolerated" by the staff. There are some units in which a patient cannot get enough "support" and one large unit in which he can be "lost" in a crowd of other patients. Being lost, of course, may be therapeutically beneficial or not, depending upon the nature of the patient's condition. Conversely, there are wards that are conducive to the formation of intimate relationships among patients.

Where do the images of such therapeutic dimensions come from? In part, they derive from the psychiatrist's perceptions of certain common-sense features of the wards. Some wards, for instance, actually have high censuses of patients; some are of considerable physical size; some possess high ratios of personnel to patients; some have male aides; some tend to have more youngsters, while others tend to have numerous old people. But the therapeutic dimensions also derive, without question, from each psychiatrist's personal experiences—beginning early in residency—with treating patients upon certain wards. Through empirical experience he has discovered that certain wards seem beneficial, ineffective, or injurious for certain kinds of patient. He may also have discovered that certain wards are of dubious benefit for most of his patients, and he therefore scarcely uses them.

Although some psychotherapists tend to map the hospital according to a rather limited set of therapeutic dimensions, we have actually seen them operate with somewhat different dimensions for each patient or at least for each type of patient. Consequently it is more accurate to say that each has a different map of the hospital for each of his patients. He will try to have his patient placed initially on a certain ward according to what he judges that patient needs most, whether it be "contact," confrontation with "reality," or something else. Of course, more than one therapeutic dimension may be simultaneously relevant to his treatment. (Actually, although the therapist may request that his patient be assigned initially to a given ward, the disposition depends on the ROD's judgment at the time of admission. The ROD tends to go along with the request if it seems reasonable and if a bed is available. Often neither condition obtains.)

In other words, the psychotherapist takes into account only, or primarily, those aspects of the wards that appear relevant to his patient's condition. In so doing, he purposely ignores aspects important for treating other patients. This way of relating patients and wards places a premium upon the psychiatrist's ability to grasp the therapeutic possibilities of various wards. Even the most unimaginative pronounce given wards as useful, or not, for given kinds of treatment. The more ingenious the psychiatrist, the more therapeutic possibilities he is able to divine. With further experience, he may learn to imagine yet others. Each time that he brings in a different kind of patient, new therapeutic possibilities are likely to be revealed.

When such a psychiatrist has been successful in placing his patient upon a given ward, he has completed a considered action. He has had in mind how the environment may and may not affect his patient. But he may go further: He can attempt to control that setting to maximize its beneficial effects. He attempts to do so in two principal ways. First, he leaves "orders" that promote certain desirable possibilities for his patient. He may leave either written or verbal orders that his patient be treated with consistent firmness; be given "lots of contact"; or be forced to "confront reality" by certain treatments. A second technique for shaping the environment involves the psychiatrist's management of his patient's privileges. By expanding or contracting these privileges, the psychiatrist can transform the ward into different kinds of *milieu* for his patient. Thus a ward can be made relatively open by giving the patient opportunities to walk around the hospital or to visit friends on other wards. The patient may be cut off from communication with his family or allowed extensive telephone privileges. Even the most closed ward can be rendered relatively open for a patient by manipulating his privileges. Probably every attending man, regardless of his psychiatric ideology, attempts to manage the environments of his patients through proper orders and privileges, but the psychotherapeutically oriented shape those environments according to therapeutic designs.

Actually, the matter is much more complicated for at least two further reasons. Since most patients whom the psychotherapists treat at the hospital have not previously been treated in their offices, the therapists must frequently spend days or weeks observing patients— either directly or indirectly through pursuing reports—in order to judge what is wrong and what would be appropriate treatment. A certain amount of trial and error, manipulation of orders nd privileges, and selective placement upon various wards may therefore take place. Another complication is that, after a therapeutic program has been decided upon, the patient's progress or retrogression usually calls for a reshaping of the therapeutic environment. For instance, when the patient has responded well to "firm control" by the nursing staff, the *milieu* can be made more "permissive" because the patient has developed "internalized controls."

This changing relationship of patient and environment is indeed a very important matter. It is important that one understand that the psychiatrist has a notion of "phasing" that has less to do with the patient's outward behavior than with his internal changes. (In later chapters, we shall discuss what happens when the nursing staff views a patient's phasing differently from his psychiatrist.) When a patient leaves one stage and enters another, the therapist has alternative options: He may reshape the *milieu* for his patient, or he may transfer him to a more appropriate ward. A patient who has "pulled himself together" sufficiently to have regained control over himself may either be allowed additional privileges or be transferred to more open and freer wards progressively until he leaves the hospital. Whether the psychiatrist chooses to transfer his patient or to reshape the ward setting, he is taking the *milieu* into account therapeutically.

Where then does psychotherapy fit into his treatment? One must keep in mind the wide spectrum of patients whom these physicians are called upon to hospitalize. Some patients are so bizarre, so sick, that psychiatrists rely upon ward settings more than upon their own face-to-face contacts with them. But at the other extreme, a patient may receive more benefit from some type of psychotherapy than from experiences on the ward. In any event, as we shall see in later chapters, the perceived relations between ward and psychotherapy are often very subtle. To take only one instance: A psychiatrist may place his patient on a given ward because he believes it possesses certain qualities; he may gather from nursing notes and conversation with the head nurse how his patient is responding to the *milieu;* he may further check this information through his therapeutic sessions; he may recognize certain processes taking place as a result of those sessions; he may pass on certain information and leave certain orders as a result of the sessions— and thus attempt to reshape his patient's environment.

On general ideological grounds, these physicians would insist to a man that psychotherapy is far more important than ward setting. They would deny that they are *milieu*therapists. They believe that there can be no basic change in a patient without adequate psychotherapy. But what is true in theory is not entirely relevant to their kinds of hospital practice. Few of their patients continue in office therapy after hospitalization. Nor are they really expected, although frequently advised or urged, to continue. For most hospitalized patients, the psychotherapists, like the somaticists, are willing to settle for less lofty aims. The principal aim is to get the patient back to society sufficiently improved to function better than previously. Hopefully the patient need not later return to the hospital, but perhaps he will. For these chronic or less "treatable" patients, the psychiatrist is often willing to admit that the hospital environment is more important than face-to-face therapy —or equally important or indistinguishable in impact—since each aspect of the total treatment is relevant.

This style of hospital practice can be visualized as if it were an elaborate game of chess: The therapist seeks to gauge his patient's therapeutic movement and relates that movement to various therapeutic strategies of his own; whether in shaping the environment, in transferring the patient from one environment to another, or in managing his therapeutic sessions with the patient. The analogy with the chess game, of course, is most striking when the therapist moves his patient around the hospital according to some over-all therapetuic plan.

Not that he fails to do certain conventional things: He may handle some patients very much as do the somaticists. For instance, he may use drugs, shock treatment, and a minimum of "talking" therapy for elderly depressives. Yet he tends to order less EST and relies less on drugs than do the somaticists. He tends to try psychotherapy, including ward strategy, with most patients before relying on EST. He is accused, by somaticists, of a disposition to let patients run through Blue Cross money without substantial improvement. Whether that is true or not, these psychiatrists are certainly less concerned to get patients speedily home. They have no firm philosophy that the quickest treatment is the best treatment, although, as we have said, with some patients they reach this conclusion; but in general they have more faith in longer psycho-therapy and somewhat lengthier stays in the hospital.

This kind of hospital practice necessarily casts the psychothera-pist into dramatic roles. He finds himself unable strategically to use the hospital without becoming a diplomat. Except in his simplest maneuvers, he cannot take ward settings for granted or merely utilize routine nursing care. Of course he frequently does, but to the extent that he wishes to control his patient's environment with more subtlety, he must make arrangements and have understandings with the nursing personnel that involve diplomatic negotiation. While somaticists must also negotiate, the psychotherapists must do much more of it because they cannot so easily rely on stable understandings and routine arrange-ments. To control what goes on around their patients they must nego-tiate, dicker, and "play ball," as well as order, caution, advise, and ex-press wishes.

These therapists do not, however, necessarily have an unduly high regard for nurses and aides, nor do they attribute to such per-sonnel great psychiatric understanding or capacity for comprehending treatment. The psychotherapists vary in the specific ways they handle nurses. Some spend much time talking with nurses; some display higher regard for them; some pay little or no attention to aides; some give more direction to the personnel in deportment toward the patient. Some are certainly good at this diplomatic game they must play with the nursing staff, but others are rather inept or perhaps too busy with bur-geoning office practices to care. Whatever the variations in their hand-ling of nurses, they share a single view of the *psychiatric* nurse: Some are better than others but mainly because of "intuition" or some gift for spontaneous understanding of certain patients, rather than because of genuine intellectual understanding. What is true of nurses is even more true of aides, who are classified as better or worse on grounds of interest in and concern with patients and because of native emotional capacities (they are maternal, warm, and so forth). Unquestionably, much that happens in the hospital and to patients stems from this view of the nursing personnel, in conjunction with the personnel's failure to recognize that not merely some, but virtually all, the psychiatrists share this view.

When organizing his patient's treatment, the psychotherapist must cope with certain inherent institutional problems discussed earlier in this chapter. He may reason that his patient belongs most properly on 2W, but if 2W is full his patient may have to be housed on 3EW. Later he may calculate that his patient should be transferred to a less restricted ward—but simultaneously the 3EW staff may discover that it cannot tolerate his patient. The psychiatrist may then find his patient actually transferred to a more closed unit. Then he is likely to complain that PPI, with its fast-moving turnover, cannot handle lengthier periods of therapy; that, although its personnel can be permissive with patients, they cannot maintain "a firm line"; that PPI would be a better hospital if his patients were not exposed to the talk of EST patients; that PPI's rules and regulations are designed more for keeping order than for true therapy. But it is striking that this group of psychiatrists generally finds the hospital rather a good locale for its practice. These men criticize and carp, and they have trouble with the staff and administration from time to time, yet their criticism of the hospital is neither acrid nor severe. They do not have clear conceptions of how a more nearly ideal hospital would operate. On the whole, PPI suits their styles of hospital practice. If this attitude were not evident from interviews with them, we might have guessed it anyhow, for not one ex-resident has chosen to practice elsewhere in preference to PPI.

One final question about this style of practice requires an answer: How did these therapists learn to use the hospital as they do, since the chess game in which they are engaged is not simply a logical outcome of psychodynamic training and supervision? The answer is not difficult to find. From the moment that the young physician steps onto PPI's floors during his first weeks of residency, he hears of and sees the supposed therapeutic deficiencies and virtues of the various wards. He becomes aware of how very differently the attending men use the wards, whether for good or ill. As administrator of a ward, he finds himself in the midst of these conflicting views. He also has experience of the wards as a supervised resident, for he treats hospitalized service patients for three years. He finds himself maneuvering his patients around the hospital, just as ex-residents do. As important as anything else, however, is the absence of any clear alternative model for practicing at the hospital. He rejects what he believes is the somaticists' use of the hospital. (He typically enters residency with a bias against EST and is not supervised by somaticists.) The more idiosyncratic uses of the hospital, which will be described later, the resident does not recognize at all. To the extent that he enters into conversation with the few therapists who use the hospital differently, he notices specific strategies with particular patients, but he does not recognize that those strategies flow from models different from his own. This blindness is all the more noteworthy since some of his supervisors have never practiced in this kind of hospital, and some have not treated hospitalized patients for several years. All in all, the whole

weight of the resident's training and experience biases him toward combining psychotherapy and ward strategy.

A few ex-residents use the hospital quite differently because—
like some attending men trained elsewhere—they possess strong alternative models for organization of hospital treatment. It is significant
that a few attending men who were trained elsewhere organize treatment exactly as do the ex-residents—mainly because they entered practice with no strong commitments to alternative models of hospital treatment. We turn now to the careers and hospital strategies of psychotherapeutically oriented men who fall into neither group of psychiatrists
already discussed.

The Staff's Organization of Treatment

We have caught occasional glimpses of personnel developing modes of
treatment behind the backs of attending physicians. The conditions
under which they do are worth noting because they reveal something
about work coordination in this kind of hospital. We already know that
somaticists give permission for supplementary handling of their patients
when the staff believes such efforts can help. An irate staff may take its
case against a somaticist to central administration when a youthful
patient is receiving EST without visible salutary results. But the staff may
also embark, under certain conditions, upon its own therapeutic program
without the explicit knowledge or consent even of a co-operative
psychotherapist. The staff may grow restless because a patient "is not
moving," is not showing any progress, and indeed seems to be retro-
gressing. Sometimes the physician, disagreeing with the staff's analysis,
persists doggedly in his own program, so that the staff feels it must
institute a supplementary program. When a physician rufflles the feelings of the staff by not letting members in on his program, and if his
program—whatever it may be—seems not to be producing results, then
conditions are almost perfect for supplementary programing. Furthermore, if the physican seems genuinely confused, seems not to have
"doped out" his patient, or has confessed bafflement, then the staff
members may reach consensus about a reasonable line of action and
may pursue it even if he rejects their advice. Immensely troublesome
patients are likely to be regarded as "manipulating" their physicians,
"just as they do to us." Having lost faith in the "manipulated" physician's
efforts to control his patient, the staff is inclined to develop its own
program. In all such instances, consensus may be imperfect, but it involves at least several people, including the head nurse. Among parties

to the agreement may be the ward resident, the ward co-ordinator, and even members of the central administration. Consensus is reached not only through informal chats at the station but in actual formal conclave. Weekly conferences also tend occasionally to draw paternal unit co-ordinators into the therapeutic act, providing that they cannot dissuade the staff from giving the offending physicians a few more days grace.

Among the conditions that propel the staff into its own programing is one characterized by much fanfare: when patients become so enmeshed in mutual problems that the staff feels individual programs are no longer either manageable or therapeutically realistic. During our stay at PPI, there occurred a famous incident known as "the adolescent scarification." To the staff's mounting dismay, a number of adolescents continued for days to slash their own hands and wrists, and no action seemed able to stop this distressing fad. The staffs of the wards involved never achieved genuine consensus, so that the continued "sacrification" spawned a number of individualistic and group programs. The attending physicians regarded staff action variously, according to their respective philosophies. Some openly accused staff members of throwing therapy out of the window in favor of control, but there is little reason to believe that these personnel were actually concerned only with safety and management. Not only was the principle of fair play at stake (Mary should be transferred; keeping her here is not fair to Joan, who imitates her), but direct therapeutic responsibility to patients was also involved. In reply to accusations that they were simply overanxious, frightened, and concerned for ward orderliness, the personnel charged that the psychiatrists were ineffective with their patients—and that something must be done. Harsh judgment was made of various psychiatrists precisely on the grounds that they refused to act as a therapeutic body when the situation called for collaboration rather than individual programs.

Educational Technology: New Myths and Old Realities

Anthony Oettinger, Sema Marks

Many people believe that technology will revolutionize education. A Republic Steel advertisement tells us:

> Someday a single computer will give individual instruction to scores of students—in a dozen subjects at the same time. . . . The computer will very probably revolutionize teaching—and learning—within a decade. It is already happening in its early stages.
>
> Computerized instruction can practically (and pleasurably) allow each student to learn more, faster, but always at his own pace. Individualized instruction, the ultimate dream of effective education, is well within the range of possibility.[1]

We are also told that through its capacity to individualize instruction, the computer will reduce discipline problems, eliminate the need for compensatory education, solve the dropout problem, and free the teacher from administrative tasks. And all this is around the corner. Or is it? R. Louis Bright, associate commissioner for the U. S. Office of Education's Bureau of Research, has been quoted as saying that "computers will be ready for massive use in the classrooms of American elementary and secondary schools 'in three to four years.' "[2]

Our conclusions, however, after a study of the impact of technology on education under the Harvard/IBM Program on Technology and Society, are somewhat less enthusiastic.

Consider, for example, the claim cited above, that technology will usher in "individualized instruction, the ultimate dream of effective education." The sustained differences between persistent glorification of individuality as a goal of education and as a desired quality of pedagogical technique, and the equally persistent autocracy and regimentation of the classroom deserves examination. It turns out, as one might have expected, that the meaning of "individualized instruction" is in fact exceedingly fuzzy and of little value as anything but a flag. This, however, is not apparent in much of the literature on the upcoming "technological revolution" where the term is used with great abandon and little definition. Moreover, even if we were to assume a

Excerpted from *Harvard Educational Review* 38 (Fall, 1968):697–717.

limited notion of individualized instruction, there would still remain very serious problems of implementation.

A full description of these problems would need to touch upon every aspect of the school and its environment. Short of that, however, one may appreciate some of the difficulties of "individualization" by looking at the more general problem of technological innovation in the schools. The reasons for the discrepancy between ultimate promise and immediate possibility become apparent through a comparative examination of the properties of a system receptive to technological innovation and the properties of school systems.

"Individualized Instruction"

Many psychologists now officially agree that there are individual differences in learning capacities. There obviously is also increasing consciousness that contemporary education does not serve equally the needs and interests of all groups in our society. Current educational talk is thus all for individualized instruction. But what does "individualization" mean?

A case can be made for defining it as something like personalizing or customizing, namely taking a mass-produced object and stamping it with gold initials or heaping chrome on fins to give the illusion of individual tailoring. This is the sense in which current experimental computer programs greet you with "Good morning, Johnny" by filling in the blank "Good morning, ———" with the name you had to give to identify yourself to the machine in the first place. This is more genteel than "Do not fold, spindle, or mutilate!" "Hey you!" or "Good to see you, 367-A-45096." It is, however, just as superficial, even when randomly selected variations heighten the effect of spontaneity.

A loftier interpretation postulates that individualizing means giving full scope to idiosyncrasy, to the freedom to pursue whatever subject suits one's fancy in a manner entirely of one's own choosing.

To current practitioners, individualization means much less than pure idiosyncrasy but usually more than the golden initials. Precisely what it means is rather in doubt:

> During the past decade, the term "individualizing instruction" has become a watchword with educational reformers. Two recent yearbooks of educational organizations have had this term as title. . . . Oddly, both volumes were written as though everyone knows what individualization means since neither of them offers a working definition of the term. In point of fact, there is great confusion.[3]

In spite of or because of its obscure meaning individualized instruction is held up as a panacea for the ills of education. Speaking on the IPI (Individually Prescribed Instruction) Project at the Oakleaf School, Bright explains why federal officials are so enthusiastic about it:

> ———Youngsters of all ability levels would learn more. And they would enjoy school far more, thus reducing discipline problems.
> ———There would be no need for compensatory education for deprived children, on which the Federal government now is spending $1 billion of its $4 billion annual education budget.
> ———The dropout problem would largely be licked.
> ———Teachers would cease being mere dispensers of information and would be free to tutor students individually and encourage youngsters to think and to express themselves.
> ———Parents could take children out of school for vacations any time during the year without disrupting their learning process.[4]

The IPI people themselves describe their work in a much more modest and scholarly fashion:

> The project's concern for the individualization of rates of progression should not be taken as a judgment that this represents an attack on the most important aspect of individual differences. It represents a decision to make a rather intensive study of a school program which concentrates on this one aspect. Other aspects such as differences in interests and in other personal qualities may be equally important or even more important, but this project, at least for the present, will concern itself largely with the differentiation of rates.[5]

Lindvall and his co-workers thus clearly recognize that progression at one's own rate is only one facet of any reasonable concept of individualized instruction. In this case, the misrepresentations arise when others equate the part and the whole for public exposure and consumption.

The extent to which a student may deviate from a given course, in either content or style is also limited. The IPI program specifies a sequence of behaviorally defined objectives for each subarea in the subjects involved.

> Each objective should tell exactly what a pupil should be able to do to exhibit his mastery of the given content and skill . . .
>
> Objectives should be grouped in meaningful streams of content . . .
>
> Within each stream or area the objectives should, to the extent possible, be sequenced in such an order that each one will build on those that precede it and, in turn, be a prerequisite to those that follow. The goal here is to let the objectives constitute a "scale" of abilities . . .

Individually Prescribed Instruction lesson materials must be geared exactly to the instructional objectives.[6]

If, as is true of all computerized systems of "individualized" instruction now visible as prototypes as well as of many others based on explicit definitions of "behavioral objectives" (BO's), the intent is to instruct students in such a manner that all will achieve a final level of competency which meets (or surpasses) the same set of minimally acceptable performance criteria, with variation only in style, speed, or level of achievement, the object cannot be the cultivation of idiosyncrasy. It is, rather, what an industrial engineer might call mass production to narrow specifications with rigid quality control. Each pupil is free to go more or less rapidly exactly where he is told to go.

Semantic perversion therefore tends to mask the fact that the techniques now being developed may have great value in training to very narrow and specific "behavioral objectives" but do not address themselves to the many broader but just as basic problems of education. Training to minimal competence in well-defined skills is very important in a variety of military, industrial, and school settings. It is not, however, the whole of what the educational process should be.

Let us assume for the moment that an effective curriculum has been designed which does in fact provide for the types and ranges of learner variability encompassed by the school. What about implementing it?

Allowing students to go to their own rates creates certain problems even when all students are directed toward the same prescribed narrow goals. In a continuous progress, nongraded environment, the children move onward according to their readiness to proceed. Each child spends a different amount of time with each of different instructional resources. The task of matching time, instructors, facilities, and students already requires much effort and expense in present educational institutions. It is still more difficult when scheduling is on a "continuous progress" basis.

Patrick Suppes of the Brentwood School has found that when students are given the opportunity to progress at will, "the rate at which the brightest children advance may be five to ten times faster than that of the slowest children."[7] Although he began with a group of students "very homogeneous in initial measures of ability" (IQ range from 122 to 167, with a mean of 137.5), after a year and a half the spread was "almost two years."[8]

A computer simulation done by the System Development Corporation points out that two schools in different parts of the country which had independently experimented with a continuous progress plan for four years "independently decided to place their slowest students back in a lockstep group plan."[9]

One reason why the lockstep system has persisted for so long may be that it minimizes the teacher's information-processing problems. Students progress in unison; they are given identical assignments and they take tests simultaneously. In the continuous progress plan school, on the other hand, at any one time each student may be working at a point in the curriculum different from every other.

Thus, each student's status must be tracked individually. To complicate the matter still further, the records must be kept in "real-time," i.e., *at any time*, not just weekly or by marking periods, the student's status as a learner must be available to the decison-maker, be it computer or human guidance counselor. An effective monitoring device and evaluation scheme must be built in, because otherwise it would be impossible to know when to schedule a student for, say, extra help. Extrapolation from the SDC simulation suggests that "with a population of 900 students, there would be from 30 or 40 changes between courses and about 300 mastery tests daily."[10]

Although classroom scheduling by computer is advertised as a fait accompli, this is true only in the rather restricted sense of assigning students to conventional classroom groups and insuring that the number of groups matches the number of available teachers, and that these groups and teachers fit into available classrooms. The whole operation typically takes place once a term. This, however, is a far cry from keeping track of individual students week by week, day by day, hour by hour, or minute by minute, and matching them in turn with resources themselves parceled out in smaller packages than teachers per semester or rooms per semester. Keeping an accurate real-time list of teachers, rooms, and media is a major inventory control problem, of a type at the edge of the state of the computer art.

Thus, we remain at quite some distance from implementing truly individualized instruction in the classroom and begin to become aware of the difficulties of integrating technology into the schools on a large scale.

Systems and Schools

Computers are not now the great individualizers of instruction and may never even be useful in the schools unless the schools are drastically reorganized and appropriately funded to absorb reform. The discrepancy between ultimate promise and immediate possibility becomes apparent in a comparative examination of properties of school systems and the properties of other social systems that have proved to be receptive to innovation.

It is difficult to comprehend the boundaries of the so-called "school system." One of the most striking features of the educational network is the complexity of multifarious linkages between various elements of society and the school system.

A change in the school hours affects not only pupils and school personnel but every child's mother. You introduce the "new math" and shake up every parent in town. Ability grouping invites federal court decisions prohibiting it. If part of the high school burns down, it may be cheaper for local taxpayers to build a new one because the state contributes toward costs of new construction but not of renovation. An experiment with new curricula raises the specter of low performance on college boards. And, most obviously, the people who make up every other institution from the family to the Presidency are products of the school.

Granted the complexity of the system, it becomes obvious that any change in the schools which alters or even threatens to alter established linkages between the school and any other segment of society will meet at best with the delays inherent in explaining any change to those affected by it and at worst with stony resistance. Whenever one of the segments of society with which schools interact sees it in its interest to press for change in the schools, then the schools, if anxious to accept the change, must in turn still make their peace with other linked segments of society; if the change seems undesirable to the schools themselves but the pressures are strong, the schools are likely to adopt evasive tactics which suggest the form of change without commitment to its substance.

There is, in fact, widespread critical opinion that this indeed is what happens. We read, for instance, that:

> Boston—and other cities—like to talk innovation. Innovation has become fashionable and profitable. The federal government will pay for almost anything billed as new or experimental. In the past two years more than two billion dollars have gone to programs associated with education for "disadvantaged youth." Around the urban schools are magnificent necklaces of special programs, head starts, pilot schools, enrichment classes, but the body of education and the results produced remain almost unchanged. In Boston, which has enough trial programs and experiments to fill a book, the life of the average child in the average classroom is virtually unaffected. The teachers, the curriculum, the school committee are the same. The books are the same. The attitudes are the same.[11]

A visit to a place we shall call Small City provided an example of this phenomenon. Overhead projectors were introduced into a brand new high school to meet the emergency created because blackboards had not been delivered before the opening of school. School officials provided enough overhead projectors to have approximately one for every two classrooms. These remained even after the blackboards came, but older teachers who had complained all along that they needed a pilot's license to use these gadgets, promptly abandoned their use. Although we were told that the younger teachers had been enthusiatic about the new devices, we saw no evidence of anyone using them in any classroom.

Not all failures to integrate new hardware into the educational system result from the intransigence of teachers, as the following observation suggests:

> The shop seemed well-equipped with the standard wood-working hand tools and also with an impressive array of power tools, including three lathes, a planer, a joiner, a sander, and a drill press. Had we been walking through on a more superficial tour, we would have remained deeply impressed, but when the shop teacher caught our glance toward the equipment, he quickly volunteered the information that the tools had been standing there for a year and a half and were unconnected to any power source. He also pointed to a stack of electrical cabling conduits on top of one of the cabinets, which he said represented some $800 worth of electrical equipment necessary to connect his power tools, but had lain. in its resting place for an equally impressive number of months. With some bitterness, he attributed this sad state of affairs to the fact that the entire school system has only four electricians who, at Christmas time, damn well had to go and get the mayor's Christmas tree lit up. He also told us that the work benches, which were new, had been on order for ten years. The machine tools, he said, had been ordered a long time ago and appeared at a time when he had given up hope, but this manna was unaccompanied by the juice necessary to wash it down.[12]

Unfortunately there is a rather large step to take between the act of recognizing that because the schools are tied to many apron strings they find it hard to change and the acquisiton of sufficient knowledge about the strings, what they are made of, how they are interconnected, who pulls them, how much they can stretch, etc., to provide first, understanding, and second, rational control and direction toward agreed upon and well-defined goals. This particular aspect of the school system does not augur well for the introduction of technology. If we compare the organizational structure of the schools with the structure of organizations which have successfully integrated advanced technology into their functioning, it becomes obvious that the educational system is far more complex than anything we have hitherto tackled—air defense systems, moon shots, and air, rail, or communication networks notwithstanding —and that, in addition, we have far less knowledge of its component parts.

The system which is amenable to the introduction of technology is characterized by (1) enough independence from the other systems related to it for interactions with these systems to be satisfactorily accounted for or ignored; (2) well-developed and reliable research and design tools; and (3) most important, goals which are both well known and specifiable.

School systems, on the other hand, are closely tied to society. Research findings on significant educational issues are fragmented and contradictory, and we have already noted the difficulty of defining as obvious a goal as individualization.

> It sometimes appears that existing American political and social systems have built-in defenses against being treated as systems, for purpose of analysis or problem solving. Socially and politically, we have substantial decentralization and localization in our decision-making structure (much different than the hierarchical structure in the defense establishment).[13]

There is nothing in education remotely approximating the Secretary of Defense or the Joint Chiefs of Staff. Rather, there are 27,000 local autonomous school districts and corresponding school boards.

> The schools are over-centralized in the sense that universalistic practices, the standardized curriculum, and the conduct of programs of school-community relationships from the central office and board result in obvious difficulties in adapting to the different problems of varying neighborhoods . . . In Chicago, the local area superintendent is to "run his own district," but control over budget, staffing, and so on is still left downtown. The schools are also under-centralized in the sense that it is difficult for decisions made at the top of the organization to become operationalized lower in the organization.[14]

It is difficult, for example, to find an appropriate audience in the schools much less to find a source of funds and still less a boss to satisfy:

> This problem of identifying and determining how most effectively to address each audience is much more severe in the civil sector than it is in the military environment. The hierarchical and authoritarian structure, as well as the often classified nature of military systems contracts, precludes much public debate and minimizes the number and variety

of audiences for the report. Yet, almost all civil systems work must be responsive to many sets of requirements and many audiences—a problem which constitutes much of the so-called communications gap between defense systems people and civil servants.[15]

In contrast to the military environment, where decisions often depend on obscure knowledge and security regulations further narrow the scope of debate on a given proposal, schools are a familiar experience for everyone and consequently nearly everyone has an opinion about them. Clearly, at least the school board must be convinced of the value of going ahead with an innovation; in Boston, for instance, one would have to deal with Mrs. Hicks. Appearing at a meeting in Dorchester "she declared that there will be no redistricting, that the state suggestions were 'made by a computer which didn't take into consideration the emotions of the citizens.' "[16] This kind of barrier is impervious alike to the crew-cut ex-merchant of death and the bearded academic zealot.

Even if the decison to innovate were handed down from the school board, the task of integrating and adopting the new technologies would be left in the hands of the teachers.

> If there is one thing the teacher, particularly the female teacher, is not, it is an engineer. Indeed, it is difficult to think of two world views further apart than those symbolized by the Golden Rule on the one hand and the slide rule on the other. The one calls to mind adjectives such as romantic, warm, tender-minded, naïve; the other calls to mind adjectives such as realistic, cold, tough-minded, efficient. One is essentially feminine, the other masculine. These two lists of adjectives undoubtedly exaggerate the real differences to be found between these two groups, but they do give us pause when we consider the likelihood of increasing the dialogue between the tender-minded teachers and the tough-minded technicians. To say that they do not speak the same language is a gross understatement.[17]

In addition, "if classroom teachers are only mildly interested in particular techniques, it is unlikely that those techniques will enjoy rapid and widespread use."[18] These observations are consistent with our own concerning resistance to the use of overhead projectors cited earlier.

If, indeed, it makes sense to introduce advanced technology into the classroom—and we will assume this purely for the sake of the present argument—then massive education and re-education, by in-service training or during sabbaticals, will be necessary to produce a breed of teachers who can feel at home with technical devices. Yet no viable mechanisms have yet been developed for the retraining of teachers. As Davies says succinctly, "in-service teacher training is the slum of American education."[19] But even if there were people in the schools who could deal with the new technology, it is the children who matter in the last analysis.

Equipment to date does not meet the demands of the school. Although the manufacturers would like to convey the impression that all one need do to install a computer system is "plug it in," implementing the "new technology" is a nontrivial task even in firmly established computer installation. A recent editorial in *Datamation* colorfully describes the results of listening "to the siren song of the salesman":

> Those moans, groans, sobs and whimpers you hear from the big corner office down the hall from the beautiful, clean, glass-enclosed shrine they call the machine room are coming not from children but grown men, grizzled veterans of the edp wars, pioneering heroes who are trying to make their large-scale third-generation systems work.
>
> The problems and the agonies have to be lived with to be believed . . .
>
> Remember, this is 1967. Third generationsville. The people we're talking about have been through the conversion snarl before. They are experienced and knowledgeable. What in the hell is going on here anyway?[20]

Reliability is a problem with even the most modest of devices, as anyone will testify who has had a piece of chalk board in his hand or who has cursed a skipping ball point pen. The schools are not accustomed to dealing with anything less reliable or flexible than the blackboard.

> The blackboard is literally at the teacher's fingertips. He can write on it, draw on it, immediately erase what he has written, or preserve it for days. He can scrawl key words on it, produce a detailed diagram, or write out a series of essay questions. He can use the board himself; or ask his students to use it. He can place material on it in advance, or use it to capture the fleeting and ephemeral thoughts emerging from a discussion. Given this flexibility, it is no wonder that the chalk-smudged sleeve has become the trademark of the teacher.[21]

Perhaps the best example of equipment in common use that must meet the same standards of reliability and cheapness as educational equipment is the telephone. The instrument is so widespread that it must lend itself to operation by practically anyone, under the most varied environmental conditions; and it is frequently subject to vandalism. Just how major are even the most innocent-looking engineering improvements necessary to achieve this degree of reliability may be illustrated by the example of the telephone dial, which has been in continuous development for well over twenty-five years.

A new dial has been designed with slightly less noisy gears than the dial now in existence. It is to be somewhat more reliable and longer lived than its predecessor and somewhat less disturbing as a contributor to room noise. This "minor" change is the product of a year and a half spent by three design engineers and an expenditure of about two million dollars for retooling the manufacturing plant! The difference between a laboratory prototype and a reliable instrument amenable to wide distribution under severe conditions of use must therefore be measured in large multiples of such human and dollar costs.

Current experience with teletype terminals for computers suggests that tomorrow's logs may well include entries about chewing gum in the type mechanism. Those with graphic terminals are learning that a deposit of ear wax interferes with the operation of light-pens. Since the grass always looks greener on the other side of the fence, we may look with confidence toward the early development by biomolecular genetic engineers of earless and therefore waxless pupil systems.

Our general conclusion is that the observed combination of institutional rigidity with infant technology will preclude really significant progress in the next decade if significant progress is interpreted, in accord with contemporary literature, as widespread and meaningful adoption, integration, and use of technological devices within the schools. In addition, this discussion should suggest the enormous difficulties that will have to be overcome if educational technology is to be introduced in any decade in the twentieth century.

An Example

To illustrate concretely some of the general arguments made up to this point, we would like to examine one specific instance of the use of technology in education: a language laboratory currently operating in the Watertown, Massachusetts, Public Schools.

The Language Laboratory

The choice of the language laboratory as an example deserves some explanation. It is a good example of a branch of educational technology whose adoption is sufficiently recent for the sound of drumbeats and promises still to reverberate, while, at the same time, enough language laboratories are now in enough schools for a realistic assessment to be possible.

Since it, too, has been touted as leading to individualization, we should be aware of the possibilities for perversion. The Raytheon brochure advertising their "Random Access Teaching Equipment" states:

> RATE systems are tailored to the individual student's progress, as each position permits the instructor to gauge the progress of all students on an individual basis. Therefore, the entire class is not limited to the learning capacity of the slowest members, thus permitting fast progress through any given area of instruction when possible.

A trip out to Watertown High School, where the system is operative, produced the following set of Language Laboratory Procedures:

Watertown High School Language Laboratory Procedures

1. The equipment in the laboratory is not like ordinary tape recorders. The principles involved are quite different. *Please do not ask unnecessary questions about its operation.* [Italics added.]
2. . . . . .
3. No books, pencils, pens, papers, pocketbooks are to be taken to the booths. People asigned to the first row will leave their belongings on the bookcase at the left front of the room under the windows. Those assigned to rows B through E will leave their materials in the bookcase under the blackboard at the opposite side of the room. Take only yourself to the booth.
4. You will stand quietly behind the chair at your booth until the teacher asks you to sit. Then sit in as close to the desk as possible.
5. *No one is an individual in the laboratory.* [Italics added.] Do nothing until instructions are given by the teacher. Then listen carefully and follow directions exactly.
6. If you find anything out of order in your booth, report it to your teacher immediately. This is *very expensive* equipment. You must take pride in it by giving it the best of care.

Good luck to you!

Perhaps the statement that "no one is an individual in the laboratory" is an overstatement. We learned, for example, that the laboratory contains student booths, each equipped with a tape holder. The system provides the option to submit up to five independent inputs to the students. We were told, however, that this capacity is rarely used. There is difficulty, noted by the students as well as by the teachers, in picking materials that are relevant to what goes on in the classroom. The problem of multimedia integration, reflected in such time-worn complaints as that the reading in the textbook has nothing to do with the lectures, will not be automatically ameliorated by the introduction of more elaborate technology. The point is simple: if it is hard to pick one set of tapes, it is still harder to pick five and to monitor the progress of students proceeding on five different tracks.

We are told by Robert Locke, senior vice president of McGraw-Hill that the "language labs have taken over the drill and left the teacher to do the things she's trained to do. . . The children, of course, have gained enormously because now they can be exposed to the language as it ought to be spoken, and they can practice their own speech without the embarrassment of doing it in front of the whole class. It's like singing in the shower."[22]

However, the fact remains that one teacher can give each of thirty students at most one and a third to two minutes of attention in a forty to sixty minute period. Consequently, private schools tend to design their language laboratories for fifteen rather than thirty students. The common notion that the introduction of technology necessarily changes education from a labor-intensive to a capital-intensive activity is therefore not borne out in this case.

Neither has the laboratory eliminated the problem of student motivation. One language coordinator confided to me: "The language laboratory is a magnificent environment for daydreaming. Kids who are used to having blaring transitor radios around them every waking moment have trained themselves to ignore anything coming into their ears, and therefore hear very little of what comes out of the earphones they wear in the language lab."

The difficulties in the path of realizing individualization are not grandiose, but rather are the accumulation of a myriad of minor frustrations and inadequacies which, in the aggregate, create a problem whose complexity lies far beyond that of any system design problem with which modern technology has successfully grappled to date.

Hard design lessons must be learned to produce equipment that will stand up under the kind of use that appears to be normal in schools. The phenomenon is not restricted necessarily to secondary schools or to schools which are in an area where the auditorium must be padlocked to maintain security. One problem, for example, is that students will pull wires out of head sets! While it is standard on many appliances designed for home, industrial, or military use to supply control knobs that are held on a shaft by a spring and therefore pull off with a reasonable amount of force, this a clearcut invitation—if not necessarily to vandalism—then at least to absent-minded, but nonetheless destructive fiddling.

The operating problems are brought home by a casual look at the teacher's log. It shows the following sprinkling of entries:

> Not working at all; not audio-active; tape cartridge doesn't play; no hook for headset; button missing; could not hear tape; blue ink marks on tape drive; scratches on tape drive; some spots of missing paint on deck; blue ink mark on desk.

Thus the likelihood that Watertown will be affected substantially by such new technology within the next decade is exceedingly small, for the problems of engineering the transition from laboratory to mass production have only barely begun to be faced; the economies of scale necessary to bring costs within reason can be realized only through massive production and standardization; teaching materials to be used with such systems exist only in bits and pieces; and the people capable of forwarding the state of this art are woefully few. Moreover, no one has yet faced the scheduling problems entailed by even this limited amount of individualization. As the evidence of the Systems Development Corporation studies and the Brentwood experiment points out, the rate of spread of even an initially uniform group of students is enormous. As a consequence, just as Watertown has been unable to take advantage even of the restricted amount of flexibility provided by its language laboratory equipment, so it is highly probable that Watertown or any other school in the next decade will be unable to take advantage even of the pacing flexibility of computers without the kind of major administrative revolution that seems conclusively blocked by other factors in so short a time span.

The Longer Range

It is curious that, in an era where the great and undeniable power of science and technology in certain realms is seen by some with ecstasy and by others with horror, we should be stuck through plain, old-fashioned *ignorance*. What holds back progress in education and in other types of social problems is not that the scientific method has failed us, but rather that it has so far revealed very little of systematic value in attaining the goals of education even if one could assume some measure of agreement on their definition.

We are dealing with problems of an order of complexity for which available mathematical and analytical tools leave us quite unprepared. Worse yet, the elementary building blocks arrayed in such monumental complexity are themselves mysterious. Contemporary psychology can tell us essentially nothing about the details of individual learning processes. Contemporary social and political science can tell us essentially nothing about the dynamic processes that come to play in the transition from one form of social organization to another. Static, descriptive accounts abound, but the dynamics of social science is still *in utero*.

Attempting to design an educational or any other social system with our contemporary scientific apparatus is rather like giving Lucretius an imperial grant to make the bomb starting with his atomic theory. Whether we are two thousand years or thirty years ahead of ourselves makes little difference, and we cannot predict with any degree of reliability how much time it will take for physical, biological, and social science to progress far enough.

We should not, therefore, persist in a naive illusion that science has answers which education can exploit if only it will organize itself properly and do the right incantations. Having owned up to this, our choice of actions is relatively simple, at least in outline.

We may, on the one hand, choose to continue playing the game with the trappings but without the substance of science. Consciously taken, this cynical approach has, as indicated throughout the essay, considerable short-term political value. Its longer range implications, however, are admirably spelled out by Brewster Denny:

> Perhaps the greatest danger which science poses for democracy as far as the processes of government are concerned is scientism—a cult of faith in the mechanistic superiority of the scientific method, in the trappings of science, in the mystery and the mystique of science. This is profane perversion of science—cheap, anti-intellectual, and denies the very basic creative faith on which science is founded. Perversion it may be, but man's pathetic desire to put decision and responsibility in a mechanism, or a process, or a machine may at last have found in the period of big government and big science methodologies and technologies of decision-making which will take man off the hook for good.[23]

If, on the other hand, we are prepared to admit that we are playing in ignorance, this realization need hold no special terror. This, after all, has been the condition of mankind for millenia. However, this admission urges strongly against any form of strong coordinative planning and prescription on *substantive* matters. Based on deep ignorance, such planning has a much higher probability of being disastrous than of leading to correct or useful solutions.

However wasteful in appearance, it seems best to encourage as much diversity as possible, as many different paths, as many different outlooks, as many different experiments, as many different initiatives as we can afford once the demands of education have been balanced against those of other needs of our society. We should, in short, plan for the encouragement of diversity, at least in technique.

It seems vital to encourage greater freedom of choice in a situation which, however diverse in appearance because of the 27,000 school districts, has in fact a dreary monotony. Vesting all educational authority in the federal government makes no sense whatever under the preceding arguments, but letting our schools continue as local monopolies perpetuates on the local level a crime we would not tolerate and do not tolerate nationally.

There may be other alternatives for providing a kind of large-scale evolutionary effect with enough units at stake to create a fair probability that lots of different paths will be taken, and that illuminating controversy will rage. In other words we are groping for a definition of a reasonable setting for educational experimentation, but we think it vital to shy away from prescriptions of either goal or technique.

We should have a chance to fiddle around with both goals and techniques, and we should give people enough freedom and options so they need not feel like unwilling victims of any particular experiment. We should pursue independence, diversity, professional competence, and integrity; we should encourage following through on longitudinal studies and critical comparisons, upping R & D on higher education from present a pitiful 0.2 per cent, and so on.

Critical comments on all the foregoing are cordially invited. As you can see we are quite unable to make any wise, ringing, and optimistic proposal for the future.

Notes

1. *Scientific American,* 216 (September, 1967), 13.
2. "Enormous Role Seen for Computer," *Washington Monitor,* November 27, 1967, p. 78.
3. Glen Heathers, "Individualized Instruction," in U.S. Congress, Senate, Committee on Labor and Public Welfare, Subcommittee on Education, *Notes and Working Papers Concerning the Administration of Programs Authorized Under Title III of Public Law 89–10, The Elementary and Secondary Education Act of 1965 as Amended by Public Law 89–750* (Washington: U.S. Government Printing Office, 1967), chapter 7, section B, p. 178. This report is hereafter cited as *Notes and Working Papers.*
4. "Individual Teaching Plan Excites Experts," *Boston Globe,* October 5, 1967, p. 42.
5. C. M. Lindvall (ed.), *Defining Educational Objections,* report of the Regional Commission on Educational Coordination and the Learning Research and Development Center (Pittsburgh, Pa.: University of Pittsburgh Press, 1964), p. 4.
6. Research for Better Schools, *Individually Prescribed Instruction* (Undated manuscript, Philadelphia, Pa.), pp. 3–4.
7. Patrick Suppes, "The Uses of Computers in Education," *Scientific American,* 215 (September, 1966), 218.
8. Patrick Suppes, *Accelerated Program on Elementary School Mathematics —The Second Year,* Technical Report no. 86 (Stanford, Calif.: Institute for Mathematical Studies in the Social Sciences, 1965), p. 11.
9. John F. Cogswell, *Analysis of Instructional Systems* (Santa Monica, Calif.: System Development Corp., TM–1493/201/00, 1966), p. 183.
10. *Ibid.,* p. 42.

11. Peter Schrag, *Village School Downtown: Politics and Education—A Boston Report* (Boston: Beacon Press, 1967), p. 117.

12. Anthony G. Oettinger, "Visit to a Small City" (Unpublished memorandum, 1967), pp. 20–21.

13. John S. Gilmore, *et al., Defense Resources in the Civil Sector,* prepared for the U.S. Arms Control and Disarmanent Agency (Washington: U.S. Government Printing Office, 1967), p. 65

14. David Street, "Public Education and Social Welfare in the Metropolis," Working Paper no. 69 (Chicago: Center for Social Organizational Studies, 1966), p. 22.

15. Gilmore, *et al., Defense Systems,* pp. 53–54.

16. Schrag, *Village School Downtown,* p. 126.

17. Philip W. Jackson, "The Teacher and the Machine: Observations on the Impact of Educational Technology," prepared for the Committee for Economic Development, September, 1966, p. 7.

18. *Ibid.,* p. 8.

19. Don Davies, "Teacher Education," in *Notes and Working Papers,* chapter 15, section B, pp. 295–304.

20. "EDP's Wailing Wall," *Datamation,* 13 (July, 1967), 21.

21. Jackson, "The Teacher and the Machine," pp. 3–4.

22. Robert W. Locke, "Educational Technology," talk prepared for delivery at a Convention of the Chicago Educational Publishers Association, November 16, 1966, p. 8.

23. Brewster C. Denney, "Science and Democracy: Politics as Usual in the Nuclear Age?" talk prepared for delivery at the inaugural meeting of the Sigma Xi Club, Richland, Wash., October 12, 1967, pp. 14–15.

Chapter VI

Authority and Control

The basic problem in every organization is the recruitment and retention of members, and the motivation and compliance of these members to perform organizationally prescribed roles. Hence, the exercise of social control in organizations is designed to elicit and to monitor work performances in accordance with organizational goals as well as to insure the coordination of work (Katz and Kahn, 1966, pp. 199–222).

Social controls in organizations are manifested in several ways. First, the division of labor defines the parameters of decision making for organizational members, including the amount of decisional discretion allocated to each position (Simon, 1965). Second, the compliance structure is designed to govern the members' performance of organizational tasks which is accomplished through the development of a system of rewards and sanctions. Third, mechanisms of socialization serve to indoctrinate members to organizational ideologies and the appropriate performance of their roles.

Underlying all mechanisms of social control in organizations is the exercise of power. One expression of power is authority which indicates compliance of subordinates to the legitimate orders of superiors. The allocation of authority and power by organizations to various staff positions and the exercise of control over organizational activities by the staff often reflect the goal commitments and technologies employed by human service organizations.

In human service organizations a distinction needs to be made between the amount of power members exercise over other members and the amount of power members exercise over clients. For example, the authority structure which regulates the relationship between superiors and subordinates does not always regulate the relations between lower level staff and clients. When lower level staff are likely to have more frequent contacts with clients than superiors, they tend to exercise greater power and control over the fate of the client in the organization even though they do not possess the expertise (Belknap, 1956; Greenblatt, Levinson, and Williams, 1957; McCleery, 1961; Street, Vinter, and Perrow, 1966). This phenomenon occurs in those human service organizations where the visibility of staff-client relations is low, thereby hindering direct supervision of staff performance.

In the first selection Smith deals with some of the social control dilemmas confronting human service organizations in which lower level staff possess considerable power and autonomy. This tendency which characterizes "front-line organizations" occurs when (1) the locus of organizational initiative is located in front-line units, (2) each unit performs its tasks independently of other units, and (3) there are barriers to the direct supervision of the unit's activities.

Using the state mental hospital as an illustrative case, Smith describes how the ward system of the hospital through its monopoly communications, initiatives regarding patient care, management, and services as well as treatment goals for patients, becomes a center of power for influencing organizational policy. Smith's analysis discloses how organizational functionaries, who hold responsibility for policy making and the provision of services, are unable to exercise their responsibility.

In a comparative study of five correctional institutions for delinquents, Zald examines the ways in which organizational goals influence differences in organizational control structures. Three types of institutional goals are identified: custodial, treatment, and a combination of both. He demonstrates how differences in the relative dominance of these goals lead to differences in the distribution of power and control among executives and various staff groups. He finds that those staff groups who perform tasks which are essential to the organization's dominant goals tend to have the greatest decisional power and authority over inmate activities.

Becker deals with the authority problems of the public school teacher in her relations with other teachers, principals and parents. For each of these relationships he considers (1) the teacher's conception of her rights and prerogatives, (2) the teacher's problems in obtaining and maintaining acceptance of this role conception on the part of others, and (3) the teacher's methods in handling such problems. Becker's analysis illuminates some of the unique problems and pressures confronting human service professionals. Not only must they cope with authority relations internal to the organization, but at the same time deal with challenges to their legitimate authority from those outside the organization. He demonstrates how the authority system of the public school regulates the interactions among teachers and principals, and shows how this same system of influence is ineffectual in governing the schools' relations with parents.

Rosengren reports a study of 87 large government hospitals and 45 small private hospitals in which the relations between structural and supervisory forms of control are investigated. He explores in detail the relationships between organizational size and sponsorship, structures, operational policies, and styles of administrative supervision. He finds that highly bureaucratized hospitals tend to have limited supervision over employees, while less bureaucratized hospitals have greater supervisory control. When there is a minimum of supervisory control over employees, social control tends to be patterned into a well developed division of labor—specialization of tasks, procedures of work and communication. In the absence of these structural patterns, supervisory strategies of control over employees appear to be more pervasive and extensive. The control of patients in the highly bureaucratized hospitals was exercised through treatment technologies that were highly standardized, reliable, and predictable while in the nonbureaucratized hospitals, treatment technologies were less standardized, reliable, and predictable and therefore could not serve as mechanisms of control over patients.

References

Belknap, I. 1956. *Human Problems of a State Mental Hospital.* New York: McGraw-Hill.

Greenblatt, M., Levinson, D. J., and Williams, R. H. (eds.), 1957. *The Patient and the Mental Hospital.* Glencoe, Ill.: Free Press.

Katz, D., and Kahn, R. L. 1966. *The Social Psychology of Organizations.* New York: John Wiley and Sons, Inc.

McCleery, R. H. 1961. "Policy Change in Prison Management." In Amitai Etzioni (ed.), *Complex Organizations: A Sociological Reader.* New York: Holt, Rinehart and Winston.

Simon, H. A. 1965. *Administrative Behavior: A Study of Decision-Making Process in Administration Organization.* 2nd ed. New York: The Free Press of Glencoe.

Street, D., Vinter, R. D., and Perrow, C. 1966. *Organization For Treatment: Comparative Study of Institutions for Delinquents.* New York: The Free Press.

Front-Line Organization of the State Mental Hospital

Dorothy E. Smith

As sociological research extends into new types of organization, departures from accepted features of organization stimulate reflection on established theoretical positions. The state mental hospital presents an anomaly which has been widely reported, namely the ability of a subordinate group in the hospital, the ward attendants, to resist programs of reform initiated by a centralized leadership.[1] The exercise of significant control over policy by a subordinate group is a marked exception to established theories of the distribution of power in large-scale organizations, and in particular to that formulation of the tendencies of power to become centralized, Michels's "iron law of oligarchy."[2] So strikingly different is the tendency in state mental hospitals that one theorist in the field[3] has argued that there is a general tendency in large-scale organizations for power to influence policy to become concentrated at the lower levels of the organizational hierarchy.

The iron law of oligarchy asserts that in any organization the power to determine organizational policy tends to become vested in a small group of leaders. In stating this position, Michels drew attention to a discrepancy between the formally democratic structure of policy determination in radical political parties and the actual distribution of power. Formally, power to determine policy rested with the membership of the party, the leaders acting only as representatives of their electoral constituency. But Michels noted that power generally became concentrated in a small number of more or less permanent leaders who were able to wield extensive control over party policies. He described it as an "iron law," because he believed it to arise from the nature of organization as such and despite formal commitment to democratic process.

In his studies of prison organization, McCleery[4] drew attention to the way in which communication structures influence the distribution of power in an organization. Information is a basic element in the exercise of effective control, and a communication structure creates differential access to messages traveling in that structure as well as differential

Reprinted from *Administrative Science Quarterly* 10 (December, 1965): 381–99.

opportunities for initiating messages. When all the information needed to make decisions about a given task is available within a given status structure, so that the exchange of information for corrections (the "feedback" cycle) can be completed without reference to external sources for information of policy decisions, the structure will have a high degree of autonomy. If its task is a major part of the total organizational activity, its power to influence policy will be considerable.

The situation analyzed by McCleery presents a close parallel to that of the state mental hospital. The distinctive difference is in the characteristic locus of power. The analyses of both Michels and McCleery suggest that its coordinates can be located in terms of the communication structure. An examination of the way in which the work of the state mental hospital is organized should therefore disclose patterns of communication that result in a tendency for power to be distributed to the periphery. This analysis of the ward system of the mental hospital points out those conditions that lead to the development of the ward as an information "pocket." From the analysis certain general structural characteristics can be abstracted, which typify what is here called a "front-line" organization.[5]

Characteristic Features of the Ward System
of the State Mental Hospital

As a way of arranging the location and grouping of inmates, the ward system of the state mental hospital results in a structure with characteristic features.

Locus of Initiative. In the state mental hospital, the primary locus of initiative is the ward. Outside the custodial organization, an individual is self-mobilizing, so that the locus of initiative, as far as the ordering of his daily life is concerned, can be said to be the individual. Within the custodial organization, the initiative is transferred from the individual inmate to the organization, and in particular to that segment of the organization known as the ward. Ward attendants are responsible for the coordination of services to the inmate on the ward. Cooking and laundering are normally centralized, but ward attendants are in charge of distribution to patients. The inmate's ward membership determines his physician. His access to recreational and other leisure activities is regulated by his ward membership. Ward attendants are normally responsible for the full round of ward management and patient care, whether the work is performed by them or by the patients under their supervision. In addition, the transfer of initiative from the patient to the custodial organization involves the ward attendants in problems of order which go beyond those of simple regulation. Ward attendants are responsible for the inmates' conformity to institutional and relevant societal norms; for seeing that patients are properly dressed, washed, fed, and so on, and that they maintain—within limits set by the standards specific to the ward—a minimum of restraint in their behavior to other patients. Thus the locus of initiative in patient management and the coordination of services to the patient is the ward, and the next level up in the attendant hierarchy is only minimally involved in these processes.

With respect to the treatment goals of the organization the locus of initiative is also distributed to the periphery. In principle, objectives of treatment are formulated for the individual, and methods of treatment must be adjusted to the individual case. But the traditional practice of the state mental hospital allocates a patient to a ward according to criteria involving considerations of the type of behavioral problem he presents coupled with estimates of his probable response to an active treatment program. This implies a general categorization of treatment objectives for the group of patients assembled on a ward. The treatment goals for patients on a custodial ward, for example, may be a minimal level of functioning within the hospital, in contrast to the goal of discharge for patients on an intensive treatment unit. Accordingly, treatment goals and methods are differentiated as different ward policies.

Task Independence. In the state mental hospital the tasks of care and housekeeping, and the management of the inmate's daily routine are contained within the ward; they do not have to be adjusted to the work of other wards and have no consequences for the success or failure of other wards. Moreover, the type of specialization among wards does not increase interdependence, but instead intensifies the detachment that results from the lack of comparability in types of care and treatment provided in different wards.[6] Except for wards handling difficult cases, wards do not provide services upon which other wards depend. Thus although the work of each ward contributes to the total work of the hospital, direct task dependence among the different wards is lacking.

Obstacles to Supervision. On the ward of a general medical hospital, many services are provided directly to the bedside, creating considerable traffic through the ward. In addition, an increased specialization of nursing tasks has resulted in a devolution of household and even some aspects of the physical care of patients to other occupational roles; and specialized nonroutine services required by many patients bring specialists on different technical problems into the ward. To this is added the traffic of outside visitors during the regular visiting hours. The wards of medical hospitals are thus relatively public places, and ward practice is exposed to the informal surveillance which arises as a by-product of other activities.[7]

In contrast to this, the wards of a state mental hospital, whether they conform to the cottage plan or are some variant of the corridor plan, are designed for security. They are therefore secluded from the casual visitation of those who might pass through on their way to some other place. Wards normally constitute more or less self-contained units.Even though certain services may be shared with adjacent wards, the number of persons who might have business there is small. Since most wards are locked, only visitors officially privileged with keys can take the ward by surprise. Visitors to the hospital are seldom admitted to the ward and then only to selected wards and to specified parts. Relatives of patients are provided with waiting rooms and visiting facilities in rooms adjacent to the wards. The ward is therefore insulated from the "natural" processes of control that arise from exposure to the public process.

Lack of visible results also makes supervision difficult. In the absence of other means of control and information, the differential visibility of the ward work assumes special significance. Those aspects of inmate welfare connected with cleanliness and tidiness, with ward order and decorum are highly visible to inspection; whereas, deviations from standards of individualized care and from a responsible usage of power over the inmate are less visible. Use of force and forcible means of control, beyond what is needed to restrain the patient, the arbitrary use of authority, exploitation of the patient's services, verbal abuse and teasing are visible only to those present. Other more nebulous areas of individual care—particularly those indicated by the prescription "Tender Loving Care" are visible primarily by the patient. Even physical injuries that require medical treatment do not yield unambiguous evidence of how they occurred.

The Ward as an Information Pocket

The wards are linked to the central administration through a hierarchy of offices, the basis of which is territorial. At the ward level, a charge nurse or attendant presides over a number of attendants. A number of adjacent wards are grouped into an area supervised from a single office. The area office reports to the central nursing office, and the central nursing office to the hospital superintendent.[8]

McCleery's description of the highly centralized form of the prison structure of controls stresses the relationship between the centralization of control at the apex of the custodial hierarchy and the flow of communication upward from the lower levels.

All communications flowed upwards, leaving each supervisor

better informed than his subordinate and limiting the information on lower levels on which discretion could be based.[9]

In the large state mental hospital the communications flow is reversed. Each ward constitutes a pocket of information. Information about ward affairs circulates freely among attendants at the ward level. The center of the ward structure is the office, where the charge sits at the conjunction of the ward system and the hospital system. The windows of this office ordinarily look out over the dayroom, where patients are located when they are not doing anything else. To the ward office come patients making request of various kinds, the doctor to see patients, attendants completing errands or awaiting further instructions. The telephone through which all calls come to the ward is here. The ward is thus the place at which there is the most information about the patient and ward practice. This information is not readily accessible to persons who do not participate directly in ward affairs. Written reports combined with inspections contribute to the information available at the next level up. But the lack of interdependence among wards means that this information does not add in jigsaw puzzle fashion into a more complete picture, available only to the higher-level position and resulting in a distinctive strategic advantage, as is the case in the prison.

Front-Line Organization

Characteristics

These aspects of the structure of the state mental hospital can be generalized as a type of organization which is here called a "front-line organization" and which has the following distinctive characteristics:

1. The locus of organizational initiative is in front-line units, whether these are individual positions or segments of the organization.

2. Each such unit performs its task independently of other like units.

3. There are obstacles to the direct supervision of the activities of such units.

These characteristics can be compared with the assumption of Michels and other theorists.

Locus of Organizational Initiative. Michels held that oligarchic tendencies are:

immanent . . . in every kind of human organization which strives for the attainment of definite ends.[10]

He argued that successful organization of a "fighting party" necessitated the emergence of an oligarchic structure of control.[11] In so doing he implied a specific relationship between a centralized structure of control and the type of action in which the organization is engaged. His generalization of the "iron law" of oligarchy thus rests on the assumption that all organizations striving for "the attainment of definite ends" are engaged in fundamentally similar types of action and confront fundamentally similar exigencies.

In current organizational theory it is assumed that the fundamental problem of formal (or planned) organization is securing its ability to act as a unit in a fluctuating or otherwise problematic environment. Michels was concerned with the "fighting party." The simple illustrations of organizational action used as paradigms by exponents of this theoretical approach are of a similar form of action—rolling a stone up a hill,[12] fighting a fire,[13] making a boat.[14] This type of action is one in which a number of individuals cooperate to achieve a specific objective in an environment that makes the success of the venture problematic because of its changing or obstructive character. The central problem of organization thus becomes: How is it possible to get a number of men to act as if they were one man? In March and Simon's work on organizations, this analogy is made explicit by a metaphor likening the coordinative system of an organization to the central nervous system.[15]

Coordination as a process of integrating organization activity is ordinarily identified as the function of the line of command. This type of control structure may thus be conceived as the administrative response to the problem of securing effective corporate action and is specifically related to the integration of specialized functions and their mobilization for corporate action. It is through the line that the decisions made at executive positions at the top become effective as organizational acts.

In the front-line organization, however, the locus of initiative is among individual participants or small work groups at the periphery of the organization. There is a decentralization of the executive process.[16] Tasks are initiated for the organization at the front-line level rather than by directives traveling through a chain of command; for example, in medical practice, the objectives of treatment are formulated individually for each patient. Or the situation of action at the front line is so constantly in flux, and responses to its fluctuations must be so rapidly introduced, that decisions cannot be referred back to a centralized command.

The combat fighter is not routinized and self-contained. Rather his role is one of constant improvisation, regardless of his service or weapon. Improvisation is the keynote of the individual fighter or combat group. The impact of battle destroys men, equipment, and organization that need constantly to be brought back into some form of unity through on-the-spot improvisation. In battle the planned division of labor breaks down.[17]

The unit tends to develop a monopoly of information about the environment with which it interacts; therefore for coordination and mobilization, it approaches a closed system. The initiation and carrying out of tasks does not need inputs of information from other sources, nor do decisions have to be referred to a higher authority, so the unit can operate without the direct participation of superordinates.

Task Independence. The unit is responsible for a complete task (or set of tasks), and the units are not dependent upon each other as part of a serially organized division of labor or for services each may provide. For example, the individual bank clerk[18] is responsible for the cycle of activities initiated by each customer, and the way in which he performs this task can neither impede nor facilitate the work of other clerks. The work structure does not necessitate patterns of cooperative interaction between units: "The work flow processes are unique in that they do not tie the employees together. Most employees have relatively discrete jobs."[19] In contrast, the work flow of the restaurant, as described by Whyte,[20] mobilizes the whole or a considerable segment of the organization.

In the front-line organization individuals or work groups are largely functionally autonomous. This lack of interdependence prevents overlap in the functioning of different units; consequently, access to information tends to be monopolized by the single work group and cannot be fed into the system through communication channels linking units with centralized structures of authority.

The work structure tends to confine informal relations to the work group by reducing opportunities for contact between different work groups. The extent to which ingroup solidarities develop depends on other factors, such as the frequency and intensity of interaction.[21] But the individual performance is constantly exposed to the view of other members of the work group, so that the individual's ability to control his own role definition is reduced, although the ability of the group to control the role definitions of its members vis à vis the organization may be considerable. The individual participant is more exposed, therefore, to corrections by his fellows. Informal standards developed in the group are more effectively enforced than organizational standards, and this informal structure of enforcement may be discontinuous with the organizational process of control.[22]

Obstacles to Supervision. Work groups responding to emergencies or to rapidly changing situations are not readily accessible to supervision; for these may make it necessary to take action without consulting a centralized command. One principle of modern military strategy, for example, assumes that communications will be broken and that small front-line units must be capable of maintaining their own "organizational impetus."[23]

Physical distance may make it difficult to maintain adequate communications. Bowra has suggested that this is one reason why efforts to unify the Greek city states were unsuccessful. The mountainous terrain which separated them made adequate and reliable communications too difficult.[24] In spite of modern communications technology, distance still has an effect by limiting information to what may be reliably transmitted by the means of communication.

Separation of the locus of actions may give the operator in the front-line unit substantial autonomy. For example, on the newspaper Warren Breed describes in his analysis of social control in the newsroom,[25] there was considerable ideological divergence between editorial policy and the beliefs of staff reporters. For policy and campaign stories, and assigned stories, official policy generally prevailed, but for "beat" stories and stories which the reporter initiated, he had substantial autonomy:

When we come to the beat story . . . it is clear that the function of the reporter changes. *No editor comes between him and his beat* (police department, city hall, etc.), *thus the reporter gains the "editor" function.* It is he who, to a marked degree, can select which stories to pursue, which to ignore. Several cases developed in interviews of beat men who smothered stories they knew would provide fuel for policy—policy they personally disliked or thought injurious to the professional code (italics added).[26]

Separation of loci of action geographically or temporally increases the need for the special provision of controls, since access to information requires special procedures and is not supplemented by knowledge of the context from informal access and face-to-face interaction. Or the work process may be of a kind which is not readily codeable for reports or which for other reasons cannot be readily evaluated in a systematic and routine fashion. Large-scale organizations have developed complex structures of accounting and reporting to ensure the regular and reliable supply of information. But, as March and Simon have pointed out:

The person who summarizes and assesses his own direct perceptions and transmits them to the rest of the organization becomes an important source of informational premises for organizational action. The "facts" he communicates can be disbelieved, but they can only rarely be checked. Hence, by the very nature and limits of the communication system, a great deal of discretion and influence is exercised by those persons who are in direct contact with some part of the "reality" that is of concern to the organization.[27]

Quite apart from the problems of falsification and error, the extent to which judgment enters into the process of encoding is an important source of control. Ideally, there is the minimum leeway for judgment, but although the development of standardized rules is sometimes simply a problem of developing the appropriate set of rules, in other cases the criteria are and must remain ambiguous,[28] and the individual's or group's standards of judgment become operative.

Effect of Structure on Communications

These features of the structure of front-line organizations have definite consequences for the distribution of information and the flow of communication in the organization. If, as in the state mental hospital, there is some form of line organization, it will not conform to the classic model as Barnard has formulated it:

The special system of status associated with chains of command or hierarchy of authority depends upon each position being a "communication center," the inferior command being associated with restricted areas or fields, the higher command being more comprehensive.[29]

This is based on a view of the corporate process as one in which objectives are formulated for the organization as a whole and the tasks specified as components necessary to their attainment are divided up successively and delegated downward at each level of the organization. In the pure type (but we must remember that no actual organization conforms to the pure type) the exchange of information for corrections involves the whole organization. Positions at the periphery have access only to a segment of the total picture. Each higher position has a strategic advantage over subordinate positions, and only those occupying positions at the center can gain a perspective of the process as a whole.[30]

By contrast, in the front-line type of organization, the organization confronts its objectives distributively rather than as a corporate unit. The definition of objectives and the exchange of information for corrections can be completed without reference to higher-level positions or to a more complete perspective of the functioning of the organization. Because of the relative inaccessibility of front-line units to direct supervision, the information available at these points is not readily available to higher-level positions. Therefore the front-line unit occupies the strategic position in the structure and is capable of discretionary action with respect to organizational goals.

Relations Between Front-Line and Center

These characteristics of front-line organization do not imply the absence of a formally centralized leadership. Indeed the formal model of a front-line organization is incomplete without specifying the relationship between front-line units and centralized positions of responsibility.

An organization as a corporate group controls certain resources both of personnel and of plant, equipment and funds. Control of the corporate process as a whole necessitates centralized positions of responsibility where policy is formulated for the organization as a whole. In a front-line organization the locus of responsibility for organizational performance and policy making at the center is peculiar in being divorced from the locus of organizational initiative in units at the periphery.

Because of this separation, policies are not made in the form of definite concrete objectives to be attained at some more or less definite time in the future. They tend rather to be statements of general principles or rules to be followed at the front line. Perrow notes that the goals of the general medical hospital are not stated as concrete objectives but are ideological in character. He points out that different representative groups in the hospital formulate the goals of the hospital in different ways.[31] Thompson and Bates have also drawn attention to the ambiguity of the goals of hospitals and universities.[32] In the mental health field, the discussion of organizational goals is commonly in terms of a "philosophy of treatment." The ideological or ambiguous terms in which policy is formulated for the organization by persons in positions of leadership are, I suggest, a function of the requirement that *objectives* be set at the front line.

The power of the front-line unit to influence policy results from two factors: (1) the ability of the unit to take action that will commit the organization to some significant degree without involving other organizational segments in the decision-making process; and (2) the insulation of the unit from processes of control, both vertical and horizontal. Thus when actions of front-line units may also have consequences of any significance to the organization, or when a major part of the work of the organization is entrusted to units of this kind, their ability to determine effective standards of performance becomes important as a means of influencing organizational policy.

The dilemma of those occupying central positions is that they are responsible for making policy and maintaining standards of performance for the organization as a whole, while occupying positions from which this responsibility can least effectively be exercised as authority. The devolution of power (as information) to peripheral positions, makes the reliability of procedures for transmitting information questionable and trust of those who initiate action for the organization at the front-line level of vital importance. Furthermore, the detachment of the units from other segments of the organization may be paralleled by a development of normative detachment and unreliability arising from phenomena of drift. This is particularly likely when the units are required to act in a constantly changing environment, since each decision commits the unit in unforeseen ways. Also, when the work of the unit involves interaction with persons who are not members of the organization, and with those who, from the perspective of the organization, are irresponsible, the processes of interaction may result in commitments in the form of obligations to outsiders as well as to a course of events.[33]

The operative policies[34] of the organization must emerge from an interaction between central and front-line positions. The extent to which the policies pursued by front-line units conform to the policies formulated by persons in positions at the center should then be a function of how well the structures and processes of control are adapted to dealing with this special problem of control.

Structures of Control in Front-Line Organizations

As Michels formulated the "iron law of oligarchy" it is a "tendency" arising from the fact of organization for the attainment of definite ends. The term "tendency," is here taken to mean that given certain specified conditions, certain specific consequences will follow unless a further and usually unspecified factor intervenes to prevent it. In this case, this further factor must clearly be some form of structure and process of control which represents a successful internal adaptation of the organization to its peculiar problem. In the oligarchic type of organization the problem to be solved is to ensure that the development of power located in centralized positions is responsive to the membership, which is the formal locus of policy making. The sense in which the ITU, as analyzed in *Union Democracy*,[35] constitutes a deviant case is that the institutionalization of a two-party system provides an effective means of membership control over union leadership. It does not, however, result in a change in the locus of organizational initiative, which is the prerogative of whichever group of leaders occupies the central positions.

Structures and processes of control may be expected to vary systematically with the problems of internal control that are characteristic of different organizational forms. The control structures of front-line organizations should show special features which represent administrative responses to the irresponsible tendencies of front-line units. From the specification given of a front-line organization, two main inferences may be drawn:

1. That a front-line organization will be likely to develop mechanisms of control adapted to regulating and restricting the autonomy of front-line units.

2. If such mechanisms fail to develop or are ineffective, the operative policies of the organization will be decided at the front line rather than at the center.[36]

There is space here only to suggest what some alternative control structures might be:

Intensive Supervision

One possibility is to increase the quantity of information coming up from the front line to the central administration by such devices as requiring the maintenance of extensive records on all aspects of front-line activity and the use of both routine and spot inspection. These techniques of supervision are characteristic of state mental hospitals. Kaufman has recorded the same phenomenon as a response to problems of regulating the performance of forest rangers.[37] These methods of control are most appropriate when the front-line tasks are largely routinized and the exercise of initiative is limited. Their major disadvantage is that the maintenance of elaborate records may actually interfere with the performance of the tasks. In addition an organizational preference for this form of control may markedly inhibit the development of initiative.

Charismatic Leadership

When front-line units exercise active initiative, it becomes of greater importance to have persons in formal positions of leadership at the front line who through training and indoctrination have internalized organizational goals and are competent to assume responsibility for maintaining adequate standards. One way of doing this—although its viability as an organizational form is questionable—is based on a central charismatic position of leadership with a discipular relationship with front-line agents. The occupant of the central position plays the role of a moral leader. Control of front-line agents is maintained by intensive ideological conversations, which expose front-line performance to the corrections and advice of the leader.[38]

Professional Control Structure

A professional type of control structure appears to be particularly relevant to the problem of front-line organization. Processes of training and indocrination controlled by the profession provide the individual with skills, knowledge, and internalized standards, which enable him to act in accordance with professional standards of performance in situations insulated from supervision. The professional role, moreover, incorporates a responsibility for realizing professional goals and normally endows the individual with authority enabling him to direct and regulate the performance of other front-line actors.[39] Moreover when positions at the center and front line are filled by persons with common professional membership—as is generally the case in professional organizations—then the structure of controls becomes stronger because of the cross-cutting alignment of the professional colleague group, which provides a direct link between center and periphery. The formal status of the full professional permits some decentralization of responsibility. It also provides guarantees of individual competence and commitment, which lessen the special problems of trust characteristic of this organizational form.

Summary

The state mental hospital has been presented as an exception to the iron law of oligarchy formulated by Michels. It has been suggested that differences in the distribution of power could be accounted for in terms of differences in the communication structure. The structure and processes of the ward system of the state mental hospital have been described with special reference to their consequences for the communication structure. It has been shown how the ward unit tended to emerge as a pocket of information, and three aspects of state mental hospital structure were abstracted as characteristics of a "front-line" organization:

1. The locus of organizational initiative is front-line units.

2. The task of each unit is performed independently of other like units.

3. There are obstacles to the direct supervision of the activities of such units.

When a major part of the task of an organization is allocated to front-line units, the major locus of responsibility for organizational performance in positions at the center becomes divorced from the locus of organizational initiative in units at the periphery. Front-line organizations thus present distinctive problems of control. To be effective, structures of organizational control must incorporate appropriate responses. Some alternative structures of control have been presented with special emphasis on the relevance of a professional structure to this type of organization.

Notes

1. There is an extensive literature dealing with the attitudes and culture of the mental hospital attendant which, in studying the moral and psychological bases of resistance, takes for granted the attendant's ability to assert his preferences over those of the formal authority. Other writers have concerned themselves specifically with the problem of the power of attendants. Those are: I. Belknap, *Human Problems of a State Mental Hospital* (New York: McGraw-Hill, 1956); J. and E. Cumming, "Social Equilibrium and Social Change in the Large Mental Hospital," in M. Greenblatt, D. J. Levinson, and R. H. Williams (eds.), *The Patient and the Mental Hospital* (Glencoe, Ill.: Free Press, 1957); D. Mechanic, Sources of Power of Lower Participants in Complex Organizations, *Administrative Science Quarterly,* 7 (December 1962), 349–364; F. Miyamoto, "Factors Facilitating Institutional Change in a State Mental Hospital," paper presented at the annual meeting of the Pacific Sociological Society, May, 1962; T. J. Scheff, "Control over Policy by Attendants in a Mental Hospital," *Journal of Health and Human Behavior* 2 (1961), 93–105.

2. R. Michels, *Political Parties* (Glencoe, Ill.: Free Press, 1915).

3. Miyamoto, *op. cit.*

4. See Richard H. McCleery, "Policy Change in Prison Management," in A. Etzioni, (ed.), *Complex Organizations: A Sociological Reader* (New York: Holt, Rinehart and Winston, 1961).

5. This study is based on eighteen months of field research in a California state mental hospital. I am very grateful to the staff and patients of the hospital for their help and friendship.

6. Peter M. Blau and W. Richard Scott, *Formal Organizations: A Comparative Approach* (San Francisco, Calif.: Chandler, 1962), p. 183. These authors have drawn attention to the differences between "parallel" and "interdependent" types of specialization. The operations of an automobile plant are an example of the interdependent type. The parallel form of specialization is exemplified by the department store where different but no interdependent services are provided by the various sales departments. The state mental hospital would be an instance of parallel specialization.

7. T. Burling, E. M. Lentz, and R. N. Wilson, *The Give and Take in Hospitals* (New York: G. P. Putnam, 1956), p. 111. Cf. their description of a general hospital ward. Among the personnel who may visit the wards of a general medical hospital on regular business are food service personnel, dietitians, social service workers, physiotherapists, laboratory technicians, and maids. Each of these cate-

gories reports to a separate department in the hospital. See also Jane Jacobs, *The Death and Life of Great American Cities* (New York: Random House, 1962), p. 36. She draws attention to the social controls provided by sidewalk traffic.

The social controls which arise as a simple by-product of the presence of a passer-by (i.e., a non-participant, present but not engaged) is an aspect of the public process which is particularly important in maintaining public morality. This is not because the passer-by is necessarily prepared to act as its representative. He may not even be aware of any reason for disapproval; or disapprove if he is aware. But to escape the imputation, he will have to give some special signal indicating complicity or distinct withdrawal of interest. The glance of a passer-by can catalyze a self-examination even when a person is not guilty of wrongdoing.

8. This is a slightly simplified model of an actual structure. In the case studied, the position of clinical director intervened between central nursing office and hospital superintendent. The simpler model appears to be representative of this segment of the control structure of state hospitals. Compare, for example, Belknap, *op. cit.*, pp. 40–41.

9. Richard H. McCleery, *op. cit.*, p. 381.

10. Michels, *op. cit.*, p. 14.

11. *Ibid.*, pp. 46–47.

12. Chester I. Barnard, *The Functions of the Executive* (Cambridge, Mass.: Harvard University, 1956), p. 28.

13. H. A. Simon, *Administrative Behavior* (New York: Macmillan, 1961), p. 106.

14. J. G. March, and H. A. Simon, *Organizations* (New York: John Wiley, 1958).

15. *Ibid.*, p. 26.

16. J. D. Thompson, and F. L. Bates, "Technology, Organization and Administration," in J. D. Thompson, P. B. Hammond, R. W. Hawkes, B. H. Junker, and A. Tuden (eds.), *Comparative Studies in Administration* (Pittsburgh: University of Pittsburgh, 1959).

17. Morris Janowitz, *The Sociology of Military Establishments* (New York: Russell Sage Foundation, 1959), pp. 37–38.

18. C. Argyris, *Organization of a Bank* (New Haven, Conn.: Yale University, 1954).

19. *Ibid.*, p. 57.

20. W. F. Whyte, The Social Structure of the Restaurant, *American Journal of Sociology* 54 (January 1949).

21. Cf. George C. Homans, *The Human Group* (New York: Harcourt, Brace, 1950).

22. For a description of informal processes of control in maintaining conformity to unofficial work norms in the bank wiring room, see R. J. Roethlisberger, and W. J. Dickson, *Management and the Worker* (Cambridge, Mass.: Harvard University, 1939).

23. Janowitz, *op. cit.*, pp. 36–37.

24. C. M. Bowra, *The Greek Experience* (New York: World Publishing, 1957).

25. Warren Breed, Social Control in the Newsroom: A Functional Analysis, *Social Forces* 33 (May 1955).

26. *Ibid.*

27. March and Simon, *op. cit.*, p. 165.

28. This problem is, of course, a familiar one to the researcher in the social sciences.

29. Chester I. Barnard, "The Functions of Status Systems in Formal Organization," in R. K. Merton, A. P. Gray, B. Hockey, and H. C. Selvin (eds.), *Reader in Bureaucracy* (Glencoe, Ill.: Free Press, 1952).

30. Here is Barnard's vivid description of this process: The general executive states that 'this is the purpose, this the objective, this the direction, in general terms, in which we wish to move, before next year.' His department heads, or the heads of his main territorial divisions, say to their departments or suborganizations: 'This means for us these things now, then others next month, then others later, to be better defined after experience.' Their subdepartment or division heads say: 'This means for us such and such operations now at these places, such others at those places, something today here, others tomorrow there.' Then district or bureau chiefs in turn become more and more specific, their sub-chiefs still more so as to place, group, time, until finally purpose is merely jobs, specific groups, definite men, definite times, accomplished results. But meanwhile, back and forth, up and down, the communications pass, reporting obstacles, difficulties, impossibilities, accomplishments; redefining, modifying purposes level after level. Chester I. Barnard, *The Functions of the Executive* (Cambridge: Harvard, 1938), pp. 231–232.

31. C. Perrow, *Authority, Goals, and Prestige in a General Hospital* (Ph.D. dissertation in sociology, University of California, Berkeley, 1960).

32. J. D. Thompson, and F. L. Bates, Technology, Organization, and Administration, *Administrative Science Quarterly* 2 (December 1957).

33. For an analysis of this process, see P. Selznick, *TVA and the Grass Roots* (Berkeley, Calif.: Universiy of California, 1949).

34. "Operative" policies or goals is Perrow's term for those goals which an organization actually pursues as a consequence of its normal procedures and practice and are to be distinguished from its "official" goals—i.e., those to which it publicly adheres. Cf. C. Perrow, The Analysis of Goals in Complex Organizations, *American Sociological Review* 26 (December 1961), 854–866.

35. S. M. Lipset, M. A. Trow, and J. S. Coleman, *Union Democracy* (Glencoe, Ill.: Free Press, 1956).

36. The power of the state mental hospital attendant can thus be viewed as resulting from a failure to develop effective controls.

37. H. Kaufman, *The Forest Ranger* (Baltimore, Md.: Johns Hopkins, 1960).

38. See, for example, Jules Henry's description of the structure and processes of control at the Sonia Shankman Orthogenic School in "Types of Institutional Structure" in Greenblatt, Levinson, and Williams *op. cit.*

39. Barr and his associates suggest that increased professionalization among teachers has reduced the need for intensive supervision and made it possible for the teacher to exercise greater initiative in the classroom. Cf. A. S. Barr, W. H. Burton, and L. J. Brueckner, *Supervision: Democratic Leadership in the Improvement of Learning* (New York: Appleton-Century, 1947). Janowitz, *op. cit.*, p. 36, in describing the front-line organization of segments of the modern army, emphasizes the importance of developing a professional type of leadership to take charge of such units.

Organizational Control Structures in Five Correctional Institutions

Mayer N. Zald

Like universities and mental hospitals, most correctional institutions are organizations that have multiple goals. One can characterize the goals of any given correctional institution in terms of the relative importance of custodial or treatment purposes; some institutions have almost purely custodial goals, some have "mixed goals," and some have almost purely treatment goals.

Custodial goals are operative when an organization devotes a large part of its energies and resources to the control and containment of inmates; treatment goals are operative when a large part of organizational resources and energies are devoted to the rehabilitation and positive social change of inmates.

Organizational goals are conceptualized as the analytic independent variable; action necessary to implement custodial or treatment goals leads to, or requires, differences in organizational control structures.

Two institutions whose goals are approximately the same might differ sharply in structure and practice, however, if they employ different methods. A mental hospital, for example, which utilizes mainly electroconvulsive and other neurological therapies has different staff-patient relationships and practices than one using primarily psychotherapy. In treatment institutions for delinquents there are important differences in structure required by individual treatment (psychotherapy, casework, or counseling) as contrasted with milieu treatment (interpreting behavior and changing the individual through his relationship with others).

This study concentrates on the relationship between custodial and treatment goals and aspects of organizational control structures—the pattern of departmentalization and the distribution and balance of power among executives and employees of five institutions for delinquents.[1] My central assumption is that implementation of custodial or treatment goals requires different relationships between institutions and the local community, between various groups of employees, and

Reprinted from *American Journal of Sociology* 68 (November, 1962):451–65.

between employees and inmates. These differences directly affect the control structure of the institution.[2]

The control structure of an organization can be described in terms of the distribution of power and the channels for utilizing power.[3] The pattern and amount of departmentalization and interdepartmental relationships are part of the structure of control because they reflect the way in which responsibility (and control) is delegated. The balance of power among executive and staff groups reflects both the formal delegation of control and the informal seizure of control by some executives and groups. My general thesis is that institutions with dominant treatment goals differ in their control structure from those with dominant custodial goals; the more complex departmental structure and tasks require a wider distribution of power among the executives and a different allocation of power among both executives and staff groups.

Two major hypotheses are examined:

Hypothesis 1: *In mixed-goal and treatment institutions power is distributed among executives; whereas in more custodial institutions power is not distributed, only the superintendent possesses power.* Internal practices required in treatment institutions are more complex, less routinized, and more individualized than those in custodial institutions. Similarly, because he must obtain a larger amount of resources per inmate than his counterpart in custodial institutions, and because he must defend the relatively open quality of his program, the superintendent of an institution with treatment goals must concern himself more with external affairs than his counterpart in a custodial institution.

Differences in the relative dominance of custodial and treatment goals among institutions lead to differences in the substantive bases of decisions and imply differences in the importance attached to various activities (e.g., containment, counseling, etc.). Therefore, aside from the extent to which executive power is shared, difference in goals between institutions leads to the allocation of power to executives who differ in their values and goal commitments, that is, to a difference in the balance of power. In a mixed-goal institution, the executive responsible for internal activities is likely to pursue custodial goals and the executive concerned with external affairs ostensibly will pursue treatment goals. Such an arrangement placates the demands of specialized publics for a rehabilitative program at the same time that it insures attainment of basic custodial goals. In a treatment institution, however, the executive responsible for internal control must be fully committed to treatment goals.

Differences in the basic goals of the institution lead not only to differences in the criteria on which decisions are based but also to differences in the amount of power held by various groups within the institution, because custodial and treatment goals require different staff groups to be in control of decisions about discipline and activities for inmates.

Hypothesis 2: *In custodial institutions the influence and authority of the cottage parent is likely to be relatively high and that of a social service worker relatively low. The reverse will tend to hold true in individual treatment institutions; since milieu treatment attempts to involve more of the staff in the decision-making process, a "team" concept results and a general sharing of power is likely. In all institutions teachers are relatively isolated from the major operating problems of the organization and are likely to have little influence.*

Although social service workers have power in both the individual- and milieu-treatment institutions, they differ in their relationship to the other staff members. In a milieu institution the social service staff can make its influence felt only through other staff members; in individual-treatment institutions social service workers may function relatively independently of the rest of the staff. I shall explore both the power of staff groups and the kinds of relationships existing among staff groups.

Before the data pertaining to these hypotheses are presented, the sample institutions must be briefly described.

The Sample Institutions

From a large number of institutions whose goals were known on a reputational basis by experts,[4] five were selected for intensive study.[5] In Table 1 the goals, number of inmates and employees, and type of control (public or private) of each institution are shown.

Each of these institutions, particularly those with treatment goals, had been subject to processes of change and conflict in recent times. All of them formally stressed some form of rehabilitation goals (as has been true historically for institutions for delinquents). But institutions with such older or traditional concepts of rehabilitation as "training" also stressed custodial aims. The description of each institution which follows locates the goals with reference to the relative dominance of custody and treatment and highlights important features of each institution's operation.

Dick Industrial School[6] stressed discipline, training, and containment in its goal statements. Operating its own farm, Dick was an isolated, custodial institution.

Regis Home, the smallest institution in the study, was run by a Catholic religious order. Although some boys received individual counseling, Regis aimed primarily at educating and training the boys.

TABLE I

Five Sample Institutions, by Goals, Size, and Control, Public or Private

	Size	
Goals	Small	Large
Custodial		Dick Industrial School 260 Inmates 65 Staff members Public
Mixed	Regis Home 56 Inmates 13 Staff members Private	Mixter Training School 400 Inmates 177 Staff members Public
Treatment	Inland School 60 Inmates 40 Staff members Private	Milton School for Boys 200 Inmates 117 Staff members Public

The Home was located in an urban community and sent its boys to twenty schools in the community.[7] Discipline was firm, although less punitive than at Dick, and all counseling, especially in regard to sexual practices, had to conform to the tenets of the governing religious order.

Mixter, a mixed-goal institution, was the largest in the study. Mixter represents a benign custodial type which minimizes repressive sanctions while not fully developing a treatment program.

Milton, which stressed a milieu approach, and Inland, which stressed individual treatment, were the two institutions in the sample with relatively dominant treatment goals. They differed from each other in that Milton was a large public institution while Inland was a small private institution. Milton had changed to a milieu approach after a decade and a half of growth and conflict. Its milieu approach was intended to eliminate tensions between professional and lay personnel by having them consult often with each other as well as to implement treatment philosophy.

Because Milton was a public institution and had to accept all delinquents sent to it, it was not able to dispense with custodial goals as completely as Inland. Inland defined itself as a "residential treatment center" and its personnel placed a great deal of stress on the delinquent's progress in counseling.

To summarize, I consider Dick to have had the most custodial goals of the institutions in the sample, followed by Regis and Mixter. Although Inland was able to dispense with custodial emphases to a greater extent than Milton, both Milton and Inland were clearly institutions with dominant treatment goals. With this array of institutions it is possible to compare smaller institutions with larger; public institutions with private; and institutions with custodial, mixed, and treatment goals.[8]

Departmental Structure and Administrative Power Balance

The hypothesis that power is more widely distributed among executives in treatment institutions than in custodial ones rests on the greater complexity of organization tasks and on the greater external demands on the superintendent in the former. Without delegating authority, the superintendent would have an overextended span of control. Formal delegation of authority often takes place through the creation of departmental structures, and institutions with different basic goals and methods set up different types of departmental patterns. Since departmental structures also affect the relations among staff groups, before presenting data which bears directly on the first hypothesis, I will discuss the departmental structures of the five institutions as they relate to correctional institutions in general.

Such custodial institutions as Dick and, to a lesser extent, Regis operate on a routine and repetitive basis and require little departmentalization.[9] When containment and control of inmates are achieved, organizational goals are fulfilled. Thus, the co-ordination of the staff is required primarily for physical movement of inmates and for rotation of personnel shifts. The executive can easily maintain an extended span of control.

Both Dick and Regis had simple formal structures. Of course, Regis' small size as well as its basically routine operation accounted for its lack of departmentalization. Dick was partially departmentalized; only the academic school and the farm had effective departmental heads. Even though each of the five cottages had a nominal leader, all cottage parents often reported directly to the superintendent. No attempt was made to delegate control of the cottages to a department head, and there was little supervision of cottage parent activity. Furthermore, the departmentalization of the farm did not stem from a desire to implement more complex programs for the boys or to control employee relations with inmates; it occurred only after Dick's farm production was criticized by a citizen's committee and was an attempt to insure an adequate variety of food. Although Dick was larger than Inland, it had less departmentalization, suggesting that size alone does not account for the degree of departmentalization. Moreover, the superintendent and assistant superintendent at Dick had little difficulty in meeting role demands, indicating that under prevailing conditions further departmentalization was not required.

In contrast to custodial institutions, such mixed-goal and treatment institutions as Mixter, Milton, and Inland cannot operate as routinely, and more complex combinations of personnel must be coordinated. Both Mixter and Inland had multiple department structures, a form which is most likely to occur when each of the diverse tasks of the institution is relatively autonomous. In an institution with mixed goals, for instance, cottage life, education, treatment, recreation, and maintenance might each be in a separate and unintegrated department. Such an institution as Inland, operating under individual treatment philosophy, also allows departments to function independently, since the relevance of activity in the school or cottage to the rehabilitative process is not stressed, and high integration of departments thus is not required.

Although the larger size of Mixter resulted in more subsystem divisions than in Inland, the basic structure in both institutions was similar. Social service, training and education, cottage life, and business and maintenance each comprised separate departments, no one of which had control over the others. At Mixter the superintendent took responsibility for integrating the activities of the various departments, while at Inland the assistant director performed this function.

The departmental structure at Mixter permitted the superintendent to have a reasonable span of control, while at Inland the assistant superintendent was not so fortunate. The emphasis on individual relations to inmates, inmate voluntarism, and non-routinized programs, as well as his role as chief disciplinarian, overextended the range of control of the assistant superintendent. Although Inland had less than one-fourth the number of employees of Mixter and two-thirds as many as Dick, and although its over-all departmental structure was similiar to that of Mixter's, the lack of a highly routinized program led to continuous operating pressures on the assistant superintendent.

Milieu-treatment institutions operate on criteria that are more consistently applied throughout the institution than in either mixed-goal or individual-treatment institutions, in this respect resembling custodial institutions. But the milieu institution differs from the custodial institution in its attempt to rationalize greater areas of organizational activity, in the complex combination of personnel, and in the substantive basis of the decisions it makes.

Milton was divided into two major divisions, the business and maintenance division and the clinical division. Under the direction of a psychiatrist, the clinical division had responsibility for all activity with the inmates. The social service staff, which in multiple departmental structures usually gives direct service to clients but only consultant service to the rest of the staff assumed responsibility for the supervision of the cottage staff. The social service staff and the cottage parents worked together on cottage committees to make decisions about the boys. The basic therapeutic role was not defined as a one-to-one relationship between a clinical staff member and a delinquent but was, theoretically, the relationship between the boy and all staff members with whom he had contact. But, although the school and vocational training areas were under the direction of the clinical director, they were not as fully incorporated into the unitary authority structure as the cottage area. The "dual-division" structure that operated at Milton permitted to a greater extent than a multiple-department structure the centralized control over all activity in which inmates are involved. Personnel dealing with treatment were placed directly in control of the day-to-day operating staff of the institution.[10]

These patterns of departmentalization establish the official range of hierarchical positions in an institution, but they do not reveal the actual amount of power or influence that a group or individual may exercise. My first proposition deals with the distribution of power among executives.

In my analysis I was able to compare the staff members' perceptions of the distribution of power among executives within an institution as well as to compare the power of executives in similar positions in different institutions.[11] Employees of the institutions were asked to rate the amount of influence possessed by each of the members of the executive core.[12] Table 2 presents the proportion of staff attributing "high influence" to each of them.[13]

In Dick and Regis, the more custodial institutions, a large proportion of the staff thought only the superintendent had "a great deal of say," while in Mixter, Milton, and Inland, the staff believed that the superintendent and at least one other member of the executive core had a great deal of influence. In fact, the data in Table 2 indicate that at Inland and Milton a larger proportion of the staff regarded the assistant superintendent rather than the superintendent as having "a great deal of

TABLE 2
Distribution of Perceived Executive Power
Staff Perception of High Influence of Various Members of Executive Core

	Percent of High Influence[a]				
Executives Rated	Dick	Regis	Mixter	Milton	Inland
Superintendent	79	100	59	52	62
Assistant director	34	11	23	65	81
Head of social service	11	0	19	12[b]	19
Head of cottage parents . . .	10[c]	[d]	52	26	3
Principal of school	15	[d]	8	7	5
Total number	(62)	(9)	(155)	(108)	(37)

[a]Percentages are given for the highest point of a five-point scale ("A great deal of say").
[b]Business manager substituted for head of social service at *Milton*.
[c]Farm manager substituted for head of cottage parents at *Dick*.
[d]No head of cottage parents or school principal at *Regis*.

influence." These data add credibility to our first hypothesis. It may be noted that both the school principals and social service directors were consistently perceived as having little power.

One might ask, however, if these findings necessarily related to the goals and departmental structures of these institutions or were merely accidentally associated in these institutions. The personalities of the superintendents, the size of the institutions, and—in the case of Regis—the structure of the religious order were variables which might have contributed to the great amount of power attributed to superintendents at Dick and Regis and to the smaller amount of power attributed to them at Mixter, Milton, and Inland.

In accounting for the magnitude of difference between the treatment and custodial superintendents one cannot ignore these factors. The small size of Regis minimized the need for delegation and decentralization of decision-making, while the particular personality of the superintendent at Dick contributed to the staff perception of his role as highly concentrated in power.

While the personality attributes of the superintendents of custodial institutions contributed to the image of their high power, the converse seemed to be true in the treatment institutions. The superintendent at Milton felt that his training did not qualify him to make decisions about the treatment of children, leading him to defer often in judgment to the professionals on his staff. On the other hand, although Inland's director had training that might be considered appropriate, his interpersonal relations were characteristically very tense, and the assistant director instead gained the allegiance and loyalty of the staff.

To say that such factors minimize the magnitude of the difference in patterns of power between custodial and treatment institutions is not to vitiate the over-all pattern. The creation of more than one office with authority in treatment institutions necessitates a wider disribution of power. To act effectively each department must have the right to make some decisions, and professional treatment personnel in particular must be given more power. Furthermore, the superintendents may have to spend a good deal of time on matters not directly concerned with the internal operation of the institution, such as the relationship of the institution to the community, etc.

If executive power is shared in mixed-goal or treatment institutions, among whom is it shared? The clinical director and assistant director at Milton and Inland, respectively, were attributed high power by the staff, while at Mixter the head of the cottage-life department was perceived as the second in command. The attribution of high power to the clinical director at Milton and to the assistant director was in line with their official status, and both attempted to implement treatment goals. But the division of power between the superintendent and the head of cottage life at Mixter did not correspond to their official status, and might appear to have indicated a bifurcation of power between rehabilitational and custodial goals, the superintendent representing rehabilitative programs and the head of cottage life custodial programs. But this separation was more apparent than real: although the superintendent claimed to be committed to rehabilitational goals, in practice he concentrated his attention on benign custodial aims. Moreover, the head of cottage life, though custodially oriented, was opposed to using means which he considered overly repressive. In fact, there was little conflict between the superintendent and the head of cottage life; the superintendent felt that the head of cottage life was doing a much better job than two social workers who had previously held the position and "couldn't stand the pressure." Contrary to my expectations, the two men's approaches were not so far apart—I underestimated the pressures for consensus among major executives.

The attribution of high power to the head of cottage life at Mixter was due to his official position inasmuch as the training director was officially the second in command (52 percent attributed "a great deal of say" to the head of cottage life, whereas only 23 percent attributed "a great deal of say" to the training director). Power was given to the head of cottage life because he guaranteed control and containment in a situation in which repressive sanctions were banned. The head of cottage life and his assistants acted as roving police, backing up the cottage parents in their decisions and controlling situations beyond the scope of cottage parent power. Of course, the director of cottage life also had to co-ordinate a staff of approximately seventy men. But the problems of co-ordination were relatively routine and were partly delegated to the assistant cottage-life supervisors. By itself, the role of co-ordinator would not have called for granting a high degree of power to the head of cottage life.

I have argued that the clinical director at Milton, the assistant director at Inland, and the head of cottage life at Mixter were in particularly central positions for organizational control; but except for discussing the position of the training director at Mixter, I have not analyzed why other executives were not attributed high power. In all of the institutions the school principal and the director of social service influenced the over-all operation of the institution only by their consultant relationship to the superintendent or assistant superintendent. Although they could influence considerably the operation of their own departments, their influence on the rest of the institution was indirect.

It would be a mistake, however, to conclude that the principals or the social service directors were powerless or that their positions did not vary somewhat from institution to institution. Approximately 50 percent of the staff at Mixter and Inland perceived the heads of social service to have "a great deal of say" or "considerable say," the highest two categories in our list of alternatives. Field observations indicated that the assistant director at Inland relied on the head of social service for many clinical decisions, while the superintendent at Mixter consulted more with the head of social service than he did with the training director. The influence of the social service director, especially at Inland, was related to the importance of his position for pursuing treatment aims.

The Balance of Power of Staff Groups

The balance of power among cottage parents, social service workers, and teachers, like the balance of power among executives, is a function of the goals of the organization. I hypothesized that the influence of social service personnel is likely to be higher in treatment institutions than in custodial institutions, while the power of cottage parents is likely to be higher in custodial than in individual treatment institutions. Since the milieu institution requires a team organization, a more general sharing of power is likely.

To measure the power of the various groups in making decisions about clients, I asked the staff of each institution to judge the amount of influence cottage parents, social service workers, and teachers had in making judgments about how the boys should be handled (Table 3).[14]

The statistical differences clearly indicate that a larger proportion of the staff attributes high influence to social service workers in treatment institutions than in custodial institutions. The smallest proportion attributes high influence to social service workers at Dick and Regis, a larger proportion attributes high influence to them at Mixter, and the largest proportion attributes high influence to social service workers at Inland and Milton. Cottage parent power tends to decline as we move from custodial to individual-treatment institutions, however, the cottage-committee structure at Milton, where cottage parents shared in decision-making, led to the cottage parents there being thought of as having high influence by a larger proportion of the staff than at any of the other institutions.

On the other hand, teachers were attributed a relatively low amount of influence in all the institutions. Data in Table 2 indicate that the school principals also were seen as having little influence in the institutions, suggesting that the academic schools had little over-all authority or control in operating the institutions. The school personnel were not central to the definition of institutional philosophy and were restricted to an unproblematic area of institutional operation.

It was originally anticipated that within custodial institutions a larger proportion of the total staff would believe the cottage parents have high influence. This was not so perceived by the social service staff. As it turned out, only 11 percent more of the staff at Dick perceived the cottage parents to have "a great deal of influence," while at Mixter

TABLE 3
Distribution of Perceived Group Power
Staff Perception of High Influence of Social Service Workers,
Cottage Parents, and Teachers

	Percent of High Influence				
Groups Rated	*Dick*	*Regis*	*Mixter*	*Milton*	*Inland*
Social service	39	22	49	76	76
Cottage parents	50	33	34	70	8
Teachers	23	a	11	17	19
Total number	(62)	(9)	(155)	(108)	(37)

aNo teachers at *Regis.*

15 percent attributed more power to social service than to cottage parents. Two factors may account for my incorrect prediction. First, as low-paid, low-status staff at the bottom of the administrative hierarchy, the cottage parents tended to make decisions within the bounds of discretion set by the administrators. Although cottage parents in custodial institutions had more discretion about the discipline and more influence on the discharge of inmates, they did not formulate basic rules and procedures. On the other hand, even in the custodial institutions the higher salaried and more educated social service staff members, although they did not make decisions about individual boys, were able to influence the executives in the formulation of policy.

Second, although in the more custodial institutions cottage parents had high discretion to discipline and grade the boys, this power was shared with other staff members who worked with the boys. At Dick, any person who worked with the boys was allowed to paddle or punish them. At Mixter, while the cottage parent gave each boy 50 percent of his monthly grade (which was the basis on which he was discharged), teachers and detail supervisors made up the rest of the grade. By contrast, at Milton the cottage committee meted out serious discipline, and the cottage parent on duty had a range of possible sanctions not available to teachers or supervisors.

TABLE 4
Percentage of Total Staff and of Cottage Parents at Milton and Inland
Perceiving High Degree of "Helpfulness" of Social Service Advice

Group	Milton	Inland
Total staff:		
Total number	108	37
Percent	61	43
Cottage parents:		
Total number	35	7
Percent	71	29

It is interesting to note that the over-all amount of power attributed to all staff groups was higher at Milton than at any other institution, and lowest at Dick and Regis. (The question permitted all groups to be ranked high, under the assumption that more or less power may be mobilized, depending on both the number of decisions and the number of people involved in decisions in an organization.) This may indicate that milieu treatment requires more decisions and involves more people than custodial institutions, leading to a higher actualization of potential power within the organization.

The data in Table 3 quite clearly indicate the power of social service workers in treatment institutions. Role definitions, however, vary in different institutions so that power expresses itself or is used in very different ways. In the individual-treatment institution the authority of social service is based to a large extent on the staff perception of the prevailing treatment philosophy and on the social service workers' control over decisions made about individual clients. In the milieu institution, although social service workers can make many decisions, they also are required to work through and with other staff members.

In Table 4 are given the proportions of (*a*) all staff and (*b*) cottage parents alone at Milton and Inland who viewed social service advice as helpful.[15] The data clearly indicate the utility of social service to other personnel at Milton. The entente that existed between cottage parents and social service workers in the milieu institution was especially strong; over twice the percentage of cottage parents at Milton as compared with cottage parents in Inland found social service guidance to be of help. Although the ratio of clinical personnel to other personnel was approximately the same at Milton and Inland, the constant attempt of clinical personnel at Milton to accomplish their aims through the milieu program led them to be useful resources for others.

Through a comparative study of five institutions for delinquents I have explored the effects of goals and related methods on organizational control structures. After describing the five sample institutions and their departmental structures my analysis based on questionnaire and field data has supported two propositions. (1) As organizational complexity increases and organization-community relations lead to greater external commitments by the superintendent, the chief executive must share power. In a mixed-goal institution it is likely that power is shared with a person with basically custodial aims, while in institutions with dominant treatment goals power must be given to a person concerned with treatment goals. (2) The balance of power among groups is also a function of organizational goals: social service personnel acquire great influence in treatment institutions, while cottage parent influence is less, except when the major focus of the institution is on the group-living situation, as in the milieu institution.

This analysis has assumed that the structure of control evolves to solve problems of good implementation; without an organizational structure to support and control staff behavior, organizational objectives are not met. My analysis has been primarily static comparing institutions at one point in time. A study of any one institution would show that goals are often in flux as forces internal and external to the organization press for redefinitions or extensions of emphasis. Moreover, in correctional institutions movement toward greater treatment or custodial emphasis brings about opposite pressures from groups with divergent perspectives. Even though the basic pattern of departmentalization may be relatively stable, an ebb and flow of power among groups and among executives is likely to occur as compensating policies and mechanisms are introduced.

Notes

1. There have been few studies from a sociological point of view of institutions for delinquents. For a case study see Robert D. Vinter and Roger Lind, *Staff Relationships and Attitudes in a Juvenile Correctional Institution* (Ann Arbor: School of Social Work, The University of Michigan, 1958). For current approaches to the study of prisons and mental hospitals, see George Grosser (ed.), *Theoretical Studies in Social Organization of the Prison* ("SSRC" Pamphlet, No. 15 [New York: Social Science Research Council, 1960]); Donald Cressey (ed.), *The Prison: Studies in Institutional Organization and Change* (New York: Holt, Rinehart & Winston, 1961); and Milton Greenblatt, Daniel J. Levinson, and Richard H. Williams (eds.), *The Patient and the Mental Hospital* (Glencoe, Ill.: Free Press, 1957).

2. Goals also have more indirect consequences for the attitudes of employees toward inmates, the amount and pattern of conflict, and the role problems of employees. On the patterns of conflict in correctional institutions see my "Power Balance and Organizational Conflict in Correctional Institutions for Delinquents," *Administrative Science Quarterly*, 7 (June, 1962), 22–49. On the role problems of employees see Cressey, "Contradictory Directives in Complex Organizations: The Case of the Prisons," *Administrative Science Quarterly*, 4 (June, 1959), 1–19.

3. The concept of organizational control structure used here is more inclusive than that used by Arnold Tannenbaum and his associates. They include only the distribution of influence among groups in their definition of the control structure, in effect assuming or ignoring the patterned channels through which influence is utilized. See Arnold S. Tannenbaum and Robert L. Kahn, "Organizational Control Structure: A General Descriptive Technique as Applied to Four Local Unions," *Human Relations*, 10 (May, 1957), 127–40; and Tannenbaum and Basil Georgopoulos, "The Distribution of Control in Formal Organizations," *Social Forces*, 38 (October, 1957), 44–50.

4. One representative of the United States Children's Bureau and a professor of social work interested in correctional institutions helped to pick the initial sample. They were asked to name a wide variety of institutions with specific reputations for emphasis on custodial or treatment programs. The reputations of institutions are obviously composites of their goals and their operating procedures. The use of reputations as an index of goals would make my argument circular because I would be using a consequence of structure analytically as a determinant of structure. Institutional goals were independently and directly measured by using data obtained from official statements of goals, interviews with executives, and staff responses to questionnaire items. These measurements indicated that my judgments of goals based on reputations were largely supported (see "Multiple Goals . . . ," *op. cit.*, pp. 64–114). Furthermore, if one uses as a measure of treatment goals the input of treatment personnel, it is clear that our most custodial institution had the lowest

ratio of social service workers to inmates, 1 to 125, whereas our most treatment-oriented institution had a ratio of 1 to 12. The underlying model is a rational and unfolding one; persons in authority have responsibility for implementing goals and take action to pursue those goals, including hiring appropriate personnel. Personnel in interaction then help to change definitions of goals.

5. The selection of institutions met four requirements: (1) an array of institutions among the custodial-treatment dimension; (2) institutions of different sizes as a control measure; (3) both public and private institutions; and (4) institutional goals related to the action program of the organization.

I did not attempt to select a representative sample but aimed instead at maximizing comparison of the effects of goals. Comparison of the five institutions to the universe of institutions in the United States indicates that, in fact, they are not representative of the universe of institutions. Institutions with low inmate-staff ratios and high per capita costs are overrepresented, indicating most likely an over-representation of treatment institutions (*ibid.*, pp. 51–54). But the institutions selected to fulfill the requirements of my comparative design.

6. The institutions have been given false names to preserve guaranteed anonymity. The first two or three letters of each name serve as a mnemonic device for some salient aspect of the institutional program.

7. Since there was no attempt to contain delinquents at Regis, its inclusion in the study might be questioned. To fill the required cells of the design of my study a small institution emphasizing containment was sought. Since none was available, excluding Regis would have left an important gap in the comparisons. Its small size permits comparisons with Inland School, and its emphasis on education and respect reflects a parallel with older concepts of rehabilitation.

8. The absence from the sample of large private or small public institutions means that comparisons for the variables of size and control are confounded. My primary comparisons, however, deal with the custodial-treatment dimension, and I believe these missing data do not seriously affect the basic analysis of the effects of custodial and treatment goals.

9. A department is defined as a relatively self-contained subsystem of an organization. A group of workers can be considered members of a department when there is a designated liaison or responsible supervisor for the group. Workers performing similar tasks but relating individually to the superintendent, assistant superintendent, or another executive are not considered members of a department.

10. In "The Reduction of Role Conflict in Institutional Staff," *Children*, 5 (1958), 65–69, Lloyd Ohlin has described a similar structural development in a girls' training institution; caseworkers were given administrative responsibility for the management of the cottages. One result of such a change is to partially shift conflict from an interrole to an intrarole level.

11. Several kinds of data were collected in all five institutions. (1) Historical records and institutional publications were examined. (2) Loosely structured observations of organizational practices and conferences were carried out over a two-week period in each institution. (3) Extended interviews with members of the executive core (the superintendent, assistant superintendent, and heads of major departments) were conducted. (4) Questionnaires were distributed to all staff members, yielding a response rate of 85 percent or more in each of the institutions. The interrelationship of measures and observations is stressed. In no case was a datum accepted as veridical when it did not jibe with other data.

12. Respondents were asked: "In general, how much say or influence in the

way——is run would you say each of the following individuals or groups has? (Put one check on each line.)" Respondents checked a five-point scale.

13. To the extent that "real power" is overtly expressed, employee ratings of the power of executives is a legitimate reflection of the amount of power wielded. To the extent that power relations are masked or indirect, we would expect employee perception of power to be based on the actual amount of influence of the executive core, and power to be conceived of as a "whole"—as a general attribute. Herbert Simon ("Introduction to the Theory and Measurement of Influence," *American Political Science Review*, 49 [1955], 431–51) and Nelson Polsby ("Community Power: Three Problems," *American Sociological Review*, 24 [1959], 796–803) have both argued that a general influence rating may conceal the differentiated power wielded in different contexts. Nevertheless, a general measure of attributed power has some validity and has the merit of methodological simplicity.

14. Respondents were asked: "How much influence do each of the following groups have in making decisions about *how the boys should be handled?*" Respondents checked a four-point scale.

15. Respondents were asked: "How much help are the people in social service in advising how to work with the boys?" Three alternatives were used.

The Teacher in the Authority System of the Public School

Howard S. Becker

Institutions can be thought of as forms of collective action which are somewhat firmly established.[1] These forms consist of the organized and related activities of several socially defined categories of people. In service institutions (like the school) the major categories of people so defined are those who do the work of the institution, its functionaries, and those for whom the work is done, its clients. These categories are often subdivided, so that there may be several categories of functionaries and several varieties of client.

One aspect of the institutional organization of activity is a division of authority, a set of shared understandings specifying the amount and kind of control each kind of person involved in the institution is to have over others: who is allowed to do what, and who may give orders to whom. This authority is subject to stresses and possible change to the degree that participants ignore the shared understandings and refuse to operate in terms of them. A chronic feature of service insti-

Reprinted from *Journal of Educational Sociology* 27 (November, 1953): 128–41.

tutions is the indifference or ignorance of the client with regard to the authority system set up by institutional functionaries; this stems from the fact that he looks at the institution's operation from other perspectives and with other interests.[2] In addition to the problems af authority which arise in the internal life of any organization, the service institution's functionaries must deal with such problems in the client relationship as well. One of their preoccupations tends to be the maintenance of their authority definitions over those of clients, in order to assure a stable and congenial work setting.

This article deals with the authority problems of the metropolitan public school teacher. I have elsewhere described the problems of the teacher in her relations with her pupils,[3] and will here continue that discussion to include the teacher's relations with parents, principals, and other teachers. The following points will be considered in connection with each of these relationships: the teacher's conception of her rights and prerogatives, her problems in getting and maintaining acceptance of this conception on the part of others, and the methods used to handle such problems. The picture one should get is that of the teacher striving to maintain what she regards as her legitimate sphere of authority in the face of possible challenge by others. This analysis of the working authority system of the public school is followed by a discussion which attempts to point up its more general relevance. The description presented here is based on sixty long and detailed interviews with teachers in the Chicago public schools.[4]

Teacher and Parent

The teacher conceives of herself as a professional with specialized training and knowledge in the field of her school activity: teaching and taking care of children. To her, the parent is a person who lacks such background and is therefore unable to understand her problems properly. Such a person, as the following quotation shows, is considered to have no legitimate right to interfere with the work of the school in any way:

> One thing, I don't think a parent should try and tell you what to do in your classroom, or interfere in any way with your teaching. I don't think that's right and I would never permit it. After all, I've a special education to fit me to do what I'm doing, and a great many of them have never had any education at all, to speak of, and even if they did, they certainly haven't had my experience. So I would never let a parent interfere with my teaching.

Hers is the legitimate authority in the classroom and the parent should not interfere with it.

Problems of authority appear whenever parents challenge this conception, and are potentially present whenever parents become involved in the school's operation. They become so involved because the teacher attempts to make use of them to bolster her authority over the child, or because they become aware of some event about which they wish to complain. In either case the teacher fears a possible challenge of her basic assumption that the parent has no legitimate voice with regard to what is done to her child in school.

In the first instance, the teacher may send for the parent to secure her help in dealing with a "problem child." But this is always done with an eye to possible consequences for her authority. Thus, this expedient is avoided with parents of higher social-class position, who may not only fail to help solve the problem but may actually accuse the teacher of being the source of the problem and defend the child, thus materially weakening the teacher's power over her children:

> You've got these parents who, you know, they don't think that their child could do anything wrong, can't conceive of it. If a teacher has to reprimand their child for something they're up in arms right away, it couldn't be that the child did anything wrong, it must be the teacher. So it's a lot of bother. And the children come from those kind of homes, so you can imagine that they're the same way.

The teacher feels more secure with lower-class parents, whom she considers less likely challengers. But they fail to help solve the problem, either ignoring the teacher's requests or responding in a way that increases the problem or is personally distasteful to the teacher.

> [They] have a problem child, but you can't get them to school for love or money. You can send notes home, you can write letters, you can call up, but they just won't come.
>
> If you send for [the child's] parents, they're liable to beat the child or something. I've seen a mother bring an ironing cord to school and beat her child with it, right in front of me. And, of course, that's not what you want at all.

This tactic, then, is ordinarily dangerous in the sense that the teacher's authority may be undermined by its consequences. Where it is not dangerous, it tends to be useless for strengthening authority over the child. This reinforces the notion that the parent has no place in the school.

Parents may also become involved in the school's operation on their own initiative, when they come to complain about some action of the school's functionaries. Teachers recognize that there are kinds of activity about which parents have a legitimate right to complain, for which they may legitimately be held responsible, although the consequences of the exercise of this right are greatly feared. They recognize, that is, that the community, in giving them a mandate to teach, reserves the right to interfere when that mandate is not acted on in the "proper" manner. As Cooley put it:

> The rule of public opinion, then, means for the most part a latent authority which the public will exercise when sufficiently dissatisfied with the specialist who is in charge of a particular function.[5]

Teachers fear that the exercise of this latent authority by parents will be dangerous to them.

One form of this fear is a fear that one will be held responsible for any physical harm that befalls the child:

> As far as the worst thing that could happen to me here in school, I'd say it would be if something awful happened someplace where I was supposed to be and wasn't. That would be terrible.

This, it is obvious, is more than a concern for the child's welfare. It is also a concern that the teacher not be held responsible for that welfare in such a way as to give the parents cause for complaint, as the following incident makes clear:

> I've never had any trouble like that when the children were in my care. Of course, if it happens on the playground or someplace where I'm not there to watch, then it's not my responsibility, you see. . . . My children have had accidents. Last year, two of the little boys got into a fight. They were out on the playground and Ronald gave Nick a little push, you know, and one thing led to another and pretty soon Nick threw a big stone at Ronald and cut the back of his head open. It was terrible to happen, but it wasn't my fault, I wasn't out there when it happened and wasn't supposed to be. . . . Now, if it had happened in my room when I was in there or should have been in there, that's different, then I would be responsible and I'd have had something to worry about. That's why I'm always careful when there's something like that might happen. For instance, when we have work with scissors I always am on my toes and keep looking over the whole room in case anything should happen like that.

Another area in which a similar fear that the parents will exercise their legitimate authority arises is that of teaching competence; the following incident is the kind that provokes such fears:

> There was a French teacher—well, there's no question about it, the old man was senile. He was getting near retirement. I think he was sixty-four and had one year to go to retire. The parents began

382 Human Service Organizations

to complain that he couldn't teach. That was true, of course, he couldn't teach any more. He'd just get up in front of his classes and sort of mumble along. Well, the parents came to school and put so much pressure on that they had to get rid of him.

The teachers' fear in these and similar situations is that intrusion by the parents, even on legitimate grounds, will damage their authority position and make them subject to forms of control that are, for them, illegitimate—control by outsiders. This fear is greatest with higher class groups, who are considered quick to complain and challenge the school's authority. Such parents are regarded as organized and militant and, consequently, dangerous. In the lower-class school, on the other hand:

> We don't have any PTA at all. You see, most of the parents work; in most families it's both parents who work. So that there can't be much of a PTA.

These parents are not likely to interfere.

To illustrate this point, one teacher told a story of one of her pupils stabbing another with a scissors, and contrasted the reaction of the lower-class mother with that to be expected from the parents of higher status whose children she now taught:

> I sure expected the Momma to show up, but she never showed. I guess the Negroes are so used to being squelched that they just take it as a matter of course, you know, and never complain about anything. Momma never showed up at all. You take a neighborhood like the one I'm teaching in now, why, my God, they'd be sueing the Board of Education and me, and there'd be a court trial and everything.

It is because of dangers like this that movement to a school in such a neighborhood, desirable as it might be for other reasons, is feared.[6]

The school is for the teacher, then, a place in which the entrance of the parent on the scene is always potentially dangerous. People faced with chronic potential danger ordinarily develop some means of handling it should it become "real" rather than "potential," some kind of defense. The more elaborate defenses will be considered below. Here I want to point to the existence of devices which teachers develop or grow into which allow them some means of defense in face-to-face interaction with the parent.

These devices operate by building up in the parent's mind an image of herself and of her relation to the teacher which leads her to respect the teacher's authority and subordinate herself to it:

> Quite often the offense is a matter of sassiness or back-talk. . . .
> So I'll explain to the parent, and tell him that the child has been sassy

and disrespectful. And I ask them if they would like to be treated like that if they came to a group of children. . . . I say, "Now I can tell just by looking at you, though I've never met you before, that you're not the kind of a person who wants this child to grow up to be disrespectful like that. You want that child to grow up mannerly and polite." Well, when I put it to them that way, there's never any argument about it. . . . Of course, I don't mean that I'm not sincere when I say those things, because I most certainly am. But still, they have that effect on those people.

The danger may also be reduced when the teacher, over a period of years, grows into a kind of relationship with the parents of the community which minimizes the possibilities of conflict and challenge:

> If you have a teacher who's been in a school twenty years, say, why she's known in that community. Like as not she's had some of the parents as pupils. They know her and they are more willing to help her in handling the children than if they didn't know who she was.

If the teacher works in the same neighborhood that she lives in she may acquire a similar advantage, although there is some evidence that the degree of advantage is a function of the teacher's age. Where she is a middle-aged woman whose neighborhood social life is carried on those women of similar age who are the parents of her pupils, the relationship gives her a distinct advantage in dealing with those same women in the school situation. If, however, she is a younger woman, parents are likely to regard her as "a kid from the neighborhood" and treat her accordingly, and the danger of her authority being successfully challenged is that much greater.

In short, the teacher wishes to avoid any dispute over her authority with parents and feels that this can be accomplished best when the parent does not get involved in the school's operation any more than absolutely necessary. The devices described are used to handle the "parent problem" when it arises, but none of them are foolproof and every teacher is aware of the ever-present possibility of a parent intruding and endangering her authority. This constant danger creates a need for defenses and the relations of teacher and principal and of teachers to one another are shaped by this need. The internal organization of the school may be seen as a system of defenses against parental intrusion.

Teacher and Principal

The principal is accepted as the supreme authority in the school:

> After all, he's the principal, he is the boss, what he says should go, you know what I mean. . . . He's the principal and he's the authority, and you have to follow his orders. That's all there is to it.

This is true no matter how poorly he fills the position. The office contains the authority, which is legitimated in terms of the same principles of professional education and experience which the teacher uses to legitimate her authority over parents.

But this acceptance of superiority has limits. Teachers have a well-developed conception of just how and toward what ends the principal's authority should be used, and conflict arises when it is used without regard for the teachers' expectations. These expectations are especially clear with regard to the teacher's relationships with parents and pupils, where the principal is expected to act to uphold the teacher's authority regardless of circumstances. Failure to do this produces dissatisfaction and conflict, for such action by the principal is considered one of the most efficient defenses against attack on authority, whether from parents or pupils.

The principal is expected to "back the teacher up"—support her authority—in all cases of parental "interference." This is, for teachers, one of the major criteria of a "good" principal. In this next quotation the teacher reacts to the failure of a principal to provide this:

> That's another thing the teachers have against her. She really can't be counted on to back you up against a child or a parent. She got one of our teachers most irate with her, and I can't say I blame her. The child was being very difficult and it ended up with a conference with the parent, principal, and teacher. And the principal had the nerve to say to the parent that she couldn't understand the difficulty, none of the other teachers who had the child had ever had any trouble. Well, that was nothing but a damn lie, if you'll excuse me. . . . And everybody knew it was a lie. . . . And the principal knew it too, she must have. And yet she had the nerve to stand there and say that in front of the teacher and the parent. She should never have done that at all, even if it was true she shouldn't have said it. [Interviewer: What was the right thing to do?] Well, naturally, what she should have done is to stand behind the teacher all the way. Otherwise, the teacher loses face with the kids and with the parents and that makes it harder for her to keep order or anything from then on.

This necessity for support is independent of the legitimacy of the teacher's action; she can be punished later, but without parents knowing about it. And the principal should use any means necessary to preserve authority, lying himself or supporting the teacher's lies:

You could always count on him to back you up. If a parent came to school hollering that a teacher had struck her child, Mr. D———— would handle it. He'd say, "Why, Mrs. So-an-So, I'm sure you must be mistaken. I can't believe that any of our teachers would do a thing like that. Of course, I'll look into the matter and do what's necessary but I'm sure you've made a mistake. You know how children are." And he'd go on like that until he had talked them out of the whole thing.

Of course the teacher would certainly catch it later. He'd call them down to the office and really give them a tongue lashing that they wouldn't forget. But he never failed them when it came to parents.

Not all principals live up to this expectation. Their failure to support the teacher is attributed to cowardice, "liberalism," or an unfortunate ability to see both sides of a question. The withholding of support may also, however, be a deliberate gesture of disapproval and punishment. This undermining of the teacher's authority is one of the most extreme and effective sanctions at the principal's command:

[The teacher had started a class project in which the class, boys and girls, made towels to be given to the parents as Christmas presents.] We were quite well along in our project when in walked this principal one day. And did she give it to me! Boy! She wanted to know what the idea was. I told her it was our Christmas project and that I didn't see anything the matter with it. Well, she fussed and fumed. Finally, she said, "Alright, you may continue. But I warn you if there are any complaints by fathers to the Board downtown about one of our teachers making sissies out of their boys you will have to take full responsibility for it. I'm not going to take any responsibility for this kind of thing." And out she marched.

Teachers expect the same kind of support and defense in their dealings with pupils, again without regard for the justice of any particular student complaint. If the students find the principal a friendly court of appeal, it is much harder for the teacher to maintain control over them.[7]

The amount of threat to authority, in the form of challenges to classroom control, appears to teachers to be directly related to the principal's strictness. Where he fails to act impressively "tough" the school has a restless atmosphere and control over pupils is difficult to attain. The opposite is true where the children know that the principal will support any action of a teacher.

The children are scared to death of her [the principal]. All she has to do is walk down the hall and let the children hear her footsteps and right away the children would perk up and get very attentive. They're really afraid of her. But it's better that way than the other.

Such a principal can materially minimize the discipline problem, and is especially prized in the lower-class school, where this problem is greatest.

The principal provides this solid underpinning for the teachers' authority over pupils by her daily acts of "toughness," daily reaffirmations of his intention to keep the children "in line." The following quotation contrasts successful and unsuccessful principal activity in this area:

> For instance, let's take a case where a teacher sends a pupil down to the office. . . . When you send a child down to this new principal, he goes down there and he sits on the bench there. . . . Pretty soon, the clerk needs a messenger and she sees this boy sitting there. Well, she sends him running all over the school. That's no punishment as far as he's concerned. Not at all.
>
> The old principal didn't do things that way. If a child was sent down to the office he knew he was in for a rough time and he didn't like it much. Mr. G—— would walk out of his office and look over the children sitting on the bench and I mean he'd look right through them, each one of them. You could just see them shiver when he looked at them. Then he'd walk back in the office and they could see him going over papers, writing. Then, he'd send for them, one at a time. And he'd give them a lecture, a real lecture. Then he'd give them some punishment, like writing an essay on good manners and memorizing it so they could come and recite it to him the next day by heart. Well, that was effective. They didn't like being sent to Mr. G——. When you sent someone there that was the end of it. They didn't relish the idea of going there another time. That's the kind of backing up a teacher likes to feel she can count on.

The principal is expected to support all teachers in this way, even the chronic complainers who do not deserve it:

> If the principal's any good he knows that the complaints of a woman like that don't mean anything but he's got to back her just the same. But he knows that when a teacher is down complaining about students twice a week that there's nothing the matter with the students, there's something the matter with her. And he knows that if a teacher comes down once a semester with a student that the kid has probably committed a real crime, really done something bad. And his punishments will vary accordingly.

The teacher's authority, then, is subject to attack by pupils and may be strengthened or weakened depending on which way the principal throws the weight of his authority. Teachers expect the principal to throw it their way, and provide them with a needed defense.

The need for recognition of their independent professional authority informs teachers' conceptions of the principal's supervisory role. It is legitimate for him to give professional criticism, but only in a way that preserves this professional authority. He should give "constructive" rather than "arbitrary" orders, "ask" rather than "snoop." It is the infringement of authority that is the real distinction in these pairs of terms. For example:

> You see, a principal ought to give you good supervision. He ought to go around and visit his teachers and see how they're doing—come and sit in the room awhile and then if he has any constructive criticism to make, speak to the teacher about it privately later. Not this nagging bitching that some of them go in for, you know what I mean, but real constructive criticism.
>
> But I've seen some of those bastards that would go so far as to really bawl someone out in public. Now that's a terrible thing to do. They don't care who it's in front of, either. It might be a parent, or it might be other teachers, or it might even be the kids. That's terrible, but they actually do it.

Conflict arises when the principal ignores his teachers' need for professional independence and defense against attacks on authority. Both principal and teachers command sanctions which may be used to win such a conflict and establish their definition of the situation: i.e., they have available means for controlling each other's behavior. The principal has, as noted above, the powerful weapon of refusing to support the teacher in crucial situations; but this has the drawback of antagonizing other teachers and, also, is not available to a principal whose trouble with teachers stems from his initial failure to do this.

The principal's administrative functions provide him with his most commonly used sanctions. As administrator he allocates extra work of various kinds, equipment, rooms, and (in the elementary school) pupils to his teachers. In each category, some things are desired by teachers while others are disliked—some rooms are better than others, some equipment newer, etc. By distributing the desired things to a given teacher's disadvantage, the principal can effectively disicipline her. A subtle use of such sanctions is seen in this statement:

> Teacher: That woman really used to run the school, too. You had to do just what she said.
> Interviewer: What did she do if you "disobeyed?"

> Teacher: There were lots of things she could do. She had charge of assigning children to their new rooms when they passed. If she didn't like you she could really make it tough for you. You'd get all the slow children and all the behavior problems the dregs of the school. After six months of that you'd really know what work meant. She had methods like that.

Such sanctions are ineffective against those few teachers who are either eccentric or determined enough to ignore them. They may also fail in lower-class schools where the teacher does not intend to stay.[8]

The sanctions teachers can apply to a principal who respect or protect their authority are somewhat less direct. They may just ignore him: "After all if the principal gets to be too big a bother, all you have to do is walk in your room and shut the door, and he can't bother you." Another weapon is hardly a weapon at all—making use of the power to request transfer to another school in the system. It achieves its force when many teachers use it, presumably causing higher authorities to question the principal's ability:

> I know of one instance, a principal of that type, practically every teacher in her school asked to leave. Well, you might think that was because of a group that just didn't get along with the new principal. But when three or four sets of teachers go through a school like that, then you know something's wrong.

Finally, the teachers may collectively agree on a line of passive resistance, and just do things their way, without any reference to the principal's desires.

In some cases of extreme conflict, the teachers (some of whom may have been located in the school for a longer period than the principal) may use their connections in the community to create sentiment against the principal. Cooperative action of parents and teachers directed toward the principal's superiors is the teachers' ultimate sanction.

The principal, then, is expected to provide a defense against parental interference and student revolt, by supporting and protecting the teacher whenever her authority is challenged. He is expected, in his supervisory role, to respect the teacher's independence. When he does not do these things a conflict may arise. Both parties to the conflict have at their disposal effective means of controlling the other's behavior, so that the ordinary situation is one of compromise (if there is a dispute at all), with sanctions being used only when the agreed-on boundaries are overstepped.

Colleague Relations

It is considered that teachers ought to cooperate to defend themselves against authority attacks and to refrain from directly endangering the authority of another teacher. Teachers, like other work groups, develop a sense that they share a similar position and common dangers, and this provides them with a feeling of colleagueship that makes them amenable to influence in these directions by fellow teachers.

Challenging of another teacher so as to diminish her authority is the basic crime:

> For one thing, you must never question another teacher's grade, no matter if you know it's unjustified. That just wouldn't do. There are some teachers that mark unfairly. A girl, or say a boy, will have a four "S" report book and this woman will mark it a "G". . . . Well, I hate to see them get a deal like that, but there's nothing you can do.

Another teacher put it more generally: "For one thing, no teacher should ever disagree with another teacher or contradict her, in front of a pupil." The result in terms of authority vis-a-vis students is feared: "Just let another teacher raise her eyebrow funny, just so they [the children] know, and they don't miss a thing, and their respect for you goes down right away." With regard to authority threats by parents it is felt that teachers should not try to cast responsibility for actions which may provoke parental interference on another teacher.

Since teachers work in separate rooms and deal with their own groups of parents and pupils, it is hard for another teacher to get the opportunity to break these rules, even if she were so inclined. This difficulty is increased by an informal rule against entering another teacher's room while she is teaching. Breaches of these rules are rare and, when they do occur, are usually a kind of punishment aimed at a colleague disliked for exceeding the group work quotas or for more personal reasons. However, the danger inherent in such an action—that it may affect your own authority in some way or be employed against you —is so feared that it is seldom used.

In short, teachers can depend on each other to "act right" in authority situations, because of colleague feeling, lack of opportunity to act "wrong," and fear of the consequences of such action.

Discussion

I have presented the teacher as a person who is concerned (among other things) with maintaining what she considers to be her legitimate authority over pupils and parents, with avoiding and defending against challenges from these sources. In her view, the principal and other teachers should help her in building a system of defenses against such challenges. Through feelings of colleagueship and the use of various kinds of sanctions, a system of defenses and secrecy (oriented toward preventing the intrusion of parents and children into the authority system) is organized.

This picture discloses certain points of general relevance for the study of institutional authority systems. In the first place, an institution like the school can be seen as a small, self-contained system of social control. Its functionaries (principal and teachers) are able to control one another; each has some power to influence the others' conduct. This creates a stable and predictable work setting, in which the limits of behavior for every individual are known, and in which one can build a satisfactory authority position of which he can be sure, knowing that he has certain methods of controlling those who ignore his authority.

In contrast the activities of those who are outside the professional group are not involved in such a network of mutual understanding and control. Parents do not necessarily share the values by which the teacher legitimates her authority. And while parents can apply sanctions to the teacher, the teacher has no means of control which she can use in return, in direct retaliation.

To the teacher, then, the parent appears as an unpredictable and uncontrollable element, as a force which endangers and may even destroy the existing authority system over which she has some measure of control. For this reason, teachers (and principals who abide by their expectations) carry on an essentially secretive relationship vis-à-vis parents and the community, trying to prevent any event which will give these groups a permanent place of authority in the school situation. The emphasis on never admitting mistakes of school personnel to parents is an attempt to prevent these outsiders (who would not be subject to teacher control) from getting any excuse which might justify their intrusion into and possible destruction of the existing authority system.

This suggests the general proposition that the relations of institutional functionaries to one another are relations of mutual influence and control, and that outsiders are systematically prevented from exerting any authority over the institution's operations because they are not involved in this web of control and would literally be uncontrollable, and destructive of the institutional organization, as the functionaries desire it to be preserved, if they were allowed such authority.[9]

Notes

1. Cf. E. C. Hughes, "The Study of Institutions," *Social Forces*, 20 (March, 1942), 307–10.

2. See my earlier statement in "The Professional Dance Musician and His Audience," *American Journal of Sociology*, 57 (Sept., 1951), 136–144.

3. Howard S. Becker, "Social-Class Variations in the Teacher-Pupil Relationship," *Journal of Educational Sociology*, 25 (April, 1952), 451–465.

4. Details of method are reported in Howard S. Becker, "Role and Career Problems of the Chicago Public School Teacher," (unpublished Ph.D. dissertation, University of Chicago, 1951).

5. Charles Horton Cooley, *Social Organization* (New York: Charles Scribner's Sons, 1927), p. 131.

6. See Howard S. Becker, "The Career of the Chicago Public School Teacher," *American Journal of Sociology*, 57 (March, 1952), 475.

7. Cf. *The Sociology of Georg Simmel*, trans. Kurt Wolff (Glencoe: Free Press, 1950), p. 235: "The position of the subordinate in regard to his superordinate is favorable if the latter, in his turn, is subordinate to a still higher authority in which the former finds support."

8. See Becker, "The Career of the Chicago Public School Teacher," *op. cit.*, 472–473.

9. Cf. Max Weber: "Bureaucratic administration always tends to be an administration of 'secret sessions': in so far as it can, it hides its knowledge and action from criticism. . . . the tendency toward secrecy in certain administrative fields follows their material nature: everywhere that the power interests of the domination structure toward *the outside* are at stake . . . we find secrecy." In H. H. Gerth and C. Wright Mills, *From Max Weber: Essays in Sociology* (New York: Oxford University Press, 1946), p. 233.

Structure, Policy, and Style:
Strategies of Organizational Control

William R. Rosengren

Studies of formal organizations turn more and more to the strategies of control that organizations use to make their employees or clients tractable to the organization. Investigations of control in formal organizations often focus upon two conceptually divergent though empirically related issues. One deals with the kinds of internal structures that develop in organizations—the division of labor, task specialization, and systems of communication.[1] Included here are studies which view the structural

Reprinted from *Administrative Science Quarterly* 12 (June, 1967):140–64.

properties of organizations as derived from the goals of the organization and the degree of autonomy it enjoys. A related approach takes account of size as a determinant of organizational structure.[2] Studies such as these are generally consistent with Weberian concepts, especially in their focus upon structural arrangements and how they are effected. The second issue is related to the strategies of administrative leadership and influence that control participants in desired ways—whether by loose or close supervision, by manipulation of rewards, by the degree of democratization of decision making, and so forth.[3] This aspect of organizational behavior has been investigated in case studies of single organizations undergoing change, reorganization, or other crisis situations.

Only recently, however, has the study of organizational control included both structural characteristics and supervisory styles. The contention here is that structural characteristics in organizations can themselves be regarded as mechanisms of control. Therefore, if participant control can be achieved either through structural characteristics or supervisory strategies, then it is of interest to find how these two means of control are related.

The distinction between supervisory or administrative strategies of control and organizational structure is noted in the difference between influence and authority. Authority is customarily regarded as legitimized power over others residing in organizational structure. Influence, conceived as nonlegitimized power, is more nearly what is meant by supervisory style, although the capactiy to exercise influence over others can hardly be sharply distinguished from the prerogatives that attach to an office. Shils, for example, has argued that even in orderly bureaucracies, authority acquires a "charisma of status," which gives the office holder an increment of power beyond that which attaches to the position.[4] Thus, while structural arrangements may define the limits within which participants *must* act, the potential for supervisory influence allows discretion as to the boundaries within which incumbents *may* act.

This article is concerned with the relationship between the structure of offices and supervisory styles as they relate to control of participants in organizations. More specifically, this study examines some relationships between size and sponsorship, specialization of tasks, operational policies, and supervisory control styles in 132 psychiatric hospitals.

Organizations Studied

A questionnaire was sent to the chiefs of psychiatric service in the 270 hospitals approved for psychiatric residency training in 1961 by the

American Medical Association, with military hospitals excluded.[5]Responses were received from 152, or 56.3 percent, of these hospitals. Of this number, 12 were eliminated from the sample because they reported no in-patient psychiatric services and eight because they returned questionnaires with internal errors or inconsistencies. Of the total sent out, therefore, 48.8 percent were used.

Two indicators of the representatives of the sample were used: the geographic location of the hospitals and the size of the in-patient populations. Location was determined on the basis of the nine standard census areas of the United States. The differences between the number sent and the number returned in eight areas ranged from 0.1 percent to 2.1 percent. The greatest difference (−5.0 percent) was found in the Middle Atlantic area. On the basis of returns, identified by postmark, this area appeared to be underrepresented largely because of fewer responses from the large metropolitan center in the area. For size the mean inpatient census among the 270 to which questionnaires were sent was 1,205; and the mean census among the 132 usable returns was 1,210. On the strength of these two factors, the hospitals on which this report is based might be regarded as representative of the sample.

Concepts, Indicators, and Methods of Analysis

Organizational Size and Autonomy

Organizational size. The number of in-patients served was chosen as the criterion for size. In-patient populations ranged from 20 to 12,000 with a break in the frequency distribution between 400 and about 1,000; 52 hospitals served patient populations under 400, and 80 served clienteles near 1,000 and above. On the basis of this distribution, a distinction between small and large hospitals is made in the discussion that follows.

Organizational autonomy. Differences in the relationship of the hospital to its external environment were indicated by type of sponsorship. Seven kinds of sponsorship were reported: state and municipal hospitals, private institutions operated on a proprietary basis, private hospitals functioning on a nonprofit basis, Veterans' Administration hospitals, hospitals under religious order or denominational control, and hospitals affiliated with a medical school. Because of the relatively small number of institutions in the municipal, private proprietary, and denominational categories (see Table 1), the analysis of data is based upon a comparison of *government* hospitals ($N = 87$) with *private* hospitals ($N = 45$).

The distinction between government and private hospitals is

reinforced by the correlation with size; only seven of the government hospitals were small, and none of the private hospitals were large ($X^2 = 1050.037$). The correlation between size and sponsorship was so great that these two variables are here treated as one; references to "small" hospitals imply private sponsorship, and references to "large" hospitals imply government sponsorship. In examining relations between these variables and control mechanisms, tests of independence are based *strictly* on the small-large distinction.

Neither the distinction between government versus private sponsorship—nor its correlate of size—is fully adequate as a test of the degree of organizational autonomy. Organizational autonomy is better

TABLE 1
Organizational Size and Sponsorship

Sponsorship	Number of Patients*							
	20-200	201-500†	501-850	851-1150‡	1151-1500	1501-2500	2501 plus	N
Governmental								
Municipal/county	2	1	0	5	2	0	0	10
State	1	0	0	2	16	19	24	62
Veterans administration ..	2	1	0	1	8	3	0	15
Private								
Private proprietary	9	0	0	0	0	0	0	9
Private philanthropic	10	2	0	0	0	0	0	12
Religious-denominational ..	6	0	0	0	0	0	0	6
University/medical school ..	16	2	0	0	0	0	0	18

*52 small hospitals (under 500); 80 large hospitals (over 850).
†The largest census in this category was 481.
‡The smallest census in this category distinction was 918.

thought of as marking differences in the kinds of environmental pressures to which institutions in each category might be exposed. Government hospitals might be expected to have greater constraints imposed upon their structure of offices and communication patterns than private institutions. On the other hand, sponsors of private organizations might be expected to grant more autonomy in the structural arrangements for work, and exercise more control over operational policies in the organizations they support.[6]

Internal Structures

Four aspects of internal structure were taken into account, all of which bear directly upon the issue of participant control.

Work assignments. The first relates to the work assignments. Each chief of service reported the work activities of employees in each occupational category. These included psychotherapy group therapy sessions, research, standardized patient assessment procedures, family counseling, administrative work, and others. In some hospitals, employees in each occupational category were held responsible for only a single task with different work assignments for each category of staff. In others, however, the work assignments within each occupational category were characterized by multiple and overlapping tasks that cut across occupational and professional lines. The mean number of work assignments was four. A distinction was therefore made between those organizations in which the mean number of assignments was four or more, and those in which it was three or less. The hospitals in which the work assignments were highly specific and which involved a minimum of overlap across occupational categories, that is, characterized by *specialized tasks* are here called *specialized systems*. Those characterized by a broad range of work assignments within occupational groups and therefore overlap across occupational categories, that is, *unspecialized tasks,* are called *unspecialized systems.*

Thus, in specialized systems occupational categories could be sharply distinguished on the basis of distinctive tasks in the organization, whereas in unspecialized systems, occupational title would be less of a distinguishing mark of work role. For example, in the unspecialized systems social workers and psychologists were as likely to provide individual psychotherapy as were psychiatrists; whereas in specialized systems psychotherapy was more often the exclusive task of psychiatrists.

Formal communication. The second aspect of structure involved the relative emphasis placed upon *formal* as opposed to *informal* communication. Formal communication included not only reliance upon information from regularly scheduled staff meetings, but also upon routinely prepared and regularly written reports, data from standardized testing procedures, and from existing records and documents. Informal communication included coffee-room discussions among staff, observation of patient and employee behavior, hastily written notes not intended as permanent hospital records, and other procedures unspecified as to procedure or content.

Communication across levels. The third structural feature was the range of occupational levels in the organization having direct communication with the chief of services. In some hospitals, the chief exchanged information principally with high-level professional personnel —psychiatrists, other physicians, psychologists, and social workers. In these organizations communications with line nurses, ward attendants, and other lower-level clinical personnel were routinely channelled through an employee at an intermediate staff level. This pattern of information flow is referred to as *lateral* communication. In other hospitals the chief exchanged information directly with lower-level staff members as well as with those of higher professional status. This suggests a less precise and less specified communication of information, with somewhat greater opportunity for contact and communication among all staff members than in lateral communication. This type of communication is called *institutional communication*.

Extent of communication. Finally, each respondent reported the kinds of information for which employees in each occupational category were held responsible. Such responsibilities included clinical information about patients, information about behavior in the routines of hospital life, about the family situation of patients, and about personnel and administrative matters. The mean number of communication responsibilities in the 132 hospitals was four, with a range from one to eight. Those hospitals with a score of four or more were said to have *diffuse communication* systems; those with a score of three or less, *restricted communication* systems. In a diffuse communication system employees in each occupational category were responsible for a wide range of information, much of it similar to that for which other employees were responsible. In such a system, ward attendants were as likely to be knowledgeable about patient psychodynamics as psychiatrists. On the other hand, ward attendants working in restricted communication systems would be likely to be responsible only for knowledge about patient behavior in hospital routines, while psychiatrists would be responsible only for psychodynamics.

In structural terms then, one implication of these distinctions is that those organizations with specialized tasks, and lateral, formal, and restricted communication have a greater potential for participant control than organizations with unspecialized tasks, and institutional, informal, and diffuse communication. In so far as these indicators may suggest a distinction between bureaucratic and unbureaucratic organizations, they suggest that bureaucracies have a greater structural capacity for control than less bureaucratic institutions.

Operational Policies

Patient care. Three indicators of operational policies were used. The first was the emphasis on *Traditional treatment* as contrasted with *Innovative treatment* of patients. Hospitals with traditional treatment emphasized electric-shock, drug therapy, and arts and crafts—all of which entail specific and routinized technique. Those with more innovative treatment favored treatments such as group therapy, manipulation of peer relationships among the patients, and interpersonal relations between staff and patients—treatments in which technique and implementation are less specifically prescribed and routinized.

Patient subculture. A second indicator of operational policy was the extent to which subcultural forms of patient conduct were judged to be organizationally relevant. The forms of patient misconduct usually found in in-patient hospitals that were taken into account are listed in Table 2. Each respondent indicated by "yes" or "no" whether each form of patient behavior was regarded as sufficiently important to be of interest and concern. Those institutions above the mean (3.5) were said to have a *relevant patient subculture;* those below the mean were said to have an *irrelevant patient subculture.*

TABLE 2

Questionnaire Items on Patient Subculture

Do you expect staff members in your hospital to be concerned about:
1. Leadership persistently exercised by a small group of patients?
2. Myths or stories which the patients tell about the hospital and the staff?
3. Special jargon or "catch" phrases among the patients?
4. Trading forbidden foods and other articles of value among the patients?
5. Periodic patient misconduct?
6. Ways of "hazing" new patients as they enter the hospital?
7. Ways of "getting around" rules and regulations?
8. Periodic fads and fashion in dress, recreation, and so forth among the patients?

Reaction to patient subculture. Lastly, regardless of the extent of the hospital's concern about patterned deviations among the patients, each respondent indicated how such forms of patient behavior were treated. The reactions of the hospitals are listed in Table 3. A distinction was made between reactions that involved the adjustment of the hospital system itself, allowing indigenous forms of patient conduct to persist (marked "*s*" in Table 3), as compared with the implementation of administrative tactics and policies to eliminate the behavior, or to dominate or control the patients (marked "*p*" in Table 3). Reactions allowing the patient subculture to persist, here called *permissive patient control,* led to methods such as the use of ward representatives, relaxation of hospital rules when they appeared to conflict with the patients' customary behavior, and ward meetings and discussions among the patients. Reactions leading to direct organizational intervention to control patients, here termed *suppressive patient control,* included suppressing patient misconduct through therapists or other personnel, filling loop-

TABLE 3

Questionnaire Items on Reactions to Patient Subculture

Which of the following methods are used in your hospital to deal with the kinds of patient behavior you indicated to be present in your institutions?

1. Use of patient ward representatives or patient government, (s).*
2. Handle through the use of therapists or oher personnel on an individual basis, (p).†
3. Filling loopholes in administrative procedures, (p).
4. Adding more ward personnel when possible, (p).
5. Relaxing hospital rules where they appear to conflict with the patients' forms of conduct, (s).
6. Ward meetings and discussions among the patients, (s).
7. Making regulations effective, (p).

---

* s = allowing patient conduct to persist.
† p = controlling patient conduct.

holes in rules and procedures, adding more ward personnel to achieve greater supervision, and making regulations generally more effective.

Supervisory Style

The supervisory style characterizing the exercise of discretionary power in these hospitals was indicated by (1) the extent of organizational control over employee conduct, and (2) the kinds of standards and criteria against which adequate work performance was judged.

Employee control. The first indicator was whether employees were subject to scrutiny and control in relation to the wide range of behaviors listed in Table 4.[7] Hospitals attempting to maintain control over only the few kinds of behaviors directly related to the work situation, that is, having *limited employee control* were interested in working hours, consumption of alcohol, and the cleanliness of employees' work places. Hospitals, attempting to control a broad scope of employee conduct, whether directly or indirectly related to the work situation, that is, having *pervasive employee control* exercised control in relation to the forms of address workers used in talking with one another, how much leisure time employees spent with superiors and subordinates, faithfulness of employees to their spouses, and in other ways.

Job criteria. The second indicator of supervisory style was related to the criteria the service chief used to evaluate employee performance. Criteria such as the ability to supervise subordinates and to execute

TABLE 4

Questionnaire Items on Employee Control

Do you feel that your organization has a responsibility to take account of and supervise your employees with respect to the following kinds of behaviors?

1. Employees' working hours.
2. How much alcohol employees consume.
3. The kind of temperament employees exhibit on the job.
4. How much importance employees attach to getting along with other people.
5. How employees divide up their work day among their various duties.
6. The type of clothing employees wear at work.
7. The form of address employees use in talking with their colleagues.
8. How much leisure time employees spend with their subordinates.
9. The tidiness of employees' office or work places.
10. How faithful an employee is to his wife.
11. How much leisure time employees spend with their superiors.
12. The amount of work employees take home with them.

---

directions efficiently, and the level of formal education are here called *categoric criteria.* Those which emphasized previous work history and experience, creativity and initiative, and ability to get along with people, are here called *interpersonal criteria.* Workers in limited-control institutions might be expected to know and to conform to the prevailing rules of relevance more than persons in pervasive-control organizations, in which the limits of conduct relevance would be less precise and circumscribed.

The analysis, then, is based upon (1) *organizational size and sponsorship,* comparing large governmental hospitals with small private ones; (2) *structural controls* including specialization of tasks and operational policies; and (3) *supervisory style,* as shown by the scope of organizational control over employee conduct and the criteria by which employees were judged.

These dimensions of organization are considered in their bearing on the control of organizational members. Specifically, it is argued that hospitals with specialized tasks, formal, lateral, and restricted communication patterns, with traditional treatment, with irrelevant patient subculture and suppressive patient control patterns have great structural capacity for control. Finally, it is assumed that interpersonal criteria of work competence and pervasive employee control result in greater pressures toward employee control than categoric criteria and limited employee control.

The aim of the following analysis is to determine the relations between structural and supervising forms of control within the two size and sponsorship categories of organizations.

Findings

To the extent that the dimensions of organizational structure and dynamics may be related to a bureaucratic conception of organizations, the following associations might be expected among these variables:

1. The *structural* characteristics most conducive to achieving participant control will occur more frequently in large government hospitals than in small private ones. Specifically, specialized tasks, and formal, lateral, and restricted communication will characterize large government hospitals.
2. The *operational* structures most conducive to maximizing participant control, i.e., traditional treatment, will vary independently of specialization of tasks and forms of communication systems.[8]
3. Hospitals with specialized tasks (and other structural characteristics conducive to control) will exercise more pervasive employee control than organizations with structural dimensions less conducive to maximum control.
4. Hospitals with structural arrangements likely to maximize employee control will also attempt to maximize control over patients, i.e., will have relevant patient subcultures and suppressive patient control.

With expectations such as these guiding the analysis of data, the findings are reported as they bear upon them. Associations are tested by means of chi-square analysis.

Size and Sponsorship, and Structural Controls

There were marked associations between size and diffuse-restricted communication ($X^2 = 62.490$), and between size and lateral-institutional communications ($X^2 = 56.000$). Restricted communication—limited and prescribed kinds of information for each level of employees —was the typical pattern in the large governmental hospitals. The reverse, diffuse communication, characterized small private hospitals.[9] Similarly organizational size and sponsorship was associated with lateral-institutional communication. Information appeared to pass to and from all occupational levels in the smaller institutions, whereas it was limited more strictly to rank equals in the larger hospitals ($X^2 = 61.684$). The close association between size and sponsoreship precludes an explanation of this finding; however, these findings *are* in accord with the expectations about communication systems and specialization of tasks in large government organizations, which are derived from a classical conception of bureaucracy.[10]

Contrary to what might have been anticipated, however, specialized tasks were found no more frequently in the large hospitals than in the small ones, nor were unspecialized task assignments characteristic of the smaller hospitals. Therefore, although large size and government sponsorship appeared to result in structural control by restricted communication and the limitation of participants to lateral communication, they were not otherwise important determinants of structural conrol mechanisms.

Task Specialization and Communication Systems

Hospitals with specialized tasks were characterized by lateral communication, while those with unspecialized tasks more often had institutional communication ($X^2 = 7.526$). Furthermore, those with specialized tasks relied on formal means of communication, but those with unspecialized tasks used more informal methods of communication ($X^2 = 15.272$). There was no significant difference, however, between the specialized and unspecialized hospitals as to restricted-diffuse communication responsibilities ($X^2 = 1.550$).

The data indicated, therefore, that maximization of control through specialization of tasks tended to be associated with control through the systems of communication and information flow in these organizations. It should be emphasized, however, that the relations between task assignments and communication lines were more marked in the small private hospitals than in the large ones. The relevance of size as an intervening variable was observed throughout this study.

Specialization of Tasks and Operational Policies

The data on the specialization of tasks and operational policies are shown in Table 5. There was a consistent association between specialization of tasks and type of treatment; again, however, the association was more marked in the small hospitals than in the large hospitals. In both cases, however, hospitals with specialized tasks tended to favor traditional treatment, whereas those with unspecialized tasks emphasized innovative treatment. Therefore, maximization of structural control through specialization of tasks, especially in the small hospitals, was associated with control of patients through the operational system of the hospitals. Perhaps the most striking difference is that hospitals with specialized tasks tended to maximize patient control; whereas hospitals with unspecialized tasks showed minimal recourse to organizational constraints designed to control and dominate patterned deviations, despite the high relevance of these deviations.

There was, therefore, a consistent association between the struc-

TABLE 5
Task Specialization and Operational Policies in Relation to Size*

Operational Policies	Specialized Hospitals†	Unspecialized Hospitals‡	x^2	p
Small hospitals *(N* = 52)				
Innovative treatment *(N* = 31)	25.8	74.2	24.122	.001
Traditional treatment (*N* = 27)	70.3	29.7	6.166	.05
Relevant patient subculture (*N* = 28)	39.2	60.8	5.181	.05
Suppressive patient control (*N* = 22)	81.8	18.2	11.988	.001
Large hospitals (*N* = 80)				
Innovative treatment (*N* = 41)	36.5	63.5	15.542	.001
Traditional treatment (*N* = 38)	65.7	34.3	2.033	---
Relevant patient subculture (*N* = 42)	50.0	50.0	2.115	---
Suppressive patient control (*N* = 45)	68.8	31.2	5.464	.05

*Data are shown in percentages, with the N for each indicator of operational policy used as the base. Only the top two cells of each four-fold contingency are reproduced in the table. Frequencies in the reciprocal lower two cells may be computed by subtracting from two N's under structure of offices.
†N = 28 for small hospitals; N = 46 for large hospitals.
‡N = 24 for small hospitals; N = 34 for large hospitals.

ture of offices, indicated here by specialization of tasks, and operational policies, these associations being somewhat more marked in the small private hospitals. In general, the structural mechanisms of control inherent in the specialization of tasks were consistent with those in the systems of communication. Lastly, both of these control-implementing structures were found in close association with operational policies that maximized structured control over patients.

Supervisory Styles, Specialization of Tasks, and Operational Policies

The association between the employee control and work criteria was sufficiently marked ($X^2 = 7.713$) to suggest that they related to similar ways of expressing supervisory influence. That is, if there was pervasive employee control, employees were also likely to be subject to interpersonal criteria of work competence. In view of this, data are reported only in terms of employee control, although similar patterns were found for standards of work competence. The findings are reported in Table 6.

There were marked differences in specialization of tasks, systems of communication, and operational policies—all significantly related to the prevailing style of supervisory control. Specifically, hospitals with pervasive employee control tended to have unspecialized tasks as well as institutional, informal, and diffuse communication. On the other hand, organizations with limited employee control tended to have more specialization of tasks as well as more restricted and formalized communication.

Those hospitals in which the style of supervision was characterized by limited employee control stressed traditional treatment, regarded indigenous patterns of patient subculture as irrelevant, and reacted to patterned deviations by suppressive patient control. On the other hand, hospitals with pervasive employee control had unspecialized tasks, valued innovative treatment, found the patient subculture highly relevant, although they reacted to this by permissive patient control.

The point to be emphasized here is that when employee control was patterned into structured specialization of tasks, procedures for work, and systems of communication, then supervisory control of employees was minimal. When the structural patterns for employee control were absent, supervisory strategies of control appeared to elicit pervasive and extended patterns of employee control. In short, employee control appeared to be patterned into specialization of tasks in specialized hospitals, but was imposed by processes of supervisory influence in hospitals not having structural characteristics making for employee control.

A related though somewhat different issue is the contrasting kinds of operational policies found in these two types of organizations. The hospitals with specialized tasks favored traditional treatment, which involves the intrusion of objects between patients and employees— drugs, machines, implements, and consensually validated theory systems. Under such circumstances, relationships between patients and employees are likely to be routinized—perhaps to the point of depersonalization. Employees in such organizations are required to invest less of their personal selves (though perhaps more of their professional selves), in the processes of work. Hence, organizations in which such treatment policies are found—quite apart from their specialization of tasks—are presented with only a narrow scope of employee conduct to be controlled. But the innovative treatment in hospitals with unspecialized tasks allows patients and employees to be in continuous contact and interaction without the intervention of either a studied and symbolic professional repertoire or an elaborate machine technology. Therefore, employees in unspecialized hospitals may have more of their personal selves in their work, and therefore to present organizational authorities with a greater variety of behaviors for supervisory control.[11]

Finally, although these associations were the general pattern,

TABLE 6

Internal Structures and Operational Policies in Relation to Employee Control in Small and Large Hospitals*

Structure and Operation	All Hospitals				Small Hospitals (N=52)					Large Hospitals (N=80)					
	Pervasive Control (N=73)	Limited Control (N=59)	X^2	P	N	Pervasive Control (N=32)	Limited Control (N=20)	X^2	P	N	Pervasive Control (N=41)	Limited Control (N=39)	X^2	P	N
Internal structures															
Specialized tasks	32.4	67.6	35.536	.001	74	39.3	60.7	12.568	.001	28	28.3	71.7	23.001	.001	46
Restricted communication	47.3	52.7	4.331	.05	74	42.9	57.1	†	–	7	47.8	52.2	2.117	–	67
Lateral communication	50.8	49.2	.898	–	61	43.3	56.7	10.065	.01	30	58.1	41.9	.930	–	31
Formal communication	36.6	63.4	21.809	.001	71	30.4	69.6	12.055	.001	23	39.6	60.4	6.537	.01	48
Operational policies															
Innovative treatment	73.6	26.4	21.538	.001	72	71.0	29.0	7.130	.01	31	73.2	26.8	12.560	.001	41
Traditional treatment	35.4	64.6	7.556	.01	65	25.9	74.1	23.342	.001	27	42.1	57.9	3.904	.05	38
Relevant patient subculture	72.8	27.2	18.595	.001	70	78.6	21.4	11.038	.001	28	69.0	31.0	8.258	.01	42
Supressive patient control	49.2	50.8	2.009	–	67	40.5	59.5	7.048	.01	22	48.9	51.1	.226	–	45

*Data are shown in percentages, with the N's for each indicator of structure and policy used as the base. Only the two top cells for each four-fold contingency are reproduced in the table. Frequencies in the reciprocal lower two cells may be computed by subtracting from the two N's listed under types of administrative style.

†Expected frequency in cell too small to compute X^2.

there remains the persisting issue of organizational size as an intervening variable, between structural and supervisory means of control.

Supervisory Controls and Organizational Size

The patterns just discussed were generally consistent in both large and small institutions, but there was sufficient variation related to size to justify reporting associations between style of employee supervision and structural characteristics separately in the large and small hospitals. These data are also shown in Table 6.

First, limited employee control was associated with specialized tasks and with suppressive patient control in both the large and small hospitals; pervasive employee control was the prevailing supervisory style in those institutions with unspecialized task assignments and permissive patient control. That is, pervasive employee control was associated with permissive patient control, and limited employee control with suppressive control of patients.

Aside from this, the principal difference between the large and small organizations was in operational policies. In *both* the large and small hospitals with pervasive employee control, innovative forms of treatment tended to be highly valued. However, while smaller hospitals with pervasive employee control devalued traditional treatment, the larger hospitals placed considerable emphasis on traditional treatment *as well* as upon more innovative treatment. Also, high relevance of the patient subculture was associated with pervasive employee control in both the large and small establishments, but permissive patient control was strongly related to pervasive employee control *only* in the small organizations.

The style of supervisory control was related to the specialization of tasks in both large and small hospitals, but was related to differences in operational policies somewhat more strongly only in the small hospitals. Thus, the control of clients appeared to be linked to the control of employees through operational policies in the small hospitals, but through specialization of tasks in the large organizations. That is, large hospitals relied operationally upon those forms of treatment which themselves function as control mechanisms over patient behavior. Therefore, although they may have incorporated innovative treatment into their operational policies, thus indicating a tendency away from suppressive patient control, they also retained those structural features (traditional treatment) which tended toward suppressive patient control.

The implication of this, therefore, is that in the small hospitals, the coincidence of unspecialized tasks and pervasive employee control was accompanied by a decrease in control over patients both in operational strategies and supervisory constraint. While there was a similar congruence between unspecialized tasks and pervasive employee control in the large hospitals, those operational structures conducive to the maintenance of suppressive patient control were retained.

Summary and Discussion

This study was concerned with the relation of organizational size and sponsorship, organizational structures and operational policies and styles of administrative supervision. Both structural characteristics and styles of supervision have been regarded as mechanisms for maintaining participant control.

Summary

The data indicated that restricted communication responsibilities characterized large governmental institutions. Because of the correlation between size and sponsorship it is possible only to speculate as to whether this characteristic is related to size or sponsorship. It could be argued that increased size places both ecological and internal limitations on the access employees have to information. It may also be contended that the extra-organizational responsibiliites of government agencies lead to more restricted communication responsibilities than in private organizations.

In the associations between specialization of tasks and communications also, small hospitals with specialized tasks had formal and restricted communication, while those with unspecialized tasks had informal and diffuse communication. The patterns in the large hospitals were less clear. Furthermore, specialized hospitals implemented traditional kinds of treatment, whereas unspecialized hospitals emphasized innovative treatment. Here again the association was somewhat more marked in the smaller hospitals than in the large ones.

Size and sponsorship, however, are not as closely related to organizational structures and operational policies as styles of supervisory control. Hospitals with pervasive employee control tended to have unspecialized tasks and innovative treatment; those with limited employee control had specialized tasks and traditional treatment.

Interpretation Based on Weberian Model

The association between types of internal structures and the character of operational policies is of further interest when considered from the point of view of hospitals using treatment based upon a body of rational-technical knowledge, the implementation of which is likely in itself to result in client control. All formal organizations are to some extent faced with an imperfect body of knowledge and a clientele that is not entirely compliant. The absence of a body of reliable knowledge makes orderly specialization of tasks hard to devise; consequently, task assignments become unspecialized and employee control a structural problem. The lack of client control associated with this presents organizations with a further control problem. It would appear, then, that an understanding of the control of organizational employees can hardly be separated analytically from the control of clients.

In specialized hospitals, the control of employees appeared to be achieved by structural means, and the control of patients by treatment programs in which methods, tactics, and techniques were recurrent, reliable, and predictable. These organizations were also conducted as if indigenous forms of inmate behavior were not relevant except in so far as the hospital had devised specific structural means to control such patterned deviations. In short, the presence of a technology resting upon rational-technical knowledge seemed to lead to the control of both patients and staff through structural mechanisms with a minimum of reliance upon supervisory control strategies. In specialized hospitals, policies were based less upon predictable and recurrent knowledge and were therefore less likely to result in the structural mechanisms conducive to patient or employee control. This seemed to be correlated with a highly relevant patient subculture, and resulted in reacting to patient deviations in a less controlling and constraining way. An explanation of these attributes of the unspecialized organizations may be that a drift away from specialized to unspecialized organizations may be accompanied by the emergence of what might be called a humanitarian organizational ethic that rejects the use of force and coercion.

Therefore, while the specialized hospitals were mobilized structurally to maximize patient control, the scope of employee control was limited. In contrast, unspecialized hospitals had neither the structural nor the supervisory mechanisms to maintain control over patients, and employees were the principal targets for supervisory control. In Goffman's terms, the specialized hospitals were "total" for clients, but "minimal" for employees, whereas structurally unspecialized hospitals were "minimal" for patients, but "total" for employees.[12] The distinction emphasized here between structural and supervisory means of control implies alternate ways of achieving consistency in the ways in which participants engage in the tasks of organizations. If organizations conformed to an ideal construct of bureaucracy, it does not seem likely that the exercise of supervisory controls would be found empirically. In such a case, control of both client and staff would occur through self-control, effected by the rationality of knowledge and the consequent systematic specialization of tasks. But with partial client autonomy and an imperfect division of labor, means of control will be devised outside the organizational structure.

In this study, supervisory style appeared to function as the mechanism of control over the employees, while operational policies functioned as the mechanism of control over clients.[13] One implication of this is that the intrusion of styles of supervision into organizations and the adaptation of operational policies to control problems represent defective structural arrangements. This becomes an even more plausible explanation when these seeming incongruities are viewed from the perspective of a conceptually pure model of bureaucratic organization. A second implication relates to the emphasis upon pervasive employee control in the unspecialized organizations, and suppressive client control in the specialized ones. This apparent anomaly might reflect organizational priorities not revealed by the data presented. In both cases, however, such implications lead logically to the conclusion that these patterns deviate from what organizations *ought* to be—in both structural and supervisory ways—were it not for the fact that they fall short of what a bureaucratic model of organizations prescribes. There is a different point of view, however, which warrants consideration.[14]

Interpretation Based on Non-Weberian Models

In contrast to the previous position, it could be argued that the relationships between structural and supervisory control of clients and staff are not unexpected. Such an argument rests upon the assumption that organizations need not conform in all respects to a classical model of bureaucracy to be judged orderly and understandable. Such a position assumes that organizations may have different, although equally legitimate, conceptions of their work; and that they work upon materials, with chosen means, with differing degrees of tractability and uniformity. Given variations in these respects, it seems reasonable to expect that organizations will be confronted with different kinds of control problems and will deal with them in different ways.

Bennis contends that the traditional bureaucratic form seems peculiarly suited to organizations that deal not with persons in their more humanized capacities but rather with objects, or with persons seen as objects.[15] To this extent, the associations between unspecialized tasks, innovative treatment, and permissive patient control might be understandable—although the pattern of employee control remains unexplained. There is, in addition, a large body of literature dealing with the therapeutic milieu in hospitals, in which the goals of the organization seem to necessitate deviations from the traditional bureaucratic form.[16]

More recently, Perrow has taken the position that differences in organizational structure arise as a consequence of the organization's perception of the materials to be worked upon.[17] One aspect of this model consists of a continuum along which materials range from well-understood, uniform, and stable (the custodial institution), to not well-understood, nonuniform and unstable (the elite psychiatric agency). The conception of organizations derived from such a model is that the institution dealing with unknown and unstable human materials will be characterized by high supervisory power, high interdependence of groups, high supervisory discretion, and flexible polycentralized authority. This cluster of characteristics—regarded as systematic and orderly from the perspective of Perrow's model—are not inconsistent with the characteristics of unspecialized hospitals found here. Conversely, the organization dealing with well-understood and stable materials is characterized by low supervisory power, low group interdependence, low-administrative discretion, and by formal-centralized authority, patterns consistent with the structural and supervisory controls found in the specialized hospitals.

Another pertinent conception of organizations is that outlined by Burns and Stalker.[18] They contrast the properties of "mechanical" and "organic" management systems. The mechanical system (similar to specialized here) appears particularly suited to the maintenance of organizational stability in the face of stable external conditions, accommodates programmed decision making, and allows the individual employee more freedom than does the organic. Furthermore, the administrator is less apprehensive and concerned about what others in the organization are doing, and employee loyalty is achieved through a *"presumed* [italics mine] community of interest with the rest of the working organization," whereas in the organic system it arises out of a "commitment to the concern's task."[19]

The Perrow and the Burns and Stalker models account for differences in the structural arrangements in organizations that may not be consistent with a classical Weberian conception of organizations. They differ, however, in that Perrow regards perceptions of the materials worked upon as determinants of structural arrangements, whereas Burns and Stalker regard the contingencies of "innovation" as the more important.

The structural properties, operational activities, and styles of supervisory controls examined in this paper can be regarded as deviations from an ideal type, and therefore incongruous and inconsistent. On the other hand, more recent models of organizations make it possible to understand deviations from a pure bureaucratic model.

The differential effect of size may be critical in choosing one explanation rather than the other. The increased use of organizations as units of analysis may provide the opportunity to document an explanation for at least two findings of this study which are of interest to students of formal organizations: (1) the inverse relation between the employee and client control, and (2) specification of the variant relationships between structural and supervisory controls.

Notes

1. See for example, S. N. Eisenstadt, Bureaucracy, Bureaucratization, and De-bureaucratization, *Administrative Science Quarterly*, 4 (1959), 302–320; A. Etzioni. "Organizational Control Structure," in J. March (ed.), *Handbook of Organizations* (Chicago: Rand-McNally, 1965); Sol Levine and P. E. White, Exchange as a Conceptual Framework for the Study of Interorganizational Relationships, *Administrative Science Quarterly*, 5 (March 1961), 583–601; Richard L. Simpson and H. W. Gulley, Goals, Environmental Pressures, and Organizational Characteristics, *American Sociological Review*, 27 (June 1962), 344–351; James D. Thompson and W. D. McEwen, Organizational Goals and Environment: Goal-Setting as an Interactional Process, *American Sociological Review*, 23 (February 1958), 23–31; T. Burns and G. Stalker, *The Management of Innovation* (London: Tavistock, 1961); Michael Crozier, *The Bureaucratic Phenomenon* (Chicago: University of Chicago, 1965); James Thompson (ed.), *Approaches to Organizational Design* (Pittsburgh: University of Pittsburgh, 1966); Stanley H. Udy Jr., Administrative Rationality, Social Setting, and Organizational Development, *American Journal of Sociology*, 68 (November 1962), 299–308.

2. Some studies conclude that bureaucratization increases with size; others find the reverse. Cf. Theodore R. Anderson and S. Warkov, Organizational Size and Functional Complexity: A Study of Administration in Hospitals, *American Sociological Review*, 26 (February 1961), 23–28; Theodore Caplow, Organizational Size, *Administrative Science Quarterly*, 1 (March 1957), 484–505; Frederick W. Terrien and D. L. Mills, The Effects of Changing Size upon the Internal Structure of Organizations, *American Sociological Review*, 20 (February 1955), 11–14; Oscar Grusky, Corporate Size, Bureaucratization, and Managerial Succession, *American Journal of Sociology*, 67 (November 1961), 261–269; Robert H. Guest. Managerial Succession in Complex Organizations, *American Journal of Sociology*, 68 (July 1962), 47–54; Louis Kriesberg, Careers, Organization Size, and Succession, *American Journal of Sociology*, 68 (November 1962), 355–359.

3. For example, Amitai Etzioni, *A Comparative Analysis of Complex Organizations* (New York: The Free Press, 1961); also "Organizational Control Structure," in J. March, *op. cit.;* Peter Blau, *The Dynamics of Bureaucracy* (Chicago: University of Chicago, 1955); Peter Blau and W. Richard Scott, *Formal Organizations* (San Francisco: Chandler, 1962); Richard McCleery, *Policy Change in Prison Management* (East Lansing: Michigan State University Governmental Research Bureau, 1957).

4. Edward Shils, Charisma, Order, and Status, *American Sociological Review*, 30 (April 1965), 199–213.

5. One of the problems connected with data from questionnaires is whether the respondents have taken seriously the task of completing such questionnaires. The indications used in this study were whether each respondent had reported the in-patient census in rounded-off figures, and whether he had gone beyond what was contained in the questions, and added further information. In the first instance, 33 questionnaires contained in-patient census figures which might be regarded as rounding or guessing about the in-patient census. Of these, however, 21 included other indications of respondent seriousness: erasures indicating correction or recalculations, explication of response, notations written on the questionnaire, or extensive comments and explanations written on the blank page which accompaied each questionnaire. Among the total 132 questionnaires, 83 percent contained such additions, explications, or corrections. In addition, 70 percent of the respondents wrote under separate cover commenting on the study and asking for publications and reports when available. In so far as such indicators are meaningful, most respondents appear to complete the questionnaire thoughtfully and seriously. Also although findings are reported by a single respondent from each organization, the chief of services, though not a disinterested observer in his own institution, is a person in a position to know the kinds of information asked for.

6. See Leonard Mayo, Relationships Between Public and Voluntary Health and Welfare Agencies, *American Journal of Public Health*, 49 (October 1959), 1307–1313.

7. The items were drawn from: Edgar H. Schein and J. S. Ott, The Legitimacy of Organizational Influence, *American Journal of Sociology*, 67 (May 1962), 682–689.

8. Studies about the relevance of bureaucracy to administration may have led to a neglect of its relevance for work functions. Weber has written, "The concept of administrative authority would include all the rules which govern the behaviour of the administrative staff, as well as that of the members vis-à-vis the corporate group." Cf. M. Weber, *Basic Concepts in Sociology* (London: Peter Owen, 1962), p. 113.

9. One factor which may account for this pattern was the difference in the physical settings between the large and small organizations. The small institutions tended to operate with all employees in a single building. Many of the larger hospitals, however, included several buildings, each with different activities, and in some instances, the hospital's work spaces were not even on the same grounds.

10. The coincidence of authority communication patterns is discussed by T. Hopkins, "Bureaucratic Authority: The Convergence of Weber and Barnard," in A. Etzioni (ed.), *Complex Organizations* (New York: Winston, 1961), pp. 82–98.

11. Similar patterns were found with respect to types of work performance criteria. Hospitals in which categoric standards were used—educational level and ability to "take orders"—tended to be bureaucratically organized and to value therapies such as electric shock, and also exercised maximal control over clients. But hospitals which evaluated employee competence on the basis of interpersonal criteria tended to be less bureaucratic and to value less traditional forms of care, and also exercised less constraint over patients.

12. E. Goffman, *Asylums* (New York: Doubleday-Anchor), 1961.

13. Differences in the control functions of structure, policy, and style, in organizations of different size raises the possibility that optimum size categories may be found within which control of employees *is* achieved within the division of labor

itself. In such a case, one might expect that the use of control would not be necessary and that administrative styles would be mild and unobtrusive. It might further be expected that within such optimal size categories, the classic separation of policy from administration might indeed be found, since the operational aspects of the organization would not need to be mobilized to serve both goal achievement and system maintenance functions at the same time.

14. A further causal sequence suggested by an editorial reader is that administrators begin their work with a "technological theory," the implementation of which requires a particular style of administration. This then results in the emergence of the appropriate organizational structures through which the available technology can best be administered. Comparative and longitudinal studies of organizational growth would be one means of putting this to the test.

15. The importance of shifts in values in the structure and function of organizations is suggested in W. Bennis, Beyond Bureaucracy, *Trans-Action*, 2 (July/ August 1965), 31–35.

16. See for example, Mark Lefton, S. Dinitz, and B. Pasamanick, Decision-Making in a Mental Hospital: Real, Perceived, and Ideal, *American Sociological Review*, 24 (1959), 822–829; Robert Rapoport, *et al.*, *Community as Doctor* (London: Tavistock, 1960); W. Rosengren, Communications, Organization, and Conduct in the "Therapeutic Milieu," *Administrative Science Quarterly*, 9 (June 1964), 70–90; A. Stanton and M. Schwartz, *The Mental Hospital* (New York: Basic Books), 1954.

17. Charles Perrow, "Hospitals: Technology, Structure, and Goals," in J. March (ed.), *op. cit.;* also "A Framework for the Comparative Analysis of Organizations," paper presented at the Annual Meetings of the American Sociological Association, Miami, 1966.

18. T. Burns and G. Stalker, *op. cit.*

19. *Ibid.*, pp. 121–122.

Chapter VII

Professionals and Nonprofessionals

Most human service organizations employ and rely upon vast cadres of professional personnel to implement their service goals. Likewise, service professionals in varying degrees require organizations as contexts for their practice. This mutual dependence between service professions and human service organizations exists for a number of reasons. As we point out in the Introductory Chapter, human service organizations require professionals because (1) they possess the technical expertise necessary to implement their service delivery systems; (2) they assist in legitimating organizational goals and provide liaison with relevant publics in the acquisition of needed resources; and finally (3) professionals help to certify that clients, students, patients, or inmates have achieved the new status for which they have been processed or changed.

The degree to which the organization serves as a context for professional practice is one element that distinguishes the established professions from the semi-professions (Etzioni, 1969). The established professions are more autonomous and less constrained by the organization than the semi-professions. For example, teachers, social workers, and nurses, in contrast to physicians and lawyers, do not have complete autonomy to deal with students, clients, or patients in the manner in which their professional expertise and education might prescribe. Perhaps what is most potentially problematic for semi-professionals is the fact that organizational functionaries have the freedom to establish limits, prescriptions, and proscriptions on the nature, type, and quality of service to be rendered.

The established professions enjoy greater prestige and monopoly over their work, and have greater opportunities for practice both within and outside organizations. Their professional careers, therefore, are less dependent on the organization. In contrast the semi-professions are locked into organizations, and their professional career patterns are frequently synonymous with their organizational careers. Moreover, the semi-professions are limited in their pursuit of professional practice outside of organizations with respect to the variety and range of organizations requiring their professional expertise.

The presence of professionals in bureaucratic organizations in general, and human service organizations in particular, create a set of unique problems for both the professions and bureaucratic organizations.

First, an inherent dilemma in the interaction between professionals and bureaucratic organizations is the degree of accommodation between professional norms and values and organizational demands and exigencies. The critical issue is the extent to which professional norms and values will determine organizational structure and service delivery patterns, or the extent to which organizational demands and exigencies will influence professional practice.

Second, a potential conflict exists in professional-organizational interaction because professions and bureaucracies are organized on fundamentally different principles. The sources of incompatibility have been usually related to differences in organizational versus professional norms, goals, and operating procedures, and divergent authority patterns of organizational hierarchy and professional expertise. As a consequence of these antithetical principles some authors have argued that the professional is confronted with making choices between commitments to his profession and to the organization (Scott, 1966; Merton, 1968: 249–260; Goldner and Ritti, 1967; Mills, 1951; Clark, 1962).

Recognizing this basic incompatibility between professional and bureaucratic models of organization, several patterns of accommodation have been identified. These include the relaxation of bureaucratic rules and procedures which minimize conflict and strain, i.e., debureaucratization (Katz and Eisenstadt, 1960; Katz, 1964; Scott, 1965); and structural and role separation between professional tasks and administrative tasks (Goss, 1961, 1963; Engel, 1970).

In making the distinction between uniform and non-uniform tasks a central part of his analysis, Litwak's article suggests the necessity for nonhierarchical structures to accommodate the work of professionals which requires the exercise of discretion, autonomy, and flexibility in dealing with nonstandardized and highly idiosyncratic tasks.

He develops a model of organization variant from Weber's monocratic model of rational-legal bureaucracy, termed "professional" bureaucracy. This model is compared with Weber's and a human relations model of bureaucracy. The author points out the conditions under which each model is most efficient in achieving organizational goals and the types of professional practice ideally suited to each organizational climate.

The professional model essentially combines the formal properties of monocratic bureaucracy and the human relations model. Since the structural characteristics of these two models are antithetical, Litwak argues that "mechanisms of segregation" are necessary in order to maintain these divergent social forms and to minimize conflict. Four mechanisms of segregation are presented: (1) role separation, (2) physical distance, (3) transferral occupations, and (4) evaluation procedures.

The literature on the relationship between professions and bureaucratic organizations has been predominantly concerned with dysfunctional consequences of bureaucracy on professional practice. Freidson's provocative essay turns our attention to the other face of the bureaucratic-professional dichotomy. Rather than viewing professional organization as a superior alternative to bureaucratic organization, Freidson shows that in the case of the medical profession and the large medical hospital, ". . . many of the rigid, mechanical, and authoritarian attributes, and much of the inadequate coordination said to characterize the health services," may develop from the dominance of professional organization and not from its bureaucratic dimensions.

In particular, Freidson suggests that much of the depersonalization of clients in the medical hospital may be attributed to the dominance of the medical profession. This may be equally true in other human service organizations characterized by dominant professions. Moreover, we would add that the depersonalization of clients in human service organizations may also stem from the lack of meaningful involvement and participation of clients in the service delivery system itself as well as from professional dominance in the organization.

One mechanism that has been developed to facilitate the participation of clients in human service organizations has been the employment of indigenous nonprofessionals. The increasing presence of nonprofessional personnel in such organizations has created new constraints, pressures, and organizational demands for conflict resolution (Meyer, 1969).

Katan presents a conceptual framework for analyzing the roles of nonprofessionals and the organizational factors related to their differential deployment in seven different human service organizations. He begins with the identification of eight motives human service organizations have used for employing nonprofessionals, and the types of organizational role expectations held for their performance. From these motives Katan describes three different types of role models for the nonprofessional: conformist, mediator, and innovator.

A test of a series of propositions regarding the types of work performed by nonprofessionals revealed a preponderance of mediating activities between client groups and the organization. Moreover, he found that the experiences gained by nonprofessionals in dealing with various external groups were rarely utilized within the organization. Rather the performance of simple and routine tasks along with mediating activities with community groups constituted the core activities of this group of nonprofessionals. He attributes his findings to four factors: (1) the lack of appropriate organizational mechanisms for involving nonprofessionals in planning and decision-making structures; (2) the lack of motivation among nonprofessionals to assume innovative roles as well as the lack of organizational mechanisms to induce and facilitate such involvements; (3) the depression effect of professionals on the work performed by nonprofessionals, and (4) the absence of activated pressure groups to stimulate organizational change and innovation.

References

Blau, P. M., and Scott, W. R. 1962. *Formal Organizations: A Comparative Approach*. San Francisco: Chandler Publishing Company.

Clark, B. 1962. *Educating The Expert Society*. San Francisco: Chandler Publishing Company.

Engel, G. V. 1970. "Professional Autonomy and Bureaucratic Organizations." *Administrative Science Quarterly* 15:12–21.

Etzioni, A. (ed.). 1969. *The Semi-Professions and Their Organizations*. New York: The Free Press. He includes nurses, social workers and teachers among the "semi-professions."

Goldner, F. H., and Ritti, R. R. 1967. "Professionalization as Career Immobility." *American Journal of Sociology* 72:489–502.

Goss, M. E. W. 1961. "Influence and Authority Among Physicians in an Out-Patient Clinic." *American Sociological Review* 26:39–50.

———. 1963. "Patterns of Bureaucracy Among Hospital Staff Physicians." Pp. 170–94 in Elliot Freidman (ed.), *The Hospital in Modern Society*. Glencoe: Free Press.

Katz, E., and Eisenstadt, S. N. 1960. "Some Sociological Observations on the Response of Israeli Organizations to New Immigrants." *Administrative Science Quarterly* 5:113–33.

Katz, F. 1964. "The School as a Complex Social Organization." *Harvard Educational Review* 34:428–55.

Merton, R. K. 1968. *Social Theory and Social Structure*. New York: The Free Press.

Meyer, H. J. 1969. "The Nonprofessional, The Agency, and The Social Work Profession: Some Sociological Comments." in C. Grosser, et al. (eds.), *Nonprofessionals in Human Service*. San Francisco: Jossey-Bass.

Mills, C. W. 1951. *White Collar*. New York: Oxford University Press.

Scott, R. W. 1965. "Reactions to Supervision in a Heteronomous Professional Organization." *Administrative Science Quarterly* 10:65–81.

————. 1966. "Professionals in Bureaucracies-Areas of Conflict." Pp. 265–75 in Howard M. Vollmer and Donald L. Mills (eds.), *Professionalization*. Englewood Cliffs, New Jersey: Prentice-Hall, Inc.

Models of Bureaucracy Which Permit Conflict

Eugene Litwak

In the present article an attempt will be made to suggest some conditions for polar models[1] of bureaucracy. This will in turn permit some specifications of an intermediate model of bureaucracy which may more clearly fit contemporary urban society.

The two models of bureaucracy to be contrasted are that which stresses secondary relations and organizational rules (i.e., as Weber's), and that which stresses primary-group relations and organizational goals[2] (as in the "human-relations" approach). Weber's model is most efficient when the organization deals primarily with uniform events and with occupations stressing traditional areas of knowledge rather than social skills. The human-relations model will be most efficient for dealing with events which are not uniform (research, medical treatment, graduate training, designing) and with occupations emphasizing social skills as technical aspects of the job (as that of psychiatric social worker, salesman if there is little differentiation in the products, and politician).

However, for most organizations in our society a theoretical model of bureaucratic organization must be developed that combines the central and conflicting features from both types. Since they are conflicting, what characterizes this third model and distinguishes it from the other two is a need for "mechanisms of segregation." These permit mutually antagonistic social forms to exist side by side in the same organization without ruinous friction.

The Uniform and the Non-uniform

Weber's model of bureaucracy[3] can be characterized by: impersonal social relations, appointment and promotion on the basis of merit, au-

Reprinted from *The American Journal of Sociology* 67 (September, 1961): 177–84.

thority and obligations which are specified a priori and adhere to the job rather than the individual (i.e., separation of work from private life), authority organized on a hierarchical basis, separation of policy and administrative positions, the members of the bureaucracy being concerned with administrative decisions, general rules for governing all behavior not specified by the above, and, finally, specialization. If the organization is large and structured by these ideal conditions, it will be more efficient[4] than any other kind of organization. Weber's theoretical model assumes that the organization will be dealing with uniform situations.

By "uniform" two things are meant: The task to be dealt with is recurrent (in time as well as among many people) and important, exemplified in such occupations as that of: research scientist or developmental engineer, as opposed to supervisor of an assembly line; doctor or surgeon providing treatment in areas of medicine where little is known (neurosurgeon), as opposed to one dealing with standardized problems; soldier in combat, as opposed to in peacetime; administrator of a large organization producing a rapidly changing product (e.g., chemicals, electronic apparatus, pharmaceuticals, or missiles), as opposed to one dealing with standardized procedures, such as a public utility or a large governmental agency administering well-established regulations.

The importance of distinguishing between the uniform and the non-uniform as well as noting Weber's assumption of uniformity can best be seen if the criticisms of his model are reviewed.[5] The critics point out that the larger the organization, the more likely is it to encompass diverse social situations and people. If a general rule is developed for each situation, the rules would be so numerous as to defy learning. If rules are not developed, then either the administrator will apply rules which are not appropriate or substitute for them his private system of values. In all cases there is likely to be a drop in efficiency when general rules are used and the task is not uniform.

The same point can be made with regard to the hierarchy of authority and delimitation of duties and privileges of the office, for both are only special cases of general rules. Thus, for maximum efficiency, a hierarchy or delimitation of jobs should be based on merit. Setting up a hierarchy based on merit is a relatively simple matter when dealing with one uniform event. However, if the event is relatively unique, it is difficult for any one hierarchy to suffice for all tasks in the organization. Yet this is the assumption which must be made in all cases where Weber's specifications are applied to organizations dealing with the non-uniform. Since this is too heroic, the individuals concerned might do better to internalize the values of the organization and reach *ad hoc* rather than a priori decisions as to job hierarchy and boundaries.

In his pioneering work, Pelz investigated a large industrial concern whose parts were classified into several groups: those dealing with non-uniform events (i.e., scientists and engineers) and those working with relatively uniform events (central staff and manufacturing).[6] He found that among those in the occupations dealing with non-uniform tasks there was a higher correlation between their motivation to work and productivity when they were free to make their own decisions. In contrast, among those working on uniform tasks there was a higher correlation between motivation and productivity when they were restricted in making decisions. Permitting each individual to control decisions on the job indicates a trend toward a colleague rather than a hierarchical relationship. Pelz's study supports the point of view advocated here, that is, there are differential efficiencies in organizational structure depending on whether the task is uniform or not.

Somewhat the same analysis holds with regard to specialization, which is efficient where there are relatively constant problems. Where there are many problem areas and where they change rapidly, the demand for specialization may lead to premature organizational closure and great inflexibility in deciding, as in the armed forces where a rapidly changing technology has made traditional specialties obsolete. Many argue that the clinging to the traditional specialties has led to a dangerous lag in military preparedness as well as wasteful conflict between specialties.[7]

Weber's demand for impersonality also assumes uniform events. Individuals faced with non-uniform events which are not clearly covered by rules are insecure. In such situations, they must be able to call on colleagues in whom they put great trust[8] if they are to perform efficiently. In other words, in the ambiguous situation brought about by non-uniform events, frequently personal primary group relations conduce to more efficiency than would impersonal ones.

Finally, it can be argued that the separation of policy and administrative decisions is inefficient when the organization is confronted with non-uniform situations. Such separation implies that general rules can be laid down a priori to guide administrative decisions along common lines of policy. As suggested above, such general rules become impossibly complex when the organization faces non-uniform situations. Internalizing organizational policy and localizing discretion (combining administrative and policy decisions) would then be more efficient.

In short, where organizations deal with non-uniform events, a model of bureaucracy may be more efficient which differs in degree from Weber's in at least six characteristics: horizontal patterns of authority, minimal specialization, mixture of decisions on policy and on administration, little a priori limitation of duty and privileges to a given office, personal rather than impersonal relations, and a minimum of general rules. This form of organization generally characterizes the "human-relations" model described as ideal by many contemporary industrial psychologists.

Social and Traditional Job Skills

Weber also implicitly assumes in his discussion of bureaucracy that occupations stressing traditional areas of knowledge (as compared to social skills) dominate the organization. By traditional areas of knowledge is meant, say, knowledge of engineering, of chemistry, of economics, of the law, of company rules, and the like. By social skills or abilities is meant the actual capacity to communicate with others, to motivate them to work, to co-operate with others, and to internalize the values of the organization.

Granted Weber's assumptions about traditional areas of knowledge, his model of bureaucracy does not necessarily lead to efficiency when the job requirements stress social skills.

Personal and impersonal.—Weber's strictures concerning the importance of impersonal social relations are far from self-evident when social abilities rather than traditioal knowledge are at issue. The capacity to motivate others to work, to co-operate and to communicate with others, to internalize the norms of the organization, might well increase, not decrease, as a consequence of positive emotional involvement. Thus, studies of psychiatric wards, involving professions whose chief technical tools are social, suggest that greatest efficiency requires some positive emotional involvement.[9] Weber's analysis tends to overlook the virtues of close personal relations, concentrating on negative features. Since in an advanced bureaucratic society these latter are minimized,[10] many of Weber's objections to close personal relations are not so important.

Strict delimitation of obligation and duties to the office.—Weber's view that in an efficient organization there should be a strict delimitation of obligations and duties to a specified office assumes that the work can be shut off from private life (e.g., the family). This assumption has considerable validity when one is dealing with the traditional areas of knowledge. However, it is questionable when the chief technical demand of the job is for social skills. This is so because family and friends are major sources for the development of social skills. Therefore, experience in primary groups is likely to enter into one's life at work.[11] More generally, where it is difficult to separate work from other situations, such as family life, the organization must seek to control the latter for the sake of efficiency. The development in large organizations, such as the DuPont Corporation, of family counseling services can be understood in this light.

Separation of policy and administrative decisions.—The inability to isolate work from other situations also makes it difficult, if not impossible, to keep decisions on policy and administration separate. To do so would require that administrative decisions have a code of ethics of their own. Thus an engineer working on a bomb, a dam, or an automobile can say how good an engineer he is in terms of common engineering standards and somewhat independently of organizational policy. By contrast, the psychiatric social worker, because her major technical tool is social skills, finds such distinctions hard to maintain: is participation of the client or the avoidance of physical punishment an administrative technic or the agency's policy? When such distinctions are hard to make, it is more efficient to inculcate policy and give the professional discretion with regard to "administrative" decisions.

Specialization and generalization.—In part, Weber's assumptions regarding efficiency of specialization would not hold where social skills are the technique required for the job. The ability to communicate with others is general in every area of work and is the same for the engineering administrator, the accounting administrator, and every other administrator. The need to train "generalists" for administration is seen in the systematic efforts to move promising executives to a variety of departments in the company.[12] It can also be noted that the most recent recommendation concerning the curriculum in schools of social work (dealing with occupations whose chief technical tool is social abilities) was to drop the specialties and train all students in the basic social skills.[13]

Thus, in some technical fields there has been increasing specialization, while in the fields characterized by administration and by the demand for social skills there has been increasing generalization; and the total picture may indeed suggest the growth of both specialization and generalization.

Hierarchial and horizontal relations.—Hierarchical relations may well lead to efficiency when the job is defined by traditional areas of knowledge. However, there is some evidence that participation in making decisions is crucial where it is necessary to motivate people to identify themselves with organizational goals, to co-operate in their social relations, and to communicate.[14] Since these involve social skills, participation in making decisions is important where jobs are chiefly defined by those abilities. Put differently, jobs characterized by social skills might be carried out most efficiently under a horizontal structure of authority, that permits all individuals to participate equally in decisions.[15]

Specifications for a Third Model of Bureaucracy

To point out the weaknesses of Weber's model is not to suggest its elimination. Quite the contrary; this article argues that there are several models of organization with differential efficiences depending on the nature of the work and the types of tasks to be performed. In this regard, at least three types have been suggested: Weber's, that found in "human relations," and what may be called the "professional bureaucracy."[16] The third model, not discussed as yet, is characterized by the degree to which the organization must deal with events both uniform and not uniform, or by the need to have jobs requiring great social skills as well as jobs requiring traditional areas of knowledge. Perhaps the outstanding illustrations of the third type would be a large hospital, a graduate school, or a research organization. To more systematically highlight the difference between the three models, Table 1 has been presented.

It can be seen from Table 1 that the chief distinguishing characteristic of the professional model is its inclusion of contradictory forms of social relations. This model is particularly relevant to contemporary society where most large-scale organizations have to deal with uniform and non-uniform tasks[17] or with occupations that demand traditional knowledge as well as social skills.[18]

Granted this assertion, one of the key theoretical and empirical problems facing the student of complex organizations is the study of "Mechanisms of Segregation"—the procedures by which potentially contradictory social relations are co-ordinated in some common organizational goals.[19] That this central issue might be clearly seen as well as to suggest possible paths of inquiry, four mechanisms of segregation will be discussed in greater detail.

1. *Role separation as a mechanism of segregation.*—One way of co-ordinating contradictory forms of behavior is to restrict primary group behavior to one set of individuals and formal relations to another.[20] This is a well-known procedure, in part recognized in Parsons' analysis of current occupational structure.[21] One partcularly relevant illustration of role segregation comes from Blau's analysis of bureaucracy.[22] Using the analogy of the civil service, he suggests that all

TABLE 1

Characteristics of Three Models of Bureaucracy

Characteristic	Weber's Model*	Human Relations†	Professional Model‡
Impersonal relations	Extensive	Minimal	One part extensive One part minimal
Appointment on merit	Extensive	Extensive	Extensive
A priori specification of job authority ..	Extensive	Minimal	One part extensive One part minimal
Hierarchical authority	Extensive	Minimal	One part extensive One part minimal
Separation of policy and administrative decisions	Extensive	Minimal	One part extensive One part minimal
General rules to govern relations not specified by above dimensions	Extensive	Minimal	One part extensive One part minimal
Specialization	Extensive	Minimal	One part extensive One part minimal

* This model would be most efficient where tasks are uniform and involve traditional areas of knowledge, such as: governmental agencies given little discretion by law—police force, enforcing traffic and criminal law, the army during peacetime, processing most income tax returns; and private concerns with constant products and technologies—public utilities such as gas, water, and electricity.

† This model would be most efficient where tasks are relatively not uniform or involve social skills; to illustrate: situations which are so non-uniform that government cannot lay down highly specified laws but rather sets up commissions with broad discretionary powers—National Institutes of Mental Health, National Labor Relations Board, etc.; and situations involving the selling of undifferentiated products—large advertising firms.

‡ This model would be most efficient where the job requires dealing with both uniform and non-uniform events or with social skills as well as traditional areas of knowledge; e.g., situations requiring standardized administrative tasks and great professional autonomy—large hospitals, large graduate schools, large research organizations—and situations requiring both knowledge of administrative details as well as high interpersonal skills—large social work agencies or psychiatric hospitals.

hiring and firing functions be handled by a special group which has no responsibilities for production or administration. In this way, the potential contradiction between positive affect and objectivity can be minimized, while the virtues are maximized.

Another principle of segregation by role is illustrated by Melman in his study of a large auto concern organized into several large gangs, with each being given a production goal.[23] The management paid individuals on the basis of their gang's endeavor. Within the gang the management made little effort to deal with the non-uniform everyday problems of man-to-man supervision. This was left to the gang, with its own mechanisms of supervision.

However, the setting-up of gangs and the over-all policy of expansion and contraction of goals of production (relatively uniform problems dealing with traditional areas of knowledge) were based on a hierarchy of authority. Thus, within the same organization there were two kinds of decision systems. On the one hand, there was a centralized hierarchy of authority and, on the other hand, local discretion. There was little conflict between the two systems because management and workers had agreed in advance that interaction between one set of roles was to be handled by local discretion, but between another set of roles by centralized authority. Since the roles were clearly differentiated, it was possible to do this with minimal friction.

2. *Physical distance as a mechanism of segregation.*—A mechanism of segregation suitable only in limited cases is physical separation. Perhaps the most dramatic use of this procedure is illustrated by recent developments in research departments in business concerns.[24] The purer the research, that is, the more non-uniform the event, the more likely will physical distance be put between the departments of research and production. The Bell Laboratories, a subsidiary of American Telegraph and Telephone Company, which is a case in point, tends to fit the "human-relations" model of bureaucracy,[25] while the part of it dealing with the production of telephones and the installation of telephones is, comparatively speaking, more likely to follow Weber's model. Conflict between the two systems is minimized by their being kept physically apart.

Though the mechanism of physical separation permits a solution, it is inadequate because, as studies of larger organizations indicate, there are within the same job or closely interrelated jobs both uniform and non-uniform events, or there is within the same job the demand for knowledge and for social skills. In such cases, mechanisms of physical separation are, by definition, inappropriate.

3. *Transferral occupations as mechanisms of segregation.*— Where the organization is based on technological innovation, such as the modern industrial concern, the advances of science might transform an event from non-uniform to uniform, or vice versa. This means that there must be certain occupations whose major function is to switch areas of work from one set of social relations to another without contaminating the atmospheres of either. For instance, the engineer must frequently be in a position to take the pure scientist's work and put it on the production line. This means that he must move between the world of science, with its colleague relationships, to the world of production, with its formal hierarchical relations, without permitting the attitudes to mix.[26]

Transferral occupations have unique problems and become central when the assumption is made that organizations consist of potentially conflicting modes of behavior working harmoniously toward some over-all goal. As such, transferral occupations deserve considerable attention on the part of those interested in elaborating bureaucratic theory.

4. *Evaluation procedures as mechanisms of segregation.*—Highly related to the transferral occupations are the procedures of evaluation. If the organization contains contradictory social relations and, at the same time, is subject to constant changes, then there must be some procedure for determining points at which one kind of social relations should be replaced by another. Melman indicates that management has set up occupations for evaluating all new machines for eventual incorporation into the organization.[27] In an analogous manner, the organizations containing conflicting social relations will operate more efficiently if they have procedures for deciding at what point there should be a shift from one form of social relation to another. This is in contrast to the common assumption that the structure is permanent. Focusing on evaluation will be a major concern for future research if the model of bureaucracy geared to organizational change suggested here is to be effected.

This now sums up consideration of some possible mechanisms of segregation. It also indicates why a key area for advancing the theory of complex organizations is the study of ways by which contradictory forms of organizational structure exist side by side without ruinous friction.

Notes

1. The term "model" is not being used in a rigorous sense: all that is meant is that a given organizaion may have unique dimensions, no rules being specified to predict the interrelations between the dimensions.

2. *From Max Weber: Essays in Sociology*, trans. and ed., H. H. Gerth and C. Wright Mills (New York: Oxford University Press, 1946), pp. 196–203. Similarly, James G. March and Herbert A. Simon differentiate between process and purpose theories of organization (*Organizations* [New York: John Wiley & Sons, 1958], p. 29).

3. These do not exactly duplicate Weber's statement, but they are sufficiently close to do no violence to it (see Weber, *op. cit.*, pp. 196 ff.).

4. The terms "efficiency" and "productivity" are deliberately left undefined since many well-known problems of value would require extensive consideration if a formal definition were attempted. But it is here assumed that efficiency is defined in terms of some central set of liberal social values which have dominated our society within the last two hundred years; and that when the value problems revolving around the definition of efficiency are more fully solved they will not be inconsistent with this usage.

5. Julian Franklin, *Man in Society* (New York: Columbia University Press,

1955), I, 941–42; Peter M. Blau, *Bureaucracy in Modern Society* (New York: Random House, 1956), pp. 58, 62; Robert K. Merton, "Bureaucratic Structure and Personality," in *Reader in Bureaucracy*, ed. R. K. Merton, A. P. Gray, B. Hockey, and H. C. Selvin (Glencoe, Ill.: Free Press, 1952), p. 364; Philip Selznick, "A Theory of Organizational Commitment," in *Reader in Bureaucracy*, pp. 194–202.

6. D. C. Pelz, "Conditional Effects in the Relationship of Autonomy and Motivation to Performance," (August, 1960) (mimeographed). The development of colleague relations among scientists and members of graduate departments of universities would also provide evidence on the point.

7. It is frequently said that, because of their commitment to a specialty, members of the armed services tend to overlook the general problem of defense in favor of their own immediate tasks, with a consequent loss for the basic goals of defense (see H. L. Wilensky and C. N. Lebeaux, *Industrial Society and Social Welfare* [New York: Russell Sage Foundation, 1958], pp. 235–65).

8. Blau, *op. cit.*, pp. 63–64. This point is buttressed by the studies of combat troops or miners engaged in dangerous operations, both cases involving great uncertainty and severe risk where, apparently, strong primary group relations are effective (see E. A. Shils and M. Janowitz, "Cohesion and Disintegration in the *Wehrmacht* in World War II," in *Public Opinion and Propaganda* [New York: Dryden Press, 1954], pp. 91–108).

9. D. A. Hamburg, "Therapeutic Aspects of Communication and Administrative Policy in the Psychiatric Section of a General Hospital," in *The Patient and the Mental Hospital*, ed. M. Greenblatt, D. S. Levinson, and R. H. Williams (Glencoe, Ill.: Free Press, 1959), pp. 91–107, and P. Barrabee, "The Community, the Mental Hospital and the Aged Psychotic," *ibid.*, pp. 530–35. For a general statement relating primary group relations to communication, see E. Katz and P. F. Lazarsfeld, *Personal Influence* (Glencoe, Ill.: Free Press, 1955), pp. 15–30.

10. E. Litwak, "The Use of Extended Family Groups in the Achievement of Social Goals," *Social Problems*, 7 (Winter, 1959–60), 184–85.

11. This point is clearly illustrated in Jules Henry's analysis of an institution for child treatment which provides twenty-four-hour care on the assumption that successful treatment concerns every aspect of life. He notes how much the therapist's own life becomes involved with that of the patient ("Types of Institutional Structures," *The Patient and the Mental Hospital*, pp. 73–91).

12. M. Janowitz, *The Professional Soldier* (Glencoe, Ill.: Free Press, 1960), pp. 166–71.

13. The stress toward generalization can also be noted among ward personnel in psychiatric wards (R. A. Cohen, "Some Relations between Staff Tensions and the Psychotherapeutic Process," *The Patient and the Mental Hospital*, pp. 307–8).

14. For a review of the literature see March and Simon, *op. cit.*, p. 81.

15. Hamburg (*op. cit.*, pp. 95–96) points out that where nurses, ward attendants, and patients are permitted to participate in decision-making—among other things—the efficiency of the ward goes up, there is a smaller labor turnover, fewer aggressive actions of the patients, etc. This is not to rule out the importance of vertical relations but only to suggest that they are least likely to lead to efficiency in bureaucratic organizations where jobs require social skills.

16. See Robert Vinter, "Notes on Professions and Bureaucracy" (unpublished manuscript, September, 1960).

17. One assumption which should be made explicit is that non-uniform events will constitute a major factor in organizational analysis in the foreseeable

future. This assumption rests on the following considerations: (*a*) scientific advance not only reduces prior areas of ignorance to known uniformities but reveals new areas; (*b*) as Talcott Parsons suggests (*The Social Systems* [Glencoe, Ill.: Free Press, 1951], pp. 44–45), the processes of socialization are inevitably imperfect, and as a consequence one must always assume the idiosyncratic to be part of any model of human behavior; and (*c*) a society committed to technological advance must be prepared for constant social change, and for dealing with phenomena for which it has no prior uniform modes of interaction.

18. The assumption is made that jobs calling for social abilities will constitute a significant proportion of all jobs in the foreseeable future. This assumption is based on investigations such as were made by Nelson N. Foote and Paul K. Hatt who in their paper, "Social Mobility and Economic Advancement" (*American Economic Review*, 43 [May, 1953], 364–67), suggest a shift from the primary extractive and secondary manufacturing industries to the tertiary, quaternary, and quinary industries consisting largely of human services. It also rests on analyses such as made by Reinhard Bendix (*Work and Authority in Industry* [New York; John Wiley & Sons, 1956], pp. 216 ff.), who points out that as the organization becomes larger, personal relations become important as technical features of the job.

19. To stress mechanisms which permit the coordination of potentially conflicting relations is not to deny that there are certain relations which can never be reconciled. Thus, one important aspect of organizational analysis (the resolution of conflict rather than its co-ordination), not included in this discussion, would have involved an analysis of physical violence, strikes, arbitration, propaganda, etc.

20. Robert K. Merton, in "The Role-Set: Problems in Sociological Theory" (*British Journal of Sociology*, 8 [June, 1957], 106–20), suggests by analogy several additional mechanisms of segregation which will not be discussed here.

21. Parsons points out the need to keep the family separated from the occupational life, one of the major devices being to keep the family physically isolated by a division of labor by sex ("The Social Structure of the Family," *The Family: Its Function and Destiny*, ed. Ruth N. Anshen [New York: Harper & Bros., 1949]).

22. Blau, *op. cit.*, pp. 64–66.

23. Seymour Melman, *Decision Making and Productivity* (Oxford: Basil Blackwell, 1958), pp. 92–135; also see Blau, *op cit.*, p. 66, and Ralph J. Cordiner, *New Frontiers for Professional Managers* (New York: McGraw-Hill Book Co., 1956), pp. 40–80.

24. Between 1953 and 1956 there was an estimated 67 per cent increase in the total amount of money spent for research in America ($5.4 billion to $9 billion). Business concerns whose major purpose was not research increased their expenditures almost 50 percent (from $3.7 billion to $6.5 billion) (see *Reviews of Data on Research and Development* [National Science Foundation, No. 10, NSF-58-10, May, 1958], pp. 1–2). There seem to be no estimates of business expenditures or research which go past 1953; however, estimates of federal expenditures for research, which might be correlated with business expenditures, are that between 1940 and 1958 the federal government expanded its research budget almost three times (*Proceedings of a Conference on Research and Development and Its Impact on the Economy* [National Science Foundation, NSF-58-36, 1958]).

25. The Bell Laboratories will frequently hire scientists with the explicit provision that they are free to work on the problems they like and in the manner, within reason, they choose, with the restriction that any resulting product belongs to the company. As a consequence, social relations within the laboratory may be like a

university's colleague relationship—non-hierarchical, personal, informal, face to face, with few a priori rules on duties and obligations.

26. The same phenomena can be seen in the mass media if the analysis of Katz and Lazarsfeld and Inkeles can be taken as a given. These men see two elements in the mass media: (a) the formal organization which broadcasts messages, and (b) the small primary groups which receive and interpret them. Katz and Lazarsfeld suggest that these two diverse and somewhat antithetical worlds are breached by the opinion leader, and Inkeles argues (to a lesser extent) that they are breached by the agitator. Like the engineer, the opinion leader and the agitator move between the two worlds without contaminating either (see Elihu Katz and Paul F. Lazarsfeld, *Personal Influence* [Glencoe, Ill.: Free Press, 1955], pp. 162–208; Alex Inkeles, *Public Opinion in Soviet Russia* [Cambridge, Mass.: Harvard University Press, 1951], pp. 38–135).

27. Melman, *op. cit.*

Dominant Professions, Bureaucracy, and Client Services

Eliot Freidson

For at least a century we have been treated to the use of the word "bureaucracy" as an epithet. Indeed, we have tended to take as self-evidently true the assertion that the rationalization and systematization of work, governed by formal administrative authority and written rules, leads to a fragmentation of experience, a loss of meaning, and a sense of alienation. Bureaucratic principles have come to dominate the process of industrial production and increasingly dominate the commercial organization of sales and many personal services. Even more recently, in the case of health, education, and social welfare services, bureaucratization has been growing. In such settings, too, where the organization justifies its existence by the benefits it provides clientele, clients are said to suffer a sense of helplessness, anxiety, and resentment over the way the organization of services has led to their depersonalization and loss of dignified identity. The culprit is thought to be the organizing principle of bureaucracy—orderly, systematic administrative procedures designed to ensure that work is done efficiently, honestly and fairly.

In contrast to the negative word "bureaucracy" we have the word

Reprinted from William R. Rosengren and Mark Lefton, eds., *Organizations and Clients: Essays in the Sociology of Service* (Columbus, Ohio: Charles E. Merrill Publishing Co., 1970), pp. 71–92.

"profession." This word is almost always positive in its connotation, and is frequently used to represent a superior alternative to bureaucracy. Unlike "bureaucracy," which is disclaimed by every organization concerned with its public relations, "profession" is claimed by virtually every occupation seeking to improve its public image. When the two terms are brought together, the discussion is almost always at the expense of "bureaucracy," and to the advantage of "profession." The principles underlying the two are said to be antithetical, the consequences of one being malignant and the other benign.

Over the years the literature has emphasized the differences between the two. Parsons pointed out that Max Weber, in his classic discussion of rational-legal bureaucracy, failed to distinguish between the authority of administrative office (generic to rational-legal bureaucracy) and the authority of expertise (generic to profession).[1] Making use of that distinction in the context of a study of a gypsum plant, Gouldner suggested that conventional, monocratic, and "punishment-centered" bureaucratic rules may not be so effective in ordering human effort in organizations as may rules based on expertise and consented to by all parties involved.[2] Elaborating on Gouldner's discussion, Goss[3] and Smigel[4] have developed conceptions of "advisory" and "professional" bureaucracy in which expertise is critical in creating and enforcing the rules. Many other writers, Thompson[5] and Blau[6] among them, have suggested that the principles of expertise and professionalization may constitute more efficient and more personally satisfying modes of organizing work than the classical principles of rational-legal administrative coordination. By virtually all writers, expertise and professions are equated with a flexible, creative and equalitarian way of organizing work, while bureaucracy is associated with rigidity, and with mechanical and authoritarian ways. There are, however, two important problems overlooked by that literature.

First, it seems to assume that technical expertise, unlike "arbitrary" administrative authority, is in some way neutrally functional and therefore so self-evidently true as to automatically produce cooperation or obedience in others and the efficient attainment of ends. In Gouldner's analysis, for example, we are told that so long as the *end* of technical expertise is accepted by workers, the expert's recommendation of means to that end will also be accepted automatically or at least without serious question in a "representative" or "expert" bureaucracy.[7] The implication is that when all workers can participate in setting ends in a complex organization, technical expertise can guide the way production is carried out without the necessity of exercising "punishment-centered" authority. Similarly, the implication in Parsons' comparison[8] of the authority of office with the authority of expertise is that while the former arbitrarily compels obedience, the latter is in some way naturally compelling by virtue of the fact that it is expertise and not office which is giving "orders."

But as I have shown elsewhere,[9] the authority of expertise is in fact problematic, requiring in its pure functional form the time-consuming and not always successful effort of persuading others that its "orders" are at once true and appropriate. As a special kind of occupation, professions have attempted to solve the problem of persuasion by obtaining institutional powers and prerogatives which at the very least set limits on the freedom of their prospective clients, and which on occasion even coerce their clients into compliance. The expertise of the professional is institutionalized into something similar to bureaucratic office. The implications of this fact have not been considered in the literature comparing "bureaucratic" and "professional" modes of organizing the performance of work.

Second, virtually all past work has compared an organization as a whole, from top to bottom and across all specialized tasks organized by bureaucratic administration, with a single specialized work group or profession within that larger organization and the way its members are ordered by their occupational norms. Such comparison illogically contrasts a whole with a part. What is required logically is comparison between (1) the ordering and mobilization of *all* types of workers in the organization's division of labor by office-holders who have administrative but not necessarily technical or productive expertise with (2) the ordering of the *complete* division of labor in an organization by the principle of technical expertise independent of bureaucratic office.

As I shall point out in this article, holding in mind characterizations of rational-legal, monocratic bureaucracies as wholes, when one looks at the *total* collection of workers among which professionals are found in some organizations, and when one examines how their interrelations are ordered by the authority of professional expertise, one finds distinctive properties which qualify considerably the significance of traditional contrasts between the consequences of bureaucracy and of profession on the experience of both workers and clients, and on the distribution of services to clients. I wish to suggest that the division of labor has a social organization distinct from any "external" or "artificial" authority imposed on it by "administrators." That social organization is constituted by the relations which occupations within a division of labor have to each other. Such relations are not merely determined by the functional interdependence of those occupations, but also by the social characteristics of the occupations themselves. The social organization of the division of labor is especially distinctive, I believe, when occupations with a special professional status are involved. Indeed, a division of labor ordered by professional rather than by administrative authority contains within it mechanisms and consequences similar to those described as the pathologies of bureaucracy.

Concentrating on the field of health, which is the most highly professionalized area of work to be found in our society, I shall suggest that many of the rigid, mechanical, and authoritarian attributes, and much of the inadequate coordination said to characterize the health services, may stem more from its professional organization than from its bureaucratic characteristics. In my discussion I shall deal with the influence of such organization on client experience as well as on the division of labor as such. Starting with a concrete organizational setting, I will point out how one kind of professional organization produces a non-bureaucratic but nonetheless real rigidity and authoritarianism which may be as much if not more responsible for the tribulations of the patient than the specifically bureaucratic elements of the health organization. Furthermore, I will point out how the place of the dominant profession in the health-related division of labor influences other workers, the emphasis of health services, and the facility with which the client receives services. But I must clarify what I mean by the word, "profession."

Profession as Organized Autonomy

A great many words have been consumed by discussions of what a profession is—or rather, what the best definition of "profession" is.[10] Unfortunately, discussion has been so fixed on the question of definition that not much analysis has been made of the significance and consequences of some of the elements common to most definitions. The most critical of such underexamined elements are organizational in character, dealing with the organization of practice and of the division of labor. Such elements are critical because they deal with facets of professional occupations which are independent of individual motivation or intention, and that may, as Carlin has suggested for law,[11] minimize the importance to behavior of the personal qualities of intelligence, ethicality and trained skill imputed to professionals by most definitions. The key to such institutional elements of professions, I believe, lies in the commonly invoked word, "autonomy." Autonomy is said to mean, "the quality or state of being independent, free and self-directing."[12] In the case of professions, autonomy apparently refers most of all to control over the content if not the terms of the work. That is, the professional is self-directing in his work.

From the single condition of self-direction, or autonomy, I believe we can deduce or derive virtually all the other institutional elements that are included in most definitions of professions. For example, an occupational group is more likely to be able to be self-directing in its work when it has obtained a legal or political position of privilege that protects it from encroachment by other occupations. This is one of the functions of licensure,[13] which provides an occupation with a legal monopoly over the performance of some strategic aspect of its work so as to effectively prevent free competition from other occupations. In the United States, for example, the physician is virtually the only one who can legally prescribe drugs and cut into the body. Competitors are left with being able to talk to the patients and to lay hands *on* the body, but they may not penetrate the body chemically or physically.

Second, an occupational group is not likely to be able to be self-directing if it cannot control the production and particularly the application of knowledge and skill to the work it performs. This is to say, if the substance of its knowledge and skill is known to and performed by others, the occupation cannot be self-directing because those others can legitimately criticize and otherwise evaluate the way it carries out its work, thereby limiting autonomy by having the last word. The extended period of education controlled by the profession is an exclusively segregated professional rather than liberal arts school, and in a curriculum which includes some *special* theoretical content (whether scientifically proven or not), may be seen to represent a declaration that there is a body of special knowledge and skill necessary for doing the occupation's work which is not presented in colleges of arts and sciences or their specialized departments. The existence of such self-sufficient schools in itself rules out as *legitimate* arbiters of the occupation's work those with specialized training in the same area, but training received from some other kind of school. The professional school and its curriculum also, of course, constitute convenient institutional criteria for licensure, registration, or other exclusionary legal devices.

Third, a code of ethics or some other publicly waved banner of good intentions may be seen as a formal method of declaring to all that the occupation can be trusted, and thus persuades society to grant the special status of autonomy. The very existence of such a code implies that individual members of the occupation have the personal qualities of professionalism, the imputation of which is also useful for obtaining autonomy. Thus, most of the commonly cited attributes of professions may be seen either as consequences of their autonomy, or as conditions useful for persuading the public and the body politic to grant such autonomy.

Autonomy and Dominance in the Division of Labor

Clearly, however, autonomy is not a simple criterion. One can think of many occupations which are autonomous merely by virtue of the esoteric character of their craft or the circumstances in which they work. Nightclub magicians and circus acrobats, for example, form autonomous occupations by virtue of their intensive specialization in an area of work that is itself narrowly specialized without at the same time constituting part of an interdependent division of labor. Other occupations are fairly autonomous because their work takes place in a mobile or physically segregated context such as to prevent others from observing, and therefore evaluating and controlling performance. In these cases we have *autonomy by default.* An occupation is left wholly to its own devices because there is no strong public concern with its work, because it works independently of any functional division of labor, and because its work is such (in complexity, specialization or observability) as to preclude easy evaluation and control by others. Where we find autonomy by default, we find no formal institutions in existence which serve to protect the occupation from competition, inter-vention, evaluation and direction by others. Should interest in such an autonomous occupation be aroused among other workers or in society, its autonomy would prove to be fragile indeed without the introduction of such institutions. In short, most stable and relevant to professions is *organized autonomy.*

When we turn to look at occupations engaged in such a complex division of labor as is found in the field of health, however, we find that the only occupation which is truly autonomous is medicine itself.[14] It has the authority to direct and evaluate the work of others without in turn being subject to formal direction and evaluation by them. Para-doxically, its autonomy is sustained by the *dominance* of its expertise in the division of labor. It is true that some of the occupations it dominates —nursing for example—claim to be professions. So do other groups which lack either organized autonomy or dominance claim the name— schoolteachers and social workers, for example. Surely there is a critically significant difference between dominant professions and those others who claim the name but do not possess the status, for while the members of all may be committed to their work, may be dedicated to service, and may be specially educated, the dominant profession stands in an entirely different structural relationship to the division of labor than does the subordinate. To ignore that difference is to ignore some-thing major. One might call many occupations "professions" if one so chooses, but there is a difference between the dominant profession and the others. In essence, the difference reflects the existence of a *hierarchy of institutionalized expertise*. That hierarchy of office to be found in rational-legal, monocratic bureaucracies, can have the same effect on the experience of the client as bureaucracy is said to have. Let me briefly indicate how.

The Client in the Health Organization

Unlike education, where most services are given within complex organizations, in the field of health most personal services have been given in settings that are, organizationally, analogous to small shops. For a number of reasons, however, the proportion of personal health services given in complex organizations like hospitals seems to be increasing. And it is the service in such organizations that has been most criticized for dehumanizing care. But is it bureaucratic office or institutionalized expertise which produces the client experience underlying that criticism?

Some of the complaints, such as the cost of hospitalization, reflect the method of financing medical care in the United States rather than the organization as such. Other complaints—such as those about poor food, noise, and general amenities—seem to reflect the economic foundation and capital plant of the institution rather than its organization. For our present question, two sets of complaints seem most important—those related to the physical treatment for sickness, and those related to the discomforts of being in a patient role in medical organizations.

Clearly many complaints about the depersonalization of the client in the medical organization are complaints about what some technical ostensibly therapeutic procedures do to people.[15] Simply to be strapped on a rolling table and wheeled down corridors, into and out of elevators, and, finally, out into an operating room for the scrutiny of all is to be treated like an object, not a person. To be anesthetized is to become literally an object without the consciousness of a person. And to be palpitated, poked, dosed, purged, cut into, probed, and sewed is to find oneself an object. In such cases, it is the technical work of the profession, not "bureaucracy," which is responsible for some of the unpleasantness the client experiences in health organizations. That unpleasantness is partly analogous to what is supposedly suffered by the industrial worker when the machine he works on requires him to make limited, repetitive motions at some mechanically paced speed. It is directly analogous to what is suffered by the raw materials shaped by worker and machine in productive industry.

Such discomfort may easily be excused by the outcome—that is, improvement or cure is generally thought to be a product well worth the discomfort of being treated like an object. The problem, though, is to determine exactly how much of that treatment has any necessary bearing at all on the technical outcome. There is no doubt that some of the management of the patient has little or no bearing on the purely technical requirements for treatment. Some practices bear on the bureaucratic problem of administering services to a number of individuals in a manner that is fair, precise, predictable and economical. Other practices bear on the convenience of the staff, medical or otherwise, and while they may be justified by reference to staff needs as workers, such justification has no bearing on staff expertise as such. Without denying the role of formal bureaucratic organization in creating some of the problem, it is the role of the professional worker himself I wish to examine more closely if only because, in medical and other organizations, the professional worker is specifically antibureaucratic, insisting on controlling the management of treatment himself. The question is, how do professional practices contribute to the unhappy experience of the patient?

The best way of beginning to answer that question seems to lie in recalling the difference I made between an object and a person. An object does not possess the capacity for understanding, and its behavior cannot be influenced by communication or understanding. When a person is treated *as if* he were an object, he will nonetheless behave on the basis of his understanding of that treatment. Naturally, his understanding is formed in part by what he brings with him into the treatment setting. It is also formed by the sense he himself can make of what is happening to him in the treatment setting. Since the treatment setting is presumably dominated by specialized, expert procedures, however, the most critical source of his information and understanding lies in the staff and its ability and inclination to communicate with the patient. If the staff does not communicate to the patient the meaning of and justification for what is done to him, it in essence refuses him the status of a responsible adult, or of a person in the full sense of the word.

The extent to which the staff withholds information from the patient, and avoids communicative interaction with him, has been a common criticism of the operation of such medical organizations as hospitals.[16] The complaint is that no one tells the client what is going to be done to him, why, and when. And after he has been treated, no one tells him why he feels the way he does, what can be expected subsequently, and whether or not he will live or die. The charge is that so little information is provided him that the patient cannot evaluate the meaning of the manner in which he is being treated. Experience is mysteriously meaningless, including long waits for something unknown to happen, or for something that does not happen; being awakened for an apparently trivial reason; being examined by taciturn strangers who enter the room unintroduced; perceiving lapses in such routines as medication and feeding without knowing whether error or intent is at issue. Surely this experience is little different from that of Kafka's antibureaucratic hero of *The Castle*.

In commercial organizations, "personalized forms," and other superficial means are employed to acknowledge their clients' status as responsible adults capable of intelligent choice and self-control. In the hospital situation, explanations by the staff would supply such acknowledgements, yet they do not occur. Part of the reason may stem from the necessity to treat clients in batches standardized by their technical status and by the services they require. Some reason may also be found in understaffing and overwork, which excuses the minimization of interaction with some in order to maximize it with those who have more "serious" problems. But these reasons do not explain why *bureaucratic* solutions to the problem of communication are not adopted—for example, distributing brochures explaining and justifying hospital routines, describing the experiences of "typical" cholycystectomies, mastectomies, or heart patients from the first day through convalescence, and including answers to "commonly asked questions." The prime reason for the failure to communicate with the patient does not, I believe, lie in underfinancing, understaffing, or bureaucratization. Rather, they lie in the professional organization of the hospital, and in the professional's conception of his relation to his clients.

In the medical organization, the medical profession is dominant. This means that all the work by other occupations which is related to the service of the patient is subject to the order of the physician.[17] The dominant profession alone is held competent to diagnose illness, treat or direct the treatment of illness, and evaluate the service. Without medical authorization, little can be done for the patient by paraprofessional workers. The client's medication, diet, excretion, and recreation are all subject to medical "orders." So is the information given to the patient. By and large, without medical authorization paramedical workers are not supposed to communicate anything of significance to the patient about what his illness is, how it will be treated, and what the chances are for improvement. The physician himself is inclined to be rather jealous of the prerogative, and is not inclined to authorize other workers to communicate information to the patient. Consequently, the paraprofessional worker who is asked for information by a patient is inclined to pass the buck like any bureaucrat—"You'll have to ask your doctor," the patient is told.

The dominant professional, then, is jealous of his prerogative to diagnose and forecast illness, holding it tightly to himself. But while he does not want anyone else to give information to the patient, neither is he himself inclined to do so. A number of reasons are advanced for this disinclination—the difficulty of being sure about diagnosis and precise about prognosis being perhaps the most neutral and technical of them all. Another reason is the physician's own busy schedule—that he does not have the time to spend in conversation with the patient, that more serious cases need his attention. But the reasons of uncertainty and of time-pressure are rather too superficial to dwell on. In the former case, the fact of uncertainty can constitute a communication, though as Davis has shown[18] it can be asserted to avoid communication; in the latter case, the task can merely be delegated if the doctor is lacking time. For our present purposes, the most revealing argument against communication is based on characteristically professional assumptions about the nature of clients as such. The argument, which goes back at least as far as Hippias' defensive remarks in the Hippocratic Corpus, asserts that, lacking professional training, the client is too ignorant to be able to comprehend what information he gets, and that he is in any case too upset at being ill to be able to use the information he does get in a manner that is rational and responsible.[19] From this it follows that giving information to the patient does not help him, but rather upsets him and creates additional "management problems" for the physician. Thus, the patient should not be treated like an adult, but rather like a child, given reassurance but not information. To do otherwise would only lead to the patient being upset and making unnecessary trouble for the staff. Characteristically, the professional does not view the client as an adult, responsible person.

In addition, it is worth pointing out the implications of the professional insistence on faith or trust rather than persuasion. The client, lacking professional training, is thought to be unequipped for intelligent evaluation of or informed cooperation with his consultant. Essentially, he is expected either to have faith in his consultant and do what he is told without searching questions, or else to choose another consultant in whom he does have faith. To question one's doctor is to show lack of faith and is justifiable grounds for the doctor to threaten to withdraw his services. Such insistence on faith, I believe, rests on more than the purely functional demands of an effective therapeutic or service relationship. It also neutralizes threat to status. The very special social position of institutionalized privilege that is the profession's is threatened as well as demeaned by the demand that advice and action be explained and justified to a layman. If the professional must justify himself to a layman, he must use grounds of evidence and logic common to both professional and layman, and cannot use esoteric grounds known and subscribed to by the profession alone. Insistence on faith constitutes insistence that the client must give up his role as an independent adult and, by so neutralizing him, protects the esoteric foundation of the profession's institutionalized authority.[20]

Other Workers in the Professional Organization

Thus, far, I have pointed out that in medical organizations if the client is alienated the source is professional rather than bureaucratic authority.[21] Some alienating characteristics of professional authority may lead to practices with a curiously bureaucratic look to them, including such notorious practices as passing the buck, and such a notorious problem as (in the form of requiring doctor's orders) red tape. In this organization the client's position is similar to that which he is said to suffer in civil service bureaucracies—handled like an object, given little information or opportunity for choice, and unable to feel like a responsible adult. And what of the subordinate worker in this setting dominated by a profession?

As I noted at the beginning of this article, it has been felt by many writers that the worker as well as the client suffers from the bureaucratization of production by a monocratic administration. Lacking identification with the prime goals of the organization, lacking an important voice in setting the formal level and direction of work, and performing work which has been so rationalized as to become mechanical and meaningless, functioning as a minute segment of an intricate mosaic of specialized activities which he is in no position to perceive or understand, the worker is said to be alienated. In contrast to the bureaucratized worker, however, the professional is said to be committed to and identified with his work so that it retains meaning for him, becoming in fact a central life interest. This may be true for dominant professions, but what of the other occupations working in the organization which the professional dominates? Are they not prone to alienation?

By and large, this question has not been asked in past studies, for the emphasis has been more on the positive response of "professionalism" than on the negative responses of alienation. What evidence there is, however, indicates that there are serious problems of worker morale in professional settings. Available studies are fairly clear about the existence of hierarchy in the professional health organization, and about a decrease of participation in decision-making the farther down the hierarchy one goes. Neither the ends nor the means of their work seem to be a matter for legitimate determination by lower level workers, though of course they do have their sometimes very strong informal influence on such determination. Furthermore, even in situations where the stated official expectation is free participation by all workers in conferences about the running of such units as wards, participation has been observed to be quite unequal.[22]

The paraprofessional worker is, then, like the industrial worker, subordinated to the authority of others. He is not, however, subordinated solely to the authority of bureaucratic office, but also to the positively superior knowledge and judgment of professional experts. In some studies this authority is characterized as a kind of stratification,[23] in others as a function of status.[24] In very few if any of such studies is that status or stratification said to be of administrative or bureaucratic origin. It is instead largely of professional origin. In a few studies the notion of alienation has been specifically cited.[25] Clearly, while there is no comparative evidence to allow us to determine whether more or fewer workers are alienated from professional than from bureaucratic organizations, neither hierarchical nor authoritarian tendencies are missing in the professional organization of the division of labor, nor are alienation, absenteeism, low morale and high turnover insignificant problems. Just as is true for the patient, so is it true for the worker that the professionally organized division of labor has pathologies similar to those said to stem from bureaucracy.

Substantive Bias in Client Services

Thus far I have compared the influence of professional authority with the influence of bureaucratic authority on the experience of both client and worker in the physically limited corporate body we usually call an organization. Since, however, inter-organizational relations may themselves be seen as organization, and since the production of particular goods and services is rarely limited to the confines of a single corporate body, requiring a variety of functions from outside "the" organization, it seems useful to continue my comparison in the rather broader context of planning and coordinating service as such. I have already noted that the common assumption is that the expert authority has a neutral, functional foundation rather than, like bureaucratic authority, the foundation of arbitrary office. If this is so, then we should expect that the influence of expert authority on the support and planning of services would be highly functional, lacking arbitrary bias from the special vantage of bureaucratic office. Our expectation is not so met in health services. There, the dominant profession exercises great influence on the disposition of resources which make services available for clients. The character of that influence does stem from professional views of the purely functional considerations of what service is needed to accomplish some desired end, but those views have been distorted by the lenses of a special occupational perspective.

To understand how resources get distributed to the varied health services sought or required by the client, we must keep in mind the fact that the medical division of labor is not functionally complete. It is composed solely of those occupations and services controlled by the dominant profession. Outside of it are some which perform work that is functionally and substantively related to the profession, but not subject to the profession's authority. In matters of health in the United States, such occupations as dentistry, optometry, chiropracty and clinical psychology exemplify by their independent existence the functional incompleteness of the medically ordered division of labor. Furthermore, these are occupational groups whose work is often at least partly related to health problems, but which are not recognized medical occupations— schoolteachers, specialized training and guidance personnel, social workers, and even ministers may be cited here. These are not part of the medically ordered division of labor either. Thus, while the profession stands as the supreme authority in the medical division of labor, the medical division of labor does not encompass all health-related activities of the large health-related division of labor. Nonetheless, the distribution of support and resources tends to move disproportionately through the medical division of labor.

I have argued for the distinction of a type of profession that has ultimate authority over its work in such a way that it is self-directing or autonomous, and dominant in a division of labor. In the case of medicine, a strategic facet of its authority is its delineation of pathology, of the definitions of health and illness which guide the application of knowledge to human ills. The physician is the ultimate expert on what is health and what illness, and on how to attain the former and cure the latter. Indeed, his perspective leads him to see the world in terms of health and illness, and the world is presently inclined to turn to him for advice on all matters related to health and illness irrespective of his competence. Given the highly visible miracles medicine has worked over the past century, the public has even been inclined to ask the profession to deal with problems that are not of the bio-physical character for which success was gained from past efforts. What were once recognized as economic, religious and personal problems have found redefinitions as illness, and have therefore become medical problems.[26] This widening of medical jurisdiction has had important consequences for the allocation of resources to client services.

No philanthropies today seem to be able to attract more financial support than those devoting themselves to an illness, particularly one that affects children. If the label of illness can be attached to a problem, it receives extensive support. And it also becomes dominated by medical institutions even when there is no evidence that medical institutions have any especially efficacious way of dealing with the problem. By virtue of being the proprietor of notions of illness and health, medicine has in fact become a giant umbrella under which a disparate variety of workers (including sociologists) can be both financed and protected from overclose outside scrutiny by virtue of their semantically created connection with health. But those that do not or cannot choose to huddle under the umbrella, even though their work is health related, tend to find it difficult to obtain support.

One rather obvious consequence is the uneven distribution of resources to health-related activities. For example, it was pointed out recently that heavy financing has been given to medical research into mental deficiency, only a small amount of which is biologically or genetically caused, while *educational* facilities for the training and teaching of mental deficients have been solely underfinanced.[27] Less obvious and more important to public welfare is the extent to which this uneven distribution of resources emphasizes some hypotheses and investigatory and therapeutic models at the expense of others equally plausible. For example, it was recently pointed out that work in rehabilitation has come to be pulled in under medical supervision, the result of which has been the inappropriate emphasis on the traditional authoritarian therapeutic relationship of medicine which I have already discussed.[28] By and large, within the well-financed division of labor dominated by the profession and under its protective umbrella, most work is limited to that which conforms to the special perspective and substantive style of the profession—a perspective that emphasizes the individual over the social environment, the treatment of rare and interesting disorders over those that are common and uninteresting, the cure rather than the prevention of illness, and preventive medicine rather than what might be called "preventive welfare"—social services and resources which improve the diet, housing, way of life and motivation of the people without the necessity for each to undertake consultation with a practitioner. In short, I suggest that by virtue of its position in the public esteem, and in its own division of labor, the dominant profession of the field of health exerts a special and biased influence on the planning and financing of the services of the general field within which it is located. The prime criterion for determining that emphasis is not necessarily functional in character, but social and structural—whether or not the services can be dominated by or be put under the umbrella of the dominant profession. The consequence for the client is an array of differentially supported services which may not be adequate for his needs and interests.

Finally, I might point out that given this array of health-related services, differentially developed and supported by functional and other considerations, still further qualifications of the kind of service a client is likely to get is exercised by the dominant profession. In general, I wish to suggest that when some of the relevant services lie outside of the medical division of labor and some inside, serious problems of access to relevant care and of the rational coordination of care are created by the barriers which the profession creates between that segment of the division of labor it does dominate, and that segment it does not.

Perhaps the simplest way of discussing those barriers is to examine the process by which clients move through the division of labor. They move in part by their own choice and selection of consultants, and in part by their consultants' choice of and referral to other consultants or technicians. To the extent that the client moves through the division of labor by his own volition, he is responsible for his own care and his consultants are dependent on him for relevant information about his problem. But to the extent to which the client is being guided by consultants, the character of his experience and care is dependent on the substantive direction of his consultants' referrals, and on the exchange of information among them bearing on treatment. Here is where the professionally created barrier is found. Within the general health division of labor, the referral of clients tends to go on in only one direction—into the smaller medical division of labor, without also going from the medical into the larger system. This is also generally true of the transmission of information about the client. To put it more bluntly, teachers, social workers, ministers and others outside of the medical division of labor refer to physicians, and communicate information about the client to them, but physicians are not likely either to refer clients to them or to provide them with the results of medical investigation.[29]

By the same token, physicians do not routinely refer to clinical psychologists, optometrists, chiropractors and others outside of the medical division of labor but clearly within the health division of labor. They are likely to refer only when they are sure that solely the limited services they may order and no more will be performed—psychological testing rather than psychotherapy, spectacle fitting and sales rather than refractions, and minor manipulations for medically untreatable muscular-skeletal complaints rather than for other complaints. They are also, wittingly or not, likely to discourage such workers' referrals to them by reciprocating neither referrals nor information about their findings. And from at least one study there is evidence that they are prone to reject the patient if he comes to them from an outside source.[30]

By and large, physicians refer to and communicate extensively only with those who, within the medical division of labor, are subject to their prescription, order or direction. Indeed, physicians are likely to be very poorly informed about any of the institutional and occupational resources that lie outside of their own jurisdiction. And, as is quite natural for people who have developed commitment to their work, they are likely to be suspicious of the value of all that lies outside their domain, including the competence and ethicality of those working outside. Their commitment leads them to deprecate the importance of extramedical services and their position as a profession encourages them to restrict their activities to the medical system they control. So long as this is all their clients need or want, no harm is done save for the possibility that the professional's response to outside services may encourage those outside to avoid or delay in referring clients to the physician. If services from outside are necessary for the client's well-being, however, referral to them may be delayed or never undertaken, and the client's interests unprotected.

Profession, Bureaucracy and the Client

I began this article with the comment that "bureaucracy" has become an epithet. From what I have said about "profession" in my exposition, you might think that I am attempting to make it, too, an epithet. This is not true. It is true, however, that I have attempted to remove the word from the realm of the normative, where most usage has been prone to keep it, and to move it into a realm of reality which is subject to logical and empirical investigation. In this effort, I have chosen first to use the word to refer to a way of *organizing work* rather than, as is common, to refer to an *orientation* toward work or a *body of knowledge*. By that criterion I suggested that we might distinguish between what are commonly (and, I believe, meaninglessly) called professions, and those which are dominant, directing others in a division of labor and being themselves autonomous, subject to direction by no other. Medicine is one of those dominant professions.

After discussing the implications of this usage for the other variables commonly attached to the notion of profession, I then went on to suggest some of the ways the medical profession influences health services. First, I suggested that the experience of the client in the medical organization—particularly the hospital—is created less by the bureaucratic elements in those organizations than by the work as such and by the perspective of the dominant profession which orders the activity of most of the occupations in the organization. Second, I suggested that the experience of the worker in the medical organization suggests alienation similar to that said to exist in bureaucratically organized settings. Third, I suggested that the planning and distribution of health resources tends to be weighted by the dominant profession's structural position in the division of labor as well as by the functional problems of health and illness as such. Finally, I suggested that in the cooperative exchange and referral of clients which is a prerequisite for the expeditious delivery of all necessary health-related services, the physician neither reciprocates referrals nor communicates with those who work outside of his own division of labor. In all four cases, and perhaps in more, I suggest, the relations between clients and organizations, and the relations between clients and the services they need are influenced strongly by the dominance of a single, autonomous profession. Insofar as there is pathology, much stems from the profession, not bureaucracy.

Thus, I suggest that the dominance of client services by the principle of expertise which is embodied in a professionally ordered division of labor is, analytically and practically, fully as problematic as is dominance by the principles of rational-legal bureaucracy. Expertise institutionalized into a profession is not, as much writing seems to assume, an automatically self-correcting, purely task-oriented substitute for "arbitrary" bureaucracy. The definition of the work—that is, how the client should behave and what other workers should do—is a partial expression of the hierarchy created by the office, and of the ideology stemming from the perspective of the office as well as of the purely technical character of the work itself. And when that work involves personal services of some importance to the welfare of the client, both the ideology and the technology combine to produce bureaucracy-like consequences for his fate.

It may be said that my analysis, fixed as it has been on one profession, does not reflect all professions. This is true. Of all the established professions, only medicine has developed such an elaborate and complex division of labor. The division of labor in college teaching, for example, is positively primitive, though more so in the teaching of some subjects than others. So is the division of labor in the ministry. And in the case of law, while there is a fairly complex division of labor, most of it in the United States has as yet escaped dominance by the profession. But I believe it can be argued that medicine provides the most important even if not the most representative case of the professions because its dominance is the model toward which (and against which) ambitious occupations are now struggling. We may expect to see many more cases like medicine in the future.

Limitations on the Professional Perspective

Finally, I must say that my intent here has not been to find villains on whom to blame the problems confronting the organization and presentation of client services. Both professional and bureaucrat have, by and large, the best of intentions. Both, like everyone else, are creatures of their perspectives, and those perspectives are limited by training, by commitment, and by personal work experience which comes to be regarded as wisdom. This is not some easily remedied defect, but something inherent in the nature of social life requiring countervailing pressure from other perspectives more than better intentions from within. One serious difference between professional and bureaucrat, however, lies in the very existence of legitimate countervailing pressures.

As Parsons pointed out in distinguishing between the authority of office and the authority of expertise, a critical difference between bureaucrat and professional lies in the foundations for their authority. One is largely a creature of the organization itself and the laws which establish it, answerable to the organizational rules and to a legal order that stands outside of him, his colleagues and the organization in which he works. His client has recourse to both sets of rules and, in our society at least, has specific civil rights in that order. While it is a serious problem of our time how we can make such a formal, rational-legal order actually work efficiently, fairly, and humanely, the principles of the order are designed to protect both worker and client, giving them the basic right to be recognized as responsible adults.

Such protection does not exist unequivocally in professional organizations. Unlike the bureaucrat, who may on occasion attain autonomy by *default*, the professional has gained *organized autonomy* and is not bound by rules which stand outside of his profession. His performance, however, can produce the same barriers to communication and cooperation within a functional division of labor, the same structures of evasion and the same reduction of the client to an object which have been attributed to bureaucratic organization. In the name of health the client may be stripped of his civil status, a status which is as much if not more an element of his welfare as is his health. But unlike bureaucratic practices, which in rational-legal orders are considered arbitrary and subject to appeal and modification, professional practices are imputed the unquestioned objectivity of expertise and scientific truth, and so are not routinely subject to higher review or change by virtue of outside appeal. There is no generally accepted notion of due process for the layman—client or worker—in professional organization. And in theory, the lack of review or due process is as it should be, since the professional's arbitrary authority is not supposed to be that of bureaucratic office. In practice in the everyday world, though, there is no such thing as pure knowledge or expertise—there is only knowledge in the service of a practice.

Here is the crux of the matter. Expertise is not mere knowledge. It is the *practice* of knowledge, organized socially and serving as the focus for the practitioner's commitment. In this sense, it is not merely mechanical skill which like the cog of a machine, automatically fits itself into Durkheim's organic order. The worker does not see his work as merely different than another's. He develops around it an ideology and, with the best of intentions, an imperialism which stresses the technical superiority of his work and of his capacity to perform it. This imperialistic ideology is built into the perspective that his training and practice create. It cannot be overcome by ethical dedication to the public interest because it is sincerely believed in as the only proper way to serve the public interest. And it hardens when an occupation develops the autonomy of a profession and a place of dominance in a division of labor, and when expertise becomes an institutional status rather than a capacity. The pathology arises when outsiders may no longer evaluate the work by the rules of logic and the knowledge available to all educated men, and when the only legitimate spokesman on an issue relevant to all men must be someone who is officially certified.

Notes

1. Talcott Parsons, "Introduction," in Max Weber, *The Theory of Social and Economic Organization* (New York: The Free Press of Glencoe, 1964), pp. 58–60.
2. Alvin W. Gouldner, *Patterns of Industrial Bureaucracy* (New York: The Free Press of Glencoe, 1964).
3. Mary E. W. Goss, "Patterns of Bureaucracy Among Hospital Staff Physicians," in Eliot Freidson, ed., *The Hospital in Modern Society* (New York: The Free Press of Glencoe, 1963), pp. 170–194.
4. Erwin O. Smigel, *The Wall Street Lawyer* (New York: The Free Press of Glencoe, 1964).
5. Victor Thompson, *Modern Organization* (New York: Alfred A. Knopf, 1961).
6. Peter Blau, *The Dynamics of Bureaucracy* (Chicago: University of Chicago Press, 1959).
7. Gouldner, *op. cit.*, pp. 221–22.
8. Parsons, *op. cit.*
9. See Eliot Freidson, "The Impurity of Professional Authority," in Howard

S. Becker, *et al., Institutions and the Person: Essays Presented to Everett C. Hughes* (Chicago: Aldine Publishing Co., 1968).

10. E.g., Morris I. Cogen, "Toward a Definition of Profession," *Harvard Educational Review*, 23 (1953), 33–50.

11. Jerome Carlin, *Lawyers' Ethics* (New York: Russell Sage Foundation, 1966).

12. *Webster's Third New International Dictionary* (Springfield, Mass.: G. & C. Merriam Co., 1967), p. 148.

13. Cf. W. K. Selden, *Accreditation* (New York: Harper, Row, 1960).

14. See Eliot Freidson, "Paramedical Personnel," in *International Encyclopedia of the Social Sciences* (New York: Macmillan and Free Press, 1968), Vol. X, pp. 114–120, for a more complete discussion of the division of labor as a social organization.

15. Important in this context is Erving Goffman, "The Medical Model and Mental Hospitalization," in Erving Goffman, *Asylums* (Garden City: Doubleday and Co., 1961), pp. 321–386.

16. For example, see the following: Julius A. Roth, "The Treatment of Tuberculosis as a Bargaining Process," in A. M. Rose, ed., *Human Behavior and Social Processes* (Boston: Houghton Mifflin Co., 1962), pp. 575–588; Jeanne C. Quint, "Institutionalized Practices of Information Control," *Psychiatry*, 28 (1965), 119–132.

17. E.g., Albert F. Wessen, "Hospital Ideology and Communication Between Ward Personnel," in E. G. Jaco, ed., *Patients, Physicians and Illnesses* (New York: The Free Press of Glencoe, 1958), pp. 448–468.

18. Fred Davis, "Uncertainty in Medical Prognosis, Clinical and Functional," *American Journal of Sociology*, 66 (1960), 41–47.

19. See, for example, the material in Barney G. Glaser and Anselm L. Strauss, *Awareness of Dying* (Chicago: Aldine Publishing Co., 1965).

20. For a more extensive discussion of the professional ideology see Eliot Freidson, *Profession of Medicine* (New York: Dodd, Mead and Co., 1970).

21. For a rare study of patients using a measure of alienation, see John W. Evans, "Stratification, Alienation and the Hospital Setting," *Engineering Experiment Station Bulletin*, No. 184, Ohio State University, 1960.

22. For example, see the findings in William Caudill, *The Psychiatric Hospital as a Small Society* (Cambridge: Harvard University Press, 1958).

23. See M. Seeman and J. W. Evans, "Stratification and Hospital Care," *American Sociological Review*, 26 (1961), 67–80, 193–204, and Ivan Oxaal, "Social Stratification and Personnel Turnover in the Hospital," *Engineering Experiment Station Monograph*, No. 3, Ohio State University, 1960.

24. See E. G. Mishler and A. Tropp, "Status and Interaction in a Psychiatric Hospital," *Human Relations*, 9 (1956), 187–205, and William R. Rosengren, "Status Stress and Role Contradictions: Emergent Professionalization in Psychiatric Hospitals," *Mental Hygiene*, 45 (1961), 28–39.

25. See Rose L. Coser, "Alienation and the Social Structure: Case Study of a Hospital," in Freidson, *Hospital in Modern Society, op. cit.*, pp. 231–265, and L. I. Pearlin, "Alienation from Work: A Study of Nursing Personnel," *American Sociological Review*, 27 (1962), 314–326.

26. For an extended discussion of the relative place of notions of health and illness in modern society, see Eliot Freidson, *Profession of Medicine, op. cit.*

27. George W. Albee, "Needed—A Revolution in Caring for the Retarded," *Transaction*, 5 (1968), 37–42.

28. Albert F. Wessen, "The Apparatus of Rehabilitation: An Organizational Analysis," in Marvin B. Sussman, ed., *Society and Rehabilitation* (Washington: American Sociological Association, 1966), pp. 148–178.

29. For work bearing on these statements see Elaine Cumming *et al.*, *Systems of Social Regulation* (New York: Atherton Press, 1968). And see Eugene B. Piedmont, "Referrals and Reciprocity: Psychiatrists, General Practitioners, and Clergymen," *Journal of Health and Social Behavior*, 9 (1968), 29–41.

30. See David Schroder and Danuta Ehrlich, "Rejection by Mental Health Professionals: A Possible Consequence for Not Seeking Appropriate Help for Emotional Disorders," *Journal of Health and Social Behavior*, 9 (1968), 222–232.

The Utilization of Indigenous Workers in Human Service Organizations

Yosef Katan

The purpose of this article is to investigate two issues: the nature of the roles in which organizations utilize indigenous nonprofessionals and the organizational factors associated with their differential deployment. This investigation is a part of a more comprehensive study designed to develop an adequate conceptual framework which aids in the collection of data on several aspects of the integration of indigenous workers into human service organizations.[1]

The Movement to Employ Indigenous Workers and Its Basic Assumptions and Motives

A description and analysis of the unique characteristics of indigenous workers and of the various arguments used to justify their employment in human service organizations is needed. The list of motives serves as a basis for identifying the various role perceptions and expectations inherent in the movement to employ this specific type of worker.

The employment of nonprofessionals is not a new phenomenon. A majority of the workers employed by welfare agencies have no professional training.[2] There is some evidence that, in practice, the employment of indigenous workers did not begin in the last decade, but much earlier. However, there are two basic differences between the situation in the past and the current trend.

Article written especially for this volume.

First, agencies absorbed this type of worker in the past, mainly because of the shortage of trained manpower; but they attempted to overcome some of the perceived disadvantages by improving the selection mechanism, by introducing in-service training activities, and by encouraging the nonprofessionals to complete their academic training.[3] At present there is a positive emphasis on the worker being *indigenous* and *nonprofessional*. A worker may be indigenous through his cultural affiliations with the client group. This is a sociological orientation. It assumes that by virtue of the cultural overlap, this type of worker will possess insights into values, beliefs, morals, and customs. He will be able to communicate in the language of the clients and will therefore be more "acceptable" and more effective in the delivery of services. He also may be indigenous through his shared problem experiences with the client group. Here the assumption is that a worker, by virtue of his personal experiences in crises, or handicaps (i.e., addiction, alcoholism, mental illness, poverty) will have a better understanding of the clients' needs. The assumption is that this experience is sometimes more important and valuable than formal training and professional knowledge.

Second, the current trend to employ indigenous nonprofessionals stems neither from the organizations themselves nor from professional associations, but from an initiative of influential members of the academic community which was supported by federal agencies and was included in such legislation as the Economic Opportunity Act of 1964.[4] A review of the literature on the subject shows that the following eight motives have been used for justifying the introduction of this type of employee into organizations.

1. *Manpower Shortages.* About seventy-five percent of the workers employed by human service organizations have no academic training. The prospects for the future show that the increasing output of professional schools will not meet the demands of the expanded network of social services.[5] The hard-core unemployed persons and the residents of poor neighborhoods are seen, therefore, as an important source of manpower to overcome this shortage and facilitate further development and expansion of public services.[6]

2. *The Need to Relocate Work Within an Organization.* Given the present "gap" between rising demand and the shortage of manpower, many organizations see the use of indigenous workers as an opportunity to "farm out" tasks of a repetitive nature and creating positions requiring less skill or technical competence for nonprofessionals. This will free the professional to concentrate on those activities requiring the full capacities of his training and expertise.[7]

3. *The Desire to Solve the Problems of Poverty and Unemployment.* The hiring of indigenous workers is viewed also as one of the most effective tools for solving the problems of poverty and unemployment in the United States. This optimistic hope is based on the following premises: A human service organization is seen as a more appropriate framework for absorbing unemployed and poor persons than does industry.[8] In contrast to positions in the private economy, jobs in welfare agencies are free of many competitive performance criteria. These organizations are expected, therefore, to be more tolerant toward untrained employees and to facilitate their integration into the working force.

4. *The Desire to Change the Image of the Poor.* Several authors emphasize the possible contributions of the employment of indigenous nonprofessionals toward changing the image of the poor in society.[9] The poor are defined primarily in terms of a one-sided dependence on other groups rather than on the basis of mutual interdependence. This results in an image (or status) being defined largely in negative terms. Employment of the poor is seen as one way of bringing about a change in this image.

5. *The Desire to Provide Therapeutic Experiences.* Related to the above is the "helper therapy" principle described by Riessman.[10] Stated simply, the proposition contains two basic ideas: (a) since many indigenous workers recruited for human services jobs are likely to be school dropouts, ex-drug addicts, unemployed, delinquent, or otherwise "stigmatized" individuals, placing them in a helping role will be highly therapeutic for them; and (b) as the therapeutic benefits are realized, these people should become more effective workers and thus a positive growth force in the manpower pool of the community.

6. *The Desire to Make Services More Meaningful to the Clientele.* One of the main criticisms directed toward welfare services is their inability to supply meaningful services to the needy clientele.[11] Critics attribute this malfunction of welfare agencies to the middle-class tendencies and orientations of their professional staff and to the bureaucratic characteristics which emphasize uniform, impersonal attitudes toward the clientele. The employment of indigenous workers is viewed as a device for bridging the gap between human service organizations and their clientele and creating better communication channels between them. The nonprofessional may interpret the policy and the rules of the agency to the clientele on one hand, while informing the agency about the real needs of the clientele on the other hand.

7. *The Desire to Change Human Service Organizations.* Several students of service organizations argue that the "communication gap" is but a symptom of a more basic problem and that the malfunctions

and the unresponsiveness of the services stem from their basic structure and policy. From this point of view, the indigenous nonprofessional is seen as a potential agent of change within the organization: his specific background prepares him for understanding the sources of the organization's failure and may help him to identify and implement solutions.[12]

8. *The Desire to Increase Citizen Participation.* The movement to involve citizens in the operation of human service organizations, particularly in poverty programs, has been advocated under the rubric of "maximum feasible participation." It is held that citizens have a basic right to take part in the planning and operation of programs relevant to the basic fabric of their lives, and their employment in these organizations is viewed as one form of participation.[13]

A careful examination of these motives uncovers at least three different and even contradicting types of role expectations. These types, the conformist, the mediator, and the innovator describe the amount of change that the worker is expected to introduce into the organizational context. Although not yet based on empirical data, this typology may serve to describe more practically the operational implications associated with the utilization of nonprofessionals in organizations.

1. *Conformity.* A worker functioning within this role set will have little status within the organizational hierarchy. His duties will be narrowly defined even though they may be quite varied. His chances to influence the organizational policy will be very limited.

2. *Mediation.* This role set requires the worker to serve as a "bridge" between the client and the organization. Although he is allowed more latitude than the conformist in terms of interpretation and discretion, his main function remains that of an information channel between the clients and the organization.

3. *Innovation.* Given this role set, a worker will be expected to introduce new elements (programs or activities) into the organization. The indigenous worker may then become an instrument of change and be given discretion and autonomy to take action in accordance with the knowledge he possesses of the "real" needs of clients.

The associations between the motives for hiring indigenous workers and the role sets that workers might possess (or in which they might be cast) in organizational contexts are described in table 1.

This discussion indicates that the movement toward employing nonprofessionals offers organizations a variety of roles that nonprofessionals can perform. Therefore, it raises the fundamental issue of what organizational factors will influence the type of role that the indigenous worker will be given in the organization. In the following, we shall

TABLE 1

Motives and Role Expectancies

	Conformity	Mediation	Innovation
1. Reduce manpower shortage	X		
2. Reallocate work	X		
3. Eliminate poverty	X		
4. Change of image of client		X	
5. Provide therapeutic experiences		X	
6. Increase meaningfulness of services		X	
7. Change human service organizations			X
8. Increase participation of clients			X

construct a conceptual framework to respond to the questions surrounding this issue.

The Conceptual Framework

Two areas of study in the field of sociology of organizations can be called upon to provide the theoretical underpinning of this conceptual framework: the area of innovation and change in organizations and the relationship between organizations and their environment.

Organizational Approach to Innovation and Change

The employment of a new type of employee lacking formal education but having experience as clients provides welfare agencies with new elements foreign to certain conventional conceptions held by formal organizations. It may be worthwhile, therefore, to view the question of the utilization of nonprofessionals from the perspective of organizational approach to innovation and change and to draw some ideas and insights from studies done in this area.

These studies assumed that the internal organizational structure has a decisive impact on its ability to initiate or adopt changes and innovations. Hage and Aiken, who have explored this subject in their study on welfare agencies, find that rates of program change in organizations are negatively correlated with their degree of formalization and centralization.[14] These findings are congruent with some models of "innovative organizations" which were developed in several theoretical studies.[15] A higher degree of formalization (measured by the degree of job codification, existence of written rules specifying what should be done in each case, and existence of a supervision and control system responsible for enforcing the rules) is considered detrimental to innovation and change for several reasons. A highly formalized job provides little latitude to the worker to consider alternative actions. Moreover, the demand for workers to act according to rigid rules provides little incentive to search for new modes of action. Thus, such organizations neither encourage nor allow indigenous workers to generate new ideas but tend to lock them in conformist roles.

A high level of organizational centralization (measured by the degree of power concentration in the organization's top level) is also considered to be detrimental to innovation and change for several reasons. Introduction of indigenous workers into the organizational realm may be considered by those placed at the top as a potential threat to their position. They tend to confine these workers into positions where they can be controlled. Moreover, highly centralized organizations usually leave only a few channels open for lower level members to communicate to the people at the top. Thus, there are no real opportunities for new ideas to be transmitted from front-line workers to the organization's elite.

While these assumptions may lead to the conclusion that only in decentralized and less structured organizations will indigenous workers be allowed or even encouraged to perform innovative functions in which their unique experience and knowledge may be reflected, attention should be paid to some other structural aspects of these organizations that may impede such utilization.

Organizational decentralization and a low degree of formalization are conducive to innovativeness in the sense that they provide workers with a certain amount of autonomy, thereby allowing them to be innovative and creative. These conditions, nevertheless, may be ineffective in settings where the workers themselves are reluctant or unable to raise new ideas and to convey them to other organizational sections. In such settings, an innovative utilization of workers may require the organization to provide a definition and description of the nonprofessionals' role, specifying the innovative, nontraditional aspects, as well as training and supervisory arrangements designed to prepare and assist workers in the performance of such roles. This kind of organizational initiative may be facilitated by the presence of an executive favorably disposed toward innovative utilization of nonprofessionals. Such an executive is likely to initiate appropriate training programs, as well as to involve the indigenous workers in planning and decision-making activities. He rewards them for showing initiative and reinforces innovative utilization of these workers by other workers in the organization.

Organizations and Their Environment

An examination of some theoretical frameworks dealing with different aspects of these relationships (Selznick's co-optation theory,[16] Litwak's and Meyer's "balance theory,"[17] and Eisenstadt's concepts of bureaucratization and debureaucratization[18] may show that each provides a possible explanation for the use of the nonprofessional.

Selznick's theory claims that the idea of citizen participation or democratic management developed by some organizations is a defense mechanism geared to co-opt active groups in their environment. This theory may indicate that human service organizations tend to employ indigenous workers in order to incorporate their clients' representatives into the organization's framework placing them in subordinate conformist roles.

A possible explanation for the tendency to utilize indigenous workers in mediating roles is offered by Litwak's and Meyer's theory, which presumes that the proper functioning of an organization depends upon the existence of balanced relationships with primary groups operating within their domain, and that this balance can be attained by using appropriate linking mechanisms. From this theoretical viewpoint, organizations' tendency to employ indigenous workers can be seen as stemming from their willingness to coordinate their relationships with environmental groups. They tend, therefore, to accept these workers and to place them in mediating roles, where they can function as linking mechanisms. This utilization pattern is characteristic of organizations facing too active or too passive client groups and, therefore, the organizations are much more aware of the need for balanced relationships.

Some conditions under which the innovative nonprofessional role may emerge are described by Eisenstadt's theory which offers a typology of organization-environment relationships containing balanced as well as unbalanced situations. One of his three types, debureaucratization, describes a situation that can be created by the presence of innovative indigenous workers—elements extraneous to the organization can penetrate it and transform its structure or activities. Eisenstadt argues that the main factor which may lead to this situation is an organizational dependence on one environmental sector for mobilizing resources necessary for its existence. This argument suggests that the "innovative type" may emerge in settings where the indigenous workers represent an extraneous group commanding resources needed by the organization and wishing to exercise its potential power.

The review of these three theoretical frameworks indicates that the tendency to utilize indigenous workers as conformists will be stronger in organizations that wish to co-opt parts of their environment and have the power to do it. The "innovative" person may emerge in settings where organizations are surrounded by powerful primary groups. The emergence of the mediating type will be a result of the organizations' wish to coordinate their relationships with their clientele, without dominating or being dominated by it. The emergence of each type of nonprofessional worker may be affected by the internal structure of the organization, as well as by its external relationships. The following table, which summarizes the main theoretical assumptions presented above, describes the varied organizational implications embodied in each of the expected role sets.

Each type of nonprofessional worker represents a distinct configuration of requirements necessary for their incorporation into the organizational framework. The "conformist" type, with its emphasis on mobility patterns, achievement criteria, and in-service training, is the only type that fits into organizations with formal structure and centralized authority. But the potential contribution of the "conformist" to the organization's relationships with groups in its environment is very limited. The "mediator" demands comprehensive internal organizational changes, but his possible contribution to the improvement of the organization's external relationships are much more significant. The "innovator" poses such radical demands for organizational changes that only organizations fully dependent on external groups will be willing to accept him. On this basis, the following propositions may be offered:

1. The less structured and centralized the organization, the wider will be the scope of the roles in which indigenous workers will be allowed to engage and the stronger will be their chances to become involved in innovative and change-oriented activities at the organizational level.
2. In settings where the indigenous workers show no interest or capability of performing innovative roles by their own initiative, this pattern of utilization is dependent upon the presence of innovative and change-oriented executives and upon the existence of appropriate organizational mechanisms designed to encourage and prepare the workers to perform innovative tasks.
3. Organizational awareness of its inability to obtain access to certain community segments will lead to the tendency to use members of these segments as mediators. Their function will be to deliver

TABLE 2

The Nonprofessionals' Roles and Their Implications for Organizations.

Type of Nonprofessional Role	Implications for the Organization's Relationships with the Clientele	Implications for the Internal Organizational Structure
Conformist	1. A limited improvement in the "public image" of the organization and in its communication with clients. 2. Cooling off of certain external pressures imposed on organizations.	1. A hierarchical structure with clear patterns of nobility. 2. A set of criteria defining the preconditions for nobility in the organizational hierarchy. 3. In-service training programs designed to socialize the workers and to equip them with values, knowledge, and skills vital for ensuring their loyalty to the organization. 4. Adoption of a selection mechanism suited to the special characteristics of this occupational group.
Mediator	1. Improving communication between the organization and its clientele. 2. Cooling off external pressures imposed on organizations. 3. Outreaching to new clients and consequently broadening the organizational domain. 4. Improving the flow of information into the organization.	1. Establishing new positions in the organizational front and allocating a certain amount of autonomy to the nonprofessionals who occupy them. 2. Creating contexts for an intensive exchange of information and ideas among workers at different organizational levels. 3. Adding to the existent criteria for selecting new workers: qualifications such as experience as a client, community residence, and attachment to certain ethnic groups. 4. Developing technologies designed to deal with an increasing flow of information and larger numbers of clients.

TABLE 2 (cont.)

Type of Nonprofessional Role	Implications for the Organization's Relationships with the Clientele	Implications for the Internal Organizational Structure
Innovator	1. Improving the "Public Image" of the organization. 2. Bringing considerable reduction in the pressures imposed by clients on the organization.	1. A radical change in the structure of the organization stemming from the opening up of positions at the top for people lacking formal credentials. 2. A basic change in the existent organizational division of work, role definitions and mobility patterns. 3. Exposing the organization's secrets to a new element.

information about available services and to establish links between the organization and new clients.

4. In situations where organizations are threatened by clientele pressures, indigenous workers will be employed as conformists and mediators, absorbing part of these pressures and helping to moderate the clientele. However, under certain circumstances, such as very strong external pressure, the organization may be compelled to utilize indigenous workers in innovative capacities.

The Field Study

A pilot survey of seven human service organizations in a midwestern city has revealed that the following agencies employ indigenous workers: an Office of Economic Opportunity, a Planned Parenthood office, a co-op extension service, the city school system, a Model Cities office, a community mental health center, and a center for runaways.

Four techniques have been used for gathering the data:

a) Open interviews with almost all the professional, nonprofessional, and administrative staff members of the organizations

b) Analysis of a variety of documents including formal job descriptions of the nonprofessionals' roles, and bi-weekly or monthly reports written by them

c) Use of external informants including ex-workers in the organizations and social work students who have participated in field placement

d) Observation on activities of the indigenous workers

The Findings

The Nonprofessionals Roles

The information accumulated in the study reveals three important dimensions by which the differential utilization of nonprofessionals may be discerned.[19]

a) The kind of clients with whom the workers interact

b) The objectives of the activities performed by the workers—the goals they wish or are asked to accomplish in their interaction with the clients

c) The nonprofessional's position and location within the organizational structure

A careful examination of the nonprofessional activities in relation to the different client groups in the various settings shows that the objectives they wish to accomplish may be grouped under the following ten major categories:

1. Identification of a target—the worker discovers clients (individuals, groups, or communities) who are experiencing difficulties

2. Collection of information—the worker gathers information about the clients and their problems

3. Assessment of problems—the worker analyzes and assesses the information

4. Distribution of information—the worker provides information to the "clients" about the availability and location of resources

5. Establishment of linkages—the worker puts needy clients in touch with services that can be beneficial to them

6. Helping clients in their contact with the services—the worker participates in the negotiations between clients and agency officials and helps them to overcome bureaucratic blockages and constraints

7. Delivery of resources—the worker delivers material resources to the clients

8. Advocating—the worker plays an active part on behalf of the clients' rights; he challenges the organization's practices and demands changes

9. Education and teaching—the worker conveys knowledge and values to clients and helps them to develop certain skills

10. Counseling—the worker advises clients on how to cope with certain problems they face

Table 3 describes the range of objectives covered by the nonprofessionals in their contact with clients in each of the organizational settings. The reader will find that the ten categories are organized into three groups. The first includes more simple activities dealing with collecting information about the clients and their needs without taking any concrete action to relieve them. The second includes mediating functions—the creation of linkages between clients and the organizations and the delivery of material resources. The third represents those activities which reflect the worker's direct involvement in teaching, training, and providing personal counseling to clients.

The table indicates several interesting points. Most of the workers' activities are concentrated in the second group, that is, they function mostly as mediators between clients and organizations. (Only one setting—the schools—departs from this general trend.) Within this sphere of activities, the variations among the organizations are very small; they increase somewhat in the third group of activities. In five of the seven organizations (extension service, O.E.O., community mental health, runaway center, and the public schools) indigenous workers take part in teaching or providing counseling to clients. They, at least, potentially have a direct effect on their behavior and habits. In the other two settings (Model Cities and Planned Parenthood), the workers engage only in steering clients toward existing services and professional experts without providing any direct service to them. In addition, the table clearly shows that most of the workers' activities are concentrated at the individual client level. Fewer activities take place at the group level, and only a small number of activities are "community-oriented." These are carried out mainly by one organization—the center for runaways.

The data in Table 3 is not complete without taking into account the activities of the nonprofessionals within their own organization. The accumulated data in the field indicates that these activities may be included in the following categories:

1. Performing simple and routine tasks inside the organization office
2. Performing supervision and coordination activities
3. Taking part in planning activities and programs in the organization
4. Taking part in decision making
5. Introducing changes in the organization

Table 4 describes the involvement of the workers in each of the organizations by the above five categories of activity. In two of the categories (planning and decision making) a distinction is made between the workers' impact on their own work, and on the organization as a whole.

The table reflects several interesting trends. It appears that the workers have a considerable amount of discretion in handling their own

TABLE 3

The Range of Objectives, Clients and Targets Covered by Nonprofessionals in Each of the Organizations

	Individuals							Groups							Communities						
	PP	OEO	EX	MC	MH	SC	RC	PP	OEO	EX	MC	MH	SC	RC	PP	OEO	EX	MC	MH	SC	RC
I																					
1. Identification of a target	√	√	√					√		√				√				√	√	√	√
2. Information collection				√														√			
3. Assessment of problems and making recommendations			√		√		√	√		√											
II																					
4. Distribution of information	√	√	√	√	√		√	√	√	√	√	√		√		√		√	√		√
5. Establishment of linkages	√	√	√	√	√		√	√		√	√	√		√				√	√		√
6. Helping clients in contacts	√	√	√	√	√		√	√		√	√	√		√							
7. Delivery of resources	√	√	√	√	√		√	√		√	√	√		√							
8. Advocating	√	√	√	√	√		√	√		√	√	√		√							√
III																					
9. Education and teaching	√	√	√			√		√	√	√			√	√							√
10. Counseling			√		√		√							√							

Code: PP = Planned Parenthood
MC = Model Cities
RC = Runaways' Center
OEO = Office of Economic Opportunity
MH = Community Mental Health Center
EX = Extension Service
SC = Schools

TABLE 4

The Involvement of Workers in Activities at the Organizational Level

	PP	OEO	ES	MC	MH	SC	RC
1. Simple and routine tasks	✿	✿	✿	✿	✿	✿	✿
2. Supervising and coordination		✿			✿		✿
3. Planning							
A. In their own work	✿	✿	✿	✿	✿		✿
B. In the organization		✿	✿		✿		✿
4. Decision making							
A. In their own work	✿	✿	✿				✿
B. In the organization		✿	✿				✿
5. Introducing changes		✿					✿

activities in the field. Working within the basic framework of rules set up in each organization, the workers plan their daily activities, initiate new ones, and when facing clients, make decisions about the course of action that should be taken.

This independence in the field is not coupled with parallel activities at the organizational level. In only two settings, the center for runaways and co-op extension service, the workers translate ideas derived from their experiences with clients into the organizational planning and decision-making process. In another organization, the community mental health center, the nonprofessionals have an effect on the planning and decision-making processes occurring in the local settings where they work. They do not, however, influence the central bodies of the organization which set up its basic policy.

In O.E.S. the director, who is an indigenous worker, affects the planning and decision-making process. However, other nonprofessional staff members do not possess this capacity. Furthermore, the director himself is constrained by other factors, and his involvement in planning and decision making is quite limited.[20] These trends will be further explored by examining the third dimension: the location of nonprofessionals in the organization's hierarchy.

Table 5 shows that with the exception of the runaways' center which appears to be a special case in terms of the nonprofessionals' involvement in planning and decision-making activities, only one nonprofessional, the director of the O.E.O., occupies a position in the higher level of the organization. All the other workers are concentrated in the two lowest levels.

In O.E.O., as well as in three branches of the community mental health center, a considerable number of nonprofessionals are found in the second level, that is, in some kind of a supervisory or coordinating position. In the runaway center, the lower levels are occupied by volunteers (most of them nonprofessionals), while the permanent staff members are dispersed in the two higher levels of the organization.

TABLE 5
The Position of the Nonprofessional in the Organizations' Hierarchy

	PP	OEO	ES	MC	MH	SC	RC	Total
Fourth level	–	–	–	–	–	–	–	0
Third level	–	1	–	–	–	–	3	4
Second level	–	4	–	–	4	–	7	15
Lowest level	4	12	5	3	4	20	–	48

In sum it appears that mediating tasks in relation to clients and simple and routine tasks within the organization may be considered the common "core" of the indigenous workers' activities. Variations among organizations are actually related to the extent to which their non-professional workers perform additional activities beyond this "core": teaching and counseling clients, supervising and coordinating other workers, and participating in planning and decision-making processes. These additional activities allow workers to have a greater direct effect on the organization's behavior, and thereby to perform an "innovative" role.

Factors Affecting the Utilization of Nonprofessionals

In theorizing about the possible correlates between organizational characteristics and roles of nonprofessionals, it was proposed that agencies which vary in their internal structural characteristics, in their relationships with external groups, and in the attitudes of their executives, tend to utilize nonprofessionals differently and provide different opportunities for their involvement in innovative activities. The impact of each of these factors on the patterns of the nonprofessionals' utilization will now be examined in light of the results of the field study.

The effect of the organization's internal structure on the utilization of indigenous workers (Proposition 1)

Most of the organizations included in our study are characterized by a low level of structure and centralization. Yet in only two of them, the center for runaways and to some extent the co-op extension service, indigenous workers take part in organizational planning and decision making. In a third organization, the community mental health center, they participate in planning and decision making only at two of the organization's local settings but not in its central headquarters. Although the workers were allowed to manifest a certain degree of innovativeness in the way in which they act in the field in relation to their clients, they were not involved in the planning and decision making at the organizational level. An examination of the study data shows that three factors may explain this phenomenon. Two of them, lack of motivation among the indigenous workers themselves and the absence of appropriate organizational mechanisms designed to motivate and help them to perform innovative tasks, are mentioned in proposition 1. The third factor, the professionals' position, has been identified in this study.

Motivation of Indigenous Workers

The data on the basic role expectations of the indigenous workers show that their low degree of involvement in planning and decision making stems partly from their lack of motivation to engage in these activities. It appears that the "real" indigenous workers (that is, those who are poorly educated and have had very unstable occupational careers) possess a very limited range of expectations regarding their organizational roles, and they are satisfied with their roles in the organizations. In contrast, workers with higher educational achievements (those who have completed high school or one or two years in academic institutions) have a broader range of expectations and show interest in assuming innovative tasks at the organizational level. However, their number was very small, and they were concentrated mainly in one organization—the runaways' center. The hope that indigenous workers be able to change and innovate human service organizations ignores the possibility that people drawn from poor neighborhoods will often refrain from assuming such roles, and will tend instead to welcome conformists in the organization.

Organizational Guidance Mechanisms

Examination of the executives' attitudes shows that in four of the organizations, O.E.O., co-op extensions service, community mental health center, and the center for runaways, the executives wished to engage nonprofessionals in organizational planning and decision making in addition to their mediating roles. However, only in two of these organizations, the runaways' center and the co-op extension service, are these attitudes translated into practice. In these two settings, a close mutual relationship between the executives and the workers has enabled the indigenous workers to offer and convey ideas to higher organizational levels. In the other organizations, the lack of close contact between the directors and the indigenous workers, prevented the workers from contributing significantly to organizational decision making.

This finding runs contrary to the assumption that close contact between executives and workers is detrimental to workers' self-initiative and willingness to innovate. It shows that when these contacts do not serve solely as monitoring instruments or downward communicators, but are designed to establish close relationships with subordinates on a mutual basis, they may stimulate workers to raise new ideas and provide channels for communicating those ideas to higher organizational levels.

There is not necessarily a positive correlation between loose and remote supervision and innovative-oriented workers. On the contrary, in some organizations a lack of adequate guidance mechanisms deprives the nonprofessionals of incentives to formulate and convey new ideas based on their unique experiences.

The Effect of Professionals

When a highly decentralized organization employs a large number of professionals, they may have a decisive effect on the utilization of nonprofessionals. This situation is well reflected in the city public schools. In this setting, the nonprofessional aides working in teams with teachers are under very close professional control. The teachers, in fact, are authorized to use the aides according to their own needs and perceptions. The indigenous workers are thus denied the opportunity to construct their own roles or to influence certain facets of the educational system unless allowed or encouraged to do so by teachers or the school principal.

As the data indicate, the teachers do not encourage the aides to operate at the community or organization levels, as mediators or as change agents. Therefore, in organizations characterized by a large professional component, the professionals determine the scope of activities and targets covered by the indigenous workers.

The Effect of the External Organizational Relationships
(Proposition 2)

The executive directors in six of the organizations consider the mediating function as the main activity performed by nonprofessionals. They explain this position by pointing out the problems faced by their organizations in their attempts to gain access to certain segments in the population (individuals, groups, and communities). Indeed, it appears that in all the organizations, except the schools, the workers operate on behalf of their organizations among passive poor people, who have a variety of problems, are dispersed in different areas, and lack any sense of attachment to a "community" of people with similar problems. The main task assigned to the indigenous workers is to steer these people toward available services, and to help them to overcome bureaucratic blockages and constraints. Thus, facing a passive clientele, organizations tend to employ indigenous nonprofessionals in mediating roles.

The characteristics of the clients affect not only the approach toward the utilization patterns, but also the workers' own perception of their roles. In the absence of clear, direct guidance and of articulate self-role perception, the intense contact which the indigenous workers have with this kind of clientele plays a decisive part in forming their own attitude toward their role. One could postulate that working among individual clients having no sense of "community" will stimulate workers to emphasize individual-oriented mediating functions, while working among active cohesive groups or communities will stimulate them to stress functions designed to attain institutional change.

In summary, the examination of the effect of the clientele on the utilization of nonprofessionals indicates that in the absence of external stresses, neither the organizations nor the nonprofessionals tend to develop programs and mechanisms encouraging the indigenous workers to innovative activities at the organizational level.

Summary

The findings of this exploratory investigation seem to be important in the sense that they cast some doubt on the hope that indigenous nonprofessionals will revitalize and reinnovate human service organizations. It is found that most of them act as mediators, helping their organizations to improve communications with their existent clientele and to expand services to additional potential clients.

Several factors may explain this phenomenon: the absence of appropriate organizational mechanisms, the lack of motivation among the workers, the professionals' effect, and the absence of environmental pressures. However, the study provides only primary findings on the subject and it cannot be generalized beyond the boundaries of the cases encompassed. The next step in studying indigenous nonprofessionals' utilization should be to conduct a national empirical study embracing different kinds of agencies located in different contexts. The conceptual framework and the set of propositions developed in this exploratory study may guide such an undertaking.

Notes

1. See Yosef Katan, "The Utilization of Indigenous Nonprofessionals in Human Service Organizations and the Factors Affecting It—An Exploratory Study." A doctoral dissertation, University of Michigan, Ann Arbor, 1972.

2. For information on concrete use of nonprofessionals in social work settings before the emergence of the indigenous nonprofessionals movement see Morcella Farror and Mary L. Hemmy, "Use of Nonprofessional Staff in Work with the Aged." *Social Work* 8 (July, 1963):40–55. See also Lawra Epstein, "Differential Use of Staff: a Method to Expand Socio-Services." *Social Work* 7 (October, 1962):66–72.

3. See Carol H. Meyer, *Staff Development in Public Welfare Agencies* (New York: Columbia University Press, 1966).

4. See the United States Office of Economic Opportunity, *The Tide of Progress,* Washington, D.C., 1968.

5. See Morton Levine, "Trends in Professional Employment" in Edward Schwartz *Manpower in Social Welfare: Research Perspectives* (New York: National Association of Social Workers, 1964), pp. 12–16.

6. See Arthur Pearl and Frank Riessman, *New Careers for the Poor* (New York: The Free-Press, 1965).

7. See Robert Reiff and Frank Riessman *The Indigenous Nonprofessional. A Strategy of Change in Community Action and Community Mental Health Programs* (New York: National Institute of Labor Education, 1964).

8. See, for example, Louis Ferman *Job Development for the Hard to Employ,* Ann Arbor, University of Michigan, Institute of Labor and Industrial Relations, 1968.

9. See particularly Louis A. Coser, "The Sociology of Poverty." *Social Problems* (Fall, 1965:140–48.

10. Riessman, Frank, "The Helper Therapy Principle." *Social Work* 10 (April, 1965):27–32.

11. Numerous articles deal with this issue, see for example R. Cloward and I. Epstein, "Private Social Welfare Disengagement from the Poor: The Case of Family Adjustment Agencies" in George Broger and Francis Purcell, eds., *Community Action Against Poverty* (New Haven: College and University Press, 1967), pp. 40–63.

12. See Laura P. Houston, "Black People, New Careers and Human Services." *Social Casework* 511 (May, 1970):291–99.

13. See L. Rubin, "Maximum Feasible Participation, the Origins, Implementation and Present Status." *Poverty and Human Resources* 2 (November-December, 1967):5–8, and Ralph M. Kramer, *Participation of the Poor* (Englewood Cliffs, New Jersey: Prentice Hall), pp. 18–21.

14. Hage, Jerold, and Aiken, Michael, *Social Change in Complex Organizations* (New York: Random House, 1970).

15. See for instance Victor A. Thompson, "Bureaucracy and Innovation." *Administrative Science Quarterly* 10 (June, 1965):1–20.

16. See P. Selznick, *T.V.A. and the Grass-Roots* (Berkeley: University of California Press 1949).

17. Litwak, E., and Meyer, H. J., "A Balance Theory of Coordination between Bureaucratic Organizations and Primary Groups." *Administrative Science Quarterly* 11 (June, 1966):31–58.

18. Eisenstadt, S. N., "Bureaucracy, Bureaucratization and Rebureaucratization" in A. Etzioni, ed., *Complex Organizations* (New York: Holt, Rinehart and Winston, 1961).

19. For full details see Yosef Katan. *op. cit.*

20. *Ibid.*

Chapter VIII

Organization-Client Relations

The relationship between the organization and its clients serves to distinguish and illuminate differences between human service organizations and other types of formal organizations in several significant ways.

First, the nature of organization-client relations is crucial for the achievement of organizational goals. It is primarily through purposeful relations between staff and clients that human service organizations, particularly people-changing organizations, seek to achieve desired client changes. Hence, it is the content and quality of the relations between human service organizations and their clients that will largely determine the nature and the outcome of organizational services.

Second, unlike the clientele in other formal organizations, clients in human service organizations tend to assume multiple social roles. Not only are students, patients, and welfare clients, for example, the *recipients* of services, but they are also the *objects* that the organization attempts to change. And in many instances, clients become, albeit temporarily, members of the organization and perform crucial tasks in the overall operation of the organization (Rosengren and Lefton, 1970).

Third, since human service organizations tend to have a monopoly over the services they provide, their clients are frequently unable to "shop around," and are therefore more dependent upon the organization than clientele in other bureaucracies. This implies that clients in human service organizations potentially have little or no control over their fate in the organization. This is particularly the case whenever the client is involuntarily committed to the organization. For example, in correctional institutions and psychiatric hospitals, clients have little control over whether or not they shall remain as clients (Vinter, 1959, p. 265).

The potential imbalance in organization-client relations is further reinforced by the fact that most of the staff in human service organizations perform full-time occupational roles in the organization in contrast to clients who are only temporary members and whose involvement is at best segmental (Parsons, 1970). Obviously, the lack of client control over his fate in the organization will have the greatest consequences for those whose membership in the organization is of long duration, whose choices of service are limited or nonexistent, and those who have little or no control over the time span of their client status.

Inevitably, organization-client relations involve moral judgments of the staff about clients which may significantly influence the organizations' conception of clients and their problems, their career experiences within the organization, and their access to organizational resources. These moral judgments are based not only on the attributes associated with the clients' problems or needs, but also take into account many of their latent characteristics (i.e., socio-economic status, race, and ethnic identities).

If client cooperation, commitment and involvement are necessary for desired organization-client relations, then they must have adequate opportunities for making contributions. In general, we would agree, following Parsons (1970), that the greater the degree of equality in organization-client relations, the more likely the organization will be able to motivate and achieve client commitment for the desired change effort.

A review of the literature on organization-client relations indicates that the following conditions will contribute to the development of equality in organization-client relations: (1) the extent to which the organization is responsive to the reaction-potential of its clients in the determination and implementation of its service procedures (Lefton, 1970); (2) the extent to which there is positive staff identification with clients and their problems; (3) the extent to which clients have access to organizational resources, such as a "free choice" in the selection of professional personnel; (4) the extent to which the organization has limited control over the life space of the client; (5) the extent to which the client transacts with the organization in an organized manner (e.g., welfare rights organizations, inmate systems, student organizations) and; (6) the extent to which the organization's technology provides for a consideration of individualization and idiosyncratic attributes of its clients.

Throughout this chapter organization-client relations and staff-client relations have been used interchangeably. However, as Zald (1965:556) points out, clients may interact with one or more persons in human service organizations. For instance, in a private family service agency staff-client relations may only be organized around a single social worker and the client, while in a correctional institution or psychiatric hospital, staff-client relations typically require the inputs from many different levels of staff. In most cases, in order to mobilize client commitment to change and to execute organizational technology, the organization must coordinate a wide range of staff personnel in their relations with clients. It is in such cases that the client relates to the entire organization as a coordinated system of interaction and not solely to a single person.

The articles in this Chapter, therefore, take the organization-client system or one of its sub-parts as the focal point of analysis, and not the individual client or purveyor of services. Theoretical perspectives for conceptualizing organization-client relations and empirical studies which identify salient organizational variables that shape these relations are introduced.

Lefton and Rosengren provide a perspective of human service organizations which views the relationships between clients and organizations as critical determinants influencing organizational structure and functioning. These authors suggest that organizations may vary in their orientations toward clients along two dimensions. The first dimension refers to the range of organizational concern for the client's biographical space, and the second to the organization's interest in the time span of the client's biography. These authors then show how human service organizations differ in their orientations to clients along these two dimensions. They hypothesize that these orientations toward clients will significantly affect organizational structure, interpersonal processes and interorganizational relations.

The selection by Scott describes how incongruences between client problems and the needs of the organization significantly influence the distribution of services as well as the type of services a particular population of clients receive. He presents data on social service programs for the blind, and finds that unique environmental conditions and organizational needs for survival predispose these agencies to give precedence to their own problems over the needs of clients. As Scott demonstrates, human service organizations may attempt to optimize their own survival by selecting clients for which successful outcomes are highly probable, and/or those who possess attributes which the society highly values (i.e., youth, veterans of the armed services, middle-class social status).

Roth provides illustrative cases of how the hospital's lateral-longitudinal orientation toward clients significantly affects patient services. This occurs despite the fact that the hospital emergency service is a setting where relatively little background information is known about the client and the duration of organization-client relations is short-term. Roth demonstrates how moral judgments of clients by staff on a limited set of client attributes influence the quality of service they receive. These moral judgments, in fact, become significant determinants not only for the person's treatment, but also in evaluating his worthiness and ligitimacy as a patient.

In the selection by Rist, documentation is provided on a disturbing national dilemma which suggests how not to achieve equal educational opportunity. Although the implications of this study transcend the limited focus of this chapter, it serves to illuminate the dynamics of organization-client relations in a public school setting which have long-range and deleterious effects for the future careers of students. In this study of one classroom of black children from low-economic backgrounds, Rist demonstrates how a stratification system reflecting the larger societal values, emerges in the kindergarten years and persists throughout these students' first and second grade years. The social inequalities that exist in the larger society are introduced into the classroom through teacher expectations which significantly influence student performance. According to Rist once the student's performance becomes a part of the organization's record, it is used in such a way as to affect his future career in the organization. It is through this dynamic that self-fulfilling prophecies occur.

References

Lefton, M. 1970. "Client Characteristics and Structural Outcomes: Toward the Specification of Linkages." In William R. Rosengren and Mark Lefton (eds.) *Organization and Clients: Essays in the Sociology of Service*. Columbus, Ohio: Charles E. Merrill Publishing Company.

Parsons, T. 1970. "How Are Clients Integrated in Service Organizations?" In William R. Rosengren and Mark Lefton (eds.) *Organizations and Clients: Essays in the Sociology of Service*. Columbus, Ohio: Charles E. Merrill Publishing Company.

Rosengren, W. R. 1968. "Organizational Age, Structure, and Orientations Toward Clients." *Social Forces* 47 (September):1–11.

Vinter, R. D. 1959. "The Social Structure of Service." Pp. 242–69 in Alfred J. Kahn (ed.) *Issues in American Social Work*. New York: Columbia University Press.

Zald, M. N. (ed.). 1965. *Social Welfare Institutions: A Sociological Reader*. New York: John Wiley and Sons, Inc.

Organizations and Clients: Lateral and Longitudinal Dimensions

Mark Lefton and William R. Rosengren

This article sets forth a framework for the development of an analytic model of formal organizations which views the clients of organizations as integral factors influencing the structure and functioning of such systems. Three reasons are basic to this effort. Of first importance is the fact that our age is witness to a new phase in the organizational revolution, one which is marked by a phenomenal growth in the number, variety, and importance of formal organizations which serve people as persons, rather than catering exclusively to material needs and wishes. Second, this transition appears to involve a major shift in the criteria by which the operations of organizations must be evaluated.[1] That is, the substitution of what may be called "humanitarian" values for purely economic and administrative considerations will eventually demand organizational responsiveness to an ethic of service rather than to one of efficiency. The third consideration has to do with the fact that emphasis upon such issues as rational efficiency, internal structures of authority and control, and the maintenance of organizational autonomy, while of obvious importance for the sake of better understanding economic and administrative organizations, may be of less utility in the analysis of organizations concerned with the social and personal dilemmas of men. In addition, the existing conceptions of organizations may have to be broadened to cope with the inter-organizational demands engendered by large-scale action programs in the fields of human welfare.

There are four distinct traditions in organizational analysis, none of which, for different reasons, has yet codified the linkages between clients and formal organizational structure. The first of these is perhaps best represented by the work which owes its principal intellectual debt to Weber's original conception of bureaucracy as a form of legitimate authority.[2] The second includes those studies dealing with the impact of the demographic and ecological characteristics of the surrounding community upon the formal structure and functioning of organizations.[3] Third, the social system perspective focuses more upon the structural linkages by which the functional requisites of formal

Reprinted from *American Sociological Review* 31 (December, 1966):802–10.

organizations—seen as subsystems—are integrated with and accommodated to the institutional systems of the larger social order.[4] Finally, the fourth tradition in the study of organizations is represented by the symbolic interactionists.[5]

A diversity of organizational contexts have been examined from the perspective of Weber's ideal type, but the central focus has remained consistent with the bureaucratic model. The prime concern has been with the operating functionaries of organizations rather than with the clients they serve. The structural approach has yielded a large body of literature which compares and contrasts the formal properties of organizations with expectations derived from the ideal type.[6]

In contrast, the community structure approach has tended to focus either on cooptation, competition and other processes by which "publics in contact" are made congruent with organizational needs, or upon the manner in which organizations emerge as the demographic and ecological products of the host community.[7] A variant of this approach focuses specifically on the need for an organization to manipulate its incentive system in order to maintain the commitment of its members. Effort along these lines has attempted to link particular types of organizational incentive to varying "publics" and emphasize the strategic importance of examining an organization's sensitivity to changing motives as well as to environmental conditions.[8]

The social system approach, in its focus upon the systemic relations between organizations and the institutional sub-systems of which they are but a part, has tended to preclude a deliberate concern with the role of clients in organizations, precisely because of the level of analysis at which such concerns are generally expressed.

Finally, the symbolic interactionist approach leads to a conception of formal organizational structures and processes as having only secondary importance, providing only a contextual backdrop against which processes of self-identity, situational definitions, role emergence, and symbol verification are brought into bold relief.[9]

This brief discussion is designed to make one point: Insofar as they do not explicitly deal with the clients of organizations, the major traditions in organizational analysis remain conceptually divergent and substantially distinct.

Attempts to Relate Clients to Organizations. Congruent with the concerns indicated above, there has recently been an increased awareness on the part of several students of formal organizations of the need to regard clients as critical factors in organizational structure and functioning. For example, Parsons states: ". . . in the case of professional services there is another very important pattern where the recipient of the service becomes an operative member of the service-providing organization. . . . This taking of the customer *into* the organization has important implications for the nature of the organization."[10] But then the discussion is directed once again to a systemic analysis of the strategies by which organizations meet system-maintenance requisites without pursuit of the implications of the previous insight.

Blau and Scott explicitly identify some of the instances in which organizations might better be understood in the light of client characteristics. They say:

> It is perhaps a truism to say that organizations will reflect the characteristics of the publics they serve. A technical high school differs in predictable ways from a college preparatory school, and an upper-middle class church is unlike the mission church of the same denomination in the slums. While such differences seem to be important and pervasive, there has been little attempt to relate client characteristics systematically to organizational structures.[11]

It should be obvious that clients may present organizations with a wide range of characteristics. Any specific clientele characteristic may have a varying impact upon organizational functions, but only if such a characteristic is regarded as relevant. In this regard, organizations must select and define those client characteristics which are salient for their purposes. In a discussion of hospital structures, Perrow argues that hospitals belong to that class of organizations which attempt as their primary goal the alteration of the state of human material—such material being at once self-activating, subject to a multitude of orientations, "encrusted with cultural definitions," and embodying a wide range of organizational relevancies. Perrow then indicates the impacts that contrasting definitions of the client material are likely to have upon the technologies employed in hospitals and of their structural properties as well.[12]

The importance of contrasting definitions by organizations of the publics they serve, particularly for internal as well as external control processes, has been emphasized by Etzioni. From this perspective, a critical dimension in this respect derives from the confrontation between service as an ideology and service as an organizational instrument of manipulation and control.[13]

Another hint at the importance of clients is provided by Eisenstadt's discussion of debureaucratization. The client is here perceived as a scarce resource—a fact having implications for internal structure as well as for inter-organizational relationships. To the extent that the client does constitute a scarce resource upon which organizational survival depends, "the more (the organization) will have to develop techniques of communication and additional services to retain the clientele for services in spheres which are not directly relevant to its main goals."[14]

Finally, the symbolic interactionist tradition has recently been represented by the work of Glaser and Strauss. Their paradigm of "contexts of awareness" is designed to explain the interpersonal contingencies of dying in a hospital. A critical aspect of this scheme is the fact that staff and patients often interact in terms of very different definitions of the situation. They conclude that, ". . . in so much writing about interaction there has been much neglect or incomplete handling of *relationships* (italics ours) between social structure and interaction that we have no fear of placing too much emphasis upon those relationships . . . the course of interaction may partly change the social structure within which interaction occurs."[15]

Suggestive as these remarks are, their essentially descriptive character has precluded a realization of their points of convergence and their analytic potential. The purpose of the remainder of this study is to set forth a model of formal organizations with two uses: first, to provide a frame of reference which facilitates a synthesis of previous work dealing with clients and organizations; and second, to provide an analytical point of departure from which other hypotheses may be generated concerning relationships between organizations and their clients.

A Perspective Toward Clients and Organizations

Notwithstanding the apparently divergent interests in the works referred to above, a major theme is discernible, *viz.*, organizations have contrasting interests in their clients. Furthermore, these organizational interests in the "client biography" may vary along two major dimensions. First, such interests may range from a highly truncated span of time (as in the emergency room of a general hospital) to an almost indeterminate span of time (as in a long-term psychiatric facility or a chronic illness hospital). There is, moreover, a second range of interests which considers the client not in terms of biographical time, but rather in terms of biographical space. That is to say, some organizations may have an interest in only a limited aspect of the client as a person—as in the case of a short-term general hospital—whereas other organizations may have a more extended interest in who the client is as a product of and participant in society—as in the case of a psychiatric out-patient clinic.

The analytically important fact is that lateral and longitudinal interests in the biographical careers of clients may vary independently of one another. There are four logically different kinds of arrangements—each of which is likely to have significantly different impacts upon the internal structure and interpersonal processes of organizations, as well as upon extra-organizational relationships. The four biographical variants may be depicted as follows:

| | Biographical Interest | |
Empirical Examples	Lateral Social Space	Longitudinal (Social Time)
Acute general hospital	—	—
TB Hospital, Rehabilitation Hospital, Public Health Department, Medical School	—	+
Short-Term Therapeutic Psychiatric Hospital	+	—
Long-Term Therapeutic Hospital, Liberal Arts College	+	+

The logic of this typological system suggests that certain similarities ought to be found between those organizations manifesting a similar lateral interest in their clients, even though they may differ sharply in the extent of their longitudinal concern. Thus, for example, one would expect to find some structural similarities between a general hospital and a tuberculosis hospital, in spite of the fact that the latter has an extended longitudinal interest in the client, while the former does not. That is to say, the orientation of both institutions toward their clients, i.e., patients, is highly specific, focusing as each does upon relatively well-defined disease entities. Thus, though each organization may take account of such lateral life-space factors as occupation, family life, age, and sex, the relevance of these to the defined client problem is minimal. Conversely, those institutions which have a similar stake in the longitudinal careers of their clients should share some features in common despite possible marked differences along the lateral dimension. Thus, a long-term psychiatric hospital, for example, should logically resemble in some respects a tuberculosis hospital, even though the former has a broad lateral interest in the client, while the latter does not. And similarly, each of the four types should reflect some organizational characteristics which distinguish them.

Client Biographies and Issues of Compliance. One of the persisting theoretical issues in organizational analysis has to do with the strategies by which participants are made tractable to the internal needs of organizations.[16] This issue is of equal importance when the client becomes the focus of attention rather than the operative functionaries. The four types of client biographical interests outlined here appear to give rise to different kinds of control problems, and, therefore, to different structural arrangements for achieving compliance.

In utilizing the client as the point of departure by which to examine organizational dynamics, an immediate issue concerns the distinction between conformity and commitment as different modes of client compliance. In the former instance, clients' adherence to conduct rules in the organization is the key problem; in the latter the investment of the client in the ideology of the institution is at issue. These modes of compliance pose different organizational problems in each of the four types. Thus, the greater the laterality of the organization's interest in the client's biography, the greater is the variety of conduct alternatives on the part of the client which are regarded as organizationally relevant. This sets the stage for the emergence of contrasting control strategies. Conversely, those institutions with a minimal lateral interest in their clients are likely to be those in which the conformity of clients to organizational rules is of less concern. In extreme examples, in fact, conformity may be regarded as given and hence unproblematic, because of the physical structure of the institution, e.g., close security cells in custody prisons, or by the physical incapacitation of the client, e.g., quadriplegics in rehabilitation hospitals.

In the longitudinal institution, however, the compliance problem is of a somewhat different order since such organizations have a long-term commitment to the client's future biography which in some cases may extend beyond the time he will actually be physically present in the institution. In these circumstances, the re-arrangement of the client's future biography cannot be accomplished merely by the exercise of coercion. It would appear that for this type of institution the client is controlled by getting him to believe either in the moral goodness or in the practical fitness of the biography the organization is attempting to shape for him. This problem is often attacked by way of an elaborate ideology which the organization attempts to transmit to the client so that self-control is exercised once he is outside the physical confines of the institution.[17]

In terms of the client biography model, the patterns of conformity and commitment take the following shape:

Orientations Toward Clients		Compliance Problems	
Lateral	Longitudinal	Conformity	Commitment
—	—	No	No
+	+	Yes	Yes
—	+	No	Yes
+	—	Yes	No

In summary to this point: These problems of client control, which derive logically from a presumed differential institutional investment in the biographies of their clients (laterally and/or longitudinally), give rise to a series of different types of organizational problems and are attended by different modes of resolution.

Client Biographies and Problems of Staff Consensus. In addition to the contrasting problems of client conformity which derive from the model, the organization's concern with client biography also gives rise to contrasting problems of staff consensus. That is, organizations also may be described by the extent to which conflict between and among staff members is present with regard either to means or to ends. It is our contention that the patterns of consensus relevant to organizational means and ends are systematically related to laterally and longitudinality. Specifically, they take the following form:

Orientations Toward Clients		Difficulties Over Consensus	
Lateral	Longitudinal	Means	Ends
—	—	No	No
+	+	Yes	Yes
—	+	No	Yes
+	—	Yes	No

With respect to the non-lateral and non-longitudinal institution, the specificity of the orientation toward clients results in clear priorities and consensus as to the relative efficacy of different skills in the repair job to be done. Hence there is little ground for competing orientations to be developed. Similarly, this specificity of orientation and subsequent instant removal of the client implies that there is no compulsion to devise criteria or mechanisms for evaluating long-term outcome, the allocation of organizational resources for these purposes, nor need to establish boundaries to longitudinal responsibility.

This does not mean that stress and strain do not occur in the non-lateral/non-longitudinal organization. It means simply that they seldom become subject to *formal procedures*, but occur at the informal and extra-institutional level. Thus, claims for status are made by those whose place in the hierarchy of professional priorities is somewhere other than the top.[18] Informal negotiations are engaged in for scarce organizational resources. Power alignments develop among staff, involving agreement of a *quid pro quo* kind.[19] Moreover, such an institution is continually subject to pressures from outside, generally in the direction of pressing for greater laterality and longitudinality. Internally as well, informal negotiations develop regarding the ultimate goals and purposes of the institution, again in the direction of more broadly defining the goals of the establishment.

The most contrasting situation with regard to staff competition and conflict is to be found in the lateral and longitudinal organization, in which there is a heightened organizational response to the ubiquitous pressures for formal resolution which stem from the existence of diverse postures toward means and ends. In view of the felt need for official consensus regarding means and ends, such an organization continually devises officially established devices for making such resolutions. While the initial roots of conflict regarding means and ends may well emerge from within the context of the informal system of power alignments and personal negotiations, these issues are swifty legitimized and made subject to formal means of solution. Here is to be found a proliferation of formal systems of communication, specialized staff meetings, and increased attempts to make the organization conform to some popularized conception of bureaucracy. The not infrequent outcome is a repeated re-organization of the system of authority and decision-making, and continual addition of staff personnel with finely discriminated skills and techniques. In short, the lateral-longitudinal organization involves a continually changing formal system of authority, with a conflict culture the content of which is co-opted into the formal system.

Although there are other obvious consequences of laterality and longitudinality for the internal structure and dynamics of organizations, we turn now to a consideration of some of their consequences for one type of inter-organizational dilemma, namely, collaborative relations between organizations.

Client Biographies and Inter-Organizational Collaboration. It is useful to make the distinction between formal and informal processes of inter-organizational collaboration. We shall define formal processes as those ways in which members of organizations engage in collaboration *in their capacities as members of the organization.* By informal we mean those ways of collaborating which involve either an *intervening* organization, e.g., a professional association, or those in which the collaborators act in some capacity other than as organizational members, e.g., a voluntary community organization. Finally, we emphasize the importance of the distinction between administrative-financial concerns as compared with collaboration involving operational facilities. It seems reasonable to argue that these modes of inter-organizational collaboration are also systematically related to the character of the organization's interest in the client's biography. With respect to these distinctions we suggest specifically that the four types of organizations differ in their *propensities* for kinds of collaboration.

Orientations Toward Clients		Modes of Collaboration			
		Formal		Informal	
Lateral	Longitudinal	Operating	Admin.	Operating	Admin.
—	—	No	No	Yes	Yes
+	+	Yes	Yes	No	No
—	+	Yes	No	No	Yes
+	—	No	Yes	Yes	No

The non-lateral/non-longitudinal organization (the acute general hospital, for example), typically has little propensity for formal collaboration at either the administrative or operating levels. The specificity of its interest in the client and its concern with discriminating strategies of care tend to make such organizations isolated professional islands in the community.[20] Moreover, while this situation may result in the efficient operation of separate institutions, such efficiency does not necessarily extend to the community as a whole. In fact, the reverse may indeed be true—that is, the very efficiency of separate institutions may imply duplication of expensive services such as a cobalt machine, and may thus be detrimental for the needs of the community which they independently serve.[21]

In addition, because they do have a truncated longitudinal interest in their clients, such organizations need not devise strategies to follow their departed clients. "Checking" on clients requires the development of administrative mechanisms for getting information from other organizations which may later be responsible for the welfare of the client. In addition, such organizations normally stand as splendid pillars of financial isolation in the community, with little need (or capacity) to develop "master plans" with other organizations.[22] But again, this is only at the formal level; such organizations are involved in networks of informal relationships. In the case of the general hospital, for example, such networks may extend through the local medical society and health insurance programs in the community as well as to the local community power structure. We do not mean that the non-lateral/non-longitudinal organization does not engage in collaboration, but only that control of the kind and extent of collaboration has been co-opted by extra-organizational agencies.

On the other hand, the lateral-longitudinal organization stands as the most contrasting type. The long-term therapeutically oriented psychiatric institutional, for example, is customarily involved in a massive and sometimes conflicting set of administrative and operating linkages at both the formal and the informal level. The wide range of professional personnel it utilizes tends to extend their professional contacts into other similarly organized institutions. Further, the fact of a longitudinal interest in the client's future biography means that the organization must devise ways of establishing working relationships with other organizations which may ultimately be held responsible for the later career of the client. Thus one is likely to find that the non-lateral/non-longitudinal organization (hospital or not) has no established linkages with the juvenile court, nursing homes, family welfare agencies, the probation office, and so forth, while the administrative personnel in the longitudinal institution are often intimately tied in with a wide range of other interested institutions.[23]

In sum, there appear to be variable relations between an organization's structural extensions in time and space toward other organizations, and its functional commitments to the client.

For purposes of this article, we shall not pursue the other two types. It is rather more strategic on both theoretical and practical grounds to consider what is likely to happen when two organizations of the same type or of sharply divergent types are faced with a potential collaborative relationship. We would expect that a similarity in laterality or longitudinality would be likely to enhance formal collaboration, while contrasting types would be inhibited in collaboration and even experience open conflict.

In the field of rehabilitation, for example, one may find illustrations of these divergent types. Deliberately contrived programs of collaboration involving the consolidation of different rehabilitation agencies, such as organizations for the blind, the mentally retarded, or the physically handicapped, often founder at the operational level. This situation may be explained by the fact that rehabilitation agencies are differentially committed to the lateral careers of their clients. What appears to account for the collaborative effort in the first place is their common interest in the longitudinal dimensions of the client biography. The logical outcome of this duality leads to harmony in terms of effective dialogue at the administrative level but to a great deal of conflict and stress at the operational level. Furthermore, this condition may become characterized over time by elaborate administrative superstructures rather than by operational effectiveness.[24]

These illustrations point to but a few of the logical outcomes for collaboration problems between organizations which stem from the client biography model herein considered. We would expect that the nature of the analysis indicated would also be relevant and useful for an understanding of the organizational dilemmas encountered by such agencies as public health facilities, custodial and punishment-centered institutions, schools, and other client-oriented organizations.

Summary and Conclusion. The client biography model discussed in this article provides a framework conducive to a more systematic linkage between four major, but often divisive, orientations associated with organizational analysis; namely, the classical bureaucratic, the systemic, the communal, and the symbolic interactionist traditions. The importance of this potential is underscored by the fact that although sociologists are generally aware of the need to better integrate these orientations, attempts to do so have tended to remain implicit and have failed to specify the theoretical link between clients and organizations. This is not to say that the importance of clients in organizations has been overlooked—the point to be emphasized is that existing theories have not incorporated client characteristics in the propositions with which they deal.

The conception of relations between organizations and their clients as varying along the lateral and longitudinal dimensions may be regarded as an initial step toward just such a synthesis.

Notes

1. Warren Bennis, "Beyond Bureaucracy," *Transaction* 2 (July-August, 1965) pp. 31–35.
2. See, for example, T. R. Anderson and S. Warkov, "Organizational Size and Functional Complexity: A Study of Administration in Hospitals," *American Sociological Review* 26 (February, 1961): 23–28; Peter M. Blau, *The Dynamics of Bureaucracy*, Chicago: University of Chicago Press, 1955; Amitai Etzioni, *A Comparative Analysis of Complex Organizations*, New York: The Free Press of Glencoe, 1961; Alvin Gouldner, *Patterns of Industrial Bureaucracy*, Glencoe: The Free Press, 1954.

3. For example, Ivan Belknap and J. Steinle, *The Community and Its Hospitals*, Syracuse: Syracuse University Press, 1963; Ray H. Elling, "The Hospital Support Game in Urban Center," in Eliot Freidson, ed., *The Hospital in Modern Society*, Glencoe: The Free Press, 1963; Basil Georgopoulous and F. Mann, *The Community General Hospital*, New York: Macmillan Co., 1962; Delbert Miller, "Industry and Community Power Structure: A Comparative Study of an American and an English City," *American Sociological Review* 23 (February, 1958):9–15; Harold W. Pfautz and G. Wilder, "The Ecology of a Mental Hospital," *Journal of Health and Human Behavior* 3 (Summer, 1962):67–72; Stanley Lieberson, "Ethnic Groups and the Practice of Medicine," *American Sociological Review* 23 (October, 1958):542–549.

4. Philip Selznick, "Foundations of the Theory of Organizations," *American Sociological Review* 13 (February, 1948):25–35; *TVA and The Grass Roots*, Berkeley: University of California Press, 1953; Talcott Parsons, "Suggestions for a Sociological Approach to the Theory of Organizations," *Administrative Science Quarterly* 1 (June, 1956):63–85.

5. For example, J. Bensman and I. Gerver, "Crime and Punishment in the Factory," in A. Gouldner and H. Gouldner, eds., *Modern Society*, New York: Harcourt Brace and World, 1963, pp. 593–596; Barney Glaser and Anselm Strauss, *Awareness of Dying*, Chicago: Aldine Press, 1965; Erving Goffman, *The Presentation of Self in Everyday Life*, Edinburgh: University of Edinburgh Press, 1956; Julius Roth, *Timetables*, Indianapolis: Bobbs-Merrill, 1963.

6. For example, Michel Crozier, *The Bureaucratic Phenomenon*, Chicago: University of Chicago Press, 1964; Eugene Haas, R. Hall and N. Johnson, "The Size of Supportive Components in Organizations," *Social Forces* 42 (October, 1963): 9–17; Robert Merton, "Bureaucratic Structure and Personality," in *Social Theory and Social Structure*, Glencoe: The Free Press, 1949, pp. 151–160; Melvin Seeman and J. Evans, "Stratification and Hospital Care: I. The Performance of the Medical Interne, *American Sociological Review* 26 (February, 1961):67–80; Arthur Stinchcombe, "Bureaucratic and Craft Administration of Production," *Administrative Science Quarterly* 4 (September, 1959):168–187; Stanley Udy, Jr., "Bureaucratic Elements in Organizations: Some Research Findings," *American Sociological Review* 23 (August, 1958):415–418.

7. For example, Blau and Scott *op. cit.*, especially chapter 3, "The Organization and Its Publics," pp. 59–86; Burton R. Clark, *The Open Door College*, New York: McGraw-Hill, 1960; Charles Perrow, "Goals and Power Structures: A Historical Case Study," in Eliot Freidson, ed., *op. cit.*, pp. 112–146; Erwin Smigel, "The Impact of Recruitment on the Organization of the Large Law Firm," *American Sociological Review* 25 (February, 1960):56–66; James D. Thompson and W. McEwen, "Organizational Goals and Environment: Goal Setting as an Interaction Process," *American Sociological Review* 23 (February, 1958):23–31.

8. The classic discussion of this issue is found in James March and H. Simon, *Organizations*, New York: John Wiley, 1958; a specific statement of the relationship between incentives and organizational types is found in Peter B. Clark and J. Q. Wilson, "Incentive Systems: A Theory of Organizations," *Administrative Science Quarterly* 6 (September, 1961):129–166.

9. For example, Fred Davis, "Definitions of Time and Recovery in Paralytic Polio Convalescence," *American Journal of Sociology* 61 (May, 1956):582–587; Barney Glaser and Anselm Strauss, "Temporal Aspects of Dying as a Non-Scheduled Status Passage," *American Journal of Sociology* 71 (July, 1965):48–59; Erving

Goffman, "The Moral Career of the Mental Patient," in *Asylums*, New York: Double-day, 1961, pp. 125–170; Erving Goffman, *The Presentation of Self in Everyday Life*, Edinburgh: University of Edinburgh Press, 1956.

10. Talcott Parsons, "Suggestions for a Sociological Approach to the Theory of Organizations," in Etzioni, ed., *Complex Organizations: A Sociological Reader*, New York: Holt, Rinehart and Winston, 1961, pp. 39–40.

11. Blau and Scott, *op. cit.*, p. 77.

12. Charles Perrow, "Hospitals: Technology, Structure and Goals," in James March, ed., *Handbook of Organizations*, Chicago: Rand-McNally, 1965, pp. 650–677.

13. Amitai Etzioni, *Modern Organizations*, Englewood Cliffs: Prentice-Hall, 1964, p. 94.

14. S. N. Eisenstadt, "Bureaucracy, Bureaucratization, and Debureaucratization," in Etzioni, *Complex Organizations: A Sociological Reader*, p. 276.

15. Glaser and Strauss, *Awareness of Dying, op. cit.*, p. 284.

16. Amitai Etzioni, "Organizational Control Structure," in James March, ed., *Handbook of Organizations, op. cit.*, pp. 650–677.

17. A dimension of clients in organizations which is not pursued here has to do with the intrinsic content of the socialization process and its effects upon the individual. A major issue along these lines has to do with the consequences of con-formity for behavior expectations on the one hand, and for the internalization of values on the other. See, for example, Robert Dubin, "Deviant Behavior and Social Structure," *American Sociological Review* 24 (April, 1959):147–164; and Irving Rosow, "Forms and Functions of Adult Socialization," *Social Forces* 44 (September, 1965):35–45.

18. One of the key organizational issues which stems from lateral interests, particularly in psychiatric institutions, has to do with the presumption of rank-equality among clinical staff. See for example, Milton Greenblatt, R. York, and E. Brown, *From Custodial to Therapeutic Patient Care in Psychiatric Hospitals*, New York: Russell Sage Foundation, 1955; Mark Lefton, S. Dinitz and B. Pasamanick, "Decision-Making in a Mental Hospital: Real, Perceived, and Ideal," *American Sociological Review* 24 (December, 1959):822–829; Robert Rapoport and Rhona Rapoport, "Democratization and Authority in a Therapeutic Community," *Behavioral Sciences* 2 (April, 1957):128–133; William Rosengren, "Communication, Organiza-tion, and Conduct in the 'Therapeutic Milieu'," *Administrative Science Quarterly* 9 (June, 1964):70–90.

19. For example, Richard McCleery, "Authoritarianism and the Belief Sys-tem of Incorrigibles," in D. Cressey, ed., *The Prison: Studies in Institutional Orga-nization and Change*, New York: Holt, Rinehart and Winston, 1961, pp. 260–306; William R. Rosengren and S. DeVault, "The Sociology of Time and Space in an Obstetrical Hospital," in Freidson, *op. cit.*, pp. 266–292; Anselm Strauss, *et al.*, "The Hospital and Its Negotiated Order," in E. Freidson, ed., *op. cit.*, pp. 147–169.

20. See, for example, Ray Elling, "The Hospital Support Game in Urban Center," in Freidson, *op. cit.*, pp. 73–112; Oswald Hall, "The Informal Organization of the Medical Profession," *Canadian Journal of Economics and Political Science* 12 (February, 1946):30–44.

21. For example, J. H. Robb, "Family Structure and Agency Co-ordination: De-centralization and the Citizen," in Mayer N. Zald, *Social Welfare Institutions: A Sociological Reader*, New York: John Wiley, 1965, pp. 383–399; Oliver Williams, *et al.*, *Suburban Differences and Metropolitan Policies: A Philadelphia Story*, Phila-delphia: University of Pennsylvania Press, 1965.

22. See, for example, Charles V. Willie and Herbert Notkin, "Community Organization for Health: A Case Study," in E. Gartley Jaco, *Physicians, Patients, and Illness*, Glencoe: The Free Press, 1958, pp. 148–159.

23. For example, Sol Levine and P. White, "Exchange as a Conceptual Framework for the Study of Interorganizational Relationships," *Administrative Science Quarterly* 5 (March, 1961):583–601; Eugene Litwak and L. Hylton, "Interorganizational Analysis," *Administrative Science Quarterly* 6 (March, 1962):395–420; J. V. D. Saunders, "Characteristics of Hospitals and of Hospital Administrators Associated with Hospital-Community Relations in Mississippi," *Rural Sociology* 25 (June, 1960):229–232; James D. Thompson, "Organizations and Output Transactions," *American Journal of Sociology* 68 (November, 1962):309–324.

24. A clear example of this process can be discerned in the recent history of the National Mental Health Association. A short time ago this existed merely as a loosely held together congeries of autonomous, local mental health societies. Some of these groups were laterally and others non-laterally committed to their clientele. However, they shared in common a longitudinal interest in the careers of locally-defined client groups. The original move toward official collaboration came through the New York office and has persisted at the administrative and fund-raising level. It has now reached the point where most of the originally autonomous local societies provide little or no service to clients. They function merely as linkages in a nation-wide administrative system. It should be added, lastly, that this decline of service functions and preeminence of administrative functions had also resulted in a dramatic shift in the sources of recruitment and staffing patterns of these organizations.

The Selection of Clients by Social Welfare Agencies: The Case of the Blind

Robert A. Scott

The purpose of social welfare is to promote the social betterment of a class or group of people who are defined as disadvantaged, handicapped, or deprived. A set of common problems are attributed to such persons based upon the nature of the trait or quality which sets them apart from the rest of society. Programs of social welfare are then planned to meet the needs which arise out of these problems.

It is believed that the form and content of such programs should be determined by the needs of the client. As his needs change, the programs themselves must change; conversely, the welfare of the client should be the primary factor to consider in making any policy decisions about changes in such programs.

In reality, other factors also exert a determining influence on

Reprinted from *Social Problems* 14 (Winter, 1967):248–57.

social welfare programs. These factors are at least as important for setting policy as the clients' welfare and at times may even supersede it.
Many such factors have been identified by other investigators.[1] Two
are especially important. First, welfare services are characteristically
distributed in our society through private philanthropy or government at
its federal, state, and local levels. These programs are ordinarily incorporated in large-scale bureaucratic structures. As such, they are subject
to the pressures and forces common to all complex bureaucracies. The
preservation of the organization itself is a vital factor in setting program
policy; and standardization based upon the criteria of efficiency, production, and costs is often applied to services which are intended to
meet highly personal human needs.

Second, welfare programs must rely upon the public for their
support, whether through legislative appropriation or private fund
raising efforts. The availability of services depends, at least in part, upon
the kinds of support which the benefactors of welfare are willing to provide. When the benefactors are the body politic, funds will ordinarily be
made available for only those programs which the legislators believe are
politically tenable to support. When the benefactors come from the
private sector of society, the kinds of programs they are willing to support depend upon their personal conception of the nature of the problems of disadvantaged groups, and what they imagine constitutes a
desirable and moral solution. In either case, such conceptions are generally responsive to broad cultural themes and values, especially those
of youth, work, hope, contentment, and personal fulfillment.

At times, the personal welfare of the client, the needs of the
bureaucratic structures through which services are supplied, and the
benefactors' definition of the problems of the disadvantaged persons will
coincide. Ordinarily these factors will coincide when the client possesses
valued cultural attributes (e.g., youth, intelligence) and when valued
cultural goals (e.g., employment, independence) are realistically attained for him. More often, however, these forces do not coincide; they
may even conflict. Consequently, the public, whether through legislative
bodies or private donations, may be unwilling to support programs for
individuals with personal characteristics which are culturally devalued,
although such individuals may be the majority of the disadvantaged
group. From the point of view of organizational maintenance, it may be
untenable to undertake extensive service programs for persons who,
by virtue of their disability and other characteristics, may be unable to
make a productive contribution to the society, even though they represent a majority of those who need service programs.

Social welfare programs are, therefore, set within and responsive to a variety of organizational and community pressures, which are highly determinative of program policy and implementation. By contrast, the problems of the recipient group ordinarily are caused by factors which are entirely unrelated to those which work upon the welfare agencies. The causes of the specific problems, and therefore the needs of a handicapped person, are not the same factors which determine what kinds of welfare services are offered to them. Clients' needs and the kinds of available welfare services run in two separate orbits, which may coincide only at certain points. It cannot be assumed, therefore, that the services which are offered apply to all persons who belong to the disadvantaged group, nor can it be assumed that the persons who receive services are necessarily benefited by them.

These facts suggest a number of questions for research about the relationships between social welfare service programs, and the welfare problems of persons to whom the services are directed. First, it is necessary to determine the amount of congruence between services required by a disadvantaged group and those available to them. Second, it is necessary to determine the amount of congruence between persons who are in need of services and those who in fact receive them through existing structures. Finally, it is necessary to determine the consequences for a disadvantaged person of receiving services in existing welfare programs.

The purpose of this paper is to provide data related to the latter two questions, by examining one type of social welfare program: services for the blind. I will compare existing services in this field to the population of blind persons, in order to identify what, if any, discrepancies exist in the present distribution of services. This will be done by describing the demographic properties of the blind population of the United States at the present time; and the corresponding distribution and properties of agencies which serve it. From these data, I will also examine some of the consequences for an individual, both for himself and in relation to the community, of receiving welfare services through existing agencies.

While the remainder of this discussion will specifically deal with agencies for the blind, my remarks apply with equal cogency to many types of welfare agencies, and especially to those which provide social services to persons possessing stigmatized and unimprovable deviant qualities.[2]

Demographic Characteristic of the Blind

Approximately 955,000 persons in the civilian, non-institutionalized population of the United States under the age of 80 are blind.[3] There are a number of significant facts about the blind population. First, a majority of them are elderly. Sixty-six per cent are between the ages of 55 and 80; another 15 per cent are in the age group of 45–54; 17 per cent of all blind persons are in the age group of 18–44; and only about 2 per cent are children under 18. According to these data, two thirds of all blind persons are in age groups where retirement is either pending or a reality, and only a small minority of blind persons are in age groups where either employment or education is realistic.

Second, blindness is much more common in women than in men.[4] Seven out of ten cases of blindness occur in women, and in all age groups there are more blind women than blind men, although the sex difference is greatest in the older age groups. Taking the factors of age and sex together, one half of all cases of blindness are among women 55 years of age and older; another 20 per cent of the cases of blindness occur among women in the age group of 18–54. Elderly men account for 18 per cent of all cases, and only 12 per cent of the cases of blindness occur among men 18–54.[5]

Third, blindness is comparatively rare among children. There are estimated to be only about 27,000 blind children in the United States at the present time.[6] The blindness rate among children is only .35 per 1,000 of the population. In contrast, the rate for elderly persons is about 33 per 1,000 of the population.

Finally, the term "blindness" refers both to those who are completely without vision and to those who have severe visual impairments but who can see. Only a small number of blind persons are in fact totally blind; a majority of them have some measurable visual acuity. The available data suggest that there is a direct relationship between the amount of visual loss and age.[7] The older a blind person is, the more serious his visual loss is likely to be.

The adequacy and effectiveness of welfare programs can be judged in many ways. One such measure, which will be used in this paper, concerns their completeness. By this I mean the degree to which welfare services are provided for all or most segments of the population in need. From this point of view, service programs for the blind may be regarded as adequate insofar as they reflect, in a general way, the composition of the blind population; correspondingly, they may be regarded as inadequate insofar as they apply only to special segments of the blind population.

It is recognized that this point of view is not commonly accepted among workers for the blind. They have argued that it is more worthwhile to supply services to those blind persons for whom there is the greatest expectation of success. Accordingly, it is held that resources are more wisely devoted to the education and training of blind children than to the care of elderly blind adults; and that it is more logical to aid the employable blind than those who are not employable. This argument is based on the assumption that resources for supporting service programs are limited, and that it is therefore necessary to establish these priorities. In reality, this assumption is generally incorrect in view of the fact that enormous sums of money are expended annually for services to the blind (for further information on this point, see footnote 16). The argument also contains an erroneous implication: that there is a correspondence between the way in which an individual experiences problems of blindness and the priority which his problems are assigned by the criteria of real or imagined economic and social factors. Because there are economic and social reasons why the problems of blind children might receive priority in service programs, we cannot assume that the older blind person experiences his problems as less serious.

If services for the blind roughly reflect the age and sex distribution of the blind population, then we can expect to find a major portion of the financial and manpower resources of this field invested in programs designed to meet the needs of those who are not expected to be self-supporting, and more particularly of the elderly. Conversely, we would expect that only a small portion of those resources would be invested in programs for educating and training children and employable adults. An analysis of services for the blind in this country reveals that the situation is exactly the opposite.

I made a study of the programs of all direct service agencies listed in a substantially complete directory of agencies for the blind in this country.[8] Seven hundred and ninety-eight separate agencies were identified, 274 of which are private and 520 governmental. Only 9 per cent (71) of these agencies are concerned exclusively with elderly blind persons. By contrast, 67 per cent (529) of the agencies have programs intended primarily for children and employable adults. The remaining 23 per cent (187) are "mixed" agencies, which offer services to blind persons of all ages. The remaining one per cent (11) do not offer direct services to the blind.

An analysis was made of programs in the 71 agencies and organizations which serve elderly blind persons exclusively. There are 21 domiciles which house and care for about 1,000 elderly blind persons. The remainder of these organizations are state offices responsible for administering the federal-state program of aid to the needy blind. In the mixed agencies, programs for the elderly are almost exclusively recreational, ranging from organized recreational programs to drop-in daytime clubs.

One hundred and thirty-four separate agencies serve blind children exclusively, and 395 agencies have programs primarily concerned with vocational rehabilitation and employment. Although mixed agencies do offer some recreational services to elderly blind persons, the primary emphasis of their programs is unmistakably on children and employable adults. Of the 187 mixed agencies, only a few have a separate division for the elderly blind; by contrast there are almost none which do not have a children's division or a division for employable adults.

These data show a clear bias in work for the blind in favor of children and employable adults and against elderly blind persons. About 90 per cent of agencies in work for the blind place exclusive or primary emphasis upon serving less than one third of the blind population; and only 9 per cent of the agencies are seriously concerning themselves with the bulk of blind persons.

Another important fact is not apparent from these data. Existing programs are not geared to serve all blind persons in a given age group. Numerous services are available for the child who is educable, but there are almost no services for the multiply handicapped child. There are many services for the blind person who is thought to be employable, but few for the one who is thought to be untrainable or for whom employment is an unrealistic goal. Recreation programs for elderly blind persons are located in the agency itself, so that only those older blind persons who are mobile and independent enough to travel can take advantage of them. In effect, programs are geared to serve selected blind persons, and usually those who enjoy the highest probability for success; conversely, most service programs are ill-equipped to assist those for whom success is unlikely.

This systematic bias of work for the blind in favor of young blind children and employable blind adults, and the corresponding neglect of older blind persons, is reflected in another way—in the literature of work for the blind. An analysis was made of all articles which appeared in the *New Outlook for the Blind* (the principal professional journal of that field) from 1907 to 1963. This study showed that out of 1,069 articles, 36 per cent dealt with children, 31 per cent with rehabilitation, 15 per cent with braille reading, 17 per cent with specific services such as mobility, 21 per cent with employment, and only 2 per cent with geriatric problems. In short, 70 per cent of the blind population (the elderly) received only 2 per cent of the attention of writers in the major professional journal in work for the blind; whereas less than 30 per cent of the population (children and employable adults) were discussed in 98 per cent of the analyzed articles.

The reasons for the proliferation of services for a limited segment of the blind population are numerous and complex. I will try to discuss the most significant ones here. First, the same concepts which guided the pioneers of work for the blind 125 years ago make up a large part of contemporary theory. The demographic characteristics of the blind population then differed in several important ways from the present population. The number of persons in the general population who survived childhood and lived to old age was low, and the number of elderly blind persons was therefore correspondingly small.[9] A major cause of blindness in the adult population at that time was industrial accidents.[10] Ordinarily the eyes were the only organs involved, so that adult blind persons were healthy working people whose only handicap was blindness. Substantial numbers of children were blinded at birth because of diseases which specifically affected the eyes.[11]

Because a majority of the blind in the late nineteenth century were children and adults of working age, the concepts in this field stressed education and employment. Through the years, these concepts have not changed in response to changing social, economic, and public health conditions. In addition, workers for the blind have implicitly assumed that these problems of education and employment are inherent to the condition of blindness. They have mistaken these concepts for the problem of blindness itself. The blind to whom the concepts cannot be easily applied are viewed by workers as marginal to the "real work" in services for the blind. This work is believed to be educational and vocational; services for elderly, unemployable, or uneducable blind individuals are regarded as marginal activities. Education and employment are viewed as the only alternative solutions to the problems of the blind. If a person cannot benefit from either service, his problems are defined as unsolvable, and his case is closed. Consequently, elderly blind persons, the multiply handicapped, and the unemployable are considered apart from the "real problems" of blindness, because workers for the blind continue to employ archaic concepts in their service approach.

This tendency to employ archaic concepts can be viewed as a specific instance of a more general tendency by workers for the blind to resist any innovation or change in service programs. In the history of this field, there has been a characteristic and stubborn resistance to the adoption of any mechanical aids, educational devices, or concepts which in any way deviate from the status quo.[12] This tendency is itself a function of a complex set of factors, the nature of which can be only briefly delineated in this article. Essentially work for the blind is a low-prestige profession, one of that category of occupations called "dirty work."[13] Because the stigma associated with blindness may inadvertently rub off on workers for the blind,[14] this field is unable to attract the top persons in such fields as social work, psychiatry, psychology, education, ophthamology, and rehabilitation. In fact, in work for the blind, there is an unusual opportunity for individuals with very little formal training to attain positions of great power and responsibility.

This phenomenon has had many consequences for the field, one of which is a tendency to resist change. Many leaders in this field have power which derives from the agencies they control, and from their acquired expertise in certain specific service programs such as braille, mobility, rehabilitation, employment, or education. They lack generic professional training; consequently, it is difficult for them to move from one type of service program for the blind to another, or from services for the blind to services for other types of handicapped persons. Their expertise is highly specialized and is acquired by hard experience. Because of these limitations, little is transferable from traditional services to new ones which are proposed. Consequently, when changes are attempted in existing programs and agencies, such persons are faced with a major loss in power, status, and income. It would be impossible for them to secure comparable positions outside agencies for the blind because assignment to such positions would be based upon formal credentials such as education, rather than upon their specialized skills and acquired status in the field. The person with only a high school education who holds a powerful position in an agency for the blind stands to lose a great deal if that agency changes in any substantial way. Therefore, workers for the blind have traditionally had more intense commitment to the agencies they have built than to the persons whom they serve.[15] Concomitantly, they have tried to maintain the traditional base upon which their power rests and to rationalize these efforts by traditional concepts and theories of the field.

Another cause of client selectivity in service programs for the blind is the fact that agencies are dependent upon the public for financial support. All but a few private agencies rely upon fund-raising appeals to finance their programs, and public agencies are entirely dependent upon annual appropriations from state legislatures and from Congress. In either case, agencies for the blind are in stiff competition with one another, and with hundreds of other charities, for a share of the public's philanthropic dollars.

In this competitive situation, the success of fund-raising campaig s depends upon strong emotional appeals on behalf of the needy. In their fund-raising campaigns, agencies for the blind exploit a certain number of cultural stereotypes in our society. These stereotypes concern blindness, youth, work, and hope. The images of blind persons which are projected in these campaigns are either those of educable children, or of young, employable adults, who can be helped to overcome a serious handicap to become materially productive.[16] These appeals, therefore, leave the unmistakable but erroneous impression that blind people are young, intelligent persons who can be educated and employed. The public has come to expect results which are measurable in these terms. This consequence intensifies the agencies' search for the few blind people who in fact have these personal attributes.

At the same time, agencies are extremely reluctant to begin programs for other groups of blind persons unless there is good reason to believe that these programs will be supported by the public. It is assumed that appeals for funds to help persons from whom only modest gains can be expected, such as elderly blind persons and multiply handicapped children or adults, will not succeed in offsetting the costs of such programs. It has been argued by the agencies that funds obtained through appeals on behalf of blind children and employable adults can be partly diverted to support programs for other groups of blind persons. However, programs for children and employable adults involve enormous capital investments. These investments require increasing sums of money annually for maintenance and growth purposes. One consequence, therefore, of successful fund raising has been that more and more money is needed simply to keep programs going.

I have compared the distribution of services for the blind in this country to the demographic characteristics of the blind population, and I have tried to indicate some of the reasons there is such a discrepancy between them. Now I want to consider another question—the avowed purpose of all programs for the blind to help the individual blind person to function as independently as he can. The question therefore arises, "What is the actual impact of agency programs upon those blind persons who do receive services?"

Since there are only about 950,000 blind persons in the entire country, the number of visually impaired individuals living in any particular geographical area is usually quite small. It is estimated that there are only about 40,000 to 50,000 blind persons in all of New York City, only about 10,000 in Philadelphia, and only about 14,000 blind persons in the Boston metropolitan area.[17] Yet, there are over 700 separate agencies and organizations for the blind in this country, a majority of which are situated in large urban areas. New York City has 50 separate organizations for the blind, 38 of which offer direct services; Philadelphia has 14 major direct agencies; and there are 13 major agencies in the greater metropolitan area of Boston.[18] Since a majority of these agencies offer services only to children and/or employable adults, there is obviously a very high ratio of agencies to clients. In New York City, for example, three major agencies and six smaller ones offer direct social and educational services to an estimated 1,000 blind children living in the area. Even if we assume that none of these children are multiply handicapped (which we cannot), the agency-client ratio is very large indeed. Twenty-two different organizations and agencies provide direct rehabilitation and vocational services to an estimated 13,000 blind persons who are of working age. This figure is inflated somewhat when we consider that between 50 and 60 per cent of blind persons 18–54 years of age are women, for whom employment is not always a realistic or appropriate objective. Eleven other organizations specialize in the production and distribution of braille books and recordings for the blind. In addition, a number of state and federal services are available to the blind of New York City.

The disproportionately large number of agencies offering services has many consequences for blind persons, agencies for the blind, and for the community which supports them. One consequence is an intense and often highly spirited competition for clients among agencies for the blind. In some instances, this competition has become so keen that outside parties have had to intervene to protect the welfare of those involved. The pirating of clients is not unknown,[19] and great conflict between agencies ordinarily occurs in urban areas which have not been previously assigned to the competing agencies.

The intense and sometimes ruthless competition between these agencies for clients who fit their programs affects the agency's relationship to its clients. When an agency has the opportunity to provide services to a blind person who is suitable for its program, it is reluctant to let him go. The chances of finding a replacement for the client who leaves are not always good, and without a substantial number of clients on hand, the agency may find it difficult to justify its expenditures to the supporting public. Clients are encouraged to organize their lives around the agency. Employment is secured for them in the agency's sheltered workshop, free recreational services are provided by the agency on an indefinite basis, and residential homes are maintained for them. Gradually a greater and greater portion of the client's contact with the larger community becomes mediated, and often determined by the agency, until the blind person is literally sequestered from the community.[20] At this point, the agency completely negates its original objective, which is to help the blind persons to become independent.

Discussion

My analysis indicates that programs of services for the blind are often more responsive to the organizational needs of agencies through which services are offered, than they are to the needs of blind persons. Moreover, by sequestering certain blind persons from the community, agencies for the blind are actually contributing to the very problems which they purport to be solving. The sociological concept which most appropriately applies to this phenomena is "displacement of organizational goals." This concept describes a situation in which an organization "substitutes for its legitimate goals some other goals for which it was not created, for which resources are not allocated, and for which it is not known to serve."[21]

This phenomenon, which has been observed in a variety of organizational settings, has been attributed to a number of factors, including the selection of organizational means and policies which preclude implementation of the goals,[22] the effects of bureaucracy on the personality and motivation of those who work in it,[23] elimination of the problems for which the organization was originally established,[24] and the requirement of the bureaucratic structure for resources and manpower.[25] The findings of a larger study of work for the blind, of which the data of this paper are but one part, suggest that each of these factors plays a part in accounting for goal displacement in this field. In addition, another factor is suggested: the absence of any clear criteria by which to determine if the agency is or is not implementing its objectives.

It is generally agreed that the purpose of agencies for the blind is to help blind persons to maximize their ability to perform independently. Rehabilitation, which is a core service in any agency, seeks to restore the blind person "to the fullest physical, mental, social, vocational, and economic usefulness of which he is capable." The phrase "of which he is capable" is a crucial modifier, since there is no consensus among workers for the blind regarding what a blind person can or cannot do. In practice, this definition is often used tautologically, since any level of performance which a blind person happens to attain is regarded as the one "of which he is capable." It is difficult, and at times impossible, to know if an agency for the blind is actually attaining its goals.

Using the definitions often employed by workers for the blind, every client they serve is a successful case. By other criteria, such as amount of independent employment or degree of participation in the larger community, the conclusions with respect to the implementation of goals are more modest. In addition, when a blind person performs in a manner which everyone agrees is his maximum level of independence, it is difficult to demonstrate concretely that his independence is a result of the services which he has received. By the same token, when he is not functioning at a level believed to be his maximum, it is not known if this is because services have been inadequate, or because he is a victim of the erroneous beliefs of the larger society about blindness and its effects on human functioning. There is, therefore, a great amount of uncertainty concerning whether an agency is or is not attaining its goals. Criteria of measurement are nebulous, and so many factors might explain success or failure that it is impossible to demonstrate conclusively that a given agency has in fact implemented its goals.

A preoccupation with organizational means is one of the responses to the uncertainty which is generated by this situation. Over the years an intense interest has developed in the refinement of administrative procedures of service programs. This interest has been accompanied by a growing disinterest in the more fundamental questions concerning the necessity for a particular service, or its impact upon the client.[26] This preoccupation with administrative procedures provides workers with a feeling of certainty and accomplishment which would not otherwise exist. Since most workers for the blind are not professionally trained, and their competency to help the blind is therefore continually being challenged, we can see that this uncertainty regarding goal attainment is intensified. As a defense against this situation, workers bury themselves in the administrative details of their jobs. This preoccupation ultimately leads to the displacement of the organizations goals.

Ironically, the tendency toward the displacement of goals is not entirely dysfunctional when viewed from the perspective of the general public. There is a general resistance among most "normals" to become involved with stigmatized persons such as the blind, and avoidance is the characteristic initial response. [27] The blind have always complained that they are segregated from the rest of society, and that they are assigned a marginal and unsatisfying social role.[28] The tendency of agencies for the blind to sequester certain clients (i.e., those for whom there is the greatest probability of integration into the larger community) is consistent with the desire of the public to avoid blind persons. This response, of course, is not unique in welfare services for the blind; it applies with equal cogency to other groups of persons who are defined as disabled, handicapped, or otherwise socially undesirable.[29] The very fact that agencies for the blind exist creates a repository into which the blind may be placed by the larger community. Consequently, the fact that goals are displaced may have unfortunate consequences for particular blind persons, but not necessarily for society at large.

Finally, it should be clear that there is no nationally or regionally coordinated effort to provide services for blind persons. Since agencies must compete with one another for funds and clients, they do not ordinarily coordinate their activities with respect to the problems of the entire population in need of them. Nor, for that matter, do they even possess a clear image of the parameters of that population. A deliberately coordinated national effort is clearly indicated as one important step to remedy the present unnecessary duplication of effort among agencies which are committed to the same general goals.

Notes

1. See, for example, Harold L. Wilensky, and Charles N. Lebeaux, *Industrial Society and Social Welfare*, New York: Russell Sage Foundation, 1958, ch. VII and X.

2. Eliot Freidson, "Disability as Social Deviance," in Marvin B. Sussman (ed.), *Sociological Theory Research, and Rehabilitation*, American Sociological Association, 1966.

3. This figure has been derived from data from two separate sources. For estimates of the prevalence of blindness in the noninstitutionalized civilian population of the U.S. between the ages of 18–79 see "Binocular Visual Acuity of Adults, United States, 1960–1962," National Center for Health Statistics, Series 11, #3. For estimates of the prevalence of blindness in children, see "Annual Report," American Printing House for the Blind (APHB), Louisville, Kentucky, 1962.

4. "Binocular Visual Acuity," *op. cit.*, Table 3, p. 16.

5. *Ibid.*

6. This estimate is based upon the figures of the APHB for school-age children, and an educated guess by practitioners of works for the blind for preschool-age children.

7. "Binocular Visual Acuity," *op. cit.*

8. *Directory of Agencies Serving Blind Persons in the United States*, 14th ed., New York: American Foundation for the Blind, 1965.

9. See Harry Best, *Blindness and the Blind in the United States*, New York: Macmillan Company, 1934, ch. XII.

10. *Ibid.*, ch. I and IV.

11. *Ibid.*, ch. II and III.

12. For discussions of resistance to the adoption of the Hoover cane, see Thomas Carroll, *Blindness*, pp. 134–135; for discussions related to braille, see Robert Erwin, *As I Saw It*, AFB, 1966, pp. 1–56; for discussions related to seeing eye dogs, see W. M. Ebeling, "The Guide Dog Movement," in Paul A. Zahl, *Blindness: Modern Approaches to the Unseen Environment*, New York and London: Hofner Publishing Company, 1962; also see Hector Chevigny and Sydell Braverman, *The Adjustment of the Blind*, New Haven: Yale University Press, 1950, ch. IX.

13. Marvin Sussman, "Sociology of Rehabilitation Occupations," *Sociological Theory, Research and Rehabilitation, op. cit.*, ch. II.

14. Erving Goffman, *Stigma, Notes on the Management of Spoiled Identity*, Englewood Cliffs, N.J.: Prentice-Hall, Inc., 1963, ch. 1.

15. Chevigny and Braverman, *op. cit.*, ch. IX.

16. Such appeals have been enormously successful. I have estimated that in the state of New York alone, between $57,000,000 and $63,0000,000 are anually expended by public and private organizations for services to the blind. This figure was compiled from data from a variety of sources, including the routine annual reports of governmental-sponsored service programs, the annual reports of private agencies which are routinely filed with the Charities Registration Bureau of the State of New York, and private correspondence with the numerous other organizations who do not ordinarily make financial reports public.

17. These estimates were derived by computing the blindness rate per 1,000 of the population and then multiplying them by the number of persons living in each city.

18. For a listing of most of these agencies, see *Directory of Agencies Serving Blind Persons in the United States, 1965, op. cit.*

19. Chevigny and Braveman, *op. cit.*, ch. IX.

20. This situation also applies to other types of welfare organizations. See, for example, Erving Goffman, *Asylums, Essays on the Social Situation of the Mental Patient, and Other Inmates.* Garden City, N.Y.: Anchor Books, 1961: and Harold Orlans, "An American Death Camp," *Politics* (Summer, 1948), pp. 162–167.

21. A. Etzioni, *Modern Organization*, Englewood Cliffs, N.J.: Prentice Hall, Inc., 1964, p. 10.

22. R. Michels, *Political Parties*, Glencoe, Ill.: Free Press, 1949: P. Selznick, *TVA and the Grass Roots*, Berkeley: University of California Press, 1949.

23. Robert K. Merton, *Social Theory and Social Structure*, rev. ed., Glencoe, Ill.: Free Press, 1957.

24. S. L. Messinger, "Organizational Transformation: A Case Study of a Declining Social Movement," American Socological Review, 20 (February, 1955), pp. 3–10.

25. B. R. Clark, "Organizational Adaption and Precarious Values," American Sociological Review, 21 (1956), pp. 327–336.

26. One manifestation of this trend is the shifting focus of papers and discussions at meetings of workers for the blind. At the beginning of organized programs of services for the blind, papers at such meetings were largely devoted to basic discussions of the appropriate goals of work for the blind; at the present time they are concerned almost exclusively with perfection of the means. See *Annual Proceedings* of the American Association of Workers for the Blind.

27. Goffman, *Stigma, op. cit.*, ch. 1.

28. Alan Gowman, *The War Blind in American Social Structure*, New York: American Foundation for the Blind, 1957, pp. 5–9.

29. Goffman, *Stigma, op. cit.*, ch. 1.

Some Contingencies of the Moral Evaluation and Control of Clientele: The Case of the Hospital Emergency Service

Julius A. Roth

The moral evaluation of patients by staff members has been explored in detail in the case of "mental illness" (Scheff 1966, chap. 5; Strauss et al. 1964, chaps. 8 and 12; Belknap 1956; Scheff 1964; Goffman 1961, pp. 125–70, 321–86; Hollingshead and Redlich 1958; Szasz 1960). The assumption is made by some (especially Thomas Szasz) that mental illness is a special case which readily allows moral judgments to be made because there are no technical criteria to be applied and because psychiatric concepts in their historical development have been a pseudoscientific replacement of moral judgments. Charles Perrow (1965) stresses lack of technology as a factor which forces psychiatric practitioners to fall back on commonsense concepts of humanitarianism which open the way to moral evaluations of the clientele.

I contend that the diagnosis and treatment of mental illness and the "care" of mental patients are not unique in incorporating moral judgments of the clientele, but are only obvious examples of a more general phenomenon which exists no matter what the historical development or the present state of the technology. Glaser and Strauss (1964) put forward such a notion when they demonstrated how the "social worth" of a dying patient affects the nursing care he will receive. I would add that moral evaluation also has a direct effect on a physician's diagnosis and treatment recommendations. This is obvious in extreme cases, such as when a monarch or the president of the United States is attended by teams of highly qualified diagnosticians to insure a detailed and accurate diagnosis and has outstanding specialists flown to his bedside to carry out the treatment. I will discuss some aspects of this same process as it applies on a day-to-day basis in a routine hospital operation involving more "ordinary" patients.

The data are taken from observation of six hospital emergency services in two parts of the country—one northeastern location and one West Coast location. My co-workers and I spent several periods of time (spread over two or three months in each case) in the emergency department of each of the hospitals. In one hospital we worked as

Reprinted from *American Journal of Sociology* 77 (March, 1972):839–56.

intake clerks over a period of three months. At other times we observed areas in the emergency unit without initiating any interaction with patients, visitors, or personnel. At other points we followed patients through the emergency service from their first appearance to discharge or inpatient admission, interviewing patient and staff during the process. During these periods of observation, notes were also kept on relevant conversations with staff members.

The hospital emergency service is a setting where a minimum of information is available about the character of each patient and a long-term relationship with the patient is usually not contemplated. Even under these conditions, judgments about a patient's moral fitness and the appropriateness of his visit to an emergency service are constantly made, and staff action concerning the patient—including diagnosis, treatment, and disposition of the case—are, in part, affected by these judgments.

The Deserving and the Undeserving

The evaluation of patients and visitors by emergency-ward staff may be conveniently thought of in two categories: (1) The application by the staff of concepts of social worth common in the larger society. (2) Staff members' concepts of their appropriate work role. In this section I will take up the first of these.

There is a popular myth (generated in part by some sociological writing) that persons engaged in providing professional services, especially medical care, do not permit the commonly accepted concepts of social worth in our culture to affect their relationship to the clientele. An on-the-spot description of *any* service profession—medicine, education, law, social welfare, etc.—should disabuse us of this notion. There is no evidence that professional training succeeds in creating a universalistic moral neutrality (Becker et al. 1961, pp. 323–27). On the contrary, we are on much safer ground to assume that those engaged in dispensing professional services (or any other services) will apply the evaluations of social worth common to their culture and will modify their services with respect to those evaluations *unless discouraged from doing so by the organizational arrangements under which they work.* Some such organizational arrangements do exist on emergency wards. The rapid turnover and impersonality of the operation is in itself a protection for many patients who might be devalued if more were known about them. In public hospitals, at least, there is a rule that *all* patients themselves at the registration desk must be seen by a doctor, and clerks and nurses know that violation of this rule, if discovered, can get them into serious trouble. (Despite this, patients are occasionally refused registration, usually because they are morally repugnant to the clerk.) Such arrangements restrict the behavior of the staff only to a limited extent, however. There remains a great deal of room for expressing one's valuation of the patient in the details of processing and treatment.

One common concept of social worth held by emergency-ward personnel is that the young are more valuable than the old. This is exemplified most dramatically in the marked differences in efforts to resuscitate young and old patients (Glaser and Strauss 1964; Sudnow 1967, pp. 100–109). "Welfare cases" who are sponging off the taxpayer —especially if they represent the product of an immoral life (such as a woman with illegitimate children to support)—do not deserve the best care. Persons of higher status in the larger society are likely to be accorded more respectful treatment in the emergency ward just as they often are in other service or customer relationships, and conversely those of lower status are treated with less consideration. (The fact that higher-status persons are more likely to make an effective complaint or even file lawsuits may be an additional reason for such differential treatment.)

Of course, staff members vary in the manner and degree to which they apply these cultural concepts of social worth in determining the quality of their service to the clientele. The point is that they are in a position to alter the nature of their service in terms of such differentiation, and all of them—porters, clerks, nursing personnel, physicians—do so to some extent. Despite some variations, we did in fact find widespread agreement on the negative evaluation of some categories of patients—evaluations which directly affected the treatment provided. Those who are the first to process a patient play a crucial role in moral categorization because staff members at later stages of the processing are inclined to accept earlier categories without question unless they detect clear-cut evidence to the contrary. Thus, registration clerks can often determine how long a person will have to wait and what kind of treatment area he is sent to, and, occasionally, can even prevent a person from seeing a doctor at all. Some patients have been morally categorized by policemen or ambulance crewmen before they even arrive at the hospital—categorization which affects the priority and kind of service given.

In the public urban hospital emergency service, the clientele is heavily skewed toward the lower end of the socioeconomic scale, and nonwhite and non-Anglo ethnic groups are greatly overrepresented. Also, many patients are in the position of supplicating the staff for help, sometimes for a condition for which the patient can be held responsible. With such a population, the staff can readily maintain a stance of moral superiority. They see the bulk of the patients as people undeserving of the services available to them. Staff members maintain that they need not tolerate any abuse or disobedience from patients or visitors. Patients and visitors may be issued orders which they are expected to obey. The staff can, and sometimes does, shout down patients and visitors and threaten them with ejection from the premises. The staff demands protection against possible attack and also against the possibility of lawsuits, which are invariably classified as unjustified. There is no need to be polite to the clientele and, in fact, some clerks frequently engage patients and visitors in arguments. The staff also feels justified in refusing service to those who complain or resist treatment or refuse to follow procedures or make trouble in any other way. From time to time the clients are referred to as "garbage," "scum," "liars," "deadbeats," people who "come out from under the rocks," by doctors, nurses, aides, clerks, and even housekeepers who sweep the floor. When we spent the first several days of a new medical year with a new group of interns on one emergency service, we found that an important part of the orientation was directed toward telling the interns that the patients were not to be trusted and did not have to be treated politely. At another public hospital, new registration clerks were told during their first few days of work that they would have to learn not to accept the word of patients but to treat everything they say with suspicion.

Despite the general negative conception of the clientele, differentiations are made between patients on the basis of clues which they present. Since this is typically a fleeting relationship where the staff member has little or no background information about the patient, evaluations must usually be made quickly on the basis of readily perceivable clues. Race, age, mode of dress, language and accents and word usage, and the manner in which the client addresses and responds to staff members are all immediate clues on which staff base their initial evaluations. A little questioning brings out other information which may be used for or against a patient: financial status, type of employment, insurance protection, use of private-practice doctors, nature of medical complaint, legitimacy of children, marital status, previous use of hospital services. In the case of unconscious or seriously ill or injured patients, a search of the wallet or handbag often provides informative clues about social worth.

Some characteristics consistently turn staff against patients and affect the quality of care given. Dirty, smelly patients cause considerable comment among the staff, and efforts are made to isolate them or get rid of them. Those dressed as hippies or women with scanty clothing (unless there is a "good excuse," e.g., a woman drowned while swimming) are frowned upon and are more likely to be kept waiting and to be rushed through when they *are* attended to. We observed hints that certain ethnic groups are discriminated against, but this is difficult to detect nowadays because everyone is extremely sensitive to the possibility of accusations of racial discrimination. If a woman with a child is tabbed a "welfare case" (from her dress, speech, and manner, or in the explicit form of a welfare card which she presents), the clerk is likely to ask, "Is there a father in the house?" while better-dressed, better-spoken women with children are questioned more discreetly.

Attributes and Categories: A Reciprocal Relationship

On one level, it is true to say that the staff's moral evaluation of a patient influences the kind of treatment he gets in the emergency room. But this kind of causal explanation obscures important aspects of the network of interrelationships involved. On another, the definition of devalued or favored categories and the attributes of the patient reinforce each other in a reciprocal manner.

Take, for example, patients who are labeled as drunks. They are more consistently treated as undeserving than any other category of patient. They are frequently handled as if they were baggage when they are brought in by police; those with lacerations are often roughly treated by physicians; they are usually treated only for drunkenness and obvious surgical repair without being examined for other pathology; no one believes their stories; their statements are ridiculed; they are treated in an abusive or jocular manner; they are ignored for long periods of time; in one hospital they are placed in a room separate from most other patients. Emergency-ward personnel frequently comment on how they hate to take care of drunks.

Thus, it might seem that the staff is applying a simple moral syllogism: drunks do not deserve to be cared for, this patient is a drunk, therefore, he does not deserve good treatment. *But* how do we know that he is drunk? By the way he is treated. Police take him directly to the drunk room. If we ask why the police define him as drunk, they may answer that they smell alcohol on his breath. But not all people with alcohol on their breath are picked up by the police and taken to a hospital emergency room. The explanation must come in terms of some part of the patient's background—he was in a lower-class neighborhood, his style of dress was dirty and sloppy, he was unattended by any friend or family member, and so on. When he comes to the emergency room *he has already been defined as a drunk.* There is no reason for the emergency-room personnel to challenge this definition—it is routine procedure and it usually proves correct in so far as they know. There is nothing to do for drunks except to give them routine medications and let them sleep it off. To avoid upsetting the rest of the emergency room, there is a room set aside for them. The police have a standard procedure of taking drunks to that room, and the clerks place them there if they come in on their own and are defined as drunk on the basis, not only of their breath odor (and occasionally there is no breath odor in someone defined as drunk), but in terms of their dress, manner, and absence of protectors. The physicians, having more pressing matters, tend to leave the drunks until last. Of course, they may miss some pathology which could cause unconsciousness or confusion because they believe the standard procedure proves correct in the great majority of cases. They really do not know *how* often it does not prove correct since they do not check up closely enough to uncover other forms of pathology in most cases, and the low social status of the patients and the fact that they are seldom accompanied by anyone who will protect them means that complaints about inadequate examination will be rare. There *are* occasional challenges by doctors—"How do you know he's drunk?"— but in most cases the busy schedule of the house officer leaves little time for such luxuries as a careful examination of patients who have already been defined as drunks by others. Once the drunk label has been accepted by the emergency-room staff, a more careful examination is not likely to be made unless some particularly arresting new information appears (for example, the patient has convulsions, a relative appears to tell them that he has diabetes, an examination of his wallet shows him to be a solid citizen), and the more subtle pathologies are not likely to be discovered.

Thus, it is just as true to say that the *label* of "drunk" is accepted by hospital personnel because of the way the patient is treated as it is to say that he is treated in a certain way because he is drunk. Occasional cases show how persons with alcohol on their breath will not be treated as drunks. When an obviously middle-class man (obvious in terms of his dress, speech, and demands for service) was brought in after an automobile accident, he was not put in the drunk room, although he had a definite alcohol odor, but was given relatively quick treatment in one of the other examining rooms and addressed throughout in a polite manner.

Most drunks are men. A common negative evaluation for women is PID (pelvic inflammatory disease). This is not just a medical diagnostic category, but, by implication, a moral judgment. There are many women with difficult-to-diagnose abdominal pains and fever. If they are Negro, young, unmarried, lower class in appearance and speech, and have no one along to champion their cause, doctors frequently make the assumption that they have before them the end results of a dissolute sex life, unwanted pregnancy and perhaps veneral disease, illegal abortion, and consequent infection of the reproductive organs. The label PID is then attached and the patient relegated to a group less deserving of prompt and considerate treatment. This is *not* the same thing as saying a diagnosis of PID leads to rejection by medical personnel.

We observed one patient who had been defined as a troublemaker because of his abusive language and his insistence that he be released immediately. When he began to behave in a strange manner (random thrashing about), the police were promptly called to control him and they threatened him with arrest. A patient who was not defined as a troublemaker and exhibited like behavior prompted an effort on the part of the staff to provide a medical explanation for his actions. Here again, we see that the category into which the patient has been placed may have more effect on determining the decisions of medical personnel than does his immediate behavior.

Thus, it is not simply a matter of finding which "objective" pathological states medical personnel like or dislike dealing with. The very definition of these pathological states depends in part on how the patient is categorized in moral terms by the screening and treatment personnel.

The Legitimate and the Illegitimate

The second type of evaluation is that related to the staff members' concept of their appropriate work roles (Strauss et al. 1964, chap. 13). Every worker has a notion of what demands are appropriate to his position. When demands fall outside that boundary, he feels that the claim is illegitimate. What he does about it depends on a number of factors, including his alternatives, his power to control the behavior of others, and his power to select his clientele (more on this later).

The interns and residents who usually man the larger urban emergency services like to think of this assignment as a part of their training which will give them a kind of experience different from the outpatient department or inpatient wards. Here they hope to get some practice in resuscitation, in treating traumatice injuries, in diagnosing and treating medical emergencies. When patients who are no different from those they have seen *ad nauseam* in the outpatient department present themselves at the emergency ward, the doctors in training believe that their services are being misused. Also, once on the emergency ward, the patient is expected to be "cooperative" so that the doctor is not blocked in his effort to carry out his tasks. Nurses, clerks, and others play "little doctor" and to this extent share the concepts of the boundaries of legitimacy of the doctors. But, in addition to the broadly shared perspective, each work specialty has its own notions of appropriate patient attributes and behavior based on their own work demands. Thus, clerks expect patients to cooperate in getting forms filled out. Patients with a "good reason," unconsciousness, for example, are excused from cooperating with clerical procedures, but other patients who are unable to give requested information or who protest against certain questions bring upon themselves condemnation by the clerks who believe that a person who subverts their efforts to complete their tasks has no business on the emergency ward.

A universal complaint among those who operate emergency services is that hospital emergency rooms are "abused" by the public—or rather by a portion of the public. This is particularly the case in the city and county hospitals and voluntary hospitals with training programs subsidized by public funds which handle the bulk of emergency cases in urban areas. The great majority of cases are thought of as too minor or lacking in urgency to warrant a visit to the emergency room. They are "outpatient cases" (OPD cases), that is, patients who could wait until the outpatient department is open, or if they can afford private care, they could wait until a physician is holding his regular office hours. Patients should not use the emergency room just because it gives quicker service than the outpatient department or because the hours are more convenient (since it is open all the time). Pediatricians complain about their day filled with "sore throats and snotty noses." Medical interns and residents complain about all the people presenting long-standing or chronic diseases which, though sometimes serious, do not belong in the emergency room. In every hospital—both public and private—where we made observations or conducted interviews, we repeatedly heard the same kinds of "atrocity stories": a patient with a sore throat of two-weeks' duration comes in at 3:00 A.M. on Sunday and expects immediate treatment from an intern whom he has got out of bed (or such variations as an itch of 75-days' duration, a congenital defect in a one-year-old child—always coming in at an extremely inconvenient hour).

Directors of emergency services recognize that some of their preoccupation with cases which are not "true emergencies" is not simply a matter of "abuse" by patients, but the result of tasks imposed upon them by other agencies—for example, giving routine antibiotic injections on weekends, caring for abandoned children, giving routine blood transfusions, receiving inpatient admissions, giving gamma globulin, providing veneral disase follow-up, examining jail prisoners, arranging nursing-home dispositions for the aged. But the blame for most of their difficulty is placed upon the self-referred patient who, according to the emergency-room staff, does not make appropriate use of their service.

The OPD case typically gets hurried, routine processing with little effort at a careful diagnostic work-up or sophisticated treatment unless he happens to strike the doctor as an interesting case (in which case he is no longer classified as an OPD case). Thus, pediatric residents move rapidly through their mass of sore throats and snotty noses with a quick look in ears and throat with the otolaryngoscope, a swab wiped in the throat to be sent to the laboratory, and if the child does not have a high fever (the nurse has already taken his temperature), the parent is told to check on the laboratory results the next day, the emergency-ward form is marked "URI" (upper respiratory infection), and the next child moves up on the treadmill. If a patient or a visitor has given anyone trouble, his care is likely to deteriorate below the routine level. Often, doctors define their task in OPD cases as simply a stopgap until the patient gets to OPD on a subsequent day, and therefore a careful work-up is not considered necessary.

Medical cases are more often considered illegitimate than surgical cases. In our public hospital tabulations, the diagnostic categories highest in the illegitimate category were gynecology, genito-urinary, dental, and "other medical." The lowest in proportion of illegitimate cases were pediatrics (another bit of evidence that children are more acceptable patients than adults), beatings and stabbings, industrial injuries, auto accidents, other accidents, and "other surgical." Much of the surgical work is suturing lacerations and making other repairs. Although these are not necessarily serious in terms of danger to life (very few were), such injuries were seen by the staff as needing prompt attention (certainly within 24 hours) to reduce the risk of infection and to avoid scarring or other deformity.

It is not surprising that in surgical cases the attributes and behavior of the patients are of lesser consequence than in medical cases. The ease with which the condition can be defined and the routine nature of the treatment (treating minor lacerations becomes so routine that anyone thinks he can do it—medical students, aides, volunteers) means that the characteristics and behavior of the patient can be largely ignored unless he becomes extremely disruptive. (Even violence can be restrained and the treatment continued without much trouble.) Certain other things are handled with routine efficiency—high fevers in children, asthma, overdose, maternity cases. It is significant that standard rules can be and have been laid down in such cases so that everyone—clerks, nurses, doctors (and patients once they have gone through the experience)—knows just how to proceed. In such cases, the issue of legitimacy seldom arises.

We find no similar routines with set rules in the case of complaints of abdominal pains, delusions, muscle spasms, depression, or digestive upset. Here the process of diagnosis is much more subtle and complex, the question of urgency much more debatable and uncertain. The way is left open for all emergency-ward staff members involved to make a judgment about whether the case is appropriate to and deserving of their service. Unless the patient is a "regular," no one on the emergency service is likely to have background information on the patient, and the staff will have to rely entirely on clues garnered from his mode of arrival, his appearance, his behavior, the kind of people who accompany him, and so on. The interpretation of these clues then becomes crucial to further treatment and, to the casual observer, may appear to be the *cause* of such treatment.

It is also not surprising that "psychiatric cases" are usually considered illegitimate. Interns and residents do not (unless they are planning to go into psychiatry) find such cases useful for practicing their diagnostic and treatment skills,[1] and therefore regard such patients as an unwelcome intrusion. But what constitutes a psychiatric case is not based on unvarying criteria. An effort is usually made to place a patient in a more explicit medical category. For example, a wrist slashing is a surgical case requiring suturing. An adult who takes an overdose of sleeping pills is a medical case requiring lavage and perhaps antidotes. Only when a patient is troublesome—violent, threatening suicide, disturbing other patients—is the doctor forced to define him as a psychiatric case about whom a further decision must be made. (In some clinics, psychiatrists are attempting to broaden the definition by making interns and residents aware of more subtle cues for justifying a psychiatric referral and providing them with a consulting service to deal with such cases. However, they must provide a prompt response when called upon, or their service will soon go unused.)

It is no accident either that in private hospitals (especially those without medical school or public clinic affiliation) the legitimacy of a patient depends largely on his relationship to the private medical system. A standard opening question to the incoming patient in such hospitals is, "Who is your doctor?" A patient is automatically legitimate if referred by a physician on the hospital staff (or the physician's nurse, receptionist, or answering service). If he has not been referred, but gives the name of a staff doctor whom the nurse can reach and who agrees to handle the case, the patient is also legitimate. However, if he does not give a staff doctor's name, he falls under suspicion. The hospital services, including the emergency room, are designed primarily to serve the private physicians on the staff. A patient who does not fit into this scheme threatens to upset the works. It is the receptionist's or receiving nurse's job to try to establish the proper relationship by determining whether the case warrants the service of the contract physician or the doctor on emergency call, and if so, to see to it that the patient gets into the hands of an attending staff doctor for follow-up treatment if necessary. Any patient whose circumstances make this process difficult or impossible becomes illegitimate. This accounts for the bitter denunciation of the "welfare cases"[2] and the effort to deny admission to people without medical insurance or other readily tappable funds. (Most physicians on the hospital staff do not want such people as patients, and feel they have been tricked if a colleague talks them into accepting them as patients; neither does the hospital administration want them as inpatients.) Also, such hospitals have no routine mechanism for dealing with welfare cases, as have the public hospitals which can either give free treatment or refer the patient to a social worker on the premises. Such patients are commonly dealt with by transferring them to a public clinic or hospital if their condition permits.

The negative evaluation of patients is strongest when they combine an undeserving character with illegitimate demands. Thus, a patient presenting a minor medical complaint at an inconvenient hour is more vigorously condemned if he is a welfare case than if he is a "respectable citizen." On the other hand, a "real emergency" can overcome moral repugnance. Thus, when a presumed criminal suffering a severe abdominal bullet wound inflicted by police was brought into one emergency ward, the staff quickly mobilized in a vigorous effort to prevent death because this is the kind of case the staff sees as justifying the existence of their unit. The same patient brought in with a minor injury would almost certainly have been treated as a moral outcast. Even in the case of "real emergencies," however, moral evaluation is not absent. Although the police prisoner with the bullet wound received prompt, expert attention, the effort was treated simply as a technical matter—an opportunity to display one's skill in keeping a severely traumatized person alive. When the same emergency ward received a prominent local citizen who had been stabbed by thugs while he was trying to protect his wife, the staff again provided a crash effort to save his life, but in this case they were obviously greatly upset by their failure, not simply a failure of technical skills but the loss of a worthy person who was the victim of a vicious act. One may speculate whether this difference in staff evaluations of the two victims may have resulted in an extra effort in the case of the respected citizen despite the appearance of a similar effort in the two cases.

Staff Estimates of "Legitimate" Demands

As is common in relationships between a work group and its clientele, the members of the work group tend to exaggerate their difficulties with the clients when they generalize about them. In conversations, we would typically hear estimates of 70%–90% as the proportion of patients who were using the emergency service inappropriately. Yet, when we actually followed cases through the clinic, we found the majority were being treated as if they were legitimate. In one voluntary hospital with an intern and residency training program, we classified all cases we followed during our time on the emergency room as legitimate or illegitimate whenever we had any evidence of subjective definition by staff members, either by what they said about the patient or the manner in which they treated the patient. Among those cases suitable for classification, 42 were treated as legitimate, 15 as illegitimate, and in 24 cases there was insufficient evidence to make a classification. Thus, the illegitimate proportion was about 20%–25% depending on whether one used as a base the total of definite legitimate and illegitimate cases or also included the unknowns. In a very active public hospital emergency room we did not use direct observation of each case, but rather developed a conception of what kind of diagnostic categories were usually considered legitimate or illegitimate by the clinic staff and then classified the total census for two days according to diagnostic categories. By this method 23% of 938 patients were classified as illegitimate. This constitutes a minimum figure because diagnostic category was not the only basis for an evaluation, and some other patients were almost certainly regarded as illegitimate by the staff. But it *does* suggest that only a minority were regarded as illegitimate.

The numbers of specific undesirable or inappropriate categories of patients were also consistently exaggerated. Thus, while in the public hospital the interns complained about all the drunks among the men and all the reproductive organ infections among women ("The choice between the male and the female service is really a choice between alcoholics and PIDs," according to one intern), drunks made up only 6% of the total emergency-room population and the gynecology patients 2%. Venereal disease was also considered a common type of case by clerks, nurses, and doctors, but in fact made up only about 1% of the total E.R. census. Psychiatric cases were referred to as a constant trouble, but, in fact, made up only a little over 2% of the total. Some doctors believed infections and long-standing illnesses were common among the E.R. population and used this as evidence of neglect of health by the lower classes. Here again, however, the actual numbers were low—these two categories made up a little more than 3% of the total census. In two small private hospitals, the staffs were particularly bitter toward "welfare cases" whom they regarded as a constant nuisance. However, we often spent an entire shift (eight hours) in the emergency rooms of these hospitals without seeing a single patient so classified.

Workers justify the rewards received for their labors in part by the burdens which they must endure on the job. One of the burdens of service occupations is a clientele which makes life hard for the workers. Thus, the workers tend to select for public presentation those aspects of the clientele which cause them difficulty. Teachers' talk deals disproportionately with disruptive and incompetent students, policemen's talk with dangerous criminals and difficult civilians, janitors' talk with inconsiderate tenants. A case-by-case analysis of client contacts is likely to demonstrate in each instance that the examples discussed by the staff are not representative of their total clientele.

Control of Inappropriate Demands for Service

When members of a service occupation or service organization are faced with undesirable or illegitimate clients, what can they do? One possible procedure is to select clients they like and avoid those they do not like. The selecting may be done in categorical terms, as when universities admit undergraduate students who meet given grade and test standards. Or it may be done on the basis of detailed information about specific individuals, as when a graduate department selects particular students on the basis of academic record, recommendations from colleagues, and personal information about the student. Of course, such selection is not made on a unidimensional basis and the selecting agent must often decide what weight to give conflicting factors. (Thus, a medical specialist may be willing to take on a patient who is morally repugnant because the patient has a medical condition the specialist is anxious to observe, study, or experiment with.) But there is an assumption that the more highly individualized the selection and the more detailed the information on which it is based, the more likely one is to obtain a desirable clientele. Along with this process goes the notion of "selection errors." Thus, when a patient is classed as a good risk for a physical rehabilitation program, he may later be classed as a selection error if doctors uncover some pathology which contraindicates exercise, or if the patient proves so uncooperative that physical therapists are unable to conduct any training, or if he requires so much nursing care that ward personnel claim that he "doesn't belong" on a rehabilitation unit (Roth and Eddy 1967, pp. 57–61).

Selectivity is a relative matter. A well-known law firm specializing in a given field can accept only those clients whose demands fit readily into the firm's desired scheme of work organization and who are able to pay well for the service given. The solo criminal lawyer in a marginal practice may, for financial reasons, take on almost every case he can get, even though he may despise the majority of his clients and wish he did not have to deal with them (Smigel 1964; Wood 1967). A common occupational or organizational aspiration is to reach a position where one can be highly selective of one's clientele. In fact, such power of selection is a common basis for rating schools, law firms, hospitals, and practitioners of all sorts.[3]

If one cannot be selective in a positive sense, one may still be selective in a negative sense by avoiding some potentially undesirable clients. Hotels, restaurants, and places of entertainment may specifically exclude certain categories of persons as guests, or more generally reserve the right to refuse service to anyone they choose. Cab drivers will sometimes avoid a presumed "bad fare" by pretending another engagement or just not seeing him. Cab driving, incidentally, is a good example of a line of work where judgments about clients must often be made in a split second on the basis of immediate superficial clues—clues based not only on the behavior and appearance of the client himself, but also on such surrounding factors as the area, destination, and time of day (Davis 1959; Henslin 1968, pp. 138–58). Ambulance crewmen sometimes manage to avoid a "bad load," perhaps making a decision before going to the scene on the basis of the call source or neighborhood, or perhaps refusing to carry an undesirable patient if they can find a "good excuse" (Douglas 1969, pp. 234–78).

Medical personnel and organizations vary greatly in their capacity to select clients. Special units in teaching hospitals and specialized outpatient clinics often are able to restrict their patients to those they have individually screened and selected. The more run-of-the-mill hospital ward or clinic is less selective, but still has a screening process to keep out certain categories of patients. Of all medical care units, public hospital emergency wards probably exercise the least selectivity of all. Not only are they open to the public at all times with signs pointing the way, but the rule that everyone demanding care must be seen provides no legal "out" for the staff when faced with inappropriate or repugnant patients (although persons accompanying patients can be, and often are, prevented from entering the treatment areas and are isolated or ejected if troublesome). In addition, the emergency ward serves a residual function for the rest of the hospital and often for other parts of the medical-care system. Any case which does not fit into some other program is sent to the emergency ward. When other clinics and offices close for the day or the weekend, their patients who cannot wait for the next open hours are directed to the emergency service. It is precisely this unselective influx of anyone and everyone bringing a wide spectrum of medical and social defects that elicits the bitter complaints of emergency-service personnel. Of course, they are not completely without selective power. They occasionally violate the rules and refuse to accept a patient. And even after registration, some patients can be so discouraged in the early stages of processing that they leave. Proprietary hospitals transfer some patients to public hospitals. But compared with other parts of the medical-care system, the emergency-service personnel, especially in public hospitals, have very limited power of selection and must resign themselves to dealing with many people that they believe should not be there and that in many cases they have a strong aversion to.

What recourse does a service occupation or organization have when its members have little or no control over the selection of its clients? If you cannot pick the clients you like, perhaps you can transform those you *do* get somewhat closer to the image of a desirable client. This is particularly likely to occur if it is a long-term or repeated relationship so that the worker can reap the benefit of the "training" he gives the client. We tentatively put forth this proposition: *The amount of trouble one is willing to go to to train his clientele depends on how much power of selection he has. The easier it is for one to avoid or get rid of poor clients (that is, those clients whose behavior or attributes conflict with one's conception of his proper work role), the less interested one is in putting time and energy into training clients to conform more closely to one's ideal. And, of course, the converse.*

Janitors have to endure a clientele (that is, tenants) they have no hand in selecting. Nor can a janitor get rid of bad tenants (unless he buys the building and evicts them, as happens on rare occasions). Ray Gold (1964, pp. 1–50) describes how janitors try to turn "bad tenants" into more tolerable ones by teaching them not to make inappropriate demands. Tenants must be taught not to call at certain hours, not to expect the janitor to make certain repairs, not to expect him to remove certain kinds of garbage, to expect cleaning services only on given days and in given areas, to expect heat only at certain times, and so on. Each occasion on which the janitor is able to make his point that a given demand is inappropriate contributes to making those demands from the same tenant less likely in the future and increases the janitor's control over his work load and work pacing. One finds much the same long-term effort on the part of mental hospital staffs who indoctrinate inmates on the behavior and demands associated with "good patients"—who will be rewarded with privileges and discharge— and behavior associated with "bad patients"—who will be denied these rewards (Stanton and Schwartz 1954, pp. 280–89; Belknap 1956, chaps. 9 and 10). Prisons and schools are other examples of such long-term teaching of clients.[4]

The form that "client-training" takes depends in part on the time perspective of the trainers. Emergency-ward personnel do not have the long-time perspective of the mental hospital staff, teachers, or janitors. Despite the fact that the majority of patients have been to the same emergency ward previously and will probably be back again at some future time, the staff, with rare exceptions, treats each case as an episode which will be completed when the patient is discharged. Therefore, they seldom make a direct effort to affect the patient's future use of their services. They are, however, interested in directing the immediate behavior of clients so that it will fit into their concept of proper priorities (in terms of their evaluation of the clients) and the proper conduct of an emergency service, including the work demands made upon them. Since they do not conceive of having time for gradual socialization of the clients, they rely heavily on demands for immediate compliance. Thus, patients demanding attention, if not deemed by staff to be urgent cases or particularly deserving, will be told to wait their turn and may even be threatened with refusal of treatment if they are persistent. Visitors are promptly ordered to a waiting room and are reminded of where they belong if they wander into a restricted area. Patients are expected to respond promptly when called, answer questions put to them by the staff, prepare for examination when asked, and cooperate with the examination as directed without wasting the staff's time. Failure to comply promptly may bring a warning that they will be left waiting or even refused further care if they do not cooperate, and the more negative the staff evaluation of the patient, the more likely he is to be threatened.[5]

Nursing staff in proprietary hospitals dealing with the private patients of attending physicians do not have as authoritative a position vis-à-vis their clients as public hospital staff have; therefore, the demands for prompt compliance with staff directions must be used sparingly. In such a case more surreptitious forms of control are used. The most common device is keeping the patient waiting at some step or steps in his processing or treatment. Since the patient usually has no way of checking the validity of the reason given for the wait, this is a relatively safe way that a nurse can control the demands made on her and also serves as a way of "getting even" with those who make inappropriate demands or whom she regards as undeserving for some other reason.

In general, we might expect that: *The longer the time perspective of the trainers, the more the training will take the form of efforts toward progressive socialization in the desired direction; the shorter the time perspective of the trainers, the more the training will take the form of overt coercion ("giving orders") if the trainers have sufficient power over the clients, and efforts at surreptitious but immediate control if they lack such power.*

Conclusion

When a person presents himself at an emergency department (or is brought there by others), he inevitably sets off a process by which his worthiness and legitimacy are weighed and become a factor in his treatment. It is doubtful that one can obtain any service of consequence anywhere without going through this process. The evidence from widely varying services indicates that the servers do not dispense their service in a uniform manner to everyone who presents himself, but make judgments about the worthiness of the person and the appropriateness of his demands and take these judgments into account when performing the service. In large and complex service organizations, the judgments made at one point in the system often shape the judgments at another.

The structure of a service organization will affect the manner and degree to which the servers can vary their service in terms of their moral evaluation of the client. This study has not explored this issue in detail. A useful future research direction would be the investigation of how a system of service may be structured to control the discretion of the servers as to whom they must serve and how they must serve them. This article offered some suggestions concerning the means of controlling the inappropriate demands of a clientele. The examples I used to illustrate the relationships of power of selection and the nature of training of clients are few and limited in scope. An effort should be made to determine whether these formulations (or modifications thereof) apply in a wider variety of occupational settings.

Notes

1. The authors of *Boys in White* (Becker et al. 1961, pp. 327–38) make the same point. A "crock" is a patient from whom the students cannot learn anything because there is no definable physical pathology which can be tracked down and treated.

2. "Welfare cases" include not only those who present welfare cards, but all who are suspected of trying to work the system to get free or low-priced care.

3. I am glossing over some of the intraorganizational complexities of the process. Often different categories of organizational personnel vary greatly in their participation in the selection of the clientele. Thus, on a hospital rehabilitation unit, the doctors may select the patients, but the nurses must take care of patients they have no direct part in selecting. Nurses can influence future selection only by complaining to the doctors that they have "too many" of certain kinds of difficult patients or by trying to convince doctors to transfer inappropriate patients. These attempts at influencing choice often fail because doctors and nurses have somewhat different criteria about what an appropriate patient is (Roth and Eddy 1967, pp. 57–61).

4. Of course, my brief presentation greatly oversimplifies the process. For example, much of the teaching is done by the clients rather than directly by the staff. But, ultimately, the sanctions are derived from staff efforts to control work demands and to express their moral evaluation of the clients.

5. Readers who are mainly interested in what happens on an emergency ward should not be misled into thinking that it is a scene of continuous orders and threats being shouted at patients and visitors. Most directives are matter-of-fact, and most clients comply promptly with directions most of the time. But when the staff's directive power is challenged, even inadvertently, the common response is a demand for immediate compliance. This situation arises frequently enough so that on a busy unit an observrer can see instances almost every hour.

References

Becker, Howard S., Blanche Geer, Everett C. Hughes, and Anselm Strauss. 1961. *Boys in White*. Chicago: University of Chicago Press.

Belknap, Ivan. 1956. *Human Problems of a State Mental Hospital*. New York: McGraw-Hill.

Davis, Fred. 1959. "The Cab Driver and His Fare." *American Journal of Sociology* 65 (September):158–65.

Douglas, Dorothy J. 1969. "Occupational and Therapeutic Contingencies of Ambulance Services in Metropolitan Areas." Ph.D. dissertation, University of California.

Glaser, Barney, and Anselm Strauss. 1964. "The Social Loss of Dying Patients." *American Journal of Nursing* 64 (June):119–21.

Goffman, Erving. 1961. *Asylums*. New York: Doubleday.

Gold, Raymond L. 1964. "In the Basement—the Apartment-Building Janitor." In *The Human Shape of Work*, edited by Peter L. Berger. New York: Macmillan.

Henslin, James. 1968. "Trust and the Cab Driver." In *Sociology and Everyday Life*, edited by Marcello Truzzi. Englewood Cliffs, N.J.: Prentice-Hall.

Hollingshead, August B., and Frederick C. Redlich. 1958. *Social Class and Mental Illiness*. New York: Wiley.

Perrow, Charles. 1965. "Hospitals, Technology, Structure, and Goals." In *Handbook of Organizations*, edited by James G. March. Chicago: Rand McNally.

Roth, Julius A., and Elizabeth M. Eddy. 1967. *Rehabilitation for the Unwanted*. New York: Atherton.

Scheff, Thomas J. 1964. "The Societal Reaction to Deviance: Ascriptive Elements in the Psychiatric Screening of Mental Patients in a Midwestern State." *Social Problems* 11 (Spring):401–13.

————. 1966. *Being Mentally Ill*. Chicago: Aldine.

Smigel, Erwin. 1964. *Wall Street Lawyer*. New York: Free Press.

Stanton, Alfred, and Morris Schwartz. 1954. *The Mental Hospital*. New York: Basic.

Strauss, Anselm, Leonard Schatzman, Rue Bucher, Danuta Ehrlich, and Melvin Sabshin. 1964. *Psychiatric Ideologies and Institutions*. New York: Free Press.

Sudnow, David. 1967. *Passing On*. Englewood Cliffs, N.J.: Prentice-Hall.

Szasz, Thomas. 1960. "The Myth of Mental Illness." *American Psychologist* 15 (February):113–18.

Wood, Arthur Lewis. 1967. *Criminal Lawyer*. New Haven, Conn.: College and Universities Press.

Student Social Class and Teacher Expectations: The Self-Fulfilling Prophecy in Ghetto Education

Ray C. Rist

It is the purpose of this article to explore what is generally regarded as a crucial aspect of the classroom experience for the children involved—the process whereby expectations and social interactions give rise to the social organization of the class. There occurs within the classroom a social process whereby, out of a large group of children and an adult unknown to one another prior to the beginning of the school year, there emerge patterns of behavior, expectations of performance, and a mutually accepted stratification system delineating those doing well from those doing poorly. Of particular concern will be the relation of the teacher's expectations of potential academic performance to the social status of the student. Emphasis will be placed on the initial presuppositions of the teacher regarding the intellectual ability of certain groups of children and their consequences for the children's socialization into the school system. A major goal of this analysis is to ascertain the importance of the initial expectations of the teacher in relation to the child's

Excerpted from *Harvard Educational Review* 40 (August, 1970):411–51.

chances for success or failure within the public school system. (For previous studies of the significance of student social status to variations in educational experience, cf. Becker, 1952; Hollingshead, 1949; Lynd, 1937; Warner, *et al.*, 1944).

Increasingly, with the concern over intellectual growth of children and the long and close association that children experience with a series of teachers, attention is centering on the role of the teacher within the classroom (Sigel, 1969). A long series of studies have been conducted to determine what effects on children a teacher's values, beliefs, attitudes, and, most crucial to this analysis, a teacher's expectations may have. Asbell (1963), Becker (1952), Clark (1963), Gibson (1965), Harlem Youth Opportunities Unlimited (1964), Katz (1964), Kvaraceus (1965), MacKinnon (1962), Riessman (1962, 1965), Rose (1956), Rosenthal and Jacobson (1968), and Wilson (1963) have all noted that the teacher's expectations of a pupil's academic performance may, in fact, have a strong influence on the actual performance of that pupil. These authors have sought to validate a type of educational self-fulfilling prophecy: if the teacher expects high performance, she receives it, and vice versa. A major criticism that can be directed at much of the research is that although the studies may establish that a teacher has differential expectations and that these influence performance for various pupils, they have not elucidated either the basis upon which such differential expectations are formed or how they are directly manifested within the classroom milieu. It is a goal of this article to provide an analysis both of the factors that are critical in the teacher's development of expectations for various groups of her pupils and of the process by which such expectations influence the classroom experience for the teacher and the students.

The basic position to be presented in this article is that the development of expectations by the kindergarten teacher as to the differential academic potential and capability of any student was significantly determined by a series of subjectively interpreted attributes and characteristics of that student. The argument may be succinctly stated in five propositions. First, the kindergarten teacher possessed a roughly constructed "ideal type" as to what characteristics were necessary for any given student to achieve "success" both in the public school and in the larger society. These characteristics appeared to be, in significant part, related to social class criteria. Secondly, upon first meeting her students at the beginning of the school year, subjective evaluations were made of the students as to possession or absence of the desired traits necessary for anticipated "success." On the basis of the evaluation, the class was divided into groups expected to succeed (termed by the teacher "fast learners") and those anticipated to fail (termed "slow learners"). Third, differential treatment was accorded to the two groups in the classroom, with the group designated as "fast learners" receiving the majority of the teaching time, reward-directed behavior, and attention from the teacher. Those designated as "slow learners" were taught infrequently, subjected to more frequent control-oriented behavior, and received little if any supportive behavior from the teacher. Fourth, the interactional patterns between the teacher and the various groups in her class became rigidified, taking on caste-like characteristics, during the course of the school year, with the gap in completion of academic material between the two groups widening as the school year progressed. Fifth, a similar process occurred in later years of schooling, but the teachers no longer relied on subjectively interpreted data as the basis for ascertaining differences in students. Rather, they were able to utilize a variety of informational sources related to past performance as the basis for class-room grouping.

Methodology

Data for this study were collected by means of twice weekly one and one-half hour observations of a single group of black children in an urban ghetto school who began kindergarten in September of 1967. Formal observations were conducted throughout the year while the children were in kindergarten and again in 1969 when these same children were in the first half of their second-grade year. The children were also visited informally four times in the classroom during their first-grade year.[1] The difference between the formal and informal observations consisted in the fact that during formal visits, a continuous handwritten account was taken of classroom interaction and activity as it occurred. Smith and Geoffrey (1968) have labeled this method of classroom observation "microethnography." The informal observations did not include the taking of notes during the classroom visit, but comments were written after the visit. Additionally, a series of interviews were conducted with both the kindergarten and the second-grade teachers. No mechanical devices were utilized to record classroom activities or interviews.

The School

The particular school which the children attend was built in the early part of the 1960's. It has classes from kindergarten through the eighth grade and a single special education class. The enrollment fluctuates near the 900 level while the teaching staff consists of twenty-six teachers, in addition to a librarian, two physical education instructors, the principal, and an assistant principal. There are also at the school, on a part time basis, a speech therapist, social worker, nurse, and doctor, all employed by the Board of Education. All administrators, teachers, staff, and pupils are black. (The author is caucasian.) The school is located in a blighted urban area that has 98% black population within its census district. Within the school itself, nearly 500 of the 900 pupils (55%) come from families supported by funds from Aid to Dependent Children, a form of public welfare.

The Kindergarten Class

Prior to the beginning of the school year, the teacher possessed several different kinds of information regarding the children that she would have in her class. The first was the pre-registration form completed by 13 mothers of children who would be in the kindergarten class. On this form, the teacher was supplied with the name of the child, his age, the name of his parents, his home address, his phone number, and whether he had had any pre-school experience. The second source of information for the teacher was supplied two days before the beginning of school by the school worker who provided a tentative list of all children enrolled in the kindergarten class who lived in homes that received public welfare funds.

The third source of information on the child was gained as a result of the initial interview with the mother and child during the registration period, either in the few days prior to the beginning of school or else during the first days of school. In this interview, a major concern was the gathering of medical information about the child as well as the ascertaining of any specific parental concern related to the child. This latter information was noted on the "Behavioral Question-naire" where the mother was to indicate her concern, if any, on 28 different items. Such items as thumb-sucking, bed-wetting, loss of bowel control, lying, stealing, fighting, and laziness were included on this questionnaire.

The fourth source of information available to the teacher concerning the children in her class was both her own experiences with older siblings, and those of other teachers in the building related to behavior and academic performance of children in the same family. A rather strong informal norm had developed among teachers in the school such that pertinent information, especially that related to discipline matters, was to be passed on to the next teacher of the student. The teachers' lounge became the location in which they would discuss the performance of individual children as well as make comments concerning the parents and their interests in the student and the school. Frequently, during the first days of the school year, there were admonitions to a specific teacher to "watch out" for a child believed by a teacher to be a "trouble-maker." Teachers would also relate techniques of controlling the behavior of a student who had been disruptive in the class. Thus a variety of information concerning students in the school was shared, whether that information regarded academic performance, behavior in class, or the relation of the home to the school.

It should be noted that not one of these four sources of information to the teacher was related directly to the academic potential of the incoming kindergarten child. Rather, they concerned various types of social information revealing such facts as the financial status of certain families, medical care of the child, presence or absence of a telephone in the home, as well as the structure of the family in which the child lived, *i.e.*, number of siblings, whether the child lived with both, one, or neither of his natural parents.

The Teacher's Stimulus

When the kindergarten teacher made the permanent seating assignments on the eighth day of school, not only had she the above four sources of information concerning the children, but she had also had time to observe them within the classroom setting. Thus the behavior, degree and type of verbalization, dress, mannerisms, physical appearance, and performance on the early tasks assigned during class were available to her as she began to form opinions concerning the capabilities and potential of the various children. That such evaluation of the children by the teacher was beginning, I believe, there is little doubt. Within a few days, only a certain group of children were continually being called on to lead the class in the Pledge of Allegiance, read the weather calendar each day, come to the front for "show and tell" periods, take messages to the office, count the number of children present in the class, pass out materials for class projects, be in charge of equipment on the playground, and lead the class to the bathroom, library, or on a school tour. This one group of children, that continually were physically close to the teacher and had a high degree of verbal interaction with her, she placed at Table 1.

As one progressed from Table 1 to Table 2 and Table 3, there was an increasing dissimilarity between each group of children at the different tables on at least four major criteria. The first criterion appeared to be the physical appearance of the child. While the children at Table 1 were all dressed in clean clothes that were relatively new and pressed, most of the children at Table 2, and with only one exception at Table 3, were all quite poorly dressed. The clothes were old and often quite dirty. The children at Tables 2 and 3 also had a noticeably different quality and quantity of clothes to wear, especially during the winter months. Whereas the children at Table 1 would come on cold days with heavy coats and sweaters, the children at the other two tables often wore very thin spring coats and summer clothes. The single child at Table 3 who came to school quite nicely dressed came from a home in which the mother was receiving welfare funds, but was supplied with clothing for the children by the families of her brother and sister.

An additional aspect of the physical appearance of the children related to their body odor. While none of the children at Table 1 came to class with an odor of urine on them, there were two children at Table 2 and five children at Table 3 who frequently had such an odor. There was not a clear distinction among the children at the various tables as to the degree of "blackness" of their skin, but there were more children at the third table with very dark skin (five in all) than there were at the first table (three). There was also a noticeable distinction among the various groups of children as to the condition of their hair. While the three boys at Table 1 all had short hair cuts and the six girls at the same table had their hair "processed" and combed, the number of children with either matted or unprocessed hair increased at Table 2 (two boys and three girls) and eight of the children at Table 3 (four boys and four girls). None of the children in the kindergarten class wore their hair in the style of a "natural."

A second major criteria which appeared to differentiate the children at the various tables was their interactional behavior, both among themselves and with the teacher. The several children who began to develop as leaders within the class by giving directions to other members, initiating the division of the class into teams on the playground, and seeking to speak for the class to the teacher ("We want to color now"), all were placed by the teacher at Table 1. This same group of children displayed considerable ease in their interaction with her. Whereas the children at Tables 2 and 3 would often linger on the periphery of groups surrounding the teacher, the children at Table 1 most often crowded close to her.

The use of language within the classroom appeared to be the third major differentiation among the children. While the children placed at the first table were quite verbal with the teacher, the children placed at the remaining two tables spoke much less frequently with her. The children placed at the first table also displayed a greater use of Standard American English within the classroom. Whereas the children placed at the last two tables most often responded to the teacher in black dialect, the children at the first table did so very infrequently. In other words, the children at the first table were much more adept at the use of "school language" than were those at the other tables. The teacher utilized standard American English in the classroom and one group of children were able to respond in a like manner. The frequency of a "no response" to a question from the teacher was recorded at a ratio of nearly three to one for the children at the last two tables as opposed to Table 1. When questions were asked, the children who were placed at the first table most often gave a response.

The final apparent criterion by which the children at the first table were quite noticeably different from those at the other tables consisted of a series of social factors which were known to the teacher prior to her seating the children. Though it is not known to what degree she utilized this particular criterion when she assigned seats, it does contribute to developing a clear profile of the children at the various tables. Table 1 gives a summary of the distribution of the children at the three tables on a series of variables related to social and family conditions. Such variables may be considered to give indication of the relative status of the children within the room, based on the income, education and size of the family. (For a discussion of why these three variables of income, education, and family size may be considered as significant indicators of social status, cf. Frazier, 1962; Freeman, *et al.*, 1959; Gebhard, *et al.*, 1958; Kahl, 1957; Notestein, 1953; Reissman, 1959; Rose, 1956; Simpson and Yinger, 1958.)

Believing, as I do, that the teacher did not randomly assign the children to the various tables, it is then necessary to indicate the basis for the seating arrangement. I would contend that the teacher developed, utilizing some combination of the four criteria outlined above, a series of expectations about the potential performance of each child and then grouped the children according to perceived similarities in expected performance. The teacher herself informed me that the first table consisted of her "fast learners" while those at the last two tables "had no idea of what was going on in the classroom." What becomes crucial in this discussion is to ascertain the basis upon which the teacher developed her criteria of "fast learner" since there had been no formal testing of the children as to their academic potential or capacity for cognitive development. She made evaluative judgments of the expected capacities of the children to perform academic tasks after eight days of school.

TABLE 1
Distribution of Socio-Economic Status Factors by Seating Arrangement at the
Three Tables in the Kindergarten Classroom

	Seating Arrangement*		
Factors	Table 1	Table 2	Table 3
Income			
1) Families on welfare	0	2	4
2) Families with father employed	6	3	2
3) Families with mother employed	5	5	5
4) Families with both parents employed	5	3	2
5) Total family income below $3,000./yr** .	0	4	7
6) Total family income above $12,000./yr** .	4	0	0
Education			
1) Father ever grade school	6	3	2
2) Father ever high school	5	2	1
3) Father ever college	1	0	0
4) Mother ever grade school	9	10	8
5) Mother ever high school	7	6	5
6) Mother ever college	4	0	0
7) Children with pre-school experience	1	1	0
Family Size			
1) Families with one child	3	1	0
2) Families with six or more children	2	6	7
3) Average number of siblings in family	3-4	5-6	6-7
4) Families with both parents present	6	3	2

*There are nine children at Table 1, eleven at Table 2, and ten children at Table 3.
**Estimated from stated occupation.

Certain criteria became indicative of expected success and others became indicative of expected failure. Those children who closely fit the teacher's "ideal type" of the successful child were chosen for seats at Table 1. Those children that had the least "goodness of fit" with her ideal type were placed at the third table. The criteria upon which a teacher would construct her ideal type of the successful student would rest in her perception of certain attributes in the child that she believed would make for success. To understand what the teacher considered as "success," one would have to examine her perception of the larger society and whom in that larger society she perceived as successful. Thus, in the terms of Merton (1957), one may ask which was the "normative reference group" for Mrs. Caplow that she perceived as being successful.[2] I believe that the reference group utilized by Mrs. Caplow to determine what constituted success was a mixed black-white, well-educated middle class. Those attributes most desired by educated members of the middle class became the basis for her evaluation of the

children. Those who possessed these particular characteristics were expected to succeed while those who did not could be expected not to
succeed. Highly prized middle-class status for the child in the classroom was attained by demonstrating ease of interaction among adults;
high degree of verbalization in Standard American English; the ability
to become a leader; a neat and clean appearance; coming from a family
that is educated, employed, living together, and interested in the child;
and the ability to participate well as a member of a group.

The kindergarten teacher appeared to have been raised in a
home where the above values were emphasized as important. Her
mother was a college graduate, as were her brother and sisters. The
family lived in the same neighborhood for many years, and the father
held a responsible position with a public utility company in the city.
The family was devoutly religious and those of the family still in the
city attend the same church. She and other members of her family were
active in a number of civil rights organizations in the city. Thus, it
appears that the kindergarten teacher's "normative reference group"
coincided quite closely with those groups in which she did participate
and belong. There was little discrepancy between the normative values
of the mixed black-white educated middle-class and the values of the
groups in which she held membership. The attributes indicative of
"success" among those of the educated middle class had been attained
by the teacher. She was a college graduate, held positions of respect
and responsibility in the black community, lived in a comfortable
middle-class section of the city in a well-furnished and spacious home,
together with her husband earned over $20,000 per year, was active
in a number of community organizations, and had parents, brother, and
sisters similar in education, income, and occupational positions.

The teacher ascribed high status to a certain group of children
within the class who fit her perception of the criteria necessary to be
among the "fast learners" at Table 1. With her reference group orientation as to what constitute the qualities essential for "success," she responded favorably to those children who possessed such necessary
attributes. Her resultant preferential treatment of a select group of
children appeared to be derived from her belief that certain behavioral
and cultural characteristics are more crucial to learning in school than
are others. In a similar manner, those children who appeared not to
possess the criteria essential for success were ascribed low status and
described as "failures" by the teacher. They were relegated to positions
at Table 2 and 3. The placement of the children then appeared to result
from their possessing or lacking the certain desired cultural characteristics perceived as important by the teacher.

The organization of the kindergarten classroom according to the expectation of success or failure after the eighth day of school became the basis for the differential treatment of the children for the remainder of the school year. From the day that the class was assigned permanent seats, the activities in the classroom were perceivably different from previously. The fundamental division of the class into those expected to learn and those expected not to permeated the teacher's orientation to the class.

The teacher's rationalization for narrowing her attention to selected students was that the majority of the remainder of the class (in her words) "just had no idea of what was going on in the classroom." Her reliance on the few students of ascribed high social status reached such proportions that on occasion, the teacher would use one of these students as an exemplar that the remainder of the class would do well to emulate.

> (It is Fire Prevention Week and the teacher is trying to have the children say so. The children make a number of incorrect responses, a few of which follow:) Jim, who had raised his hand, in answer to the question, "Do you know what week it is?" says, "October." The teacher says "No, that's the name of the month. Jane, do you know what special week this is?" and Jane responds, "It cold outside." Teacher says, "No, that is not it either. I guess I will have to call on Pamela. Pamela, come here and stand by me and tell the rest of the boys and girls what special week this is." Pamela leaves her chair, comes and stands by the teacher, turns and faces the rest of the class. The teacher puts her arm around Pamela, and Pamela says, "It fire week." The teacher responds, "Well Pamela, that is close. Actually it is Fire Prevention Week."

On another occasion, the Friday after Halloween, the teacher informed the class that she would allow time for all the students to come to the front of the class and tell of their experiences. She, in reality, called on six students, five of whom sat at Table 1 and the sixth at Table 2. Not only on this occasion, but on others, the teacher focused her attention on the experiences of the higher status students.[3]

> (The students are involved in acting out a skit arranged by the teacher on how a family should come together to eat the evening meal.) The students acting the roles of mother, father, and daughter are all from Table 1. The boy playing the son is from Table 2. At the small dinner table set up in the center of the classroom, the four children are supposed to be sharing with each other what they had done during the day—the father at work, the mother at home, and the two children at school. The Table 2 boy makes few comments. (In real life he has no

father and his mother is supported by ADC funds.) The teacher comments, "I think that we are going to have to let Milt (Table 1) be the new son. Sam, why don't you go and sit down. Milt, you seem to be one who would know what a son is supposed to do at the dinner table. You come and take Sam's place."

In this instance, the lower-status student was penalized, not only for failing to have verbalized middle-class table talk, but more fundamentally, for lacking middle-class experiences. He had no actual father to whom he could speak at the dinner table, yet he was expected to speak fluently with an imaginary one.

Though the blackboard was long enough to extend parallel to all three tables, the teacher wrote such assignments as arithmetic problems and drew all illustrations on the board in front of the students at Table 1. A rather poignant example of the penalty the children at Table 3 had to pay was that they often could not see the board material.

> Lilly stands up out of her seat. Mrs. Caplow asks Lilly what she wants. Lilly makes no verbal response to the question. Mrs. Caplow then says rather firmly to Lilly, "Sit down." Lilly does. However, Lilly sits down sideways in the chair (so she is still facing the teacher). Mrs. Caplow instructs Lilly to put her feet under the table. This Lilly does. Now she is facing directly away from the teacher and the blackboard where the teacher is demonstrating to the students how to print the letter, "O."

The realization of the self-fulfilling prophecy within the classroom was in its final stages by late May of the kindergarten year. Lack of communication with the teacher, lack of involvement in the class activities and infrequent instruction all characterized the situation of the children at Tables 2 and 3. During one observational period of an hour in May, not a single act of communication was directed towards any child at either Table 2 or 3 by the teacher except for twice commanding "sit down." The teacher devoted her attention to teaching those children at Table 1. Attempts by the children at Table 2 and 3 to elicit the attention of the teacher were much fewer than earlier in the school year.

In June, after school had ended for the year, the teacher was asked to comment on the children in her class. Of the children at the first table, she noted:

> I guess the best way to describe it is that very few children in my class are exceptional. I guess you could notice this just from the way the children were seated this year. Those at Table 1 gave consistently the most responses throughout the year and seemed most interested and aware of what was going on in the classroom.

Of those children at the remaining two tables, the teacher commented:

> It seems to me that some of the children at Table 2 and most all the children at Table 3 at times seem to have no idea of what is going on in the classroom and were off in another world all by themselves. It just appears that some can do it and some cannot. I don't think that it is the teaching that affects those that cannot do it, but some are just basically low achievers.

The Students' Response

The students in the kindergarten classroom did not sit passively, internalizing the behavior the teacher directed towards them. Rather, they responded to the stimuli of the teacher, both in internal differentiations within the class itself and also in their response to the teacher. The type of response a student made was highly dependent upon whether he sat at Table 1 or at one of the two other tables. The single classroom of black students did not respond as a homogenous unit to the teacher-inspired social organization of the room.

For the high-status students at Table 1, the response to the track system of the teacher appeared to be at least three-fold. One such response was the directing of ridicule and belittlement towards those children at Tables 2 and 3. At no point during the entire school year was a child from Table 2 or 3 ever observed directing such remarks at the children at Table 1.

> Mrs. Caplow says, "Raise your hand if you want me to call on you. I won't call on anyone who calls out." She then says, "All right, now who knows that numeral? What is it, Tony?" Tony makes no verbal response but rather walks to the front of the classroom and stands by Mrs. Caplow. Gregory calls out, "He don't know. He scared." Then Ann calls out, "It sixteen, stupid." (Tony sits at Table 3, Gregory and Ann sit at Table 1.)

> Jim starts to say out loud that he is smarter than Tom. He repeats it over and over again, "I smarter than you. I smarter than you." (Jim sits at Table 1, Tom at Table 3).

> Milt came over to the observer and told him to look at Lilly's shoes. I asked him why I should and he replied, "Because they so ragged and dirty." (Milt is at Table 1, Lilly at Table 3.)

> When I asked Lilly what it was that she was drawing, she replied, "A parachute." Gregory interrupted and said, "She can't draw nothin'."

The problems of those children who were of lower status were compounded, for not only had the teacher indicated her low esteem of them, but their peers had also turned against them. The implications for the future schooling of a child who lacks the desired status credentials in a classroom where the teacher places high value on middle-class "success" values and mannerisms are tragic.

It must not be assumed, however, that though the children at Tables 2 and 3 did not participate in classroom activities and were systematically ignored by the teacher, they did not learn. I contend that in fact they did learn, but in a fundamentally different way from the way in which the high-status children at Table 1 learned. The children at Table 2 and 3 who were unable to interact with the teacher began to develop patterns of interaction among themselves whereby they would discuss the material that the teacher was presenting to the children at Table 1. Thus I have termed their method of grasping the material "secondary learning" to imply that knowledge was not gained in direct interaction with the teacher, but through the mediation of peers and also through listening to the teacher though she was not speaking to them. That the children were grasping, in part, the material presented in the classroom, was indicated to me in home visits when the children who sat at Table 3 would relate material specifically taught by the teacher to the children at Table 1. *It is not as though the children at Table 2 and 3 were ignorant of what was being taught in the class, but rather that the patterns of classroom interaction established by the teacher inhibited the low-status children from verbalizing what knowledge they had accumulated.* Thus, from the teacher's terms of reference, those who could not discuss must not know. Her expectations continued to be fulfilled, for though the low-status children had accumulated knowledge, they did not have the opportunity to verbalize it and, consequently, the teacher could not know what they had learned. Children at Table 2 and 3 had learned material presented in the kindergarten class, but would continue to be defined by the teacher as children who could not or would not learn.

A second response of the higher status students to the differential behavior of the teacher towards them was to seek solidarity and closeness with the teacher and urge Table 2 and 3 children to comply with her wishes.

> The teacher is out of the room. Pamela says to the class, "We all should clean up before the teacher comes." Shortly thereafter the teacher has still not returned and Pamela begins to supervise other children in the class. She says to one girl from Table 3, "Girl, leave that piano alone." The child plays only a short time longer and then leaves.

> The teacher has instructed the students to go and take off their coats since they have come in from the playground. Milt says, "Ok y'al, let's go take off our clothes."

> At this time Jim says to the teacher, "Mrs. Caplow, they pretty flowers on your desk." Mrs. Caplow responded, "Yes, Jim, those flowers are roses, but we will not have roses much longer. The roses will die and rest until spring because it is getting so cold outside."

> When the teacher tells the students to come from their desks and form a semi-circle around her, Gregory scoots up very close to Mrs. Caplow and is practically sitting in her lap.

> Gregory has come into the room late. He takes off his coat and goes to the coat room to hang it up. He comes back and sits down in the very front of the group and is now closest to the teacher.

The higher-status students in the class perceived the lower status and esteem the teacher ascribed to those children at Tables 2 and 3. Not only would the Table 1 students attempt to control and ridicule the Table 2 and 3 students, but they also perceived and verbalized that they, the Table 1 students, were better students and were receiving differential treatment from the teacher.

> The children are rehearsing a play, Little Red Riding Hood. Pamela tells the observer, "The teacher gave me the best part." The teacher overheard this comment, smiled, and made no verbal response.

> The children are preparing to go on a field trip to a local dairy. The teacher has designated Gregory as the "sheriff" for the trip. Mrs. Caplow stated that for the field trip today Gregory would be the sheriff. Mrs. Caplow simply watched as Gregory would walk up to a student and push him back into line saying, "Boy, stand where you suppose to." Several times he went up to students from Table 3 and showed them the badge that the teacher had given to him and said, "Teacher made me sheriff."

The children seated at the first table were internalizing the attitudes and behavior of the teacher toward those at the remaining two tables. That is, as the teacher responded from her reference group orientation as to which type of children were most likely to succeed and which type most likely to fail, she behaved toward the two groups of children in a significantly different manner. The children from Table 1 were also learning through emulating the teacher how to behave toward other black children who came from low-income and poorly educated homes. The teacher, who came from a well-educated and middle-income family, and the children from Table 1 who came from a background similar to the teacher's, came to respond to the children from poor and uneducated homes in a strikingly similar manner.

The lower-status students in the classroom from Tables 2 and 3 responded in significantly different ways to the stimuli of the teacher.

The two major responses of the Table 2 and 3 students were withdrawal and verbal and physical in-group hostility.

The withdrawal of some of the lower-status students as a response to the ridicule of their peers and the isolation from the teacher occasionally took the form of physical withdrawal, but most often it was psychological.

> Betty, a very poorly dressed child, had gone outside and hidden behind the door. . . . Mrs. Caplow sees Betty leave and goes outside to bring her back, says in an authoritative and irritated voice, "Betty, come here right now." When the child returns, Mrs. Caplow seizes her by the right arm, brings her over to the group, and pushes her down to the floor. Betty begins to cry. . . . The teacher now shows the group a large posterboard with a picture of a white child going to school.

> The teacher is demonstrating how to mount leaves between two pieces of wax paper. Betty leaves the group and goes back to her seat and begins to color.

> The teacher is instructing the children in how they can make a "spooky thing" for Halloween. James turns away from the teacher and puts his head on his desk. Mrs. Caplow looks at James and says, "James, sit up and look here."

> The children are supposed to make United Nations flags. They have been told that they do not have to make exact replicas of the teacher's flag. They have before them the materials to make the flags. Lilly and James are the only children who have not yet started to work on their flags. Presently, James has his head under his desk and Lilly simply sits and watches the other children. Now they are both staring into space. . . . (5 minutes later) Lilly and James have not yet started, while several other children have already finished. . . . A minute later, with the teacher telling the children to begin to clean up their scraps, Lilly is still staring into space.

> The teacher has the children seated on the floor in front of her asking them questions about a story that she had read to them. The teacher says, "June, your back is turned. I want to see your face." (The child had turned completely around and was facing away from the group).

> The teacher told the students to come from their seats and form a semi-circle on the floor in front of her. The girls all sit very close to the piano where the teacher is seated. The boys sit a good distance back away from the girls and away from the teacher. Lilly finishes her work at her desk and comes and sits at the rear of the group of girls, but she is actually in the middle of the open space separating the boys and the girls. She speaks to no one and simply sits staring off.

The verbal and physical hostility that the children at Tables 2 and 3 began to act out among themselves in many ways mirrored what the Table 1 students and the teacher were also saying about them. There are numerous instances in the observations of the children at Tables 2 and 3 calling one another "stupid," "dummy," or "dumb, dumb." Racial overtones were noted on two occasions when one boy called another a "nigger," and on another occasion when a girl called a boy an "almond head." Threats of beatings, "whoppins," and even spitting on a child were also recorded among those at Tables 2 and 3. Also at Table 2, two instances were observed in which a single child hoarded all the supplies for the whole table. Similar manifestations of hostility were not observed among those children at the first table. The single incident of strong anger or hostility by one child at Table 1 against another child at the same table occurred when one accused the other of copying from his paper. The second denied it and an argument ensued.

In the organization of hostility within the classroom, there may be at least the tentative basis for the rejection of a popular "folk myth" of American society, which is that children are inherently cruel to one another and that this tendency toward cruelty must be socialized into socially acceptable channels. The evidence from this classroom would indicate that much of the cruelty displayed was a result of the social organization of the class. Those children at Tables 2 and 3 who displayed cruelty appeared to have learned from the teacher that it was acceptable to act in an aggressive manner toward those from low-income and poorly educated backgrounds. Their cruelty was not diffuse, but rather focused on a specific group—the other poor children. Likewise, the incidence of such behavior increased over time. The children at Tables 2 and 3 did not begin the school year ridiculing and belittling each other. This social process began to emerge with the outline of the social organization the teacher imposed upon the class. The children from the first table were also apparently socialized into a pattern of behavior in which they perceived that they could direct hostility and aggression towards those at Table 2 and 3, but not towards one another. The children in the class learned who was vulnerable to hostility and who was not through the actions of the teacher. She established the patterns of differential behavior which the class adopted.

First Grade

Though Mrs. Caplow had anticipated that only twelve of the children from the kindergarten class would attend the first grade in the same school, eighteen of the children were assigned during the summer to the first-grade classroom in the main building. The remaining children either were assigned to a new school a few blocks north, or were assigned to a branch school designed to handle the overflow from the main building, or had moved away. Mrs. Logan, the first-grade teacher, had had more than twenty years of teaching experience in the city public school system, and every school in which she had taught was more than 90 percent black. During the 1968–1969 school year, four informal visits were made to the classroom of Mrs. Logan. No visits were made to either the branch school or the new school to visit children from the kindergarten class who had left their original school. During my visits to the first-grade room, I kept only brief notes of the short conversations that I had with Mrs. Logan; I did not conduct formal observations of the activities of the children in the class.

During the first-grade school year, there were thirty-three children in the classroom. In addition to the eighteen from the kindergarten class, there were nine children repeating the first grade and also six children new to the school. Of the eighteen children who came from the kindergarten class to the first grade in the main building, seven were from the previous year's Table 1, six from Table 2, and five from Table 3.

In the first-grade classroom, Mrs. Logan also divided the children into three groups. Those children whom she placed at "Table A" had all been Table 1 students in kindergarten. No student who had sat at Table 2 or 3 in kindergarten was placed at Table A in the first grade. Instead, all the students from Table 2 and 3—with one exception—were placed together at "Table B." At the third table which Mrs. Logan called "Table C," she placed the nine children repeating the grade plus Betty who had sat at Table 3 in the kindergarten class. Of the six new students, two were placed at Table A and four at Table C. Thus the totals for the three tables were nine students at Table A, ten at Table B, and fourteen at Table C.

The seating arrangement that began in the kindergarten as a result of the teacher's definition of which children possessed or lacked the perceived necessary characteristics for success in the public school system emerged in the first grade as a caste phenomenon in which there was absolutely no mobility upward. That is, of those children whom Mrs. Caplow had perceived as potential "failures" and thus seated at either Table 2 or 3 in the kindergarten, not one was assigned to the table of the "fast learners" in the first grade.

The initial label given to the children by the kindergarten teacher had been reinforced in her interaction with those students throughout the school year. When the children were ready to pass into the first grade, their ascribed labels from the teacher as either successes or failures assumed objective dimensions. The first-grade teacher no longer had to rely on merely the presence or absence of certain behavioral and attitudinal characteristics to ascertain who would do well and who would do poorly in the class. Objective records of the "readiness" material completed by the children during the kindergarten year were available to her. Thus, upon the basis of what material the various tables in kindergarten had completed, Mrs. Logan could form her first-grade tables for reading and arithmetic.

The kindergarten teacher's disproportionate allocation of her teaching time resulted in the Table 1 students' having completed more material at the end of the school year than the remainder of the class. As a result, the Table 1 group from kindergarten remained intact in the first grade, as they were the only students prepared for the first-grade reading material. Those children from Tables 2 and 3 had not yet completed all the material from kindergarten and had to spend the first weeks of the first-grade school year finishing kindergarten level lessons. The criteria established by the school system as to what constituted the completion of the necessary readiness material to begin first-grade lessons insured that the Table 2 and 3 students could not be placed at Table A. The only children who had completed the material were those from Table 1, defined by the kindergarten teacher as successful students and whom she then taught most often because the remainder of the class "had no idea what was going on."

It would be somewhat misleading, however, to indicate that there was absolutely no mobility for any of the students between the seating assignments in kindergarten and those in the first grade. All of the students save one who had been seated at Table 3 during the kindergarten year were moved "up" to Table B in the first grade. The majority of Table C students were those having to repeat the grade level. As a tentative explanation of Mrs. Logan's rationale for the development of the Table C seating assignments, she may have assumed that within her class there existed one group of students who possessed so very little of the perceived behavioral patterns and attitudes necessary for success that they had to be kept separate from the remainder of the class. (Table C was placed by itself on the opposite side of the room from Tables A and B.) The Table C students were spoken of by the first-grade teacher in a manner reminiscent of the way in which Mrs. Caplow spoke of the Table 3 students the previous year.

Students who were placed at Table A appeared to be perceived by Mrs. Logan as students who not only possessed the criteria necessary for future success, both in the public school system and in the larger society, but who also had proven themselves capable in academic work.

These students appeared to possess the characteristics considered most essential for "middle-class" success by the teacher. Though students at Table B lacked many of the "qualities" and characteristics of the Table A students, they were not perceived as lacking them to the same extent as those placed at Table C.

A basic tenet in explaining Mrs. Logan's seating arrangement is, of course, that she shared a similar reference group and set of values as to what constituted "success" with Mrs. Caplow in the kindergarten class. Both women were well educated, were employed in a professional occupation, lived in middle-income neighborhoods, were active in a number of charitable and civil rights organizations, and expressed strong religious convictions and moral standards. Both were educated in the city teacher's college and had also attained graduate degrees. Their backgrounds as well as the manner in which they described the various groups of students in their classes would indicate that they shared a similar reference group and set of expectations as to what constituted the indices of the "successful" student.

Second Grade

Of the original thirty students in kindergarten and eighteen in first grade, ten students were assigned to the only second-grade class in the main building. Of the eight original kindergarten students who did not come to the second grade from the first, three were repeating first grade while the remainder had moved. The teacher in the second grade also divided the class into three groups, though she did not give them number or letter designations. Rather, she called the first group, the "Tigers." The middle group she labeled the "Cardinals," while the second-grade repeaters plus several new children assigned to the thrid table were designated by the teacher as "Clowns."[4]

In the second-grade seating scheme, no student from the first grade who had not sat at Table A was moved "up" to the Tigers at the beginning of second grade. All those students who in first grade had been at Table B or Table C and returned to the second grade were placed in the Cardinal group. The Clowns consisted of six second-grade repeaters plus three students who were new to the class. Of the ten original kindergarten students who came from the first grade, six were Tigers and four were Cardinals. Table 2 illustrates that the distribution of social economic factors from the kindergarten year remained essentially unchanged in the second grade.

By the time the children came to the second grade, their seating arrangement appeared to be based not on the teacher's expectations of how the child might perform, but rather on the basis of past perforcance of the child. Available to the teacher when she formulated the seating groups were grade sheets from both kindergarten and first grade, IQ scores from kindergarten, listing of parental occupations for approximately half of the class, reading scores from a test given to all students at the end of first grade, evaluations from the speech teacher and also the informal evaluations from both the kindergarten and first-grade teachers.

TABLE 2
Distribution of Socio-Economic Status Factors by Seating Arrangement
in the Three Reading Groups in the Second-Grade Classroom

	Seating Arrangement*		
Factors	*Tigers*	*Cardinals*	*Clowns*
Income			
1) Families on welfare	2	4	7
2) Families with father employed	8	5	1
3) Families with mother employed	7	11	6
4) Families with both parents employed	7	5	1
5) Total family income below $3,000./yr.** .	1	5	8
6) Total family income above $12,000./yr.** .	4	0	0
Education			
1) Father ever grade school	8	6	1
2) Father ever high school	7	4	0
3) Father ever college	0	0	0
4) Mother ever grade school	12	13	9
5) Mother ever high school	9	7	4
6) Mother ever college	3	0	0
7) Children with pre-school experience	1	0	0
Family Size			
1) Families with one child	2	0	1
2) Families with six or more children	3	8	5
3) Average number of siblings in family	3-4	6-7	7-8
4) Families with both parents present	8	6	1

*There are twelve children in the Tiger group, fourteen children in the Cardinal group, and nine children in the Clown group.
**Estimated from stated occupation.

The single most important data utilized by the teacher in devising seating groups were the reading scores indicating the performance of the students at the end of the first grade. The second-grade teacher indicated that she attempted to divide the groups primarily on the basis of these scores. The Tigers were designated as the highest reading group and the Cardinals the middle. The Clowns were assigned a first-grade reading level, though they were, for the most part, repeaters from the previous year in second grade. The caste character of the reading groups became clear as the year progressed, in that all three groups were reading in different books and it was school policy that no child could go on to a new book until the previous one had been completed. Thus there was no way for the child, should he have demonstrated competence at a higher reading level, to advance, since he had to continue at the pace of the rest of his reading group. The teacher never allowed individual reading in order that a child might finish a book on his own and move ahead. *No matter how well a child in the lower reading groups might have read, he was destined to remain in the same reading group. This is, in a sense, another manifestation of the self-fulfilling prophecy in that a "slow learner" had no option but to continue to be a slow learner, regardless of performance or potential.* Initial expectations of the kindergarten teacher two years earlier as to the ability of the child resulted in placement in a reading group, whether high or low, from which there appeared to be no escape. The child's journey through the early grades of school at one reading level and in one social grouping appeared to be pre-ordained from the eighth day of kindergarten.

Notes

1. The author, due to a teaching appointment out of the city, was unable to conduct formal observations of the children during their first-grade year.

2. The names of all staff and students are pseudonyms. Names are provided to indicate that the discussion relates to living persons, and not to fictional characters developed by the author.

3. Through the remainder of the paper, reference to "high" or "low" status students refers to status ascribed to the student by the teacher. Her ascription appeared to be based on perceptions of valued behaviorial and cultural characteristics present or absent in any individual student.

4. The names were not given to the groups until the third week of school, though the seating arrangement was established on the third day.

References

Adams, R. G. "The Behavior of Pupils in Democratic and Autocratic Social Climates." Abstracts of Dissertations, Stanford University, 1945.

Anderson, H. *Studies in Teachers' Classroom Personalities.* Stanford: Stanford University Press, 1946.

Anderson, H.; Brewer, J.; and Reed, M. "Studies of Teachers' Classroom Personalities, III. Follow-up Studies of the Effects of Dominative and Integrative Contracts on Children's Behavior." *Applied Psychology Monograph.* Stanford: Stanford University Press, 1946.

Asbell, B. "Not Like Other Children." *Redbook,* 65 (October, 1963), pp. 114–118.

Austin, Mary C. and Morrison, Coleman. *The First R: The Harvard Report on Reading in Elementary Schools.* New York: Macmillan, 1963.

Becker, H. S. "Social Class Variation in Teacher-Pupil Relationship." *Journal of Educational Sociology* 25 (1952):451–465.

Borg, W. "Ability Grouping in the Pupil Schools." Cooperative Research Project 557. Salt Lake City: Utah State University, 1964.

Clark, K. B. "Educational Stimulation of Racially Disadvantaged Children." *Education in Depressed Areas.* Edited by A. H. Passow. New York: Columbia University Press, 1963.

Coleman, J. S., et al. *Equality of Educational Opportunity.* Washington, D.C.: United States Government Printing Office, 1966.

Deutsch, M. "Minority Groups and Class Status as Related to Social and Personality Factors in Scholastic Achievement." *The Disadvantaged Child.* Edited by M. Deutsch, et al. New York: Basic Books, 1967.

Eddy, E. *Walk the White Line.* Garden City, N. Y.: Doubeday, 1967.

Frazier, E. F. *Black Bourgeoise.* New York: The Free Press, 1957.

Freeman, R.; Whelpton, P.; and Campbell, *A Family Planning, Sterility and Population Growth.* New York: McGraw-Hill, 1959.

Fuchs, E. *Teachers Talk.* Garden City, N. Y.: Doubleday, 1967.

Gebhard, P.; Pomeroy, W.; Martin, C.; and Christenson, C. *Pregnancy, Birth and Abortion.* New York: Harper & Row, 1958.

Gibson, G.: "Aptitude Tests." *Science,* 1965, *149,* 583.

Goldberg, M.; Passow, A.; and Justman, J. *The Effects of Ability Grouping.* New York: Teachers College Press, Columbia University, 1966.

Harlem Youth Opportunities Unlimited. *Youth in the Ghetto.* New York: HARYOU, 1964.

Henry, J. "Docility, or Giving the Teacher What She Wants." *Journal of Social Issues* 11 (1955):2.

―――. "The Problem of Spontaneity, Initiative and Creativity in Suburban Classrooms." *American Journal of Orthopsychiatry* 29 (1959):1.

―――."Golden Rule Days: American Schoolrooms." *Culture Against Man.* New York: Random House, 1963.

Hollingshead, A. *Elmtown's Youth.* New York: John Wiley & Sons, 1949.

Jackson, P. *Life in Classrooms.* New York: Holt, Rinehart & Winston, 1968.

Kahl, J. A. *The American Class Structure.* New York: Holt, Rinehart & Winston, 1957.

Katz, I. "Review of Evidence Relating to Effects of Desegregation on Intellectual Performance of Negroes." *American Psychologist* 19 (1964):381–399.

Kelly, H. and Thibaut, J. "Experimental Studies of Group Problem Solving and Process." *Handbook of Social Psychology,* Vol. 2. Edited by G. Lindzey. Reading, Mass.: Addison-Wesley, 1954.

Kohl, H. *36 Children.* New York: New American Library, 1967.

Kozol, J. *Death at an Early Age.* Boston: Houghton Mifflin, 1967.

Kvaraceus, W. C. "Disadvantaged Children and Youth: Programs of Promise or Pretense?" Burlingame: California Teachers Association, 1965. (Mimeographed.)

Lawrence, S. "Ability Grouping." Unpublished manuscript prepared for Center for Educational Policy Research, Harvard Graduate School of Education, Cambridge, Mass., 1969.

Leacock, E. *Teaching and Learning in City Schools.* New York: Basic Books, 1969.

Lewin, K.; Lippitt, R.; and White R. "Patterns of Aggressive Behavior in

Experimentally Created Social Climates." *Journal of Social Psychology* 10 (1939): 271–299.

Lynd, H. and Lynd, R. *Middletown in Transition.* New York: Harcourt, Brace & World, 1937.

MacKinnon, D. W. "The Nature and Nurture of Creative Talent." *American Psychologist* 17 (1962):484–495.

Merton, R. K. *Social Theory and Social Structure.* Revised and Enlarged. New York: The Free Press, 1957.

Moore, A. *Realities of the Urban Classroom.* Garden City, N.Y.: Doubleday, 1967.

Notestein, F. "Class Differences in Fertility." *Class, Status and Power.* Edited by R. Bendix and S. Lipset. New York: The Free Press, 1953.

Preston, M. and Heintz, R. "Effects of Participatory Versus Supervisory Leadership on Group Judgment." *Journal of Abnormal Social Psychology* 44 (1949): 345–355.

Riessman, F. *The Culturally Deprived Child.* New York: Harper and Row, 1962.

———. "Teachers of the Poor: A Five Point Program." Burlingame: California Teachers Association, 1965. (Mimeographed.)

Reissman, L. *Class in American Society.* New York: The Free Press, 1959.

Robbins, F. "The Impact of Social Climate upon a College Class." *School Review* 60 (1952):275–284.

Rose, A. *The Negro in America.* Boston: Beacon Press, 1956.

Rosenthal, R. and Jacobson, Lenore. *Pygmalion in the Classroom.* New York: Holt, Rinehart & Winston, 1968.

Sigel, I. "The Piagetian System and the World of Education." *Studies in Cognitive Development.* Edited by D. Elkind and J. Flavell. New York: Oxford University Press, 1969.

Simpson, G. and Yinger, J. M. *Racial and Cultural Minorities.* New York: Harper and Row, 1958.

Smith, L. and Geoffrey, W. *The Complexities of an Urban Classroom.* New York: Holt, Rinehart & Winston, 1968.

Smith, M. "Equality of Educational Opportunity: The Basic Findings Reconsidered." *On Equality of Educational Opportunity.* Edited by F. Mosteller and D. P. Moynihan. New York: Random House, 1971.

Warner, W. L.; Havighurst, R.; and Loeb, M. *Who Shall Be Educated?* New York: Harper and Row, 1944.

Wilson, A. B. "Social Stratification and Academic Achievement." *Education in Depressed Areas.* Edited by A. H. Passow. New York: Teachers College Press, Columbia University, 1963.

Chapter IX

Interorganizational Relations

Interorganizational relations are the variety of interactions between two or more organizations designed to enhance organizational goals. While there is a less extensive literature on interorganizational analysis as compared with intraorganizational research and theory, the increasing development of formalized relations between organizations illuminates its significance. Some well-known examples include social welfare coordinating agencies, federations of private and state colleges and universities, intergovernmental agencies, hospital confederations, and federations of churches and municipal health and welfare departments. It is useful to study interorganizational relationships in order to understand the conditions that lead to the emergence of relationships between organizations, to become sensitive to consequences of these relationships on intraorganizational structure, processes, and clientele, and to become aware of the forms of linkages which effectively join organizations to each other.

One approach to the analysis of interorganizational relations involves the study of an "organizational set" which is composed of a network of organizations in interaction with a focal organization or a class of focal organizations (Evan, 1965). Here a focal organization is embedded in an environment of input and output organizations with which it has interactions. Input organizations provide various types of resources for a focal organization, including personnel, legitimation, clients, and capital, while output organizations receive a product, new knowledge, a service, or a client system from a focal organization.

Figure I provides a description of the interactions between a focal organization and a network of organizations in its environment. The focal organization is a community juvenile delinquency project. Only two variables are used to illustrate the types of interactions between the focal organization and the network of organizations in its environment: standardized relations and awareness of interdependence. Standardized relations refers to repetitive and predictable actions, that is, client referrals, requests for information, and the like. By awareness of interdependence we mean that the focal organization and other organizations in its organizational set have formally recognized as a matter of public policy that a state of interdependence exists (Litwak and Hylton, 1962). The choice of variables is unlimited and, in part, depends upon the investigator's interests. For example, in a similar approach using the concept of organizational set to illustrate the relations between organizations, Hall (1972) included the following variables: the frequency of interaction, formalization of relationships, and whether the relationship was cooperative or conflictual. Other studies have begun to identify those variables which are important in the analysis of interorganizational analysis and the specification of conditions that would allow predictions about the direction of relationships between variables.

This illustration is only descriptive of a particular organizational set and does not deal with relations among all members of the organizational set or the complexities of these relations. Thus, for example, the focal organization has highly developed standardized relations with the police department, juvenile court, probation and parole office, the state youth corrections board, and the state correctional institution. However, high standardization does not necessarily mean high awareness of interdependence.

Other approaches to the study of relations between organizations include the study of (1) the relations between an entire network of organizations, (2) the interactions between a pair of organizations within a network, or (3) the forms of linkages organizations use to relate to other organizations.

A ubiquitous problem confronting organizations in their relations with other units is the need to maintain their functional autonomy and institutional identity (Gouldner, 1959). This is particularly problematic for human service organizations. Since these organizations are frequently required to coordinate and exchange their activities with a variety of other organizations, they are constrained to manage the problem of environmental dependence. Organizational strategies must be developed to deal with dependent relations which introduce constraints, contingencies, and problems threatening organizational domain (Thompson, 1967). What are some unique features of human service organizations that create problems in the management of interorganizational relations?

First, human service organizations frequently are faced with the dilemma of providing multiple services versus specialized services to meet client needs. While the provision of multiple services allows the organization to meet a broader spectrum of client needs, it increases the dependence of the organization on its environment and reduces its

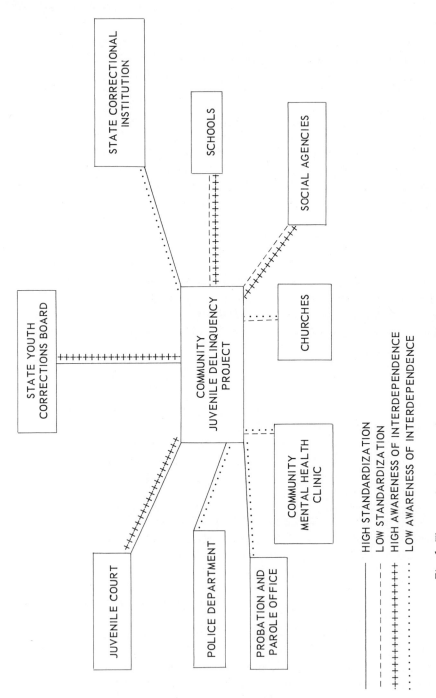

Fig. 1. The organization set and standardization of relations and awareness of interdependence

STATE CORRECTIONAL INSTITUTION

SCHOOLS

SOCIAL AGENCIES

STATE YOUTH CORRECTIONS BOARD

COMMUNITY JUVENILE DELINQUENCY PROJECT

CHURCHES

JUVENILE COURT

POLICE DEPARTMENT

PROBATION AND PAROLE OFFICE

COMMUNITY MENTAL HEALTH CLINIC

HIGH STANDARDIZATION
LOW STANDARDIZATION
+++++++++++ HIGH AWARENESS OF INTERDEPENDENCE
·············· LOW AWARENESS OF INTERDEPENDENCE

distinctiveness. On the other hand, as an organization increases its specialization it tends to become less dependent on the environment. Thus, as Litwak and Hylton (1962) point out, welfare organizations with narrowly prescribed goals, such as the American Cancer Society and the Red Cross, were able to establish distinctive markets for the recruitment of financial resources and were able to reduce their dependency on other agencies as well as resist pressures to affiliate with local Community Chest organizations.

Whenever the provision of specialized services requires the establishment of relations with other organizations providing complimentary services, the effectiveness of the focal organization may partially be determined by the type of exchanges it develops with these organizations. For example, the effectiveness of a job retraining center may be dependent upon the quality of jobs an employment placement service provides for the center's clients.

Second, an increase in specialization may require the client to transact with a wide range of organizations in order to have his needs met. Hence, the burden to locate complimentary services will invariably fall upon the client who is forced to undergo multiple and overlapping processing by the various organizations from whom he seeks services.

Third, human service organizations often emerge in response to a specific set of human needs which are identified and promoted by such bodies as community interests groups, legislators, and professional associations. As a result the services of these organizations tend to be segmental and reflect the ideologies and interests of the social groups which promote their development. Examples of such organizations would include Planned Parenthood, associations for the blind and emotionally disturbed and anti-poverty agencies. The segregation of services by client or type of service or both only intensifies the problems of coordination for these organizations.

Finally, because of political, social, and demographic changes in the social environment of human service organizations, they frequently find it necessary to develop new interorganizational relations in order to accommodate these changes (Stinchcombe, McDill, Walker, 1968). For example, pressures to serve indigent populations may require a family service agency to interact with a local community action agency or another grass-roots organization with access to such populations.

The articles in this section reflect many of the issues we have raised. In the first selection by Levine and White interorganizational relations are conceptualized as a voluntary exchange relationship between organizations for the purpose of enhancing their individual goals.

In stressing resource acquisition as the critical basis of exchange relations, Levine and White argue that research scarcity in one organization makes interorganizational exchange essential. According to their view, organizational interdependence is contingent upon three conditions: (1) the accessibility of each organization to necessary elements from external sources, (2) the objectives of the organization, and particular functions to which it allocates the elements it controls, and (3) the degree to which domain consensus exists among the various organizations. The direction in which organizational exchange occurs is highly variable, hence Levine and White assert that it may either be unilateral, reciprocal, or joint.

Litwak and Hylton present a theory of interorganizational relations which focuses on the concept of interdependence. They argue that low interdependence leads to no coordination between organizations and high interdependence leads to organizational merger. Therefore, according to their view coordination is likely to occur only under conditions of moderate independence. The type of coordinating mechanism which emerges is hypothesized to result from the interaction of three variables: the *number* of interdependent organizations, the degree of their *awareness* of their interdependence, and the extent of their *standardization* (predictability).

Aiken and Hage, in a study based on data from sixteen social welfare and health organizations, consider the joint program as the element of interorganizational relationship. The measure and degree of organizational interdependence is defined as the number of joint programs that an organization has with other organizations. Aiken and Hage show that organizations which participate in joint programs tend to be more complex, more innovative, have more active internal communication channels and somewhat more decentralized decision-making structures.

References

Evan, W. M. 1965. "Toward a Theory of Interorganizational Relations." *Management Science* 2 (August):B 217–30.

Gouldner, A. 1959. "Reciprocity and Autonomy in Functional Theory." Pp. 241–70 in Llewellyn Gross (ed.), *Symposium on Sociological Theory*. New York: Harper and Row.

Hall, R. H. 1972. *Organizations: Structure and Process*. Englewood Cliffs, New Jersey: Prentice-Hall, Inc.

Litwak, E., and Rothman, J. 1970. "Towards The Theory and Practice of Coordination Between Formal Organizations." Pp. 137–86 in William R. Rosengren and Mark Lefton (eds.), *Organizations and Clients*. Columbus, Ohio: Charles E. Merrill.

Marrett, C. B. 1971. "On The Specification of Interorganizational Dimensions." *Sociology and Social Research* 56 (October):83–99.

Purcell, F. P., and Specht, H. 1965. "The House On Sixth Street." *Social Work* (October):69–76.

Stinchcombe, A. L., McDill, M. S., and Walker, D. R. 1968. "Demography of Organizations," *American Journal of Sociology* (November):221–29.

Thompson, J. D. 1967. *Organizations in Action.* New York: McGraw Hill.

Thompson, J. D., and McEwen, W. J. 1958. "Organizational Goals and Environment: Goal-Setting as an Interaction Process." *American Sociological Review* 23 (February):23–31.

Exchange as a Conceptual Framework for the Study of Interorganizational Relationships

Sol Levine and Paul E. White

Sociologists have devoted considerable attention to the study of formal organizations, particularly in industry, government, and the trade union field. Their chief focus, however, has been on patterns within rather than between organizations. Studies of interrelationships have largely been confined to units within the same organizational structure or between a pair of complementary organizations such as management and labor. Dimock's study of jurisdictional conflict between two federal agencies is a notable exception.[1] Another is a study of a community reaction to disaster by Form and Nosow in which the authors produce revealing data on the interaction pattern of local health organizations. The authors observe that "organizational cooperation was facilitated among organizations with similar internal structures."[2] March and Simon suggest that interorganizational conflict is very similar to intergroup conflict within organizations but present no supporting data.[3] Blau has commented on the general problems involved in studying multiple organizations.[4] In pointing up the need to study the organization in relation to its environment, Etzioni specifies the area of interorganizational relationships as one of the three meriting further intensive empirical study.[5]

Health and social welfare agencies within a given community offer an excellent opportunity for exploring patterns of relationship

Reprinted from *Administrative Science Quarterly* 5 (March, 1961):583–601.

among organizations. There are an appreciable number of such organizations in any fairly large urban American community. Most of them
are small so that relatively few individuals have to be interviewed to
obtain information on their interaction. Within any community setting,
varying kinds of relations exist between official and voluntary organizations concerned with health and welfare. Thus welfare agencies may
use public health nursing services, or information on the status of
families may be shared by such voluntary organizations as the Red
Cross and the Tuberculosis and Health Association.

Facilitating communication between local organizations has
been a major objective of public health administrators and community organizers. Their writings contain many assertions about the
desirability of improving relationships in order to reduce gaps and
overlaps of medical services to the citizens, but as yet little effort
has been made to appraise objectively the interrelationships that actually exist within the community.

In the following pages we should like to present our theoretical
interpretation of interorganizational relationships together with a discussion of our research approach and a few preliminary findings, pointing up some of the substantive areas in organizational sociology for
which our study has relevance. Our present thinking is largely based
on the results of an exploratory study of twenty-two health organizations
in a New England community with a population of 200,000 and initial
impressions of data on a more intensive study, as yet unanalyzed, of
some fifty-five health organizations in another New England community
of comparable size.[6]

The site of our initial investigation was selected because we
found it fairly accessible for study and relatively independent of a large
metropolis: moreover, it contained a range of organizations which were
of interest—a full-time health department, a welfare department,
autonomous local agencies, local chapters or affiliates of major voluntary health and social welfare organizations, and major community
hospitals. Of the twenty-two health organizations or agencies studied,
fourteen were voluntary agencies, five were hospitals (three with out-
patient clinics and two without) and three others were official agencies
—health, welfare, and school. Intensive semistructured interviews were
conducted with executive directors and supervisory personnel of each
organization, and information was obtained from members of the boards
through brief semistructured questionnaires. In addition, we used an
adaptation of an instrument developed by Irwin T. Sanders to locate the
most influential leaders in the community for the purpose of determining

their distribution on agency boards.[7] The prestige ratings that the influential leaders assigned to the organizations constituted one of the independent variables of our study.

Exchange as a Conceptual Framework

The complex of community health organizations may be seen as a system with individual organizations or system parts varying in the kinds and frequency of their relationships with one another. This system is enmeshed in ever larger systems—the community, the state, and so on.

Prevention and cure of disease constitute the ideal orientation of the health agency system, and individual agencies derive their respective goals or objectives from this larger orientation. In order to achieve its specific objectives, however, an agency must possess or control certain elements. It must have clients to serve; it must have resources in the form of equipment, specialized knowledge, or the funds with which to procure them; and it must have the services of people who can direct these resources to the clients. Few, if any, organizations have enough access to all these elements to enable them to attain their objectives fully. Under realistic conditions of element scarcity, organizations must select, on the basis of expediency or efficiency, particular functions that permit them to achieve their ends as fully as possible. By function is meant a set of interrelated services or activities that are instrumental, or believed to be instrumental, for the realization of an organization's objectives.

Although, because of scarcity, an organization limits itself to particular functions, it can seldom carry them out without establishing relationships with other organizations of the health system. The reason for this is clear. To fulfill its functions without relating to other parts of the health system, an organization must be able to procure the necessary elements—cases, labor services, and other resources—directly from the community or outside it. Certain classes of hospitals treating a specific disease and serving an area larger than the local community probably most nearly approximate this condition. But even in this case other organizations within the system usually control some elements that are necessary or at least helpful to the carrying out of its functions. These may be money, equipment, or special personnel, which are conditionally lent or given. Usually agencies are unable to obtain all the elements they need from the community or through their individual efforts and, accordingly, have to turn to other agencies to obtain additional elements. The need for a sufficient number of clients, for example, is often more efficiently met through exchanges with other organizations than through independent case-finding procedures.

Theoretically, then, were all the essential elements in infinite supply there would be little need for organizational interaction and for subscription to co-operation as an ideal. Under actual conditions of scarcity, however, interorganizational exchanges are essential to goal attainment. In sum, organizational goals or objectives are derived from general health values. These goals or objectives may be viewed as defining the organization's ideal need for elements—consumers, labor services, and other resources. The scarcity of elements, however, impels the organization to restrict its activity to limited specific functions. The fulfillment of these limited functions, in turn, requires access to certain kinds of elements, which an organization seeks to obtain by entering into exchanges with other organizations.

Interaction among organizations can be viewed within the framework of an exchange model like that suggested by Homans.[8] However, the few available definitions of exchange are somewhat limited for our purposes because they tend to be bound by economics and because their referents are mainly individual or psychological phenomena and are not intended to encompass interaction between organizational entities or larger systems.[9]

We suggest the following definition of organizational exchange: *Organizational exchange is any voluntary activity between two organizations which has consequences, actual or anticipated, for the realization of their respective goals or objectives.* This definition has several advantages. First, it refers to activity in general and not exclusively to reciprocal activity. The action may be unidirectional and yet involve exchange. If an organization refers a patient to another organization which then treats him, an exchange has taken place if the respective objectives of the two organizations are furthered by the action. Pivoting the definition on goals or objectives provides for an obvious but crucial component of what constitutes an organization. The co-ordination of activities of a number of individuals toward some objective or goal has been designated as a distinguishing feature of organizations by students in the field.[10] Parsons, for example, has defined an organization as a "special type of social system organized about the primacy of interest in the attainment of a particular type of system goal."[11] That its goals or objectives may be transformed by a variety of factors and that, under some circumstances, mere survival may become primary does not deny that goals or objectives are universal characteristics of organizations.

Second, the definition widens the concept of exchange beyond the transfer of material goods and beyond gratifications in the immediate present. This broad definition of exchange permits us to consider a number of dimensions of organizational interaction that would otherwise be overlooked.

Finally, while the organizations may not be bargaining or interacting on equal terms and may even employ sanctions or pressures (by granting or withholding these elements), it is important to exclude from our definition relationships involving physical coercion or domination, hence emphasis is on the word "voluntary" in our definition.

The elements that are exchanged by health organizations fall into three main categories: (1) referrals of cases, clients, or patients; (2) the giving or receiving of labor services, including the services of volunteer, clerical, and professional personnel, and (3) the sending or receiving of resources other than labor services, including funds, equipment, and information on cases and technical matters. Organizations have varying needs of these elements depending on their particular functions. Referrals, for example, may be seen as the delivery of the consumers of services to organizations, labor services as the human means by which the resources of the organization are made available to the consumers, and resources other than labor services as the necessary capital goods.

The Determinants of Exchange

The interdependence of the parts of the exchange system is contingent upon three related factors: (1) the accessibility of each organization to necessary elements from sources outside the health system, (2) the objectives of the organization and particular functions to which it allocates the elements it controls, and (3) the degree to which domain consensus exists among the various organizations. An ideal theory of organizational exchange would describe the interrelationship and relative contribution of each of these factors. For the present, however, we will draw on some of our preliminary findings to suggest possible relationships among these factors and to indicate that each plays a part in affecting the exchange of elements among organizations.

Gouldner has emphasized the need to differentiate the various parts of a system in terms of their relative dependence upon other parts of the system.[12] In our terms, certain system parts are relatively dependent, not having access to elements outside the system, whereas others, which have access to such elements, possess a high degree of independence or functional autonomy. The voluntary organizations of our study (excluding hospitals) can be classified into what Sills calls either corporate or federated organizations. Corporate organizations are those which delegate authority downward from the national or state level to the local level. They contrast with organizations of the federated type which delegate authority upwards—from the local to the state or national level.

It appears that local member units of corporate organizations, because they are less dependent on the local health system and can obtain the necessary elements from the community or their parent organizations, interact less with other local agencies than federated organizations. This is supported by preliminary data presented in Table 1. It is also suggested that by carrying out their activities without entering actively into exchange relationships with other organizations, corporate organizations apparently are able to maintain their essential structure and avoid consequences resulting in the displacement of state or national goals. It may be that corporate organizations deliberately choose functions that require minimal involvement with other organizations. An examination of the four corporate organizations in our preliminary study reveals that three of them give resources to other agencies to carry out their activities, and the fourth conducts broad educational programs. Such functions are less likely to involve relationships with other organizations than the more direct service organizations, those that render services to individual recipients.

An organization's relative independence from the rest of the local health agency system and greater dependence upon a system outside the community may, at times, produce types of disagreements with other agencies within the local system. This is dramatically demonstrated in the criticisms expressed toward a local community branch of an official state rehabilitation organization. The state organization, to justify its existence, has to present a successful experience to the legislators—that a minimum number of persons have been successfully rehabilitated. This means that by virtue of the services the organization has offered, a certain percentage of its debilitated clients are again returned to self-supporting roles. The rehabilitative goal of the organization cannot be fulfilled unless it is selective in the persons it accepts as clients. Other community agencies dealing with seriously debilitated clients are unable to get the state to accept their clients for rehabilitation. In the eyes of these frustrated agencies the state organization is remiss in fulfilling its public goal. The state agency, on the other hand, cannot commit its limited personnel and resources to the time-consuming task of trying to rehabilitate what seem to be very poor risks. The state agency wants to be accepted and approved

TABLE 1

Weighted Rankings of Organizations Classified by Organizational Form on Four Interaction Indices

| | | | Sent to | | | | | |
| | | | Voluntary | | Hospital | | | |
Interaction Index	Sent by	N	Corporate	Federated	Without Clinics	With Clinics	Official	Total Interaction Sent
Referrals	Vol. corporate	4	4.5	5	3.7	4.5	5	5
	Vol. federated	10	3	4	3.7	3	4	3
	Hosps. w/o clinics	2	4.5	3	3.7	4.5	3	4
	Hosps. w. clinics	3	1	1	1.5	2	1	1
	Official	3	2	2	1.5	1	2	2
Resources	Vol. corporate	4	5	2	1	4	5	3.5
	Vol. federated	10	4	3	3	4	4	3.5
	Hosps. w/o clinics	2	2	4.5	4.5	5	3	5
	Hosps. w. clinics	3	1	1	2	1	2	1
	Official	3	3	4.5	4.5	2	1	2
Written and verbal communication	Vol. corporate	4	5	3	2	4	5	4
	Vol. federated	10	3	1	3	3	3	2.5
	Hosps. w/o clinics	2	2	5	4.5	5	4	5
	Hosps. w. clinics	3	4	4	4.5	1	1.5	2.5
	Official	3	1	2	1	2	1.5	1
Joint activities	Vol. corporate	4	4.5	4	3	5	3.5	5
	Vol. federated	10	3	3	5	3	1	3
	Hosps. w/o clinics	2	2	5	1	2	3.5	4
	Hosps. w. clinics	3	4.5	2	2	1	5	1.5
	Official	3	1	1	4	4	2	1.5

*Note: 1 indicates highest interaction; 5 indicates lowest interaction.

by the local community and its health agencies, but the state legislature and the governor, being the primary source of the agency's resources, constitute its significant reference group. Hence, given the existing definition of organizational goals and the state agency's relative independence of the local health system, its interaction with other community agencies is relatively low.

The marked difference in the interaction rank position of hospitals with out-patient clinics and those without suggests other differences between the two classes of hospitals. It may be that the two types of hospitals have different goals and that hospitals with clinics have a greater "community" orientation and are more committed to the concept of "comprehensive" care than are hospitals without clinics. However, whether or not the goals of the two types of hospitals do indeed differ, those with out-patient departments deal with population groups similar to those serviced by other agencies of the health system, that is, patients who are largely ambulatory and indigent; thus they serve patients whom other organizations may also be seeking to serve. Moreover, hospitals with out-patient clinics have greater control over their clinic patients than over those in-patients who are the charges of private physicians, and are thereby freer to refer patients to other agencies.

The functions of an organization not only represent the means by which it allocates its elements but, in accordance with our exchange formulation, also determine the degree of dependence on other organizations for specific kinds of elements, as well as its capacity to make certain kinds of elements available to other organizations. The exchange model leads us to explain the flow of elements between organizations largely in terms of the respective functions performed by the participating agencies. Indeed, it is doubtful whether any analysis of exchange of elements among organizations which ignores differences in organizational needs would have much theoretical or practical value.

In analyzing the data from our pilot community we classified agencies on the basis of their primary health functions: resource, education, prevention, treatment, or rehabilitation. Resource organizations attempt to achieve their objectives by providing other agencies with the means to carry out their functions. The four other agency types may be conceived as representing respective steps in the control of disease. We have suggested that the primary function determines an organization's need for exchange elements. Our preliminary data reveal, as expected, that treatment organizations rate highest on number of referrals and amount of resources received and that educational organizations, whose efforts are directed toward the general public, rate low on the number of referrals (see Table 2). This finding holds even when the larger organizations—official agencies and hospitals —are excluded and the analysis is based on the remaining voluntary agencies of our sample. As a case in point, let us consider a health organization whose function is to educate the public about a specific disease but which renders no direct service to individual clients. If it carries on an active educational program, it is possible that some people may come to it directly to obtain information and, mistakenly, in the hope of receiving treatment. If this occurs, the organization will temporarily be in possession of potential clients whom it may route or refer to other more appropriate agencies. That such referrals will be frequent is unlikely however. It is even less likely that the organization will receive many referrals from other organizations. If an organization renders a direct service to a client, however, such as giving X-ray examinations, or polio immunizations, there is greater likelihood that it will send or receive referrals.

An organization is less limited in its function in such interagency activities as discussing general community health problems, attending agency council meetings or co-operating on some aspect of fund raising. Also, with sufficient initiative even a small educational agency can maintain communication with a large treatment organization (for example, a general hospital) through exchanges of periodic reports and telephone calls to obtain various types of information. But precisely because it is an educational agency offering services to the general public and not to individuals, it will be limited in its capacity to maintain other kinds of interaction with the treatment organization. It probably will not be able to lend or give space or equipment, and it is even doubtful that it can offer the kind of instruction that the treatment organization would seek for its staff. That the organization's function establishes the range of possibilities for exchange and that other variables exert influence within the framework established by function is suggested by some other early findings presented in Table 3. Organizations were classified as direct or indirect on the basis of whether or not they provided a direct service to the public. They were also classified according to their relative prestige as rated by influential leaders in the community. Organizations high in prestige lead in the number of joint activities, and prestige seems to exert some influence on the amount of verbal and written communication. Yet it is agencies offering direct services—regardless of prestige—which lead in the number of referrals and resources received. In other words, prestige, leadership, and other organizational variables seem to affect interaction patterns within limits established by the function variable.

TABLE 2

Weighted Rankings* of Organizations, Classified by Function on Four Interaction Indices

Interaction Index	Received by	N	Received from					Total Interaction Received
			Education	Resource	Prevention	Treatment	Rehabilitation	
Referrals	Education	3	4.5	5	5	5	5	5
	Resource	5	3	4	2	4	1	3
	Prevention	5	2	1	3	2	2.5	2
	Treatment	7	1	2	1	1	2.5	1
	Rehabilitation	2	4.5	3	4	3	4	4
Resources	Education	3	4.5	5	4	5	4.5	5
	Resource	5	1.5	3	3	4	3	3.5
	Prevention	5	1.5	4	2	3	4.5	3.5
	Treatment	7	3	2	1	2	2	1
	Rehabilitation	2	4.5	1	5	1	1	2
Written and verbal communication	Education	3	4	5	4.5	5	5	5
	Resource	5	3	2	2	3	2	2.5
	Prevention	5	2	4	3	4	4	3
	Treatment	7	1	1	1	2	3	1
	Rehabilitation	2	5	3	4.5	1	1	2.5
Joint activities	Education	3	4	4	1	3	4.5	4
	Resource	5	2	1	3	4	1	3
	Prevention	5	1	2	2	2	3	1
	Treatment	7	3	3	4	1	2	2
	Rehabilitation	2	5	5	5	5	4.5	5

*Note: 1 indicates highest interaction; 5 indicates lowest interaction.

An obvious question is whether organizations with shared or common boards interact more with one another than do agencies with separate boards. Our preliminary data show that the interaction rate is not affected by shared board membership. We have not been able to ascertain if there is any variation in organizational interaction when the shared board positions are occupied by persons with high status or influence. In our pilot community, there was only one instance in which two organizations had the same top community leaders as board members. If boards play an active role in the activities of health organizations, they serve more to link the organization to the community and the elements it possesses than to link the organization to other health and welfare agencies. The board probably also exerts influence on internal organizational operations and on establishing or approving the primary objective of the organization. Once the objective and the implementing functions are established, these functions tend to exert their influence autonomously on organizational interaction.

Organizational Domain

As we have seen, the elements exchanged are cases, labor services, and other resources. All organizational relationships directly or indirectly involve the flow and control of these elements. Within the local health agency system, the flow of elements is not centrally co-ordinated, but rests upon voluntary agreements or understanding. Obviously, there will be no exchange of elements between two organizations that do not know of each other's existence or that are completely unaware of each other's functions. Even more, there can be no exchange of elements without some agreement or understanding, however implicit. These exchange agreements are contingent upon the organization's domain. The domain of an organization consists of the specific goals it wishes to pursue and the functions it undertakes in order to implement its goals. In operational terms, organizational domain in the health field refers to the claims that an organization stakes out for itself in terms of (1) disease covered, (2) population served, and (3) services rendered. The goals of the organization constitute in effect the organization's claim to future functions and to the elements requisite to these functions, whereas the present or actual functions carried out by the organization constitute *de facto* claims to these elements. Exchange agreements rest upon prior consensus regarding domain. Within the health agency system, consensus regarding an organization's domain must exist to the extent that parts of the system will provide each agency with the elements necessary to attain its ends.

TABLE 3
Weighted Rankings* of Organizations Classified by Prestige of Organization and by General Type of Service Offered on Four Interaction Indices

Interaction Index	Received by	N	Received from				Total Interaction Received
			High Prestige		Low Prestige		
			Direct service	Indirect service	Direct service	Indirect service	
Referrals	High direct	9	1	1	1	1	1
	High indirect	3	3	3.5	3	3.5	3
	Low direct	6	2	2	2	2	2
	Low indirect	4	4	3.5	4	3.5	4
Resources	High direct	9	2	2	2	2	2
	High indirect	3	3	3	3	3.5	3
	Low direct	6	1	1	1	1	1
	Low indirect	4	4	4	4	3.5	4
Written and verbal communication	High direct	9	2	2	3	1	2
	High indirect	3	3	3	1	3	3
	Low direct	6	1	1	2	2	1
	Low indirect	4	4	4	4	4	4
Joint activities	High direct	9	1	1.5	2	2	2
	High indirect	3	2	1.5	1	1	1
	Low direct	6	4	3	3	4	3
	Low indirect	4	3	4	4	3	4

*Note: 1 indicates highest interaction; 5 indicates lowest interaction.

Once an organization's goals are accepted, domain consensus continues as long as the organization fulfills the functions adjudged appropriate to its goals and adheres to certain standards of quality. Our data show that organizations find it more difficult to legitimate themselves before other organizations in the health system than before such outside systems as the community or state. An organization can sometimes obtain sufficient elements from outside the local health system, usually in the form of funds, to continue in operation long after other organizations within the system have challenged its domain. Conversely, if the goals of a specific organization are accepted within the local agency system, other organizations of the system may encourage it to expand its functions and to realize its goals more fully by offering it elements to implement them. Should an organization not respond to this encouragement, it may be forced to forfeit its claim to the unrealized aspect of its domain.

Within the system, delineation of organizational domains is highly desired.[14] For example, intense competition may occur occasionally between agencies offering the same services, especially when other agencies have no specific criteria for referring patients to one rather than the other. If both services are operating near capacity, competition between the two tends to be less keen, the choice being governed by the availability of service. If the services are being operated at less than capacity, competition and conflict often occur. Personnel of referring agencies in this case frequently deplore the "duplication of services" in the community. In most cases the conflict situation is eventually resolved by agreement on the part of the competing agencies to specify the criteria for referring patients to them. The agreement may take the form of consecutive handling of the same patients. For example, age may be employed as a criterion. In one case three agencies were involved in giving rehabilitation services: one took preschool children, another school children, and the third adults. In another case, where preventive services were offered, one agency took preschool children and the other took children of school age. The relative accessibility of the agencies to the respective age groups was a partial basis for these divisions. Another criterion—disease stage—also permits consecutive treatment of patients. One agency provided physical therapy to bedridden patients; another handled them when they became ambulatory.

Several other considerations, such as priorities in allocation of elements, may impel an organization to delimit its functions even when no duplication of services exists. The phenomenon of delimiting one's role and consequently of restricting one's domain is well known. It can be seen, for instance, in the resistance of certain universities of high prestige to offer "practical" or vocational courses, or courses to meet the needs of any but high-status professionals, even to the extent of foregoing readily accessible federal grants. It is evidenced in the insistence of certain psychiatric clinics on handling only cases suitable for psychoanalytic treatment, of certain business organizations on selling only to wholesalers, of some retail stores on handling only expensive merchandise.

The flow of elements in the health system is contingent upon solving the problem of "who gets what for what purpose." The clarification of organizational domains and the development of greater domain consensus contributes to the solution of this problem. In short, domain consensus is a prerequisite to exchange. Achieving domain consensus may involve negotiation, orientation, or legitimation. When the functions of the interacting organizations are diffuse, achieving domain consensus becomes a matter of constant readjustment and compromise, a process which may be called negotiation or bargaining. The more specific the functions, however, the more domain consensus is attained merely by orientation (for example, an agency may call an X-ray unit to inquire about the specific procedures for implementing services). A third, less frequent but more formalized, means of attaining domain consensus is the empowering, licensing or "legitimating" of an organization to operate within the community by some other organization. Negotiation, as a means of attaining domain consensus seems to be related to diffuseness of function, whereas orientation, at the opposite extreme, relates to specificity of function.

These processes of achieving domain consensus constitute much of the interaction between organizations. While they may not involve the immediate flow of elements, they are often necessary preconditions for the exchange of elements, because without at least minimal domain consensus there can be no exchange among organizations. Moreover, to the extent that these processes involve proffering information about the availability of elements as well as about rights and obligations regarding the elements, they constitute a form of interorganizational exchange.

Dimensions of Exchange

We have stated that all relationships among local health agencies may be conceptualized as involving exchange. There are four main dimensions to the actual exchange situation. They are:

1. *The parties to the exchange.* The characteristics we have thus

far employed in classifying organizations or the parties to the exchange are: organizational form or affiliation, function, prestige, size, personnel characteristics, and numbers and types of clients served.

2. *The kinds and quantities exchanged.* These involve two main classes: the actual elements exchanged (consumers, labor services, and resources other than labor services), and information on the availability of these organizational elements and on rights and obligations regarding them.

3. *The agreement underlying the exchange.* Every exchange is contingent upon a prior agreement, which may be implicit and informal or fairly explicit and highly formalized. For example, a person may be informally routed or referred to another agency with the implicit awareness or expectation that the other organization will handle the case. On the other hand, the two agencies may enter into arrangements that stipulate the exact conditions and procedures by which patients are referred from one to another. Furthermore, both parties may be actively involved in arriving at the terms of the agreement, or these terms may be explicitly defined by one for all who may wish to conform to them. An example of the latter case is the decision of a single organization to establish a policy of a standard fee for service.

4. *The direction of the exchange.* This refers to the direction of the flow of organizational elements. We have differentiated three types:

(*a*) *Unilateral:* where elements flow from one organization to another and no elements are given in return.

(*b*) *Reciprocal:* where elements flow from one organization to another in return for other elements.

(*c*) *Joint:* where elements flow from two organizations acting in unison toward a third party. This type, although representing a high order of agreement and co-ordination of policy among agencies, does not involve the actual transfer of elements.

As we proceed with our study of relationships among health agencies, we will undoubtedly modify and expand our theoretical model. For example, we will attempt to describe how the larger systems are interwined with the health agency system. Also, we will give more attention to the effect of interagency competition and conflict regarding the flow of elements among organizations. In this respect we will analyze differences among organizations with respect not only to domain but to fundamental goals as well. As part of this analysis we will examine the orientations of different categories of professionals (for example, nurses and social workers) as well as groups with varying experiences and training within categories of professionals (as nurses with or without graduate education).

In the meantime, we find the exchange framework useful in ordering our data, locating new areas for investigation, and developing designs for studying interorganizational relationships. We feel that the conceptual framework and findings of our study will be helpful in understanding not only health agency interaction but also relationships within other specific systems (such as military, industrial, governmental, educational, and other systems). As in our study of health agencies, organizations within any system may confidently be expected to have need for clients, labor, and other resources. We would also expect that the interaction pattern among organizations within each system will also be affected by (1) organizational function, (2) access to the necessary elements from outside the system, and (3) the degree of domain consensus existing among the organizations of the system. It appears that the framework also shows promise in explaining interaction among organizations belonging to different systems (for example, educational and business systems, educational and governmental, military and industrial, and so forth). Finally, we believe our framework has obvious value in explaining interaction among units or departments within a single large-scale organization.

Notes

1. Marshall E. Dimock, "Expanding Jurisdictions: A Case Study in Bureaucratic Conflict," in Robert K. Merton, Ailsa P. Gray, Barbara Hockey, Hanan C. Selvin, eds. *Reader in Bureaucracy* (Glencoe, 1952).

2. William H. Form and Sigmund Nosow, *Community in Disaster* (New York, 1958), p. 236.

3. James G. March and H. A. Simon, *Organizations* (New York, 1958).

4. Peter M. Blau, Formal Organization: Dimensions of Analysis, *American Journal of Sociology* 63 (1957), 58.

5. Amitai Etzioni, New Directions in the Study of Organizations and Society, *Social Research* 27 (1960), 223–228.

6. The project is sponsored by the Social Science Program at the Harvard School Public Health and supported by Grant 8676–2 from the National Institutes of Health. Professor Sol Levine is the principal investigator of the project and Benjamin D. Paul, the director of the Social Science Program, is coinvestigator. We are grateful for the criticisms and suggestions given by Professors Paul, S. M. Miller, Irwin T. Sanders, and Howard E. Freeman.

7. Irwin T. Sanders, The Community Social Profile, *American Sociological Review*, 25 (1960), 75–77.

8. George C. Homans, Social Behavior as Exchange, *American Journal of Sociology* 53 (1958), 597–606.

9. Weber states that "by 'exchange' in the broadest sense will be meant every case of a formally voluntary agreement involving the offer of any sort of present, continuing, or future utility in exchange for utilities of any sort offered in return." Weber employs the term "utility" in the economic sense. It is the "utility"

of the "object of exchange" to the parties concerned that produces exchange. See Max Weber, *The Theory of Social and Economic Organization* (New York, 1947) p. 170. Homans, on the other hand, in characterizing interaction between persons as an exchange of goods, material and nonmaterial, sees the impulse to "exchange" in the psychological make-up of the parties to the exchange. He states, "the paradigm of elementary social behavior, and the problem of the elementary sociologist is to state propositions relating the variations in the values and costs of each man to his frequency distribution of behavior among alternatives, where the values (in the mathematical sense) taken by these variables for one man determine in part their values for the other." See Homans, *op. cit.*, p. 598.

      10. Talcott Parsons, Suggestions for a Sociological Approach to the Theory of Organizations—I, *Administrative Science Quarterly* 1 (1956), 63–85.

      11. *Ibid.*, p. 64.

      12. Alvin W. Gouldner, Reciprocity and Autonomy in Functional Theory, in Llewellyn Gross, ed., *Symposium on Sociological Theory* (Evanston, Ill., 1959); also The Norm of Reciprocity: A Preliminary Statement, *American Sociological Review* 25 (1960), 161–178.

      13. David L. Sills, *The Volunteers: Means and Ends in a National Organization* (Glencoe, 1957).

      14. In our research a large percentage of our respondents spontaneously referred to the undesirability of overlapping or duplicated services.

Interorganizational Analysis: A Hypothesis on Co-ordinating Agencies

Eugene Litwak and Lydia F. Hylton

One major lacuna in current sociological study is research on interorganizational relations—studies which use organizations as their unit of analysis. There are some investigations, which bear tangentially on this problem, such as studies on community disasters and community power,[1] and the study of Gross and others on the school superintendency.[2] There are some explicit formulations of general rules of interorganizational analysis among some of the sociological classics of the past, such as Durkheim's discussion of organic society and, in a tangential way, Marx's analysis of class.[3] But little has been done in current sociological work to follow up the general problems of interorganizational analysis as compared to the problems of intraorganizational analysis, that is studies in bureaucracy.[4]

Reprinted from *Administrative Science Quarterly* 6 (March, 1962):395–420.

Differences Between Interorganizational
and Intraorganizational Analysis

One of the major sociological functions of organizational independence is to promote autonomy. This is important when there is a conflict of values and the values in conflict are both desired. For instance, a society might stress both freedom and physical safety. These two values may conflict in many areas of life; yet the society seeks to maximize each. One way of assuring that each will be retained, despite the conflict, is to put them under separate organizational structures; i.e., have the police force guard physical safety and the newspapers guard freedom of the press. If both safety and freedom were the concern of a single organization, it is likely that when conflict arose, one of the values would be suppressed, as, for example, where the police have control over the press.

This conflict between organizations is taken as a given in interorganizational analysis, which starts out with the assumption that there is a situation of partial conflict and investigates the forms of social interaction designed for interaction under such conditions. From this point of view the elimination of conflict is a deviant instance and likely to lead to the disruption of interorganizational relations (i.e., organizational mergers and the like). By contrast, intraorganizational analysis assumes that conflicting values lead to a breakdown in organizational structure. Thus Weber's model of bureaucracy assumed that the organization had a homogeneous policy.[5] Blau's modification of Weber's analysis (i.e., the individual must internalize the policies of the organization) assumes that the organization has a single consistent system.[6] Selznick has pointed out that deficiencies in the Tennessee Valley Authority centered around the problem of conflicting values.[7]

By distinguishing between interorganizational and intraorganizational analysis, the investigator is sensitized to the organizational correlates of value conflict and value consistency. Without such a distinction he might concentrate on showing that value conflicts lead to organizational breakdown without appreciating that interorganizational relations permit and encourage conflict without destruction of the overall society relations.

Organizational independence for autonomy is functional not only in value conflict but in most forms of social conflict. For instance, values may be theoretically consistent, but limited resources force individuals to choose between them without completely rejecting either choice. (This is one of the classic problems of economics.) Or it may be that a given task requires several specialties, i.e., a division of labor, and limited resources at times of crisis force a choice between them, although all are desirable (for example, the conflicts between the various military services). In such cases organizational independence might be given to the specialties to preserve their essential core despite competition.

A second point follows from the preceding discussion. Interorganizational analysis stresses the study of social behavior under conditions of unstructured authority. International relations between nations is the polar model for interorganizational behavior,[8] a modicum of co-ordination is necessary to preserve each nation, yet there is no formal authority which can impose co-operation. By contrast, most intraorganizational analysis is made under the assumption of a fairly well-defined authority structure. As a consequence, formal authority plays a larger role in explaining behavior within the organization than it does in interorganizational analysis with exceptions, of course, as where the society has a strong monolithic power structure and is very stable. Because of this difference, interorganizational analysis will frequently use, as explanatory variables, elements that are disregarded or minimized in intraorganizational studies.

In summary, interorganizational analyses suggest two important facets of analysis which differ somewhat from intraorganizational analysis: (1) the operation of social behavior under conditions of partial conflict and (2) the stress on factors which derive equally from all units of interaction rather than being differentially weighted by authority structure.

To point out that multiple organizations are effective in situations of partial conflict is not to suggest that they necessarily arise from such situations or that conflict is the only reason for their persistence. Multiple organizations might be the consequence of social growth. Thus in one city, there may be twenty family agencies, with no rational basis for separation except that their growth was an unplanned consequence of immediate social pressure. They might, indeed, be in the process of consolidation. Yet at any given time in a changing society, the investigator must expect to find multiple organizations because the process of centralization and decentralization are slow. Culture values also condition the development of multiple organizations. In the field of business enterprise there is a tendency to argue that a competitive situation is a good per se; even where a monopoly is more efficient, society might reject it. Within the welfare field, family agencies may be separated by religious beliefs. In short, where there is a situation of partial conflict (which all societies must have because of limited resources for maximizing all values simultaneously), where a society is constantly changing, and where cultural values dictate it, the problem of multiple organizations will be an important one. Consequently there is a need for theories dealing with interorganizational analysis—situations involving partial conflict and interactions without a structure of formal authority.

The Problem of Co-ordination

One strategic problem in interorganizational analysis concerns co-ordination, a somewhat specialized co-ordination, since there is both conflict and co-operation and formal authority structure is lacking. If the conflict were complete, the issue could be settled by complete lack of interaction or by some analogue to war. Where the conflict overlaps with areas of support, however, the question arises: What procedures ensure the individual organizations their autonomy in areas of conflict while at the same time permitting their united effort in areas of agreement?

One such mechanism is the co-ordinating agency—formal organizations whose major purpose is to order behavior between two or more other formal organizations by communicating pertinent information (social service exchange and hospital agencies), by adjudicating areas of dispute (Federal Communications Commission), by providing standards of behavior (school accrediting organizations), by promoting areas of common interest (business associations, such as the National Association of Manufacturers, restaurant associations, grocery store associations), and so forth. What characterizes all these organizations is that they co-ordinate the behavior between two or more organizations. Furthermore, the organizations being co-ordinated are independent, because they have conflicting values or because the demands of efficiency suggest organizational specialization, yet share some common goal which demands co-operation.

From this reasoning we can advance the following hypothesis: Co-ordinating agencies will develop and continue in existence if formal organizations are partly interdependent; agencies are aware of this interdependence, and it can be defined in standardized units of action. What characterizes the three variables in this hypothesis (interdependence, awareness, and standardization of the units to be co-ordinated) is the extent to which they are tied to the organizations to be co-ordinated. By contrast, if this were an intraorganizational analysis, the development of co-ordinating mechanisms might be accounted for by authority structure with little concern for the awareness of the units to be co-ordinated, without standardization, and without significant variations in interdependence. For instance, the leadership might institute co-ordinating mechanisms because they are aware of inter-dependence where the units to be co-ordinated are unaware of this; or they might introduce co-ordinating mechanisms not to increase effi-ciency of the organization but to perpetuate their own authority structure; or they might introduce co-ordinating mechanisms despite lack of standardization because they feel this might speed up the process of standardization. In other words, authority structure is im-portant in understanding intraorganizational behavior, while the var-iables suggested here for understanding interorganizational analysis may be insignificant.[9]

Study Design and Definition of Terms

In order to provide a limited test of this hypothesis, specific attention is directed to two types of co-ordinating agencies—community chests and social service exchanges. The following nine "traditional" problems of community chest and social service exchanges will be used to show how they can be accounted for by the general hypothesis about co-ordinating agencies:

1. The emergence and continuing growth of community chest pro-grams.
2. The fluctuations in financial campaigns of community chest pro-grams.
3. The resistance of national agencies such as the American Cancer Society to participating in the local community chest.
4. The ability of some agencies to exclude others from the chest—Catholic agencies exclude planned-parenthood agencies.
5. The development of dual campaigns—Jewish agencies and the Red Cross participate in local community chests as well as run inde-pendent national campaigns.
6. The decline of the social service exchange.
7. The fact that community chest agencies have adjudication functions while social service exchanges do not.
8. Principles of growth of new co-ordinating agencies.
9. The increasing encroachment of community chest agencies on mem-ber agencies' budget decisions.

If, in fact, it can be demonstrated that these diverse problems are all variations on a common theme (specified by our hypothesis), then we shall feel that our hypothesis has had initial confirmation. If nothing more, it has met the test of Ockham's razor.

To simplify the presentation, each element of the hypothesis will be examined separately. Although normally all are simultaneously involved, there are certain forms of co-ordination which more clearly represent the influence of one of these variables rather than another. In the concluding discussion, systematic consideration will be given to the simultaneous interaction among all three variables as well as alternative mechanisms of co-ordination (aside from the formal co-ordinating agency).

First it seems appropriate to define the three terms of the hypothesis—interdependence, awareness, and standardization. By interdependence is meant that two or more organizations must take each other into account if they are to accomplish their goals.[10] The definition of this term has been formally developed by Thomas who points out that there are several kinds of interdependency. The initial discussion here will concentrate on competitive interdependence (where one agency can maximize its goals only at the expense of another), while the later discussion will introduce and relate facilitative interdependence (where two or more agencies can simultaneously maximize their goals). By awareness we mean that the agency, as a matter of public policy, recognizes that a state of interdependency exists. By standardized actions we mean behavior which is reliably ascertained and repetitive in character, e.g., requests for funds, information on whether the client is served by another agency, price of goods, cost of living index, and the like.[11]

The Evidence on Interdependency

Historical Emergence and Continued Growth of Community Chests

If the factors accounting for the origin of community chest programs[12] are examined, one explanation which appears repeatedly is the complaints of donors and fund raisers that they were being confronted with too many requests for assistance and that fund raising was both time-consuming and economically wasteful.[13] It was at the urging of these donors and fund raisers that many of the community chest programs had their beginnings.

It is argued here that these complaints of the donors and their consequent demands for centralized fund raising were manifestations of the increasing interdependence of welfare agencies in the community, for what in effect had occurred was an increase in the number of agencies drawing on a limited local community fund. This meant that any given agency which drew from this common fund was depriving some other agency of a source of money, and that the same donor received many requests for funds. How much the donors' feelings of waste were a consequence of agencies' increasing interdependence on a limited and common pool of funds can be seen if one envisions the situation of few agencies and much money. In such cases no two agencies need go to the same donor. The donor, as a consequence, would not feel plagued by many requests and thus become aware of the inefficiency of many agencies carrying on independent fund raising activities.

Community chest programs have continued to grow partly because financial dependence has grown—agencies' demands for funds have grown at the same or a faster rate than national income.[14]

Fluctuations in Financial Campaigns of Community Chest Programs

If the development of co-ordinating agencies is a function of interdependency, then any fluctuation in interdependency should lead to a fluctuation in co-ordination. If the pool of resources in the community is suddenly decreased while the number of agencies remains the same or increases, then the agencies' competition for funds should increase and their interdependency increase accordingly. Such limitations of community funds occur during periods of crisis—natural catastrophies, depressions, or wars. In one major historical instance, in Cincinnati, the community chest program arose not as a result of donor pressures but was formed as a consequence of a disastrous flood.[15] The same point is made in the study of a modern catastrophe by Form and Nosow, who say, "Hence [inter]organizational integration is the most crucial dimension in disaster."[16]

Co-ordination should grow both in periods of prosperity (World War II) and depression, since greater interdependency can be expected in both these periods. Figure 1 indicates that the funds raised by community chest programs rose sharply during the early thirties (prior to governmental intervention in public relief) and again during the war years of the 1940's.[17] These are peak years as compared to the years immediately preceding and following. These data suggest that the co-ordinating agencies were strengthened during these periods and that interdependency, not the level of income, was an important factor. In summary, instead of three *ad hoc* explanations, i.e., war, depression, and catastrophe, we offer one which provides a general explanation for all three.[18]

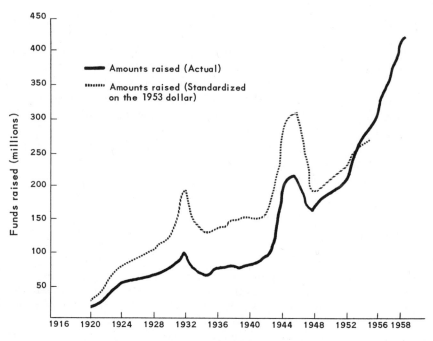

Fig. 1. Federated fund raising

Resistance of National Agencies to Local Community Chests—Fixed Markets

Interdependency should also be able to account for the fact that certain agencies are able to resist efforts to include them in the co-ordination process. The answer to such resistance should lie in part in the limited dependence of these agencies on other agencies in the community; i.e., they can raise money regardless of what other agencies in the community do. When examined, such agencies are seen to have "fixed markets" as far as fund raising is concerned. For instance, the American Cancer Society knows that in any open competition with other agencies, it will receive more funds than most other organizations, because of the public's tremendous concern with, and awareness of, the injurious effects of cancer.[19] The Red Cross is another agency which can resist, to some extent, local community chest involvement because its historic tradition has created a following among donors which amounts to a "fixed market." Fixed markets in fund raising are also enjoyed by religious agencies in cities where their members form a large element in the local community. Such agencies can generally count on receiving priority in any competition for funds. In other words, where an agency, by virtue of cultural norms (religious), historical tradition (Red Cross), or through current interest (American Cancer Society), is able to establish a "fixed money market," it is less dependent on other agencies in the community and can resist efforts at incorporation into community chest programs.

The problem of resistance to community chest programs is a variation on the same basic theme which explains the historical emergence and the fluctuation of funds raised in community chest programs.

Multiple Dependencies—Dual Campaigns and Agency Exclusions

Thus far the assumption has been that agencies are linked by one dependency relation, or if multiple dependencies exist they are consistent with each other. Where an agency has multiple relations with another and they are not consistent, i.e., some involve interdependency and some involve independence, then it will affiliate with co-ordinating agencies only on its own terms. This permits explanation of two classical problems in community chest programs—the exclusion of one agency by another and the running of dual campaigns.

For instance, Catholic agencies frequently insist that planned-parenthood agencies be excluded from community chest programs as a condition of their participation. What characterizes the Catholic agencies is mixed multiple dependencies with other agencies. Like the American Cancer Society, Catholic agencies in strong Catholic communities, have a fixed financial market. Unlike the American Cancer Society, the Catholic agencies perform services (family and recreational) that involve them in an interdependency relation with other agencies in the community. The American Cancer Society's chief service is research, which is equally valuable when done outside the confines of the community. Consequently, Catholic agencies have an incentive to join the local community chest while the Cancer Society does not. Yet, because of their financial independence, Catholic agencies can afford a policy of joining only where the situation is advantageous to them. If a Catholic agency is large, it can force the ouster of the smaller planned-parenthood organization, whose values are antithetical to theirs.

The concept of multiple and conflicting dependencies also explains why some organizations run dual campaigns. Thus Jewish agencies will frequently co-operate with the local community chest and in addition run a separate campaign. The Jewish agencies, like the Catholic agencies, may have a fixed financial market, but have local services which lead to interdependence with other agencies. In addition they have national services which are not dependent on local agencies, such as raising funds for Israel and for research on prejudice. Because of their dual service interests—local and national—their interests only partly overlap that of the local community chest. Because of their financial semi-independence they can enforce their demands for dual campaigns. Similarly, the Red Cross is also likely to run dual campaigns.

Where there are multiple dependencies, there are several possibilities which have different implications for affiliation with local co-ordination agencies. These are outlined in Table 1. Where all relations are independent of the local community, the organizations will refuse affiliation with local community chests (e.g., American Cancer Society). Where there are mixed dependencies, the organization is likely to enter the community chests only on its own terms (i.e., eliminate conflicting organizations or run dual campaigns). Where the organization has multiple dependencies and they mostly involve interdependence, there will be strong support of local co-ordinating organizations.

The Decline of Social Service Exchange

Since the 1940's there has been a steady decline in the number of social service exchanges from 320 exchanges in 1946 to 220 in 1956 to 175 in 1959.[20] If the hypothesis advanced here is correct, this decline should be a function of decreasing interdependence. To ascertain this relationship, it is necessary to know what the functions of the social service exchanges were. From the turn of the century up to the early 1930's one of the major services offered by private welfare agencies was direct material aid—money, clothing, housing, food, and the like. All agencies sought to maximize their services by providing the largest amount to the greatest number of needy. This made them interdependent, for if two agencies were both providing funds to the same individual without being aware of it, neither agency was maximizing its goals. The social service exchange served an important co-ordinating function, since any client coming to an agency could be checked through the exchange to see if he was receiving aid from another agency as well.

Two developments undermined the interdependence of the agencies and led to the decline of the social service exchange. First, the government in the middle 1930's took over most of the material assistance programs. Secondly, the private agencies turned their attention to other services with a strong emphasis on psychiatric case-

TABLE 1

Multiple Dependencies and Affiliations with Community Co-ordinating Agencies

Services	Financially Interdependent	Financially Independent (Fixed Markets)
Interdependent (local services)	Nondenominational family services generally have no fixed financial market and have local services which are interdependent with other agencies. They will affiliate most strongly.	Catholic family agencies in strong Catholic communities have a fixed market but are dependent for services. They will affiliate with co-ordinating agencies on their own terms, i.e., elimination of planned-parenthood groups.
Independent (national services)	National health organizations whose main activity is research but which have achieved no public acceptance of their importance will affiliate with community co-ordinating agencies.	National cancer associations have a fixed market (because of the public's fear of cancer) and have independence in services because these are mostly research. They will not affiliate with local community co-ordinating agencies.
Mixed interdependent and independent (both local and national services)	Agencies such as the Red Cross have both national and local services. They are becoming less independent because their tradition is fading. Therefore they enter into local community arrangements while insisting on maintaining their identity and the right to run national mass-media campaigns.	Jewish community councils in a strong Jewish community have a fixed market. At the same time they have both local services (family and recreation programs) and national services (i.e., research on antisemitism, aid to Israel, etc.) Hence they are likely to have dual campaigns.

work,[21] which did not necessitate communication between agencies. First, the client was unlikely to seek duplication of service as he might seek duplication of material benefits. Secondly, it was argued that all crucial information could be secured from the client,[22] consequently it was not necessary to have any record of prior counseling by some other agency. In addition, some theorists would argue that it would be unethical to secure information from outside sources without the client's knowledge or consent.[23] In other words, old services which were co-ordinated by the social service exchange have disappeared and the new services do not result in agency interdependence,[24] and the decline of social service exchanges can therefore be explained by the decreasing interdependence of the member agencies.

Adjudicatory Functions and Types of Interdependency

Thus far the analysis has attempted to demonstrate that a series of seemingly diverse problems might all be related to the same underlying phenomenon. A simple derivative of the interdependency hypothesis might now be taken into account. If co-ordinating agencies develop when there is agency interdependency, the type of co-ordination should vary with type of dependency. Thomas points out that there is both a competitive and a noncompetitive form of interdependency.[25] In competitive interdependency an agency seeking to maximize its goal deprives another agency of doing likewise. Thus in a community chest where there is a limited amount of social welfare funds, the more one agency receives, the less another agency will receive. By contrast, the social service exchanges dealt with a noncompetitive facilitating interdependency, where maximal goal achievement by one agency was most likely when other agencies maximized their goals as well. Interdependency explains both the rise of the community chest and the decline of the social service agencies.

However, the competitive interdependency of community chests and the facilitating interdependency of social service agencies explains one of the basic differences between these agencies—the adjudicating functions of the community chest. Where a co-ordinating agency must deal with competitive interdependence, it must have some process for adjudicating the differences which must arise. Such agencies will therefore be characterized by some judicial processes. The budget committees of community chests are frequently the core committees whose major function is to hand down judgments by approving or disapproving budget requests of competing agencies. By contrast, the social service exchanges deal with situations where member agencies have no dispute but can only increase their goal achievement by communicating through the co-ordinating agencies. This explains why social service exchanges have minor adjudicatory functions.

Growth Pattern of Co-ordinating Agencies and Some Policy Implications

Our analysis suggests that where interdependency rests on some very stable set of social relations one can anticipate the growth of the co-ordinating agencies to be constant. Since financial support is one of the most stable social conditions in a money economy such as ours, there is good reason to predict the growth and continued existence of co-ordinating agencies such as the community chest. By contrast, interdependency based on services has no such stable support, for social services frequently rest on discoveries in the social sciences. For example, psychotherapy is constantly open to the changes of scientific progress,[26] and it would be hypothesized that co-ordinating agencies dealing with such services might have a much more uncertain future. One of the policy implications which follows is that such co-ordinating agencies must be given maximum discretion to alter their functions as necessitated by new scientific developments.

Self-Awareness and Co-ordinating Agencies— The Future Role of Research

Our hypothesis stated that in addition to dependency there must be self-awareness. In dealing with financial services there seems to be little problem in our moneyed economy of self-awareness. This in part explains the early emergence of the social service exchanges and the community chest. Interdependency based on services and resting on theories of social behavior might not be so easy to observe and, once observed, difficult to raise to agency self-awareness. To do this requires some publicly certified method such as scientific research. Thus it took a scientific survey such as Buell's[27] to raise to the agency policy level the fact that many agencies were treating different problems of the same families. By not being aware of this, the agencies frequently proposed programs of action to the client which were contradictory. As the social sciences develop, it is quite probable that agencies will increasingly turn to scientific research to see whether interdependence indeed exists.

Aside from the question of research, economic theorists suggest still another factor affecting awareness of dependency. They point out that where there are many units in the field, e.g., farming, it is almost impossible to observe and communicate interdependency.[28] By contrast, where one has a few units, observability or interdependence is markedly increased. In the initial stages community welfare agencies were supported by a few wealthy individuals.[29] It was perhaps the small number of persons involved which contributed to their perception of the need for, and their ability to co-operate in, the development of community chest programs.[30] Whereas a large number of agencies will make observability of interdependence difficult, a small number reduces the need for formal co-ordinating agencies, since co-ordination can be handled informally.

Standardization of Community Chest and Encroachment on Welfare Agencies

This, in turn, points out the importance of the last term of the hypothesis —standardization of social action. In order for a co-ordinating agency to operate efficiently it must develop specialists. For such specialists to develop, however, the behavior to be co-ordinated has to be standard in character—continuing and repetitious over long periods. If, for instance, social workers in family agencies needed to consult with those in childrens' agencies, and each case was unique, there would be no real way of codifying this information or developing specialists in transmitting this information, and therefore no need for formal co-ordinating agencies. The most efficient way to handle this form of interdependence might be informal mechanisms of co-ordination—telephone conversations between workers, bringing in consultants, and the like.

In short, if one is to move from mechanisms of co-ordination to formal co-ordinating agencies, it is necessary to deal with standardized units of behavior. Conversely, to increase its efficiency, a co-ordinating agency must seek to standardize the behavior which makes up inter-agency dependency as much as possible. In this connection the growing detailed budgetary demands made by community chests on member agencies are most instructive. From the early times, where community chests asked for a rough estimate of the agencies' current budgetary needs, to the present time, where most elaborate forms are filled out for at least one year in advance, the pressure for standardization of budgetary requests has increased. The same process can be observed in social service exchanges where the drive for standardization has led to an increasingly detailed and complex categorizing of information.

However, the relationship between standardization and co-ordinating agencies is not monotonic. Thus where extreme standardization takes place, it is frequently possible to co-ordinate activities via rules or laws rather than community organization. This is ideally what the economists mean when they speak about automatic stabilizers.[31] A good illustration of how interaction between two organizations can be co-ordinated by rules are the escalator clauses in union-management contracts. It is possible to have such rules because the computation of the living cost and wage payment is standardized—rules for computing them are readily made, publicly observable, and easily checked, and if done over and over again the same results would have a high probability of occurring.

Mechanisms For Preserving Conflict

Thus far the analysis of co-ordinating mechanisms has with one exception centered on the element of co-operation or interdependence. If the interorganizational character is to be retained, there must also be some procedures for preserving autonomy and conflict. For instance, if the community chest were to concentrate just on the co-operative functions, there would be a tendency for organizational merger of member agencies or, as a minimum, the development of uniformity of services. Groups such as the community chest were originally organized around the goal of co-operation (i.e., fund raising and allocation). Group goals once set have a powerful socializing effect on members;[32] furthermore, the group tends to recruit only those who are sympathetic to its goals. Because these socialization and screening pressures for co-operation and merger have a group base, the counterpressures for preserving organizational autonomy and conflict must have an equally pervasive influence.

One type of group mechanism designated to preserve areas of autonomy and conflict is signaled by the phrase "conflict of interest." The mechanism is a law or a professional code of ethics which says that no individual can belong to two organizations which have legitimate areas of conflict. The incipient basis for this type of mechanism can be seen in the area of welfare fund raising as well. In contrast to the community chests, community councils have in recent years more and more taken the position of defending agency autonomy (i.e., arguing that the community chests does not have the right to make decisions about the nature and quality of services). If this incipient division of labor crystallizes, then a code of ethics might eventuate in which a person will be said to have a conflict of interest if he sits on the budget committee of the community chest and is a member of the community council committee for preserving professional control of services.

Another possible procedure for maintaining legitimate areas of conflict is to have a division of labor *within* the co-ordinating agency, with one group dealing with areas of co-operation and the other with areas of conflict and autonomy.[33] Thus the budget committee of the community chest is frequently dominated by lay people who exercise considerable control over fund raising and allocation. Problems of fund allocations frequently lead to questions about the respective merits of various services, however, and the nonprofessional members may lean heavily on their staff experts. The professional members are frequently educated to accept the legitimacy of multiple and competing forms of service and act as a barrier to demands for merger or premature resolution of conflicts.

Still another mechanism for preserving conflict is the use of the ideology of "tradition" as a decision rule. Where there has been a profusion of services in the past, such a decision rule acts to maintain existing states of conflict.[34] This mechanism is generally vulnerable, however, because it does not provide for innovation in a society where change is a cultural characteristic. Therefore, if this mechanism is to survive in our society, it is likely to be used as the courts use the concept of "precedent." The fiction of tradition is maintained, although, *de facto*, much innovation is permitted. There are a variety of other mechanisms of equal merit[35] which will not be explored here.

It must be pointed out that, while interorganizational co-ordination requires both co-operation and conflict, at any given time emphasis might be on one or the other. Thus, since the middle eighteen-hundreds, the major problem in welfare fund raising has been to develop co-operation between competing agencies. It is only recently, when community chests have become exceedingly strong, that attention has shifted to the problem of agency autonomy and preserving legitimate areas of conflict. By contrast, in the business world since the middle eighteen-hundreds primary attention has been paid to preserving areas of conflict between concerns (antitrust laws) and only recently has more attention been paid to the need to maintain co-operation (fair price laws, farmer subsidies, and so on). The researcher must therefore keep in mind that despite the exigencies of any particular situation, interorganizational co-ordination is characterized by the need to maintain areas both of conflict and of co-ordination.

Interaction of Interdependency, Awareness, and Standardization

Now that each variable has been discussed independently the full implications of our hypothesis can be spelled out by showing the simultaneous interaction of all three variables (interdependence, awareness, and standardization). The following rules should be kept in mind:

1. Standardization is curvilinearly related to co-ordinating agencies: too little leads to no co-ordination or *ad hoc* informal types of co-ordination, while too much means the use of rules or laws rather than co-ordinating agencies.
2. There is a monotonic relation between awareness and co-ordination, with low observability meaning little co-ordination and high observability leading to high co-ordination.
3. There is a curvilinear relation between interdependence and co-ordinating agencies: high interdependency leads to the merger of organizations, with co-ordination taking place intraorganizationally, while low interdependence leads to no co-ordination rather than to co-ordinating agencies.

To these rules one will be added. Although the number of firms is related to awareness it also affects co-ordination independently. Thus in spite of awareness of interdependence, it is more difficult to develop co-ordinating agencies where there are a large number of organizations to co-ordinate (5,000). On the other hand, where there are only a few organizations (2–4) there is no need for co-ordinating agencies, since much of the co-ordination can be handled informally by telephone or a luncheon engagement. In short:

4. There is a curvilinear relation between number of organizations and the development of co-ordinating agencies.

Since in the present paper we are interested in interorganizational analysis, and in highlighting alternative forms of co-ordination between organizations, we will confine the discussion that follows to the situation where a moderate amount of interdependency occurs.

Table 2 is a scheme for presenting the alternative forms of co-ordination, given a moderate amount of interdependency. It can be seen that co-ordinating agencies will arise when there is a moderate amount of standardization, a high awareness, and a medium number of organizations to be co-ordinated (Cell 5). This is a precise statement of our hypothesis with regard to co-ordinating agencies. However, following rules 2–4 above allows us to develop other forms of co-ordination. For instance, where there are few organizations to be co-ordinated, awareness of interdependence on other agencies, and little standardization, the case conference between workers from the two agencies might be the form of co-ordination (Cell 9). Because the worker has high awareness of dependence, she will seek aid; because the problems have not been standardized, there are no specialists who handle the matter of interagency communication; because there are few agencies involved,

TABLE 2

Types of Co-ordinating Mechanisms Resulting from the Interaction between Awareness, Standardization, and Number of Agencies under the Condition of Moderate Interdependence*

No. of organizations	High Awareness			Low Awareness		
	High standardization	Medium standardization	Low standardization	High standardization	Medium standardization	Low standardization
Large (over 200)	1. Fair price laws, directories of agencies, etc.	2.	3. Permanent arbitrators for labor grievances	10. Adam Smith's "invisible hand" theory of laissez faire," i.e., the price mechanism	11.	12. Little chance of co-ordination
Medium (10–200)	4.	5. Co-ordinating agencies—community chest	6.	13.	14. Ad hoc endorsement committees	15.
Small (2–9)	7. Dental care or unemployment information handled by family agency in small community by informal telephoning—no directories	8.	9. Case conferences or consultations between members of different organizations handled on an informal basis	16. Unstable situation leading to Cell 7. Informal co-operation between members of different organizations handled as friendship favors	17.	18. Very poor co-ordination, handled by ad hoc rules and under guise of friendship favors

* Where there is great interdependence, the tendency will be towards organizational merger and the analysis will be intraorganizational mechanisms of co-ordination. Thus under conditions of great interdependence, high awareness, high standardization, and many people, there will be a tendency for Weber's model of bureaucracy to develop, while under the same conditions but little standardization there will be a tendency for professionalistic models (i.e., hospital) to develop, etc. Where no interdependence exists there is little concern for co-ordinating mechanisms.

there is no need for formal organizational co-ordination. As a consequence, the case conference set up by the worker is likely to be the chief mechanism of co-ordination. Cell 7 would be slightly different. It has all of the features of Cell 9 except that it deals with a highly standardized event. This might be illustrated by the case worker dealing with a client who needs dental care or employment. This is a recurrent problem and simple to describe. Rules in the form of directories are available and the social worker can look up her list and give the client an address or telephone number to call. The mechanism of co-ordination is a directory. Where there are few organizations involved, this directory will either be in the social worker's head or will be a fairly informal mimeographed sheet. By contrast, if one examines Cell 1 which differs from Cell 7 in only one regard—there are many organizations involved— one would expect that the directory would take the form of a fairly substantial printed volume. Cell 1 is also the ideal place for the economist's "automatic" stabilizers or the place where behavior between concerns is regulated by self-enforcing laws, e.g., escalator clauses, unemployment insurance. By contrast, Cell 3, which differs from Cell 1 in the degree of standardization, would have laws which embodied administrative commissions to make decisions. This is because the lack of standardization means that specific rules for each decision cannot be set up, and therefore a commission which understands the general intent of the law must be set up to judge each case as it comes up. The more fully developed the commission, the more likely it is to resemble a formal co-ordinating agency, as designated in Cell 5. The more amorphous and *ad hoc* the commission, e.g., a one-man commission with little if any staff, the less likely it is to overlap with co-ordinating agencies.

All situations in Cells 1–9 are characterized by high levels of awareness as contrasted with those in Cells 10–18. Two generalizations can be made about these latter cells. Where they are characterized by high standardization and few organizations (Cell 16) they are likely to be unstable (people will become aware), because it is hypothesized that these variables are partially correlated with awareness. Secondly, they are likely to lead to *ad hoc* solutions; where agencies are interdependent but not aware of it, they are likely to co-ordinate their behavior during periods of crisis and then permit it to lapse afterward.

Cell 14 would be represented by an *ad hoc* committee, such as the endorsement committees, which were the predecessors of the community chest organizations. These endorsement committees (usually set up by the Chamber of Commerce) would provide the stamp of legitimacy for the various drives by endorsing those they judged to be responsible. In effect they were performing a co-ordinating function. Because money raising was a fairly standardized procedure and because there were only a moderate number of drives, a formal group (a committee) could be set up. Because the awareness was limited, however, the formal group was *ad hoc*—attached to the Chamber of Commerce whose major function lay elsewhere. Furthermore, the committee was not completely formalized; i.e., it did not have the professional staff and fully developed adjudicating functions of later co-ordinating agencies.

Cell 10 would best be represented by Adam Smith's "invisible hand" theory of economic behavior, e.g., the wheat or cotton farmers before government subsidies. Cell 16 can be represented by friendship favors between workers in two different agencies. Because of standardization and high interdependence the workers are likely to have contact with each other regarding their cases; however, because they are not aware of the organizational interdependence, they might view their co-operation in terms of friendship favors. This state is likely to be unstable because the high standardization and the small number of agencies are both conducive toward the development of awareness and would lead to the behavior indicated in Cell 7. By contrast, Cell 18 is likely to exhibit the same behavior—the reliance on friendship favors—but because of the low standardization is likely to be highly stable. Cell 12 has low awareness, low standardization, and many agencies (e.g., "hard core" families in New York or Chicago) and is least likely to have any form of co-ordination.

From this brief analysis of Table 2, it can be seen in what sense the co-ordinating agency is only one form of interorganizational co-ordination and how a large variety of potential mechanisms can develop depending on the nature of interaction between interdependency, awareness, and standardization.

Summary

This concludes the evidence for our hypothesis on co-ordinating agencies. Through a consideration of the concepts of interdependency, awareness, and standardization, one can show that a series of seemingly unrelated phenomena are actually closely related, e.g., the rise of community chests, the decline of social service exchanges, the reluctance of cancer agencies to join community chests, the exclusion of agencies such as planned-parenthood agencies from community chests, the increasing encroachment of community chests on welfare agency service, the fact that some co-ordinating agencies have adjudicatory functions while others do not, and the demands for co-ordination among the "hard core" families.

In addition, general rules are suggested for interrelating an entire series of co-ordinating mechanisms, e.g., committees, laws, directories, and friendship favors. This initial study does not exhaust the questions raised by the hypothesis; it is hoped that our consideration of the problem will stimulate further sociological inquiry into other aspects of interorganizational co-ordination.

Notes

1. William H. Form and Sigmund Nosow, *Community in Disaster* (New York, 1958), pp. 243–244; Floyd Hunter, *Community and Power Structure* (Chapel Hill, N. C., 1953).

2. Neal Gross, W. S. Mason, and A. W. McEachern, *Exploration in Role Analysis: Studies of the School Superintendency Role* (New York, 1958).

3. Emile Durkheim, *The Division of Labor in Society* (Glencoe, Ill., 1947). If the concept of organization is used very broadly, it could be argued that Marx provided in his theory of class conflict a view of interorganizational analysis which, according to him, explains all social behavior.

4. The systematic study of *intra*organizational analysis has proceeded at a rapid pace since the 1940's as indicated by the many studies in bureaucracy as well as the development of industrial sociology. For a review of some of this literature, see Peter M. Blau, *Bureaucracy in Modern Society* (New York, 1956). Interorganizational analysis has received no such systematic attention. This contrasts somewhat with related social sciences, where interorganizational analysis has been a major concern. For some illustrations in economics see John K. Galbraith, *American Capitalism: The Concept of Countervailing Power* (Boston, 1952), pp. 117–157; Friedrich A. Hayek, *The Road to Serfdom* (Chicago, 1944), pp. 56–127; K. William Kapp, *The Social Costs of Private Enterprise* (Cambridge, Mass., 1950); E. F. M. Durbin, *Problems of Economic Planning* (London, 1949).

5. H. H. Gerth and C. Wright Mills, eds. and tr., *From Max Weber: Essays in Sociology* (New York, 1946), pp. 196–203.

6. *Bureaucracy in Modern Society*, pp. 57–68.

7. Philip Selznick, *TVA and the Grass Roots: A Study in the Sociology of Formal Organization* (Berkeley, Calif., 1949).

8. Current relations between the United States and Russia are a case in point. These two nations do not recognize any authority superior to them. Because of the potential destructive power of atomic warfare and the interrelated character of international relations they are interdependent, i.e., each can destroy the other or each must take the other into account in order to achieve its national goals. At the same time they have conflicting ideologies, which lead them to seek to maintain regions of legitimized conflict, i.e., national sovereignty.

9. Some of the current studies in industrial organization also suggest the need to consider localized discretion and the decentralization of authority. Seymour Melman's *Decision-Making and Productivity* (Oxford, 1958), pp. 3–23, is a case in point. It is not always easy to know when a situation fits the intraorganizational or interorganizational model. Concerns such as General Electric are nominally one

organization but at times resemble a series of independent ones in coalition, while the steel industry consists of formally separated groups which for many purposes tend to act as a unit (in labor bargaining, on pricing of goods, and against political pressure groups).

10. For a more formal definition and discussion of interdependence see Edwin J. Thomas, Effects of Facilitative Role Interdependence on Group Functioning, *Human Relations*, 19 (1957), 347–366. In the definition used here the phrase "take into account" is meant in a very immediate sense for in a broad sense all organizations must take each other into account.

11. In contrast to these illustrations the diagnosis and treatment of mental illness is nonstandardized and not public in character.

12. For a detailed account of the beginnings of the federation movement see: John R. Seely *et al.*, *Community Chest* (Toronto, 1957), pp. 13–29; Frank J. Bruno, *Trends in Social Work: 1874–1956* (New York, 1957), pp. 199–206; and William J. Norton, *The Cooperative Movement in Social Work* (New York, 1927), pp. 8 ff., 112 ff.

13. Norton, *op. cit.*, pp. 50 ff., 68 ff., 113 ff.

14. An indirect measure of this is that for 1940–1955, where comparable figures were available, the amount collected by united funds (including Red Cross) increased at the same or slightly higher rate than disposable personal income. See *Trends in Giving, 1955* (New York, 1956), p. 3. The rate of increase of gross national product and united community funds is roughly similar between the period 1948 to 1958. See *Trends in Giving, 1958* (New York, 1959), p. 2 .

15. Norton, *op. cit.*, pp. 96 ff., 133 ff.

16. "While in everyday affairs organizations implicitly are dependent on one another to meet routine problems, they are rarely called out in force to function effectively *together* as one unit. Yet this is precisely what is required in a disaster— the full mobilization and cooperation of interdependent organizations, which normally operate autonomously. Hence organizational integration is the most crucial dimension in disaster" (Form and Nosow, *op. cit.*, pp. 243–244).

17. Sources of data: J. Frederic Dewhurst *et al.*, *America's Needs and Resources* (New York, 1955), p. 437; Russel H. Kurtz, *Social Work Yearbook, 1957* (New York, 1957), p. 175; *Trends in Giving, 1957, 1958, 1959* (New York, 1958, 1959, 1960). The amount of funds raised is affected by short-term crises and is therefore a more sensitive measure of organizational strength than number of organizations, which do not reflect short-term declines because of career and job commitments. Also, when the dollar value was stabilized by computing all figures on the basis of the 1953 dollar, no significant change in the character of the fluctuations occurred.

18. The reader can note from Figure 1 that there is a continued increase in funds following the Korean crisis. This period is marked by aggresive solicitations by national agencies in smaller communities leading to an increase in interdependency. In addition, smaller communities became aware of united giving because of its popularity among the larger cities. An examination of the *Annual Directory of Chests, United Funds and Councils* (UCFC) (1936 and 1956) shows that approximately one-third of the 429 community chests listed in 1936 were in towns of 25,000 or less population. In 1956, towns of this size represented better than half of the 1,182 community chests listed. Also see *United Giving in the Smaller Community* (New York, 1956).

19. For details regarding the nonparticipation of national agencies, see *Organizing a United Fund* [1953] and *United We Stand* [1958] (New York, 1954,

1959); *1958 Experience in United Funds, 1957 Experience in United Funds,* and *United Giving in the Smaller Community* (New York, 1956); and F. Emerson Andrews, *Philanthropic Giving* (New York, 1950), pp. 152 ff., 156 ff.

20. Regarding the experiences of the exchange see *Summary Report of Research on the Social Service Exchange* (New York, 1959): *Social Work Yearbook 1957,* pp. 547 ff; Norton, *op. cit.,* pp. 22–24.

21. See note 20 and *Budget $ in a Community Chest* (New York, 1953).

22. See note 20.

23. *Ibid.*

24. More recent trends in treatment suggest that social service exchanges might be reorganized around different functions.

25. *Op. cit.*

26. In this connection the tendency among some social workers and psychoanalysts to view principles of therapy as permanently fixed displays an attitude more akin to religious movements than to the spirit of scientific progress.

27. B. Buell, *et al., Community Planning for Human Services* (New York, 1952).

28. Galbraith, *op. cit.,* pp. 12–25, 35–53.

29. See note 12.

30. By contrast, current chest programs have a large mass base. However, by 1959 close to 85 per cent of the funds were collected under the aegis of business, and support for united fund drives comes from the managers of large organizations, who are relatively few in number. This estimate of 85 per cent is rough and is based on the amount given directly by corporations and the amount collected at the place of work. See *Trends in Giving, 1958,* and F. Emerson Andrews, *Corporation Giving* (New York, 1952), pp. 156–158. Like the few wealthy individuals of the past, these managers are able to see the disruptive forces in having many diverse drives.

31. E. Despres, M. Friedman, A. Hart, P. A. Samuelson, and D. H. Wallace. The Problem of Economic Instability, *American Economic Review,* 40 (1950), 505–538.

32. The socializing effects of the group on the individual has been thoroughly documented. For a recent summary see Eugene Litwak, "Some Policy Implications in Communications Theory with Emphasis on Group Factors," *Education for Social Work, Proceedings of the Seventh Annual Program Meeting* (New York, 1959), pp. 98–109.

33. For illustrations of a division of labor as a way for maintaining legitimized conflict see Blau, *Bureaucracy in Modern Society,* pp. 64–66; James D. Thompson and Arthur Tuden, "Strategies, Structures, and Processes of Organizational Decision," in James D. Thompson *et al.,* eds., *Comparative Studies in Administration* (Pittsburgh, 1959), pp. 200–202.

34. The ideology of progress rather than tradition might be used to provide for legitimate areas of conflict where the past has shown a monolithic uniformity.

35. Mechanisms might be derived by analogy from a consideration of Robert K. Merton, The Role-Set: Problems in Sociological Theory, *British Journal of Sociology,* 8 (June 1957), 106–120; and Eugene Litwak, Models of Bureaucracy Which Permit Conflict, *American Journal of Sociology,* 47 (1961), 177–184.

Organizational Interdependence and Intra-Organizational Structure

Michael Aiken and
Jerald Hage

The major purpose of this article is to explore some of the causes and consequences of organizational interdependence among health and welfare organizations. The aspect of organizational interdependence that is examined here is the joint cooperative program with other organizations. In particular, we are interested in relating this aspect of the organization's relationships with its environment to internal organizational behavior.

Thus this article explores one aspect of the general field of interorganizational analysis. The effect of the environment on organizational behavior as well as the nature of the interorganizational relationships in an organization's environment are topics that have received increasing attention from scholars in recent years. Among studies in the latter category, there are those that have attempted to describe the nature of organizational environments in terms of the degree of turbulence (Emery and Trist, 1965; cf. Terreberry, 1968) and in terms of organizational sets (Evan, 1966). Others have emphasized transactional interpendencies among organizations [Selznick, 1949; Ridgeway, 1957; Dill, 1962; Levine and White, 1961; Levine et al., 1963; Guetzkow, 1966; Litwak and Hylton, 1962; James Thompson, 1962; Elling and Halbsky, 1961; Reid, 1964.] Still others have emphasized the importance of an understanding of interorganizational relationships for such problem areas as education (Clark, 1965), medical care (Levine and White, 1963), rehabilitation and mental health (Black and Kase, 1963), delinquency prevention and control (Miller, 1958; Reid, 1964); services for the elderly (Morris and Randall, 1965); community action (Warren, 1967); and community response to disasters (Form and Nosow, 1958).

Few studies, however, have examined the impact of the environment on internal organizational processes. One such study by Thompson and McEwen (1958) showed how the organizational environment can affect goal-setting in organizations, while a study by Dill (1958) examined how environmental pressures affect the degree of managerial autonomy. Simpson and Gulley (1962) found that voluntary organiza-

Reprinted from *American Sociological Review* 33 (December, 1968):912–30.

tions with diffuse pressures from the environment were more likely to have decentralized structures, high internal communications, and high membership involvement, while those having more restricted pressures from the environment had the opposite characteristics. Terreberry (1968) has hypothesized that organizational change is largely induced by forces in the environment, and Yuchtman and Seashore (1967) have defined organizational effectiveness in terms of the organization's success in obtaining resources from the environment. Recently, James D. Thompson (1967) and Lawrence and Lorsch (1967) have suggested some ways in which elements in the environment can affect organizational behavior. There are also other studies which argue that another aspect of the environment—variations in cultural values and norms— may also affect the internal structure of organizations (Richardson, 1959; Harbison et al., 1963; Crozier, 1964). Each of these studies, then, suggests ways in which the organization's environment affects the internal nature of the organization. The purpose of this study is to show how one aspect of the organization's relationship with its environment, i.e., the interdependence that arises through joint cooperative programs with other organizations, is related to several intra-organizational characteristics. We shall do this by describing a theoretical framework about organizational interdependence and then by examining some results from an empirical study of organizational interdependence.

A second objective in calling attention to this relatively neglected area of organizational analysis is to suggest that the processes of both conflict and cooperation can be incorporated into the same model of organizational interdependence. The concept of interdependence helps us to focus on the problem of interorganizational exchanges. At the same time, the exchange of resources, another aspect of the relationships between organizations, is likely to involve an element of conflict. While Simmel has made the dialectic of cooperation and conflict a truism, as yet there has been little work that explains interorganizational cooperation and conflict. Caplow (1964) has suggested a model of conflict involving the variables of subjugation, insulation, violence, and attrition, but this model focuses neither on the particular internal conditions that give rise to interorganizational relationships nor on the consequences of them for organizational structure. These are key intellectual problems in attempting to understand exchanges among organizations.

The models of pluralistic societies described by Tocqueville (1945) and more recently by Kornhauser (1959) underscore the importance of autonomous and competing organizations for viable democratic processes. Such theoretical models assume that the processes of conflict as well as cooperation inhere in social reality. Recent American social theory has been criticized for its excessive emphasis on a static view of social processes and for failing to include conflict in its conceptual models (Dahrendorf, 1958; Coser, 1956; Wrong, 1961). The study of interorganizational relationships appears to be one area which can appropriately incorporate the processes of both conflict and cooperation. Therefore the concept of organizational interdependence becomes a critical analytical tool for understanding this process.

Most studies of organizational interdependence essentially conceive of the organization as an entity that needs inputs and provides outputs, linking together a number of organizations via the mechanisms of exchanges or transactions. (Cf. Ridgeway, 1957; Elling and Halbsky, 1961; Levine and White, 1961; Dill, 1962; James D. Thompson, 1962.) Some types of organizational exchanges involve the sharing of clients, funds, and staff in order to perform activities for some common objective (Levine et al., 1963). The measure of the degree of organizational interdependence used here is the *number of joint programs* that a focal organization has with other organizations. The greater the number of joint programs, the more organizational decision-making is constrained through obligations, commitments, or contracts with other organizations, and the greater the degree of organizational interdependence. (Cf. Guetzkow, 1966). This type of interdependence among health and welfare organizations has variously been called "functional co-operation" by Black and Kase (1963), and "program co-ordination" by Reid (1964), is considered a more binding form of interdependence and therefore a more interesting example of interorganizational cooperation. This does not suggest that the cooperation that is involved in joint programs is easily achieved. On the contrary, there are a number of barriers to establishing such interdependencies among organizations (cf. Johns and de Marche, 1951), and the probability of conflict is quite high, as Miller (1958) and Barth (1963) point out.

The reader may wonder why the concept of the joint program is apparently such an important kind of interorganizational relationship. The answer is that, unlike exchanges of clients or funds (which may only imply the *purchase* of services) or other types of organizational cooperation, a joint program is often a relatively enduring relationship, thus indicating a high degree of organizational interdependence.

The *joint program* needs to be carefully distinguished from the *joint organization*. The latter refers to the situation in which two or more organizations create a separate organization for some common purpose. For example, the Community Chest has been created by health and welfare organizations for fund-raising purposes. Similarly, Harrison (1959) has noted that the Baptist Convention was created by the separate Baptist churches for more effective fund raising. Guetzkow (1950) has described interagency committees among federal agencies, representing a special case of the joint organization. Business firms have created joint organizations in order to provide service functions. These are clearly different from the joint program because these joint organizations have separate corporate identities and often their own staff, budget, and objectives.

Some examples of joint programs in organizations other than those in the health and welfare field are the student exchange programs in the Big Ten. Harvard, Columbia, Yale, and Cornell Universities are developing a common computerized medical library. Indeed, it is interesting to note how many universities use joint programs of one kind or another. We do not believe that this is an accident; rather, it flows from the characteristics of these organizations. In our study, which includes rehabilitation centers, we have observed the attempt by one organization to develop a number of joint programs for the mentally retarded. These efforts are being financed by the Department of Health, Education, and Welfare, and evidently reflect a governmental concern for creating more cooperative relationships among organizations. Even in the business world, where the pursuit of profit would seem to make the joint program an impossibility, there are examples of this phenomenon. Recently, Ford and Mobil Oil started a joint research project designed to develop a superior gasoline. This pattern is developing even across national boundaries in both the business and nonbusiness sectors.

It is this apparently increasing frequency of joint programs that makes this form of interdependence not only empirically relevant, but theoretically strategic. In so far as we can determine, organizational interdependence is increasingly more common (Terreberry, 1968), but the question of why remains to be answered.

Theoretical Framework

The basic assumptions that are made about organizational behavior and the hypothesis of this study are shown in Figure 1. These assumptions provide the argument, or model, to use Willer's (1967) term, for the hypotheses to be tested below.

The first three assumptions deal with the basic problem of why organizations, at least health and welfare organizations, become involved in interdependent relationships with other units. The type of interdependency with which we are concerned here is the establishment of joint, cooperative activities with other organizations. If we accept Gouldner's (1959) premise that there is a strain toward organizations maximizing their autonomy, then the establishment of an interdependency with another organization would seem to be an undesirable course of action. It is the view here that organizations are "pushed" into such interdependencies because of their need for resources—not only money, but also resources such as specialized skills, access to particular kinds of markets, and the like (cf. Levine et al., 1963).

Assumptions:
  I. Internal organizational diversity stimulates organizational innovation .
  II. Organizational innovation increases the need for resources.
  III. As the need for resources intensifies, organizations are more likely to develop greater interdependencies with other organizations, joint programs, in order to gain resources.
  IV. Organizations attempt to maximize gains and minimize losses in attempting to obtain resources.
  V. Heightened interdependence increases problems of internal control and coordination.
  VI. Heightened interdependence increases the internal diversity of the organization.

Hypotheses:
  1. A high degree of complexity varies directly with a high number of joint programs.
  2. A high degree of program innovation varies directly with a number of joint programs.
  3. A high rate of internal communication varies directly with a high number of joint programs.
  4. A high degree of centralization varies inversely with a high number of joint programs.
  5. A high degree of formalization varies inversely with a high number of joint programs.

Fig. 1. Assumptions and Hypotheses About Organizational Interdependence

One source of the need for additional resources results from a heightened rate of innovation, which in turn is a function of internal organizational diversity. In several ways internal diversity creates a strain towards innovation and change. The conflict between different occupations and interest groups, or even different theoretical philosophical, or other perspectives, results in new ways of looking at organizational problems. The likely result of this is a high reate of both proposals for program innovations as well as successful implementation of them (Hage and Aiken, 1967). But organizational diversity also implies a greater knowledge and awareness of the nature of and changes in the organizational environment, particularly when organizational diversity implies not only a spectrum of occupational roles in the organization, but also involvement in professional societies in the environment by the incumbents of these occupational roles, itself a type of organizational interdependency. Together the internal conflicts and awareness of the nature of the organization's environment create strains towards organizational change.

But innovation has its price. There is a need for more resources to pay the costs of implementing such innovations—not only money, but staff, space, and time. The greater the magnitude of the change or the number of changes within some specified period of time, the greater the amounts of resource that will be needed and the less likely that the normal sources will be sufficient. Some have called organizations that successfully accomplish this task effective ones (Yuchtman and Seashore, 1967). Thus, the leaders of innovating organizations must search for other possibilities, and the creation of a joint, cooperative project with another organization becomes one solution to this problem.

This mechanism for gaining resources, i.e., the establishment of a joint program, is best viewed as a type of organizational exchange. The leaders sacrifice a small amount of autonomy for gains in staff, funds, etc. While there are strong organizational imperatives against such exchanges, since they inevitably involve some loss of autonomy, as well as necessitate greater internal coordination, the increased intensification of needs for greater resources makes such an alternative increasingly attractive. Still, another factor involved here is that some objectives can only be achieved through cooperation in some joint program. The goal may be so complicated or the distribution of risk so great that organizations are impelled to enter into some type of joint venture. Of course the creation of interdependencies with other organizations also has its costs. The organization must utilize some of its own resources in order to perform whatever coordination is necessary. Hence an organization with no surplus resources available could hardly afford a joint program. Thus there must be some slack in the resource base in the organization before any innovation or cooperative venture is likely.

This is not to argue for the perfect rationality of organizational leaders. Some decisions about change or the choice of a cooperative activity may be quite irrational, and perhaps non-logical (Wilensky, 1967). Indeed much of our argument about the conditions that lead to organizational innovation, i.e., conflict among different occupations, interest groups, or perspectives, is that this is hardly the most rational way to bring about change. Perhaps it is best to view the process as a series of circumstances that propel such events.

While we feel that this line of reasoning is a valid explanation of why organizations enter into interdependent relationships with other organizations via such mechanisms as the joint program, alternative explanations have been offered and must be considered. Lefton and

Rosengren (1966) have suggested that the lateral and longitudinal dimensions of organizational commitment to clients are factors, at least in health and welfare organizations. These are probably not the primary factors in other types of organizations, such as economic ones. However, our concern has been to attempt to find the most general argument possible to explain organizational interdependence. At the same time we have left unanswered the question of why organizations become diverse in the first place, and their framework may provide one possible answer. Reid (1964) has indicated that complementary resources are also an important factor in understanding organizational interdependence. Without necessarily agreeing or disagreeing with these points of view, we do believe that the first three assumptions in Figure 1 represent *one* causal chain showing why organizations become involved in more enduring interorganizational relationships.

The next theoretical problem is what kind of organization is likely to be chosen as a partner in an interdependent relationship. Here we assume that organizations attempt to maximize their gains and minimize their losses. This is our fourth premise. That is, they want to lose as little power and autonomy as possible in their exchange for other resources. This suggests that they are most likely to choose organizations with complementary resources, as Reid (1967) has suggested, or partners with different goals, as Guetzkow (1966) has indicated. This reduces some of the problem of decreased autonomy, because the probability of conflict is reduced and cooperation facilitated in such symbiotic arrangements (cf. Hawley, 1951). This assumption also implies that other kinds of strategies might be used by the leaders of the organization once they have chosen the joint program as a mechanism of obtaining resources. Perhaps it is best to develop interdependent relationships with a number of organizations in order to obtain a given set of resources, thus reducing the degree of dependence on a given source. Again, we do not want to argue that organizational leaders will always choose the rational or logical alternative, but rather that they will simply *attempt* to minimize losses and maximize gains. Under circumstances of imperfect knowledge, some decisions will undoubtedly be irrational.

Our last theoretical problem is consideration of the consequences for the organization of establishing interdependent relationships as a means of gaining additional resources. Such joint activities will necessitate a set of arrangements between the participating organizations to carry out the program. This will mean commitments to the other organization, resulting in constraints on some aspects of organizational behavior. This in turn will mean an increase in problems of internal coordination, our fifth assumption. It is often difficult to work with outsiders, i.e., the partner in a joint activity. In this circumstance a number of mutual adaptations in a number of different areas will become necessary. One solution to this problem is the creation of extensive internal communication channels, such as a broad committee structure which meets frequently.

But perhaps a more interesting consequence of the joint program is that it can in turn contribute to organizational diversity. There is not only the likelihood of the addition of new staff from other organizations, but, more importantly, the creation of new communication links with other units in the organization's environment. New windows will have been opened into the organization, infusing new ideas and feeding the diversity of the organization, which means that the cycle of change, with all of its consequences, is likely to be regenerated.

In this way a never-ending cycle of diversity—innovation—need for resources—establishment of joint programs—is created. What may start as an interim solution to a problem can become a long-term organizational commitment which has a profound impact on the organization. In the long run, there is the tendency for units in an organizational set to become netted together in a web of interdependencies. (Cf. Terreberry, 1968).

With these six assumptions, a large number of testable hypotheses can be deduced. Indeed this is one of the advantages of a general theoretical framework. Not only does it provide the rationale for the hypotheses being tested, but it can suggest additional ideas for future research. Since we are mainly concerned with the factors associated with high interdependency, and more particularly the number of joint programs, all of the hypotheses in Figure 1 are stated in terms of this variable.

Organizational diversity implies many different kinds of variables. We have examined three separate indicators of it: diversity in the number of occupations or the degree of complexity; diversity in the number of power groups or the degree of centralization; and diversity in the actual work experience or the degree of formalization. If assumptions I–III are correct, then the stimulation of change, and more particularly innovation brought about by each of these kinds of diversity, should be associated with a large number of programs. But this is not the only way in which these variables can be related; and that observation only emphasizes how the internal structure of the organization affects the extent of the enduring relationships with other organizations. The problems of internal coordination and the increased diversity, assumptions V and VI, are also related. Both mechanisms of coordination—communication and programming—are undoubtedly tried, but communication is probably preferred. This increases the advantages of diversity and also helps to bring about greater decentralization and less formalization. Similarly, the greater awareness of the environment, via the infusion of staff from other organizations, feeds this cycle of cause and effect relationships. Therefore, we have hypothesized that the number of joint programs varies directly with the degree of complexity (hypothesis 1) and inversely with the degree of centralization and formalization (hypotheses 4 and 5).

Since our arguments also involve statements about the stimulation of innovation, which in turn heightens the need for resources, it is clear that we would expect the degree of innovation to co-vary with the number of joint programs. This is hypothesis 2 of Figure 1. While program change is only one kind of organizational innovation, it is probably the most important, at least from the standpoint of generating needs for additional resources, and thus it goes to the heart of the argument presented in Figure 1. Program innovation in turn has consequences for the degree of centralization and formalization in the organization, but here we are mainly concerned about the relationship between the rate of organization innovation as reflected in new programs and the number of joint programs, and not about these other mediating influences.

The degree of attempted internal coordination is measured by only one variable, namely the rate of communication, but again we feel that this is an important indication of this idea. Given the desire to minimize the loss of autonomy (assumption IV), organizational members must be particularly circumspect when dealing with staff and other kinds of resources from their organizational partners. This largely reduces the options about programming and encourages the elite to emphasize communication rates. Probably special "boundary spanning" roles (Thompson, 1962) are created; these men negotiate the transactions with other organizations and in turn keep their organizational members informed. The problems of interpenetration by other organizational members will keep the communication channels open and filled with messages as internal adjustments are made. Thus this is the rationale for the third hypothesis.

Study Design and Methodology

The data upon which this study is based were gathered in sixteen social welfare and health organizations located in a large midwestern metropolis in 1967. The study is a replication of an early study conducted in 1964. Ten organizations were private; six were either public or branches of public agencies. These organizations were all the larger welfare organizations that provide rehabilitation, psychiatric services, and services for the mentally retarded, as defined by the directory of the Community Chest. The organizations vary in size from twenty-four to several hundred. Interviews were conducted with 520 staff members of these sixteen organizations. Respondents within each organization were selected by the following criteria: (a) all executive directors and department heads; (b) in departments of less than ten members, one-half of the staff was selected randomly; (c) in departments of more than ten members, one-third of the staff was selected randomly. Non-supervisory administrative and maintenance personnel were not interviewed.

Aggregation of Data. This sampling procedure divides the organization into levels and departments. Job occupants in the upper levels were selected because they are most likely to be key decision-makers and to determine organizational policy, whereas job occupants on the lower levels were selected randomly. The different ratios within departments ensured that smaller departments were adequately represented. Professionals, such as psychiatrists, social workers and rehabilitation counselors, are included because they are intimately involved in the achievement of organizational goals and are likely to have organizational power. Non-professionals, such as attendants, janitors, and secretaries are excluded because they are less directly involved in the achievement of organizational objectives and have little or no power. The number of interviews varied from eleven in the smallest organization to sixty-two in one of the larger organizations.

It should be stressed that in this study the units of analysis are *organizations,* not individuals in the organizations. Information obtained from respondents was pooled to reflect properties of the sixteen organizations, and these properties were then related to one another. Aggregating individual data in this way presents methodological problems for which there are yet no satisfactory solutions. For example, if all respondents are equally weighted, undue weight is given to respondents lower in the hierarchy. Yet those higher in the chain of command, not the lower-status staff members, are the ones most likely to make the decisions which give an agency an ethos.[1]

We attempted to compensate for this by computing an organizational score from the means of social position within the agency. A social position is defined by the level or stratum in the organization and the department or type of professional activity. For example, if an agency's professional staff consists of psychiatrists and social workers, each divided into two hierarchical levels, the agency has four social positions: supervisory psychiatrists, psychiatrists, supervisory social workers, and social workers. A mean was then computed for each social position in the agency. The organizational score for a given variable was determined by computing the average of all social position means in the agency.[2]

The procedure for computing organizational scores parallels the method utilized in selecting respondents. It attempts to represent organizational life more accurately by not giving disproportionate weight to those social positions that have little power and that are little involved in the achievement of organizational goals.

Computation of means for each social position has the advantage of avoiding the potential problem created by the use of different sampling ratios. In effect, responses are standardized by organizational location—level and department—and then combined into an organizational score. Computation of means of social position also has a major theoretical advantage in that it focuses on the sociological perspective of organizational reality.

We make no assumption that the distribution of power, regulations, or rewards is random within any particular social position. Instead, each respondent is treated as if he provides a true estimate of the score for a given social position. There is likely to be some distortion due to personality differences or events unique in the history of the organization, but the computation of means for each social position hopefully eliminates or at least reduces the variation due to such factors. By obtaining measures from all levels and all departments, the total structure is portrayed and reflected in the organizational score.

The Measurement of Organizational Interdependence. The degree of organizational interdependence is measured by the number of joint programs with other organizations. There are several possible measures of the nature and degree of organizational interdependence among social welfare and health organizations. Among these are:

1. The number of cases, clients or patients referred or exchanged.
2. The number of personnel lent, borrowed, or exchanged.
3. The number, sources, and amounts of financial support.
4. The number of joint programs.

The first two of these were used in an earlier study of interorganizational relationships (Levine and White, 1961). In our research we found that organizations such as rehabilitation workshops and family agencies simply did not keep records of the number of walk-ins or calls referred by other organizations. Similar problems were encountered with exchanges of personnel. Thus, we found great difficulty in using these measures of interdependence. While the nature and amounts of financial support are interesting and important aspects of interorganizational analysis, they are not included in this study.

We asked the head of each organization to list every joint program in which his organization had been involved in the past ten years, whether terminated or not. A profile of each program was obtained, including the name of participating organizations, goals of the program, number and type of clients or patients involved, and source of financial and other resources for the program. Only existing programs and those involving the commitment of resources by all participating organizations—such as personnel, finances, space—were included in our analysis.

Since a number of our sixteen organizations had participated in joint programs with each other, it was possible to check the reliability of their responses. We did not find any difficulties of recall for this period of time. In part this is probably because most of the joint programs, once started, tended to continue over time. Some organizations had maintained their organizational relationships for as many as twenty years. Then too, the fact that the joint program is not a minor incident in the life of an organization also facilitates recall. We did discover that organizational leaders tended to think of the purchase of services as a joint program. To solve this problem we included in our interview schedule a series of follow-up questions about the amount of staff shared and the amount of funds contributed by each organization involved in the joint program.

Another problem of measurement centered on the difficulty of defining separate joint programs. For example, there was a tendency for an organization with a history of successful relationships (those that endured for more than two years) to develop a number of joint programs with the same organization. The relationships would grow in scope and depth in much the way that one would predict from Homans' (1950) hypotheses about the interaction between people. This raised the problem of whether joint programs with the same organization should be counted as separate programs. Our solution was to count the program separately if it involved different activities. Thus a research program and an education program with the same organization, two common kinds of programs, would be counted as separate joint programs. The key in making this decision was the idea of separate activities. In fact, programs were usually developed at different dates, suggesting again that our solution was a correct one. At the same time, if an organization developed the same joint program with three organizations, this was counted only once. From a practical standpoint these attempts at refinement were not so important because it is clear that the differences in number of joint programs among the sixteen organizations in our study are so great that similar ranking would occur regardless of how one counted the programs.

The number of existing joint programs among these sixteen organizations ranged from none to 33. Rehabilitation centers had the highest average number of joint programs, although the range was quite extensive among some other kinds of organizations in our study (Table 1). The special education department and the hospitals had an intermediate range of programs. Social casework agencies and homes for

TABLE 1

Average Number of Joint Programs by Type of Organization

Type of Organizations	Number of Organizations	Average Number of Joint Programs	Range
Rehabilitation Centers	3	20.7	8–33
Special Education Department— Public Schools	1	15.0	15
Hospitals	3	8.3	6–12
Homes for Emotionally Disturbed	3	2.3	1–3
Social Casework Agencies	6	1.2	0–4
All organizations	16	7.3	0–33

the emotionally disturbed had the least number of joint programs. In every case, however, there was some variation within each organizational category.

Findings

A strict interpretation of data would allow us to discuss only the consequences of interorganizational relationships on the internal structure and performance of an organization. This is true because the period of time during which measurement of the number of joint programs, our measure of organizational interdependence, was made occurred prior to most of our measures of structure and performance. Yet the reasoning in our theoretical framework suggests that these variables are both causes and effects in an on-going process. Strictly speaking, our data reflect the consequences of increased joint programs, but we shall still make some inferences about their causes.

1. *Organizations with many joint programs are more complex organizations, that is, they are more highly professionalized and have more diversified occupational structures.* By complexity we do not mean the same thing as Rushing's (1967) division of labor, a measure of the distribution of people among different occupations, but rather the di-

versity of activities. There are essentially two aspects of complexity as we have defined it: the degree to which there is a high number of different types of occupational activities in the organization; and the degree to which these diverse occupations are anchored in professional societies.[3] One of the most startling findings in our study is the extremely high correlation between the number of different types of occupations in an organization and the number of joint programs ($r=0.87$).

The relationship between the occupational diversity of the organization and the number of joint programs in 1967 is very high, whether we use the number of occupations in 1959 ($r=0.79$), the number of occupations in 1964 ($r=0.83$), or the number of occupations in 1967 ($r=0.87$). While time sequence is not the same as causation, this does suggest that occupational diversity is not solely a function of new programs. Rather it suggests that organizations that have a high number of joint programs are organizations that have been occupationally diverse for a number of years.

The addition of joint programs evidently makes an organization aware of the need for still more specialties. One rehabilitation center used social workers in a joint program involving the mentally retarded with several other agencies. It then decided to add social workers to a number of its other programs. The addition of new specialties may also be necessary in order to help solve some of the problems of coordination created by the joint programs.

The dependent variable, number of joint programs, is quite dispersed with a range from 0 to 33 and a mean of 7.3. It is entirely possible that the unusually high correlations for some variables in Table 2 are simply a function of a highly skewed distribution on this variable. Therefore, we computed two non-parametric measures of correlation, Spearman's rank order correlation coefficient (rho) and Kendall's rank correlation coefficient (tau) for the relationship between number of occupations in 1967 and the number of joint programs as shown in Table 3. The relationship between these two variables remains strong even when using the non-parametric statistics.

The objection could be raised that the very strong relationship between number of occupational specialties and the number of joint programs may also be a function of the type of organization. In Table 1, it was shown that rehabilitation centers had the most joint programs, followed by the special education department, hospitals, homes for the emotionally disturbed, and finally social casework agencies. The observation that there is a positive relationship between these two variables is valid within three of the four categories of organizations shown in Table 4. That is, within the categories of rehabilitation centers, mental

TABLE 2

Relationships Between the Number of Joint Programs and Organizational
Characteristics

Organizational Characteristics	Pearsonian Product-Moment Correlation Coefficients between Each Organizational Characteristic and the Number of Joint Programs
1. Degree of Complexity	
Index of Professional Training	.15
Index of Professional Activity	.60**
Number of Occupations: 1967	.87****
2. Degree of Organizational Innovation: 1959–1966	
Number of New Programs	
(including new programs that are joint programs)	.71***
Number of New Programs	
(excluding new programs that are joint programs)	.74****
3. Internal Communication	
Number of Committees	.47*
Number of Committee	
Meetings per Month	.83****
4. Degree of Centralization	
Index of Participation	
in Decision-Making	.30
Index of Hierarchy of	
Authority	.33
5. Degree of Formation	
Index of Job Codification	.13
Index of Rule Observation	−.06
Index of Specificity of Job	−.06

*P<.10.
**P<.05.
***P<.01.
****P<.001.

hospitals, and homes for the emotionally disturbed the organizations
having the highest number of occupations have the most joint programs
while those having the fewest occupational specialties have the smallest
number of joint programs. Only among social casework agencies does the
relationship not hold. It might be noted that only one social casework
organization had more than one interorganizational tie.

The degree to which an organization is professionalized is also
strongly related to the number of joint programs. We measured the degree of professionalism in organizations in two ways: first, the degree to
which the organizational members received professional training; and

TABLE 3

Comparison of Pearsonian Correlation Coefficient (R), Spearman's Rank Order
Correlation Coefficient (RHO), and Kendall's Rank Correlation Coefficient
(TAU) for the Four Largest Correlations Shown in Table 2.

Organizational Characteristic	Correlation Coefficient between Number of Joint Programs and Organizational Characteristics		
	r	*rho*	*tau*
Number of Occupations: 1967	.87	.81	.74
Number of New Programs: 1959–1966 (including new programs that are joint programs)	.71	.84	.75
Number of New Programs: 1959–1966 (excluding new programs that are joint programs)	.74	.80	.70
Number of Committee Meetings per Month	.83	.61	.54

second, the degree to which organizational members are currently active
in professional activities, i.e., attending meetings giving papers, or holding offices. The measure of current professional activity was also quite
highly related to our measure of the number of joint programs
($r = 0.60$).[4] The degree of professional training had little relationship
with the number of joint programs ($r = 0.15$).[5]

2. *Organizations with many joint programs are more innovative
organizations.* The degree of organizational innovation is measured by
the number of new programs that were successfully implemented in the
organization during the eight-year period from 1959 to 1966. The correlation coefficient between joint programs and new programs is 0.71, as
shown in Table 2. Of course, there is an element of spuriousness in this
relationship, since some of the new programs are joint programs. If the
correlation coefficient is recomputed, eliminating all new programs that
are also joint programs, we find the same result ($r = 0.74$).

As in the case of number of occupational specialties in the organization, the finding based on non-parametric measures of association between each of these two measures of organizational innovation and the
number of new programs is little different from the results based on the
parametric statistical measure (See Table 3).

It could be that the above relationships between degree of or-

TABLE 4

Number of Occupations in 1967 and Number of Joint Programs
by Type of Organization

Rehabilitation Centers	Number of Occupations 1967	Number of Joint Programs
Rehabilitation Center A	27	33
Rehabilitation Center B	24	21
Rehabilitation Center C	13	8
Department of Special Education		
Educational Organization D	19	15
Mental Hospitals		
Mental Hospital E	18	12
Mental Hospital F	18	7
Mental Hospital G	11	6
Homes for Emotionally Disturbed		
Home H	11	3
Home I	10	3
Home J	7	1
Social Casework Agencies		
Casework Agency K	7	1
Casework Agency L	6	0
Casework Agency M	5	1
Casework Agency N	5	1
Casework Agency O	4	4
Casework Agency P	1	0

ganizational innovation and number of joint programs may simply be a function of complexity. We have argued that the degree of complexity gives rise not only to joint programs, but also to new programs. While there is no relationship between professional training and the number of new programs ($r = -0.18$), there are relatively strong relationships between this variable and professional activity ($r = 0.74$) as well as occupational diversity ($r = 0.67$). When the relationships between the number of joint programs and the number of new programs (excluding new programs that are joint programs) is controlled for each of these three indicators separately, the relationship between these two variables remains relatively strong (see Table 5). This illustrates that the number of new programs is related to the number of joint programs independently of these various indicators of complexity.

The key idea in our interpretation is that it is the rate of organizational innovation that intensifies the need for new resources. The higher this rate, the more likely organizations are to use the joint program as a mechanism for cost reduction in such activities. The fact that some new programs are joint programs only strengthens our argument that the joint program is a useful solution for the organization seeking to develop new programs.

This interplay between new programs and joint programs can be made clear with several examples from our study. One rehabilitation center with a high rate of new programs developed joint programs with several organizations that were primarily fund-raising organizations, as

TABLE 5

Partial Correlation Coefficients Between Number of Joint Programs and Organizational Innovation, Controlling for Indicators of Complexity

Control Variables	*Partial Correlation between Number of Joint Programs and Number of New Programs 1959–1966 (Excluding New Programs that are Joint Programs), Controlling for the Variable Indicated*
Indicators of Complexity	
Index of Professional Training	.77
Index of Professional Activity	.55
Number of Occupations: 1967	.46

a solution for funding its growth. But in turn these organizations recognized new needs and asked the organization to develop still more new programs in areas for their clients. This particular agency is presently exploring the possibility of developing special toys for the mentally retarded because one of its joint programs is with an organization concerned with this type of client.

We may also re-examine the relationships between indicators of complexity and the number of joint programs. As shown in Table 6, only the relationship between the number of occupations and the number of joint programs remains strong when the number of new programs (excluding new programs that are joint programs) is controlled (partial $r = 0.75$).

3. *Organizations with many joint programs have more active internal communication channels.* We measured the degree of internal communication in two ways. First, the number of committees in the organization and, second, the number of committee meetings per month. An active committee structure in an organization provides the potential for viable communication links in an organization. As shown in Table 4,

there was a moderately strong relationship between the number of organizational committees and joint programs ($r=0.47$) and a very strong relationship between the number of committee meetings per month and the number of joint programs ($r=0.83$).

The relationship between the number of joint programs and the number of committee meetings per month remains moderately strong when the two non-parametric measures of association are computed. (See Table 3.)

Actually the system of communication for joint programs is even more complex than this. For example, one rehabilitation agency with the largest number of joint programs had a special board with the university with which it had many joint programs and was in the process of establishing another joint board with a second university. Another rehabilitation agency created a special steering committee to suggest and supervise joint programs: the members of this committee were representatives from other organizations.

Controlling for the indicators of complexity and program change reduces the relationship between the number of committees and number

TABLE 6

Partial Correlation Coefficients between Number of Joint Programs and Indicators of Complexity, Controlling for Number of New Programs (Excluding New Programs that are Joint Programs)

Indicators of Complexity	Partial Correlation between Number of Joint Programs and Indicators of Complexity, Controlling for Number of New Programs (Excluding New Programs that are Joint Programs)
Index of Professional Training	.32
Index of Professional Activity	.11
Number of Occupations: 1967	.75

of joint programs almost to zero in every case except that of professional training. Thus, the number of committees is evidently a function of these factors. On the other hand, the very strong relationship between the number of joint programs and the frequency of committee meetings is only moderately reduced when these controls are applied as shown in Table 7. This shows that the frequency of committee meetings is not simply a function of the complexity of the organization or the degree of organizational innovation, but has an independent relationship with the number of joint programs.

4. Organizations with many joint programs have slightly more decentralized decision-making structures. In our study, staff members were asked how often they participated in organizational decisions about the hiring of personnel, the promotion of personnel, the adoption of new organizational policies, and the adoption of new programs or services. The organizational score was based on the degree of participation in these four areas of decision-making.[6] As shown in Table 2, there is a weak, positive relationship between the degree of participation in agency-wide decisions and the number of joint programs ($r=0.30$). This appears to be measuring the way resources are controlled. A second kind of decision-making concerns the control of work. We measure the degree of decision-making about work with a scale called the "hierarchy of authority."[7] This scale had a relationship with the number of joint programs in the opposite direction to our expectation ($r=0.33$). While highly interdependent organizations have slightly more decentralization of decisions about organizational resources, there is slightly less control over work in such organizations. It is difficult to account for this other than that the organizations with a high degree of program change during the period 1964–1966 had less control over work decisions in 1967 than in 1964. This suggests that the rate of change was so high in such organizations during this period that some more rigid mechanisms of social control were adopted in these organizations. Since the highly innovative organizations were also those with more joint programs, this helps to explain the reversal.

TABLE 7

Partial Correlation Coefficients between Number of Joint Programs and Indicators of Internal Communication, Controlling for Indicators of Complexity and Innovation

Control Variables	Partial Correlation between Number of Joint Programs and Number of Committees, Controlling for the Variable Indicated	Partial Correlation between Number of Joint Programs and Frequency of Committee Meetings, Controlling for the Variable Indicated
Indicators of Complexity		
Index of Professional Training	.45	.83
Index of Professional Activity	.13	.76
Number of Occupations: 1967	.11	.57
Indicator of Organizational Innovation		
Number of New Programs: 1959–1966 (excluding new programs that are joint programs)	.08	.64

TABLE 8

Partial Correlation Coefficients between Number of Joint Programs and Indicators of Centralization of Decision-making, Controlling for Indicators of Complexity, Innovation, and Internal Communication

Control Variables	Partial Correlations between Number of Joint Programs and Participation in Decision-making, Controlling for the Variable Indicated	Partial Correlations between Number of Joint Programs and Hierarchy of Authority, Controlling for the Variable Indicated
Indicators of Complexity		
Index of Professional Training	.27	.33
Index of Professional Activity	.01	.21
Number of Occupations: 1967	−.10	.31
Indicator of Organizational Innovation		
Number of New Programs: 1959–1966 (excluding new programs that are joint programs)	.20	−.28
Indicators of Internal Communication		
Number of Committees	.16	.17
Number of Committee Meetings per Month	.43	.22

Partial correlations between the number of joint programs and the degree of participation in decision-making, controlling for each of the indicators of complexity, innovation, and internal communication, are shown in Table 8.

The relatively low relationship between these two variables is reduced, and in one case reversed, when these other factors are controlled by using partial correlations. Only in the case of frequency of committee meetings is the relationship strengthened. What this means is that the degree of participation in decision-making is largely a function of some of the previously discussed variables—professional activity, number of occupations, and number of committees. Thus, it has little independent relationship with the number of joint programs.

The relationship between hierarchy of authority and the number of joint programs is little affected by indicators of complexity, but somewhat more by the indicators of internal communication. (See Table 8.) On the other hand, the relationship between these two variables is reversed when the number of new programs is controlled, and the relationship is now in the expected direction, i.e., members of organizations with many joint programs having more control over individual work tasks. This finding buttresses our earlier interpretation that it was the dramatic increase of new programs that brought about less control over individual work decisions in organizations with many joint programs.

5. *There is no relationship between formalization and the number of joint programs.* Rules and regulations are important organizational mechanisms that are often used to insure the predictability of performance. There are several important aspects of rules as mechanisms of social control. One is the number of regulations specifying who is to do what, when, where, and why; this we call job codification.[8] A second is the diligency with which such rules are enforced, this we call rule observation.[9] A third is the degree to which the procedures defining a job are spelled out; this we call the index of specificity of jobs.[10]

Two of these three indicators of formalization, the degree of rule observation and the degree of specificity of jobs, had very small inverse relationships with the number of joint programs ($r = -0.06$ in each case), but each of these is hardly different from zero. The index of job codification was directly related to the number of joint programs ($r = 0.13$), but it too is little different from zero, although it is in the opposite direction to our expectation.

We conclude from these findings that formalization is unrelated to the degree of organizational interdependence, suggesting that either this kind of internal diversity is not very important or that we do not have valid measures of this phenomenon. However, there is some problem of interpretation because there was also some movement of the highly innovative organizations toward greater formalization. For example, there is a negative partial correlation between the number of joint programs and each of the indicators of formalization, i.e., job codification (partial $r = -0.11$), rule observation (partial $r = -0.37$), and degree of specificity or jobs (partial $r = -0.29$), when the number of new programs during the period 1959–1966 is partialled out.

Controls for Size, Auspices, Age, and Technology. The sixteen organizations included in this study are, from one point of view, relatively homogeneous. All of them provide either psychiatric, social, or rehabilitation services of one kind or another. In comparison to economic organizations, they are indeed homogeneous. In addition, they are all located in a single metropolitan area. The reader might wonder, therefore, how far we can generalize from our study to other kinds of organizations or to organizations in other communities.

There are several ways in which some estimate of the generality can be made. One approach would be to divide the organizations into different categories, as was done in Tables 1 and 4. Here we emphasized the differences among a set of organizations that, considering the range of all organizations, are relatively homogeneous. The difficulty with this approach is that we are making comparisons among so few cases in each category.

An alternative approach is to look at some general variables that describe the conditions of all organizations. The size of the organization is one such variable. Similarly the auspices of the organization, i.e., whether private or public, is another. And the age of the organization may also be an important factor here. Perrow (1967) has recently suggested another variable, the degree of routinization of technology. Undoubtedly there are others, but these represent some of the variables that one is likely to encounter in the literature and, therefore, are a good starting place for controls.

Since there were such great differences in the size of organizations in the study, a rank ordering of size is used. The correlation coefficient between size and the number of joint programs is positive and moderate ($r=0.34$), which means that larger organizations have slightly more joint programs.

The auspices of the organization is measured by a dummy variable of private (1) versus public (0). The correlation coefficient between auspices and number of joint programs is 0.20, meaning that private organizations have slightly more joint programs.

The age of the organization was measured by constructing a trichotomous variable: (0), the organization was started in the post-Depression years (1938 to present); (1), the organization was started in the years following World War I (1918–1923); and (2), the organization was started prior to 1900. The correlation coefficient between age of the organization and the number of joint programs is -0.15, indicating that the younger organizations have slightly more joint programs.

Finally we looked at the type of technology, measured by the degree of routineness of work activities. By routineness of work we mean the degree to which organizational members have non-uniform work activities (Perrow, 1967; Woodward, 1965).[11] The correlation coefficient between routineness of work and the number of joint programs is -0.24, meaning that organizations with many joint programs have less routine technologies.

None of these four variables has strong relationships with the number of joint programs. When each of the relationships between the number of joint programs and the indicators of complexity, organizational innovation, internal communication, centralization, and formalization are controlled by each of these four variables separately, the relationships shown in Table 2 are little affected. (See Table 9.) This means that the factors of organizational size, auspices, age, and technology (as we have measured them) have little or no effect on the findings of this study.

Discussions and Conclusions

We now return to the issues raised at the outset of this article. How are organizational structure and interdependence related? How can the study of an organization and its environment be combined? What kinds of organizations are more cooperative and integrated with other organizations?

We noted that there is a greater degree of complexity, i.e., more occupational diversity and greater professionalism of staff, in those organizations with the most joint programs. The participation in joint programs is evidently one mechanism for adding new occupational specialties to the organization at a reduced cost. By combining the resources of the focal organization with one or more others, there is the possibility of adding new occupational specializations to the organizational roster. This is especially true because joint programs are likely to be of a highly specialized nature, providing services and activities that the focal organization cannot support alone.

The involvement of staff in interorganizational relationships introduces them to new ideas, new perspectives, and new techniques for solving organizational problems. The establishment of collegial relationships with comparable staff members of other organizations provides them with a comparative framework for understanding their own organizations. This is likely to affect their professional activities—attendance at meetings of professional societies—as well as reinforce professional standards of excellence. In these ways the involvement of organizations in joint programs has the effect of increasing the complexity of these social and health welfare organizations.

The heightened interdependence has other important implications for the internal structure of organizations. The partial or total commitment of organizational resources to other organizations is likely to affect various departments and the business office as well as the central programs of such an organization. Problems of coordination are likely to become particularly acute under such circumstances. The organization is forced to overcome these problems by heightening the frequency of internal communication. A more diverse committee structure and more committee meetings are mechanisms for handling such problems.

We would have expected that the heightened rates of communica-

TABLE 9

Partial Correlations Between the Number of Joint Programs and Indicators of
Complexity, Innovation, Internal Communication, Centralization, and Formalization,
Controlling Separately for Organization Size, Auspices, Age, and Technology

	Partial Correlation Coefficient Between Number of Joint Programs and the Organization Characteristic Indicated, Controlling for			
	Size	Auspices	Age	Tech-nology
Complexity				
Index of Professional Training	.35	.14	.16	.02
Index of Professional Activity	.56	.61	.64	.60
Number of Occupations: 1967	.88	.86	.89	.86
Innovation				
Number of New Programs: 1959-1966 (excluding new programs that are joint programs)	.73	.76	.74	.75
Internal Communication				
Number of Committees	.41	.45	.48	.48
Number of Committee Meetings per Month	.81	.82	.82	.83
Centralization				
Index of Participation in Decision-Making	.25	.27	.40	.18
Index of Hierarchy of Authority	.38	.35	.29	.33
Formalization				
Index of Job Codification	.18	.12	.07	.19
Index of Rule Observation	−.27	.00	−.10	−.02
Index of Specificity of Job	−.19	.03	−.16	.12

tion would have resulted in more decentralization than appears to be the case. It is entirely possible that the problems of internal coordination may be reflected in some attempts to tighten the power structure, thus leading to less movement towards decentralization than we had expected. Also, the problems of internal coordination may be reflected in greater programming of the organization, or at least attempts in that direction, and this may be the reason why there is a small relationship between heightened interdependency, as we have measured it, and the degree of centralization.

Diversity in occupations (the degree of complexity) and power groups (the degree of decentralization) are related to the number of joint programs, but diversity in work, as reflected in the absence of rules, is not related to this measure of interdependence. In part this may be a consequence of the sudden increase in the rate of program innovation. But it may also be that the degree of formalization is not a good measure of diversity. It is the diversity of occupations, including their perspectives and self-interests, along with the representation of these points of view in a decentralized structure, that allows for diversity with the most critical consequences.

Our assumptions help to explain the steadily increasing frequency of organizational interdependency, especially that involving joint programs. As education levels increase, the division of labor proceeds (stimulated by research and technology), and organizations become more complex. As they do, they also become more innovative. The search for resources needed to support such innovations requires interdependent relations with other organizations. At first, these interdependencies may be established with organizations with different goals and in areas that are more tangential to the organization. Over time, however, it may be that cooperation among organizations will multiply, involving interdependencies in more critical areas, involve organizations having more similar goals. It is scarcity of resources that forces organizations to enter into more cooperative activities with other organizations, thus creating greater integration of the organizations in a community structure. The long range consequence of this process will probably be a gradually heightened coordination in communities.

Notes

1. For a discussion of some of the basic differences between individual and collective properties, see Lazarsfeld and Menzel (1960) and Coleman (1964).

2. One advantage of this procedure is that it allows for the cancellation of individual errors made by the job occupants of a particular position. It also allows for the elimination of certain idiosyncratic elements that result from the special privileges a particular occupant might have received as a consequence. An alternative procedure for computing organizational means is to weight all respondents equally. These two procedures yield strikingly similar results for the variables reported in this paper. The product-movement correlation coefficients between the scores based on these two computational procedures were as follows for the variables indicated:

Hierarchy of authority 0.93
Participation in decision making 0.85
Job codification 0.89
Rule observation 0.89
Index of specificity of jobs 0.93
Index of routinization of technology 0.94
Professional training 0.90
Professional activity 0.93

3. It should be noted that our count of occupational specialties is not based on the number of specific job titles. Instead, each respondent was asked what he did

and then this was coded according to the kind of professional activity and whether it was a specialty. This procedure was used for two reasons. First, it allows for comparability across organizations. Second, it avoids the problem of task specialization where one activity might be divided into many specific and separate tasks. (See Thompson, 1964.)

4. The index of professional activity, which ranged from 0 to 3 points, was computed as follows: (a) 1 point for belonging to a professional organization; (b) 1 point for attending at least two-thirds of the previous six meetings of any professional organization; (c) 1 point for the presentation of a paper or holding an office in any professional organization.

5. The index was scored as follows: (a) high school graduates or less education, with no professional training, received a score of 0; (b) high school graduates or less education, with some professional training, received a score of 1; (c) staff members with a college degree or some college, but an absence of other professional training, received a score of 2; (d) staff members with a college degree or some college, and the presence of some other professional training, received a score of 3; (e) the presence of training beyond a college degree, and the absence of other professional training, received a score of 4; (f) the presence of training beyond a college degree, and the presence of other professional training, received a score of 5.

6. The index of actual participation in decision making was based on the following four questions: (1) How frequently do you usually participate in the decision to hire new staff? (2) How frequently do you usually participate in the decisions on the promotion of any of the professional staff? (3) How frequently do you participate in decisions on the adoption of new policies? (4) How frequently do you participate in the decisions on the adoption of new programs? Respondents were assigned numerical scores from 1 (low participation) to 5 (high participation), depending on whether they answered "never," "sometimes," "often," or "always," respectively, to these questions. An average score on these questions was computed for each respondent, and then the data were aggregated into organizational scores as described above.

7. The empirical indicators of these concepts were derived from two scales developed by Richard Hall (1963), namely, hierarchy of authority and rules. The index of hierarchy of authority was compared by first averaging the replies of individual respondents to each of the following five statements: (1) There can be little action taken here until a supervisor approves a decision. (2) A person who wants to make his own decisions would be quickly discouraged here. (3) Even small matters have to be referred to someone higher up for a final answer. (4) I have to ask my boss before I do almost anything. (5) Any decision I make has to have my boss's approval. Responses could vary from 1 (definitely false) to 4 (definitely true). The individual scores were then combined into an organizational score as described above.

8. The index of job codification was based on responses to the following five statements: (1) A person can make his own decisions without checking with anybody else. (2) How things are done here is left up to the person doing the work. (3) People here are allowed to do almost as they please. (4) Most people here make their own rules on the job. Replies to these questions were scored from 1 (definitely true) to 4 (definitely false), and then each of the respondent's answers was averaged. Thus, a high score on this index means high job codification.

9. The index of rule observation was computed by averaging the responses to each of the following two statements: (1) The employees are constantly being

checked on for rule violations. (2) People here feel as though they are constantly being watched, to see that they obey all the rules. Respondents' answers were coded from 1 (definitely false) to 4 (definitely true), and then the average score of each respondent on these items was computed. Organizational scores were computed as previously described. On this index, a high score means a high degree of rule observation.

10. The index of specificity of job was based on responses to the following six statements: (1) Whatever situation arises, we have procedures to follow in dealing with it. (2) Everyone has a specific job to do. (3) Going through the proper channels is constantly stressed. (4) The organization keeps a written record of everyone's job performance. (5) We are to follow strict operating procedures at all times. (6) Whenever we have a problem, we are supposed to go to the same person for an answer. Replies to these questions were scored from 1 (definitely false) to 4 (definitely true), and then the average score of each respondent on these items was computed as the other measures. A high score means a high degree of specificity of the job.

11. The index of routinization of technology was based on responses to the following five statements: (1) People here do the same job in the same way every day (reversed). (2) One thing people like around here is the variety of work. (3) Most jobs have something new happening every day. (4) There is something different to do every day. (5) Would you describe your job as being highly routine, somewhat routine, somewhat non-routine, or highly non-routine? The first four items were scored from 1 (definitely true) to 4 (definitely false). On the fifth item scores ranged from 1 (highly non-routine) to 4 (highly routine).

References

Barth, Ernest A. T. 1963. "The causes and consequences of inter-agency conflict." *Sociological Inquiry* 33 (Winter):51–57.

Black, Bertram J., and Harold M. Kase. 1963. "Inter-agency cooperation in rehabilitation and mental health." *Social Service Review* 37 (March):26–32.

Caplow, Theodore. 1964. *Principles of Organization.* New York: Harcourt, Brace & World, Inc.

Clark, Burton R. 1965. "Interorganizational patterns in education." *Administrative Science Quarterly* 10 (September):224–237.

Coleman, James S. 1964. "Research chronicle: The Adolescent Society." Phillip Hammond (ed.), *Sociologist at Work.* New York: Basic Books.

Coser, Lewis. 1956. *The Functions of Social Conflict.* Glencoe, Ill.: The Free Press of Glencoe.

Crozier, Michel. 1964. *The Bureaucratic Phenomenon.* Chicago: The University of Chicago Press.

Dahrendorf, Ralf. 1958. "Out of Utopia: toward a reorientation of sociological analysis." *American Journal of Sociology* 64 (September):115–127.

Dill, William R. 1958. "Environment on an influence on managerial autonomy." *Administrative Science Quarterly* 2 (March):409–443.

————. 1962. "The impact of environment on organizational development." Pp. 94–109 in Sidney Mailick and Edward H. Van Ness (eds.), *Concepts and Issues in Administrative Behavior.* Englewood Cliffs, N. J.: Prentice-Hall, Inc.

Elling, R. H., and S. Halbsky. 1961. "Organizational differentiation and support: a conceptual framework." *Administrative Science Quarterly* 6 (September): 185–209.

Emery, F. E., and E. L. Trist. 1965. "The casual texture of organizational environment." *Human Relations* 18 (February):21–31.

Evan, William M. 1966. "The organization-set: toward a theory of inter-organizational relations." Pp. 173–191 in James D. Thompson (ed.), *Approaches to Organizational Design*. Pittsburgh, Pa.: University of Pittsburgh Press.

Form, William H., and Sigmund Nosow. 1958. *Community in Disaster*. New York: Harper and Row.

Gouldner, Alvin. 1959. "Reciprocity and autonomy in functional theory." Pp. 241–270 in Llewellyn Gross (ed.), *Symposium on Sociological Theory*. New York: Harper and Row.

Guetzkow, Harold. 1950. "Interagency committee usage." *Public Administration Review* 10 (Summer):190–196.

———. 1966. "Relations among organizations." Pp. 13–44 in Raymond V. Bowers (ed.), *Studies on Behavior in Organizations*. Athens, Ga.: University of Georgia Press.

Hage, Jerald, and Michael Aiken. 1967. "Program change and organizational properties: a comparative analysis." *American Journal of Sociology* 72 (March): 503–519.

Hall, Richard. 1963. "The concept of bureaucracy: an empirical assessment." *American Journal of Sociology* 69 (July):32–40.

Harbison, Frederick H., E. Kochling, F. H. Cassell, and H. C. Ruebman. 1955. "Steel management on two continents." *Management Science* 2:31–39.

Harrison, Paul M. 1959. *Authority and Power in the Free Church Tradition*. Princeton, N.J.: Princeton University Press.

Hawley, Amos H. 1951. *Human Ecology*. New York: The Ronald Press.

Homans, George. 1950. *The Human Group*. New York: Harcourt, Brace and World, Inc.

Johns, Ray E., and David F. de Marche. 1951. *Community Organization and Agency Responsibility*. New York: Association Press.

Kornhauser, William. 1959. *The Politics of Mass Society*. Glencoe, Ill.: The Free Press of Glencoe.

Lawrence, Paul R., and Jay W. Lorsch. 1967. *Organization and Environment*. Boston: Graduate School of Business Administration, Harvard University.

Lazarsfeld, Paul, and Herbert Menzel. 1960. "On the relation between individual and collective properties." Pp. 422–440 in Amitai Etzioni (ed.), *Complex Organizations: A Sociological Reader*. New York: The Macmillan Company.

Lefton, Mark, and William Rosengren. 1966. "Organizations and clients: lateral and longitudinal dimensions." *American Sociological Review* 31 (December): 802–810.

Levine, Sol, and Paul E. White. 1961. "Exchange as a conceptual framework for the study of interorganizational relationships." *Administrative Science Quarterly* 5 (March):583–601.

———. 1963. "The community of health organizations." Pp. 321–347 in Howard E. Freeman, S. E. Levine, and Leo G. Reeder (eds.), *Handbook of Medical Sociology*. Englewood Cliffs, N.J.: Prentice-Hall.

Levine, Sol, Paul E. White, and Benjamin D. Paul. 1963. "Community inter-organizational problems in providing medical care and social services." *American Journal of Public Health* 53 (August):1183–1195.

Litwak, Eugene. 1961. "Models of bureaucracy which permit conflict." *American Journal of Sociology* 67 (September):177–184.

Litwak, Eugene, and Lydia F. Hylton. 1962. "Interorganizational analysis:

A hypothesis on coordinating agencies." *Administrative Science Quarterly* 6 (March):395–426.

Miller, Walter B. 1958. "Inter-institutional conflict as a major impediment to delinquency prevention." *Human Organization* 17 (Fall):20–23.

Morris, Robert, and Ollie A. Randall. 1965. "Planning and organization of community services for the elderly." *Social Work* 10 (January):96–102.

Perrow, Charles. 1967. "A framework for the comparative analysis of organizations." *American Sociological Review* 32 (April):194–208.

Reid, William. 1964. "Interagency coordination in delinquency prevention and control." *Social Service Review* 38 (December 1964):418–428.

Richardson, Stephen A. 1959. "Organizational contrasts on British and American ships." *Administrative Science Quarterly* 1 (September):189–207.

Ridgeway, V. F. 1957. "Administration of manufacturer-dealer systems." *Administrative Science Quarterly* 1 (June):464–483.

Rushing, William A. 1967. "The effects of industry size and division of labor on administration." *Administrative Science Quarterly* 12 (September):273–295.

Selznick, Philip. 1949. *TVA and the Grass Roots.* Berkeley, Cal.: University of California Press.

Simpson, Richard L., and William H. Gulley. 1962. "Goals, environmental pressures, and organizational characteristics." *American Sociological Review* 27 (June):344–351.

Terreberry, Shirley. 1968. "The evolution of organizational environments." *Administrative Science Review* 12 (March):590–613.

Thompson, James D. 1962. "Organizations and output transactions." *American Journal of Sociology* 68 (November):309–324.

———. 1966. *Organizations in Action.* New York: McGraw-Hill.

Thompson, James D., and William J. McEwen. 1958. "Organizational goals and environment: goal-setting as an interaction process." *American Sociological Review* 23 (February):23–31.

Thompson, Victor R. 1961. *Modern Organizations.* New York: Alfred A. Knopf, Inc.

Tocqueville, Alexis de. 1945. *Democracy in America.* New York: Alfred A. Knopf, Inc.

Warren, Roland L. 1965. "The impact of new designs of community organization." *Child Welfare* 44 (November):494–500.

———. 1967. "The interorganizational field as a focus for investigation." *Administrative Science Quarterly* 12 (December):396–419.

Wilensky, Harold L. 1967. *Organizational Intelligence.* New York: Basic Books, Inc.

Willer, 1967. *Scientific Sociology: Theory and Method.* Englewood Cliffs, New Jersey: Prentice-Hall.

Wilson, James Q. 1966. "Innovation in organization: notes toward a theory." Pp. 193–218 in *Approaches to Organizational Design.* Pittsburgh, Pa.: University of Pittsburgh Press.

Woodward, Joan. 1965. *Industrial Organization.* London: Oxford University Press.

Wrong, Dennis. 1961. "The oversocialized conception of man in modern society." *American Sociological Review* 26 (April):183–193.

Yuchtman, Ephraim, and Stanley E. Seashore. 1967. "A system resource approach to organizational effectiveness." *American Sociological Review* 32 (December):891–903.

Chapter X

Evaluating Organizational Performance

As purposefully designed goal seeking systems, organizations must engage in a continuous process of assessing their total performance as well as the performance of each of their components. The assessment process is, therefore, a key determinant of the effectiveness and adaptation level of the organization. The assessment process also includes outsiders whose evaluations may determine the degree of institutionalization and viability of the organization in its environment. Thus, there is a close interrelationship and mutual influence between the internal and external evaluation of the organization's performance.

The evaluative process in the organization is complex and aims at many levels. To mention a few: (a) the organization needs to determine the quantity and quality of its various outputs; (b) it must assess the extent to which these outputs enhance the overall goals of the organization; (c) the organization must determine the degree of success it has in producing the desired outputs (the question of effectiveness); (d) it must assess the costs involved in producing the outputs (the question of efficiency); and (e) the performance of each component and its contribution to the attainment of the organizational goals must be assessed as well. Suchman (1967) likewise identifies five categories of evaluation criteria: (1) effort—quantity and quality of the activities, (2) performance—the results of the efforts, (3) adequacy of performance—the contribution of the performance to the overall goals, (4) efficiency, and (5) process—how and why a program works or does not work.

It can be seen, then, that the evaluation of organizational performance has a dual function. First, the evaluation is aimed to assess the performance of the organization in relation to its task environment. Second, the evaluation serves as a monitoring system of staff activities by assessing the extent to which their role performances conform to the

614

norms and expectations of the service technology and the output requirements.

A distinctive attribute to organizational evaluation is its reliance on normative criteria. That is, the assessment is made against a set of criteria established by the organization or external units which reflect norms and values about the "goodness" and "desirability" of the organizational outputs, the relative importance of each of these outputs, and the desirable level of success in achieving the organizational goals (Suchman, 1967, pp. 33–34). The assessment process in the organization is, therefore, rarely value neutral and is closely linked to what we have termed the "organizational ideologies."

Another closely related attribute of organizational evaluation is the problem of assessing performance in relation to the multiple goals pursued by the organization. It is well acknowledged that the effectiveness of the organization is determined by its ability to optimize the attainment of its various system goals without seriously jeopardizing any of them (Etzioni, 1960). Thus, the complexity of the evaluation process in organizations is a result of the existence of multiple criteria as well as the interactions among them. For example, a hospital may be evaluated on several, not necessarily compatible, criteria such as the clinical quality of its medical care, patients functioning after treatment, the speed in which services are provided, and the extent of medical research and training. Note, however, that maximizing one criterion, such as clinical quality of medical care, may be at the expense of speed of service delivery.

Human service organizations encounter unique problems in the evaluation of their performance in addition to those noted above. These are experienced at several levels: (a) the determination of the evaluative criteria: (b) the methodology of the evaluation; (c) the administration of evaluation; and (d) the consequences of the evaluation.

On several occasions we noted that in comparison to other bureaucracies there is less consensus about the norms and values that underlie the goals of human service organizations, particularly since the ultimate object to be assessed are people processed through them. As a result, there is less agreement both inside and outside the organization about the desired outcomes and the criteria of success. For example, should the welfare agency be assessed by the number of needy persons whom it granted financial assistance, or in contrast, by the number of persons it has taken off the welfare rolls. The lack of consensus about measures of success is more problematic when the organization pursues multiple goals. This could be seen, for example, in the debate over the evaluation of the Head Start Program, i.e., whether it should be assessed solely on the basis of its ability to improve the cognitive capabilities of children, or also on its effects on the health and nutrition of children (Williams and Evans, 1969).

The formulation of evaluative criteria becomes exceedingly difficult as the service technology becomes more indeterminant. The uncertainty in the results of the techniques used is reflected in the inability to assess the effects of purposeful actions taken by the organization since cause-effect relations are incomplete. As a result, there is lack of clarity regarding what causal actions should be measured and with what potential consequences should they be correlated. It is not surprising, therefore, that in an assessment of a delinquency prevention program, for example, over a dozen different outcome measures were used (Meyer, Borgatta, and Jones, 1965).

Accurate evaluation of the organization's effectiveness necessitates appropriate controls over inputs and outputs, both of which are difficult to achieve in human service organizations. At the input level there are such disturbances as biased selection of clients, uncontrolled and unmeasured variability in their attributes, constraints in matching them with the tested treatments, and the like. At the output level the organization has limited controls over the client outside its jurisdiction and thus cannot isolate the outcomes it wishes to measure from the influence of extraneous factors. Moreover, the lack of input control creates problems of comparability among different cohorts of clients or the same clients over time.

The need to evaluate consequences of organizational activities on people adds unique methodological problems that threaten the validity of the evaluation process. Among these are (a) the uncontrolled maturation of people, (b) the occurrence of events not controllable by the organization (c) the addition or attrition of clients in the various treatment groups, and (d) the occurrence of various placebo effects (Campbell, 1969). Of equal importance is the fact that to varying degrees measurement instruments of human attributes and changes thereof still encounter significant problems of validity and reliability. The more indeterminant and complex the technology, the more serious are the problems. Consequently, the organization is likely to experience major difficulties in interpreting the information collected via its monitoring mechanisms. As a result human service organizations are likely to resort to very approximating measures which may not be intrinsic to the nature of the service endeavors. For example, the measurement of quality of a high school education may be approximated by such extrinsic measures as the number of graduates admitted to college, or the number of students winning prestigeous awards. The reliance on extrinsic measures, however, increases the danger that they displace the original service goals of the organization.

The danger of goal displacement is further intensified by the administrative problems human service organizations encounter in developing an effective information system (Wheeler, 1969). Without attempting to explore this very complex issue, a few factors can be briefly identified that sustain these problems: (a) the limited visibility of staff-client transactions; (b) the heavy reliance on staff judgments and impressions; (c) the strong dependency on the client as a source of information; (d) the inherent difficulties in developing objective monitoring devices; and (e) the lack of resources to introduce efficient data processing equipment. As a result, while the organization may be over burdened with bits of data, it has limited and occasionally distorted information necessary for appropriate evaluation. This critical administrative bottleneck results in the existence of deficient monitoring devices which deprive the organization of information vitally important to the evaluation process.

Finally, we need to consider the political implications or consequences of the evaluative program. Evaluation produces information which potentially could be used by decision makers in the allocation of resources to the organization as well as the distribution of power within it (Cohen, 1970). Needless to say, the organization wishes to score well on those evaluative criteria used by the external units which control the crucial resources of the organization. Invariably, then, the evaluation of the organizational performance is closely related to the legitimation it receives in its task environment. Thus, human service organizations are highly sensitive to the evaluative process and wish to control its results as much as possible. This sensitivity is coupled with the acknowledgement that once information becomes public, it could be interpreted in many ways both favorable and unfavorable to the organization. Internally, the assessment of staff performance may result in significant shifts of power and influence. Therefore, various staff groups may wish to control the nature of the information about their own activities in order to maintain or advance their position. Since much of the information tends to be judgmental, the potential for biased information and its interpretation are high.

The influence of the political context on organizational evaluation is most apparent in the assessment of new service programs and experiments such as Head Start, neighborhood health centers, manpower programs for the hard-to-employ, and delinquent rehabilitation projects. New programs tend to face external political pressures for early assessment of their performance. They are aimed at avoiding institutionaliza-

tion and therefore perpetuation of a program that consumes scarce resources and is ineffective. Nevertheless, rather than measuring success or
failure, the evaluation is often more likely to reflect the many organizational and administrative problems that emanate from the newness of the
program. Moreover, as the program becomes institutionalized it becomes
modified and altered in response to external and internal exigencies that
often are not considered in the assessment process (Weiss and Rein,
1970).

Donabedian presents an extensive review of studies aimed at
evaluating the quality of medical care. In so doing, the author provides
a critical analysis of the major issues involved in the evaluation of the
performance of any human service organization. For example, he points
to the limitations in the use of outcomes as measures of performance and
implies that the processes of providing medical care might be a better
target to evaluate. The author cogently indicates the inherent difficulties
in the use of records as sources of information since their use may result
in the assessment of the adequacy of the records themselves rather than
the quality of care. Although the use of normative criteria is frequent,
Donabedian points out that there may be substantial disagreements
about such standards. Finally, he raises the issue of the reliability problems in the use of judges as assessors.

Lerman cogently points out how the desire of the organization to
demonstrate the success of its program leads to biases in the evaluation
of its performance. Basically, the organization and its affiliated researchers tend to violate a basic scientific rule by attempting to confirm
the hypothesis that the program is successful, rather than attempting to
reject it. Lerman argues that the organization must also count its failures,
both in terms of those failing to perform as expected and those failing to
complete the treatment. Moreover, the organization cannot compare its
treated population with a control group that was worse off from the
beginning.

Finally, Borus, Brennan, and Rosen provide an example of the
application of cost-benefit analysis to the evaluation of outcomes in
human service organizations. Although this approach uses economic
criteria for assessment, it is rapidly becoming a powerful evaluation tool,
particularly since it forces the question of the program's costs as well as
its utility. Moreover, the tools of cost-benefit analysis can accurately
differentiate among cohorts of clients who benefit most or least from the
organization's services. The authors show that in the case of Neighborhood Youth Corps in Indiana, a high benefit-cost ratio was obtained for
males but not for females. Moreover, high school dropouts benefited
more than high school graduates, and so did those who stayed longer in

the program. Thus, the authors seem to challenge the prevalent negative evaluation of the program. Needless to say, cost-benefit analysis is an important tool of evaluation and could be (and has been) applied to a wide range of human service organizations.

References

Campbell, D. T. 1969. "Reforms as experiments." *American Psychologist* 24:409–29.

Cohen, D. K. 1970. "Politics and research: Evaluation of social action programs in education." *Review of Educational Research* 40:213–38.

Etzioni, A. 1960. "Two approaches to organizational analysis: A critique and a suggestion." *Administrative Science Quarterly* 5:258–78.

Meyer, H. J. Borgatta, F. F., and Jones, W. C. 1965. *Girls At Vocational High*. New York: Russell Sage Foundation.

Suchman, E. A. 1967. *Evaluative Research*. New York: Russell Sage Foundation. Pp. 33–34 and 61–66.

Weiss, R., and Rein, M. 1970. "The evaluation of broad-aim programs: Experimental design, its difficulties, and an alternative." *Administrative Science Quarterly* 15:97–109.

Wheeler, S. (ed.). 1969. *On Record*. New York: Russell Sage Foundation.

Williams, W., and Evans, J. 1960. "The politics of evaluation: The case of Headstart." *Annals* 385:118–32.

Evaluating the Quality of Medical Care

Avedis Donabedian

Definition of Quality

The assessment of quality must rest on a conceptual and operationalized definition of what the "quality of medical care" means. Many problems are present at this fundamental level, for the quality of care is a remarkably difficult notion to define. Perhaps the best-known definition is that offered by Lee and Jones[1] in the form of eight "articles of faith," some stated as attributes or properties of the process of care and others as goals or objectives of that process. These "articles" convey vividly the impression that the criteria of quality are nothing more than value judgments that are applied to several aspects, properties, ingredients or dimensions of a process called medical care. As such, the definition of

Excerpted from *The Milbank Memorial Fund Quarterly* 44 (July, 1966), pt. 2: 166–88.

quality may be almost anything anyone wishes it to be, although it is, ordinarily, a reflection of values and goals current in the medical care system and in the larger society of which it is a part.

Few empirical studies delve into what the relevant dimensions and values are at any given time in a given setting. Klein, *et al.*,[2] found that 24 "administrative officials," among them, gave 80 criteria for evaluating "patient care." They conclude that patient care, like morale, cannot be considered as a unitary concept and ". . . it seems likely that there will never be a single comprehensive criterion by which to measure the quality of patient care."

Which of a multitude of possible dimensions and criteria are selected to define quality will, of course, have profound influence on the approaches and methods one employs in the assessment of medical care.

Approaches to Assessment: What to Assess

The outcome of medical care, in terms of recovery, restoration of function and of survival, has been frequently used as an indicator of the quality of medical care. Examples are studies of perinatal mortality,[3, 4] surgical fatality rates[5] and social restoration of patients discharged from psychiatric hospitals.[6]

Many advantages are gained by using outcome as the criterion of quality in medical care. The validity of outcome as a dimension of quality is seldom questioned. Nor does any doubt exist as to the stability and validity of the values of recovery, restoration and survival in most situations and in most cultures, though perhaps not in all. Moreover, outcomes tend to be fairly concrete and, as such, seemingly amenable to more precise measurement.

However, a number of considerations limit the use of outcomes as measures of the quality of care. The first of these is whether the outcome of care is, in fact, the relevant measure. This is because outcomes reflect both the power of medical science to achieve certain results under any given set of conditions, and the degree to which "scientific medicine," as currently conceived, has been applied in the instances under study. But the object may be precisely to separate these two effects. Sometimes a particular outcome may be irrelevant, as when survival is chosen as a criterion of success in a situation which is not fatal but is likely to produce suboptimal health or crippling.[7]

Even in situations where outcomes are relevant, and the relevant outcome has been chosen as a criterion, limitations must be reckoned with. Many factors other than medical care may influence outcome, and precautions must be taken to hold all significant factors other than medical care constant if valid conclusions are to be drawn. In some cases long periods of time, perhaps decades, must elapse before relevant outcomes are manifest. In such cases the results are not available when they are needed for appraisal and the problems of maintaining comparability are greatly magnified. Also, medical technology is not fully effective and the measure of success that can be expected in a particular situation is often not precisely known. For this reason comparative studies of outcome, under controlled situations, must be used.

Although some outcomes are generally unmistakable and easy to measure (death, for example) other outcomes, not so clearly defined, can be difficult to measure. These include patient attitudes and satisfactions, social restoration and physical disability and rehabilitation.[8] Even the face validity that outcomes generally have as criteria of success or failure, is not absolute. One may debate, for example, whether the prolongation of life under certain circumstances is evidence of good medical care. McDermott, *et al.*, have shown that, although fixing a congenitally dislocated hip joint in a given position is considered good medicine for the white man, it can prove crippling for the Navajo Indian who spends much time seated on the floor or in the saddle.[9] Finally, although outcomes might indicate good or bad care in the aggregate, they do not give an insight into the nature and location of the deficiencies or strengths to which the outcome might be attributed.

All these limitations to the use of outcomes as criteria of medical care are presented not to demonstrate that outcomes are inappropriate indicators of quality but to emphasize that they must be used with discrimination. Outcomes, by and large, remain the ultimate validators of the effectiveness and quality of medical care.

Another approach to assessment is to examine the process of care itself rather than its outcomes. This is justified by the assumption that one is interested not in the power of medical technology to achieve results, but in whether what is now known to be "good" medical care has been applied. Judgments are based on considerations such as the appropriateness, completeness and redundancy of information obtained through clinical history, physical examination and diagnostic tests; justification of diagnosis and therapy; technical competence in the performance of diagnostic and therapeutic procedures, including surgery; evidence of preventive management in health and illness; coordination and continuity of care; acceptability of care to the recipient and so on. This approach requires that a great deal of attention be given to specifying the relevant dimensions, values and standards to be used in assessment. The estimates of quality that one obtains are less stable and less final than those that derive from the measurement of outcomes. They may, however, be more relevant to the question at hand: whether medicine is properly practiced.

This discussion of process and outcome may seem to imply a simple separation between means and ends. Perhaps more correctly, one may think of an unbroken chain of antecedent means followed by intermediate ends which are themselves the means to still further ends.[10] Health itself may be a means to a further objective. Several authors have pointed out that this formulation provides a useful approach to evaluation.[11, 12] It may be designated as the measurement of procedural end points and included under the general heading of "process" because it rests on similar considerations with respect to values, standards and validation.

A third approach to assessment is to study not the process of care itself, but the settings in which it takes place and the instrumentalities of which it is the product. This may be roughly designated as the assessment of structure, although it may include administrative and related processes that support and direct the provision of care. It is concerned with such things as the adequacy of facilities and equipment; the qualifications of medical staff and their organization; the administrative structure and operations of programs and institutions providing care; fiscal organization and the like.[13, 14] The assumption is made that given the proper settings and instrumentalities, good medical care will follow. This approach offers the advantage of dealing, at least in part, with fairly concrete and accessible information. It has the major limitation that the relationship between structure and process or structure and outcome, is often not well established.

Sources and Methods of Obtaining Information

The approach adopted for the appraisal of quality determines, in large measure, the methods used for collecting the requisite information. Since these range the gamut of social science methods, no attempt will be made to describe them all. Four, however, deserve special attention.

Clinical records are the source documents for most studies of the medical care process. In using them one must be aware of their several limitations. Since the private office practice of most physicians is not readily accessible to the researcher, and the records of such practice are generally disappointingly sketchy, the use of records has been restricted to the assessment of care in hospitals, outpatient departments of hospitals and prepaid group practice. Both Peterson[15] and Clute[16] have reported the prevailing inadequacies of recording in general practice. In addition,

Clute has pointed out that, in general practice, ". . . the lack of adequate records is not incompatible with practice of a good, or even an excellent quality. . . ." On the other hand, a recent study of the office practice of a sample of members of the New York Society of Internal Medicine[17] suggests that abstracts of office records can be used to obtain reproducible judgments concerning the quality of care. But to generalize from this finding is difficult. It concerns a particular group of physicians more likely to keep good records than the average. Moreover, for one reason or another, the original sample drawn for this study suffered a 61 per cent attrition rate.

Assuming the record to be available and reasonably adequate, two further issues to be settled are the veracity and the completeness of the record. Lembcke[7] has questioned whether key statements in the record can be accepted at face value. He has questioned not only the statements of the physician about the patient and his management, but also the validity of the reports of diagnostic services. The first is verified by seeking in the record, including the nurses' notes, what appears to be the most valid evidence of the true state of affairs. The second is verified by having competent judges re-examine the evidence (films, tracings, slides) upon which diagnostic reports are made. Observer error tends to be a problem under the best of circumstances.[18] But nothing can remove the incredulity from the finding by Lembcke, in one hospital, that the true incidence of uterine hyperplasia was between five and eight per cent rather than 60 to 65 per cent of uterine curettages, as reported by the hospital pathologist. In any case, the implications of verification as part of the assessment of quality must be carefully considered. Errors in diagnostic reports no doubt reflect particularly on the quality of diagnostic service and on the care provided by the hospital, in general. But the physician may be judged to perform well irrespective of whether the data he works with are or are not valid. This is so when the object of interest is the logic that governs the physician's activities rather than the absolute validity of these activities.

Much discussion has centered on the question of the completeness of clinical records and whether, in assessing the quality of care based on what appears in the record, one is rating the record or the care provided. What confuses the issue is that recording is itself a separate and legitimate dimension of the quality of practice, as well as the medium of information for the evaluation of most other dimensions. These two aspects can be separated when an alternative source of information about the process of care is available, such as the direct observation of practice.[15, 16] In most instances, however, they are confounded. Rosenfeld[19] handled the problem of separating recording from care by examining the reasons for downrating the quality of care in each patient record examined. He demonstrated that the quality of care was rated down partly because of what could have been poor recording ("presumptive" evidence) and partly for reasons that could not have been a matter of recording ("substantial" evidence). He also found that hospitals tended to rank high or low on both types of errors, showing that these errors were correlated. Since routine recording is more likely to be complete in the wards, comparison of ward and private services in each hospital by type of reason for downrating might have provided further information on this important question. Other investigators have tried to allow for incompleteness in the record by supplementing it with interviews with the attending physician and making appropriate amendments.[20-22] Unfortunately, only one of these studies (length of stay in Michigan hospitals) contains a report of what difference this additional step made. In this study "the additional medical information elicited by means of personal interviews with attending physicians was of sufficient importance in 12.6 per cent of the total number of cases studied to warrant a reclassification of the evaluation of necessity for admission and/or the appropriateness of length of stay."[22] When information obtained by interview is used to amend or supplement the patient record, the assumption may have to be made that this additional information has equal or superior validity. Morehead, who has had extensive experience with this method, said, "Many of the surveyors engaged in the present study employed the technique of physician interview in earlier studies without fruitful results. . . . The surveyor was . . . left in the uncomfortable position of having to choose between taking at face value statements that medical care was indeed optimal, or concluding that statements presented were untrue."[23] Even in an earlier study, where supplementation by interview is reported to have been used,[21] verbal information was discarded unless it was further corroborated by the course of action or by concrete evidence.[24]

Another question of method is whether the entire record or abstracted digests of it should be used as a basis for evaluation. The question arises because summaries and abstracts can presumably be prepared by less skilled persons allowing the hard-to-get expert to concentrate on the final task of evaluation. Abstracting, however, seemingly involves the exercise of judgment as to relevance and importance. For that reason, it has been used as a first step in the evaluation of quality only in those studies that use very specific and detailed standards.[7] Even then, little information is available about how reliable the process of abstracting is, or how valid when compared with a more expert reading of the chart. The study of New York internists, already referred to, demonstrated a high level of agreement between physicians and highly trained non-physicians abstracting the same office record.[17]

While the controversy about the record as a source of information continues, some have attempted to reduce dependence on the physician's recording habits by choosing for evaluation diagnostic categories which are likely to be supported by recorded evidence additional to the physician's own entries.[25] This explains, in part, the frequent use of surgical operations as material for studies of quality.

In general practice, patient records are too inadequate to serve as a basis for evaluation. The alternative is *direct observation* of the physician's activities by a well qualified colleague.[15, 16] The major limitation of this method would seem to be the changes likely to occur in the usual practice of the physician who knows he is being observed. This has been countered by assurances that the physician is often unaware of the true purpose of the study, becomes rapidly accustomed to the presence of the observer, and is unable to change confirmed habits of practice. Even if changes do occur, they would tend to result in an overestimate of quality rather than the reverse. These assurances notwithstanding, measuring the effect of observation on practice remains an unsolved problem.

Those who have used the method of direct observation have been aware that the problem of completeness is not obviated. The practicing physician often knows a great deal about the patient from previous contacts with him. Hence the need to select for observation "new" cases and situations that require a thorough examination irrespective of the patient's previous experience. Moreover, not all of the managing physician's activities are explicit. Some dimensions of care, not subject to direct observation, must be excluded from the scheme of assessment. Selective perception by the observer may be an additional problem. The observer is not likely to be first a neutral recorder of events and then a judge of these same events. His knowledge and criteria are likely to influence what he perceives, and thus to introduce a certain distortion into perception.

An indirect method of obtaining information is to study *behaviors* and *opinions* from which inferences may be drawn concerning quality. A *sociometric* approach has been reported by Maloney, *et al.*, which assumes that physicians, in seeking care for themselves and their families, exhibit critical and valid judgments concerning the capacity of their colleagues to provide care of high quality.[26] Such choices were shown to identify classes of physicians presumed to be more highly qualified than others. But both sensitivity and specificity, using as criterion more rigorous estimates of the quality of care, lack validation.

Georgopoulos and Mann[27] used what might be called an *autoreputa-tional*[28] approach in assessing the quality of care in selected community hospitals. This grew out of previous studies showing that people are pretty shrewd judges of the "effectiveness" of the organizations in which they work.[29] The hospitals were rated and ranked using opinions concerning the quality of medical care, and other characteristics, held by different categories of managerial, professional and technical persons working in, or connected with, each hospital, as well as by knowledgeable persons in the community. The responses were sufficiently consistent and discriminating to permit the hospitals to be ranked with an apparently satisfactory degree of reliability. This in spite of the generally self-congratulatory nature of the responses that classified the quality of medical care in the hospitals as "very good," "excellent," or "outstanding" in 89 per cent of cases, and "poor" in almost none. The authors provide much evidence that the several opinions, severally held, were intercorrelated to a high degree. But little evidence supports the validity of the judgments by using truly external criteria of the quality of care.

Sampling and Selection

The first issue in sampling is to specify precisely the universe to be sampled, which, in turn, depends on the nature of the generalizations that one wishes to make. Studies of quality are ordinarily concerned with one of three objects: 1. the actual care provided by a specified category of providers of care; 2. the actual care received by a specified group of people and 3. the capacity of a specified group of providers to provide care. In the first two instances representative samples of potential providers or recipients are required, as well as representative samples of care provided or received. In the third instance a representative sample of providers is needed, but not necessarily a representative sample of care. A more important aspect is to select, uniformly of course, significant dimensions of care. Perhaps performance should be studied in certain clinical situations that are particularly stressful and therefore more revealing of latent capacities or weaknesses in performance. Hypothetical test situations may even be set up to assess the capacity to perform in selected dimensions of care.[30-32] The distinctions made above, and especially those between the assessment of actual care provided and of the capacity to provide care, are useful in evaluating the sampling procedures used in the major studies of quality. By these criteria, some studies belong in one category or another, but some seem to combine features of several in such a way that generalization becomes difficult. For example, in the first study of the quality of care received by Teamster families, the findings are meant to apply only to the management of specific categories of hospitalized illness in a specified population group.[25] In the second study of this series, somewhat greater generalizability is achieved by obtaining a representative sample (exclusive of seasonal variation) of all hospitalized illness in the same population group.[23] Neither study is meant to provide information about all the care provided by a representative sample of physicians.

The degree of homogeneity in the universe to be sampled is, of course, a matter of great importance in any scheme of sampling or selection. The question that must be asked is to what extent the care provided by a physician maintains a consistent level. Do specific diagnostic categories, levels of difficulty or dimensions of care exist in which a physician performs better than in others? Can one find, in fact, an "overall capacity for goodness in medical care,"[15] or is he dealing with a bundle of fairly disparate strands of performance? One might, similarly, ask whether the care provided by all subdivisions of an institution are at about the same level in absolute terms or in relation to performance in comparable institutions. Makover, for example, makes an explicit assumption of homogeneity when he writes, "No attempt was made to relate the number of records to be studied to the size of enrollment of the medical groups. The medical care provided to one or another individual is valid evidence of quality and there should be little or no chance variation which is affected by adjusting the size of the sample."[20] Rosenfeld began his study with the hypothesis "that there is a correspondence in standards of care in the several specialties and for various categories of illness in an institution."[19]

The empirical evidence concerning homogeneity is not extensive. Both the Peterson and Clute studies of general practice[15, 16] showed a high degree of correlation between performance of physicians in different components or dimensions of care (history, physical examination, treatment, etc.). Rosenfeld demonstrated that the differences in quality ratings among several diagnoses selected within each area of practice (medicine, surgery and obstetrics-gynecology) were not large. Although the differences among hospitals by area of practice appeared by inspection to be larger, they were not large enough to alter the rankings of the three hospitals studied.

The two studies of care received by Teamster families[23, 25] arrived at almost identical proportions of optimal and less than optimal care for the entire populations studied. This must have been coincidental, since the percent of optimal care, in the second study, varied greatly by diagnostic category from 31 per cent for medicine to 100 per cent for ophthalmology (nine cases only). If such variability exists, the "diagnostic mix" of the sample of care must be a matter of considerable importance in assessment. In the two Teamster studies, differences in "diagnostic mix" were thought to have resulted in lower ratings for medicine and higher ratings for obstetrics-gynecology in the second study than in the first. That the same factor may produce effects in two opposite directions is an indication of the complex interactions that the researcher must consider. "The most probable explanation for the ratings in medicine being lower in the present (second) study is the nature of the cases reviewed." The factor responsible is less ability to handle illness "which did not fall into a well recognized pattern." For obstetrics and gynecology the finding of the second study ". . . differed in one major respect from the earlier study where serious questions were raised about the management of far more patients. The earlier study consisted primarily of major abdominal surgery, whereas this randomly selected group contained few such cases and had more patients with minor conditions."[23] In studies such as these, where the care received by total or partial populations is under study, the variations noted stem partly from differences in diagnostic content and partly from institutionalized patterns of practice associated with diagnostic content. For example, all nine cases of eye disease received optimal care because "this is a highly specialized area, where physicians not trained in this field rarely venture to perform procedures."[23]

Sampling and selection influence, and are influenced by, a number of considerations in addition to generalization and homogeneity. The specific dimensions of care that interest one (preventive management or surgical technique, to mention two rather different examples) may dictate the selection of medical care situations for evaluation. The situations chosen are also related to the nature of the criteria and standards used and of the rating and scoring system adopted. Attempts to sample problem situations, rather than traditional diagnoses or operations, can be very difficult, because of the manner in which clinical records are filed and indexed. This is unfortunate, because a review of operations or established diagnoses gives an insight into the bases upon which the diagnosis was made or the operation performed. It leaves unexplored a complementary segment of practice, namely the situations in which a similar diagnosis or treatment may have been indicated but not made or performed.

Measurement Standards

Measurement depends on the development of standards. In the assessment of quality standards derive from two sources.

Empirical standards are derived from actual practice and are generally used to compare medical care in one setting with that in another, or with statistical averages and ranges obtained from a larger number of similar settings. The Professional Activities Study is based, in part, on this approach.[33]

Empirical standards rest on demonstrably attainable levels of care and, for that reason, enjoy a certain degree of credibility and acceptability. Moreover, without clear normative standards, empirical observations in selected settings must be made to serve the purpose. An interesting example is provided by Furstenberg, *et al.*, who used patterns of prescribing in medical care clinics and outpatient hospitals as the standard to judge private practice.[34]

In using empirical standards one needs some assurance that the clinical material in the settings being compared is similar. The Professional Activities Study makes some allowance for this by reporting patterns of care for hospitals grouped by size. The major shortcoming, however, is that care may appear to be adequate in comparison to that in other situations and yet fall short of what is attainable through the full application of current medical knowledge.

Normative standards derive, in principle, from the sources that legitimately set the standards of knowledge and practice in the dominant medical care system. In practice, they are set by standard textbooks or publications,[7] panels of physician's,[22] highly qualified practitioners who serve as judges[23] or a research staff in consultation with qualified practitioners.[19] Normative standards can be put very high and represent the "best" medical care that can be provided, or they can be set at a more modest level signifying "acceptable" or "adequate" care. In any event, their distinctive characteristic is that they stem from a body of legitimate knowledge and values rather than from specific examples of actual practice. As such, they depend for their validity on the extent of agreement concerning facts and values within the profession or, at least, among its leadership. Where equally legitimate sources differ in their views, judgments concerning quality become correspondingly ambiguous.

The relevance of certain standards, developed by one group, to the field of practice of another group, has been questioned. For example, Peterson and Barsamian report that although spermatic fluid examination of the husband should precede surgery for the Stein-Leventhal syndrome, not one instance of such examination was noted, and that this requirement was dropped from the criteria for assessment.[35] Dissatisfaction has also been voiced concerning the application to general practice of standards and criteria elaborated by specialists who practice in academic settings. The major studies of general practice have made allowances for this. Little is known, however, about the strategies of "good" general practice and the extent to which they are similar to, or different from, the strategies of specialized practice in academic settings.

Some researchers have used both types of standards, normative and empirical, in the assessment of care. Rosenfeld used normative standards but included in his design a comparison between university affiliated and community hospitals. "Use of the teaching hospital as a control provides the element of flexibility needed to adjust to the constantly changing scientific basis of the practice of medicine. No written standards, no matter how carefully drawn, would be adequate in five years."[19] Lembcke used experience in the best hospitals to derive a corrective factor that softens the excessive rigidity of his normative standards. This factor, expressed in terms of an acceptable percent of compliance with the standard, was designed to take account of contingencies not foreseen in the standards themselves. It does, however, have the effect of being more realistically permissive as well. This is because the correction factor is likely to be made up partly of acceptable departures from the norm and partly of deviations that might be unacceptable.

Standards can also be differentiated by the extent of their specificity and directiveness. At one extreme the assessing physician may be very simply instructed as follows: "You will use a yardstick in relation to the quality of care rendered, whether you would have treated this particular patient in this particular fashion during this specific hospital admission."[23] At the other extreme, a virtually watertight "logic system" may be constructed that specifies all the decision rules that are acceptable to justify diagnosis and treatment.[35, 36] Most cases fall somewhere in between.

Highly precise and directive standards are associated with the selection of specific diagnostic categories for assessment. When a representative sample of all the care provided is to be assessed, little more than general guides can be given to the assessor. Lembcke, who has stressed the need for specific criteria, has had to develop a correspondingly detailed diagnostic classification of pelvic surgery, for example.[7] In addition to diagnostic specificity, highly directive standards are associated with the preselection of specific dimensions of care for evaluation. Certain diagnoses, such as surgical operations, lend themselves more readily to this approach. This is evident in Lembcke's attempt to extend his system of audits to nonsurgical diagnoses.[37] The clear, almost rule-of-thumb judgments of adequacy become blurred. The data abstracted under such diagnostic rubric are more like descriptions of patterns of management, with insufficient normative criteria for decisive evaluation. The alternative adopted is comparison with a criterion institution.

Obviously, the more general and nondirective the standards are, the more one must depend on the interpretations and norms of the person entrusted with the actual assessment of care. With greater specificity, the research team is able, collectively, to exercise much greater control over what dimensions of care require emphasis and what the acceptable standards are. A great deal appears in common between the standards used in structured and unstructured situations as shown by the degree of agreement between "intuitive" ratings and directed ratings in the Rosenfeld study,[19] and between the "qualitative" and "quantitative" ratings in the study by Peterson, *et al.*[15] Indeed, these last two were so similar that they could be used interchangeably.

When standards are not very specific and the assessor must exercise his own judgment in arriving at an evaluation, very expert and careful judges must be used. Lembcke claims that a much more precise and directive system such as his does not require expert judges. "It is said that with a cookbook, anyone who can read can cook. The same is true, and to about the same extent, of the medical aduit using objective criteria; anyone who knows enough medical terminology to understand the definitions and criteria can prepare the case abstracts and tables for the medical audit. However, the final acceptance, interpretation and application of the findings must be the responsibility of a physician or group of physicians."[38] The "logic system" developed by Peterson and Barsamian appears well suited for rating by computer, once the basic facts have been assembled, presumably by a record abstractor.[35, 36]

The dimensions of care and the values that one uses to judge them are, of course, embodied in the criteria and standards used to assess care.[39] These standards can, therefore, be differentiated by their selectivity and inclusiveness in the choice of dimensions to be assessed. The dimensions selected and the value judgments attached to them constitute the operationalized definition of quality in each study.

The preselection of dimensions makes possible, as already pointed out, the development of precise procedures, standards and criteria. Lembcke[7] has put much stress on the need for selecting a few specific dimensions of care within specified diagnostic categories rather than attempting general evaluations of unspecified dimensions which, he feels, lack precision. He uses dimensions such as the following: confirmation of clinical diagnosis, justification of treatment (including surgery) and completeness of the surgical procedure. Within each dimension, and for each diagnostic category, one or more previously defined activities are often used to characterize performance for that dimension as a whole. Examples are the compatibility of the diagnosis of pancreatitis with serum amylase levels or of liver cirrhosis with biopsy findings, the performance of sensitivity tests prior to antibiotic therapy in acute bronchitis, and the control of blood sugar levels in diabetes.

In addition to the extent to which preselection of dimensions takes place, assessments of quality differ with respect to the number of dimensions used and the exhaustiveness with which performance in each dimension is explored. For example, Peterson, *et al.*,[15] and Rosenfeld[19] use a large number of dimensions. Peterson and Barsamian,[35, 36] on the other hand, concentrate on two basic dimensions, justification of diagnosis and of therapy, but require complete proof of justification. A much more simplified approach is illustrated by Huntley, *et al.*,[40] who evaluates outpatient care using two criteria only: the percent of work-ups not including certain routine procedures, and the percent of abnormalities found that were not followed up.

Judgments of quality are incomplete when only a few dimensions are used and decisions about each dimension are made on the basis of partial evidence. Some dimensions, such as preventive care or the psychological and social management of health and illness, are often excluded from the definition of quality and the standards and criteria that make it operational. Examples are the intentional exclusion of psychiatric care from the Peterson study[15] and the planned exclusion of the patient-physician relationship and the attitudes of physicians in studies of the quality of care in the Health Insurance Plan of Greater New York.[24] Rosenfeld[19] made a special point of including the performance of specified screening measures among the criteria of superior care; but care was labeled good in the absence of these measures. In the absence of specific instructions to the judges, the study of Morehead, *et al.*,[23] includes histories of cases, considered to have received optimal care, in which failure of preventive management could have resulted in serious consequences to the patient.

Another characteristic of measurement is the level at which the standard is set. Standards can be so strict that none can comply with them, or so permissive that all are rated "good." For example, in the study of general practice reported by Clute,[16] blood pressure examinations, measurement of body temperature, otoscopy and performance of immunizations did not serve to categorize physicians because all physicians performed them well.

Measurement Scales

The ability to discriminate different levels of performance depends on the scale of measurement used. Many studies of quality use a small number of divisions to classify care, seen as a whole, into categories such as "excellent," "good," "fair," or "poor." A person's relative position in a set can then be further specified by computing the percent of cases in each scale category. Other studies assign scores to performance of specified components of care and cumulate these to obtain a numerical index usually ranging from 0–100. These practices raise questions relative to scales of measurement and legitimate operations on these scales. Some of these are described below.

Those who adhere to the first practice point out that any greater degree of precision is not possible with present methods. Some have even reduced the categories to only two: optimal and less than optimal. Clute[16] uses three, of which the middle one is acknowledged to be doubtful or indeterminate. Also, medical care has an all-or-none aspect that the usual numerical scores do not reflect. Care can be good in many of its parts and be disastrously inadequate in the aggregate due to a vital error in one component. This is, of course, less often a problem if it is demonstrated that performance on different components of care is highly intercorrelated.

Those who have used numerical scores have pointed out much loss of information in the use of overall judgments,[35] and that numerical scores, cumulated from specified subscores, give a picture not only of the whole but also of the evaluation of individual parts. Rosenfeld[19] has handled this problem by using a system of assigning qualitative scores to component parts of care and an overall qualitative score based on arbitrary rules of combination that allow for the all-or-none attribute of the quality of medical care. As already pointed out, a high degree of agreement was found between intuitive and structured ratings in the Rosenfeld study[19] and between qualitative and quantitative ratings in the study by Peterson, *et al.*[15]

A major problem, yet unsolved, in the construction of numerical scores, is the manner in which the different components are to be weighted in the process of arriving at the total. At present this is an arbitrary matter. Peterson, *et al.*,[15] for example, arrive at the following scale: clinical history 30, physical examination 34, use of laboratory aids 26, therapy 9, preventive medicine 6, clinical records 2, total 107. Daily and Morehead[21] assign different weights as follows: records 30, diagnostic work-up 40, treatment and follow-up 30, total 100. Peterson, *et al.*, say: "Greatest importance is attached to the process of arriving at a diagnosis since, without a diagnosis, therapy cannot be rational. Furthermore, therapy is in the process of constant change, while the form of history and physical examination has changed very little over the years."[15] Daily and Morehead offer no justification for their weightings, but equally persuasive arguments could probably be made on their behalf. The problem of seeking external confirmation remains.[41]

The problem of weights is related to the more general problem of value of items of information or of procedures in the medical care process. Rimoldi, *et al.*,[31] use the frequency with which specified items of information were used in the solution of a test problem as a measure of the value of that item. Williamson had experts classify specified procedures, in a specified diagnostic test setting, on a scale ranging from "very helpful" to "very harmful." Individual performance in the test was then rated using quantitative indices of "efficiency," "proficiency" and overall "competence," depending on the frequency and nature of the procedures used.[32]

A problem in the interpretation of numerical scores is the meaning of the numerical interval between points on the scale. Numerical scores derived for the assessment of quality are not likely to have the property of equal intervals. They should not be used as if they had.

Reliability

The reliability of assessments is a major consideration in studies of quality, where so much depends on judgment even when the directive types of standards are used. Several studies have given some attention to agreement between judges. The impression gained is that this is considered to be at an acceptable level. Peterson, *et al.*,[15] on the basis of 14 observer revisits, judged agreement to be sufficiently high to permit all the observations to be pooled together after adjustment for observer bias in one of the six major divisions of care. In the study by Daily and Morehead, "several cross-checks were made between the two interviewing internists by having them interview the same physicians. The differences in the scores of the family physicians based on these separate ratings did not exceed 7 per cent."[21] Rosenfeld[19] paid considerable attention to testing reliability, and devised mathematical indices of "agreement" and "dispersion" to measure it. These indicate a fair amount of agreement, but a precise evaluation is difficult since no other investigator is known to have used these same measures. Morehead, *et al.*,[23] in the second study of medical care received by Teamster families, report initial agreement between two judges in assigning care to one of two classes in 78 per cent of cases. This was raised to 92 per cent following reevaluation of disagreements by the two judges.

By contrast to between-judge reliability, very little has been reported about the reliability of repeated judgments of quality made by the same person. To test within-observer variation, Peterson, *et al.*,[15] asked each of two observers to revisit four of his own previously visited physicians. The level of agreement was lower within observers than between observers, partly because revisits lasted a shorter period of time and related, therefore, to a smaller sample of practice.

The major mechanism for achieving higher levels of reliability is the detailed specification of criteria, standards and procedures used for the assessment of care. Striving for reproducibility was, in fact, a major impetus in the development of the more rigorous rating systems by Lembcke, and by Peterson and Barsamian. Unfortunately, no comparative studies of reliability exist using highly directive versus nondirective methods of assessment. Rosenfeld's raw data might permit a comparison of reliability of "intuitive" judgments and the reliability of structured judgments by the same two assessors. Unreported data by Morehead, *et al.*,[23] could be analyzed in the same way as those of Rosenfeld[19] to give useful information about the relationship between degree of reliability and method of assessment. The partial data that have been published suggest that the post-review reliability achieved by Morehead, *et al.*, using the most non-directive of approaches, is quite comparable with that achieved by Rosenfeld who used a much more directive technique.

Morehead, *et al.*, raised the important question of whether the reliability obtained through the detailed specification of standards and criteria may not be gained at the cost of reduced validity. "Frequently, such criteria force into a rigid framework similar actions or factors which may not be appropriate in a given situation due to the infinite variations in the reaction of the human body to illness. . . . The study group rejects the assumption that such criteria are necessary to evaluate the quality of medical care. It is their unanimous opinion that it is as important for the surveyors to have flexibility in the judgment of an individual case as it is for a competent physician when confronting a clinical problem in a given patient."[23]

The reasons for disagreement between judges throw some light on the problems of evaluation and the prospects of achieving greater reliability. Rosenfeld found that "almost half the differences were attributable to situations not covered adequately by standards, or in which the standards were ambiguous. In another quarter differences developed around questions of fact, because one consultant missed a significant item of information in the record. It would therefore appear that with revised standards, and improved methods of orienting consultants, a substantially higher degree of agreement could be achieved."[19] Less than a quarter of the disagreements contain differences of opinion with regard to the requirements of management. This is a function of ambiguity in the medical care system and sets an upper limit of reproducibility. Morehead, *et al.*, report that in about half the cases of initial disagreement "there was agreement on the most serious aspect of the patient's care, but one surveyor later agreed that he had not taken into account corollary aspects of patient care."[23] Other reasons for disagreement were difficulty in adhering to the rating categories or failure to note all the facts. Of the small number of unresolved disagreements (eight per cent of all admissions and 36 per cent of initial disagreements) more than half were due to honest differences of opinion regarding the clinical handling of the problem. The remainder arose out of differences in interpreting inadequate records, or the technical problems of where to assess unsatisfactory care in a series of admissions.[24]

A final aspect of reliability is the occasional breakdown in the performance of an assessor, as so dramatically demonstrated in the Rosenfeld study.[19] The question of what the investigator does when a well defined segment of his results are so completely aberrant will be raised here without any attempt to provide an answer.

Bias

When several observers or judges describe and evaluate the process of medical care, one of them may consistently employ more rigid standards than another, or interpret predetermined standards more strictly. Peterson, *et al.*,[15] discovered that one of their observers generally awarded higher ratings than the other in the assessment of performance of physical examination, but not in the other areas of care. Rosenfeld[19] showed that, of two assessors, one regularly awarded lower ratings to the same cases assessed by both. An examination of individual cases of disagreement in the study by Morehead, *et al.*,[23] reveals that, in the medical category, the same assessor rated the care at a lower level in 11 out of 12 instances of disagreement. For surgical cases, one surveyor rated the care lower than the other in all eight instances of disagreement. The impression is gained from examining reasons for disagreement on medical cases that one of the judges had a special interest in cardiology and was more demanding of clarity and certainty in the management of cardiac cases.

The clear indication of these findings is that bias must be accepted as the rule rather than the exception, and that studies of quality must be designed with this in mind. In the Rosenfeld study,[19] for example, either of the two raters used for each area of practice would have ranked the several hospitals in the same order, even though one was consistently more generous than the other. The Clute study of general practice in Canada,[16] on the other hand, has been criticized for comparing the quality of care in two geographic areas even though different observers examined the care in the two areas in question.[42] The author was aware of this problem and devised methods for comparing the performance of the observers in the two geographic areas, but the basic weakness remains.

Predetermined order or regularity in the process of study may be associated with bias. Therefore, some carefully planned procedures may have to be introduced into the research design for randomization. The study by Peterson, *et al.*,[15] appears to be one of the few to have paid attention to this factor. Another important source of bias is knowledge, by the assessor, of the identity of the physician who provided the care or of the hospital in which care was given. The question of removing identifying features from charts under review has been raised, but little is known about the feasibility of this procedure and its effects on the ratings assigned. Still another type of bias may result from parochial standards and criteria of practice that may develop in and around certain institutions or "schools" of medical practice. To the extent that this is true, or suspected to be true, appropriate precautions need to be taken in the recruitment and allocation of judges.

Validity

The effectiveness of care as has been stated, in achieving or producing health and satisfaction, as defined for its individual members by a particular society or subculture, is the ultimate validator of the quality of care. The validity of all other phenomena as indicators of quality depends, ultimately, on the relationship between these phenomena and the achievement of health and satisfaction. Nevertheless, conformity of practice to accepted standards has a kind of conditional or interim validity which may be more relevant to the purposes of assessment in specific instances.

The validation of the details of medical practice by their effect on health is the particular concern of the clinical sciences. In the clinical literature one seeks data on whether penicillin promotes recovery in certain types of pneumonia, anticoagulants in coronary thrombosis, or corticosteroids in rheumatic carditis; what certain tests indicate about the function of the liver; and whether simple or radical mastectomy is the more life-prolonging procedure in given types of breast cancer. From the general body of knowledge concerning such relationships arise the standards of practice, more or less fully validated, by which the medical process is ordinarily judged.

Intermediate, or procedural, end points often represent larger bundles of care. Their relationship to outcome has attracted the attention of both the clinical investigator and the student of medical care organization. Some examples of the latter are studies of relationships between prenatal care and the health of mothers and infants[43, 44] and the relationship between multiple screening examinations and subsequent health.[45] An interesting example of the study of the relationship between one procedural end point and another is the attempt to demonstrate a positive relationship between the performance of rectal and vaginal examinations by the physician, and the pathological confirmation of appendicitis in primary appendectomies, as reported by the Professional Activities Study.[46]

Many studies reviewed[15, 16, 20, 23, 25] attempt to study the relationship between structural properties and the assessment of the process of care. Several of these studies have shown, for example, a relationship between the training and qualifications of physicians and the quality of care they provide. The relationship is, however, a complex one, and is influenced by the type of training, its duration and the type of hospital within which it was obtained. The two studies of general practice[15, 16] have shown additional positive relationships between quality and better office facilities for practice, the presence or availability of laboratory equipment, and the institution of an appointment system. No relationship was shown between quality and membership of professional associations, the income of the physician or the presence of x-ray equipment in the office. The two studies do not agree fully on the nature of the relationship between quality of practice and whether the physician obtained his training in a teaching hospital or not, the number of hours worked or the nature of the physician's hospital affiliation. Hospital accreditation, presumably a mark of quality conferred mainly for compliance with a wide range of organizational standards, does not appear, in and of itself, to be related to the quality of care, at least in New York City.[23]

Although structure and process are no doubt related, the few examples cited above indicate clearly the complexity and ambiguity of these relationships. This is the result partly of the many factors involved, and partly of the poorly understood interactions among these factors. For example, one could reasonably propose, based on several findings[23, 35] that both hospital factors and physician factors influence the quality of care rendered in the hospital, but that differences between physicians are obliterated in the best and worst hospital and express themselves, in varying degrees, in hospitals of intermediate quality.

An approach particularly favored by students of medical care organization is to examine relations between structure and outcome without reference to the complex processes that tie them together. Some examples of such studies have been cited already.[3-6] Others include studies of the effects of reorganizing the outpatient clinic on health status,[47] the effects of intensive hospital care on recovery,[48] the effects of home care on survival[49] and the effect of a rehabilitation program on the physical status of nursing home patients.[50,51] The lack of relationship to outcome in the latter two studies suggests that current opinions about how care should be set up are sometimes less than well established.

This brief review indicates the kinds of evidence pertaining to the validity of the various approaches to the evaluation of quality of care. Clearly, the relationships between process and outcome, and between structure and both process and outcome, are not fully understood. With regard to this, the requirements of validation are best expressed by the concept, already referred to, of a chain of events in which each event is an end to the one that comes before it and a necessary condition to the one that follows. This indicates that the means-end relationship between each adjacent pair requires validation in any chain of hypothetical or real events.[52] This is, of course, a laborious process. More commonly, as has been shown, the intervening links are ignored. The result is that causal inferences become attenuated in proportion to the distance separating the two events on the chain.

Unfortunately, very little information is available on actual assessments of quality using more than one method of evaluation concurrently. Makover has studied specifically the relationships between multifactorial assessments of structure and of process in the same medical groups. "It was found that the medical groups that achieved higher quality ratings by the method used in this study were those that, in general, adhered more closely to HIP's Minimum Medical Standards. However, the exceptions were sufficiently marked, both in number and degree, to induce one to question the reliability[53] of one or the other rating method when applied to any one medical group. It would seem that further comparison of these two methods of rating is clearly indicated."[20]

References

1. Lee, R. I. and Jones, L. W., *The Fundamentals of Good Medical Care*, Chicago, University of Chicago Press, 1933.

2. Klein, M. W., *et al.*, Problems of Measuring Patient Care in the Out Patient Department, *Journal of Health and Human Behavior*, 2, 138–144, Summer, 1961.

3. Kohl, S. G., *Perinatal Mortality in New York City: Responsible Factors*, Cambridge, Harvard University Press, 1955.

This study, sponsored by the New York Academy of Medicine, was an examination by an expert committee of records pertaining to a representative sample of perinatal deaths in New York City. Preventable deaths were recognized and "responsibility factors" identified, including errors in medical judgment and technique. The incidence of both of these was further related to type of hospital service, type of professional service and type of hospital, indicating relationships between structure and outcome as modified by the characteristics of the population served.

4. Shapiro, S., *et al.*, Further Observations in Prematurity and Perinatal Mortality in a General Population and in the Population of a Prepaid Group Practice Medical Care Plan, *American Journal of Public Health*, 50, 1304–1317, September, 1960.

5. Lipworth, L., Lee, J. A. H. and Morris, J. N., Case Fatality in Teaching and Nonteaching Hospitals, 1956–1959, *Medical Care*, 1, 71–76, April–June, 1963.

6. Rice, C. E., *et al.*, Measuring Social Restoration Performance of Public Psychiatric Hospitals, *Public Health Reports*, 76, 437–446, May, 1961.

7. Lembcke, P. A., Medical Auditing by Scientific Methods, *Journal of the American Medical Association*, 162, 646–655, October 13, 1956. (Appendices A and B supplied by the author.)

This is perhaps the single best paper that describes the underlying concepts as well as the methods of the highly structured approach developed by Lembcke to audit hospital records. Also included is an example of the remarkable effect that an "external audit" of this kind can have on surgical practice in a hospital.

8. Kelman, H. R. and Willner, A., Problems in Measurement and Evaluation of Rehabilitation, *Archives of Physical Medicine and Rehabilitation*, 43, 172–181, April, 1962.

9. McDermott, W., *et al.*, Introducing Modern Medicine in a Navajo Community, *Science*, 131, 197–205 and 280–287, January 22 and 29, 1960.

10. Simon, H. A., *Administrative Behavior*, New York: The Macmillan Company, 1961, pp. 62–66.

11. Hutchinson, G. B., Evaluation of Preventive Services, *Journal of Chronic Diseases*, 11, 497–508, May, 1960.

12. James, G., *Evaluation of Public Health*, Report of the Second National Conference on Evaluation in Public Health, Ann Arbor, The University of Michigan, School of Public Health, 1960, pp. 7–17.

13. Weinerman, E. R., Appraisal of Medical Care Programs, *American Journal of Public Health*, 40, 1129–1134, September, 1950.

14. Goldmann, F., and Graham, E. A., *The Quality of Medical Care Provided at the Labor Health Institute*, St. Louis, Missouri, St. Louis, The Labor Health Institute, 1954.

This is a good example of an approach to evaluation based on structural characteristics. In this instance, these included the layout and equipment of physical facilities, the competence and stability of medical staff, provisions made for continuity of service centering around a family physician, the scheduling and duration of clinic visits, the content of the initial examination, the degree of emphasis on preventive medicine and the adequacy of the medical records.

15. Peterson, O. L., *et al.*, An Analytical Study of North Carolina General Practice: 1953–1954, *The Journal of Medical Education*, 31, 1–165, Part 2, December, 1956.

Already a classic, this study is distinguished by more than ordinary attention to methods and rather exhaustive exploration of the relationship between quality ratings and characteristics of physicians, including education training and methods of practice. The findings of this study, and others that have used the same method, raise basic questions about traditional general practice in this and other countries.

16. Clute, K. F., *The General Practitioner: A Study of Medical Education and Practice in Ontario and Nova Scotia*, Toronto, University of Toronto Press, 1963, chapters 1, 2, 16, 17 and 18.

Since this study uses the method eveloped by Peterson, *et al.*, it offers an excellent opportunity to examine the generality of relationship between physician characteristics and quality ratings. In addition, the reader of this elegantly written volume gets a richly detailed view of general practice in the two areas studied.

17. Kroeger, H. H., *et al.*, The Office Practice of Internists, I. The Feasibility of Evaluating Quality of Care, *The Journal of the American Medical Association*, 193, 371–376, August 2, 1965.

This is the first of a series of papers based on a study of the practice of members of the New York Society of Internal Medicine. This paper reports findings concerning the completeness of office records, their suitability for judging quality and the degree of agreement between abstracts of records prepared by physicians and by highly trained non-physicians. Judgments concerning the quality of care provided are not given. Other papers in this series currently appearing in the *Journal of the American Medical Association* concern patient load (August 23), characteristics of patients (September 13), professional activities other than care of private patients (October 11), and background and form of practice (November 1).

18. Kilpatrick, G. S., Observer Error in Medicine, *Journal of Medical Education*, 38, 38–43, January, 1963. For a useful bibliography on observer error *see* Witts, L. J. (Editor), *Medical Surveys and Clinical Trials*, London, Oxford University Press, 1959, pp. 39–44.

19. Rosenfeld, L. S., Quality of Medical Care in Hospitals, *American Journal of Public Health*, 47, 856–865, July, 1957.

This carefully designed comparative study of the quality of care in four hospitals addresses itself to the problems of methods in the assessment of quality. Here one finds important information about the use of normative and empirical standards, reliability and bias in judgments based on chart review, the correlation between defects in recording and defects in practice and homogeneity in quality ratings within and between diagnostic categories.

20. Makover, H. B., The Quality of Medical Care: Methodological Survey of the Medical Groups Associated with the Health Insurance Plan of New York, *American Journal of Public Health*, 41, 824–832, July, 1951.

This is possibly the first published report concerning an administratively instituted, but research oriented, program of studies of the quality of care in medical groups contracting with the Health Insurance Plan of Greater New York. Unfortunately much of this work remains unpublished. A particular feature of this paper is that it describes, and presents the findings of simultaneous evaluation of structure (policies, organization, administration, finances and professional activities) and process (evaluation of a sample of clinical records).

21. Daily, E. F. and Morehead, M. A., A Method of Evaluating and Improving the Quality of Medical Care, *American Journal of Public Health*, 46, 848–854, July, 1956.

22. Fitzpatrick, T. B., Riedel, D. C. and Payne, B. C., Character and Effectiveness of Hospital Use, in McNerney, W. J., *et al.*, *Hospital and Medical Economics*, Chicago, Hospital Research and Educational Trust, American Hospital Association, 1962, pp. 495–509.

23. Morehead, M. A., *et al.*, *A Study of the Quality of Hospital Care Secured by a Sample of Teamster Family Members in New York City*, New York, Columbia University, School of Public Health and Administrative Medicine, 1964.

This study and its companion[25] perform a very important social and administrative function by documenting how frequently the care received by members of a union through traditional sources proves to be inadequate. These studies also make a major contribution to understanding the relationships between hospital and physician characteristics and the quality of care they provide. Considered are physician classifications by specialty status and admission privileges, as well as hospital classifications by ownership, medical school affiliation, approval for residency training and accreditation status. The interactional effects of some of these variables are also explored. In addition, the second of the two studies[23] pays considerable attention to questions of method, including representative versus judgmental sampling of hospital admissions and the reliability of record evaluations by different judges.

24. Morehead, M. A., Personal communication.

25. Ebrlich, J., Morehead, M. A. and Trussell, R. E., *The Quantity, Quality and Costs of Medical and Hospital Care Secured by a Sample of Teamster Families in the New York Area*, New York, Columbia University, School of Public Health and Administrative Medicine, 1962.

26. Maloney, M. C., Trussell, R. E. and Elinson, J., Physicians Choose Medical Care: A Sociometric Approach to Quality Appraisal, *American Journal of Public Health*, 50, 1678–1686, November, 1960.

This study represents an ingenious approach to evaluation through the use of "peer judgments" in what is believed to be a particularly revealing situation: choice of care for the physician or members of his own family. Some of the characteristics of the physicians and surgeons selected included long-standing personal and professional relationships, recognized specialist status, and medical school affiliation. An incidental pearl of information is that although nine out of ten physicians said everyone should have a personal physician, four out of ten said they had someone whom they considered their personal physician, and only two out of ten had seen their personal physician in the past year!

27. Georgopoulos, B. S. and Mann, F. C., *The Community General Hospital*, New York, The Macmillan Company, 1962.

The study of quality reported in several chapters of this book is based on the thesis that if one wishes to find out about the quality of care provided, all one might need to do is to ask the persons directly or indirectly involved in the provision of such care. Although physicians may find this notion rather naive, the stability and internal consistency of the findings reported in this study indicate that this approach deserves further careful evaluation. A second study of a nationwide sample of general hospitals will attempt to confirm the validity of respondent opinions by comparing them to selected indices of professional activities in each hospital. The findings will be awaited with great interest.

28. One of the author's students, Mr. Arnold D. Kaluzny, helped the author to coin this word.

29. Georgopoulos, B. S. and Tannenbaum, A. S., A Study of Organizational Effectiveness, *American Sociological Review,* 22, 534–540, October, 1957.

30. Evans, L. R. and Bybee, J. R., Evaluation of Student Skills in Physical Diagnosis, *Journal of Medical Education,* 40, 199–204, February, 1965.

31. Rimoldi, H. J. A., Haley, J. V. and Fogliatto, H., *The Test of Diagnostic Skills,* Loyola Psychometric Laboratory Publication Number 25, Chicago, Loyola University Press, 1962.

This study is of interest because it uses a controlled test situation to study the performance of medical students and physicians. Even more intriguing is the attempt to approach the question of the value or utility of diagnostic actions in a systematic and rigorous manner. While this particular study does not appear to contribute greatly to understanding the quality of care, this general approach appears to be worth pursuing.

32. Williamson, J. W., Assessing Clinical Judgment, *Journal of Medical Education,* 40, 180–187, February, 1965.

This is another example of the assessment of clinical performance using an artificial test situation. The noteworthy aspect of the work is the attachment of certain values ("helpful" or "harmful") to a set of diagnostic and therapeutic actions and the development of measures of "efficiency," "proficiency" and "competence" based on which actions are selected by the subject in managing the test case. Differences of performance between individual physicians were detected using this method. An unexpected finding was the absence of systematic differences by age, training or type of practice in groups tested so far.

33. Eislee, C. W., Slee, V. N. and Hoffman, R. G., Can the Practice of Internal Medicine Be Evaluated?, *Annals of Internal Medicine,* 44, 144–161, January, 1956.

The authors discuss the indices from which inferences might be drawn concerning the quality of surgical and medical management. The indices described include tissue pathology reports in appendectomies, diabetes patients without blood sugar determinations and without chest x-rays, and pneumonia without chest x-rays. A striking finding reported in this paper, and others based on the same approach, is the tremendous variation by physician and hospital in the occurrence of such indices of "professional activity."

34. Furstenberg, F. F., *et al.,* Prescribing as an Index to Quality of Medical Care: A Study of the Baltimore City Medical Care Program, *American Journal of Public Health,* 43, 1299–1309, October, 1953.

35. Peterson, O. L. and Barsamian, E. M., An Application of Logic to a Study of Quality of Surgical Care, Paper read at the Fifth IBM Medical Symposium, Endicott, New York, October 7–11, 1963.

This paper and its companion[36] present a fairly complete description of the "logic tree" approach to the evaluation of quality. Examples are given of the logic systems for the Stein-Leventhal Syndrome and uterine fibromyoma. No data are given on empirical findings using this method.

36. ———, Diagnostic Performance, in Jacquez, J. A. (Editor), *The Diagnostic Process*, Ann Arbor, The University of Michigan Press, April, 1964, pp. 347–362.

37. Lembcke, P. A. and Johnson, O. G., *A Medical Audit Report*, Los Angeles. University of California, School of Public Health, 1963 (Mimeographed).

This is an extension of Lembcke's method of medical audit to medical diagnostic categories as well as a large number of surgical operations. Although this volume is a compendium of fairly raw data, careful study can provide insights and limitations of the method used by the author.

38. Lembcke, P. A., A Scientific Method for Medical Auditing, *Hospitals*, 33, 65–71, June 16 and 65–72, July 1, 1959.

39. The dimensionality of the set of variables incorporating these standards remains to be determined.

40. Huntley, R. R., *et al.*, The Quality of Medical Care: Techniques and investigation in the Outpatient Clinic, *Journal of Chronic Diseases*, 14, 630–642, December, 1961.

This study provides an example of the application of a routine chart review procedure as a check on the quality of management in the outpatient department of a teaching hospital. Fairly often routine procedures were not carried out and abnormalities that were found were not followed up. A revised chart review procedure seemed to make a significant reduction in the percent of abnormalities not followed up.

41. Peterson, *et al.*, *loc. cit.*, attempted to get some confirmation of weightings through the procedure of factor analysis. The mathematically sophisticated are referred to their footnote on pp. 14–15.

42. Mainland, D., Calibration of the Human Instrument, Notes from a Laboratory of Medical Statistics, Number 81, August 24, 1964 (Mimeographed).

43. Joint Committee of the Royal College of Obstetricians and Gynecologists and the Population Investigation Committee, *Maternity in Great Britain*, London, Oxford University Press, 1948.

44. Yankauer, A., Goss, K. G. and Romeo, S. M., An Evaluation of Prenatal Care and its Relationship to Social Class and Social Disorganization, *American Journal of Public Health*, 43, 1001–1010, August, 1953.

45. Wylie, C. M., Participation in a Multiple Screening Clinic with Five-Year Follow-Up, *Public Health Reports*, 76, 596–602, July, 1961.

46. Commission on Professional and Hospital Activities, *Medical Audit Study Report 5: Primary Appendictomies*, Ann Arbor, The Commission on Professional and Hospital Activities, October, 1957.

47. Simon, A. J., Social Structure of Clinics and Patient Improvement, *Administrative Science Quarterly*, 4, 197–206, September, 1959.

48. Lockward, H. J., Lundberg, G. A. F. and Odoroff, M. E., Effect of Intensive Care on Mortality Rate of Patients with Myocardial Infarcts, *Public Health Reports*, 78, 655–661, August, 1963.

49. Bakst, J. N. and Marra, E. F., Experiences with Home Care for Cardiac Patients, *American Journal of Public Health*, 45, 444–450, April, 1955.

50. Muller, J. N., Tobis, J. S. and Kelman, H. R., The Rehabilitation Potential of Nursing Home Residents, *American Journal of Public Health*, 53, 243–247, February, 1963.

51. These studies also include data on the relationships between structural features and procedural end points. Examples are the effect of clinic structure on

the number of outpatient visits,[47] and the effect of a home care program on hospital admissions.[49]

52. Getting, V. A., *et al.*, Research in Evaluation in Public Health Practices, Paper presented at the 92nd Annual Meeting, American Public Health Association, New York, October 5, 1964.

53. Assuming the direct evaluation of process to be the criterion, the issue becomes one of the implications of reliability measures for validity.

54. Ciocco, A., Hunt, H. and Altman, I., Statistics on Clinical Services to New Patients in Medical Groups, *Public Health Reports*, 65, 99–115, January 27, 1950.
This is an early application to group practice of the analysis of "professional activities" now generally associated with the evaluation of hospital care. The indices used included the recording of diagnosis and treatment, the performance of rectal and vaginal examinations, the performance of certain laboratory examinations and the use of sedatives, stimulants and other medications subject to abuse. As is true of hospitals, the groups varied a great deal with respect to these indicators.

55. Myers, R. S., Hospital Statistics Don't Tell the Truth, *Modern Hospital*, 83, 53–54, July, 1954.

56. Even for hospital care the appropriate unit may include care before and after admission, as well as several hospital admissions.[3]

57. Cordero, A. L., The Determination of Medical Care Needs in Relation to a Concept of Minimal Adequate Care: An Evaluation of the Curative Outpatient Services in a Rural Health Center, *Medical Care*, 2, 95–103, April-June, 1964.

58. Butterworth, J. S. and Reppert, E. H., Auscultatory Acumen in the General Medical Population, *Journal of the American Medical Association*, 174, 32–34, September 3, 1960.

59. Evans, L. R. and Bybee, J. R., Evaluation of Student Skills in Physical Diagnosis, *Journal of Medical Education*, 40, 199–204, February, 1965.

60. Fattu, N. C., Experimental Studies of Problem Solving, *Journal of Medical Education*, 39, 212–225, February, 1964.

61. John, E. R., Contributions to the Study of the Problem Solving Process, *Psychological Monographs*, 71, 1957.

62. Duncan, C. P., Recent Research in Human Problem Solving, *Psychological Bulletin*, 56, 397–429, November, 1959.

63. Fattu, N. A., Mech, E. and Kapos, E., Some Statistical Relationships between Selected Response Dimensions and Problem-Solving Proficiency, *Psychological Monographs*, 68, 1954.

64. Stolurow, L. M., *et al.*, The Efficient Course of Action in "Trouble Shooting" as a Joint Function of Probability and Cost, *Educational and Psychological Measurement*, 15, 462–477, Winter, 1955.

65. Ledley, R. S. and Lusted, L. B., Reasoning Foundations of Medical Diagnosis, *Science*, 130, 9–21, July 3, 1959.

66. Lusted, L. B. and Stahl, W. R., Conceptual Models of Diagnosis, in Jacquez, J. A. (Editor), *The Diagnostic Process*, Ann Arbor, The University of Michigan Press, 1964, pp. 157–174.

67. Edwards, W., Lindman, H. and Phillips, L. D., Emerging Technologies for Making Decisions, in Newcomb, T. M. (Editor), *New Directions in Psychology*, II, New York, Holt, Rinehart & Winston, Inc., 1965, pp. 261–325.

Evaluative Studies of Institutions for Delinquents: Implications for Research and Social Policy

Paul Lerman

Evaluative research is usually undertaken for the purpose of gathering evidence of a program's success in achieving its avowed goals.[1] This approach can be questioned, however, unless a more basic question has first been answered in the affirmative: Is there any empirical evidence that the program under consideration is more likely to be associated with success than with failure? It is not sufficient merely to assume that assessing success is the relevant evaluative problem. One must be willing to face the possibility that the program is associated with high rates of failure. Instead of the success of a program, it might be more relevant to evaluate its failure.

This point of view can be applied to any program of interest to social workers. It is especially appropriate in studying institutions that seek to transform delinquents into law-abiding youths. This article will provide evidence that supports the following conclusion: Regardless of the type of program investigated, residential institutions for delinquents (under 18 years of age) are characterized by high rates of potential failure. On the basis of this evidence, it will be argued that researchers interested in evaluating new programs should focus on the problem of whether (and how) failure rates have been reduced—not whether an institution can claim success. In addition, this article will propose that the issue of humanitarianism be considered apart from the ideologies of treatment and success.

What Is Organizational Failure?

It has become virtually a custom in the delinquency field to measure the success of correctional organizations by determining whether boys released from custody have refrained from known law violations.[2] From an evaluative perspective this approach is quite misleading. Boys released from a residential institution who are not "renoticed" by the legal system *might* be regarded as successes, but it still must be demon-

Reprinted from *Social Work* 13 (July, 1968):55–64.

strated that their success is attributable to the organization. Boys can be successful in this respect for many reasons that have little to do with their residential experiences. It is the task of evaluative research to demonstrate that the organization was actually responsible for the boys' achievement.[3]

The crucial difference between potential and actual organizational success becomes even clearer when the boys who *are* renoticed are examined. Residential organizations will not readily agree that renoticed boys constitute evidence of the organizations' *actual* failure to rehabilitate. Rather, they argue (and correctly so) that the failure may be due to many factors—some of which may be beyond the power of the institution to control. Without further evidence, it is no less unfair to attribute the failures to the organization than to credit it with the successes. But organizations cannot claim unnoticed boys as their successes without also claiming renoticed boys as their failures. Again, it is the task of evaluative research to demonstrate that the organization was responsible for the boys' failure or success.

At the stage of formulating the evaluative problem to be investigated, interest is in estimating *potential* organizational failures. To carry out this purpose, *all the boys whom the organization cannot reasonably claim as evidence of success must be identified.*

Recontact with the criminal justice system constitutes one measure of potential failure. Although this is a crude measure, it is difficult to deny its social utility. If it is granted that there is social utility in assessing failure by indications of renewed delinquent activity, it is still appropriate to question the usual measure utilized in evaluation studies. Most delinquency studies rely on recidivist data—the reinstitutionalization of released boys. This type of measure implies that boys who are known to the police and/or courts but who were not reinstitutionalized should be counted as successes, which is a dubious practice. Sophisticated criminologists are well aware that indications of delinquency or criminality decrease in reliability as the level of enforcement takes one further away from the offense itself. Sellin, the dean of American criminology, states this position as follows:

> The difficulty with statistics drawn from later stages in the administrative process is that they may show changes or fluctuations which are not due to changes in criminality but to variations in the policies or the efficiencies of administrative agencies.[4]

In classifying boys as potential successes or failures, it is important that one avoid confounding the issue of renewed delinquent behavior with discretionary reactions to that behavior by court personnel. Whenever possible, studies must be analyzed to obtain indications of failure regardless of whether boys were reinstitutionalized. In brief, the notion of counting as successes boys whose behavior indicates that the institution has probably failed is rejected.

The importance of making these distinctions explicit can be highlighted by reviewing the results of a major current study.[5] For the past 6½ years the California Youth Authority's research department has been continually engaged in evaluating the Community Treatment Project, in which since September 1961 first-commitment youths have been randomly assigned to experimental services in their own communities or to a control situation that involves residence in an institution away from home. As of March 31, 1966, 241 in the experimental group and 220 in the control group had been paroled to Sacramento and Stockton, the two major sources of the sample; the former had been on parole for an average of 16.4 months and the latter for an average of 17.9 months. As of May 1967, 33 percent of the experimentals and 55 percent of the controls had violated parole (i.e., the boys' parole was officially revoked, they were recommitted, or they had received an unfavorable discharge from the youth authority). A more detailed analysis sustains this difference, but regardless of the refinement, the findings are quite misleading about the behavior of the two groups.

The difference in parole violation figures suggests that the experimentals as a group were less delinquent in their behavior than the controls, but this is not the case. As a matter of fact, the experimentals had more known delinquent offenses per boy than the controls (2.81 to 1.61).[6] When the seriousness of the offenses is considered, then the rates for "low serious" offenses are 1.56 per boy for the experimentals and .52 for the controls; for "medium serious" offenses, .61 per boy for the experimentals and .45 for the controls; and for "high serious" offenses, .64 per boy for both groups.[7] The authors present convincing evidence that the parole officers of the experimentals were much more likely to know about their boys' offenses than the parole officers of the controls.[8] In effect, they argue that the delinquent *behavioral output* was probably the same, but that the *rate of being noticed* was different.

The report could go a step further: It could demonstrate that the noticed offenses were reacted to differently by the experimental and control organizations. The parole violation rates differ because the modes of reacting to and handling the offenses are different. Table 1 compares the experimental and control groups by the seriousness of the offenses officially known; using known offenses as the base, the table then indicates the proportion of parole violations for each offense category for experimentals and controls. The table attempts to answer the following questions: Are noticed offenses of varying degrees of severity more or less likely to be judged parole violations when committed by the experimental group?

TABLE 1

Rates of Patrole Violation per Offense Category for Experimentals and Controls, California Community Treatment Project

Seriousness of Offense[a]	Experimentals		Controls	
	Number	Rate	Number	Rate
Low	376	.02	114	.17
Medium	146	.10	100	.40
High	156	.37	140	.44

[a]Seriousness-of-offense ratings are those used in the CTP study, but they have been trichotomized to highlight the trends. The low category includes California Youth Authority ratings 1-2, medium includes ratings 3-4, and high includes ratings 5-10.

SOURCE: Marguerite Q. Warren, Virginia V. Neto, Theodore B. Palmer, and James K. Turner, "Community Treatment Project: An Evaluation of Community Treatment for Delinquents," CTP Research Report No. 7 (Sacramento: California Youth Authority, Division of Research, August 1966). (Mimeographed.)

As the table clearly shows, the chance that an experimental boy's offense will be handled by revocation of parole is lower than for a control boy if the offense is low or moderate in seriousness; experimentals are judged similarly to the controls *only* when the offenses are of high seriousness. It is difficult not to conclude that the experimental boys have a lower parole violation rate because offenses of low and medium seriousness are evaluated differently by adults according to organizational context.

Instead of the misleading conclusion derived from using only parole violation differences, it appears that the potential rates of failure of the two programs are similar (at this point in time). The behavioral outputs of the experimentals and controls are probably the same; however, the experimentals' parole agents notice more of this behavior and therefore give the impression that the experimentals are more delinquent. But even though the behavior of experimentals attracts more notice, it is not evaluated in the same way as the behavior of the controls. This important study may have exercised excellent control over the random selection of boys; unfortunately, the ideology of treating boys in the community spilled over into the postexperimental phase. The experimental and control groups appear to differ in the behavior of the parole agents with respect to revocation of parole—not in the delinquent behavior of the boys.

In addition to officially noticed delinquent actions that are not regarded as parole violations, there is another measure of potential failure that has been disregarded: boys who do not "complete treatment." The following section will describe this additional source of measurement; a subsequent section will then provide data from published and unpublished studies that highlight the importance of measuring *all* the potential failures.

Counting All Outcomes

Before measurement of this other type of failure is discussed, the social bookkeeping of institutions must be understood. The literature on delinquency reveals a curious bookkeeping habit: Boys who do not complete treatment are usually *not counted* in evaluations of organizational effectiveness. These boys are treated statistically as if they never existed; in a sense they are dealt with as Orwellian "no-persons." It is difficult to think of such outcomes as successes, but organizations do not like to count them as failures. Therefore, these boys are set aside and ignored. If this group were small, this accounting fiction might be accepted; unfortunately, it is not. The rate of no-persons in an institutional population can exceed 30 percent. Discarding a third of an agency's budget as nonaccountable would never be tolerated; should one tolerate discarding a third of its clients?

The problem of how to count boys who are labeled as not completing treatment is especially acute in the private sector. Although private institutions for delinquents are heavily subsidized by public funds, they have been permitted an enormous amount of discretion in controlling the population they treat, especially with regard to intake and maintenance. These agencies choose the boys who will enter into residence and those who will remain in residence and complete treatment (and, of course, those who will not do so). By contrast, most public institutions, unless they are special experimental programs, are forced to accept into residence all boys the private institutions reject at intake; even if the boys do not "work out," they are usually maintained in the institution, since there are few if any other places that will take them. State training schools rarely have reason to use the classification "not completing treatment."

One private residential center in New York State studied by the author controls its population to the extent of rejecting seventeen boys for every one accepted for residential treatment. This institution (here-after referred to as "Boysville") considers many nonpsychological factors in exercising discretion at intake, i.e., age, previous record, ethnicity, space in the cottages. Having exercised this population control at intake, Boysville then proceeds to use its freedom to reject boys who "resist treatment." An unpublished study by the author of Boysville found that 31 percent (51 out of 164) of the boys in the study sample released from the institution were classified as not completing treatment. Most of these boys (40) were sent to state training schools. The average length of their stay at the private institution was sixteen months, far exceeding the customary remand period of ninety days. Had these boys been sent to nearby "Statesville" at intake, their average stay would have been only nine months.

This outcome was not unique to the specific time chosen for the Boysville study. The administrative staff was so surprised by the findings that they examined their records for a different time period. This unusual replication—conducted surreptitiously—revealed an almost identical rate of boys classified as not completing treatment released from the institution (33 percent).

Nor is this problem unique to private nonsectarian organizations in New York State; it is just more acute at Boysville. A study of High-lights, a special public organization located in New Jersey, reveals that 18 percent of the population released did not complete treatment.[9] A study of another special public program located in Michigan reveals a rate of 18 percent.[10] An unpublished study of a sectarian residential treatment center in New York State disclosed a rate of 25 percent.[11] Street, Vinter, and Perrow comment that in one treatment institution "many boys were screened out in the first three months."[12] These organizations share one characteristic: each exercised control at intake and was also able to "get rid of" boys who were "untreatable." In a less sophisticated period these boys might have been called "incorrigible."

This shift in semantic labels should suggest to the researcher the need to seek his own definition of this outcome. It is suggested that boys classified as not completing treatment have been granted "dishonorable discharges" from the institution, whereas those who have completed treatment are released as "honorably discharged." Only the latter boys can reasonably be conceived of as contributing to an organization's potential success. Redefining boys not completing treatment as dishon-orably discharged permits counting of *all* the boys admitted to an institution in evaluating its success. Once this is done, it is clear that institutions yield two types of potential failures:

TABLE 2
Potential Failures of Boysville Residential Treatment Center
by Two Counting Methods (Percentage)

Type of Failure	All Boys Released (n = 164)	Honorable Discharges (n = 113)
Internal	31	0
External[a]	23	34
Total	54	34

[a]Refers to boys officially rated as having violated the law between six and twenty-four months after their release to one of the five boroughs of New York City. Institutional records and the state files at Albany furnished the data.

1. *Internal potential failures*—boys released from residential institutions via the route of a dishonorable discharge.

2. *External potential failures*—boys released with an honorable discharge who later engage in criminal or delinquent violations.

Internal failures can easily be identified in the everyday records of residential institutions. However, the type of discharge will not be stamped on the folders. Of the fifty-one boys in the Boysville sample who

TABLE 3
Comparison of Potential Failures of Two New Jersey Public Institutions (Percentage)

Type of Failure	Highfields (n = 229)	Annandale (n = 116)
Internal	18	3
External[a]	34	59
Total	52	62

[a]The external failures include all law violators, both institutionalized and noninstitutionalized, who had been released for at least eight months.

SOURCE: H. Ashley Weeks, *Youthful Offenders at Highfields* (Ann Arbor: University of Michigan Press, 1958), pp. 46-50, 52, 60. This table does not appear in Weeks but is derived from data appearing in the cited pages.

did not receive the usual honorable discharge—release to aftercare—forty were reinstitutionalized in state training schools, five were sent to mental hospitals, and six were purportedly "released to the community," but were actually runaways who could not be found. All these boys are classifiable as dishonorably discharged; they should be counted as the institution's potential internal failures. Certainly it is unreasonable to view them as potential successes.

Adding up Failures

The profound differences that can ensue when *all* boys regardless of discharge status are counted are clearly shown in Table 2. When internal failures are taken into account, the minimum estimate of the total potential failures of Boysville is 54 per cent. (If this group of boys had been followed for a longer period of time, there is little doubt that the total failure rate would have been higher.) If the usual custom of "not counting" internal failures in either the numerator or the denominator had been followed, the estimate would have been 34 percent. Which social bookkeeping method is used obviously matters; the distinction is not just academic.

Although Boysville differs in many ways from its public neighbor, Statesville, the total potential failure rates for the two institutions are quite comparable for similar postrelease periods. The major difference between them is that Boysville's potential failure rate is derived from both internal and external sources; Statesville has an internal failure rate of only 3 percent. The total rates are similar even though Boysville and Statesville differ in their relative power to control intake and maintenance of population in addition to treatment modalities.

Is this estimate of comparable failure rates a unique finding? Reanalysis of the best evaluation study available in the literature indicates that it is not.[13] In Table 3 data obtained from Weeks's comparison of Highfields, a special public program, and Annandale, a typical state training school—both of which are located in New Jersey—are presented.

The rates of total potential failures differ by only 10 percent. However, the two institutions differed in their treatment services; Highfields boys worked away from their residence, received "guided group interaction," and stayed only four months; Annandale boys were incarcerated on a routine twenty-four-hour basis and stayed twelve months. The similarity of the failure rates is even more striking when the initial differences between the populations are taken into account: Annandale boys were more likely to have come from urban centers rather than suburban towns, were more likely to be Negro, and had longer and more intense careers as delinquents; Highfields boys tended to be younger and to have completed more years of schooling. In addition to these initial population differences, Highfields was composed of first offenders only; although the Annandale sample was also composed of first offenders, the institution itself contained knowledgeable multiple offenders. Annandale had little control over the maintenance of membership and initial recruitment, while Highfields had a great deal.

Furthermore, the two populations were exposed to different types of parole (or aftercare) services. Highfields parole officers encouraged boys to enlist in the armed services; twenty-seven Highfields boys and only seven Annandale boys entered the armed forces and thus were removed from the risk of failure. Also, Highfields boys, unlike their peers from Annandale, were discharged from postprogram supervision "within only a few months after their release."[14] More Annandale than Highfields boys were actually reinstitutionalized because of parole violations; had these boys not been under longer supervision they might not have been so easily renoticed. In general, Weeks presents an image of the Highfields population as more advantaged before, during, and after treatment. Despite these differences, the total potential failure rates are not too dissimilar and in both cases involve a majority of the boys.

Comparability of Control Groups

In investigating potential failure, it is not necessary to measure boys "before" and "after." Attempting to assess attitudinal change that can be attributed to an organizational experience is a complex affair; if the potential rates of failure are high, there is scant justification for expending money, personnel, and creative energy in this direction. However, there is one feature of the usual approach to evaluation that cannot be set aside so easily in assessing potential failure: if two organizations are being compared, then it is crucial that the population of boys be quite similar. The Highfields study by Weeks exhibits sensitivity to this requirement; unfortunately, a more recent study indicates that this sensitivity has not yet been translated into a norm of evaluative research.

In 1965, Jesness released a study, sponsored by the California Youth Authority, that attempted to compare "outcomes with small versus large living groups in the rehabilitation of delinquents."[15] The design of the study called for random assignment of 10–11-year-old boys at Fricot Ranch to either the experimental twenty-boy lodge or the control fifty-boy lodge. For unknown reasons, random processes did not appear to be operating in the actual assignments. Instead of being comparable, the two populations were discovered to have significant background differences: the experimentals were 73 percent white and the controls only 55 percent, 35 percent of the experimentals and 50 percent of the controls came from the poorest homes, and 67 percent of the experi-

TABLE 4
Successes and Failures as Reported by
William McCord and Joan McCord (Percentage)

Type of Outcome[a]	Wiltwyck (n = 65)	"New England State" (n = 228)
Complete success	43	48
Partial success	28	5
Complete failure	29	33
Don't know	0	13

[a]For definitions of categories see text.

SOURCE: William McCord and Joan McCord, "Two Approaches to the Cure of Delinquents," in Sheldon Glueck, ed., *The Problem of Delinquency* (Boston: Houghton-Mifflin Co., 1959), pp. 735-36.

mentals were from households in which the father was the main provider as compared with only 52 percent of the controls.[16]

Using revocation of parole as a measure of failure, Jesness found that the experimentals were less likely to fail than the controls up until after thirty-six months of exposure to parole. The rates are as follows: 32–48 percent after twelve months, 42–58 percent after fifteen months, and 61–70 percent after twenty-four months. After thirty-six months the rates were virtually the same—76 and 78 percent respectively.[17] Jesness concludes that the "effects of the experimental program tend to fade as the exposure period increases."[18] This may be so, but it seems even more likely that the higher failure rates of the controls reflect the fact that they were actually a higher-risk group at the outset of parole, since the group was comprised of more Negroes and Mexican-Americans and came from poorer homes than the experimentals (and probably poorer neighborhoods, too). Unless Jesness presents evidence that these critical background variables, when used as analytical controls, do not change the differential outcomes after twelve or fifteen months of parole exposure, his inference cannot be accepted. These background variables, for which Jesness does not control, have usually been strongly associated with delinquency and recidivism and these, not the institutional experiences, probably account for the differences in failure. In the language of multivariate analysis, Jesness' findings on early failure are probably spurious (i.e., the result of a third, uncontrolled variable).

Institutional Interests

Organizational personnel have a major stake in any evaluative outcome. They want to be associated with potential success, not failure. Researchers are not likely to have a similar stake in the outcome. Although researchers do not purposefully seek to devalue people or organizations, their motto is much more likely to be: "Let's find out the truth and let the chips fall where they may." Their reference group is the scientific community and their ethics are ideally guided accordingly. Administrators, on the other hand—the persons who hire researchers—usually want the evaluators to demonstrate that their operations are successful and worthy of the external community's moral and financial support. Rather than deny this conflict of interest, one ought to be aware of its existence and make sure that biases do not influence empirical studies and written reports.

Biases influenced by organizational interests are especially likely to develop when researchers give up their independence and seek ways to demonstrate program success. Consider the evaluative study of Wiltmyck reported by William and Joan McCord.[19] Employed as the institution's resident psychologists, the McCords seemed so eager to prove its success that they defined one type of *failure* as "partial success." Table 4 presents the data as reported by the McCords for Wiltwyck and "New England State School."

From the McCord text it is learned that "partial success" refers to boys who actually appeared in court for law violations but were not reinstitutionalized; "complete failures" were both noticed and reinstitutionalized. The McCords do not seem to be bothered by this odd use of labels, for they claim that Wiltwyck had a *combined* success rate of 71 percent whereas New England, a state institution, had a rate of only 53 percent. A fair appraisal of the data would suggest that there is no appreciable difference between these institutions in potential success, using this writer's definition; the 5 percent difference—in favor of New England—is small. If all law violations are counted as potential failure, regardless of court disposition, it appears that *both* institutions are characterized by high external failure.

A subtle form of bias can be found in a study reported by Black and Glick.[20] The population of primary interest was composed mainly of Jewish boys sentenced to Hawthorne Cedar Knolls School, a sectarian-sponsored residential treatment institution. Both researchers were regular employees of the Jewish Board of Guardians, the sponsoring agency. In a monograph reporting their results, the investigators described the selection of their sample as follows: "For purposes of this study the followup period was computed from the date of discharge from after-care."[21] Not surprisingly, Black and Glick report that Hawthorne Cedar Knolls had a higher success rate than a neighboring state school. They excluded from their sample not only all of the internal failures, but also all of the external failures occurring during the period of aftercare. Since the bulk of post-release failures take place within the first two years, the researchers thus eliminated the chance of finding many failures. In effect, all this study can hope to describe is the potential success rate of an unknown population that has been selectively screened for boys who might be failures. Since the researchers have gone to such lengths to minimize their potential failures, it is reasonable to conclude that they were unwilling to face up to the possibility that their organization, like the state school, is characterized by a high rate of internal and/or external failure.

Implications for a Humanitarian Policy

The consistent finding that treatment programs have not yet been proved to have an appreciable impact on failure rates should not be misinter-preted. For even though institutions for delinquents are probably not highly successful—regardless of treatment type—there is no reason to go back to harsher methods of child handling. It can be argued, rather, that even when boys are kept for only four months and treated with trust (as at Highfields), there is no evidence that this "coddling" will yield greater failure rates.

The case for a humanitarian approach needs to be divorced from any specific mode of treatment. People can be nice to boys with and without engaging in psychotherapy. This point is implicit in the recent work by Street, Vinter, and Perrow.[22] But we should not delude ourselves into adopting the unsubstantiated position that a humanitarian organization for delinquent boys yields lower rates of potential failures. With our present state of knowledge, it makes more sense to advocate a more humanitarian approach on the ground that it does not increase the *risk* of potential failure.

If it is decided to advocate humanitarianism in its own right, the social policy issue becomes much clearer. Given the fact that social work is still unable to influence appreciably the rates of failure of institu-tions for court-sentenced delinquents, should not ways be sought to make the total criminal-delinquent system more humane? In the name of treatment, boys have actually been sentenced for two and a half years (as at Boysville) for offenses that might bring an adult a sentence of only thirty, sixty, or ninety days. Surely it is time that youths were dealt with as humanely, and with similar regard for equity and due process of law, as adults.[23]

If lighter sentences do not increase the risk of failure, then why not be more humane and equitable? Keeping boys in the community is undoubtedly a lighter sentence than sending them away. But California has found that this probably does not increase the risk of failure. Actually, the California Community Treatment Program has evolved a series of graded punishments. If youngsters in this program misbehave or do not obey the youth officer, they are *temporarily* confined. During the first nineteen months of the program, 57 of 72 experimental cases were placed in temporary confinement a total of 183 times; this was an average of three times each, with an average length of stay of twelve days per confinement.[24] As earlier analysis disclosed, the risk of post-program failure is not increased by using this kind of approach. It is even conceivable—although this has not been demonstrated—that keeping these boys out of all long-term institutions in itself constitutes treatment and that this treatment may have a payoff much later, when the boys become adults. Spending less time in an all-delinquent community might yield more conforming adults.

Even if communities are not willing to follow the California community approach, one can still argue for shorter "lock-ups." Highfields kept first offenders for only four months, yet the risk of failure was not increased. As long as society is still determined to "teach boys a lesson" by locking them up (or sending them away), why not extend the idea of shorter confinements to a series of graded punishments for offenses? Adults are sentenced for thirty, sixty, or ninety days—why not children? Perhaps we might even come to advocate taking the institutional budgets allocated for food, beds, and clothing (based on lengthy stays) and spending them on boys and their families in their own homes. It is doubtful whether this would add to the risks, but the program would be a great deal more fun to study and run than the old failures.

Whether one embraces the perspective offered here, it is certainly time to address the problem of social accountability, regardless of the type of program. Social welfare institutions are too heavily subsidized, indirectly and directly, for social workers not to take the responsibility for knowing what has happened to the people served. A good start can be made by keeping track of all the people not completing treatment, discontinuing service, dropping out of programs, and running away. Rigorous and nondeceptive social bookkeeping may yield discomforting facts about agency success and reputation. It is hoped that we will be aware of defensive reactions and remind ourselves that we entered social work to serve *people* in trouble—not established agencies, ideologies, and methods.

Notes

1. Herbert H. Hyman, Charles R. Wright, and Terrence K. Hopkins, *Application of Methods of Evaluation: Four Studies of the Encampment for Citizenship* (Berkeley and Los Angeles: University of California Press, 1962), pp. 3–88.

2. For example, *see* Bernard C. Kirby, "Measuring Effects of Treatment of Criminals and Delinquents," *Sociology and Social Research,* Vol. 38, No. 6 (July-August 1954), pp. 368–375; Vernon Fox, "Michigan Experiment in Minimum Security Penology," *Journal of Criminal Law and Criminology,* Vol. 41, No. 2 (July-August 1950), pp. 150–166; William McCord and Joan McCord, "Two Approaches to the Cure of Delinquents," in Sheldon Glueck, ed., *The Problem of Delinquency* (Boston: Houghton-Mifflin Co., 1959); Bertram J. Black and Selma J. Glick, *Recidivism at the Hawthorne Cedar Knolls School,* Research Monograph No. 2 (New York: Jewish Board of Guardians, 1952); H. Ashley Weeks, *Youthful Offenders at Highfields: An Evaluation of the Effects of the Short-Term Treatment of Delinquent Boys* (Ann Arbor: University of Michigan Press, 1958).

3. This type of research demands careful attention to design to provide evidence that the experimental program had a greater impact on attitudes and values that, in turn, influenced postrelease behavior. This requires control groups and "before-after" measures. At the level of evaluative research herein referred to, in which *potential* outcomes are being assessed, attitudinal measures before and after are *not* necessary. As noted later on, comparability of groups continues to be important at *all* levels of evaluative research. *See* Hyman, Wright, and Hopkins, *op. cit.,* for a general statement of the problems. *See* Weeks, *op. cit.,* for the best-detailed example of evaluative research regarding institutions for delinquents.

4. Thorstein Sellin, "The Significance of Records of Crime," in Marvin E. Wolfgang, Leonard Savitz, and Norman Johnston, eds., *The Sociology of Crime and Delinquency* (New York: John Wiley & Sons, 1962), p. 64.

5. Marguerite Q. Warren, Virginia V. Neto, Theodore B. Palmer, and James K. Turner, "Community Treatment Project: An Evaluation of Community Treatment for Delinquents," CTP Research Report No. 7 (Sacramento: California Youth Authority, Division of Research, August 1966). (Mimeographed.)

6. *Ibid.,* p. 64.

7. *See ibid.,* Table 15, p. 68. For an explanation of the ranking of offenses by seriousness on which these figures are based, *see* Table 1 of this article.

8. *Ibid.,* p. 65.

9. Weeks, *op. cit.*

10. Fox, *op. cit.*

11. Personal communication from Robert Ontell, former study director of Mobilization For Youth's Reintegration of Juvenile Offenders Project, 1962.

12. David Street, Robert D. Vinter, and Charles Perrow, *Organization for Treatment: A Comparative Study of Institutions for Delinquents* (New York: Free Press, 1966), p. 196. This information is presented in a parenthetical comment about "Inland," a private institution. How many of the boys released as not completing treatment are actually excluded or included in this study is difficult to estimate. This study focuses on the attitudes of institutionalized boys about their experiences in residence. It would have been extremely valuable to know whether the screened-out boys differed in their responses to the attitudinal questions. It would also have been valuable to know whether the runaways also differed. Such information might have provided evidence that the attitudinal measures had validity. Presumably boys "resisting treatment" (i.e., those who were screened out

or ran away) should have responded differently to questions about themselves and the institutional staff. These kinds of missing data are quite central to the argument concerning the institutional "effectiveness" of Inland.

13. Weeks, *op. cit.*, pp. 41–62.

14. *Ibid.*, p. 61.

15. Carl F. Jesness, "The Fricot Ranch Study: Outcomes with Small vs. Large Living Groups in the Rehabilitation of Delinquents," Research Report No. 47 (Sacramento: California Youth Authority, Division of Research, October 1, 1965). (Mimeographed.)

16. *Ibid.*, p. 52.

17. *Ibid.*, pp. 85–90.

18. *Ibid.*, p. 89.

19. McCord and McCord, *op. cit.* The Wiltwyck sample is composed only of Negro boys between the ages of 8 and 12 (at intake) who presented no "deep-seated psychiatric problems." "New England," on the other hand, is much more heterogeneous and has older boys. The data regarding the Wiltwyck sample can be found in Lois Wiley, "An Early Follow-up Study for Wiltwyck School." Unpublished master's thesis, New York School of Social Work, 1941.

20. Black and Glick, *op. cit.*

21. *Ibid.*, p.4.

22. *Op. cit.*

23. *See* David Matza's insightful description of youthful appraisals of the juvenile court system in the discussion of the "Sense of Injustice," in Matza, *Delinquency and Drift* (New York: John Wiley & Sons, 1964).

24. Marguerite Q. Grant, Martin Warren, and James K. Turner, "Community Treatment Project: An Evaluation of Community Treatment of Delinquents," CTP Research Report No. 3 (Sacramento: California Youth Authority, Division of Research, August 1, 1963), p. 38. (Mimeographed.)

A Benefit-Cost Analysis of the Neighborhood Youth Corps

Michael E. Borus, John P. Brennan, Sidney Rosen

Congress passed the Economic Opportunity Act in August 1964 "to mobilize the human and financial resources of the Nation to combat poverty in the United States." Among the provisions of the law was one for the establishment of the Neighborhood Youth Corps (NYC). The NYC, by providing "useful work experience opportunities for unemployed young men and women," had a two-fold purpose. First, it attempted to increase the enrollee's employability or to enable his education to be resumed or continued. Second, it sought to enable public agencies and private non-

Reprinted from *Journal of Human Resources* 5 (Spring, 1970):139–59.

profit organizations to "carry out programs which will permit or contribute to the conservation and development of natural resources and recreational areas."[1] Today the Neighborhood Youth Corps, with over 600,000 enrollees annually, is the largest federal manpower training program.

The Neighborhood Youth Corps consists of three separate programs: (1) an in-school program to provide part-time employment for youths attending high school, (2) a summer program also designed primarily for young people who attend school, and (3) an out-of-school program which primarily serves dropouts. This study will deal only with the last.

Our major concern will be to measure the benefits accruing to society from the NYC program. As stated above, the Economic Opportunity Act established multiple objectives for the NYC. We will consider two types of these societal benefits: (1) the increase in the level of aggregate output—the usual benefits in analyses of manpower programs, and (2) the increase in employability (ability to earn) of NYC participants. Our primary measure of both types of benefits will be the change in the earnings of NYC participants after program participation.

Under certain conditions the program will yield the same dollar estimates of success for both these benefits, i.e., when the program affects only the productivity of the participants and the effects are accurately reflected by changes in earnings. It is possible, however, that secondary effects, such as displacement, will cause a divergence between the two estimates of program success. For instance, some of the increase in post-program earnings of NYC participants may be at the expense of other workers, causing the increase in aggregate output to be less than the employability benefits which accrue directly to the participants. Thus, to evaluate the success of the NYC program it is necessary to estimate each type of benefit separately. Then, if a single aggregate measure of program success is desired, weights might be assigned to each of the benefit measures and they could be summed. Notice, however, that this procedure departs from the standard practice of benefit-cost evaluations of manpower programs since it implicitly assigns non-zero weights for transfers of earnings.

Using the two benefit measures, we will seek to determine if the NYC program has effectively prepared the participants to be more productive or, as some have asserted, has only been an income maintenance or public works program for the period of participation. We will also seek to determine if the post-program benefits vary with the characteristics of the participants. Finally, any benefits found will be related to program costs.

Monetary and time constraints have limited the scope of the study to an examination of the program as it existed prior to December 31, 1966, in five urban areas of Indiana.[2] Further, the study is concerned only with the economic effects of the program. The effects of the NYC on social and psychological phenomena which did not have economic manifestations are not treated in this presentation.

Data Sources

All of the information on the sample members was taken from existing records. The choice of Indiana as the site for this study enabled us to make use of the "wage reporting data" collected by the Indiana Employment Security Division. All of the earnings information was obtained from this state source. These data cover total earnings, as reported by employers, for all employment covered under the Unemployment Compensation Act during calendar 1967. In Indiana, all employers of four or more persons are covered by the Act except for agricultural employers, nonprofit organizations, and governmental units. Also excluded are individuals who work as domestics, who are self-employed, or who work for immediate relatives. Approximately 66 percent of the Indiana workforce was covered by the Act in 1967.[3] Since our study deals with urban areas, it is likely that a higher proportion of our sample was employed in covered firms.

We made extensive use of basic NYC forms in the collection of demographic, termination, and cost information on the participants. Finally, we received program descriptions and supplementary information on sample members from the project staff in each of the areas.

Projects Studied

The projects studied were similar in many respects. Each had many different nonprofit and government work stations to which enrollees were assigned. In Gary and Evansville, for example, enrollees could work at any of more than 60 different stations.

Most of the jobs were with government agencies—for example, city hospitals, police departments, housing authorities, health departments, park departments, the state Employment Security Division, and the federal Department of Labor and Social Security Administration. The remainder were placed with private nonprofit organizations such as Goodwill Industries, the American Cancer Society, and local settlement houses. In each of the projects the enrollees worked as aides, assistants, or helpers to full-time regular employees; types of work ranged literally from A to Z—from automotive aides to zoo aides. Some of the more numerous or interesting jobs were clerical aides, dog catcher aides, driving permit aides, food service aides, library aides, landscape assistants, laboratory assistants, maintenance aides, nurse's aides, photography and developing aides, recreational aides, rodent control aides, sewer aides, teacher aides, and truck driver aides.

A major difference between projects was in the instruction they provided for participants. Projects in Fort Wayne, Gary, and South Bend included remedial education; no formal educational instruction was provided for the out-of-school program participants in the other areas during 1966.

The projects also started at different times and were of varying sizes. Starting dates and total number of enrollees by the end of 1966 for each project were: South Bend, May 1965, 362; Gary, August 1965, 830; Evansville, February 1966, 281; Indianapolis, June 1966, 199; and Fort Wayne, September 1966, 39.

The Sample

Our experimental group of NYC participants in each area was selected from the population of all those youths who were eligible for the program, reported to work for at least one day, and left the program by December 31, 1966. The control group came from those persons who had submitted applications prior to December 31, 1966, and were found to be eligible for the program, but who did not enroll because (1) they were put on a waiting list and never called, (2) they could not be reached for a job assignment, or (3) they did not report when assigned a job.[4] A total of 1,085 individuals (836 enrollees and 249 eligible nonparticipants) met one of these three sets of criteria and had files containing necessary demographic and other information. After consultation with program counselors and staff personnel, 315 persons (232 or 27.8 percent of the program participants, and 83 or 33.3 percent of the control group members) were not included in the study. Among those eliminated were persons who had met the other goal of the program, i.e., they had obtained further training or education. These youths constituted 11.5 percent of the experimental group and 25.3 percent of the control group.[5] An additional 11.5 percent of the experimental group and 6.4 percent of the control group were removed because they had died, entered the armed forces, or moved out of the state thus making "wage reporting data" unavailable. Also, 3.0 percent of the experimental group and 0.8 percent of the control group were eliminated because of physical or mental handicaps existing prior to the program which prevented them from holding regular jobs. We felt that the NYC program was not designed for the problems of these persons; to include them in our study would tend to cloud our findings.

Finally, in our original sampling we eliminated 49 persons who had gone to jail in 1967, on the basis that their crimes had been committed before they were selected for the NYC program. After further discussion with the NYC staff, however, we discovered that most of these individuals had committed their crimes during or after the NYC programs. Thus, because we felt that their incarcerations accurately reflected their future post-program labor market experience, we attempted to include them and were successful in getting the records of 33 individuals, all members of the experimental group. Thus we have mistakenly omitted 16 people—14 from the experimental group and two from the control group.

TABLE 1
Characteristics of the Sample

Characteristics	NYC Participants	Control Group	Total Sample
Female	51.2%	57.8%	52.6%
Average years of school completed ..	10.2 yrs.	10.0 yrs.	10.1 yrs.
Average age at time of interview ...	18.2 yrs.	18.0 yrs.	18.1 yrs.
Married	13.8%	13.9%	13.8%
Average number of family members..	6.0	6.4	6.1
English not spoken at home	6.1%	4.8%	5.8%
Interviewed in 1965...........	60.1%	26.5%	52.9%
Number by area:			
Evansville...............	75	21	96
Fort Wayne	5	6	11
Gary	320	75	395
Indianapolis	75	42	117
South Bend	129	22	151
Average number of hours in program .	520.3 hrs.	0 hrs.	408.1 hrs.
Nonwhite	73.0%	72.3%	73.0%
Average 1967 Earnings	$953.46	$675.63	$893.57
Number in sample	604	166	770

We ended up with a sample of 770 persons of whom 78.4 percent were participants in NYC programs. Table 1 presents the individual characteristics which we hypothesized would affect earnings and the benefits society would derive from the NYC program.[6] In age, education, marital status, race, family size, and language spoken at home, the averages for the participants and the control group were almost identical. The only sizable differences were in interview date and sex. Sixty percent of the participants and only 27 percent of the control group applied to the NYC program in 1965; 49 percent of the participants were men—

seven percentage points more than among the control group. To account for these differences, multiple regression techniques were used in comparisons to test whether these characteristics significantly affected the dependent variables.

Benefits of the NYC in Increased Aggregate Output

We were concerned with two types of societal benefits which may accrue from the NYC program: the increase in productive ability of society and the increase in the productive ability of the program participants.

It is very difficult to measure the influence of a particular manpower program on the level of aggregate production. The NYC, by providing work experience to the youths, allows them to learn skills and "acceptable" work habits such as appearing for work on time, accepting supervision, and accepting responsibility. It may also make them more acceptable to employers by providing them with a label of "steady workers." If these improvements occur, they should be reflected in greater earnings in the post-program period.

The increase in earnings is usually considered to equal the increase in the level of aggregate production of the society. This requires the assumption that marginal productivity and wages are closely related so that changes in earnings will also reflect increments in national product. This assumption is not sufficient, however, since one also needs to assume that the experimental group does not displace other workers. Unfortunately, we lack evidence to prove that displacement did not occur. Consequently, any increase in earnings experienced by the participants probably should be viewed as the upper extreme of possible increases in aggregate product.[7]

Average Post-program Increase in Earnings

Total 1967 earnings as reported by the Indiana Employment Security Division was the dependent variable in our analysis. These were the earnings of the sample in the first or second year after they had been interviewed for the program and after all of the participants had left it. Using simple averages, we found that the NYC participants earned $278 more in 1967 than did members of our control group. We hypothesized, however, that this difference might have reflected the demographic differences between the two groups, and therefore we used regression techniques to take account of them. We began by regressing 1967 earnings on the variables described in Table 1.[8] Equation 1 in Table 2 presents the results of this analysis.

TABLE 2
Regression of 1967 Earnings on Demographic and Program Characteristics

Variables	Equation 1	Equation 2	Equation 3	Equation 4
Intercept	−11,331.27[a]	−13,299.78[a]	−13,295.58[b]	−9,580.36[b]
Female	−976.28	−1,006.81	−970.11	−617.07
	(121.69)	(122.10)	(116.06)	(146.44)
Education in years	−995.53	−900.93	−897.07	−1,782.17
	(312.87)	(314.79)	(311.13)	(494.89)
Education in years^2	57.46	52.29	51.64	98.68
	(16.21)	(16.32)	(16.13)	(25.37)
Age at the interview	1,791.63	1,957.79	1,981.28	2.014.24
	(889.72)	(890.30)	(874.68)	(863.68)
Age at the interview^2	−48.30	−52.90	−53.47	−54.88
	(24.19)	(24.20)	(23.78)	(23.48)
Married	178.17	185.05		
	(170.11)	(169.67)		
No. of household members	21.31	19.96		
	(17.70)	(17.66)		
English not spoken at home	278.12	229.88		
	(238.76)	(239.06)		
Interviewed in 1965	113.87	23.31		
	(144.98)	(149.99)		
Lived in Fort Wayne	75.97	108.51		
	(487.53)	(486.41)		
Lived in Gary	66.45	56.54		
	(193.22)	(192.74)		
Lived in Indianapolis	88.00	141.26		
	(213.93)	(214.63)		
Lived in South Bend	81.75	144.26		
	(224.03)	(225.12)		
Enrollee	135.61	0.78		
	(139.67)	(151.44)		
No. of hours in program		0.329	0.332	−4.20
		(0.145)	(0.118)	(2.21)
Female X Hours				−0.922
				(0.251)
Education X Hours				1.12
				(0.472)
Education^2 X Hours				−0.0592
				(0.0250)
N	770	770	770	770
R^2	0.0888	0.0937	0.0996	0.1228
F	6.35	6.30	15.18	12.96
df	14 and 755	15 and 754	6 and 763	9 and 760

[a] The following characteristics enter into the intercept: males, single persons, persons who speak English at home, persons interviewed for the program in 1966, persons living in Evansville, and nonenrollees.

[b] Males are included in the intercept.

In Equation 1 three sets of variables were statistically significant at the .05 level: sex, education and age. Men earned significantly more than women and the effects on earnings of further education declined until about the ninth grade and then increased. Earnings also increased until about age 19 and then declined slightly. The other variables had the expected signs but were all clearly not statistically significant, i.e. P > .10. The coefficient of the variable for enrollment indicated that the average NYC participant in the sample earned $136 more than did the average control group member, but this was only significant at P = .33. Thus we were forced to conclude that on the average the NYC out-of-school program did not have a demonstrably significant effect on the earnings of the program participants.

Post-program Benefits Associated with Length of Participation in NYC

An earlier study, using simple cross tabulations, had found that the effects of NYC participation varied with the length of participation in the NYC program.[9] Therefore we next added a variable for hours of participation in the NYC program to those of the first equation.[10] This equation is presented as Equation 2 in Table 2.

The variable for hours of participation was significant at the P = .02 level, indicating that length of time in the program was significantly related to 1967 earnings. Those individuals who remained in the program the longest had the greatest gains associated with NYC participation. Each additional hour in the program was associated with increased earnings of $.33. Thus, while the earnings gain associated with NYC participation was small for those persons with short stays in the program, it was quite substantial for those in the program for long periods.[11]

In an attempt to determine whether the importance of length of NYC participation differed with the characteristics of the participants, we sought to reduce the size of Equation 2. We sequentially deleted the last significant variable until only those variables significant at P ≤ .05 remained. This gave us Equation 3. We then added to this equation sets of demographic and interaction variables. The interaction variables were formed as the product of a demographic variable and the number of hours of program participation. Each of the sets of demographic variables in Equation 1 and its interaction term(s) were added to Equation 3, were tested for statistical significance, and then were removed. The two sets of interaction variables which were found to be significant at P ≤ .05 were then added to the equation to form Equation 4 of Table 2.

In this equation the gain in post-program earnings from NYC

participation was dependent on the number of hours in the program and the sex and education of the participants. When we differentiated Equation 4 by hours of participation for men (i.e., $\partial Y/\partial \text{Hours} = -4.20 + 1.12 \text{ Education} - 0.0592 \text{ Education}^2$), we found the earnings gain for male participants was approximately \$1.08 for each hour of participation in the program if they had completed the ninth or tenth grades, \$.97 per hour if they had completed only the eighth grade, and \$.96 and \$.72 per hour if they had completed the eleventh or twelfth grades, respectively. Thus there were very high returns for each hour of participation by the male enrollees.

For the women participants, the increments in earnings resulting from the program were negligible. They were approximately \$.92 less than those of the men (the coefficient of Female $\times$ Hours). Those with ninth and tenth grade educations had the highest gain in 1967 earnings, but this was only about \$.16 for each hour of participation. Those who had a year more or a year less education appear to have gained nothing in terms of future earnings by participating in the Neighborhood Youth Corps. Thus the increase in earnings of \$.33 per hour of participation found in Equation 2 was the average of widely differing gains associated with NYC enrollment.[12]

As in most analyses of manpower programs, however, the true meaning of the observed relationships is not clear. Our equations took account of many important demographic characteristics, but we were not able to control for such important factors as intelligence and motivation. Consequently it is impossible to know with certainty whether increased participation in the NYC leads to higher earnings or whether there is another independent variable which is correlated with both earnings and length of stay. It is possible that those persons who remain the longest in the program are the ones who possess other characteristics, not included in our equations, which would make them more competitive in the labor market even in the absence of their NYC participation.[13] We believe, however, that the NYC does impart positive labor market qualities to the participants and that the effect is real. Later we will discuss a possible method to test this belief.

Benefits from Participant Work During the Program

One of the objectives of the NYC program is to undertake socially useful services which would not otherwise be provided and which could represent a benefit to society in terms of an increase in aggregate output.[14] It is possible, however, that much of the work done by NYC participants does not in fact produce any socially desirable product in addition to that which would have been produced in the absence of the program. The most obvious reason for no increment in output is displacement whereby the NYC enrollees take work away from others. We are unable to measure the extent of displacement but believe it to be small.

More important, it seems to us, the payments to participants in the Neighborhood Youth Corps may be merely transfer payments for "make work." While some NYC enrollees are performing work which in a competitive market would command their earnings, others are providing little if any useful services which would not otherwise have been provided if there were no program. For example, a teacher's aide may release the time spent by a teacher on routine paperwork and allow her to devote more time to instruction, but in other instances the aide may do nothing but sit in the back of the room doing completely irrelevant busy work. In the first situation there is an increase in aggregate output while in the latter there is none.

Finally, we feel that some of the sample would have had employment were they not in the NYC program, but we lack the data to measure the increase in their earnings during the NYC program.[15] We also do not know to what extent the jobs left by these persons were filled from among the unemployed, as will be discussed below.

Thus we have not been able to estimate the effect on aggregate output of the work done by the NYC participants in our sample during the program. Therefore we use two extremes. At one extreme the during-the-program benefits equal $1.31 per hour of program participation, the average wage and fringe benefits paid to the sample participants. At the other extreme they are equal to zero.

Resource Costs of the NYC

We were able to determine only the costs for the average participant in the Neighborhood Youth Corps projects we examined. Regression analysis of how the costs varied with the characteristics of the participants was impossible, given the data available to us.

For each of the projects, we collected the accounting reports of expenditures by the project sponsor. By dividing the total wage payments by $1.25, the amount per hour each participant was paid, we were able to calculate the total number of hours of work experience provided by each project for the period to the end of 1966. We divided the amounts spent on each of the major cost categories by this total hours figure to find the average cost per participant hour. These costs are presented in Table 3.[16]

TABLE 3

Costs per Hour of Work Experience for Five Neighborhood Youth Corps Out-of-school Programs in Indiana, 1965-66

Expenditure Item	Evansville	Fort Wayne	Gary	Indianapolis[a]	South Bend	Average for Five Programs
Enrollee wages	$1.25	$1.25	$1.25	$1.25	$1.25	$1.25
Employer cost of fringe benefits for enrollees	.05	.05	.06	.05	.05	.06
Total of other costs	.67	2.85	.48	.92	.96	.61
Total project costs	1.97	4.15	1.79	2.22	2.25	1.91
Adjusted total costs excluding enrollee wages & fringe benefits[b]	.71	2.93	1.08	1.12	1.00	1.08
Adjusted total project costs[b] . . .	2.01	4.23	2.39	2.42	2.30	2.39
Total hours of work experience	108,062	3,808	744,474	81,834	128,069	213,249

[a]The program conducted in Indianapolis during the summer of 1966 was both a summer program and an out-of-school program: 170 of the 269 youths enrolled returned to school in the fall of 1966. It was not possible, however, to remove the costs of this group. Therefore, the Indianapolis figures are not strictly out-of-school program costs.

[b]Estimated charges for services performed by the ISES and the administrative costs of the U.S. Department of Labor have been added.

Opportunity Costs

The largest expenditures of the NYC program were for the wages and fringe benefits paid to enrollees. Whether these reflect real cost is dependent on the assumptions made about the value of the participants' alternative activities. We feel that there were no opportunity costs for the NYC programs, and we think that most of the youths in the program would have taken any non-NYC jobs paying more than $1.31 an hour if such jobs were offered to them. The basic component of the NYC program is to provide job experience. Anyone who could gain job experience while earning more than $1.31 would not be acting rationally, at least in economic terms, by staying in the program. Thus only production from those jobs which paid less than $1.31 per hour might be foregone because of the NYC program. We feel, however, that the skills required for these jobs were so minimal that they could be filled easily from among the large number of unemployed youth who were not in the program. Therefore we believe that no production was lost.

If, however, the market was felt to approach perfect competition, there were no rents paid for participation in the NYC program, and our assumption about absorption of the unemployed was dropped, the approximately $1.31 per hour payment would reflect the maximum opportunity cost of the program. Consequently we include estimates with and without this amount in Table 3.

Marginal Costs

The project sponsor's costs were considerably higher in Fort Wayne than in the other cities. This project was just beginning when we examined it; therefore it had incurred many of the high fixed costs but had yet to enroll very many participants. Undoubtedly the average costs were reduced as overhead costs were subsequently spread over more enrollees.

The cost per hour was almost identical in all of the other cities, however, although the average length of participation differed greatly (the average length of participation of sample members was 676 hours in Gary and only 120 hours in Indianapolis). Therefore the cost per additional hour of participation appears constant once the program is under way. Consequently the average adjusted cost figures in Table 3 represent our best estimate of both the average costs and the marginal costs to society of the NYC program.

A Comparison of the Benefits and Costs in Aggregate Output

Table 4 presents the benefits to society of the NYC program for the members of our sample in terms of increased aggregate output. The increase

TABLE 4

Benefits to Society of the Neighborhood Youth Corps Out-of-school Program in Indiana Assuming a Service Life of Ten Years and a Discount Rate of 10 Percent[a]

Enrollee Output During Program Is Considered a Benefit						
Years of Education Comp pleted	Length of Program Participation					
	100 Hours		500 Hours		1,000 Hours	
	Male	Female	Male	Female	Male	Female
8 years	$728	$161	$3,638	$ 855	$7,276	$1,611
9 years	798	231	3,988	1,156	7,977	2,312
10 years	795	228	3,973	1,140	7,946	2,281
11 years	719	153	3,595	763	7,190	1,525
12 years	570	4	2,852	19	5,704	38

Enrollee Output During Program Is Excluded						
Years of Education Completed	Length of Program Participation					
	100 Hours		500 Hours		1,000 Hours	
	Male	Female	Male	Female	Male	Female
8 years	$597	$ 30	$2,983	$150	$5,966	$ 301
9 years	667	100	3,333	501	6,667	1,002
10 years	664	97	3,318	485	6,636	970
11 years	588	22	2,940	108	5,880	215
12 years	439	−127	2,196	−636	4,393	−1,272

[a]To calculate the benefits for different service lives or discount rates, multiply by the following factors: service life of 5 years − 0.6169; service life of 15 years − 1.2379; discount rate of 5 percent − 1.2289; discount rate of 15 percent − 0.8340.

in post-program output was calculated by projecting the annual earnings increases associated with short, intermediate, and long stays in the NYC, derived from Equation 4. The projections assume that the earnings gains remain constant for ten years, that the increase in earnings is received evenly during the year, and that future earnings should be discounted at an annual rate of 10 percent. These arbitrary assumptions are similar to those used in a number of other studies, and Table 4 includes the necessary data to calculate the benefits for other sets of assumptions.

A more important assumption made in calculating the post-program benefit estimates was that there would be no secondary effects in the period. Since some displacement of other workers by the enrollees would be likely, particularly if the program served as a screening device for employers seeking "steady workers," the calculated estimates probably overstate the actual benefits to society. Unfortunately, there is no way to determine empirically the degree of overstatement.

The post-program benefits were added to two sets of calculations for the increase in output during the program. The top half of Table 4 represents the benefits for society if the increase in the output of the participants during the program is equal to their earnings. The lower half of the table represents the benefits for society if the output produced during the program is not considered to be an addition to aggregate production. The difference between the two parts of the table is that the $1.31 per hour which has been added in the top half to represent increased output during the program is removed in the lower half.

Table 5 presents benefit-cost ratios based on these benefit calculations and on the average adjusted costs presented in Table 3. The values of both sets of benefits estimated in Table 4 are compared with the cost of the program when it includes wage costs of $1.31 per hour and when they are excluded, the two extreme cases for opportunity cost. Thus benefit-cost ratios are calculated for four combinations of possible benefits and costs and should present a range of possible values.

A Comparison of the Employability Benefits and Costs

The benefits of the NYC program may be defined in an entirely different framework—in equity terms. In the Economic Opportunity Act, society made a commitment to increase the employability of unemployed youths. The NYC, by providing work experience for the youths, seeks to increase their earnings in the post-program period. Similarly, the NYC may increase the earnings of the youths while they are in the program. As discussed earlier, however, we believe that some of the youths would be employed for the period of the program, but we lack the data to determine the actual increase in earnings. It would undoubtedly lie between nothing and $1.31 per hour.

Thus the figures of Table 4 also represent the benefits to society of the NYC program in terms of increased earnings for the program participants. This definition of benefits, however, requires important differences in the interpretation of the table. Table 4 represents the upper limit of increases in aggregate output since displacement is assumed not to exist. But displacement is of no concern when only the employability of the NYC participants is considered. Likewise, the problem of whether the payments to the participants during the program reflect real output or are "make work" is unimportant when employability is the criterion of success. Therefore the figures presented in the top half of Table 4 are probably close to the actual changes in employability and those of the

TABLE 5
Societal Benefit-Cost Ratios for the Neighborhood Youth Corps
Out-of-school Program in Indiana

Years of Education Completed	Output During Program Is Considered a Benefit[a]				Output During Program Is Excluded[b]			
	No Opportunity (Wage) Costs		Opportunity (Wage) Costs Included		No Opportunity (Wage) Costs		Opportunity (Wage) Costs Included	
	Male	Female	Male	Female	Male	Female	Male	Female
8 years	6.7	1.5	3.0	.7	5.5	.3	2.5	.1
9 years	7.4	2.1	3.3	1.0	6.2	.9	2.8	.4
10 years	7.4	2.1	3.3	1.0	6.1	.9	2.8	.4
11 years	6.7	1.4	3.0	.6	5.4	.2	2.5	.1
12 years	5.3	.0	2.4	.0	4.1	c	1.8	c

[a]Benefits from the top half of Tabel 4.
[b]Benefits from the lower half of Table 4.
[c] No part of the costs are recovered.

lower half represent the lower bound of possible benefits. In terms of aggregate output, however, Table 4 presents the most optimistic esti-mates of benefits from the NYC program, since it assumes no displace-ment, and could greatly overstate the benefits of the program.

With these differences in mind, Table 5 may also be used to weigh the employability effects of the NYC program. Only the columns where wage costs are included should be used for this purpose. Wage costs represent funds which could be used in other programs to increase the earnings of poor youth. Thus they should be considered as costs of the Neighborhood Youth Corps program in terms of employability consid-erations.

The Findings

From Tables 4 and 5 we reached the following conclusions:

1. The benefits for society from enrolling male participants in the NYC program were considerably larger than they were from enrolling women. Assuming that the costs of the program were the same for both groups, we found for a ten-year period that the NYC program had a ratio of benefits to costs of at least two for almost all male participants. The ratio for the women, by contrast, was below one except with the most favorable assumptions, which indicated that for them society was unlikely to derive benefits proportionate to the resources it devoted to the program.

2. The benefits of the NYC program for society were greatest

when persons who had completed only nine or ten years of schooling were enrolled. The benefits from high school graduates were below those from high school dropouts. Again assuming the same costs for all types of participants, we found that enrolling participants who completed only the ninth or tenth years of school instead of high school graduates would lead to substantially greater success per dollar of cost for the program.

3. For individual participants, the longer they were in the program, the greater were the benefits they derived. Each individual received payments and fringe benefits of $1.31 for each hour he worked. We felt that this was at least equal to what he would have earned were he not in the program.

More importantly, we found that, for male participants and for female participants who were high school dropouts, the longer they were in the program, the greater was the increase in post-program earnings which they derived from the program. Thus the implication is that to increase the earnings of individual participants, it would be desirable to encourage each enrollee to continue in the program as long as possible. Of course there will be a limit to the length of profitable participation. When we introduced the quadratic form of length of participation into Equation 2, the benefits reached a peak at approximately 1,446 hours. While this functional form was not statistically significant, it makes it clear that a lifetime stay in the NYC is not the answer to the problems of low earnings. Rather, we are suggesting that society will benefit if the youths who drop out of the program after a month or two are encouraged to remain in the program longer.

Discussion of the Findings

The findings of this study differ considerably from those of previous evaluations of the NYC. Levitan has contended that the Neighborhood Youth Corps is only an "aging vat"—an income maintenance program which serves as a holding action until the participants reach an age at which they become employable. He based this contention "on the fact that unemployment rates among youth decline as they mature into adulthood."[17] If the NYC were an "aging vat," however, we would have found age to be an important determinant of earnings, and when we included it in Equation 1, the coefficient of the variable representing hours of participation would have become nonsignificant.[18] In contrast, we found that although age was statistically significant when we added it in the quadratic forms, length of participation meanwhile remained significant $P = .02$. Thus we conclude that the NYC program definitely is not just an "aging vat."

Similarly, our findings that males gain much more than do females from participation in the NYC contradicts the findings of Walther and Magnusson. They found that training was more apt to be effective with female than with male enrollees. However, their conclusion was based on simple tabulations of the employment status and wage rates, approximately one year after application to the program, of a predominantly Negro sample in southern and border cities.[19] Our study deals with earnings for the entire year rather than a point in time, includes a somewhat greater proportion of whites, studies programs in the North, and takes account of a number of demographic characteristics in the regression analysis. Any of these factors may have caused the disparity between findings.

Finally, a basic problem with any retrospective analysis of the type we made is determining causality. We found that earnings increased as length of time in the program increased. We have interpreted this to mean that the Neighborhood Youth Corps causes earnings to increase. We feel that the longer a youth has participated in the program, the more likely he is to have learned such desirable traits as getting to work on time, reporting regularly for work, neatness in appearance, ability to communicate with middle class persons, ability to accept supervision, and ability to accept responsibility. These basic prerequisites to getting and keeping a job are often missing in the high school dropout from a poor family. In addition, we believe that the longer an individual is in the program, the more acceptable he becomes to major employers. Employers who invest in training their employees want to minimize their turnover. Long-term participation in the NYC program may be considered by these employers to be an indication of stability. Therefore we feel that the youths with the longest participation are more likely to get good jobs.

It is possible, however, that the qualities which were associated with remaining in the program may also have been associated positively with earnings. In this case those individuals who remained in the program were also the ones who would have had the greatest expected earnings in the absence of the program. Unfortunately, without data, it is not possible for us to prove that this was not the flow of causality. In the ideal experimental design one would randomly assign individuals to the program and then terminate them randomly from it at different times. Such a design is obviously not feasible in terms of program operation. We suggest, however, that individuals should be encouraged to remain in the NYC program longer. A comparison can then be made of their earnings gains and those of our sample. If our interpretation of causality is correct, average gains from the NYC program should increase.

Notes

1. "Statement of Purpose," *Economic Opportunity Act of 1964,* Public Law 88–452. Title I, Part B, 78 STAT 512; USC 2731. The 1966 amendments to the Act also allow employment in private industry. These amendments were not in operation during the period we studied.

2. These areas are Evansville, Fort Wayne, Gary, Indianapolis, and South Bend. Several hundred persons were enrolled in other small programs in smaller towns throughout Indiana, but these programs were not examined because data collection costs and time would have been disproportionately high. Programs were also conducted in East Chicago and Terre Haute, but there were not sufficient numbers of control group members to allow a meaningful analysis.

3. Statistics supplied by Unemployment Insurance Service, U.S. Department of Labor.

4. We are aware that there may have been self-selection which would lead the control group to have greater or lower expected earnings than those of the participants. We would have preferred a randomly selected control group, of course, but this was not possible since we were making a retrospective study of a program over which we had no control.

5. Almost all of the control group who obtained further education or training (92 percent) returned to school. In many cases they returned prior to being called for NYC assignment, and this was their reason for not entering the program. On the other hand, among the experimental group, 74 percent of those getting further education or training returned to school and all of them did so after leaving the program.

6. Most of the variables were those which are normally used to explain changes in earnings. Two require further explanation: We hypothesized that those persons who came from households where English was not spoken, primarily Mexican-Americans in our sample, would have labor force behavior and experience different from the other sample members. We also included a variable to show the year in which the individual was interviewed for the program. Those persons interviewed in 1965 had a longer period in which to adapt to the labor market prior to the measurement of their earnings in 1967. Also, in 1965, the NYC program was new and may have been somewhat different from the program which existed the following year.

7. For a further discussion of displacement and other secondary effects, see Einar Hardin and Michael E. Borus, "An Economic Evaluation of the Retraining Program in Michigan: Methodological Problems of Research," *Proceedings of the American Statistical Association, Social Statistics Section, 1966* (Washington: 1967), pp. 133–37.

8. We also felt that the race of the sample member would affect his earnings. Data were unavailable on the race of 60 persons in our sample, and therefore we did not introduce race at this stage.

9. Dunlap and Associates, *Survey of Terminees from Out-of-School Neighborhood Youth Corps Projects,* Vol. 1 (Darien, Conn.: 1968), p. 71.

10. The files of 77 of the NYC participants recorded the length of course participation expressed only in terms of days attended. For these persons we estimated the number of hours by multiplying the days by 6.793, the average number of hours for the 366 NYC participants who had both clock hours and days recorded.

11. We also added the square of hours of NYC participation to Equation 2 to determine if this relationship was curvilinear. This equation indicated that the gain associated with increased participation reached a maximum at approximately 1,446 hours. The regression coefficient for the squared term was not statistically significant ($P = .20$).

12. We also tested whether race was a significant determinant of post-program earnings by adding binary variables representing race and the interaction of race and the hours of participation to Equation 3 for a reduced sample of 710 for whom we had racial data. We found that the coefficient of the variable for race was significant at $P = .02$. Nonwhites in our sample had earnings in 1967 which were $323 below those of whites. The interaction of race and hours in the program was highly nonsignificant, indicating that whites and nonwhites had the same gains from the NYC program. The coefficients of the other variables in Equation 3 changed very little and were all significant at $P \leqslant .08$.

13. Another possible problem lies in our source of data. Nearly one-half of our sample members (48 percent of both the experimental and control groups; 58 percent of the women and 37 percent of the men) had no reported earnings in 1967. According to other studies of NYC participants, these figures were not unusually high. Many of the girls in this age group leave the labor force because of family responsibilities. Nationally, unemployment is exceptionally high among male teenagers with this background. Also, although we attempted to eliminate them from the sample, some of the young men may have entered military service since they were in the prime age groups. As discussed earlier, however, certain types of employment are not covered by the unemployment compensation laws. Of particular relevancy to our sample was the lack of coverage of domestics and of employees of small firms, nonprofit organizations, and government. It is possible that some of those with no reported earnings were in these categories. To test the importance of such a situation we reduced the size of our sample to include only the 401 persons who had reported earnings in 1967. We then regressed the earnings of these individuals on the six variables of Equation 3. All of the regression coefficients were significant at $P \leqslant .01$ and the regression coefficient of hours of participation was $.74. This would appear to indicate that the use of "wage reporting data" was not the cause of our finding that post-program earnings increase with length of NYC participation.

14. They could also be considered as negative costs, but since they were explicitly mentioned as objectives of the Economic Opportunity Act, we decided to include them among the benefits.

15. Unfortunately we did not have data on the earnings of the control group during the period of the NYC program since the unemployment insurance records are purged after six quarters. With these data we could have calculated the actual increase in earnings of the NYC participants.

16. There was some variation in costs because expenditures were not properly assigned to the NYC program. In Evansville, Fort Wayne, and South Bend, recruitment and job development, referral, placement, and follow-up were carried out by the project staff. In Gary and Indianapolis these functions were performed by the Indiana State Employment Service (ISES). In Gary counseling was also done by the ISES staff. Yet these were integral parts of the NYC program and while the bookkeeping entries for the expenditures involved were assigned to the ISES, they more properly belonged to the NYC. We added these costs to the totals for Indianapolis and Gary. The unadjusted costs presented in Table 3 also did not take

into account the administrative cost incurred in the regional and national offices of the U.S. Department of Labor. This would include expenditures on such items as program planning, proposal review, fiscal monitoring and accounting, project evaluation, and research. On the basis of figures on the entire NYC program provided by the Department of Labor, it appears that the cost of these services was approximately 2 percent of the total costs. While these costs could not be attributed directly to particular projects, we felt it appropriate that the adjusted figures in Table 3 should include this 2 percent administrative cost.

17. Sar A. Levitan, "Neighborhood Youth Corps," *Examination of War on Poverty Staff and Consultants Report*, Subcommittee on Employment, Manpower, and Poverty, Committee on Labor and Public Welfare, U.S. Senate, 90th Cong., 1st sess., Vol. 1, Washington, p. 55.

18. This would have occurred since the equation would then be comparing the post-program earnings of groups with differing lengths of participation while holding age constant.

19. R. Walther and M. Magnusson, *A Retrospective Study of the Effectiveness of the Out-of-School Neighborhood Youth Corps Programs in Four Urban Sites*, report submitted to the Manpower Administration, U.S. Department of Labor, Washington, 1967, pp. 44–47.

Chapter XI

Organizational Innovation and Change

The dilemma between change and stability is ubiquitous in formal organizations. On the one hand, as open system organizations encounter continuous stimuli for change both from the external environment and internally. On the other hand, change always involves costs to the organization primarily in terms of its inability to recover past investments made to attain existing modes of operations. That is, a major source of organizational "inertia" is not only the costs of the change or innovation itself, but also the potential loss of past investments, i.e., "sunk costs" (March and Simon, 1958).

    The concept of change refers to the introduction of new organizational attributes or tasks not previously in existence in the organization which necessitate a significant reallocation of resources. Hence change in this context denotes the modification of organizational variables and not change in the individuals who function in the organization (Katz and Kahn, 1966, pp. 390–91). Organizational change can be planned (i.e., innovation) in the sense that the organizational variables to be modified have been identified in advance, and the objectives of the desired change have been explicitly stated. The change process may, however, be unplanned in the sense that organizational responses to external and internal exigencies result in unanticipated consequences. For example, in promoting the professionalization of its staff, the organization may inadvertently set barriers for serving the poor (Cloward and Epstein, 1965).

    The tendency of organizations toward internal inertia on the one hand, and their increasing dependence on their environment on the other hand, suggests that increasingly organizational change is externally induced (Terreberry, 1968). Thus, the rate of change and innovation is likely to increase as changes in the environment increase, thereby making existing organizational attributes less effective in attaining organizational goals and maintaining organizational survival. In particular, changes in client attributes and needs, new developments and advances in service technologies and knowledge, emergence of new organizations competing for similar resources and outputs, and changes in the bases of support for the organization will generate strong pressures on the organization to modify its existing programs. For example, the discovery of the polio vaccine rendered obsolete the original goals of the National Foundation for Infantile Paralysis (Sills, 1957), and population shifts in central cities have altered radically the input of students into public schools.

The responsiveness of the organization to these pressures and the ability to initiate a process of change is a function of a complex set of interrelated variables. First, the organizational intelligence system will determine whether the need for change is perceived by the members of the organization. An organization lacking an effective intelligence system and important boundary spanning roles tends to be insensitive to changes in the environment and to new developments in knowledge (Wilensky, 1967), and thus is less open to innovation.

Second, organizational goals and ideologies serve as filtering devices of environmental stimuli and new ideas. When the organization is highly committed to a narrow set of ideologies, it is less likely to initiate change particularly when the stimuli for change challenge these ideologies. An example of such an organization resisting changes in its goals is the Woman's Christian Temperance Union (Gusfield, 1955). Despite changes in the public's attitude toward drinking, the WCTU refused to change its goals because of ideological rigidity. In contrast, the Y.M.C.A. has been successful in adapting to environmental changes, partly because its organizational goals were broadly defined as well as being open to inputs from its clientele (Zald and Denton, 1963).

Third, as noted in Chapter III, the executive leadership of the organization plays a crucial role in affecting the "openness" of the organization to innovation. Typically, major organizational changes can be initiated only after an executive substitution whereby the new executive serves as a change agent or mobilizes support for the change efforts. The importance of the executive leadership is highlighted by the fact that significant organizational changes invariably result in major shifts in the distribution of resources and power in the organization. Therefore, the greater the effects of the potential change on the power structure of the organization, the greater the resistance to change (McCleery, 1957). Hence, successful introduction of change in the organization often necessitates the mobilization of power, both external and internal, in support of the change efforts.

Finally, every significant organizational innovation requires the availability of uncommitted organizational resources that can bear the costs of the innovation (Thompson, 1965). These resources must include money, personnel, time, skill, and tolerance for initial failures.

This discussion implies that the ability of an organization to introduce change also necessitates an administrative structure that is receptive to innovation. Thompson (1965) suggests that the organization must devaluate authority and positional status, increase structural looseness or decentralization, encourage free communication and collegial relations, and reward the generation of new ideas. Similarly, since innovation inherently implies engagement in activities that have a high degree of nonconformity and uncertainty, Litwak (1961) proposes that a human relations model is most suitable for encouraging innovation. In addition, Wilson (1963) proposes that the rate of innovation will also be a function of the diversity in the organization.

Resistance to change and the methods to overcome it have been the major preoccupation of a large group of social scientists often identified with the "human relations" approach to organizations. The underlying premise of such an approach is that organizational change can be achieved mainly through changing the behavior of the organization's members (e.g., Lippitt, Watson, and Westley, 1958; Bennis, Benne, and Chin, 1961; Jacques, 1951; Argyris, 1962). This is accomplished primarily through power-equalization whereby management shares its power with those who must implement the innovation, and encourages lower level staff to participate in the decisions about the proposed change (Leavitt, 1965). T-group training has been the major mechanism used to achieve power-equalization.

Nevertheless, as Gross, Giacquinta, and Bernstein (1971) point out, such an approach deals almost exclusively with the initial resistance to change, and minimally with any of the organizational parameters that will ensure successful implementation of the change. We take the view that successful implementation of change in the organization will be accomplished when it can be translated into a series of tasks, incorporated in the organizational technology, and supported by an appropriate division of labor. This implies that the staff must have the knowledge and skill to perform according to the innovation requirements; that the organization must have the necessary resources to accomplish the new tasks; and that the administrative structure must be compatible and supportive of the new task requirements (Gross, Giacquinta, and Bernstein, 1971).

Human service organizations encounter some distinctive issues in relation to organizational change. In contrast to many other organizations, human service organizations increasingly face a turbulent environment characterized by changes in population, community values and expectations, bases of support, and proliferation of other human service organizations. Hence, the environment presents continuous pressures on these organizations to change. Paradoxically, however, human service organizations may fail to respond effectively to these challenges for several reasons.

First, the lack of competition for consumers of the organization's services reduces a major source of pressure for change and leads to inertia. Second, as noted in Chapter X, many human service organizations lack an effective intelligence system to monitor their environment, as well as assess the effectiveness of their own outputs. The organization, hence, may fail to comprehend changes and developments in its environment. In particular, as a result of the use of inadequate and extrinsic measures of performance, the organization may be satisfied with its service outputs irrespective of their effectiveness. Third, human service organizations tend to rely on ideologies in the face of uncertainty. Yet, the greater the reliance on ideologies, the less receptive the organization will be to innovation. Fourth, many human service organizations are highly dependent on external funding and regulatory groups. Yet, the dependence on external groups for resources and support may create barriers to organizational change and innovation.

From our perspective, the major problem human service organizations encounter is the implementation of the innovation, particularly in terms of a new service technology. As Perrow (1965) argues so cogently in the case of mental hospitals, changes in goals and structure cannot alter the basic service modalities of the hospital unless they are accompanied by a viable treatment technology. Hence, we propose that lack of an effective new service technology has been a primary factor in the failure of many human service organizations such as schools and social service agencies to develop significant and viable program innovation. We should also add that in those instances where such a technology exists, the organization may find that external constraints set by key interest groups prevent its adequate implementation.

Hasenfeld identifies some of these dilemmas in his study of the failure of the Community Action Centers to institutionalize an innovative social service model. He attributes the failure to four unresolved organizational and administrative problems: (1) the inability to develop stable bases of support in the community; (2) failure to establish crucial and systematic service linkages with other social service agencies; (3) lack of an effective intelligence system; and (4) difficulties in developing effective staff-client relations.

The article by Corwin, in turn, attempts to examine both interorganizational and intra-organizational properties associated with successful innovation. Based on the analysis of forty-two public schools and ten universities participating in the Teacher Corps Program, Corwin identifies several factors associated with innovation: (1) the quality and interdependence of the boundary personnel of the university and the school—the competence of the university faculty and their political liberalism were key factors in implementing successful innovation; (2) the extent of internal control exercised by the schools through centralization of decision making, emphasis on rules and procedures, and teachers' emphasis on pupil control—this finding is at variance with the findings by Hage and Aiken; (3) the degree of dissonance between the change agents (i.e., interns and school teachers). Contrary to the expectations, dissonance was negatively associated with the introduction of innovation. Overall, Corwin's study indicates that the ability of an organization to change may be a function of its position and linkage with the larger social context.

Hage and Aiken identify intra-organizational properties that are associated with the rate of adoption of new programs in sixteen social service agencies. Their findings indicate that a high rate of program change is associated with a high degree of staff participation in agency-wide decisions, a low degree of job codification, and a high degree of job satisfaction. In addition, they find that the larger the size of the organization and the more time the client spends in it, the higher the rate of program change. This study implies that a human relations model of organization as formulated by Litwak (1961) is most conducive to the adoption or implementation of change.

References

Argyris, C. 1962. *Interpersonal Competence and Organizational Effectiveness*. Homewood, Ill.: Dorsey Press.

Bennis, W. G., Benne, K. D., and Chin, R. (eds.). 1961. *The Planning of Change*. New York: Holt, Rinehart and Winston.

Cloward, R., Epstein, I. 1965. "Private social welfare's disengagement from the poor: The case of family adjustment agencies." Pp. 623–43 in M. Zald (ed.) *Social Welfare Institutions: A Sociological Reader*. New York: Wiley.

Gross, N., Giacquinta, J. B., and Bernstein, M., 1971. *Implementing Organizational Innovations*. New York: Basic Books.

Gusfield, J. R. 1955. "Social Structure and Moral Reform: A Study of the Woman's Christian Temperance Union." *American Journal of Sociology* 61:221–32.

Jacques, E. 1951. *The Changing Culture of a Factory*. London: Tavistock.

Katz, D., and Kahn, R. 1966. *The Social Psychology of Organizations*. New York: Wiley.

Leavitt, H. J. 1965. "Applied Organizational Change in Industry: Structural, Technological, and Humanistic Approaches." Pp. 1143–70 in J. G. March (ed.) *Handbook of Organizations*. Chicago: Rand McNally.

Lippit, R., Watson, J., and Westley, B. 1958. *The Dynamics of Planned Change.* New York: Harcourt, Brace and World.

Litwak, E. 1961. "Models of bureaucracy which permit conflict." *American Journal of Sociology* 67:177–84.

McCleery, R. H. 1957. *Policy Change in Prison Management.* East Lansing: Michigan State University Press.

March, J. G., and Simon, H. A. 1958. *Organizations.* New York: Wiley.

Perrow, C. 1965. "Hospitals, Technology, Structure and Goals." Pp. 910–71 in J. G. March (ed.) *Handbook of Organizations.* Chicago: Rand McNally.

Sills, D. L. 1957. The Volunteers. Glencoe, Ill.: The Free Press.

Terreberry, S. 1968. "The evolution of organizational environments." *Administrative Science Quarterly* 12:590–613.

Thompson, V. 1965. "Bureaucracy and Innovation." *Administrative Science Quarterly* 1:1–20.

Wilensky, H. 1967. *Organizational Intelligence.* New York: Basic Books.

Wilson, J. Q. 1963. "Innovation in organization: notes toward a theory." Pp. 193–218 in J. D. Thompson (ed.) *Approaches to Organizational Design.* Pittsburgh: University of Pittsburgh Press.

Organizational Dilemmas in Innovating Social Services: The Case of Community Action Centers

Yeheskel Hasenfeld

In the aftermath of the War on Poverty, two major competing theories have been put forward to explain the seeming failure of the Community Action Programs. One theory, most explicitly stated by Moynihan (1969), attributes the failure to the unsubstantiated sociological assumptions on the causes of poverty upon which the programs were based, and the ambiguous and conflicting set of objectives they attempted to accomplish (Moynihan, 1965). The competing theory attributes the failure of the Community Action Programs to the political conflicts they generated (Marris and Rein, 1967) and the reluctance to support them, if not the antagonism, of the national and local political establishments (Krosney, 1966).

The study reported here does not attempt to validate either theory. Rather, it suggests that both perspectives fail to adequately consider the organizational and administrative problems that beset these programs and hampered the development of effective service de-

Reprinted from *Journal of Health and Social Behavior* 12 (September, 1971): 208–16.

livery systems. As new organizations attempting to establish innovative social services for the poor, each Community Action Program was called upon to create appropriate organizational mechanisms to implement its mandate. This process of translating an organizational mission into an operative client-servicing system involved a series of critical decisions about the nature of the clientele, the mobilization and allocation of resources, development of ties with other organizations in the community, establishment of a service technology, and the recruitment and training of personnel. Selznick (1957) terms this process the "institutionalization" of the organization. Studies of social service agencies suggest that the degree of institutionalization of the agency is a major factor in determining its effectiveness (Clark, 1956; Vinter, 1967). This is, the ability of the agency to successfully resolve the above-mentioned organizational problems will determine the nature and quality of the service it will offer its clients.

The same perspective needs to be applied to understand the character of the Community Action Programs. Specifically, we feel that the precariousness of many such programs can be attributed, at least in part, to four basic organizational problems they have encountered: (1) the inability to develop stable bases of support in the community; (2) failure to establish crucial and systematic service linkages with other social service agencies, (3) lack of an information system to guide their service functions, and (4) difficulties in developing effective staff-client relations (cf. Kravetz, 1968).

The findings reported here are based on an intensive study of four Community Action Centers (CAC's), in a large metropolitan area. Each center was located in a high-poverty area, and served approximately 850 new clients per month. Information available on the operation and services offered by centers in other cities indicates that the centers studied were quite typical of many urban Community Action Centers (Marris and Rein, 1967; Perlman and Jones, 1967). Data sources for this study included (1) participant observation of the centers for approximately one year, (2) data on clients from a random sample of case files, (3) systematic observations of a sample of client-staff transactions, (4) formal interviewing at all staff levels, and (5) content analysis of agency documents.

Service Objectives

The founders of the Community Action Centers envisioned some of the following service objectives (Kravetz, 1965):

1. To link low-income people to critical resources, such as education, manpower training, counseling, housing, and health.

2. To increase the accessibility of available critical services often beyond the reach of the poor or blocked off by erroneous definitions of their real needs.
3. To create competent communities by developing in and among the poor the capacity for leadership, problem-solving, and participation in the decision-making bodies that affect their lives.
4. To restructure community service institutions to assure flexibility, responsiveness, and respect toward the problems faced by the poor.

To implement these objectives, the CAC was given the major task of seeking out the poor, assessing and evaluating their needs, and officially defining them as "poor." In so doing, the CAC attempted to link the clients and negotiate their referral with a range of agencies and services in the community not hitherto available to the poor, or not previously responsive to their needs. In this respect the CAC functioned as a "broker" organization, utilizing its knowledge, resources, and service linkages to enlist the services of other social welfare agencies on behalf of its clients.

Clearly, even a modest implementation of these objectives presupposed the ability of CAC to enlist the support and legitimation of the agencies and social groups in the environment in which it operated. Yet, the centers encountered serious difficulties in winning this support.

The Inability of the CAC to Develop Stable Bases of Support

The effects of funding problems. The ability of the CAC executive staff to mobilize resources and develop strategies to enhance its acceptance in the community was seriously constrained by its controlling organizations: the Office of Economic Opportunity (OEO) and the city government. The survival of the agency was obviously determined by its ability to compete successfully for OEO funds. Such competition involved not only the need to secure a stable flow of funds for ongoing activities, but also to bid successfully for new fiscal resources. As an agency controlled by the city government, the CAC was under constant political pressure to obtain an ever-increasing share of Federal funds. This was made difficult by the precariousness of the new "antipoverty" ideology that produced serious fiscal discontinuities and uncertainties at the Federal level. These in turn led to continuous *ad hoc* changes in the parameters determining resource allocations to local antipoverty programs.

The CAC executive staff were, therefore, forced to concentrate on what they termed "playing the funding game." Decisions by the executive staff formulating CAC's goals, policies, and activities had to be based largely on funding contingencies. This decision pattern inevitably led to a serious breakdown between the planning and the operating levels of the agency. That is, planning-level activities of the CAC tended to become divorced from those at the operating level since they often had to be governed by funding contingencies and uncertainties rather than by the goal of optimizing effective services to the clients. In particular, the need to formulate general program goals that would be "attractive" in courting fund resources left those at the operation level without a coherent and realistic set of objectives.

Community support. Although the CAC derived its main legitimation from the city government, it was unable to draw support from other critical groups in the community. As shown by Table 1, the staff at the centers perceived those community groups that controlled crucial re-

TABLE 1
CAC Staff Perception of Degree of Support (in Percent)
Program Received from Various Community Groups[a]

	Degree of Support		
Community Group	*A Great Deal*	*Some*	*Little*
The Poor	72	15	13
City Officials	58	26	16
Private Industry	44	29	27
Private Social Service Agencies	35	35	30
State Legislature	28	34	38
Public Social Service Agencies	25	18	57
The Mass Media	23	16	61

[a]Based on responses by 69 staff persons.

sources—the public and private social service agencies, private industry, the mass media, and the state legislature—as providing only limited support to the program. In contrast, the poor themselves, who were obviously powerless, were perceived to support the program strongly.

Several factors have led to the emergence of such a pattern: (1) The CAC executive leadership found it more expedient to rely on the mayor's office for legitimation than to enter into complex and uncertain negotiations to win the support of other groups in the community; (2) the identification of the CAC with the mayor and his political interests considerably narrowed the range and scope of the political support of various community groups for the program; and (3) some of the community groups, such as the various social service agencies, competed with the CAC to obtain OEO funds, and objected to the CAC monopoly on antipoverty programs in the city.

Although the poor were perceived to support the program, relations between the CAC and local resident groups were also precarious. To be sure, the CAC initiated and stimulated the mobilization of local community groups in an effort to implement the goal of "maximum feasible participation of the poor" (see Rubin, 1967). In so doing, however, the CAC executive leadership faced a fundamental dilemma of maintaining its overall stability and coherence while coping with conflicting interests, ideologies, and goals among the community groups it had mobilized.

This dilemma was reinforced by the low level of integration within these citizen groups, which increased the rancor of the conflicts between them and the CAC (Gamson, 1966). Many of the local community representatives had no tradition of regularized participation as partisans in policy decision-making processes; the CAC leadership also lacked experience in negotiating with such groups. In fact, in launching such an experiment of "citizen participation," the CAC had no bases of knowledge from which to draw operating guidelines, and had to "muddle through" the new and unpredictable consequences of "maximum feasible participation." These pressures led the CAC to retreat and seek the protection of the city government and OEO guidelines, thus becoming more and more identified as another established and omnipotent city agency.

A seriously debilitating outcome resulted because the local community representatives, perceiving themselves blocked from participation at the policy level, sought to permeate the agency at its operating level. Their success in doing so deprived the CAC client service system of a buffer against continuous environmental pressures. Community representatives intervened on behalf of clients and dissatisfied personnel, and in the daily management of activities. This undermined administrative efforts to rationalize internal work patterns. Moreover, meetings of the local governing boards of the CAC, when not the scene of personal quarreling among the members, often transformed themselves into staging grounds for attacks against the city. This situation continuously drained the energies and resources of the CAC administrators who tried to work with them.

The Lack of Service Linkages with Other Social Service Agencies

In creating a domain of service, the CAC had to establish a network of exchange relations with a wide range of other social service agencies in the community. The need for cooperative interagency relations is especially crucial for agencies like the CAC in which people-processing functions predominate. That is, staff services in such agencies consist largely of identifying the clients' needs and problems and matching them with appropriate services provided by other community resources.

An elementary precondition for the effectiveness of the CAC was, therefore, the development of multiple exchange relations with other social welfare agencies that would insure service delivery for a wide range of clients' problems and needs. This was especially important since the centers attempted to serve those types of clients who were customarily rejected by existing welfare agencies, who were unable to initiate contacts with such organizations, and who manifested multiproblems requiring coordinated efforts by many units. Nevertheless, our findings show that the centers were ineffective in this endeavor and developed an extremely limited range of exchange relations with other agencies. The only effective referrals they developed were with a medical clinic and an employment placement project, both expressly funded by OEO to serve the centers' clients. As indicated by Table 2, the four centers referred 50 per cent or more of their clients to either of these units.

It is apparent from Table 2 that the centers were deprived of critical service linkages with such agencies as the Welfare Department, local schools, the police, the housing commission, and a host of other agencies that were continuously involved in the lives of the people whom the centers were attempting to help. Nor did the centers succeed in developing vital exchanges with other antipoverty agencies such as Neighborhood Legal Services, Home Services, College-Work Study Program, and various training programs designed for the "hard-core unemployed."

Furthermore, even when the CAC utilized outside agencies such as Civil Service, the State Employment Commission, private employers, and social service agencies as potential contributors for their clients, these agencies made no established arrangements to facilitate transfer of clients and delivery of services to them.

In short, the most crucial resources necessary to insure successful referrals of the Centers' clients, namely linkages with other human service agencies, were severely curtailed. Several factors were responsible for this organizational problem:

1. In order to defend their own domain, the potential referral agencies tended to limit the flow of new service demands upon them. To serve new populations would have taxed their resources, thereby undermining their ability to meet commitments to their existing constituencies.
2. Because of the similarity of goals and functions between the CAC

TABLE 2
Type and Frequency of Referrals (in Percent)
Made by Four Community Action Centers[a]

	Center			
Referral Target	*East*	*West*	*North*	*South*
Employment				
[b] Employment Placement Project	53	33	18	30
State Employment Commission	12	19	25	23
Other Employment Agencies	2	18	–	9
Financial				
Department of Welfare	c	2	3	2
[b] CAC Financial Aid Service	–	2	–	c
Medical				
[b] Medical Clinic	18	15	33	22
Other				
Other OEO Programs	1	2	6	4
Other Social Service Agencies	2	2	6	3
General Counseling	11	6	8	6
Total	100	100	100	100
	(557)	(354)	(309)	(562)

[a] Percentages are rounded off.
[b] Indicates agency is funded by OEO.
[c] Less than 1 percent.

and such agencies, the latter saw themselves competing with the CAC for control of new resources made available through national and local commitments to combat poverty.

3. The executive leadership of the CAC lacked the resources, and failed to use the limited resources it did control, to bargain for privileged exchange relations with various social service agencies.

4. Some of these agencies, such as family service agencies, were unable to adapt to the needs of the poor and withdrew from cooperation with the CAC (Cloward and Epstein, 1965).

5. The lack of organized constituent support and the constraints from local and national regulatory groups made it impossible for the centers to become effective advocates for the poor vis-à-vis other welfare agencies.

6. Finally, the development of viable interorganizational exchange relations necessitated, as a prerequisite, that the CAC obtain information and successfully monitor its environment. Yet the CAC had no adequate information system to routinely collect and disseminate

to staff information about potentially available external resources. As we shall note below, here, too, the CAC had no existing models upon which to draw in designing such a system.

The Inadequacy of the CAC's Information System

The inability of the CAC to develop better service linkages and utilize external resources resulted partly from an inadequate information system. Specifically, the CAC linked an adequate system through which to collect, validate, and communicate information about external resources to personnel. Most staff thus remained uninformed about resources that might be readily accessible. Moreover, even when inventories of external resources were made available to staff, no adequate information retrieval system existed to enable staff to identify the prerequisites clients had to meet to qualify for such services. In addition, no mechanisms existed to update and correct existing inventories. In fact, any research for resources by staff tended to be based on rumors or on *ad hoc* and unvalidated information.

This pattern can be noted from Table 3. In all four centers, with the slight exception in North Center, staff were most likely to obtain information about community resources either through calling the potential resource or by relying on information from coworkers. Needless to say, both devices seriously curtailed the range of the resources the staff could consider and the amount and quality of the information they could obtain about them.

It should be emphasized that this problem pervades most social service agencies (Lemert, 1969; Erikson and Gilbertson, 1969). However, it became most acute in the CAC because of its relative newness and because of its major service function—referring clients to appropriate resources.

TABLE 3
Devices Used by Staff in Each Center (in Percent) to Obtain Information
on Community Resources

Device Used	Center			
	East	West	North	South
Call Referral Target	40	35	27	39
Rely on Past Experience and Training	4	15	17	13
Communication with Coworkers	40	35	21	26
Check Social Service Directory	16	15	35	22
Total	100	100	100	100
Number of Responses	(25)	(20)	(34)	(46)

The lack of a coherent and efficient information system permeated other vital aspects of the organization, particularly vis-à-vis clients. The entire system of intake—gathering, recording, and retrieving information about the client—was designed mainly to meet the external reporting needs of the agency. Minimal attention was paid to the information requirements necessary for proper service decisions for the client.

When transacting with clients, staff had to conform to the information requirements set out for them, and from which they rarely deviated. In so doing, they collected much information that was irrelevant to the immediate service needs, while at the same time important needed information about the client was not obtained.

A factor contributing to these information failures was the inability of the CAC to develop a follow-up system on its clients. In the centers studied, workers received cases to follow-up on a somewhat random basis, with little prior knowledge of the client himself. Although workers were instructed to check with the client whether he had been served or still needed further services, the purpose of the follow-up itself was vague. The time lapse between the client's visit to the center and the follow-up attempt varied widely. The feedback obtained from the follow-up, if any, was usually retained in the client's case file and not communicated to other parts of the organization for proper action.

Structural Problems in the CAC's Staff-Client Relations

Having dealt with some of the critical dilemmas the CAC faced in establishing itself in the community, we shall now assess their impact on the internal structure, procedures, and techniques used by the CAC to process its clients.

Our findings indicate that staff had strong commitments to serve the poor, and a desire to break away from what they termed "bureaucratized" patterns of services. Moreover, many staff members in the CAC exerted consistent efforts in that direction. Yet these commitments and efforts could not neutralize the impact of those organizational and environmental forces that pushed the CAC to adopt a "public welfare department" model of people processing. In other words, the centers (1) developed highly routinized procedures to process clients, (2) reduced the range of client problems to a very narrow set of categories, (3) minimized the number and intensity of staff-client contacts, (4) concentrated on eligibility determination in client processing, and (5) greatly reduced the worker's accountability for the welfare of the client.

The essence of the processing technology derived from the "public welfare department" model could best be described by examining the structure and content of the transactions between staff and clients in the centers. Based on our systematic observations of these transactions and an analysis of clients' case files, we found a number of basic characteristics of such encounters:

1. Transactions between staff and clients almost invariably followed a highly routinized pattern, in which the nature of the encounter was rigidly controlled by the demands of the intake forms that staff had to fill out. Consequently, in most instances the transaction tended to curtail the individualization of the client or his problem.

2. The encounter itself was, typically, a rather fleeting event. Workers were seldom able to make serious attempts to explore the client's situation beyond the minimum requirements of the intake forms, and a wide range of problems or potential problems that would have needed exploring for the referral to be meaningful were seldom touched upon. Workers addressed themselves almost exclusively to the literal terms of the problem or request as initially presented by the client. Thus, for example, a client who came for medical assistance might have disclosed in the interview that she was experiencing a financial hardship because of desertion by her husband and could not keep her job for lack of a child-care arrangement. Yet her only referral would be to the medical clinic, with no further follow-up.

3. The decision process of defining the client's problem or "need" was simplified. Workers relied mainly on the client's definition of the situation and tended to classify his problems within a very narrow range of categories: employment and health. Thus the staff did not consider a vast amount of individual variations and idiosyncrasies. Yet the stream of clients who came to the CAC presented a wide gamut of human problems and needs.

Therefore, it is not surprising to find that, irrespective of the client's presented problem or the referral decision, staff tended to explore the client's biography only as required by the intake form. Systematic observations in two of the centers, for example, showed that the amount of staff exploration did not vary significantly with the type of referral decision. This pattern can be readily seen from Table 4, which indicates that, irrespective of the referral decision, 60 per cent or more of the clients had their biographies explored less than or as much as required by the standardized intake form. The only exception occurred in the greater exploration of the employment background of clients in North Center.

4. Table 4 also suggests that the referral decision was equally simplified and routinized. Decisions about client referrals were made essentially on the basis of age, sex, income, and presenting problems.

Utilizing such a small amount of information about the client led to significant errors in the referral decisions. Clients were occasionally referred to agencies for which they were not eligible on the basis of other attributes, or to agencies that could not handle their underlying problems. Concomitantly, clients often were excluded from the services of various other agencies because the CAC staff lacked the knowledge about these agencies, or about the client's attributes, background, or other characteristics. Thus, clients on occasion were referred to the same agencies that had previously failed to serve them.

5. CAC staff seldom took an active role in engineering the actual routing of clients to the referral agencies. Staff were thus deprived of any meaningful feedback about the adequacy of their referral decisions, which increased the probability of misreferrals. Lack of an active staff role left the clients on their own to negotiate a favorable response from the agencies to which they had been referred.

6. Finally, transactions between staff and clients were so structured that staff accepted a responsibility to the client limited only to the duration of the encounter. Seldom were staff members made accountable for a client beyond the initial intake and disposition. In fact, in all four centers 70 per cent or more of the clients had only one contact with

TABLE 4
Extent of Routine Biographical Exploration[a] (in Percent)
By Type of Referral in East and North Centers

Type of Referral	No. of Cases	Area Explored				
		Employment	Finance	Education	Health	Family Relations
East Center						
Employment Placement Project	(31)	71	90	90	100	87
State Employment Comm.	(24)	79	96	83	100	83
Other Employers	(24)	62	96	87	100	83
Medical Clinic	(16)	88	75	88	87	81
Other Referrals	(11)	90	90	80	100	100
North Center						
Employment Placement Project	(42)	42	78	74	96	55
State Employment Comm.	(36)	50	75	69	94	67
Medical Clinic	(5)	100	60	100	100	60
Other Referrals	(16)	44	69	81	87	56
General Counseling	(11)	66	66	100	100	78

[a]Explored less than or as much as required by the intake form.

their centers. This indicated that once the client was referred to another agency, the staff ceased to monitor his subsequent career.

It should be emphasized that the foregoing pattern of staff-client encounters did not necessarily result from inadequate performance or lack of commitment to the clients. Quite the contrary: While the CAC staff recognized the serious limitations inherent in their transactions with clients, they indicated a sense of frustration in their efforts to modify them. Partly, such a sense of defeatism resulted from the staff's awareness that regardless of the problems clients might display, only a few referral channels were actually available. The lack of systematic linkages with external resources other than the medical clinic and the employment placement project implied that the centers' referrals of clients did not assure a positive response by these agencies. This, in turn, reinforced the passivity of the centers' staff, who tended to share with clients the sense that these external agencies were not effective and came to accept the idea that many clients would not follow through on the referral decisions.

Conclusions

The ideological thrust supporting the establishment of the CAC stemmed from an increased concern among reform groups that the existing welfare system systematically degraded and denied its benefits to many of the urban poor. In particular, there was increased awareness that many of the services designed to help the poor had failed to do so because of the many organizational barriers they presented to the poor. Among these were complicated eligibility criteria, overspecialization and segmentation of services, and lack of coordination and consistency among agencies.

The CAC, in turn, was conceived as an "organizational weapon" that would force changes in the welfare arena. Through its advocacy for a new service ideology toward the poor, the CAC was to undermine the legitimacy and mandate of the existing welfare agencies, pressing them to re-examine their goals and become more responsive to the needs of the poor.

In some measure, the endeavors of the CAC indeed caused changes to take place in the welfare arena. By highlighting the needs of the urban poor that had hitherto remained invisible, the CAC pressured the existing welfare agencies to respond to these needs and to develop new programs. Moreover, through its own example, the CAC moved other welfare agencies to employ indigenous workers and afford their clients a voice in policy decision-making. Yet, at the same time, the CAC experienced organizational difficulties that seriously jeopardized its mission and led it to assume the same characteristics as those of the agencies it wished to modify.

Our analysis indicates that the precariousness of the CAC occurred despite the effort of the staff to effectively serve the poor. The staff alone could not neutralize the adverse structural and environmental conditions that shaped the character of the CAC. Thus, it is at this structural level that intervention must occur if the CAC is to play more than a marginal role in the efforts to combat poverty.

References

Clark, B. 1956. "Organizational adaptation and precarious values." *American Sociological Review* (June):327–336.

Cloward, R. A., and I. Epstein. 1965. "Private social welfare's disengagement from the poor: The case of family adjustment agencies." Pp. 623–643 in Mayer N. Zald (ed.), *Social Welfare Institutions: A Sociological Reader*. New York: Wiley.

Erikson, K. T., and D. E. Gilbertson. 1969. "Case records in the mental hospital." Pp. 389–412 in Stanton Wheeler (ed.), *On Record: Files and Dossiers in American Life*. New York: Russell Sage Foundation.

Gamson, W. 1966. " Rancorous conflict in community politics." *American Sociological Review* (February):71–81.

Kravetz, S. L. 1965. "Community action programs: past, present, future." *American Child* (November):1–6.

———. 1968. "The community action programs in perspective." Pp. 259–283 in Warner Bloomberg Jr. and Henry J. Schmadt (eds.), *Power, Poverty, and Urban Policy*, Beverly Hills: Sage Publications.

Krosney, Herbert. 1966. *Beyond Welfare: Poverty in the Supercity*. New York: Holt, Rinehart.

Lemert, E. M. 1969. "Record in the juvenile court." Pp. 355–387 in Stanton Wheeler (ed.), *On Record: Files and Dossiers in American Life*. New York: Russell Sage Foundation.

Marris, Peter, and Martin Rein. 1967. *Dilemmas of Social Reform*. New York: Atherton Press.

Moynihan, D. P. 1965. "What is community action?" *Public Interest* 7 (Fall):3–8.

———. 1969. *Maximum Feasible Misunderstanding*. New York: Free Press.

Perlman, Robert, and David Jones. 1967. *Neighborhood Service Centers*. Washington: U.S. Department of Health, Education, and Welfare.

Rubin, L. 1967. "Maximum feasible participation: the origins, implications and present status." *Poverty and Human Resources Abstracts* 2 (November-December):5–18.

Selznick, Philip. 1957. *Leadership in Administration*. New York: Harper.

Vinter, R. D. 1967. "The juvenile court as an institution." Pp. 84–90 in *President's Commission on Law Enforcement and Administration of Justice, Task Force Report: Juvenile Delinquency and Youth Crime*. Washington: U.S. Government Printing Office.

Strategies for Organizational Innovation

Ronald G. Corwin

The capacity of modern man to control his destiny in a changing organizational society hinges on his collective ability to deliberately change the key formal organizations. Many attempts to intervene in organizations have been recorded in the human relations literature (Roethlesberger and Dickson, 1939; Coch and French, 1948; Likert, 1961; Bennis, 1966; cf. Leavitt, 1965). This literature reports several attempts to modify organizational structure, usually as a means of improving the task performance of the people (e.g., Morse and Reimer, 1956; Ginzberg and Reilly, 1957; Chapple and Sayles, 1961). However, compared to the importance of the topic, with notable exceptions (McCleery, 1957; Burns and Stalker, 1961; Aiken and Hage, 1970) sociologists have devoted scant attention to the frequent attempts being made today to intervene in organizations (Blau and Scott, 1962). Virtually no consideration has been given to the relative effectiveness of different strategies of reforming organizations. Perhaps because social theorists customarily attributed an independent life to social systems, which often seem beyond the control of man, they have been preoccupied with unplanned social change.

But, the literature can nevertheless suggest some critical concepts and types of variables that might help identify sociological intervention strategies and compare their relative effectiveness. Writers representing diverse and overlapping streams of thought have stressed several types of variables. It has been postulated that an organization can be more easily changed:

> If it is invaded by liberal, creative and unconventional outsiders with fresh perspectives (Gouldner, 1954; McCleery, 1957; March and Simon, 1958; Clark, 1960; Carlson, 1962; Shepard, 1967; Pareto, 1968);
>
> If those outsiders are exposed to creative, competent, flexible socialization agents (Giddings, 1897; Baldwin, 1911; Thomas and Znaniecki, 1918–1920; Cooley, 1922; Dewey, 1922; G. H. Mead, 1934; Newcomb, 1943; Clausen, 1968);
>
> If it is staffed by young, flexible, supportive, and competent boundary personnel, or "gatekeepers" (Tarde, 1890; Kroeber, 1944; Menzel, 1960; Riley and Riley, 1962; Rogers, 1962; Berelson and Steiner, 1964);

Reprinted from *American Sociological Review* 37 (August, 1972):441–54.

If it is structurally complex and decentralized (Durkheim, 1933; Cillie, 1940; March and Simon, 1958; Loomis, 1959; Burns and Stalker, 1961; Wilson, 1963; Berelson and Steiner, 1964; Greiner, 1965; Leavitt, 1965; Carroll, 1967; Sapolsky, 1967; Thompson, 1967; Aiken and Hage, 1968; 1970; Clark, 1968; Evans, 1968);

If it has the outside funds to provide the "organizational" slack necessary to lessen the cost of innovation (Guetzkow, 1965);

If its members have positions that are sufficiently secure and protected from the status risks involved in change (Thompson, 1967);

If it is located in a changing, modern, urbanized setting where it is in close cooperation with a coalition of other cosmopolitan organizations that can supplement its skills and resources (Litwak and Hylton, 1962; Putney, 1962; Wayland, 1964; Clark, 1965; Evans, 1965; Terreberry 1965; Becker and Stafford, 1967; Evan and Black, 1967; Aiken and Hage, 1968; Turk, 1970).

These variables pertain to characteristics of new members, of the socialization agents, of the boundary personnel, of the organizational structure, of the resource pool, of the members' status and of the organization's social and interorganizational context. The antecedents can be traced to several overlapping macro-theories of change identified by Hagen (1962); Moore (1963); Smelser (1967); Applebaum (1970), and others.

Setting of the Study

Because many government programs are attempting to manipulate precisely the structural variables which theory suggests are important, they should be of central interest to sociologists. The data reported here were taken from a larger, longitudinal study of the Teacher Corps, a nationwide, multi-million dollar government program whose aim is to promote educational reforms in low income schools through innovative teacher training programs, especially by opening a path to teaching for liberal arts graduates and members of minority groups who otherwise might not have entered the profession.[1] Because it was designed to attack complex social problems on a national scale, the program has tried to mobilize a coalition of organizations, each of which contributes special resources and skills to improve teaching in low income schools.

A special two-year internship allows interns to be employed in several cooperating public schools, while attending college parttime. Colleges of education are expected to experiment with curriculum and personnel policies, and to establish cooperative relationships with schools and communities and with other departments in the university. In the words of one Teacher Corps brochure, the program seeks to use the team approach for training purposes, to provide for special and continuous supervision of interns, to incorporate the spirit of the Peace Corps, to establish a closer relationship between theory and practice, to set up a route into teaching for some who might otherwise have been excluded, and to involve the community as a training ground by extending the walls of the classroom into the community. The program is divisible into two main parts and several components: a pre-service program for interns, which includes graduate courses in education as well as some observation of schools and/or the community; and a tri-partite, in-service period consisting of university study, a practical internship in poverty schools and experience with poverty children and their families in the community.

Typically, a group of thirty to fifty liberal arts graduates (interns) and several experienced teachers who serve as team leaders receive about eight weeks of special pre-service training at a college or university. Following pre-service the group is broken into four to six teams composed of three to eight interns and one team leader. Each team is assigned to a school serving a poverty area, usually an elementary school where they spend 60 percent or more of their time on a weekly basis. In the beginning they may work with small groups of students on specific lesson plans. As they gain experience, their tasks become more complex. They have experimented with cross-age tutoring, socio-drama, multi-ethnic centers, black history courses, multi-lingual programs, etc. They are expected to spend about 20 percent of their time with academic coursework at the university, which includes inter-disciplinary work in the social sciences as well as in colleges of education, and leads to teacher certification and a masters degree in two years. Finally, the interns are supposed to devote about 20 percent of their time on community activities, conducting surveys, working with social agencies, visiting parents, and participating in civic and (sometimes) political activities to familiarize themselves with the environment in which their students have grown up, and to try to bridge the gap between the school and the low income community it serves.

There has been a pervasive goal conflict between the national office, which stresses the objective of educational reform (Graham, 1968), and the local schools which attempt to use the resources provided by the Teacher Corps to supplement their existing programs. The assumptions of this program are at variance with the traditional training model, which holds veteran professionals responsible for socializing the novices. Interns have been led to view themselves as autonomous colleagues of the experienced teachers and as agents of change, a view that is not shared by most teachers and many professors, who insist on placing the interns in traditional teacher-trainee roles. More fundamentally, the entire program attempts to act as a unique type of change agent, consisting of a complex network of organizations acting in concert and designed to promote innovation within member organizations and in organizations outside the immediate network. Generally, the literature has overlooked organizations in the role of agents of change intent on changing other organizations. But the literature on interorganizational relationships (Aiken and Hage, 1968) provides a starting point, and the Teacher Corps can be used as one strategic case.

Procedures

The Sample

Ten universities with Teacher Corps programs and forty-two cooperating schools were visited for one week by teams of interviewers during the fall and winter of 1968–1969.[2] The ten programs were purposively selected from thirty-five scheduled for operation in the fall of 1968, and represented a range of types and reputed quality.[3] Rural and urban programs in every region of the country are represented in the sample; four of the programs service Negro children and two service Mexican-Americans and Indians.

Indicators and Measures

Thirty-seven indicators were used to guide the collection of data treating some of the concepts and variables identified earlier. In effect, these indicators represent the independent variables in this analysis. A more detailed account of them and the rationale for their selection is presented elsewhere (Corwin, forthcoming). It will suffice here to acknowledge the problems involved in relating concepts to indicators, and the looseness of fit between the two in the social sciences (see Torgerson, 1958). The thirty-seven variables, which were assumed to be proxies for more complex phenomena, in turn were operationalized in terms of measures presented in Figure 1. They are grouped in the table according to the face validity initially used.

The dependent variable is technological change in schools. Each school was given a score based on all reported or observed intended and unintended changes, weighted for the "innovativeness" of each change (rated by two judges). Each innovation was scored on a three-point scale on each of five dimensions: new classroom methods, new materials, changed relationships with clientele, the addition of implementing per-

Figure 1: Indicators

I. INDICATORS ASSOCIATED WITH CHARACTERISTICS OF NEW MEMBERS

1. Mean political liberalism of interns

A nine-item Likert scale assessing political attitudes toward public policies (e.g., toward the welfare state). Split-half reliability, $r = .60$ adapted from a scale developed by Peterson.

2. Interns' emphasis on pupil control

Five Likert items concerning attitude toward the rights of students to govern their own conduct and to participation in school policy decisions. Mean inter-item correlation, $r = .33$.

3. Difference in political liberalism of teachers and interns

Mean difference in (1).

4. Proportion of interns with liberal arts major

Percent of all interns in the school who have liberal arts major

5. Quality of interns' undergraduate college

Colleges in the program rated on a combined index of college resources (e.g., percent of Ph.D.'s and five other indicators) and selectivity of the student body. Based on work by Nash (1969) and Cass and Birnbaum (1970–71).

6. Mean percentage difference in status of interns and teachers in education, race, and sex

Percentage differences between teachers and interns in each school based on race, sex, education level and length of time in the region.

II. INDICATORS ASSOCIATED WITH CHARACTERISTICS OF THE BOUNDARY PERSONNEL

7. Proportion of university faculty who consider themselves very liberal politically

Proportion of respondents in each school or college who identified themselves as radical or highly liberal (as opposed to moderately liberal or moderately or highly conservative); significantly correlated with scale distributions.

8. Political liberalism of the team leader

Same as above (7).

9. Competence of the school principal

Ratings of interns' supervisors by interns and other teachers in the school on six Likert-type items. Mean inter-item correlation $r = .56$.

Figure 1 (cont.)

10. Political liberalism of the classroom teachers

Same as (1).

11. Principals' support of the program

One Likert item describing interns', team leaders' and classroom teachers' opinions on the principal's support of the program.

12. Tenure of the principal

Total number of years in the school.

III. INDICATORS ASSOCIATED WITH CHARACTERISTICS OF THE SOCIALIZATION AGENTS

13. Interns' satisfaction with university faculty

The mean scores of interns on a six-item Likert scale assessing their esteem toward their professors. (Mean inter-item correlation $r = .48$ adapted from a scale developed by Peterson).

14. Quality of the university

Same as (5).

15. Quality of school

Combined ratings of interns and teachers on four Likert items concerning level of satisfaction with the quality of teachers, administration, materials and pupils in the school. (Mean inter-item correlation, $r = .61$).

16. Competence of the team leader

Same as (9).

17. Teachers' emphasis on pupil control

Same as (2).

18. Proportion of teachers who prefer creative teachers

Proportion in each school who prefer the "creative" type of teacher over three other types described in short paragraphs; types differ on the emphasis placed on subject matter and on the exercise of adult authority (developed by Sieber and Wilder, (1967).

IV. INDICATORS ASSOCIATED WITH THE ORGANIZATIONAL STRUCTURE

19. Centralization of decision making within the school

Combined estimate of teachers and principals about where in the school or system final decisions are made about seven issues (such as permission to use team teaching).

20. Size of the university

Student enrollment.

21. Size of the school

Student enrollment.

22. Proportion of teachers who participated in the proposal

Based on self reports, by school.

Figure 1 (cont.)

V. INDICATORS OF RESOURCES AVAILABLE

23. Ratio of federal funds allocated for the program per intern — Total funds divided by number of interns.

VI. INDICATORS OF STATUS SECURITY

24. Proportion of program funds controlled by the local school — Percent of total Teacher Corps budget allocated to school.
25. Proportion of teachers who are members of union — Based on self report, by school.
26. Professional orientation of classroom teachers — School means on a 16 item Likert scale measure four role segments: orientation to the client and to colleagues, and emphasis on teachers' decision-making authority, and on knowledge as a basis of competence; split-half reliability $r_n = .65$.
27. Client orientation of teachers
27. Client orientation of teachers — Sub scale of the above (26).
28. Administrative orientation of classroom teachers — Six Likert items concerning an individual's expressed loyalty to the school administration. Split-half reliability, $r = .81$ (Corwin, 1970).
29. Quality of teachers' undergraduate college — Same as (5).
30. Proportion of teachers with an M.A. degree — Based on self reports, by school.
31. Rules and procedures orientation of classroom teachers — School means on two sub-scales consisting of twelve Likert items, loyalty to the administration ($r_n = .81$) and emphasis on rules and procedures ($r_n = .84$).

VII. INDICATORS OF THE SOCIAL AND INTER-ORGANIZATIONAL CONTEXT

32. Cooperation between the school and college — From a content analysis of interviews, each school was assigned a weighted score based on three dimensions: the frequency of its contact with the local college, the quality of the relationship and the amount of cooperation.
33. Modernization of the state — Level of economic and social modernization of each of the ten states in which the programs are located, based on a six component index developed through a factor analysis by Herriott and Hodgkins (1969).
34. Number of other training programs at the college — Highest number reported.
35. Size of the city — U.S. Census, metropolitan area.

sonnel, and extra-curricular activities. The weighting was based on the assumption that changes requiring altered or new social relationships and those affecting the basic curriculum are of greater importance than additive changes or changes in extra-curricular activities or other peripheral activities. Thus, team teaching, the introduction of black history, mixed-age grouping, and the use of indigenous laymen, received higher weights than did the use of films or the establishment of a new photography club, for example. A similar procedure was used for weighting secondary changes which, in addition to the above dimensions, included reports of improved attitudes on the part of students or professors or teachers. A school's score, then, is a product of the number of planned and unplanned innovations times the weights assigned to each dimension of change that applied to that innovation.[4]

Analysis

The analysis of data was organized around three steps. First, the degree and direction of association among the dependent and independent variables was computed. In addition to examining these relations, this step was undertaken to reduce the number of independent variables by eliminating any found to correlate highly with others.

The second step was to submit the thirty-seven independent variables to factor analysis. As was noted earlier, the explanatory perspectives used to delineate indicators overlap considerably; and the indicators themselves were selected and grouped primarily on face validity. The objective of the factor analysis was to identify inductively the common factors underlying the thirty-seven independent variables. The result was that (a) concepts were refined by identifying constructs more closely fitting the indicators and measures, and (b) the explanation of organizational innovation was clarified by reducing the multiplicity of independent variables to a few salient and more abstract factors.

The third step in the analysis was to examine the amount of variance in the dependent variable explained by the emergent factors individually and collectively. This step was accomplished through regression analysis.

Intercorrelation Among the Variables

The magnitude of correlations among the independent variables ranges from .00 to −.98. There was not a sufficiently high correlation among a significant number of variables to warrant, making many substitutions.

The Independent Factors

All variables were submitted, ungrouped, to an oblique factor analysis. This procedure yielded seven dimensions (see Table 1).

The first factor refers to the social context of the training program. Four of the components refer to characteristics of the university (its size and quality); two pertain to characteristics of the local community and region (size and modernization). Large and competent organizations probably are characteristically found in modernized social settings.

The second factor reflects the teaching staff's cosmopolitanism and independence of judgment. The teachers' professionalism refers to the emphasis they place on their right and technical competence to make decisions, especially their responsibility for the students' welfare. The fact that such teachers do not exhibit a strong sense of loyalty to the school administration, coupled with their political liberalism, are qualities indicative (a) of their ability to act independently of established authority structures and (b) of their receptivity to social change.

The third factor pertains to the amount of emphasis the organization places on maintaining internal control through controlling pupils, rules, and centralized decision making; the difficulty of maintaining control is probably associated with organizational size. The proportion of program funds, controlled by the schools indicates the amount of control they exercise over the program (relative to the college's influence).

Factor four pertains to the school administration's competence and the administrative support given to the program. It consists of the principal's competence rating, his years of experience, the quality of his school, and his willingness to support the program.

The nature of the interorganizational relations between the schools and colleges is tapped by factor five. Characteristics of the boundary personnel hold the key to the relationship. The factor includes the competence and liberalism of the university faculty and of the team leader at the school and the amount of cooperation between the two institutions.

The sixth factor concerns the status of the teaching staff, as reflected in their level of formal education, the quality of their undergraduate college, and the strength of their influence on the program proposal.

The last factor is comprised of the interns' characteristics, most of which reflect basic differences between them and the typical classroom teacher in the sample. The interns tended to be more liberal politically, to have graduated from better colleges and to place less emphasis on pupil control; and the two groups differed typically in race, sex, and level of education.

Explaining the Variance in Organizational Innovation

The seven factors account for 51 percent of the variance (Table 2). Three factors account for most of the explained variance (48 percent): (1) the quality and interdependence of the boundary personnel, which refers to characteristics of the university faculty and team leaders, including the cooperation between them ($B = .59$) (2) the organizational control exercised by the school ($B = -.23$); and (3) the uniqueness of the outside change agents ($B = -.39$). The status of the teaching staff ($B = -.10$), the quality and modernization of the context ($B = -.16$), the competence of the administration ($B = .11$) and the professionalism and social liberalism of the staff ($B = .01$) contribute little to the explanation once the first three factors have been considered.

Discussion

Relationship to the University. The most salient factor, then, is the quality and interdependence of the boundary personnel. This factor consists of four variables: the competence of the university faculty members (as rated by the interns); the faculty members' political liberalism (based on their own self-identity); the extent of cooperation between the school and the university (assessed from a content analysis of the interviews); and the competence of the experienced teacher-supervisors, the team leaders (based on the combined ratings of teachers and interns). In this connection, an inspection of Table 1 suggests that interns' ratings of the faculty members' competence ($r = .53$) and the faculty's political liberalism ($r = .66$) are probably more important than either the university's prestige or its resources. Perhaps the better universities are too socially remote and too well integrated into the academic system to have developed the interest or competence for this kind of problem. Also, the better colleges tend to attract more liberal arts majors ($r = .61$) from better undergraduate colleges ($r = .70$)—factors which already have been reported to be negatively associated with innovation (not reported in tables).

The overriding importance of the university faculty supports the contention of some writers that organizations change primarily in response to an outside stimulus. But, more specifically, it reinforces the generally acknowledged significance of interorganizational relationships, and underscores the crucial role played by boundary personnel in par-

TABLE 1

Component Loadings of Seven Factors Yield by an Oblique Factor Analysis*

1. Quality & Modernization of Context

Size of university	(−.79)	(r = .32)
Quality of university	(−.90)	(r = −.17)
Modernization of region	(−.91)	(r = .13)
No. of other training programs	(−.69)	(r = −.02)
Federal funds allocated per intern	(−.63)	(r = .39)
Size of city	(−.94)	(r = .19)

2. Professionalism & Social Liberalism of Staff

Professional orientation—teachers	(.83)	(r = −.05)
Administrative orientation—teachers	(−.42)	(r = .28)
Liberalism—teachers	(.43)	(r = −.12)
Client orientation—teachers	(.86)	(r = −.05)
Liberalism of the team leader	(.57)	(r = .43)

3. Organizational Control by the Schools

Teachers' emphasis on pupil control	(.81)	(r = −.11)
Rules & procedures orientation—teachers	(.43)	(r = .04)
Centralization of decision-making	(.75)	(r = .33)
Proportion of program funds locally controlled	(.63)	(r = −.33)
Size of school	(−.65)	(r = −.09)

4. Competence of the Administration

Principals' support for program	(−.72)	(r = −.05)
Competence of the principal	(−.86)	(r = −.15)
Quality of the school	(−.75)	(r = −.07)
Tenure of the principal	(.22)	(r = .02)

5. Quality & Interdependence of Boundary Personnel

Interns' satisfaction with university faculty	(.66)	(r = .53)
Proportion of university faculty who consider themselves very liberal politically	(.37)	(r = .66)
Cooperation between school & college	(.93)	(r = .35)
Competence of the team leader	(.29)	(r = −.01)

6. Status of Teaching Staff

Proportion of teachers with MA degree	(−.91)	(r = .10)
Quality of teachers' undergraduate college	(−.44)	(r = .14)
Proportion of teachers in the union	(−.63)	(r = .25)
Proportion of teachers who participate in proposal	(−.52)	(r = −.26)

7. Uniqueness of Outsiders

Political liberalism of interns	(−.62)	(r = −.32)
Proportion of interns with liberal arts major	(−.92)	(r = −.19)
Interns' emphasis on pupil control	(.57)	(r = .20)
Difference in political liberalism between teachers & interns	(−.46)	(r = −.16)
Quality of interns' undergraduate college	(−.73)	(r = .12)
Difference in status of teachers & interns based on education, race, & sex	(−.56)	(r = −.32)

* The first figure (in parentheses) refers to the factor component loading from the rotated matrix. The second figure (in parentheses) refers to the zero-order correlation between each independent variable and the dependent variable.

ticular, in this case represented by the school's team leaders and the university faculty members. In this sense, the findings support the diffusion approach with its emphasis on the importance of the openness of boundary personnel to change. While the technical competence of the occupants of both boundary roles appears to be important, the attitude climate set by the university faculty seems to be even more important.[5]

The dominating role of the university can be attributed to several sources. First, compared to schools, universities are more cosmopolitan, relying on regional or national financial and recruiting bases, and exporting their products throughout the nation and the world. In addition to this institutional base, faculty members probably tend to be more professionalized than teachers and less tied into the local political structure. Moreover, they have less investment in the existing technology of the schools (as opposed to their investment in their own institutions). Finally, the fact that universities are the prime contractors for this program, the program director being a faculty member, enhances the university's influence. However, this leverage for change, no matter how great, cannot be applied unless there is a channel through which the university can exert its influence, that is, a working relationship between the universities and schools. Competent and receptive team leaders are a necessary component of such a channel.

Comparison with Other Environmental Conditions. To put it another way, the major dimension of the environment contributing to innovation is the amount of cooperation between the school and the university. With that factor controlled, modernization of the state makes only a small contribution. There is some support for the contention that innovation can be promoted by adding outside resources, although in this case the volume of total funds is less important ($r_p = .11$) than the relative level of funding provided for each new trainee ($r_p = .40$). (Figures not reported in the tables.) There is, however, slightly more change in schools associated with larger universities ($r = .32$), but these variables are relatively unimportant compared to other factors examined. That the number of training programs at the university is inversely associated with program change ($r_p = -.40$) (not reported) suggests that the proposition that change occurs more readily in otherwise changing environments needs to be reconsidered. Perhaps we should allow for a ceiling effect, that is, the fact that it is also more difficult for a given program to make additional changes when there is already a high rate of change.[6]

Organizational Control. The second critical factor is the extent of internal control exercised by schools, consisting of four variables: centralization of the school system's decision-making structure; stress which

TABLE 2

Seven Factors Correlated with the Introduction of New Technologies
into Schools: Oblique Step-Wise Regression Analysis ($N = 43$)

No.	Factors (Title)	r.	R^2	R^2 added	Par- tial	T- Value	Beta Weight	F
5	Quality & Interdependence of Boundary Personnel	.64	.405	—	.600	4.37	.588	27.22
3	Organizational Control Exercised by the Schools	—.26	.445	.040	—.301	1.84	—.228	2.79
7	Uniqueness of Outside Change Agents	—.13	.475	.030	—.304	1.86	—.388	2.18
6	Status of Teaching Staff	.07	.493	.018	—.095	.56	—.095	1.34
1	Quality & Modernization of Context	.17	.503	.010	.155	.91	.161	.69
4	Competence of Administration	.08	.507	.004	.093	.55	.109	.31
2	Professionalism & Social Liberalism of Staff	—.10	.507	.000	.019	.11	.014	.01

classroom teachers and administrators place on rules and procedures; emphasis which teachers place on pupil control (i.e., strict discipline); and the proportion of program funds controlled by the schools.

This factor reflects the other side of the coin, i.e., the capacity of the cooperating, host organization to filter and shape the changes proposed by the cooperating outside organization. The first two variables form a "containment dimension," through which an organization develops the capacity to control its members and which determines how effectively it can regulate its members' reactions to proposed changes. Note that these two variables operate in opposite directions and that the positive correlation between the centralization of the decision-making structure and technological change ($r = .33$) is at variance with the widely held assumption that decentralized systems are more adaptable. The higher administration was usually responsible for introducing this program to the schools. Under these conditions, the more that power is concentrated at the top, the more effective the program will be (Griffiths, 1964). In other words, a centralized organization does not for that reason necessarily resist change; rather, centralization gives it the capacity to select and enforce innovations as well as to resist them. At the same time, where teachers emphasize classroom discipline, it probably both reflects and reinforces strong administrative control.

The tendency for innovations to decline as the proportion of funds controlled by the local schools increases ($r = -.33$) reflects the conflict in goals between these two institutions. Control over the funds is a lever for coopting the program. Schools tried to use funds to supplement their existing programs rather than to innovate. There may have been a slight tendency for the more competent principals to gain more control over program funds ($r = .22$) (not reported). While it is probably true that educational decisions are moving up and out, placing initiative outside the local system (Clark, 1965), local school boards often maintain final veto power over changes they do not want.

The Role of Dissonant Change Agents. The third factor reflects the amount of dissonance between the change agents and the members of the host organization. But contrary to the theory, the correlation is negative. Independent field observations and interviews also confirmed that interns were often a source of friction and tension in the local schools, and that schools tended to react defensively when even a few of these critical, liberal, change-oriented newcomers were introduced.[7] Perhaps the resulting conflict was not entirely counter-productive. There were small positive correlations between innovation and (a) the amount of conflict between interns and other members of the program ($r = .26$), and (b) the number of teachers reporting that the program had created problems for them ($r = .22$) (not reported). These correlations support the notion that conflict often accompanies change. But the fact that the correlations are not higher also suggests that conflict does not necessarily produce extensive change under certain circumstances.

Professional Competence. Finally, despite the theoretical importance one might attribute to variables relating to the professionalism and competence of the administrators and teachers, these variables were less important than the characteristics of other boundary personnel more directly associated with the program. Teachers' participation in the proposal is the other side of administrative centralization discussed above and is related to the dimension of teachers' competence. Their participation had only a minor effect; and contrary to usual expectations and findings from other studies (Aiken and Hage, 1970), the small effect which does appear is negative ($r = -.26$). The power equalization model presumes that changes are produced from the consent of the parties involved. However, some innovations are forced into a system, which arouses the incumbents' suspicion or opposition. This was often the case in this program. When subordinates fail to agree on the objectives or strategies of these proposed changes, but are relatively professionalized, their participation in the decisions places them in a better position to sabotage the innovation (Mulder, 1971); and under conditions when their participation is only nominal, the strategy can backfire by producing unrealistic expectations (Lefton, Dinitz and Pasamanick, 1959). Thus, this strategy can inhibit as well as promote innovation, depending on the initial balance of power, the degree of consensus, and the status threat involved.

It appears that neither (a) status security, as reflected in the teachers' competence, or (b) their professionalism promote change, judging from the negative correlation in the first instance and the low correlation in the second. Perhaps even more important note that, in view of the theoretical importance often attributed to the more generic social context, the characteristics which made up the quality and the modernization of the school context did not explain much. Again, the more immediate organization context reflected in the cooperation with the university, appeared to take precedence over these more general context variables.

These latter findings may have implications for the current decentralization issue concerning demands for community control being made by ghetto residents in large cities. On the one hand, the data support critics' contentions that the professionalism and technical competence of teachers in itself is no assurance that efforts will be made to improve the schools. On the other hand, administrative decentralization could reduce the capacity of central administrators to impose change from the top down; and more important, perhaps the whole controversy over the schools' relationship with their communities has eclipsed an equally important relationship—namely the relationship of the schools with innovative universities.

Summary and Discussion

The findings should be interpreted with caution in view of the necessarily crude ways in which some of the complex concepts were measured. But a comparative analysis of alternative explanations, despite its tentativeness, points the way to more systematic models of organizational innovation. Toward this end, by drawing on the assumptions of other writers (Gouldner, 1970; Gerard, 1957; Clark, 1968) and by extrapolating from the tentative findings reported here, we shall offer some general propositions:

> 1. *the way an innovation is conceived and implemented is a product of a combination of forces inside and outside the organization.* Organizations exist in an environment of constraint; and therefore, the success or failure of an innovation will vary with the context in which it is introduced. This might include characteristics such as the quality of the institutions involved and modernization of the region,

but at least in this case the data indicated that the characteristics of the general organizational network were the environment's most salient aspects. More specifically, technological innovation was a product of a balance of power between strong but interdependent organizations. The necessary ingredients include: (a) a dominant outside organization staffed by competent and liberal members; (b) competent, receptive boundary personnel in the host organization; and (c) functional interdependence and channels for cooperation to take place. These conditions can be reformulated to apply to characteristics of the organizational set itself: i.e., there will be more technological change in organizational networks in which there is unequal balance of power, but a high degree of interdependence among the organizations, and in which boundary roles are staffed by cosmopolitan, liberal, and professionally competent members.

2. *characteristics of both occupation and organization must be taken into account in order to explain innovation.* That is, the outcomes of attempts to change an occupation are conditioned by the characteristics of its organizational context, such as the centralization of the decision-making structure and standardization; whereas organizational innovations are influenced by the characteristics of the occupational group, such as in this instance, the teachers' emphasis on pupil control. However, in this study, the competence, professionalism and social liberalism of the rank-and-file professionals in the host organization were less important than either the comparable characteristics of the boundary personnel or the characteristics of the organizational structure.

3. *a split develops between the established leaders of the profession and a new generation.* The latter is identified with outside leaders, who stand to gain from new roles that promise to open new channels of success and to circumvent the status monopoly controlled by traditionalists. Conversely, since the proposed changes would redistribute existing tasks that were formerly the responsibility of other units, the newcomers are resisted; a dialectic develops in which the traditional, conservative procedures are reasserted or slightly adapted in order to compete with new procedures.

This last point deserves further comment. An attempt to influence the change process by introducing change agents as an independent force can be effective only under limited conditions, which were not present in this case. Even with the two most influential factors controlled, the more liberal the interns in a school, the less innovation that occurred. This fact indicates that their ineffectiveness was not simply a product of the institutional balance of power, but was inherent to the strategy itself as employed in this program. The program's tactics of course, provide an extreme test of the replacement approach. The attempt to marry the change-agent roles to the apprenticeship system placed the interns in a precarious position between two powerful organizations. They were representatives of the outside organization in the schools (i.e. the university), but could count on little direct support from remote university professors; while, they were directly supervised by defensive teachers. Sensing this resistance to them, and often finding the schools conservative toward change, in most programs a vocal minority of interns resorted to confrontation tactics. However, the conflict theory of change presumes a balance of power which did not exist in this case. As inexperienced newcomers to the profession, still in training and temporarily assigned to schools under direct supervision of experienced teachers, the interns could not gain leverage within the schools—even though, ironically, these very characteristics enabled them to maintain the autonomy which encouraged them to take risks involved in promoting change. Nor did the interns constitute a sufficiently critical mass in any of the schools to provide power from numbers or to promote the development of a strong peer group. They were so outnumbered and overwhelmed by the structural defenses available to school administrators and teachers that the schools were able to neutralize their efforts. Indeed, the interns' militancy gave the teachers little latitude to compromise without jeopardizing their authority, which created a win-lose situation. Teachers retaliated by completely withdrawing their support for interns' proposals. Thus, while some change accompanied conflict, the fact that interns had little leverage from which to wage a successful conflict helps explain the negative correlation between technological change and the proportion of liberal arts interns in the program.

This suggests that two additional conditions must be present which were not present in this case: (a) the change agents must be introduced in sufficiently large numbers, and (b) at more than one echelon in the hierarchy. The impact might have been modified either by assigning a higher ratio of interns to each school, or by recruiting interns into the administrative ranks. But in any event, the experience in this program suggests that caution should be exercised in using the replacement strategy for innovation without further examining the conditions under which it can be successful.

In conclusion, explaining technological innovation requires a *combination* of several conceptual approaches. The pattern of variables identified here has moved beyond the framework which initially guided the study design. It appears that there is a great deal of both truth and fiction in the various streams of thought which served as the original guidelines. The various types of variables seem to supplement one another. But, even in combination, the variables explored here explain only part of the total variance. Some strategies may be more effective than others, but the crucial element seems to be the way they interact. The conditions under which any given strategy is applied, that is, the situation into which an innovation is introduced, seems to be as crucial as the strategy itself. Perhaps the fundamental dimension underlying the variables considered here is the way local organizations are insulated from, or integrated into, the larger context. Thus, decentralization gives local interests leverage over unwanted changes, while centralization more closely links the system to the broader system, as do institutional cooperation and liberal and competent boundary personnel. Future research will have to give more attention to the conditions which enable organizations to maintain functional autonomy within an increasingly interdependent, changing society (Gouldner, 1959, Katz 1968).

Notes

1. Chi square analyses of a battery of opinion items and scales indicated that, compared to other new teachers (N=162) and experienced teachers (N=578), the interns (N=158) more closely conformed to a liberal, humanitarian, ideal type of teacher. Specifically, they came disproportionately from professional, technical, and managerial homes; expressed less loyalty to the school administration; were more politically liberal and held less conservative opinions; were more likely to want to work in radically integrated schools; more often expected to continue teaching in poverty area schools; identified more closely with students' interests; subscribed to a more *laissez faire* attitude toward student discipline in the classroom; placed more emphasis on developing the creative capacities of children and allowing them to do what they think is important (compared to teaching knowledge of subject matter or respecting authority or following instructions); and expressed more confidence in the ability of their pupils to learn and to graduate from high school.

2. The following universities were included in the study: University of Miami, St. Cloud State College, Pacific Lutheran University, Livingston State University, University of Missouri at Kansas City, University of Southern California, University of Nebraska at Omaha, New Mexico State University, Temple University, and East Tennessee State University. The total questionnaire sample includes: 266 interns, 872 classroom teachers, 53 team leaders, 60 principals and other school administrators, 100 graduate students in education not in the Teacher Corps, and 45 university faculty members, deans, and program directors. On the second visits questionnaires were returned by 117 interns, 24 team leaders, 107 teachers cooperating in the program, 26 principals and other administrators, and 31 university faculty members and program directors. Nine-hundred and thirty-two persons were interviewed on the first visit and 186 were interviewed twice. The average rate of questionnaire return on the first visit was 73%, and for the second visit, 92%. In addition to the four experimental schools at each location, a "comparison" school was included in the study, which was not participating in the Teacher Corps but which was matched as closely as possible to the participating schools (on the basis

of their mean proportion of students from families at the poverty level, racial compositions of faculty and student body, and proportion of teachers with advanced degrees). These do not, of course, constitute a control group in any rigorous sense; and in any event, space precludes systematic discussion of these results here except to note that the results do not change the conclusions and added too little to the interpretation to warrant inclusion here. However, anticipating the following analysis, one finding may be worth noting here: on the measure of "organizational flexibility," the comparison schools were more *receptive* to change than the participating schools; but on the measure of innovation, they were actually undergoing *less actual change*. From our interviews and observations, it appeared that on the one hand, the receptivity of the comparison schools had not been dampened by the aggressiveness of interns who had threatened teachers in the participating schools; organizational flexibility was inversely correlated with the predisposition of the interns to take initiative, the proportion who were males, who majored in the liberal arts, who identified themselves as politically very liberal, and who preferred the creative type of teacher. These characteristics account for 58 percent of the variance; while characteristics of the schools and teachers accounted for only 6 percent. On the other hand, Teacher Corps teams, under the leadership of team leaders and with the cooperation of universities, often provided a catalyst to translate the potential for change into action, a factor that was not present in the comparison schools.

3. The reputed quality of the local program was based on ratings by the staff at the national Teacher Corps headquarters in Washington and by a panel which rated programs for refunding. In view of the small number of cases, it was decided to avoid programs that were reportedly failing and would not be likely to produce any change at all. None of the programs was rated poor at the time of selection and all were ranked in the upper third of the programs. The cooperating *schools* at each program were selected on a random basis when more than four schools were participating.

4. Elizabeth Hanna supervised this phase of the coding. The term, innovation, has been used in a variety of ways (cf. Hage and Dewar, 1971; Becker and Whisler, 1967). It is viewed here as a variable pertaining primarily to a deliberate change in structural relationships and procedures in a particular organization that could lead secondarily to changed outputs. Carroll (1967) used a comparable procedure to rate the innovativeness of curriculum changes in a medical school in terms of the extent of restructuring of relationships among the faculty and students required by the change. Another procedure was used by Evan and Black (1967) who asked respondents to describe one proposal that had been implemented and one that had been rejected by management. Most other investigators have used check lists to indicate the presence or absence of specific types of innovations (Becker and Stafford, 1967) or have asked executives to list the number of new programs and services implemented (Hage and Aiken, 1967; Hage and Dewar, 1971). The latter investigators used follow-up questions to distinguish an expansion of existing services from new programs.

5. Even with the proportion of interns having liberal arts degrees and the amount of cooperation between the school and college controlled, the liberalism of the university faculty continues to contribute .50 to the R^2; whereas once these three variables have been controlled, faculty members' competence adds little more (R^2 added = .02).

6. The number of other training programs ranged from one (at one university) to six (at two others); the typical college of education had between three and four separate training programs.

7. That the presence of unconventional, change-oriented newcomers created problems in the schools is reflected in three other analyses. The characteristics of interns contributed to the explanation of both (a) the number of conflict incidents reported among members of the program, and (b) the proportion of teachers reporting that the program had created problems for them. The difference in the liberalism of the interns and teachers, and the proportion of liberal arts majors were both correlated with each variable. The defensiveness of schools in the face of this conflict is also revealed in (c) parallel effects which the presence of liberal newcomers appears to have had in promoting organizational inflexibility; five characteristics of the interns explain more than half the variance ($R^2 = .55$).

References

Aiken, Michael, and Jerald Hage. 1968. "Organizational interdependence and intra-organizational structure." *American Sociological Review* 33 (December):912–929.

———. 1970. *Social Change in Complex Organizations*. New York: Random House.

Appelbaum, Richard J. 1970. *Theories of Social Change*. Chicago: Markham.

Baldwin, J. M. 1911. *The Individual and Society*. Boston: Gorham.

Becker, Selwyn, and Frank Stafford. 1967. "Some determinants of organizational success." *Journal of Business* 40 (October):511–518.

Becker, Selwyn, and Thomas L. Whisler. 1967. "The innovative organization: a selective view of current theory and research." *Journal of Business* 40 (October): 462–469.

Bennis, Warren, 1966. *Changing Organizations*. New York: McGraw-Hill.

Berelson, Bernard, and Gary Steiner. 1964. *Human Behavior: An Inventory of Scientific Findings*. New York: Harcourt, Brace, and World.

Blau, Peter M., and Richard Scott. 1962. *Formal Organizations*. San Francisco: Chandler.

Burns, Tom and G. M. Stalker. 1961. *The Management of Innovation*. London: Tavistock Publications.

Carlson, Richard O. 1962. *Executive Succession and Organizational Change: Place-Bound and Career-Bound Superintendents of Schools*. Chicago: Midwest Administrative Center.

Carroll, Jean. 1967. "A note on departmental autonomy and innovation in medical schools." *Journal of Business* 49 (March):531–534.

Cass, James, and Max Birnbaum. 1970. *Comparative Guide to American Colleges, 1970–1971 Edition*. New York: Harper and Row.

Chapple, E. D., and L. R. Sayles. 1961. *The Measure of Management*. New York: Macmillan.

Cillie, Francois. 1940. *Centralization or Decentralization: A Study of Educational Adaptation*. New York: Columbia University Press.

Clark, Burton R. 1960. *The Open Door College: A Case Study*. New York: McGraw-Hill.

———. 1965. "Interorganizational patterns in education." *Administrative Science Quarterly* 10 (September):224–237.

Clark, Terry. 1968. "Institutionalization of innovations in higher education: four conceptual models." *Administrative Science Quarterly* 13 (June):1–25.

Clausen, John A. 1968. "A historical and comparative view of socialization theory and research." Pp. 18–72 in John A. Clausen (ed.), *Socialization and Society*. Boston: Little, Brown, and Co.

Coch, L., and J. R. P. French. 1948. "Overcoming resistance to change." *Human Relations* 1:512–533.

Cooley, C. H. 1922. *Human Nature and the Social Order.* New York: Scribner's.

Corwin, Ronald G. 1970. *Militant Professionalism: A Study of Conflict in High Schools.* New York: Appleton-Century-Crofts.

Forthcoming. *Reform and Organizational Survival: The Teacher Corps as an Instrument of Educational Change.* New York: Wiley-Interscience.

Dewey, John. 1922. *Human Nature and Conduct.* New York: Holt.

Durkheim, E. 1933. *The Division of Labor.* Trans. by G. Simpson. New York: Free Press.

Evan, William. 1965. "Superior-subordinate conflict in research organizations." *Administrative Science Quarterly* 10 (June):52–64.

Evan, William, and G. Black. 1967. "Innovation in business organizations: some factors associated with success or failure of staff proposals." *Journal of Business* 40 (October):519–530.

Evans, Richard. 1968. *Resistance to Innovation in Higher Education.* San Francisco: Jossey-Bass.

Gerard, R. W. 1957. "Problems in the institutionalization of higher education: an analysis based on historical materials." *Behavioral Science* 2 (April):134.

Giddings, F. P. 1897. *The Theory of Socialization.* New York: Macmillan.

Ginzberg, Eli, and Ewing Reilly. 1957. *Effecting Change in Large Organizations.* New York: Columbia University Press.

Gouldner, Alvin. 1954. *Patterns of Industrial Bureaucracy.* New York: Free Press.

――――. 1959. "Organizational analysis." Pp. 400–428 in Robert K. Merton, et al. (eds.), *Sociology Today.* New York: Basic Books.

――――. 1970. *The Coming Crisis of Western Sociology.* New York: Basic Books.

Graham, Richard. 1968. "The teacher corps: one place to begin." *NASSP Bulletin* (October):49–61.

Greiner, L. E. 1965. "Organization change and development." Unpublished Ph.D. dissertation, Harvard University.

Griffiths, Daniel E. 1964. "Administrative theory and change in organizations." Pp. 425–436 in Matthew Miles (ed.), *Innovation in Education.* New York: Columbia University Press.

Guetzkow, Harold. 1965. "The creative person in organizations." Pp. 35–49 in Gary A. Steiner (ed.), *The Creative Organization.* Chicago: University of Chicago Press.

Hage, Jerald, and Michael Aiken. 1967. "Program change and organizational properties: a comparative analysis." *American Journal of Sociology* 73 (March):503–519.

Hage, Jerald, and Robert Dewar. 1971. "The prediction of organizational performance: the case of program innovation." Paper read at the American Sociological Association Meetings, Denver, August, 1971.

Hagen, Everett E. 1962. *On the Theory of Social Change.* Homewood, Illinois: Dorsey Press.

Herriott, Robert E., and Benjamin Hodgkins. 1969. *Sociocultural Context and the American School: An Open-Systems Analysis of Educational Opportunity.* Center for the Study of Education, Florida State University, January.

Katz, Fred. 1968. *Autonomy and Organization.* New York: Random House.

Kroeber, Alfred L. 1944. *Configurations of Culture Growth.* Berkeley: University of California Press.

Leavitt, Harold J. 1965. "Applied organizational change in industry: structural, technological, and humanistic approaches." Pp. 1144–1170 in James March (ed.), *Handbook of Organizations.* Chicago: Rand McNally.

Lefton, Mark, Simon Dinitz, and Benjamin Pasamanick. 1959. "Decision-making in a mental hospital." *American Sociological Review* 24 (December):882–889.

Likert, Rensis. 1961. *New Patterns of Management.* New York: McGraw-Hill.

Litwak, Eugene, and Lydia Hylton. 1962. "Interorganization analysis: a hypothesis on coordinating agencies." *Administrative Science Quarterly* 6 (March): 395–420.

Loomis, Charles P. 1959. "Tentative types of directed social change involving systematic linkage." *Rural Sociology* 24 (December):383–390.

McCleery, Richard. 1957. *Policy Change in Prison Management.* East Lansing, Mich.: Government Research Bureau, Michigan State University.

March, James G., and Herbert A. Simon. 1958. *Organizations.* New York: John Wiley and Sons.

Mead, G. H. 1934. *Mind, Self, and Society.* Chicago: University of Chicago Press.

Menzel, Herbert. 1960. "Innovation, integration, and marginability: a survey of physicians." *American Sociological Review* 25 (October): 704–713.

Moore, Wilbert E. 1963. *Social Change.* Englewood Cliffs, New Jersey: Prentice-Hall.

Morse, Nancy, and E. Reimer. 1956. "The experimental change of a major organizational variable." *Journal of Social Psychology* 52:120–129.

Mulder, Mauk. 1971. "Power equalization through participation?" *Administrative Science Quarterly* 16 (March):31–39.

Nash, George. 1969. "A description of the 1444 accredited four-year institutions of higher education." Bureau of Applied Social Research: Columbia University, January (mimeo).

Newcomb, Theodore N. 1943. *Personality and Social Change.* New York: Dryden Press.

Pareto, Vilfredo, 1968. *The Rise and Fall of the Elites.* Totawa, New Jersey: The Bedminster Press.

Peterson, Richard E. *College Student Questionnaire,* Princeton, New Jersey: Educational Testing Service.

Putney, Snell, and Gladys I. Putney, 1962. "Radical innovation and prestige." *American Sociological Review* 27 (August):548–551.

Riley, John W. Jr., and Matilda White Riley. 1962. "Sociological perspectives on the use of new educational media." Pp. 27–49 in Wilbur Schramm (ed.), *New Teaching Aids for the American Classroom.* Washington, D.C.: U.S. Government Printing Office.

Roethlesberger, F. J., and W. J. Dickson. 1939. *Management and the*

Worker. Cambridge, Mass.: Harvard University Press.

Rogers, Everett M. 1962. *Diffusion of Innovations.* New York: Free Press of Glencoe.

Sapolsky, Harvey M. 1967. "Organizational structure and innovation." *Journal of Business* 40 (October):497–510.

Shepard, Herbert A. 1967. "Innovation-resisting and innovation-producing organizations." *Journal of Business* 40 (October):470–477.

Sieber, Sam D., and David E. Wilder. 1967. "Teaching styles: parental preferences and professional role definitions." *Sociology of Education* 40 (Fall): 302–315.

Smelser, Neil J. 1967. *Sociology: An Introduction.* New York: John Wiley and Sons.

Tarde, Gabriel de. 1890. *Laws of Imitation* (rev. ed., 1962). Gloucester, Mass.: Peter Smith Publisher.

Terreberry, Shirley. 1965. "The evolution of administrative environments." *Administrative Science Quarterly* 12 (March):590–613.

Thomas, W. I., and F. Zaniecki. 1918–1920. *The Polish Peasant in Europe and America.* Boston: Richard C. Badger.

Torgerson, Warren S. 1958. *Theory and Methods of Scaling.* New York: John Wiley.

Thompson, James O. 1967. *Organizations in Action.* New York: McGraw-Hill.

Turk, Herman. 1970. "Interorganizational networks in urban society: initial perspectives and comparative research." *American Sociological Review* 35 (February):1–18.

———. 1964. " Structural features of American education as basic factors in innovation." Pp. 587–613 in Matthew B. Miles (ed.), *Innovation in Education.* New York: Columbia University Press.

Wilson, James Q. 1963. "Innovation in organization: notes toward a theory." Pp. 193–218 in J. D. Thompson (ed.), *Approaches to Organizational Design.* Pittsburgh: University of Pittsburgh Press.

Program Change and Organizational Properties

Jerald Hage and Michael Aiken

A major problem in the study of organizations is the analysis of organizational change. One of the difficulties in studying change is the determination of an adequate definition of organizational change.[1] Etzioni has suggested that most organizational studies implicitly, if not explicitly, involve the study of change of some variable or property.[2] This difficulty has been labeled by Parsons as the problem of change within a system

Reprinted from *American Journal of Sociology* 72 (March, 1967):503–18.

as opposed to change of the system.[3] The difficulty lies in determining which kind of change results in a change of the organizational system. New techniques may be adopted, new models may be tried, and new rules and policies may be formulated; yet these are changes that do not necessarily imply fundamental changes in the organizational system. We shall offer a tentative solution to this problem by limiting our analysis to one kind of change within the system— the adoption of new programs or services. This kind of change appears to be an important one albeit not the only kind because it can imply changes in techniques, rules, or even goals. We are interested in studying the relationship between different organizational properties and the rate of program change, and we assume that the rate of program change, as well as other organizational properties, can be conceived most advantageously as variables in a system. We assume that a change in one variable leads to a change in other variables. If different rates of program change are related to different configurations on other organizational properties, then we can speak of different systems. This is our approach to the problem of studying organizational change.

In our study, we have measured the rate of program change in sixteen organizations over a five-year period.[4] This rate is then related to other organizational properties, for example, job satisfaction, codification of rules, decision making, which are measured cross-sectionally, not longitudinally. While this prevents our making any statements about cause and effect, it does allow us to examine how different rates of program change are associated with various organizational properties.

To this end, we studied sixteen social welfare organizations staffed largely by professionally trained personnel. These organizations provide a particularly interesting testing ground for hypotheses relating rate of program change to other organizational properties, since the organizations provide services for the physically handicapped, emotionally disturbed, or mentally retarded. It might be assumed that each agency would attempt to add as many new programs as resources allow, but this was not the case. Some welfare organizations were primarily concerned with the quantity of client service. Given additional financial resources, these organizations would probably either reduce the case load of staff members or increase the number of clients serviced. For example, a county children's welfare department had added only one new program in the previous five years and had no plans for future changes. This agency was primarily concerned with reducing the case loads of its social workers. The rationale was not to improve the quality of service but, rather, to reduce turnover among its social workers, since the case load was usually high in this agency, well beyond typical limits.

Similarly, the head of a private home for emotionally disturbed children reported that no new programs had been added in his agency in the previous five years. In contrast, some welfare organizations were primarily concerned with the quality of client service. These organizations would probably use additional financial resources to add new programs or techniques. A county mental hospital, the organization in our study with the highest rate of program change, had added eight new programs in the past five years, including a sheltered workshop, a training program in group therapy for the attendants, and a placement service. In addition, there were already plans afoot for future changes. Similarly, a private home for emotionally disturbed boys had added six new programs in the last five years and had plans for still more. One of the greatest concerns in this organization was that the case load might increase, since the agency head felt that the major emphasis should be placed on improving the quality rather than the quantity of client service. The contrasting policies of these organizations cut across the different kinds of goals and are reflected in the varying rates of program change among the sixteen organizations. The rate of program change by type of organization is shown in Table 1. While rehabilitation centers have the greatest incidence of program change, and social casework agencies the least, there are still considerable variations among these categories of organizations that ostensibly have similar goals. Furthermore, the crucial question is whether a rehabilitation center with a low rate of program change has organizational characteristics that are similar to a social casework agency with a low rate of program change.

The assumption of an organization as a system implies that certain organizational configurations are most likely to be associated with a high rate of program change. This also implies that if a high rate of program change occurs in an organization, it is likely to bring about changes in the working conditions of the organization.[5] Our data are not longitudinal, and thus it becomes impossible to stipulate any cause or effect relationships.[6] That is, we are unable to stipulate if program change brings about alternatives in other organizational properties or if new programs are introduced because of the presence of some other organizational characteristics. While our study is framed in the latter sense, this is simply for the convenience of the presentation of our findings. We would like to know organizational scores at both the beginning and end of the five-year period to unravel this problem, but unfortunately we only know organizational characteristics at the *end* of the five-year period.

Our purpose in this paper, then, is to relate the organizational characteristics of complexity, centralization, formalization, and job satisfaction to the rate of program change. We hypothesize that the rate

TABLE 1

Average Number of Program Changes by Type of Organization

Type of Organization	Number of Organizations	Average Number of Program Changes	Range
Rehabilitation centers.....	3	4.67	3–6
Hospitals..............	3	4.67	3–8
Special education department—public schools...	1	4.00	4
Homes for emotionally disturbed..............	3	2.67	0–6
Social casework agencies ..	6	1.33	0–3

of program change is positively related to the degree of complexity and job satisfaction, and negatively related to the degree of centralization and formalization.[7] The rationale for each hypothesis is discussed below as the data are examined.

Study Design and Methodology

The data upon which this study is based were gathered in sixteen social welfare agencies located in a large midwest metropolis in 1964. Ten agencies were private; six were either public or branches of public agencies. These agencies were all the larger welfare organizations that provide rehabilitation, psychiatric services, and services for the mentally retarded as defined by the directory of the Community Chest. The agencies vary in size from twelve to several hundred. Interviews were conducted with 314 staff members of these sixteen organizations. Respondents within each organization were selected by the following criteria: (*a*) all executive directors and department heads; (*b*) in departments of less than ten members, one-half of the staff was selected randomly; (*c*) in departments of more than ten members, one-third of the staff was selected randomly. Non-supervisory administrative and maintenance personnel were not interviewed.

This sampling procedure divides the organization into levels and departments. Job occupants in the upper levels were selected because they are most likely to be key decision makers and to determine organizational policy, whereas job occupants in the lower levels were selected randomly. The different ratios within departments insured that smaller departments were adequately represented. Professionals, such as psychiatrists, social workers, rehabilitation counselors, etc., are included because they are intimately involved in the achievement of organizational goals and are likely to have organizational power. Non-professionals, such as attendants, janitors, and secretaries are excluded because they are less directly involved in the achievement of organizational goals and have little or no power. The number of interviews varied from seven in the smallest to forty-one in one of the largest agencies.

It should be stressed that in this study the units of analysis are organizations, not individuals in the organizations. Information obtained from respondents was pooled to reflect properties of the sixteen organizations, and these properties are then related to one another.[8] Aggregating individual data in this way presents methodological problems for which there are yet no satisfactory solutions. For example, if all respondents are equally weighted, undue weight is given to respondents lower in the hierarchy. Yet those higher in the chain of command, not those lower in the chain of command, are most likely to make the decisions which give an agency its ethos.[9]

We attempt to compensate for this by computing an organizational score from the means of social position within the agency. A social position is defined by the level or stratum in the organization and the department or type of professional activity. For example, if an agency's professional staff consists of psychiatrists and social workers, each divided into two hierarchical levels, the agency has four social positions: supervisory psychiatrists, psychiatrists, supervisory social workers, and social workers. A mean was then computed for each social position in the agency. The organizational score for a given variable was determined by computing the average of all social position means in the agency.[10]

The procedure for computing organizational scores parallels the method utilized in selecting respondents. It attempts to represent organizational life more accurately by not giving disproportionate weight to those social positions that have little power and that are little involved in the achievement of organizational goals.

Computation of means for each social position has the advantage of avoiding the potential problem created by the use of different sampling ratios. In effect, responses are standardized by organizational location—level and department—and then combined into an organizational score. Computation of means of social position also has a major theoretical advantage in that it focuses on the sociological perspective of organizational reality. We consider an organization to be a collection of social positions which we call jobs, not simply an aggregate of individuals. Ideally, sociological properties are more than a summation of psychological properties. We feel that our computation procedures are, hopefully, more consistent with a "sociological imagination."

Organizational Properties and Rate of Program Change

Following the work of Pugh *et al.*, we find it useful to make a distinction between structural variables and performance variables as two special kinds of organizational properties.[11] The former refers to the arrangements of positions or jobs within the organization, for example, the utilization of different professional specialties or the degree of complexity, the distribution of power or the degree of centralization, the utilization of rules or the degree of formalization. The latter refers to the outcomes of the arrangements of positions, for example, the rate of program change, the degree of job satisfaction, the volume of production. In addition we examine a personality characteristic of the individuals who work in the organization, namely, their attitudes toward change. Since we are interested in rates of program change, it is entirely possible that this is affected not only by the structural and performance characteristics of the organization but also by the general orientations of the individual members. Admittedly these are not the only distinctions that can be made, but they provide a useful framework for distinguishing among major kinds of variables, helping to isolate the characteristics that are part of the system.

Structural Variables: The Degree of Complexity

Since the publication of the English translation of Durkheim's *The Division of Labor*, the degree of complexity, or specialization, has been a key concept in the organizational literature.[12] Yet, this variable has seldom been systematically related to other organizational properties. For our purposes, we define organizational complexity with three alternative empirical indicators: occupational specialties, the length of training required by each occupation, and the degree of professional activity associated with each occupation. The greater the number of specialties, the greater the length of training required by each occupation; and the greater the degree of professional activity, the more complex the organizational structure. The term "specialization" has frequently been used to describe both this phenomenon and the minute parceling of work such as that of an assembly line where training of job occupants is minimized. From our perspective, the latter is the opposite of complexity. In order to avoid terminological confusion, we prefer to use the word "complexity" to refer to the former phenomenon, since we feel that this is more consistent with Durkheim's usage of the term.[13]

    A recently published axiomatic theory hypothesizes a direct relationship between complexity and the rate of program change.[14] There are several reasons why these two properties should be related in this way. The addition of new programs frequently necessitates the addition of new occupations. Job occupants of such occupational specialties often have a particular organizational perspective which leads to the introduction of still other new programs. Further, the professional activities of job staff members function as communications links between the organization and its competitors, providing a source of information about new ideas and techniques. In addition, conflicts among the different occupational specialties in an organization act as a further dynamic force for the creation of new programs. The more professionalized the occupations, the greater the struggle to prove the need for expansion.[15]

In our interviews with staff members of organizations, each respondent was asked to describe the nature of his duties, the extent of his training, and the amount of his professional activity. Just as the number of jobs reflects the complexity of the organization, it was our belief that the more the training required, the more the probable complexity of the job itself, so that this needed to be considered as well. Furthermore, the more the professional activity of the job occupants, the more likely there would be continued increases in the complexity of the job. On the basis of the respondents' answers to our questions, three indicators of organizational complexity were computed. The first indicator is the number of occupational specialties, which was measured by counting the numbers of different kinds of work that exist in an agency. There is a correlation of .48 between the number of occupational specialties and the rate of program change. A variety of occupational perspectives is associated with a higher rate of change.

We have already stated that we are unable to determine causation because our data are taken at one point of time. Since occupational specialties more than any of our other variables can be closely linked to the programs that are added, we reconstructed the number of occupational specialties that existed in each organization prior to 1959, the beginning of the five-year period we used for measuring the rate of program change. While the number of occupational specialties was altered in several organizations, the correlation between these two properties remained virtually unchanged ($r = .45$).[16]

The amount of professional training is another indicator of the complexity of organizations. This was measured by computing an index reflecting the degree of formal training and other professional training for each social position in the organization.[17] As can be seen from Table 1, there is a weak but positive correlation between the organization score of professional training and the rate of program change ($r = .14$). Thus the amount of professional training in an organization is positively associated with the rate of program change.

To measure the extent of the extra-organizational professional activity of members of each organization, the respondents were asked to report the number of professional associations to which they belonged, the proportion of meetings attended, the number of papers given, and offices held, all of which represent professional involvement.[18] The higher this score, that is, the greater the extra-organizational professional activities of members of the organization, the more likely it was to have a high rate of program change, as shown in Table 2 ($r = .37$). It should be noted that the amount of professional involvement is more highly related to program change than the amount of professional training.

Involvement in extra-organizational professional activities evidently heightens awareness of programmatic and technological developments within a profession.[19] Professionally active job occupants introduce new ideas into the organization, and the outcome is a high rate of program change. Similarly, new programs require the addition of new job occupants who are highly trained. A plausible line of reasoning is that greater extra-organizational professional activity implies a greater emphasis on the improvement of the quality of client service, whether the clients are emotionally disturbed or mentally retarded. Such an emphasis requires a continual application of new knowledge, whether reflected in new programs or in new techniques. The number of occupational specialties and the amount of extra-organizational professional activity were themselves related; the correlation coefficient was .29. The sheer presence of different occupational perspectives, implying the idea of occupational conflict, appears to heighten professional involvement, as was suggested by Durkheim.[20]

Structural Variables: The Degree of Centralization

There are many debates in the organizational literature about the relative merits of centralization as opposed to decentralization of decision making. On the one hand, Weber argued that strict hierarchy of authority increased both the volume of production and the efficiency of an organization.[21] On the other hand, the human relations specialists have argued that decentralization increases job satisfaction and reduces resistance to change.[22] Both arguments are probably correct.

In our study the staff members were asked how often they participated in organizational decisions regarding the hiring of personnel, the promotions of personnel, the adoption of new organizational policies, and the adoption of new programs or services.[23] The organizational score was based on the average degree of participation in these four areas of

TABLE 2

Rate of Program Change and Other Organizational Properties

	Pearson Product-Moment Correlation Coefficients of Each Organizational Characteristic with Rate of Program Change *
Structural variables:	
1. Degree of complexity:	
a) Measure of the number of occupational specialties	.48
b) Measure of the amount of extra-organizational professional activity	.37
c) Measure of the amount of professional training	.14
2. Degree of centralization:	
a) Measure of the degree of participation in organizational decision making	.49
b) Measure of hierarchy of authority	— .09
3. Degree of formalization:	
a) Measure of the degree of job codification ..	— .47
b) Measure of the degree of rule observation ..	.13
Performance variables:	
1. Degree of satisfaction:	
a) Measure of job satisfaction	.38
b) Measure of expressive satisfaction	— .17
Personality variables:	
1. Motive of self-interest and negative attitudes toward change	— .04
2. Motive of values and positive attitudes toward change	— .15

* The measures of association reported here are Pearson product-moment correlation coefficients. The units of analysis in this report are the sixteen organizations in our study, not our 314 individual respondents. Product-moment correlation coefficients are highly sensitive to even slight modifications of numerical scores with so few cases. We rejected the use of non-parametric measures of association because our scales are lineal and not ordinal; non-parametric statistics necessitate our "throwing away" some of the magnitude of variations in our data. Since these sixteen organizations represent a universe of organization, tests of statistical significance are inappropriate.

decision making. As can be seen from Table 2, the greater the participation in agency-wide decisions, the greater the rate of program change in the organization ($r = .49$). Decentralization allows for the interplay of a variety of occupational perspectives. As Thompson has suggested, a centralized organization is one in which change can be, and frequently is, easily vetoed.[24]

Agency-wide decisions are not the only kind that are made. Other decisions are those concerning the performance of a specific job. Agency-wide decisions are basically decisions about the control of resources, while job decisions are basically decisions about the control of work. It is at least logically possible that the centralization of the former kind of decision making can be associated with the decentralization of the latter kind of decision making. We measure the degree of decision making about work with a scale called the "hierarchy of authority."[25] This scale was found to have little relationship with the rate of program change, although it was in the predicted direction ($r = .09$). It is the centralization of decisions about organizational resources, not the centralization of work control, that is highly related to low rates of this kind of organizational change.

Structural Variables: The Degree of Formalization

Rules or regulations are important organizational mechanisms that may be used to insure the predictability of performance. There are two aspects of the use of rules as a mechanism of social control; one is the number of regulations specifying who is to do what, where, and when; we call this the degree of job codification. Another is the diligency in enforcing these rules that specify who is doing what, where, and when; this we call rule observation. The latter is important because many organizations may not enforce all regulations. The degree of formalization is defined as both the degree of job codification as well as the degree of rule observation.

While it has been commonplace to argue that bureaucracies retard change, there have been few studies that have examined this proposition in a comparative framework. One of the essential elements of bureaucracy is its emphasis on formalization. Our hypothesis is that the two aspects of formalization outlined above retard the adoption of new programs because they discourage individual initiative.[26] Clearly codified jobs that are closely supervised to insure conformity also reduce the search for better ways of doing work. Such a use of rules encourages ritualistic and unimaginative behavior.

The two indexes of formalization were constructed on the basis of a factor analysis of scales developed by Hall.[27] At best these scales are only rough indicators of the degree of formalization in an organization. As indicated by Table 2, job codification is inversely related to the rate of organizational change ($r = -.47$). The relationship between the degree of rule observation and the rate of program change is much weaker and is in a direction opposite from our prediction ($r = .13$).

In order to determine whether each of the observed relationships between each of our indicators of various structural properties and the rate of program change are spurious, multiple and partial correlation analyses are introduced.

As shown in Table 3, only two of these variables have strong and independent relationships with the rate of program change: the degree of job codification ($rp = -.47$) and the degree of participation in decision making ($rp = .39$). It should be noted that the β weights for participation in decision making are greater (.555), however, than the β weights for job codification ($-.379$).

The number of occupational specialties and the degree of hierarchy have moderate but independent relationships with the number of program innovations, although the latter variable is related in the opposite direction when the other six variables are controlled. The degree of extra-organizational activity, the degree of professional training, and the degree of rule observation have little relationship with the number of program innovations after controlling for the other factors, although rule observation remains virtually unchanged.

Performance Variables: The Degree of Satisfaction

Since the famous French and Coch experiment, the advocates of the human relations approach to organizational analysis have emphasized the importance of morale as a factor in understanding differential acceptance of change and, therefore, implicitly differential rates of program change.[28] We developed two different measures of morale—an index of job satisfaction and an index of satisfaction with expressive relations.[29] There is a correlation of .38 between job satisfaction and rate of program change. On the other hand, satisfaction with expressive relations is negatively correlated, albeit the size of the correlation is small ($r = -.17$). This suggests a plausible explanation for several contradictory viewpoints in the literature concerning morale and organizational change. The work of Coch and French suggests a positive relationship between morale and change, but a series of studies by Mann, Hoffman, and others at the University of Michigan have noted that change creates social strain in the organization.[30] One may infer, not necessarily from our data, that job satisfaction may be a necessary precondition for the introduction of changes, but after this change has been introduced it may have disruptive and negative effects on social relationships among members in an organization. It is also plausible to argue that the organizational conditions that facilitate the introduction of change, namely, occupational diversity and decentralization, reduce satisfaction with expressive relationships because of the conflicts they engender.

TABLE 3

Multiple and Partial Correlation Analysis of the Number of Program Changes
and Other Organizational Properties

Organizational Properties	*Partial Correlation Coefficient**	*β Coefficients in Standard Form†*
1. Degree of complexity:		
a) Measure of the number of occupational specialties‡	+ .24	+ .202
b) Measure of the amount of extra-organizational professional activity	+ .08	+ .104
c) Measure of professional training	− .10	− .137
2. Degree of centralization:		
a) Measure of the degree of participation in organizational decision making	+ .39	+ .555
b) Measure of hierarchy of authority	+ .23	+ .231
3. Degree of formalization:		
a) Measure of degree of job codification	− .47	− .379
b) Measure of degree of rule observation	+.15	+ .134
Coefficient of determination	....	.558
Multiple correlation coefficient	....	.75

* These are the partial correlation coefficients between each variable and the rate of program change, controlling for the other six structural variables. Thus, each is a sixth-order partial correlation coefficient.

† These are β coefficients in standard form, i.e., β weights.

‡ This is the number of occupational specialties as of 1959, before the program changes discussed in this paper were introduced.

Personality Variables: General Orientation to Change

It is argued by some social psychologists and psychologists that all collective properties of organization, such as the degree of centralization, the degree of formalization, or the degree of complexity, are ultimately reducible to psychological factors. Since this is a common argument, we attempted to measure several personality variables that might account for differences in organizational rates of program change. It could be argued that change occurs in organizations because the organization has a high proportion of individuals who are favorably oriented to social change. Selznik has suggested the idea of selective recruitment of certain personality types; that is, when an organization needs new job occupants, the attempt is made to recruit individuals who have personality attributes consistent with organizational needs.[31] Mann and Hoffman have hypothesized the obverse of this process, namely, that individuals who cannot tolerate change will leave changing organizations and seek work in more stable ones.[32] Finally, Homans and others have argued that sociological variables are fundamentally reducible to psychological variables.[33] While we do not accept this argument, we included measures of individual orientations toward change developed by Sister Marie Augusta Neal in an attempt to test the validity of such assertions.[34]

The Neal batteries of self-interest motives, value motives, pro-change motives, and anti-change motives were factor analyzed and yielded two clear factors; one factor contains items representing attitudes of self-interest and a negative attitude toward change, while the second factor contains items representing attitudes of ideals and a positive orientation toward change. We would expect the former to be *negatively* associated with rate of program change and the latter to be *positively* associated with program change. We found only a modest relationship between these measures of attitudes toward change and the amount of organizational program change.

The measure of self-interest and anti-change was virtually unrelated to program change ($r = -.04$), while the measure of ideals and pro-change was related to program change opposite from the expected direction ($r = -.15$).

An organization can have a high proportion of job occupants who are favorably disposed toward change in their personal orientations, and yet the organization does not necessarily adopt new programs. The reverse pattern is equally true.

What this suggests is that the personality attributes included in our study add little to our understanding of organizational change as we have measured it. On the other hand, there is the possibility that there are other personality variables that are appropriate for the understanding of organizational change.

It would be desirable to know the relative importance of performance variables, such as job satisfaction and the structural properties, but the limited size of our universe of organizations ($n = 16$), makes a multiple correlational and partial correlational analysis (reported in Table 3) for all the variables that we have measured inappropriate. It should be understood that there is a very strong relationship between the degree of centralization and job satisfaction in particular.[35] At the same time, the concept of a system assumes that there is this high degree of interdependence. The precise importance of each of these variables must be determined with a much larger number of organizations and preferably with longitudinal measurements.

Contextual Variables, Organizational Properties, and Rate of Programs Change

The fact that there are varying rates of program for our different kinds of agencies, as indicated in Table 1, suggests that there may be disparate situations faced by each of our organizations. The rate of technological change may be faster in rehabilitation than in social casework agencies.

In particular, the organizations in our study vary considerably in their ease of access to resources, whether personnel or finances. They differ considerably in their age and autonomy. These and other indicators of their environmental situation can have an impact on the organization and its ability to adopt new programs. By studying the impact of such variables as auspices, size, and function, it becomes possible to view the process by which organizations are likely to develop one or another system. It also allows us some insight into the generalizability of our findings. If one of these variables accounts for most of the observed relationship between the rate of program change and the organizational properties, then we are aware of a significant limitation on our findings.

In a recent review of the organizational literature, Pugh and his associates suggest a number of contextual variables that can be used either as controls or as independent variables when examining the relationships among organizational properties. The variables that they discuss are: origin and history, ownership and control, size, charter technology, location, resources, and interdependence.[36] Presumably, each of these factors could have an impact on the characteristics of the organization, including the rate of program change. In particular, there is always the possibility that any of the relationships reported in Table 2 are simply a function of some of these contextual variables. For example, there is a standard organizational hypothesis that increasing size means more centralization and formalization, and, therefore, one might expect large organizations to have low rates of program change as a consequence. Another standard hypothesis is that older organizations are likely to be more bureaucratic and therefore to have lower rates of change.

To explore the relative importance of these environmental factors for the relationships discussed above, we employed partial correlations. A fourth-order partial correlation was computed between each of the organizational properties and rate of program change, controlling for *size*, auspices, age of organization, and major function.

Size represents the rank order of organizations by number of employees in the organization; it is the same as the contextual concept discussed by Pugh *et al.*

Auspices, that is, whether the organization is public or private, is similar to their concept of ownership and control. Since none of our organizations is a business, most of the analytical distinctions that they discussed do not apply. It should be noted that "auspices" not only includes the idea of the nature of the accountability of the chief executive, but it suggests the sources of revenue, an idea contained in the concept of resources. The public agencies are largely tax supported, while the private agencies rely upon donations, grants, and fees. In other words, the distinction between public and private carries many implications; therefore, the word "auspices" appears to be a more appropriate one than either ownership or resources.

The age of the organization is only one aspect of the organization's origin and history, but it is an attempt to measure some of the ideas discussed by Pugh *et al.*

Finally, function is our attempt to divide a relatively homogeneous universe of organizations into at least two kinds of goals and technologies. We separated our organizations into those that deal with their clients for a relatively short period of time, the typical casework situation found in the social welfare agencies, and into those that deal with their clients for a relatively long period of time, the sheltered workshop, the school, and hospital situations. The one-hour interview and the total institution reflect different kinds of technology, at least in terms of the intensiveness, even though all of our agencies are concerned with providing rehabilitative and psychiatric services. [37]

Location and interdependence are two contextual variables discussed by Pugh *et al.* that are not included in our analysis. Location is impossible to include because all of our agencies are in the same metropolitan area. We feel that interdependence is an exceedingly important contextual variable, but we are still in the process of collecting data on it. A separate analysis of this contextual variable and its impact will be made at a later date.

Not all of the four contextual variables are related to the rate of program change. Both age ($r = -.03$) and auspices ($r = -.06$) were unrelated to this kind of organizational change as we have measured it. But size ($r = -.61$) and function ($r = .58$) were highly related to the rate of program change. The larger the size of the organization and the more time the client spends in the organization, the higher the rate of program change. Since these contextual factors are themselves interrelated (larger organizations were much more likely to be total institutions) and since these factors do have an impact on rate of program change, the question remains whether the relationships between our dependent variable and the other organizational properties will be maintained if we simultaneously control for all four of the contextual variables. To put it another way, we want to know if our results are a consequence of organizational arrangements or a consequence of the environmental situations.

The partial correlation analysis is reported in Table 4. If this table is compared with Table 1, it will be noted that the correlations remain approximately the same when size, age, auspices, and function are controlled, except for two measures: the number of occupational specialties and the hierarchy of authority. Function has a very high correlation with

TABLE 4

Rate of Program Change and Other Organizational Properties When Size, Auspices, Age of Organization, and Function are Controlled

	*Partial Correlations with Rate of Program Change**
Structural variables:	
1. Degree of complexity:	
a) Measure of the number of occupational specialties†	.00
b) Measure of the amount of professional activity	.11
c) Measure of the amount of professional training	.14
2. Degree of centralization:	
a) Measure of the degree of participation in decision making	.46
b) Measure of hierarchy of authority	—.37
3. Degree of formalization	
a) Measure of the degree of job codification	—.33
b) Measure of the degree of rule observation	—.02
Performance variable:	
Degree of satisfaction:	
a) Measure of job satisfaction	.27
b) Measure of expressive satisfaction	—.19

     * There are fourth order partial correlations, i.e., the partial correlation coefficients between each factor listed and the rate of program change, controlling for size, auspices, age of organization, and function.
     †This is the number of occupational specialties as of 1959, before the program changes discussed in this study were introduced.

the number of occupational specialties, while size and auspices have moderately high correlations. The more time the client spends in the organization, the greater the number of occupational specialties ($r = .67$). If the organization is public, there are likely to be more occupational specialties than if it is private, suggesting different availability of funds ($r = .39$). Similarly, larger organizations have more occupational specialties ($r = .41$). When function, size, and auspices are held constant, the relationship between number of occupational specialties and rate of change disappears. This suggests a process when the time ordering of these variables is considered.

    The function of the organization, its size, and its auspices affect the number of specialties it has; this in turn is associated with the rate of program change. The partial correlation analysis makes clear, however, that the number of occupational specialties has little independent effect in explaining the variation in rate of program change once auspices, size, age, and function are held constant.

In contrast, the partial correlation between rate of program change and hierarchy of authority, holding constant the four contextual factors, has the predicted negative relationship with rate of program change. In fact, the relationship is stronger after controlling for these contextual factors.

In general, the observed relationships between rate of program change and the organizational properties remain, even after simultaneously controlling for these contextual factors. That is, even though the context or environment affects the organization, most of the organizational properties examined are still related to the rate of program change.

Another way of determining the generalizability of these findings is the examination of other studies of organizations to see if they found similar results. In a study of large business firms in the United States, Chandler suggests that increases in complexity as measured by product diversification led to the decentralization of decision making.[38] This was especially likely to occur after the introduction of professional managers. These firms were also more likely to allocate a much larger proportion of their budget to research, indicating a higher rate of program change. Woodward's study of some ninety industrial firms in South Essex, England, suggests that those firms that made small batches of products or custom models were more likely than the assembly-line manufacturers to have professional managers, skilled labor, decentralized decision making, higher job satisfaction, and less routinization of procedures.[39] While this study does not have a direct measure of the rate of program change, both of these studies are at least supportive of the findings reported here.

Conclusions and Discussion

Our findings suggest the following two stories about the rate of program change. One line of reasoning is as follows: Given that there is a high rate of program change, there is likely to be relatively decentralized decision making because of the necessity for discussions about the problems of change. There is a variety of decisions involving the allocation of personnel and funds attendant to the addition of new programs. In addition, the implementation of programs inevitably indicates contingencies not considered and engenders conflicts that must be resolved. Similarly, the high rate of program change will necessitate the relaxation of rules in order to solve the problems of implementation. There will be conflicts between the demands of the new program and previous regulations that will make rule observation difficult. The addition of new programs is likely to attract better-trained and active professional personnel who will like the challenge of change. And new programs can require, in many cases, new skills or areas of expertise relative to the organization. The high rate of job satisfaction can flow from the satisfaction of being a member of a dynamic organization. But the high rate of change creates strain in interpersonal relationships.

Another line of reasoning is as follows: If an organization is relatively decentralized, it is likely to have a variety of information channels which allow the consideration of both the need for new programs and their appropriateness. The sheer number of occupational specialties also increases the diversity of informal channels of communication. This is likely to lead to conflict among competing ideas for organizational resources. In contrast, the amount of job codification reduces the diversity of informal channels of information by circumscribing the occupants' perspectives, including the recognition of needs and the choice of remedies. Given that an organization is complex, decentralized, and non-formalized, then it is likely to be high in rate of program change. Such an organization is also likely to have high job satisfaction but low satisfaction with expressive relations. High job satisfaction evidently facilitates the introduction of changes, but the changes themselves are evidently disruptive of interpersonal relationships. The structural arrangements that facilitate change seem to generate conflicts among staff members. The diversity of occupational specialties, the power struggles in a decentralized arrangement of decision making, and the lack of clear work boundaries—consequences of the lack of formalization—are all conducive to organizational conflicts that are manifested in dissatisfaction with expressive relationships.

The nature of our data does not allow us to choose between these two lines of reasoning. It is our belief that both are correct and reflect again the system nature of organizations. However, future research should be directed to verifying which line of reasoning is more pervasive, but this will require longitudinal studies. Our analysis indicates that rate of program change is associated with configurations on other organizational properties, supporting the basic assumption that an organization is best viewed as a system of variables. While program change is only one kind of change within the system, future research should be directed to the question of whether other changes within the system, such as changes in rules as opposed to changes in degree of job codification, changes in who makes decisions as opposed to changes in emphasis on hierarchy, changes in techniques as opposed to changes in technology, can be analyzed in the same way. We feel that this study provides an illustration of how change within the system and change of the system can be differentiated.

Our analysis indicated that different empirical indicators of the three structural properties of organizations, that is, centralization, complexity, and formalization, are related differently to the rate of change in new programs, at least among the sixteen organizations in this study. The number of occupational specialties in the organization, an indicator of complexity, is a better predictor of program change than professional training or professional activity. Participation in agency-wide decision making is a more powerful predictor of organizational change than the degree of hierarchy of authority. Finally, the degree of job codification, an indicator of formalization, is a more powerful predictor of program change than the rule observation.

A partial correlation analysis simultaneously controlling for size, auspices, age of organization, and function demonstrated that most of the organizational properties have associations with rate of program change which are independent of variations in these contextual factors. However, function and auspices, to a lesser extent, were so strongly related to the number of occupational specialties that the relationship between number of occupational specialties—one indicator of complexity—and rate of program change disappears. Future research should attempt to consider additional contextual variables besides the ones included here.

A major theme contained in this paper is that it is important to view organizations from a sociological viewpoint. Our method for drawing the sample and the procedure for computing scores for organizational properties conceive of organizations as a collection of social positions (or jobs), not simply as an aggregate of individuals. Several different collective properties of organizations were found to be related to the rate of change. When individual orientations toward change were measured, they were found to be relatively unrelated to the rate of organizational change, at least as we have defined it. Our findings are supportive of Durkheim's famous phase that "social facts must be explained by other social facts." That is, we were able to explain the rate of organizational change better with other organizational properties, such as degree of centralization, degree of complexity, or degree of formalization, than with measures of attitudes of organizational members toward change. Certainly this does not constitute definitive proof, but it does suggest that emphasis on structural and performance variables in organizations may be a more fruitful way to study organizational change.

Notes

1. See Jerald Hage, "Organizational Response to Innovation" (unpublished Ph.D. thesis, Columbia University, 1963), chap. iii, for a discussion of several different kinds of change.

2. Amitai Etzioni (ed.), in Introduction to section on "Organizational Change," *Complex Organizations: A Sociological Reader* (New York: Holt, Rinehart & Winston, 1961), pp. 341–43.

3. Talcott Parsons, *The Social System* (Glencoe, Ill.: Free Press, 1951), chap. xii.

4. Executive directors were asked: "How many new programs or services have you added in the last five years?" In many cases the new programs did not involve the addition of new personnel or new funds but, instead, represented reallocation of existing resources. The question used a standard interval of time so that the rate could be expressed as a number. It might also be noted that the choice of an interval of time is not an easy one. We selected an interval of five years as a minimum because any shorter period is too likely to be subjected to random or episodic fluctuations.

5. In other words, all hypotheses are reversible; see Hans Zetterberg, *On Theory and Verification in Sociology* (rev. ed.; Totowa, N.J.: Bedminster Press, 1963), p. 11.

6. We are presently engaged in the second logical step of research, namely, the attempt to predict the future rate of program change on the basis of organizational properties measured prior in time.

7. For a discussion of why these properties should be related as hypothesized, see Jerald Hage, "An Axiomatic Theory of Organization," *Administrative Science Quarterly,* 10 (December, 1965), 289–321.

8. A very common error in statistical analysis is the failure to realize that assumptions must be made not only about the unit of analysis, usually the individual, but also about the time and place. Few studies systematically examine these three factors together, yet each is important. Most studies should be qualified with reference to a specific time and place.

9. For a discussion of some of the basic differences between individual and collective properties, see Paul Lazarsfeld and Herbert Menzel, "On Individual and Collective Properties," in Etzioni (ed.), *op. cit.,* pp. 422–40; and James S. Coleman, "Research Chronicle: The Adolescent Society," in Phillip E. Hammond (ed.), *Sociologists at Work* (New York: Basic Books, 1964).

10. One advantage of this procedure is that it allows for the cancellation of individual errors made by the job occupants of a particular position. It also allows for the elimination of certain idiosyncratic elements that result from the special privileges a particular occupant might have received as a consequence.

An alternative procedure for computing organizational means is to weigh all respondents equally. These two procedures yield strikingly similar results for the variables reported in this paper. The product moment correlation coefficients between the scores based on these two computational procedures were as follows for the variables indicated:

Hierarchy of Authority . . . . ·70
Actual participation in decision making . . . . ·90
Job codification 68
Rule observation 88
Job satisfaction 89

11. D. S. Pugh *et al.*, "A Scheme for Organizational Analysis," *Administrative Science Quarterly*, 8 (1963), 289–316.

12. Emile Durkheim, *The Division of Labor in Society* (New York: Macmillan Co., 1933), Part I; also Preface to 2d ed.

13. See Victor Thompson, *Modern Organization* (New York: Alfred A. Knopf Inc., 1964), chap. iii.

14. See Hage, "An Axiomatic Theory," *op. cit.*, p. 303.

15. Durkheim, *op. cit.*, pp. 267–70.

16. It should be noted that our count of occupational specialties is not based on the number of specific job titles. Instead, each respondent was asked what he did and then this was coded according to the kind of professional activity and whether it was a specialty. This procedure was used for two reasons. First, it allows for comparability across organizations. Second, it avoids the problem of task specialization where one activity might be divided into many specific and separate tasks (see Thompson, *op. cit.*).

17. The index was scored as follows: (*a*) An absence of training beyond a college degree and the absence of other professional training received a score of 0; (*b*) an absence of training beyond college degree and the presence of other professional training received a score of 1; (*c*) a presence of training beyond a college degree and the absence of other professional training received a score of 2; (*d*) a presence of training beyond a college degree and the presence of other professional training received a score of 3.

18. The index of professional activity, which ranged from 0 to 3 points, was computed as follows: (*a*) 1 point for belonging to a professional organization; (*b*) 1 point for attending at least two-thirds of the previous six meetings of any professional organization; (*c*) 1 point for the presentation of a paper or holding an office in any professional organization.

19. See Victor Thompson, "Bureaucracy and Innovation," *Administrative Science Quarterly*, 10 (June, 1965), 10–13.

20. Durkheim, *op. cit.*; although he was discussing the characteristics of city life, the argument is that much more compelling in the context of an organization where interaction is facilitated.

21. Max Weber, *The Theory of Social and Economic Organization*, trans. Henderson and Parsons (Glencoe, Ill.: Free Press, 1947), pp. 334–40.

22. The classic study is, of course, Lester Coch and John French, Jr., "Overcoming Resistance to Change," *Human Relations*, 1 (1948), 512–32. For a review of the literature and organizational experiments reflecting this dilemma between satisfaction and production, see Nancy Morse and Everett Reimer, "The Experimental Change of a Major Organizational Variable," *Journal of Abnormal and Social Psychology*, 52 (1955), 120–29.

23. The index of actual participation in decision making was based on the following four questions: (1) How frequently do you usually participate in the decision to hire new staff? (2) How frequently do you usually participate in the decisions on the promotion of any of the professional staff? (3) How frequently do you participate in decisions on the adoption of new policies? (4) How frequently

do you participate in the decisions on the adoption of new programs? Respondents were assigned numerical scores from 1 (low participation) to 5 (high participation), depending on whether they answered "never," "seldom," "sometimes," "often," or "always," respectively, to these questions. An average score on these questions was computed for each respondent, and then the data was aggregated into organizational scores as described above.

24. Thompson, 'Bureaucracy and Innovation," *op. cit.*, pp. 13–18.

25. The empirical indicators of these concepts were derived from two scales developed by Richard Hall, namely, hierarchy of authority and rules (see his "The Concept of Bureaucracy: An Empirical Assessment," *American Journal of Sociology*, 69 [July, 1963], 32–40). The index of hierarchy of authority was computed by first averaging the replies of individual respondents to each of the following five statements: (1) There can be little action taken here until a supervisor approves a decision. (2) A person who wants to make his own decisions would be quickly discouraged here. (3) Even small matters have to be referred to someone higher up for a final answer. (4) I have to ask my boss before I do almost anything. (5) Any decision I make has to have my boss's approval. Responses could vary from 1 (definitely false) to 4 (definitely true). The individual scores were then combined into an organizational score as described above.

26. Robert K. Merton, "Bureaucratic Structure and Personality," in Etzioni, *op. cit.*, pp. 48–61.

27. Hall, *op. cit.* The index of job codification was based on the following five questions: (1) I feel that I am my boss in most matters. (2) A person can make his own decisions without checking with anybody else. (3) How things are done here is left up to the person doing the work. (4) People here are allowed to do almost as they please. (5) Most people here make their own rules on the job. Replies to these questions were scored from 1 (definitely true) to 4 (definitely false), and then each of the respondent's answers was averaged. Thus, a high score on this index means high job codification.

The index of rule observation was computed by averaging the responses to each of the following two statements: (1) The employees are constantly being checked on for rule violations. (2) People there feel as though they are constantly being watched, to see that they obey all the rules. Respondent's answers were coded from 1 (definitely false) to 4 (definitely true), and then the average score of each respondent on these items was computed. Organizational scores were computed as previously described. On this index, a high score means a high degree of rule observation.

28. Coch and French, *op. cit.*

29. We used a satisfaction scale developed by Neal Gross, Ward Mason, and Alexander McEachern, *Explorations in Role Analysis* (New York: John Wiley & Sons, 1958), Appendix B. When factor analyzed, this battery provided the following scales: job satisfaction, satisfaction with expressive relations, satisfaction with salary, and satisfaction with time. The index of job satisfaction was computed on the basis of responses to the following six questions: (1) How satisfied are you that you have been given enough authority by your board of directors to do your job well? (2) How satisfied are you with your present job when you compare it to similar positions in the state? (3) How satisfied are you with the progress you are making toward the goals which you set for yourself in your present position? (4) On the whole, how satisfied are you that (your superior) accepts you as a professional expert, to the degree to which you are entitled by reason of position, training, and

experience? (5) On the whole, how satisfied are you with your present job when you consider the expectations you had when you took the job? (6) How satisfied are you with your present job in light of career expectations?

The index of expressive satisfaction was computed from responses to the following two questions: (1) How satisfied are you with your supervisor? (2) How satisfied are you with your fellow workers?

30. See Floyd C. Mann and Lawrence Williams, "Observations on the Dynamics of a Change to Electronic Data-processing Equipment," *Administrative Science Quarterly,* 5 (September, 1960), 217–57; and Floyd Mann and T. Hoffman, *Automation and the Worker* (New York: Henry Holt, 1960). The same point is made in several other studies of organizational change; see, for example, Harriet Ronken and Paul Lawrence, *Administering Changes* (Cambridge, Mass.: Harvard Graduate Business School, 1952); and Charles Walker, *Toward the Automatic Factory* (New Haven, Conn.: Yale University Press, 1957).

31. Philip Selznick, "Critical Decisions in Organizational Development," in Etzioni, *op. cit.,* pp. 355–62.

32. See Mann and Hoffman, *op. cit.*

33. George Homans, "Bringing Men Back In," *American Sociological Review,* 29 (December, 1964), 809–19.

34. Four scales that purport to measure attitudes toward change developed by Sister Marie Augusta Neal, *Values and Interests in Social Change* (Englewood Cliffs, N.J.: Prentice-Hall, Inc., 1965), were used.

35. See Michael Aiken and Jerald Hage, "Organizational Alienation," *American Sociological Review,* 31 (August, 1966), 497–507, for a discussion of this relationship.

36. D. S. Pugh *et al., op. cit.* See Hage, "An Axiomatic Theory," *op. cit.,* pp. 304–6, for hypotheses concerning these contextual variables.

37. Size was based on a rank order of all salaried employees. Rank ordering was used because we had an extremely skewed distribution. Auspices is a natural dichotomy between tax supported and non-tax supported. Age was treated as a trichotomy because all the organizations were founded either prior to 1900, between 1919 and 1923, or after the Great Depression period. Function was measured by creating a dummy variable based on the amount of contact per week between the agency and the client. An hour or less per week, the typical casework interview, was treated as low client involvement. The sheltered workshops, the rehabilitation agencies, and the total institutions were categorized as high-involvement agencies. Ideally more distinctions would be describable, but with only sixteen organizations additional refinement becomes impossible.

38. A. D. Chandler, Jr., *Strategy and Structure* (Cambridge, Mass.: M.I.T. Press, 1962).

39. Joan Woodward, *Industrial Organization: Theory and Practice* (London: Oxford Press, 1965), chap. ii, pp. 23–25.

Index

743